UMI ANNUAL COMMENTARY

PRECEPTS FOR LIVING®

MISSION STATEMENT

*We are called
of God to create, produce, and distribute
quality Christian education products;
to deliver exemplary customer service;
and to provide quality Christian
educational services, which will empower
God's people, especially within the Black
community, to evangelize, disciple,
and equip people for serving Christ,
His kingdom, and church.*

UMI
Urban Ministries, Inc.
The African American Christian Publishing
& Communications Co.

UMI ANNUAL SUNDAY SCHOOL LESSON COMMENTARY
PRECEPTS FOR LIVING 2018–2019
INTERNATIONAL SUNDAY SCHOOL LESSONS
VOLUME 21
UMI (URBAN MINISTRIES, INC.)

Melvin Banks Sr., Litt.D., Founder and Chairman

C. Jeffrey Wright, J.D., CEO

Yvonne Hawkins, Chief Content Officer

Bible art: Fred Carter

Get the Precepts for Living® eBook!

Are you among those joining the digital revolution by reading books using a Kindle, iPad, NOOK, or other electronic readers? If so, there's good news for you! UMI is keeping up with the latest technology by publishing its annual Sunday School commentary, *Precepts for Living*, in the leading eBook formats: Kindle (Amazon), NOOK (Barnes & Noble), and iBooks (Apple).

To buy an eBook copy of *Precepts for Living*, visit our website at preceptsforlivingonline.com to find download links and step-by-step instructions.

If you've purchased *Precepts for Living* for your e-reader, be sure to leave a rating and a review at the iTunes, B&N, or Amazon store sites to tell others what you think. Also, spread the word on your favorite social networking sites, and follow us on social media on Facebook @ facebook.com/urbanministriesinc, @umichicago on Twitter, and @UMI on Instagram.

PRECEPTS
FOR
LIVING®

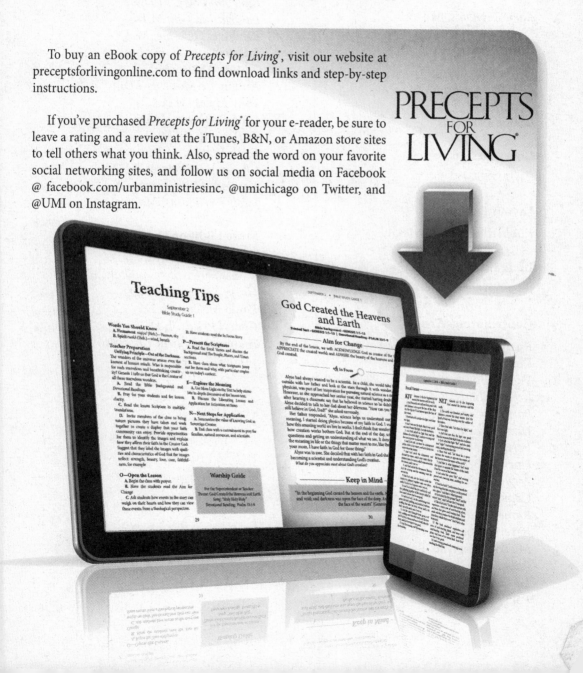

CONTRIBUTORS

Editor

Adonijah Okechukwu Ogbonnaya, Ph.D.

Developmental Editor/Contributing Writer

Allen Reynolds, M.Div

Copy Editors

William McGee
Beth Potterveld, M.A.
Geri Tucker
Barbranda Walls

Cover Design

Larry Taylor

Layout Design

Kimberly Applewhite, B.A.

Bible Illustrations

Fred Carter

Contributing Writers

Essays/In Focus Stories
Kimberly Baker, M.S.
Valerie Boyer, B.S.
Kelvin Childs, B.A.
Patricia Carroll, DTS
Danielle Echols, M.A.
Bertram Melbourne, Ph.D.
Harvey Kwiyani, Ph.D.
Angela Lampkin, Ph.D.
Courtney Mayberry, B.A.
Ramon Mayo, M.A.
Beverly Moore, M.Div
Mwikali Munyao, B.A.
Rabbi Jason Sobel
La Verne Tolbert, Ph.D.
Porsha Williams, M.Div

Bible Study Guide Writers

Philippe Andal, M.Div
Stephen Artis, M.Div
Jaimie Crumley, M.Div
JD Denkins, M.Div
Malcolm Foley, M.Div
LaQruishia Gill, M.Div
Kimberly Gillespie, M.A.
Joshua Mitchell, D.Min
Beverly Moore, M.S.
Antoinette Mosley, M.Div
Tony Myles, M.B.A.
Gina Robinson, M.Div
CaReese Rials, M.A.
Faith Waters, M.Div.
Charmaine Webster, M.Div
Katrina White Brown, M.A.
Jeremy Williams, M.Div

More Light on the Text

J. Ayodeji Adewuya, Ph.D.
Moussa et Assita Coulibaly, Ph.D.
Harvey Kwiyani, Ph.D.
Paula McGee, Ph.D.
Cheryl Price, Ph.D.
Alajemba Reuben Unaegbu, M.A.

Dear Precepts Customer,

Celebrate with us!
This edition of *Precepts For Living*® marks the 20th year we have prepared and distributed these annual Bible study guides. We launched *Precepts* with great anticipation that followers of Christ would have a compelling resource to explore God's Word and apply it to the many and varied issues we face every day, especially those of African Americans.

Your response through the years—like that of thousands of other customers—indicates that *Precepts* is meeting a genuine need in your life and in the lives of many others.

Help us celebrate!
Here's a practical way you can help us celebrate. Many people still do not know about *Precepts For Living*®. You can help us spread the Good News!

Tell a friend! Better yet, purchase and give a gift of *Precepts* to a friend or relative— in your family, church, or community.

These annual Bible studies in *Precepts For Living*® provide a solid foundation to understand the Bible and discover God's purpose and will for us in this life. And remember, people use these Bible studies not only on Sunday morning, but also for personal and small group studies at home and in the church and community.

HERE ARE WAYS TO GET PRECEPTS FOR LIVING
Your Local Bookstore
Your Church Headquarters
Online: www.urbanministries.com
UMI Telephone: 800-860-8642
UMI Fax: 708-868-7105
UMI Mail: Dept. 4860/PO Box 87618 Chicago, IL 60680-0618

Thanks for your support!
Help us spread the Word.

Sincerely,

Melvin Banks, Sr.
Founder, Chairman

Dear Precepts Customer,

It is our privilege to present the 2018–2019 Precepts for Living®. As you encounter God's Word through these lessons, we anticipate that you will find this resource to be indispensable.

Precepts for Living® comes to you in four versions: the Personal Study Guide (the workbook), the E-Book version, a large print edition, and Pastor's Edition. You will also notice that the biblical text for each lesson includes the New Living Translation in addition to the King James Version. This contemporary translation will enhance your textual understanding when you compare it side by side to the classic English translation. It is very helpful in illuminating your understanding of the text.

Precepts for Living® is designed to be a witness through our learning and sharing more of the Bible. Our intent is to facilitate innovative ways for pursuing a deeper understanding and practice of God's Word. One of the ways we strive to do this is by highlighting the larger narrative of God's work in salvation as a key part of understanding each biblical passage. We believe it is important to help you understand not only the particulars of the text but also the broad extent of God's revelation to us as well. This panoramic approach enhances our ability to witness to others about the saving power of Jesus Christ.

This year we explore the themes of Creation, Worship, Discipleship & Mission, and Covenant. Each year of Bible study offers great potential for a more intimate and transformative walk with God.

We want to continually refine Precepts for Living® as we endeavor to meet our customers' needs. We are always looking for ways to enhance your study of the Bible, and your comments and feedback are vital in helping us. If you have questions or suggestions, we encourage you to please e-mail us at precepts@urbanministries.com or mail your comments to UMI, Precepts for Living®, PO Box 436987, Chicago, IL 60643-6987.

May God draw you closer to the fullness of life with Him through this book.

God's blessings to you,

Adonijah Okechukwu Ogbonnaya

Adonijah Okechukwu Ogbonnaya, Advanced Teachers' Certificate, B.A. Bible and Philosophy, M.A. Theological Studies, M.A. Religion, Ph.D. Theology and Personality
Editor

Uncovering the Benefits of Precepts

It is a great privilege to participate in Christian education and play a significant role in the spiritual formation of fellow Christians in our churches. *Precepts for Living*® is a resource that is designed to help you lead others toward greater knowledge and practice of following Jesus Christ. To that end, please take full advantage of the substantive offerings provided to you in this year's commentary.

In this 20th anniversary edition we have revamped the "Lesson in Our Society" and "Make it Happen" sections into "Liberating Lesson" and "Application for Activation" sections, respectively. We want the liberating lesson to help you think about collective application and perspective beyond the individual level and the "Application for Activation" to help you think about personal ways to live out the lesson themes and draw closer to God.

From the standpoint of your vocation as a teacher, it is very important to be aware of the great responsibility that goes along with your position. James 3:1 reminds us that we have such a great opportunity in front of us that we run the risk of greater judgment if we are derelict in our duties. In the Gospels, Jesus is often referred to as "teacher." Being a teacher means participating in one of the church's greatest tasks, one that the ancient church called "catechesis." This is a strong word that helps us understand the great influence we have when we help our students learn about God's Word. It carries with it the idea of imparting the entirety of the faith to Christians. While many teachers might not be familiar with this word, the truth is that every time we help others learn about God's Word and ways, we are participating in this great task of the church that has been with us from the beginning. Unfortunately, this gets lost amid other concerns. As a teacher, you have an opportunity to energize or revitalize this aspect of your church's ministry. Reflect on how you have prepared for the challenge.

What is the goal when you use Precepts for Living® to open up the riches of the Bible to your students? It is beyond the mere acquisition of information. We want students to receive revelation that becomes application. Certainly we want our students to grow in knowledge, but the knowledge we seek to pass on does not solely comprise Bible facts but includes a larger sense of comprehension where the information and doctrine conveyed is oriented toward a faithful life of discipleship. That is why it is called *Precepts for Living*®, and not Precepts for Knowing.

The "People, Places, and Times," "Background," "In Depth," and "More Light on the Text" sections are there to help you provide insight and understanding of the text. But the sections include more than a simple compilation of information. In each lesson, you will also see "In Focus" stories and "Liberating Lesson" and "Application for Activation" sections serving as catalysts for applying the biblical text to life situations. It is very important that we as teachers pass on knowledge that will enable our students to deepen their devotion to God in an upward focus and encourage them to better embody that devotion in a way that makes their lives a living witness to the world. Our hope from every lesson should be to inspire students to become the best living examples of the Scriptures with the understanding that their lives may be the only Bible some people ever read.

To best take advantage of this commentary, utilize the essays to emphasize quarterly themes and enhance the classroom experience.

We believe this commentary is a great tool to help form fully devoted followers of Christ, and we invite you to wholeheartedly partake in all of the resources provided here. May God be glorified as you play your part in this great task of the church!

Creative Teaching

New Features
Precepts for Living® 2018-2019
20th Anniversary Edition

New Liberating Lesson Section

In each lesson there is a "Liberating Lesson" to replace the "Lesson In Our Society." This section is dedicated to highlighting parallels and or applications to modern life that are reflected in the Bible. This section challenges us to consider how the scriptures relate to our modern society and asks us to respond individually, collectively, and as a community to God's Word. There is a special emphasis on social justice or justice implications in Christian Scripture that the Liberating Lesson brings to the forefront.

New Application for Activation Section

In each lesson there is an "Application for Activation" to replace the "Make It Happen." This section provides guidance for practical application the reader or the local church could pursue in response to the lesson to take the lesson from information to living activation.

New Teaching Tips Essays

Take advantage of our new Teaching Tips Essays, which give insight for engaging your class and helping your students grow each quarter. They are tailored for adult learners, but many of the concepts work for instructing other ages as well. Below are some additional tips for making your students effective disciples of Jesus.

Variety in Perspective Essays

The Perspective Essays for the quarters in the 20th anniversary edition include a scholarly essay, devotional, personal reflection, and a Jewish Insight.

More Tips for Teachers

• Energizing the Class. If the class does not seem as enthusiastic or energy is low, after you open with prayer, have everyone stretch to the sky or outward. Then tell the class to shake off the low energy, and open up their hands to receive the love of God that is right there. You can always have a 30-second meet-and-greet time. This usually helps to wake people up so you can begin class on a higher energy level.

• Two Teachers in One Class—Bring Out the Best in Both. Taking turns works in some classes, but in others it creates tension and favorites. Encourage teachers to study together, and then divide the segments of the lesson. Perhaps one will teach the introduction while the other teaches a section of the text. Encourage them to also become a true team with each contributing throughout the lesson.

• Remember. Everyone cannot read or write on the same level. Use different teaching techniques and styles when teaching. How you learn affects how you teach, so be open and willing to learn and teach through various media.

• Avoid Study in Isolation. People often "get it" when they are involved with more than talking about the lesson. Why not allow the class to see the connections themselves? Try using a chart to have adult students work in pairs or groups to compare and contrast Bible people such as David and Solomon or Ruth and Orpah, Naomi's daughters-in-law. To help the students get started, suggest specific categories for comparisons such as lifestyles, families, or public ministry. As class members search the Scriptures, they will learn and remember much more than if you told them about either person individually.

• Group Studies. Have the class form groups, and have each group read the Scripture lesson and a section of the Background for the text. Have each group create a two-minute skit about the Scripture to share with the class. Encourage the groups to use their imaginations and energy. You may want to have at least one "leader" in a group if you have more than two or three reserved people in your class.

• Volunteers. Many classes begin with reading the lesson. When class members have studied, this activity is more "bringing minds" together than about the actual lesson. Still some classes can benefit from dramatic and creative reading of Bible passages at any point in the lesson. When the passage under study lends itself, assign parts to volunteers. This need not be formal—standing up isn't even critical. This strategy works best in passages that have a story such as the conversation between Moses and his father-in-law, Jethro, or Paul confronting the merchants in Thessalonica. Assign one person to each speaking character in the Bible text. Feel free to be creative with giving the class roles as "the crowd." Make sure to assign a narrator who will read the nonspeaking parts. It is fun, it is fast, and it makes for memorable Bible reading.

• Materials. You may want to have large sheets of paper, markers, glue or tape, newspapers, and magazines available on a weekly basis for the various activities.

• Additional Methods. Write the theme on a large poster board or sheet of paper, and ask each person to write a word or draw a picture that best describes the theme. Read the themes aloud, and discuss any of the pictures before you begin your class discussion or activities. If you have a very large class or time is limited, only select a few words or pictures for discussion. You can either lead the discussion or invite members of the class to do so.

• Websites. Connect with us by logging onto www.urbanministries.com. Follow us on social media on Facebook at facebook.com/urbanministriesinc, @umichicago on Twitter, and #UMI on Instagram.

• Email us at precepts@urbanministries.com, and send us some of your favorite Teaching Tips for ages 18 and older that you want to share with others. If yours is selected, we will post them under our Teaching Tips sections for Precepts. If you have ice-breaker activities, please submit them as well. Your submissions should be no longer than 125 words.

• Closing. At the end of the lesson, give your class the assignment of looking for scenes from films or television, advertisements, or parts of songs that either demonstrate the coming week's "In Focus" story, "Liberating Lesson" section, or "Application for Activation" section. Encourage them to be creative and to come up with an explanation of how their contribution helps make the truth of the lesson come to life.

• Prayer. Have a Prayer Request Board for people to write their prayer requests on each Sunday. You may want to make this a weekly activity. Have someone read the prayer request and let the class decide which prayer requests they will pray for during the week. One Sunday School teacher has his class write their prayer requests on sheets of paper and place them in the middle of the floor once a year. He then shares with the class that he will write them all down in a prayer journal that he keeps and prays over them at least once a week. Be creative and create your own prayer journal or prayer tradition(s) within your class.

TABLE OF CONTENTS

Fall Quarter 2018

Winter Quarter 2018-2019

2016–2019 Scope and Sequence—Cycle Spread

	FALL	WINTER	SPRING	SUMMER
YEAR ONE 2016–17	**GOD SOVEREIGNTY** **Sovereignty of God** Isaiah Matthew Hebrews Revelation	**CREATION** **Creation: A Divine Cycle** Psalms Luke Galatians	**LOVE** **God Loves Us** Psalms Joel Jonah John Romans Ephesians 1 John	**CALL** **God's Urgent Call** Exodus Judges Isaiah Jeremiah Ezekiel Amos Acts
YEAR TWO 2017–18	**COVENANT** **Covenant with God** Genesis Exodus Numbers 1 Samuel 2 Samuel Nehemiah Jeremiah Ezekiel 1 Corinthians Titus Hebrews	**FAITH** **Faith in Action** Daniel Matthew Acts Ephesians Colossians 1 Timothy James	**WORSHIP** **Acknowledging God** Genesis Exodus Leviticus 2 Chronicles Psalms Luke John 2 Corinthians Hebrews Revelation	**JUSTICE** **Justice in the New Testament** Matthew Luke Romans 2 Corinthians Colossians
YEAR THREE 2018–19	**CREATION** **God's World and God's People** Genesis	**LOVE** **Our Love for God** Exodus Deuteronomy Joshua Psalms Matthew Mark Luke Philippians 2 Thessalonians James 2 John	**CALL** **Discipleship and Mission** Matthew Luke Romans	**COVENANT** **Covenant in God** Ruth 1 Samuel Matthew Luke John Ephesians Hebrews Romans

God's World and God's People

In Genesis, the book of beginnings, God is revealed as the Creator, Sustainer, Judge, and Redeemer, who brought all things into being. The fall quarter surveys the book of Genesis in developing sessions on God's creation of the universe, earth, and people. It also details how God continues to co-labor with sinful humanity in reconciling and re-creating order in all things.

UNIT 1 • God Created the World

This unit has five sessions. They concentrate on God's creating the universe, earth, and people and then declaring all things created good. Although God created and sustains all life, humankind is special to God and unique. Session Four explores how God established the institution of marriage and the process of reproduction in order to populate the earth. Session Five explains how humankind chose to do wrong and thus introduced sin into God's perfectly created world.

Lesson 1: September 2, 2018
God Created the Heavens and Earth
Genesis 1:1–13

The wonders of the universe amaze even the keenest of human minds. Who is responsible for such marvelous and breathtaking creativity? God is the Creator of all these marvelous wonders.

Lesson 2: September 9, 2018
God Created Plants and Animals
Genesis 1:14–25

People's life experiences sometimes lead them to question whether the universe is ordered or unpredictably chaotic. How do the diverse parts of nature work together? God brought order to the universe God made, establishing the heavenly bodies and filling the sea, sky, and land with diverse and abundant life.

Lesson 3: September 16, 2018
God Created People
Genesis 1:26–31; 2:4–7

How the world and humans came to be is explored and questioned by many people. Where did people come from? God created people as the highest form of creation made in the image of God, and people are supported by all of God's creation.

Lesson 4: September 23, 2018
God Created the Family
Genesis 2:18–24; 4:1–2

Humans often wonder what their purpose is in life and how they relate to all that is around them. What is our purpose and where do we fit in? God created families to support and care for one another and to care for all of God's creation.

Lesson 5: September 30, 2018
God Creates, Humans Sin
Genesis 3:8–17, 20–24

Irresponsible rebellion pervades our world. Why is disregard for rules, which are necessary for ordered life, so pervasive? Although God created a perfect place for Adam and Eve, their unwillingness to trust and obey God led to the Fall, making humanity prone to disobedience.

UNIT 2 • God Destroys and Re-Creates

This unit has four sessions. Noah and his family are presented in the first two sessions as righteous followers of God, who help repopulate and restore the earth after the destruction caused by the great flood. The biblical couples, Abraham and Sarah, and Isaac and Rebekah, who worked with God in the cycle of continuing creation, are studied in the last two sessions of the unit.

Lesson 6: October 7, 2018
Noah's Steadfast Faith
Genesis 6:9–22

Faithfulness is a needed quality of life, but it is difficult to achieve. How can persons be faithful in difficult situations? Noah is an empowering example of someone who remained faithful to what God asked him to do regardless of the opposing circumstances and consequences.

Lesson 7: October 14, 2018
God Is Always Working
Genesis 10:1; 11:10, 27, 31–32; 12:1–4

Many tasks seem daunting or even impossible for mere human effort. How can mere humans accomplish such challenging and important work? Genesis teaches that God worked over many generations from Noah to Abraham in order to bring blessings to the entire world.

Lesson 8: October 21, 2018
Abraham and Sarah Trust God's Promise
Genesis 18:9–15; 21:1–7

Because of past promises that were not fulfilled, we find it hard to trust future promises. What can help us have faith and confidence to depend on important promises that shape our lives? Although Abraham and Sarah had to wait a long time for God's promise of a son to be born to them to shape all people of the earth, God showed them that this promise was trustworthy.

Lesson 9: October 28, 2018
Isaac and Rebekah Continue the Legacy
Genesis 24:12–21, 61–67

People often must face decisions that will change their lives forever. How can we make the most of the opportunities life gives us? Rebekah took initiative in answering the call to become the wife of Isaac and thus to play an important role in the unfolding of God's promises.

UNIT 3 • God Blesses and Creates Regardless

This unit has four sessions. We will explore how God blessed humble Isaac in enemy territory, and consider how Jacob deceitfully obtained the blessing God had already destined for him, later established a right relationship with God, and finally was blessed by God to marry and produce children with the wife he loved and for whom he long labored.

Lesson 10: November 4, 2018
A Troubled Birth
Genesis 25:19–34

We are often discouraged when our lives do not go smoothly but are disrupted by human conflict and struggle. How can our efforts amount to anything worthwhile when riddled with human frailty and error? In spite of their selfish actions, God was present in the lives of Esau and Jacob.

Lesson 11: November 11, 2018
Jacob Receives Isaac's Blessing
Genesis 27:5–10, 18–19, 21–29

Deceiving others is a way that people get what they want. Does human deception erase the worth of human accomplishment? Even though the deception used by Rebekah and Jacob disrupted their family, God still worked through their situation to accomplish the planned and promised divine redemption of fallen humanity.

Lesson 12: November 18, 2018
Jacob Forms a Relationship with God
Genesis 28:10–22

In the midst of human turmoil, we grow weary and can lose sight of the purpose for our lives. How can we escape the confusion to refresh and reorient ourselves to get back on track? God created an opportunity for the weary Jacob to reconnect with his spiritual mission and resources for him to begin his life's journey with renewed vigor.

Lesson 13: November 25, 2018
God Blesses Jacob and Rachel
Genesis 30:22–32, 43

Obstacles and loss often block our efforts to accomplish something worthwhile. How can we overcome these setbacks in order to live lives that count for good? God intervened to help Jacob overcome seeming defeat by not only gaining many possessions but also escaping the wrath of a selfish and deceptive father-in-law.

This World is God's World

by Allen Reynolds

God is God Alone

In the beginning God created the heavens and the earth. The first sentence of the first verse, of the first book of the Bible is the foundation for everything that follows. The book of Genesis tells the story of the foundation of the world and the beginning of humanity's relationship with God. Coming from the Hebrew word for beginning, Genesis sets the stage for the biblical narrative and introduces us to the God who created everything by speaking it into existence. God is all-powerful. God has no rival, no equal, no limitations, and no boundaries. The names used for God in Genesis reveal God's character because God decided to be in relationship with humans. Names like *Adonai*, the Lord, let us know that God owns everything; everything belongs to God. Names like *Elohim*, the Almighty God, let us know that God is supreme, multifaceted, and greater than anything. God creates the heavens, the sun, moon, stars, galaxies, and planets all by speaking them into existence.

God Creates Humanity

The focus of Genesis quickly shifts from God's relationship with creation in general to God's relationship with humanity. God creates man and woman giving them authority over all the rest of creation on earth. God tells Adam and Eve to be fruitful and multiply, fill the earth and subdue it giving the man and woman purpose. Adam and Eve sin by disobeying God, and it immediately invites shame, blame, and broken relationship into the world. God removes the family from the Garden of Eden, cutting them off from the tree of life. The sin that has infected humanity continues to grow and cause death, straining humanity's relationship with God to the point where God decides to destroy His creations on earth with the Flood. God has the right to allow destruction of what He creates because it belongs to Him. Yet, in His mercy, God preserves Noah, his family and all the animals in the Ark. God had already set the plan for redemption in motion, so that all creation would be reconciled to Him and filled with His glory instead of wickedness; so that humanity would be the children of God instead of the enemies of God.

God is Sovereign

God is the Creator of everything. God has the authority, power, and right to be destroyer of anything because God is the Creator. Often in the modern church, we give too much credit to the kingdom of darkness and its ability to destroy people's lives with everything that is not like God. But the Old Testament perspective is clear that it is God alone who has the right to allow destruction of His creation.

The risk of freedom for humanity is that people can choose to obey or depart from right

relationship with God. Anything less than perfect relationship with the one who is life is sin. Sin will always destroy God's beautiful creation if left unchecked. However, the evidence of God's mercy is that He never destroys creation entirely, He always leaves a remnant to redeem and re-create. While sin naturally leads to death, God steps in to strip the weeds of sin from choking the life out of our gardens. Mercy cuts down the weeds in God's garden. Grace takes the seeds of Eden and plants a new garden where there are no weeds.

God's created family—Adam and Eve— needed intervention to keep them from destroying themselves. The effects of sin were seen quickly with one son murdering the other. The destruction of the family began to destroy the land as humanity sought to satisfy its need for purpose apart from God.

God's Covenant Family

Despite the failings of each generation from Noah and his children to Abraham and Sarah to Isaac and Rebekah to Jacob and his wives and children, God never sees the family of faith as beyond redemption. God chooses a family to bring forth redemption. In eternal wisdom, God picks Abram and makes him a promise. God will bless Abram, give him land, and allow his descendants to be as numerous as the stars in the heavens. Through Abram's seed, all humanity will be blessed. Yet as Abram becomes Abraham, the father of many nations, and his family becomes the family of promise, the reality of humanity continues to complicate the process to fulfillment of the promise. First Abraham and his wife Sarah have a hard time believing the promise can come to pass so they try to help God. The result is that Abraham fathers Ishmael with Hagar. When Sarah does give birth to Isaac, the son of promise, Abraham's faith is tested. But the family, the children of God, God's people must continue to show the redemptive power of God until ultimate redemption can come.

4

When Isaac is of marrying age he has to find a wife to continue the family. His servant is told to find a wife on his behalf from among his father's people, a woman of good character to partner with him in bringing forth the promise and walking in the blessing of "being fruitful and multiplying" of keeping the covenant between Abraham and the Lord. Isaac's wife Rebekah becomes the mother of twin boys, Esau and Jacob, and the latter becomes greater than the former. Jacob schemes and tricks his way into receiving his brother's birthright and blessing even though God had already promised he would receive it. The family is broken yet again as Esau seeks revenge and Jacob flees into the wilderness.

While in the wilderness—in the place of isolation, shame, fear, and lack—Jacob meets God. In the place of Jacob experiencing the results of his sin against his brother and trying to get God's blessing through deceitful means, Jacob reaches the end of his own strength. Rather than showing up to condemn him, God shows up to begin a conversation. The conversation causes conviction: Jacob sees the heavens open and the presence of the angels leaves him in awe of God. Then God promises him that where he lays now will be his land, that he will be fruitful, multiply, fill the land, and possess it. God will protect him on his journey. God renews the initial command he gave to Adam and Eve with a promise that God will help Jacob begin to fulfill it on a smaller scale. Yet Jacob has no idea that God will use his seed to bring forth the ultimate Seed of Redemption: Jesus Christ. God had already made a promise before Jacob was born, already worked the divine plan to redeem and re-create before the destruction of sin even began.

God's Family by Faith

God brings forth His sinless Son from that family of chosen relationship, the one who would redeem the family and renew creation by calling forth a new family of faith. A family by choice. An adopted family that could inherit and lead the care of creation that was promised to humanity in the Garden of Eden. That family is known today as the church. We are God's family, sons and daughters of the Spirit by grace through faith. God's grace continues to find us in our broken places, our wilderness, our shame and sin, and call us into new life in right relationship with Him through Jesus Christ. God's grace and new relationship with Jesus Christ teach us how to properly care for creation. Yet the church is only the beginning of God's manifest kingdom on earth as it is in heaven. The church is simply the chosen vessel that God wants to use to reconcile all creation back to right relationship with Him and itself. Although the church is still being perfected until the day the Lord Jesus returns, in every place the children of God gather, share, and serve there is a glimpse of the revelation of the kingdom, the renewal of the promise, the reconciliation of the family, and the redemption of all creation.

Allen Reynolds M.Div, is the Editor of Adult & Customized Content at UMI.

In the Beginning...
Life Lessons in Genesis

by Kimberly Baker, M.S.

The Discipline of Teaching

As students and teachers of God's Word, it is important that we are able to demonstrate good spiritual discipline. An important part of that discipline is the study of Scripture. As teachers, we owe it to our students to be well prepared so that we can help them in their walk with Christ.

I can think of no better way than through the study of the Holy Bible. As educators, we have the responsibility to make the words of the Bible "come alive on the pages." Through research and proper exegetical exercise, we are able to accomplish this. We must properly prepare the text so that our students understand the message that God wants to convey to us.

Paul tells us in 2 Timothy 2:15 to "Study to shew thyself approved unto God, a workman that needeth not to be ashamed, rightly dividing the word of truth" (KJV). The word "study" in Greek means "to make effort, be prompt, give diligence." When we study the Bible, we have to focus on making sure that we are looking at the Scripture in its proper perspective. That means using available tools to get a clear understanding of what that Scripture means. But first and foremost, we must allow the Scripture to interpret itself before seeking outside resources.

The Biblical Story

The Bible tells a story. In essence, it tells us the history of salvation. From the beginning of time, Jesus Christ, our Savior, was coming to redeem us from a life of sin and death. The Bible tells the story of how this came to pass. Key events and people in the Bible help us to understand the great sacrifice that God made so that we can see Him again one day.

The Bible is full of lessons that we need to learn to understand the truth. For clarity, we need to begin our study at the beginning. Genesis, the first book of the Bible, sets the tone and the pace for the story. It introduces us to key concepts and themes that continue throughout the Bible. Although many themes are introduced in Genesis, four are key to our understanding of the Bible: Covenant, Sin and Redemption, Salvation, and Faith. Let's take a look at each so that we can understand their importance to our lives and those of our students.

Theme 1: Covenant

A covenant is defined as a binding agreement between two parties that creates a new relationship. Oftentimes, a promise is involved as well. In a biblical covenant, the agreement is between God and man. The covenantal relationship is carried throughout the entire Bible.

The explanation of covenant begins in Genesis 6 with Noah. God was about to destroy the world and everything in it. He decided that Noah, along with his family and two of every animal species should be saved, so He instructed Noah to build an ark to survive the coming flood. Once the ark was built, Noah's family and the animals entered and were shut in for forty days and nights. When the waters subsided, the ark was opened and all that were inside came out. God promised Noah that He would never destroy the earth with water again (Genesis 9:8–17). He gave them a symbol, the rainbow, as a seal of what He had promised.

The concept of covenant continues in Genesis 12 with Abram. God instructed Abram to leave the land he was in and go to an unfamiliar land. God was going to bless him and make his name great. Without hesitation, Abram prepared his family and belongings, and journeyed to unfamiliar territory. He did not know where he was going, but he trusted God enough to do as told. As a result, God changed Abram's name to Abraham, which means "father of many nations." God was going to make Abraham a great nation with many descendants. This was a miracle in itself because Abraham had no children. God kept His Word and a son was born to Abraham and Sarah in their mature age.

God was establishing the lineage of Abraham that would have some of the greatest people of the Bible, such as Jacob, Joseph, David, and ultimately Jesus Christ. These men went on to further establish the covenant with God's people and prepare their ancestors for Jesus.

The theme of covenant is significant because it helps us to understand what God is doing in the midst of His people and demonstrates His love for us. God will always remain true to His Word, and we must be truthful on our end. He prepared the way to send His Son to earth so that sin and death are no longer powerful over us. The Great Covenant will be fulfilled in the return of Jesus Christ.

Theme 2: Sin and Redemption

The next theme we see in Genesis is Sin and Redemption. God created Adam and Eve, placed them in the garden, and gave them full responsibility to tend to the garden and all its contents. The only instruction they received was not to eat of the tree in the middle of the garden (Genesis 2:17). The serpent came along to speak with Eve and told her that what God had said was not the truth. She disobeyed the

Lord and ate the forbidden fruit. Because of this act, sin entered the world. Adam and Eve had sinned against God and defied Him. Now, they had to leave the comfort of the only home that they had ever known and were forced to fend for themselves.

Death had entered the world; separation was present. But a Redeemer was in place! Jesus Christ was to come and take eternal sin and the consequence of death from us (Genesis 3:15). He would come and die on the cross to restore our relationship with God. But till then a mediator, in the form of a priest, would intercede on behalf of the people. Sin would still be present, but now we had another opportunity to get it right in the eyes of God.

Salvation would be possible because of what Jesus was coming to the earth to do. We first see mention of salvation with Noah and his family. When God decided He was going to destroy the earth and its inhabitants, He secured Noah and his family in the ark. The ark was their salvation as it protected them during the Flood and kept them from facing death.

As born-again believers, we must understand that salvation comes through Jesus and Jesus Christ alone (Acts 4:12). Since one of the most important themes in Scripture is salvation, we as teachers must be clear on this topic. Our students must realize that accepting and acknowledging Jesus Christ as Lord and Savior is the only way to expect to see Him again.

Theme 3: Faith

Faith is interwoven throughout the Bible. We can see the first mention of this theme in Genesis. According to the Word of God, part of faith is belief in the one, true God without actually seeing Him. Faith is a gift from God (Ephesians 2:8-9). We obtain faith by the power of our own freewill. It distinguishes who belongs to God and who does not. Faith keeps us until the end, because we know that we will see Him again and live with Him forever. We must be steadfast in our faith, the very thing that keeps us going from day to day.

Our first example of this great faith is Noah. He was told by God to build an ark to protect himself and his family from the rain that was going to destroy everything. Noah had never seen rain, but by faith, he built the ark and had it ready to go when destruction came. As believers, we have to understand that God loves us and will give us His best. But we must strive to be obedient and live by faith.

Abraham also exhibited faith. By faith, Abraham moved his entire family from the familiar to the unfamiliar. God promised and gave him a son, Isaac, despite the obstacles that appeared to be present. By faith, Abraham prepared to sacrifice his son of the promise. Because of Abraham's faith, God established a covenant with Abraham that would last for generations, culminating with the birth of Jesus Christ.

The book of Genesis provides us with a wealth of insight as to who God is. When studying Genesis, note the many "firsts" that occur. All of them help us to realize who we are and who we may become. Our students will find great value in the work that we do to help them understand these important principles, as they provide guidelines for how we should live. Our students must never shy away from any book in the Old Testament, because we need to understand our beginning in order to embrace our future.

Kimberly Baker, M.S., has served churches for more than 20 years as a teacher, curriculum writer, and director of Christian Education and is a contributing writer for *Precepts for Living* from Chicago, Illinois.

God's World, God's People

by Bertram Melbourne, Ph.D.

Identity and Origin

Life, my friend, is a vast ocean on which we sail indiviually in our small crafts. The vastness and complexities of life tend to overwhelm us. To make sense of life—navigate its seas and oceans, trek its plains and flatlands, ascend its hills and mountains, or descend its slopes and valleys—there are certain fundamental issues we must resolve and questions we must answer.

Two such puzzling yet essential questions that have plagued humans are, "Who am I?" and "Where did I come from?" They concern identity and origin. There are two fundamentally differing approaches to them. Based on Darwin's theory of natural selection and random arrival of the right circumstances, evolution teaches that life began by the chance interaction of the proper gases resulting in a unicellular organism that over millions of years produced all life, including humans. Scripture, on the other hand, proposes that God created the universe and life. In the former, life is without design or designer; for the latter, God masterminded it all.

Genesis 1:26 sheds light on these significant issues. Speaking to the issue of identity, the text illuminates origin. First, it identifies us as creatures and products of a divine intent. Second, it speaks to humans originating with God, not by chance. There was a designer. Genesis says this designer, a power greater and higher than ourselves, created us in God's own image. This designer is God. I support the latter: The

beauty, grandeur, intricate design, and pattern evident in humans could not have happened coincidentally.

This point concerning design is important. If we follow the notion of the evolutionists, then human beings are the products of chance. Accidentally the gases that produced life came together. Fortuitously, a unicellular organism living in water began to multiply and developed a backbone. By happenstance this creature developed into an amphibian that later became an ape that evolved into a monkey and then became a human being, and it suddenly stopped there. Not only are all these stages not verifiable, there is neither credible evidence for their existence nor any plausible rational explanation exists for the intricate design, orderliness, and intelligence observed in humans and our environment. It is not an unplanned occurrence that 100,000 miles of blood vessels are able to encircle the world four times yet are contained in an average 136-pound body.

Contrarily, when one accepts that we are creatures designed and fashioned by the loving hand of a kind, compassionate, just, forgiving, and beneficent God, it makes all the difference in the world. It allows us to see that thought, design, love, tenderness, compassion and care went into the process. When we view things from this perspective we have an explanation for the structure, intricate design, order, and intelligence we encounter in humans. We are designed by a Creator who formed us in

His own image. This not only gives us value, it boosts our self-image, understanding, self-confidence, self-esteem, and self-worth. It means we can hold our heads high and walk with dignity and pride for we are not just children of God, we are made in God's very own image and likeness. This means the world. It says we are products of the Creator of the universe, shaped by His own loving hands. This says I have value and can walk with pride. It gives me someone bigger and higher than me with whom to identify.

God Creates Family

Each human grapples with some fundamental issues of life. We find ourselves facing problems and hardships. We want answers that are not always forthcoming. Some of us live in families that we don't like and/or don't like us. Many have families who love them but they don't reciprocate that love, or vice versa. Others have families who care and provide for them while some have no such luck. Many have been in charge of themselves for as long as they can remember. Some children live in families with mothers and fathers while others have only one parent, and still others have none. Why such great incongruences in life?

Genesis 1:27 (HCSB) says "So God created man in His own image; He created him in the image of God, He created them male and female." This passage confirms the idea that humans were created by God in God's image. Yet, another notion is inherent in the text that is key. It speaks a truth that all need to hear though none can explain its details. I think this is where faith begins and is indispensable.

This text not only presents a tremendous reality about God—and humans. It informs that God created humankind in God's image, but for humans to epitomize that image, they had to be made male and female. The natural question is, "How is this possible?" Sadly, we must respond that we don't know all the details. God only reveals to us what He chooses to, and sometimes we simply do not know. God is a mystery, or according to theologian Rudolf Otto "the mysterium tremendum." Job's inference is appropriate: "Canst thou by searching find out God?" We must wait for and trust God's revelations.

Now, if we accept the notion that humans are products of God's hand who created us male and female to represent the Godhead, then we see something more about us and our roles in society. As we represent God in the way we were made, even so we represent Him in society and in the socialization of children. As parents, we exemplify the totality of God to our children whom we must train to love, honor, and respect God. Parents represent God to their children. It is therefore incumbent upon parents to set principled examples and to train children to obey them, which represents obedience to God. The family structure is the incubator for nurturing, training, and grounding children to reflect God's image and prepare for life in heaven. This is a tremendous responsibility that reflects the trust and honor God reposes in parents.

God is Sovereign Over Everything

Genesis 1:31a says after the creative act God saw everything He had made and said it was very good. Now, if God is good and contains no evil and if He made everything and declared them very good upon completion, where then did evil and sin come from? Moreover, if God is of purer eyes than to behold evil and cannot look upon iniquity (Habakkuk 1:13), and if sin separates God and humans (Isaiah 59:2), would God have created evil?

Does Isaiah 45:7 shed any light on this matter? This is a very fascinating text. After a cursory glance at it, one could indeed conclude that God created evil. It reads, "I form light, and create darkness; I make peace, and create evil: I the Lord do all these things." Taken literally, we would have to concede that God is responsible for all disasters, calamities, diseases, droughts, injustices, difficulties people encounter, and all the woes we confront in human existence. One could argue that God takes responsibility for the good things in the world and if Christians attribute excellence to God, why not also admit that He created evil as this text says? Did God create evil?

It is important to consider the context of the passage. In its context, the passage speaks of Cyrus the Persian who was God's chosen instrument to accomplish God's purposes. Zoroastrianism was then the dominant religion of Persia and took a dualistic approach to things. Most prominent was its two gods Ahura Mazda, responsible for good/light, and Ahriman, responsible for evil/darkness. What appears to occur in this text is that rather than attributing creation of evil to God, it says that Persians had a god responsible for light and one for darkness, but God is creator of both since He is the supreme being. Here God is held responsible for what God allows. Even if one permits the translation "evil," it is not a reference to evil in the sense of sin but in the sense of a god by that name worshiped by the Persians, and by extrapolation references disasters.

Genesis 1:31 says that when creation came from the hands of God, everything was very good. Yet, today they are not. God did not want to create beings who were forced to believe His every word and obey His every command. Thus, God created creatures with the power of choice. A choice to obey would result in a world without evil and sin. A choice to disobey would result in sin and evil. Both in heaven and on earth, God's creatures exercised their choice not to obey. What we have experienced since then has been the consequence of that choice. We were deceived once but we should not remain deceived.

God did not create evil. But God is sovereign over everything. God created a perfect world. Lucifer, with his choice to disobey, occasioned sin in heaven. He brought his disobedience to earth where Adam and Eve followed him in disobedience that resulted in the loss of the beauty and innocence of earth, and caused the pain and suffering we all know. The injustice and wrongs people experience are directly related to Lucifer's failed plan and human sin. He has become a master of the art of doing bad things to good people and encouraging them to blame a good God. Beware! Don't take the bait.

Yet, all is not lost. God did not abandon us in our plight. He chases after us and still endows us with the awesome task of creating life through procreation. Through this kind of relationship children can begin to understand what it means to be sons and daughters of God and what it will mean one day to rejoin the family of God. The whole object of human existence and the plan of salvation is the re-creation of humans in God's image.

Sources:

Achtemeier, Paul J., gen. ed. *Harper's Bible Dictonary*. San Francisco: HarperSanFrancisco, 1971.

Alexander, Desmond T. and David W. Baker, Dds. *Dictionary of the Old Testament: Pentateuch*. Downers Grove: InterVarsity Press, 2003.

Cragie, P.C. *The Book of Deuteronomy. The New International Commentary on the Old Testament*. Grand Rapids, MI: Wm. B. Eerdmans Publishing Co., 1976.

Freedman, David N., ed. *The Anchor Bible Dicionary*, Vol. 1. New York: Doubleday, 1992.

http://www.dailymail.co.uk/health/article-10976/Circulatory-Blood-vessels.html

https://www.livescience.com/36470-Human-population-weight.htm

https://www.livescience.com/474-controversy-evolution-works.html

http://www.pbs.org/wgbh/evolution/

Bertram Melbourne, Ph.D., is Professor of Biblical Language and Literature & Chair, D.Min. Committee at Howard University School of Divinity in Washington, DC.

The Adult Learner is a Voluntary Learner

by La Verne Tolbert, Ph.D.

While younger students are often brought to the classroom by their parents or guardians, adult learners are voluntary learners. Sunday after Sunday, week after week young adults, adults, and seniors attend class of their own volition. No one makes them go to Sunday School or Bible Study! These learners complete assignments, not for grades, but to deepen their relationship with God. Because they are so passionate about studying God's Word, these learners are a joy to teach!

The wise teacher is aware that adult learners bring a lifetime of experiences and knowledge. They may have wisdom gleaned from years in the workplace. Or, they may have excelled academically by completing college or earning postgraduate degrees. Whatever the path, these learners have stored within them years of practical wisdom from their family relationships, work, church, and community involvement.

Why not add to the richness of your classroom by inviting these learners to join with you in exploring God's Word? First, get to know your learners. Who are the men and women sitting in your classroom? Beyond learning their first and last names, how much do you know about their background? When topics surface that relate to their experiences,

it's great to rely upon these experts sitting right in your room.

Teacher as Coach

Think less of "talking" as a teacher and envision yourself more as a coach or a cheerleader. Rather than asking questions that require a simple "Yes" or "No" or asking questions such as "who, what, when, and where," perhaps ask questions that may promote contemplation and discussion. "How might you have felt if you were in this circumstance?" or "Have you experienced an event that's similar to today's lesson?" Invite adult learners to display their knowledge. Their perspective adds to the lesson and the information they share may be just what's needed to help someone else in the class.

One of the most exciting young adult Bible studies I attended began with the "teacher" presenting a brief 10-minute introduction to the Bible lesson. He began by demonstrating his vulnerability as he recounted a recent experience. He was driving, lost his temper, and nearly experienced road rage. Of course, he felt that he was in the right! He used this account to introduce how Jesus must have felt ministering in an environment where He was wronged.

Then, this teacher did something very unusual for the rest of the class session. He took the microphone, stepped off the platform, and went from one person to the next, allowing adult learners the opportunity to comment, quote Scriptures, give examples, and more. For the remainder of the class, students did the teaching!

More importantly, these young adults felt valued because their contributions were welcomed in class. I understood why this teacher's class was so well attended. While this method may not work for every session, there's a lesson we all can learn as teachers. Never underestimate these voluntary learners and the potential they have to enrich the learning experience.

La Verne Tolbert, Ph.D., is the author of *Teaching Like Jesus: A Practical Guide to Christian Education in Your Church* (Zondervan).

MADAM C.J. WALKER
(c. 1867-1919)

Sarah Breedlove's parents were former slaves who sharecropped in the Louisiana Delta. They had died by the time she was seven years old, so Sarah was shifted from one family to the next until she went to live with her sister Louvina and Louvina's husband, Willie Powell.

Willie began abusing her, so she ran away and married Moses McWilliams when she was just fourteen years old. They had one daughter, Lelia, before McWilliams' death.

Sarah worked hard as a laundrywoman to provide for herself and Lelia, and her daughter's education. She joined the St. Paul African Methodist Episcopal Church where she sang in the choir.

She was greatly influenced by some of the Christian women who were members of that church. At this time she developed a scalp ailment that caused her to start losing her hair. Sarah began experimenting with various ingredients to create products specifically for the hair of African American women.

In St. Louis, she met and married Charles Joseph ("C.J.") Walker and began calling herself and her company Madam C.J. Walker. Mr. Walker was a newspaperman with a talent for marketing. He started placing advertisements for her hair products in African American newspapers throughout the United States. She was hired by Annie Turnbo Malone, a successful African American haircare entrepreneur, as a commission agent in 1905. When her brother died, she moved to Denver, Colorado. After branching out with her own business, she and her husband toured to various cities demonstrating the "Walker Method" of haircare using hot combs, brushing, and her special hair pomade. Madam C.J. Walker had a great vision for the growth of her company but her husband disagreed. They divorced. However, he stayed on as a sales agent. One of his ideas was door-to-door marketing, which was very good for the growth of the business.

By 1906, the company had grown greatly. She brought on her daughter Lelia, (later A'Lelia Walker), who had just graduated from college. Lelia ran the business from the office while Madam Walker traveled throughout the country, Latin America, and the Caribbean to market her products and develop new ones. She also started a college to train women in how to use and sell the products. By 1910, she had 1,000 sales agents and moved Walker Manufacturing Company to Indianapolis, Indiana. The company continued growing.

After all the suffering, poverty, and hardship she had endured, Madam C.J. Walker was the first woman, black or white, to become a millionaire based upon her own achievements.

Sources:
"Madam C.J. Walker Biography." Biography.com A&E Television Networks, https://www.biography.com/people/madam-cj-walker-9522174.
"Madam C.J. Walker." Black Inventor On-Line Museum. http://www.blackinventor.com/pages/madamewalker.html .

Teaching Tips

Words You Should Know

A. Firmament *raqiya'* (Heb.)—Heaven, sky.

B. Spirit *ruakh* (Heb.)—Wind, breath.

Teacher Preparation

Unifying Principle—Out of the Darkness. The wonders of the universe amaze even the keenest of human minds. Who is responsible for such marvelous and breathtaking creativity? Genesis 1 tells us that God is the Creator of all these marvelous wonders.

A. Read the Bible Background and Devotional Readings.

B. Pray for your students and for lesson clarity.

C. Read the lesson Scripture in multiple translations.

D. Invite members of the class to bring nature pictures they have taken and work together to create a display that your faith community can enjoy. Provide opportunities for them to identify the images and explain how they affirm their faith in the Creator God. Suggest that they label the images with qualities and characteristics of God that the images reflect: strength, beauty, love, care, faithfulness, for example.

O—Open the Lesson

A. Begin the class with prayer.

B. Have the students read the Aim for Change.

C. Ask students how events in the story can weigh on their hearts and how they can view these events from a theological perspective.

D. Have students read the In Focus Story.

P—Present the Scriptures

A. Read the Focal Verses and discuss the Background and The People, Places, and Times sections.

B. Have the class share what Scriptures jump out for them and why, with particular emphasis on today's context.

E—Explore the Meaning

A. Use More Light on the Text to help stimulate in-depth discussion of the lesson text.

B. Discuss the Liberating Lesson and Application for Activation sections

N—Next Steps for Application

A. Summarize the value of knowing God as Sovereign Creator.

B. End class with a commitment to pray for families, natural resources, and scientists.

Worship Guide

For the Superintendent or Teacher
Theme: God Created the Heavens and Earth
Song: "Holy Holy Holy"
Devotional Reading: Psalm 33:1–9

God Created the Heavens and Earth

Bible Background • GENESIS 1:1–13
Printed Text • GENESIS 1:1–13 | Devotional Reading • PSALM 33:1–9

Aim for Change

By the end of the lesson, we will: ACKNOWLEDGE God as creator of the universe; APPRECIATE the created world; and ADMIRE the beauty of the heavens and the earth God created.

 **In Focus**

Alyse had always wanted to be a scientist. As a child, she would take her telescope outside with her father and look at the stars through it with wonder. Her father, a physicist, was part of her inspiration for pursuing natural science as a major in college. However, as she approached her senior year, she started having doubts about science after hearing a classmate say that he believed in science so he didn't believe in God. Alyse decided to talk to her dad about her dilemma. "How can you be a scientist and still believe in God, Dad?" she asked nervously.

Her father responded, "Alyse, science helps us understand our world, not give it meaning. I started doing physics because of my faith in God. I wanted to understand how this amazing world we live in works. I don't think that wondering and investigating how creation works bothers God. But at the end of the day, science is about asking questions and getting an understanding of what we see. It does not try to understand the meaning of life or the things that matter most to me, like the love I have for you and your mom. I have faith in God for those things."

Alyse was in awe. She decided that with her faith in God she could stay on her path to becoming a scientist and understanding God's creation.

What do you appreciate most about God's creation?

Keep in Mind

"In the beginning God created the heaven and the earth. And the earth was without form, and void; and darkness was upon the face of the deep. And the Spirit of God moved upon the face of the waters" (Genesis 1:1–2, KJV).

"In the beginning God created the heavens and the earth. The earth was formless and empty, and darkness covered the deep waters. And the Spirit of God was hovering over the surface of the waters" (Genesis 1:1-2, NLT).

Focal Verses

KJV Genesis 1:1 In the beginning God created the heaven and the earth.

2 And the earth was without form, and void; and darkness was upon the face of the deep. And the Spirit of God moved upon the face of the waters.

3 And God said, Let there be light: and there was light.

4 And God saw the light, that it was good: and God divided the light from the darkness.

5 And God called the light Day, and the darkness he called Night. And the evening and the morning were the first day.

6 And God said, Let there be a firmament in the midst of the waters, and let it divide the waters from the waters.

7 And God made the firmament, and divided the waters which were under the firmament from the waters which were above the firmament: and it was so.

8 And God called the firmament Heaven. And the evening and the morning were the second day.

9 And God said, Let the waters under the heaven be gathered together unto one place, and let the dry land appear: and it was so.

10 And God called the dry land Earth; and the gathering together of the waters called he Seas: and God saw that it was good.

11 And God said, Let the earth bring forth grass, the herb yielding seed, and the fruit tree yielding fruit after his kind, whose seed is in itself, upon the earth: and it was so.

12 And the earth brought forth grass, and herb yielding seed after his kind, and the tree yielding fruit, whose seed was in itself, after his kind: and God saw that it was good.

13 And the evening and the morning were the third day.

NLT Genesis 1:1 In the beginning God created the heavens and the earth.

2 The earth was formless and empty, and darkness covered the deep waters. And the Spirit of God was hovering over the surface of the waters.

3 Then God said, "Let there be light," and there was light.

4 And God saw that the light was good. Then he separated the light from the darkness.

5 God called the light "day" and the darkness "night." And evening passed and morning came, marking the first day.

6 Then God said, "Let there be a space between the waters, to separate the waters of the heavens from the waters of the earth."

7 And that is what happened. God made this space to separate the waters of the earth from the waters of the heavens.

8 God called the space "sky." And evening passed and morning came, marking the second day.

9 Then God said, "Let the waters beneath the sky flow together into one place, so dry ground may appear." And that is what happened.

10 God called the dry ground "land" and the waters "seas." And God saw that it was good.

11 Then God said, "Let the land sprout with vegetation—every sort of seed-bearing plant, and trees that grow seed-bearing fruit. These seeds will then produce the kinds of plants and trees from which they came." And that is what happened.

12 The land produced vegetation—all sorts of seed-bearing plants, and trees with seed-bearing fruit. Their seeds produced plants and trees of the same kind. And God saw that it was good.

13 And evening passed and morning came, marking the third day.

The People, Places, and Times

Creation. The act of God by which the universe came into being is Creation. The Bible's chief account of Creation is Genesis 1:1–2:3. Instead of divine combat and struggle with a willful prehistoric force as other ancient cultures believed, Genesis tells of the sole, sovereign Master of the universe directing the work of Creation by verbal command. God is shown here making the world in six days and resting on the seventh. Bible scholars differ on whether the "days" were 24-hour days or longer periods.

Background

Genesis is the first book in the Bible, the first book in what is called the Torah, or Law, for the Jewish people. Genesis sets the foundation for understanding the rest of the Scriptures. In Genesis 1, we see the power of God as Creator of the universe who creates from nothing, bringing order to the chaos of nothingness. God exists apart from creation as God alone, not marked by time, space, or any other measurement. God is self-existent, all-powerful, and eternal. God also establishes cycles and patterns that make up nature and assigns the functions of each aspect of creation, from time to growth. Through creation, God shows that He is both orderly and creative. It is important to know that God calls not only creation itself good but also the relationships He establishes for the created order. The goodness and order of these relationships in the created world are challenged by the introduction of sin into the world.

Is there a story of how something started that has particularly affected you?

At-A-Glance

1. God is Creator (Genesis 1:1–2)
2. God Creates Light (vv. 3–5)
3. God Creates Heaven (vv. 6–8)
4. God Creates Earth (vv. 9–13)

In Depth

1. God is Creator (Genesis 1:1–2)

God exists in eternity beyond time and space (Isaiah 57:15). God is eternal and limitless, but the book of Genesis begins with the account of Creation. God creates all that exists in the visible world, the heavens and the earth. The beginning here is the start of history, as eternity does not have a beginning or ending. God has not entered Creation, time, or space, but is acting on it by creating at this point in the story. God is Spirit and is the source of everything. God created the world and goes through the process of bringing order to it. This account of Creation in Genesis helps us know that God is the one who has created everything, and the one who can bring order to formless chaos. The earth was undifferentiated nothingness, as the Scripture says "without form, and void" (from v. 2). God is also revealed here as Spirit. God is not a created being, but Creator of the universe by God's Spirit. The Spirit of God moved in darkness before speaking light into manifestation in verse 3.

What impact does knowing about God's creativity have on your own understanding of creativity?

2. God Creates Light (vv. 3–5)

God speaks creation into existence. The power of God's Word is that whatever God commands must be. God speaks and creation obeys. The first thing God speaks into the visible world is light. We know from science that nothing is visible to human eyes without light.

God creates light and calls the light good; God is pleased with His creation. Then God separates light from darkness and gives them names, Day and Night, and purpose. Everything that God creates has a purpose because God gives purpose to it. God creates the cycle of night and day to define how time will be viewed on earth.

What roles have light and darkness played in your life?

3. God Creates Heaven (vv. 6–8)

God speaks heaven into existence as a firmament or barrier. The word for heaven here refers to the space between the ground and the upper atmosphere, what we would typically call the sky, but also could mean more than that. The sky separates the earth and its waters from waters in earth's upper atmosphere and the vast expanse of space beyond it. This continues God's pattern of creating and establishing order, creating boundaries between things in the created world so that the world can exist in established relationships instead of jumbled chaos.

How can natural boundaries be seen as good on the earth?

4. God Creates Earth (vv. 9–13)

In earth-shaking fashion, God calls the waters on the earth together—and the land up from the waters. God gives them purpose by naming them seas and earth and calling them and their relationship with one another good. God's creative intentionality is on full display. Then, God creates plant life; He calls it to grow out of the earth and gives each plant the ability to reproduce by using its seed. Each plant produces according to its own kind; that is to say an orange tree produces oranges instead of apples. There is intentional diversity in God's creation. Not every plant is the same, but they all reproduce according to their species. God once again calls these creations and their relationships with the rest of the earth good.

How does knowing that God created diversity influence what we think of as differences in life?

Search the Scriptures

1. Why do you think the Scripture keeps repeating the phrase "God saw that it was good," after God creates each part of the universe (Genesis 1:4, 10, 12)?

2. Why do you think God calls plants to grow out of the earth instead of simply speaking them into existence (v. 11)?

Discuss the Meaning

1. God creates by speaking everything into existence. What impact does that have on how we view the power of God's Word?

2. How do you reconcile your understanding of science with your faith as a Christian? Do you believe in any aspects of evolution? Why, or why not?

Liberating Lesson

The Bible makes it clear that God is the Creator of the universe. God not only is the source of everything created, but He gives everything purpose and function. Yet God is distinctive in making different parts of creation unique, even allowing the earth to bring forth plants that naturally reproduce. God is purposeful and intentional in establishing diversity and boundaries in nature. As a result of the perfect wisdom of God, the visible world has good relationships between all created things despite their differences. We can observe this and conclude that we as humans should also value and appreciate the purpose of all things in nature from plants to animals, day and night, and water and land. We can also use God's example of setting boundaries in our lives as perhaps good for us.

Application for Activation

Pause a moment to take in nature. Go for a walk, look at the sky, tend to a garden. Be intentional this week about engaging the natural world and thanking God for creation. Understand that God is the source of your life; everything that exists gives important meaning to what you can experience with your senses—sight, sound, smell, taste, and touch.

Reflect on beginnings. What good is there in the beginning of something in your life? How can you work with people in your community to begin something new for everyone's benefit, such as a community garden? How can you show your appreciation for God's goodness in nature?

Follow the Spirit

What God wants me to do:

_____

_____

_____

_____

Remember Your Thoughts

Special insights I have learned:

_____

_____

_____

_____

More Light on the Text

Genesis 1:1–13

1 In the beginning God created the heaven and the earth. 2 And the earth was without form, and void; and darkness was upon the face of the deep. And the Spirit of God moved upon the face of the waters.

The opening statement of the Bible declares, "In the beginning God created the heaven and the earth." There are a few important embedded assumptions in this statement that are foundational to the Christian understanding of the universe. The first assumption is that "the beginning" here speaks to the beginning of history, the start of time. God exists in eternity beyond time. God does not have a beginning or end, God simply is. The beginning here gives context to the account of God creating the universe that follows. This beginning is the edge of human understanding that looks forward toward Creation; and the other side of the beginning looks backward, prior to human history, into the expanse of eternity mentioned in John 1:1: "In the beginning was the Word..."

The word for God here in Genesis is the Hebrew word *Elohim*, which is plural, which many Christian scholars argue is a revelation of God as Triune (Father, Son, and Holy Spirit).

The word "created" here is the Hebrew *bara'* (**bah-RAH**), which communicates God being the source of Creation. This statement reveals the position of God as creator and an attribute of God as creative. The Bible contends that God is responsible for the existence of the heavens and the earth. It did not happen by accident or without intention. God created the universe on purpose. The opening statement of Genesis gives context for the story that follows; this is a story about God in relationship with heaven and earth.

The Bible assumes God exists; it is not a matter of debate or uncertainty: It is a given. Prior to the Enlightenment in 18th century Europe, this was an assumption that almost every culture in human history shared. Until the 20th century, there was no significant atheism that denied the existence of God. We understand, as believers, that without God nothing exists. Without the decision of faith that God exists the rest of the Scriptures cannot be understood and the relationship that we have with God is incomprehensible. It is impossible to please God, let alone communicate or have right relationship with God, without this foundational assumption of God's existence (Hebrews 11:6). This is the departure point for atheists: If one does not acknowledge the existence of God, then they cannot easily relate to God. In an increasingly secular, pluralistic society, Christians must know it is a faith decision to believe in God. God exists, and everything else flows from God's existence. If God exists, it does not matter if humans believe in God or not, or if they question God. They are still subject to God because He created everything and transcends humanity (Job 38).

In Genesis 1:2, we are told Creation was "without form, and void," which conveys the truth of the Earth being in an early stage of chaos. The text presents the Creation as undifferentiated and disordered. The Creation is not yet capable of producing life. The text goes on to report the gradual unfolding and development of the Creation. The Spirit "moved" This is the first reference to the Spirit of God in the Bible. The term for spirit, *ruakh* (**ROO-akh**), also translated as "wind or breath," can be thought of as something like moving air. In this instance, the Spirit of God is present and ready to bring order to the formless Creation and to prepare the earth for habitation.

The implications of this verse in our modern context are remarkable. Many people debate whether there is a gap in time between verse 1 and verse 2 because it moves from creation to chaos that is reorganized. Some then contend that this is a re-creation in verse 2. The text itself does not worry about such a possibility. God created ex nihilo or from nothing.

Some Christian apologists argue that this verse leaves room for evolution, that God creating would manifest as the evolutionary process: from nothingness taking form into somethingness as God speaks. Scientists are consistently astounded by the extreme circumstances that had to be fulfilled for our universe to exist as we know it—trillions of variables that had to act together in specific ways for the universe to function the way it does. The Scripture however is simply advancing the account of God and Creation. The account reveals another function of God: to bring order to chaos.

3 And God said, Let there be light: and there was light. 4 And God saw the light, that it was good: and God divided the light from the darkness. 5 And God called the light Day, and the darkness he called Night. And the evening and the morning were the first day.

Just the word "light," translating the common Hebrew word *'or* (**ORE**), implies God, because He Himself is Light (1 John 1:5). Today we know human, plant, and animal life are all impossible without light. He spoke every aspect of known visible light into being, and it was so. What God commands, happens (Psalm 33:9). This sets a precedent for the power of the Word of God that is carried out through the rest of Scripture. All that exists came into existence by the spoken word of God (Hebrews 11:3).

It is also important to note that in Genesis 1, God creates by differentiating. God establishes order and right relationships by creating boundaries, an action of God that plays a major role in much of Bible. Boundaries and order are good; in creation they create right relationships between things. God separates light from darkness, day from night, and brings order to the chaos.

"Darkness" is from the Hebrew word *khoshek* (**kho-SHEK**). Though some contend that darkness always represents evil, at Creation God takes the darkness that covered the formless void and calls it "night" (Heb. *layil*, **LAH-yil**). Today, we know sleep is a vital part of life; humans not only need sleep but the rest of creation requires regular rest cycles as well. The absence of balanced light and darkness cycles is a major cause of seasonal affective disorder (SAD), and light therapy is often used to treat it and other forms of seasonal depression. The light and darkness forms day and night. God continues to differentiate His creation and assign specific functions. He created for His world "morning" and "evening." The combined cycle creates the very first complete "day" or *yom* (Heb. **YOME**), a word that contains a concept of time.

The debate is hot over the use of the word "day" in Genesis 1. Depending upon the context, it may mean what we conventionally understand to be a 24-hour period, or it may refer to an epoch or a period of time. God's perspective on time is not the same as a human perspective; a day to God could be thousands of years to humanity (2 Peter 3:8). In this text, it certainly refers to God's decision to act within a certain time frame. God dwells in eternity but acts in history for the sake of Creation. With that in mind, we must think of the text as indicating that God created within a particular frame of time, which could have been seven days, epochs, or periods of work. The seventh "day" was designated as rest (Exodus 31:15). Whichever it was, we must remember that the aim of the text is to tell us that the one true God created everything, not to determine when He performed this act.

The order of the day/night cycle here can be easily overlooked: first evening and then morning. The view of night as the beginning of a day continues throughout the Bible. The night to day cycle of counting days is reflected in the development of Israel's calendar and that of other nearby cultures that were organized on a lunar calendar. One implication of this cycle is daily hope; the darkness will always give way to the light within the same day (cf. Psalm 30:5). Creation moves from darkness to light.

6 And God said, Let there be a firmament in the midst of the waters, and let it divide the waters from the waters. 7 And God made the firmament, and divided the waters which were under the firmament from the waters which were above the firmament: and it was so. 8 And God called the firmament Heaven. And the evening and the morning were the second day.

At this stage of Creation, the waters separate, apparently making the distinction between liquid and vapor forms, and the atmosphere as we know it is called into existence. "Firmament" (Heb. *raqiya'*, **rah-KEE-ah**) is used only seventeen times in the Old Testament. Although the word can refer to where birds fly (Genesis 1:20), it usually refers to more than air. It is used as being "heavenly" in Psalm 150:1: "Praise ye the LORD. Praise God in his sanctuary: praise him in the firmament of his power."

Reinforcing these uses of *raqiya'*, God called the atmosphere "heaven" (Heb. *shamayim*, **shaw-MAH-yim**), a word that is used 420 times in the Bible. Although "Heaven" is most often used like "firmament" to refer to God's abode or a divine place beyond Earth (Genesis 22:15; Psalm 8:1; Psalm 11:4), *shamayim* is also a place where birds fly (Genesis 7:3; Job 35:11) and clouds can be seen (Job 38:37).

9 And God said, Let the waters under the heaven be gathered together unto one place, and let the dry land appear: and it was so. 10 And God called the dry land Earth; and the gathering together of the waters called he Seas: and God saw that it was good. 11 And God said, Let the earth bring forth

grass, the herb yielding seed, and the fruit tree yielding fruit after his kind, whose seed is in itself, upon the earth: and it was so. 12 And the earth brought forth grass, and herb yielding seed after his kind, and the tree yielding fruit, whose seed was in itself, after his kind: and God saw that it was good. 13 And the evening and the morning were the third day.

One might think of "gathering together" as implying an orderly, even gentle act. However, the thought of the oceans of the world being gathered, while at the same time being separated from dry land, doesn't necessarily evoke the image of a gentle act. Rather, it brings to mind a violent, explosive, even volcanic act of giant mountainous upheavals combined with equally deep gouging from the various waterways and bodies of water.

It is interesting to note that all the earth's vegetation wasn't created instantly but grew out of the soil. For all the water and dry land in the world to be sorted out in a day, the evolutionary timescale for wear and tear on rocks from water must have been radically increased. This could only have been done by God's power. "Brought forth" is from the Hebrew word *yatsa* (**yah-TSAH**), which has several meanings including "growing vegetation" (Psalm 104:14). It is not surprising that God could grow trees overnight or order land and soil into existence from a formless void. Verse 12 points out that growth is a purposeful part of God's creation. Although God could have simply spoken or created each type of plant life, God instead allows each to grow from the earth through reproduction. The herbs yield seed and the trees yield fruit after their kind. Each part of creation is created to reproduce itself; God sets in motion a cycle of reproduction, and calls it good. Seeds are the means by which God chooses to let creation multiply. Growth and multiplication are part of God's creation before and after the introduction of sin and death.

It is awesome that God declares the natural world He has created as good, and the relationships and cycles in the natural world good. Scripture highlights the order of nature as valuable even before humankind is introduced to creation: The universe and the earth have value to God on their own as good creations. The complex systems we know today that make up the natural world are extremely delicate yet function consistently in orderly cycles as God created them to do. The natural sciences—such as biology, astronomy, chemistry, and physics—are all designed to help humanity understand the wonderful world that God has created.

Sources:

Achtemeier, Paul J., ed. *Harper's Bible Dictionary.* New York: HarperCollins Publishers, 1985. 192–93, 377.

"Seasonal Affective Disorder," American Psychological Association. http://www.apa.org/helpcenter/seasonal-affective-disorder.aspx.

Say It Correctly

Firmament. **FUHR**-muh-ment.
Genesis. **JEH**-nuh-ses.

Daily Bible Readings

MONDAY
In Your Suffering Trust the Creator
(1 Peter 4:15–19)

TUESDAY
Renewed by the Creator
(Colossians 3:8–11)

WEDNESDAY
God Provides the Water
(Isaiah 41:17–20)

THURSDAY
The Wind and Water Obey Voice of Jesus
(Mark 4:35–41)

FRIDAY
God Sends the Rain to Everyone
(Matthew 5:43–48)

SATURDAY
God Is Great; God Is Good
(Psalm 33:1–9)

SUNDAY
God Created the Heavens and Earth
(Genesis 1:1–13)

Notes

Teaching Tips

September 9
Bible Study Guide 2

Words You Should Know

A. Heaven *shamayim* (Heb.)—The place of stars, sun, and moon, and of the birds, plus the abode of God.

B. Signs *'oth* (Heb.)—Omens or miraculous signs to people.

Teacher Preparation

Unifying Principle—Turn On the Lights! People's life experiences sometimes lead them to question whether the universe is ordered or unpredictably chaotic. How do the diverse parts of nature work together? Genesis 1 shares that God brought order to the universe He made—establishing the heavenly bodies and filling the sea, sky, and land with diverse and abundant life.

A. Read the Bible Background and Devotional Readings.

B. Pray for your students and lesson clarity.

C. Read the lesson Scripture in multiple translations.

D. Option: Brainstorm a list of reasons to support God's declaration that creation was "good."

O—Open the Lesson

A. Begin the class with prayer.

B. Have the students read the Aim for Change.

C. Have the students read the In Focus story.

D. Ask students how events that occur in the story can weigh on their hearts and how they can view these events from a theological perspective.

P—Present the Scriptures

A. Read the Focal Verses and discuss the Background and The People, Places, and Times sections.

B. Have the class share what Scriptures jump out for them and why, with particular emphasis on today's context.

E—Explore the Meaning

A. Use More Light on the Text to help provide more in-depth discussion of the lesson text.

B. Discuss the Liberating Lesson and Application for Activation sections.

N—Next Steps for Application

A. Summarize the value of knowing God as Sovereign Creator.

B. End class with a commitment to pray for families, natural resources, and scientists.

Worship Guide

For the Superintendent or Teacher
Theme: God Created Plants and Animals
Song: "So Will I"
Devotional Reading: Psalm 136:1–9

God Created Plants and Animals

Bible Background • GENESIS 1:14–25
Printed Text • GENESIS 1:14–25 | Devotional Reading • PSALM 136:1–9

—————————— Aim for Change ——————————

By the end of the lesson, we will: EXPLORE the Bible's description of God creating light and life; CONSIDER the order and connection of all of God's creation; and RECOGNIZE the diversity and breadth of God's creation.

 In Focus

Felicia tucked her granddaughter Ayesha into her bed. As usual, Ayesha had a question to delay bedtime. "G-ma, why does it get dark outside?"

Felicia hesitated for a second. "Well, the sun goes down, and we have to rest."

Ayesha looked puzzled. "But G-ma, we still stay up after the sun goes down. The new baby stays up after it has been dark for a long time!"

Felicia responded, "Yes, that's true, but everything that lives has to rest sometime. The birds outside, the class hamster at your at daycare, even your little brother. He sleeps during the day when you're learning and your mom is at work. Although you're right. I wish he slept more at night!" They giggled. Felicia explained further, "God created both night and day. We can learn and work and play during the day, but at night we can rest just like all the other creatures."

"Does that mean I have to go to sleep?" Ayesha asked.

"Yes, baby. You are God's creation, too. And you also have to sleep sometime. But before you to sleep, let me show you one of my favorite things about the night." Felicia pulled back the curtain from the window by Ayesha's bed. "Look at the moon and stars from your window. See how bright and beautiful they are!"

Why do you think God creates a separation between day and night? Is it important? Why or why not?

—————————— Keep in Mind ——————————

"And God said, Let there be lights in the firmament of the heaven to divide the day from the night; and let them be for signs, and for seasons, and for days, and years" (Genesis 1:14, KJV).

"Then God said, "Let lights appear in the sky to separate the day from the night. Let them be signs to mark the seasons, days, and years" (Genesis 1:14, NLT).

Focal Verses

KJV **Genesis 1:14** And God said, Let there be lights in the firmament of the heaven to divide the day from the night; and let them be for signs, and for seasons, and for days, and years:

15 And let them be for lights in the firmament of the heaven to give light upon the earth: and it was so.

16 And God made two great lights; the greater light to rule the day, and the lesser light to rule the night: he made the stars also.

17 And God set them in the firmament of the heaven to give light upon the earth,

18 And to rule over the day and over the night, and to divide the light from the darkness: and God saw that it was good.

19 And the evening and the morning were the fourth day.

20 And God said, Let the waters bring forth abundantly the moving creature that hath life, and fowl that may fly above the earth in the open firmament of heaven.

21 And God created great whales, and every living creature that moveth, which the waters brought forth abundantly, after their kind, and every winged fowl after his kind: and God saw that it was good.

22 And God blessed them, saying, Be fruitful, and multiply, and fill the waters in the seas, and let fowl multiply in the earth.

23 And the evening and the morning were the fifth day.

24 And God said, Let the earth bring forth the living creature after his kind, cattle, and creeping thing, and beast of the earth after his kind: and it was so.

25 And God made the beast of the earth after his kind, and cattle after their kind, and every thing that creepeth upon the earth after his kind: and God saw that it was good.

NLT **Genesis 1:14** Then God said, "Let lights appear in the sky to separate the day from the night. Let them be signs to mark the seasons, days, and years.

15 Let these lights in the sky shine down on the earth." And that is what happened.

16 God made two great lights—the larger one to govern the day, and the smaller one to govern the night. He also made the stars.

17 God set these lights in the sky to light the earth,

18 to govern the day and night, and to separate the light from the darkness. And God saw that it was good.

19 And evening passed and morning came, marking the fourth day.

20 Then God said, "Let the waters swarm with fish and other life. Let the skies be filled with birds of every kind."

21 So God created great sea creatures and every living thing that scurries and swarms in the water, and every sort of bird—each producing offspring of the same kind. And God saw that it was good.

22 Then God blessed them, saying, "Be fruitful and multiply. Let the fish fill the seas, and let the birds multiply on the earth."

23 And evening passed and morning came, marking the fifth day.

24 Then God said, "Let the earth produce every sort of animal, each producing offspring of the same kind—livestock, small animals that scurry along the ground, and wild animals." And that is what happened.

25 God made all sorts of wild animals, livestock, and small animals, each able to produce offspring of the same kind. And God saw that it was good.

The People, Places, and Times

Heaven. In the ancient Near Eastern understanding of the world, Heaven referred to the firmament, or the massive transparent dome that covers the earth. The blue color of the sky was attributed to the chaotic waters that the firmament separated from the earth (Genesis 1:7). The earth was thus surrounded by "waters" above and below (Deuteronomy 5:8). The firmament was thought to be substantial; when the windows of the firmament were opened, rain fell (Genesis 7:11–12). In Hebrew, the word for "heaven" is always plural. Similarly, the Greek word for "heaven" in the New Testament also frequently appears in the plural. The use of the plural probably does not mean that the ancient Hebrews conceived of more than one heaven. Heaven is the place of the stars, sun, moon, and birds. It is also the abode of God (Deuteronomy 26:15) and where God is enthroned (Psalm 11:4).

Background

Genesis is the first book in the Bible, the first book in what is called the Torah or Law for the Jewish people. After narrating the radical separation of light from darkness, heavens from earth, and earth from the seas, Genesis 1 continues with God's creation of living things and the celestial bodies that we see every day and night. The action in the chapter accelerates upward, as God works from the non-living to the living, scaling the ladder of existence from the Earth itself to the soul/body hybrid of humanity. God is always asserting His own authority over the things and people that He creates. The weight of these claims is truly felt when one recognizes that the text is written not only for Israelites (and Christians) seeking to understand their own history, but distinguishes it from ancient Near Eastern and African religions, in which the sun, moon, stars, and animals were seen as gods themselves. Most important in these verses is the constant reminder of the power, sovereignty, and authority of God the Creator. The delineation of days exhibits God's orderly work, and the sheer scope of this work ought to fill the reader with awe. What a mighty God we serve, who can create the multifaceted universe that we sense and experience daily and who continues to sustain not only its natural processes but us! When this is the picture of God at the forefront of our minds, it is obvious that all that God created is rightfully subordinated to Him.

Is there anything that tempts you to believe that it is more powerful than God? Does Scripture suggest otherwise?

At-A-Glance

1. The Creation of Celestial Bodies (Genesis 1:14–19)
2. The Creation of Sea Creatures (vv. 20–23)
3. The Creation of Land Creatures (vv. 24–25)

In Depth

1. God Creates the Celestial Bodies (Genesis 1:14–19)

God speaks the sun, the moon, and the stars into existence, specifically for the telling of time. When one remembers that the sun is so huge that more than 1.3 million Earths could fit inside of it and that staring into it can quickly damage one's eyes, it is no surprise that many cultures throughout human history have attributed supernatural power to the sun. But Genesis tells us that each of these great bodies is created for the good of the rest of creation, specifically humans, the only ones to whom days, years, signs, and seasons each have lasting and significant meaning. Notable in this text is the fact that the sun and moon are not even named, instead referred to as the greater and lesser lights. This characterization further emphasizes that though these great bodies in the sky appear physically imposing, they were created by God for His glory and for our good—not as powerful apart from God.

In what situation in your life was it difficult to see how God could possibly work things out for His glory and your good?

2. The Creation of Sea Creatures (vv. 20–23)

God continues with His creation by calling forth sea creatures and birds. The objects of Day 5 of Creation are the first to be blessed and commanded. Here we see a hint that this is the beginning of history where creatures are concerned, as God does not fill the Earth instantly but rather commands and enables His animal creations to partner with Him in that work. God, by His power, infuses them with life and the means to reproduce according to their kind, or species.

God also creates "the great whales," or sea monsters, a staple of ancient mythology that are often depicted as at odds with the gods. Instead, there is no competition here. Power lies firmly in the hands of the Creator.

What are the "sea monsters" of our culture— things that war with God for control of the lives of those around us?

3. The Creation of Land Creatures (vv. 24–25)

Day 6 is the last day of creation and the climax of it. On this day, God creates the beasts of the field in the same manner that He created the birds and reptiles. His command here is not to the sea, however, but to the earth, commanding it to produce life, a work that is only possible through the matchless power of the Word of God. We know through experience and experimentation that death and non-life do not naturally produce life, so it may appear as though God is commanding the impossible. But that ignores the sheer creative power

of the Word of God, which commands and, by virtue of that command, makes things so. The combination of that command to the Earth and the term "beast of the earth" show us that what may appear to be animals coming up from the dirt is truly a miracle wrought by a magnificent God.

Are there any elements of your life that have grown routine but, upon further examination, are actually miraculous works of God?

Search the Scriptures

1. Why do you think the stars get so little attention in the text? How does that relate to a Christian understanding of astrology?

2. What do you think it meant for God to "bless" the animals, keeping in mind He did not bless inanimate objects nor plants?

Discuss the Meaning

1. What impact does God calling animals forth from the earth have on how we perceive the natural world?

2. How does our belief in God as Creator of the material universe—plants, trees, birds, and animals—affect our attitudes toward the preservation of our forests and endangered species?

Liberating Lesson

God created the universe not out of any loneliness or necessity, but rather as a display of His power and grace. Such principles extend to His creation of living things. We must not forget that no matter how physically imposing His creation may be—whether we consider the vastness of space, the depths of the ocean, the immensity of a blue whale, or the ferocity of a lion—there is one who is above and in control of all of them. This logic applies to the intricacies of our life situations. We are tempted daily to look to creation for comfort and stability instead of the Creator who gave those things the life and influence they exert. Let our view of Creation constantly lead our thoughts and gaze upward to God, the Eternal Craftsman.

Application for Activation

When you see the birds of the air, reptiles, or other animals, thank God for His creation and for the joys of life. Remember that the world around you is not a random, naturalistic combination of pre-existent matter but rather the meticulous work of a loving, sovereign God. Let the taste of a good meal, the joy and beauty of a sunrise or sunset, and the aroma of a sweet-smelling bouquet conduct your joy upward to the God who created them and to Christ, who died so that your joy might be full. As we look forward to the new heaven and new earth, we must remember that it will not be merely a spiritual reality but an embodied one. Take time this week to enjoy something in nature, and consider how it glorifies God. Let each day be filled with joy and gratitude that God would adorn His creation with such splendid glory.

Follow the Spirit

What God wants me to do:

_____

_____

_____

_____

Remember Your Thoughts

Special insights I have learned:

_____

_____

_____

More Light on the Text

Genesis 1:14–25

14 And God said, Let there be lights in the firmament of the heaven to divide the day from the night; and let them be for signs, and for seasons, and for days, and years: 15 And let them be for lights in the firmament of the heaven to give light upon the earth: and it was so. 16 And God made two great lights; the greater light to rule the day, and the lesser light to rule the night: he made the stars also. 17 And God set them in the firmament of the heaven to give light upon the earth, 18 And to rule over the day and over the night, and to divide the light from the darkness: and God saw that it was good. 19 And the evening and the morning were the fourth day.

Although man didn't exist yet, God knew for whom His creation was planned, and He knew man would need not just the abundant and self-replicating supply of nourishment that he provided on Day 3, but also the sun, moon, and stars to give us light and help us keep track of time. These lights are given for three purposes: signs, seasons, and days/years. Signs (Heb. 'oth, OATH) means that God would sometimes use the lights to give miraculous signs or omens to people. There are many examples of this throughout the Old and New Testament: the plague of darkness in Egypt (Exodus 10:21), the sun standing still (Joshua 10:12–13), Magi's star over Bethlehem (Matthew 2:9), the darkness at the Crucifixion (Matthew 27:45). "Seasons" refers not so much to the four seasons we recognize today but to agricultural growing seasons, essential knowledge for agrarian societies. "Days and years" refers to using the sun, moon, and stars to calculate a calendar, essential for all societies to plan and function beyond a daily routine.

The creation of the sun, moon, and stars visible from Earth to specifically delight humanity and serve its needs continues the purposeful progression of God's custom-designed habitat for humanity. In the ancient context, other religions viewed the sun and moon as deities, but here they are objects designed by God to serve humanity. This can be viewed in direct contrast to other religions that speak robustly about stars in their astrology. In the biblical account of Creation, stars are a small but important component. God knew humans (whom He had not created yet) would need to keep track of time and be able to navigate the Earth. Having already created light, He made these particular elements of created light appear in the sky (the "firmament of heaven") and begin their appointed tasks (vv. 16–18).

It is interesting to note that the sun, moon, and stars appeared after God created light.

20 And God said, Let the waters bring forth abundantly the moving creature that hath life, and fowl that may fly above the earth in the open firmament of heaven.

Now that the structure of our habitat was complete, it was time for it to be occupied. By divine design the entire variety of both air and sea creatures came into being as complete, living, and unique organisms. This use of "firmament" (Heb. *raqiya'*, **raw-KEY-ah**) underscores the use of the atmosphere as a place for birds to fly. In His wisdom, God not only provided for our initial and future needs, but also for the needs of all the creatures intended for an environment of sustainable survival and enjoyment.

21 And God created great whales, and every living creature that moveth, which the waters brought forth abundantly, after their kind, and every winged fowl after his kind: and God saw that it was good. 22 And God blessed them, saying, Be fruitful, and multiply, and fill the waters in the seas, and let fowl multiply in the earth. 23 And the evening and the morning were the fifth day.

Not only did God fill the earth's waters and skies with life, but by a separate command He caused them to procreate. Just as He knew humanity would need the earth's grain and fruit for nutrients and need to keep track of time, God also desired animals to be a productive part of the divinely ordered ecosystem.

The use of the Hebrew word translated "whales" (*tannim*, **tan-NEEM**) says much about who God is and His place over His creation. Elsewhere this word is translated "dragons" or "sea monsters"; they are dangerous, powerful, and live in desolate places (Deuteronomy 32:33; Isaiah 34:13; Ezekiel 29:3). However, the reader of this text can see that God is more powerful than such a monster because He is the one who created it. Even creatures that seem only to cause destruction and disorder are under God's authority and worship Him (Psalm 148:7).

God's blessing was significant because it was His first. His second blessing would be on the first human male and female (Genesis 1:28)— also before a command to procreate. An almost duplicate blessing with the same procreative context would be bestowed on Noah and his family when they were told to replenish the population of the earth after the Flood (9:1, 7).

24 And God said, Let the earth bring forth the living creature after his kind, cattle, and creeping thing, and beast of the earth after his kind: and it was so. 25 And God made the beast of the earth after his kind, and cattle after their kind, and every thing that creepeth upon the earth after his kind: and God saw that it was good.

From the Creation account, we see that God planned from the beginning for all natural life to be productive and sustainable. There were no recalls to redesign or reinvent; from the beginning God planned everything with perfection. There is again order and pattern, God created each type of animal for intentional diversity and with the ability to live and thrive in its environment. God declared land animals to be good.

"Good" (Heb. *tov*, **TOVE**) in regards to animal life also includes the meaning "satisfactory" or "delicious" as in food (Genesis 41:22). Prior to the fall of man and the Flood, humans didn't eat meat (Genesis 1:28–30). After the Fall, however, everything changed, and God actually ordained meat as food. Immediately after blessing Noah and telling him to replenish the earth's population, God said in Genesis 9:3: "Every moving thing that liveth shall be meat for you" (from Genesis 9:3). The only injunction at the time was not to eat meat with lifeblood still in it (v. 4). (More rules were to come, but never again was meat banned from humanity's diet.) Although there are exceptions and everyone has individual tastes, by far the majority of food from plant and animal sources created by God is not only nutritious and necessary, but pleasurable to eat.

God was satisfied with His creation. What a loving and thoughtful God we serve! Indeed, all that God does is good!

Sources:
Achtemeier, Paul J., ed. *Harper's Bible Dictionary.* New York: HarperCollins Publishers, 1985. 192–93, 377.
Johnson, Ashley S. "Creation." *Condensed Biblical Cyclopedia, Blue Letter Bible,* July 1, 2002. http://blueletterbible.org/study/cbc/cbc01.html
Ryrie, Charles C. *Ryrie NIV Study Bible.* Chicago. IL: Moody Press, 1984. 7, 8.

Daily Bible Readings

MONDAY
Creation, Testament of God's Steadfast Love
(Psalm 136:1–9)

TUESDAY
Jesus, Agent of God's Creation
(Hebrews 1:1–4)

WEDNESDAY
All Creatures Depend on God
(Psalm 104:24–30)

THURSDAY
Plants Witness to the Lord's Work
(Job 12:7–13)

FRIDAY
Gifts from the Father of Lights
(James 1:17–18)

SATURDAY
God Makes All Creatures Clean
(Acts 11:5–9)

SUNDAY
God Created Heavenly Lights and Animals
(Genesis 1:14–25)

Teaching Tips

Words You Should Know

A. Likeness *demut* (Heb.)—Resemblance, fashion, or being similar to.

B. Dominion *radah* (Heb.)—To rule or prevail against.

Teacher Preparation

Unifying Principle—Creation is a Very Good Thing. How the world and humans came to be is explored and questioned by many people. Where did people come from? According to Genesis, God created people as the highest form of creation made in the image of God and people are supported by all of God's creation.

A. Read the Bible Background and Devotional Readings.

B. Pray for your students and lesson clarity.

C. Read the lesson Scripture in multiple translations.

D. Option: Compare and contrast the concepts of "dominion" and "domination." What are the differences? Why are these differences important in our relationships with the rest of creation, especially in human relationships?

E. Option: Select and review hymns that testify to God's good Creation.

O—Open the Lesson

A. Begin the class with prayer.

B. Have the students read the Aim for Change.

C. Have the students read the In Focus story.

D. Ask students how events named in the story can weigh on their hearts and how they can view these events from a theological perspective.

P—Present the Scriptures

A. Read the Focal Verses and discuss the Background and The People, Places, and Times sections.

B. Have the class share which Scriptures stand out for them and why, with particular emphasis on today's context.

E—Explore the Meaning

A. Use In Depth or More Light on the Text to help provide more in-depth discussion of the lesson text.

B. Discuss the Liberating Lesson and Application for Activation sections.

N—Next Steps for Application

A. Summarize the value of knowing God created humanity to steward the earth.

B. End class with a commitment to pray for families, animals, and godly relationships.

Worship Guide

For the Superintendent or Teacher
Theme: God Created People
Song: "I Need You to Breathe"
Devotional Reading: Psalm 103:1–5, 11–14

God Created People

Bible Background • GENESIS 1:26–2:7
Printed Text • GENESIS 1:26–31; 2:4–7 | Devotional Reading • PSALM 103:1–5, 11–14

———— Aim for Change ————

By the end of the lesson, we will: EXAMINE God's role for humanity in the created world; EVALUATE ourselves and others as part of God's creation; and REFLECT on our role as stewards in God's creation.

———— In Focus ————

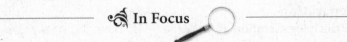

Michael knew his entire life that one day he would have to take over his dad's business. Chapman Contracting Services had helped people fix, upgrade, and renovate their homes on the west side of the city for decades. People had come to expect that if something was going wrong, Mr. Chapman would know how to take care of it, and they were slow to trust outsiders with their home projects. When Michael was just a teenager, his dad told him someday the responsibility would be his to care for his community. Now that Michael Sr., the famous "Construction Chapman," had trouble seeing and walking, it was time for Michael Jr. to take over.

"Son, remember that this family business is an institution in this community. Most of these homes for six blocks have something in them that my hands installed. It's a big responsibility, but I know I raised you to represent the Chapman name well, and care for our community well. I believe God has blessed us for so long because we've been committed to this work and treating people right. Can you handle all that?"

"Dad, you didn't just tell me from the time I was thirteen I was made for this; you let me work with you once I was old enough to hold a hammer. I'm ready to take care of the community just like you did." Michael Sr. smiled; he knew his community and his legacy would be in good hands, the hands of his son whom he had raised for this responsibility. *What is our responsibility as creations made in God's image and likeness?*

———— Keep in Mind ————

"God created humankind in his image, in the image of God he created them; male and female he created them" (Genesis 1:27, KJV).

"So God created human beings in his own image. In the image of God he created them; male and female he created them." (Genesis 1:27, NLT).

Focal Verses

KJV

Genesis 1:26 And God said, Let us make man in our image, after our likeness: and let them have dominion over the fish of the sea, and over the fowl of the air, and over the cattle, and over all the earth, and over every creeping thing that creepeth upon the earth.

27 So God created man in his own image, in the image of God created he him; male and female created he them.

28 And God blessed them, and God said unto them, Be fruitful, and multiply, and replenish the earth, and subdue it: and have dominion over the fish of the sea, and over the fowl of the air, and over every living thing that moveth upon the earth.

29 And God said, Behold, I have given you every herb bearing seed, which is upon the face of all the earth, and every tree, in the which is the fruit of a tree yielding seed; to you it shall be for meat.

30 And to every beast of the earth, and to every fowl of the air, and to every thing that creepeth upon the earth, wherein there is life, I have given every green herb for meat: and it was so.

31 And God saw every thing that he had made, and, behold, it was very good. And the evening and the morning were the sixth day.

2:4 These are the generations of the heavens and of the earth when they were created, in the day that the LORD God made the earth and the heavens,

5 And every plant of the field before it was in the earth, and every herb of the field before it grew: for the LORD God had not caused it to rain upon the earth, and there was not a man to till the ground.

6 But there went up a mist from the earth, and watered the whole face of the ground.

NLT

Genesis 1:26 Then God said, "Let us make human beings in our image, to be like us. They will reign over the fish in the sea, the birds in the sky, the livestock, all the wild animals on the earth, and the small animals that scurry along the ground."

27 So God created human beings in his own image. In the image of God he created them; male and female he created them.

28 Then God blessed them and said, "Be fruitful and multiply. Fill the earth and govern it. Reign over the fish in the sea, the birds in the sky, and all the animals that scurry along the ground."

29 Then God said, "Look! I have given you every seed-bearing plant throughout the earth and all the fruit trees for your food.

30 And I have given every green plant as food for all the wild animals, the birds in the sky, and the small animals that scurry along the ground—everything that has life." And that is what happened.

31 Then God looked over all he had made, and he saw that it was very good! And evening passed and morning came, marking the sixth day.

2:4 This is the account of the creation of the heavens and the earth. When the LORD God made the earth and the heavens,

5 neither wild plants nor grains were growing on the earth. For the LORD God had not yet sent rain to water the earth, and there were no people to cultivate the soil.

6 Instead, springs came up from the ground and watered all the land.

7 Then the LORD God formed the man from the dust of the ground. He breathed the breath of life into the man's nostrils, and the man became a living person.

7 And the LORD God formed man of the dust of the ground, and breathed into his nostrils the breath of life; and man became a living soul.

The People, Places, and Times

Adam. In Genesis, God created man and woman in His image, separating them from the animals, to rule the earth. Yahweh (God) formed Adam from the earth, set him over the Garden of Eden, and allowed him to have dominion over everything God created.

Background

These verses display two complementary accounts of the creation of humankind. Scholars debate whether the two accounts are a combination of multiple accounts or authors, but such speculation obscures the text's purpose and the questions that it seeks to answer. To view these verses as a compilation rather than a unified work is to give too much credence to a hypothetical situation. Humankind, the pinnacle of God's creation, was created in God's image and likeness, a dignity corrupted but not eradicated by the Fall. The panoramic view of Genesis 1 comes to a sharp focus on the first human couple beginning in Genesis 2:4, lingering on God's meticulous shaping of His beloved vice-regents.

Here we see two complementary, not contradictory images of God. Genesis 1:1–2:3 reveals God to be transcendent, exerting His power and influence over the breadth of creation. Genesis 2:4 reveals God to be the immanent "God with us", who cares deeply about even the small details of human life. These twin descriptions point forward to the incarnate Jesus Christ, who in His human life also exhibited the power and influence worthy of His transcendent divinity. The same one born from the humanity of Mary controlled the weather, healed disease, and exorcised demons. One must not view God's transcendence and immanence as contradictory but as necessarily entwined. It is only as both transcendent and immanent that God both cares deeply about our problems and has the power to overcome them.

At-A-Glance

1. Mankind: Vice-Regents Over Creation (Genesis 1:26–31)
2. Mankind: Living Dirt (vv. 4–7)

In Depth

1. Mankind: Vice-Regents Over Creation (Genesis 1:26–31)

Here, God gives men and women dominion over the rest of creation. This is one of the meanings of the "image" and "likeness" of God in which we have been created. Theologians from the early church through the Reformation have debated whether "image" and "likeness" reveal different aspects of human destiny but they are two sides of the same coin. The author of Genesis means for us to know that humans were created to be like God. While God as creator is radically different from us creatures, our possession of moral abilities, mind, will, and spiritual desires makes it possible for us to pursue holiness, the core of who God is. The image and likeness of God are also integral components of human nature, meaning no one can reduce or remove that dignity from us. To attempt to do so is to deny the mandates of creation. Instead, we as human beings are commanded to care for one another and to exert loving authority over earthly creation.

God's final declaration of "very good" over His creation reminds us of the original goodness of mankind along with the rest of creation. This is a picture of complete perfection, harmony, and order, the Hebrew *shalom*. It remains the mandate to mankind to seek this harmony by the power of the Holy Spirit and in the name of Christ.

What does this Scripture tell us about our environmental responsibilities?

2. Mankind: Living Dirt (2: 4–7)

The second, more focused account of the creation of mankind adds detail to the bird's-eye view offered in Genesis 1. We are reminded that we owe every gift of our creation to God. We are also reminded of the humble nature of our material origin: the dirt of the ground. As in our redemption by the Cross, Creation preaches a dual message to humanity: We are creatures of both great dignity and great humility. As Christ died for us and proclaimed our worth, so we also remember our dignity as created in the image of God. But also as our sin provided the purpose of Christ's death, Genesis reminds us that we are of the earth. The text even engages in wordplay to remind us of the similarity between the words "man" (Heb. *adam*, **ah-DOM**) and the "ground" (Heb. *adamah*, **ah-dom-AH**) from which we are formed.

Are you tempted to think more highly of yourself or more lowly?

Search the Scriptures

1. Why do you think the second account of our creation outlines the forming of our bodies before the in-breathing of our soul/spirit?

2. In this creation story, what distinguishes humanity from the beginning?

Discuss the Meaning

1. What does it mean for us to be made in God's image and likeness?

2. How do we know what we are responsible for in our community and environment?

Liberating Lesson

American history has attempted to tell African Americans that they are not bearers of the image of God. From seventeenth- and eighteenth-century attempts to frame African Americans and whites as different species to current suggestions that African Americans are dangerous or unintelligent, the powers and principalities that we battle have attempted to deny African Americans the complicated, dignified, and humble humanity that God has bestowed upon all of us indiscriminately. These attempts, however, whether they were as brutal as lynching or as subtle as the mis-education of students, cannot reduce or diminish what God has declared. Integral to the Good News of Jesus Christ is a leveling of humanity: All have sinned and all are in need of a Savior. There is no distinction. Similarly, within the body of Christ, these distinctions fade in the light of our union with Christ and with each other in Christ.

Application for Activation

In your daily life, whether it is work, school, or some other endeavor, make an effort to treat everyone you meet with the dignity that they deserve. As you make personal or even political decisions, remember that you do so not only for your own good but for the good of the diverse body of Christ. Consider how you can pray that God's glory would be exhibited through the many human vessels around you, including yourself. Interrogate your own assumptions about groups of people: If you think that some groups of people are less intelligent than others, less susceptible to the Gospel than others, or inferior in any other way, you are implicitly denying them the dignity of the image of God. Instead, look to the second greatest commandment: Love your neighbor as yourself.

Follow the Spirit

What God wants me to do:

_____

_____

_____

_____

Remember Your Thoughts

Special insights I have learned:

_____

_____

_____

_____

More Light on the Text

Genesis 1:26–31, 2:4–7

26 And God said, Let us make man in our image, after our likeness: and let them have dominion over the fish of the sea, and over the fowl of the air, and over the cattle, and over all the earth, and over every creeping thing that creepeth upon the earth.

Day 6 was the pinnacle of God's creation in that humanity was created, which is the setting for verse 26. There has been much scholarly debate regarding the plural language God used here (e.g., "let us," "our image," "our likeness").

Some scholars believe the language refers to God consulting with other divine beings (e.g., the angels), meaning those who are not God were called to participate in the act of creation. Other scholars suggest the plural language refers to the majesty, attributes, and powers within the Godhead (the Father, Son, and Holy Spirit); God was addressing His Spirit, who was present and active at the beginning of creation (Genesis 1:2).

The Hebrew word for "image" is *tselem* (**TSEH-lem**), which appears only seventeen times in the Bible. Ten times it refers to various types of physical images or idols, which leads to better understanding of why Paul exhorts us to not worship humanity or creation made in the image of God (Numbers 33:52, 2 Chronicles 23:17, Ezekiel 7:20, Amos 5:26, Romans 1:23). Two passages in Psalms (39:6, 73:20) refer to shadows using the word *tselem*, and the other five occurrences are in Genesis (1:26, 27, 5:3; 9:6). The limited use of this word in Scripture has made its interpretation difficult.

The Hebrew word for "likeness" is *demut* (**deh-MOOT**). As used here, the term means "resemblance, fashion, or being similar to." Because we realize that God does not have a physical form, it is implied that the resemblance is one of mental and/or spiritual attributes that humanity shares with the Creator. Conceivably, then, the "likeness" or "image" of God toward man serves as a mirror to the rest of the world of God's divine nature.

27 So God created man in his own image, in the image of God created he him; male and female created he them. 28 And God blessed them, and God said unto them, Be fruitful, and multiply, and replenish the earth, and subdue it: and have dominion over the fish of the sea, and over the fowl of the air, and over every living thing that moveth upon the earth.

Immediately after God blessed the first two humans, He gave them power and authority. A study of the phrase "have dominion" (Heb. *radah*, **rah-DAH**, to rule or prevail against) reveals that God gave humanity authority and stewardship over everything He created. Similar to the command to be fruitful and multiply that God gave the animals in verse 22, God's command to humanity draws upon His relationship with us as sovereign Creator. Thus, people are created in God's image to rule over God's creation on Earth on God's behalf. The purpose and function of humans involves the responsibility of caring for and cultivating creation. They are also told to be fruitful, multiply, and replenish (Heb. *mala,'* **mah-LAH**, "to fill") the earth and subdue it, speaking to God's desire for humanity to use godly wisdom to produce and reproduce so that God's image, likeness, and knowledge cover the earth and rule over it through humanity.

29 And God said, Behold, I have given you every herb bearing seed, which is upon the face of all the earth, and every tree, in the which is the fruit of a tree yielding seed; to you it shall be for meat. 30 And to every beast of the earth, and to every fowl of the air, and to every thing that creepeth upon the earth, wherein there is life, I have given every green herb for meat: and it was so. 31 And God saw every thing that he had made, and, behold, it was very good. And the evening and the morning were the sixth day.

One of the first communications between human beings and God was for them to see the many provisions God had for them. In other words, God was saying, "See all the provisions I have made for you." Look and know how far God has gone to prepare for your survival and sustenance.

What were they to see? They were to see what God had given them for their well-being.

The word "given" is translated from the Hebrew word *nathan* (**nah-THAN**). God was thoughtful in providing for the care of creatures. This, indeed, speaks to God's generosity.

Another reference to God's provision is the use the word *'oklah* (Heb. **ok-LAW**), which KJV translates as "meat," but means simply "food" or "something to eat." .Just as verse 29 deals with God's good provision for human beings, verse 30 deals with God's provision for the animals, both groups are given food to eat.

Verse 31 is the conclusion of God's creative activity. God beheld all of creation including His special creation of humanity and called it "very good." This was additional emphasis from the creation of the other five days. With the addition of man to its order, Creation was complete and the natural order of the universe was exceedingly good in the eyes of God.

2:4 These are the generations of the heavens and of the earth when they were created, in the day that the LORD God made the earth and the heavens,

The verse says the same thing twice in reverse order: "the heavens and…the earth were created" and "made the earth and the heavens." This style is an ancient form of memory aid for the oral culture that recited these verses (see Genesis 5:1, 10:1, 25:12). The term "generation" (Heb. *toledah*, **toe-leh-DAH**), which can be translated literally as "what comes after" or "what emerges from," describes something that is generated from something else. Thus, it does not describe the origin of the universe but what immediately follows or arises from the heavens and earth. Therefore, in Genesis 2:4–7, we have a more detailed description of what God did on the sixth day of creation to supplement the account in Genesis 1:24–31.

The combined name "the LORD God" (Heb. *yehovah elohiym*, **yeh-ho-VAH eh-low-HEEM**) establishes the unity of these two terms for God, the personal name (Yahweh) and the title (Elohim). Names were regarded not merely as labels but as symbols or keys to the nature or essence of the being or the thing (cf. Genesis 2:19). Yehovah is another way of writing YHWH (Yahweh), meaning "to be or I AM," revealing God as self-existent; and Elohim revealing God's majesty.

5 And every plant of the field before it was in the earth, and every herb of the field before it grew: for the LORD God had not caused it to rain upon the earth, and there was not a man to till the ground. 6 But there went up a mist from the earth, and watered the whole face of the ground.

The verse distinguishes between perennial wood plants that continue from year to year ("plant," Heb. *siach*, **SEE-akh**) and the green plants that spring up anew each year ("herb," Heb. *'eseb*, **EH-seb**). The herbs spring up as the result of rains or of seeds sown by people. The word "field" (Heb. *sadeh*, **sah-DEH**), or garden, designates the open field of arable land or a definite portion of ground. Thus the planting of the garden is eluded to here.

The phrase "there was not a man to till the ground" plays with the fact that the words "man" (Heb. *adam*, **ah-DOM**) and "ground" (Heb. *adamah*, **ah-dah-MAH**) are similar in the Hebrew. The term "mist" (Heb. *'ed*, **ADE**), or vapor, communicates a sense of enveloping. Moisture came up to water or envelop the earth.

7 And the LORD God formed man of the dust of the ground, and breathed into his nostrils the breath of life; and man became a living soul.

People consist of two elements: a physical, material side ("formed man of the dust"), showing that they have something in common with the physical environment, and an inner personality ("breathed into his nostrils the breath of life"), showing that they have something in common with God. These two elements form one being. The human body consists entirely of basic substances similar to those found in the earth. Here, God gives the man the "breath" (Heb. *neshamah*, **neh-shah-MAH**) of life in a special way that indicates that he exists on a much higher level than all other forms of life (cf. Genesis 1:26–27). He is related to the physical world by virtue of his formation from the substance of the earth. At the same time, he is related to the nonphysical world because he has special breath from God and because he was created in the image and likeness of God.

Say It Correctly

Dominion. doe-MIN-yuhn.

Daily Bible Readings

MONDAY
God Glorified in the Heavens
(Psalm 104:1–4)

TUESDAY
People Created in God's Likeness
(Ephesians 4:17–24)

WEDNESDAY
Light of the Gospel
(2 Corinthians 4:1–6)

THURSDAY
Living in the Light of God
(1 John 1:5–10)

FRIDAY
Observe and Keep the Sabbath Holy
(Deuteronomy 5:12–15)

SATURDAY
The Seventh Day, Hallowed and Blessed
(Genesis 2:1–3)

SUNDAY
God Created People
(Genesis 1:26–31; 2:4–7)

Notes

_____

_____

_____

_____

Teaching Tips

Words You Should Know

A. Help *'ezer* (Heb.)—To aid or uplift.

B. Cleave *dabaq* (Heb.)—To adhere, to follow closely.

Teacher Preparation

Unifying Principle—Relationships are Important. Humans often wonder what their purpose is in life and how they relate to all that is around them. What is our purpose, and where do we fit in? According to Genesis, God created families to support and care for one another and to care for all of God's creation.

A. Read the Bible Background and Devotional Readings.

B. Pray for your students and lesson clarity.

C. Read the lesson Scripture in multiple translations.

D. Option: Give students a picture of a multibranched tree with many limbs. Ask them to create natural or spiritual family trees, writing names of individuals on branches and limbs. Ask a few volunteers to highlight individuals from their family trees and describe their influence in the family, particularly as it relates to spiritual guidance.

O—Open the Lesson

A. Begin the class with prayer.

B. Have the students read the Aim for Change.

C. Have the students read the In Focus story.

D. Ask students how events named in the story can weigh on their hearts and how they can view these events from a theological perspective.

P—Present the Scriptures

A. Read the Focal Verses and discuss the Background and The People, Places, and Times sections.

B. Have the class share which Scriptures stand out for them and why, with particular emphasis on today's context.

E—Explore the Meaning

A. Use In Depth or More Light on the Text to help provide more in-depth discussion of the lesson text.

B. Discuss the Liberating Lesson and Application for Activation sections.

N—Next Steps for Application

A. Summarize the value of knowing God as Sovereign Creator.

B. End class with a commitment to pray for marriages, children, and relationships between men and women.

Worship Guide

For the Superintendent or Teacher
Theme: God Created the Family
Song: "I Need You to Survive"
Devotional Reading: Leviticus 19:11–18

God Created the Family

Bible Background • GENESIS 2:18–24; 4:1–2
Printed Text • GENESIS 2:18–24; 4:1–2 | Devotional Reading • LEVITICUS 19:11–18

——— Aim for Change ———

By the end of this lesson, we will: DISCOVER God's intention for family; AFFIRM sexual differences as part of God's good creation; and COMMIT to loving our families with mutual respect.

——— 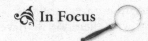 In Focus ———

"I don't need your help, I can do it myself. I've got this," Ernest said sharply to his wife, Diane. They had been trying for an hour to put together his new bird fountain and were frustrated. They had attended a workshop at church on ways to beautify and care for the community, and Ernest had decided he would build a large bird fountain for their backyard as a result.

"Fine, I was just trying to be helpful. You don't have to be so mean about it," Diane said. As Ernest struggled to put a small piece into the fountain, he realized his hands were too big. "Diane's hands would be the perfect size…" he said to himself. He paused for a minute, took a deep breath, and called as sweetly as he could, "Hey babe, can you come help me with this? I need your hands!"

"Oh, so now you want my help? Always think you know everything until you need something," remarked Diane.

"I'm sorry, honey, I just get so focused. I'm glad for a helpmate like you." Ernest said smiling.

"You're lucky I love you," Diane responded. "Let me read the directions."

Why is it difficult for us to recognize our need for help sometimes? Why can it be difficult to ask those closest to us for help?

——— Keep in Mind ———

"Therefore shall a man leave his father and his mother, and shall cleave unto his wife: and they shall be one flesh" (Genesis 2:24, KJV).

"This explains why a man leaves his father and mother and is joined to his wife, and the two are united into one" (Genesis 2:24, NLT).

Focal Verses

KJV

Genesis 2:18 And the LORD God said, It is not good that the man should be alone; I will make him an help meet for him.

19 And out of the ground the LORD God formed every beast of the field, and every fowl of the air; and brought them unto Adam to see what he would call them: and whatsoever Adam called every living creature, that was the name thereof.

20 And Adam gave names to all cattle, and to the fowl of the air, and to every beast of the field; but for Adam there was not found an help meet for him.

21 And the LORD God caused a deep sleep to fall upon Adam, and he slept: and he took one of his ribs, and closed up the flesh instead thereof;

22 And the rib, which the LORD God had taken from man, made he a woman, and brought her unto the man.

23 And Adam said, This is now bone of my bones, and flesh of my flesh: she shall be called Woman, because she was taken out of Man.

24 Therefore shall a man leave his father and his mother, and shall cleave unto his wife: and they shall be one flesh.

4:1 And Adam knew Eve his wife; and she conceived, and bare Cain, and said, I have gotten a man from the LORD.

2 And she again bare his brother Abel. And Abel was a keeper of sheep, but Cain was a tiller of the ground.

NLT

Genesis 2:18 Then the LORD God said, "It is not good for the man to be alone. I will make a helper who is just right for him."

19 So the LORD God formed from the ground all the wild animals and all the birds of the sky. He brought them to the man to see what he would call them, and the man chose a name for each one.

20 He gave names to all the livestock, all the birds of the sky, and all the wild animals. But still there was no helper just right for him.

21 So the LORD God caused the man to fall into a deep sleep. While the man slept, the LORD God took out one of the man's ribs and closed up the opening.

22 Then the LORD God made a woman from the rib, and he brought her to the man.

23 "At last!" the man exclaimed. "This one is bone from my bone, and flesh from my flesh! She will be called 'woman,' because she was taken from 'man.'"

24 This explains why a man leaves his father and mother and is joined to his wife, and the two are united into one.

4:1 Now Adam had sexual relations with his wife, Eve, and she became pregnant. When she gave birth to Cain, she said, "With the LORD's help, I have produced a man!"

2 Later she gave birth to his brother and named him Abel. When they grew up, Abel became a shepherd, while Cain cultivated the ground.

The People, Places, and Times

Adam/adamah. Adam was the Biblical name given to the first man created. The Hebrew word *adamah* makes reference to the earth from which he was formed. The concept of "redness of color" is inherent in the name *Adam/adamah*. The word *adamah* is also used to refer to the soil with which pottery is made (Isaiah 45:9) and the altars (Exodus 20:24) during the days of Moses. The word *adam* appears in three primary contexts in the Old

Testament. The most common usage for 'adam is in reference to all of humanity. The word is also used to refer to a specific man. Lastly, as a proper name, Adam is the first man and a city beside Zaretan on the Jordan River (Joshua 3:16).

Eve. The name of the first woman created, Eve means "life." She and Adam are the original ancestors of all people. Her giving in to temptation from the serpent's scheme illustrates the ease with which all human beings may fall into sin. Unlike Adam, Eve is only used in reference to Adam's wife.

Background

Genesis 2 (beginning at verse 4) differs from chapter 1 in that it provides a narrative of the Creation that begins with humanity. God creates the first man, then the garden, animals, and the woman. Genesis 2 sets the stage for the story of humanity's fall from grace. It provides an explanation of the human condition and why humanity has a troubled relationship with God. Genesis 2:15–17 explains the reasoning behind placing the man in the Garden of Eden. Adam had a vocation (to till the land), a permit (to freely enjoy the fruit of the land), and a prohibition (against eating from the tree of the knowledge of good and evil). Genesis 1:26 presents humans as primarily spiritual and powerful, made in God's image. In Genesis 2, however, we learn the spiritual and natural duality of humans. God formed man from the dust of the ground and breathed life into his nostrils. His formation from dust anticipates his work as a tiller of soil and his return to the earth after death. The divine breath in his nostrils indicates that life-breath belongs to God; a person without life-breath returns to God.

We also learn God determined human relationships during Creation. Man needed a helper. In Genesis 4, we meet the second generation of humanity, the extension of the family.

They arrive through the sexual relationship between members of the preceding generation, and they continue the behavior of transgression against God and each other found in the first generation.

How is your destiny intertwined with that of your relatives?

At-A-Glance

1. Humans Need Help (Genesis 2:18–20)
2. Woman is Man's Helpmate (Genesis 2:21–24)
3. Family Matters (Genesis 4:1–2)

In Depth

1. Humans Need Help (Genesis 2:18–20)

God created a complete world. The world included the 'adam, the Garden, rivers, and trees. As a perfect God surveyed what should have been a perfect creation, something was missing. God formed every kind of animal and the birds of the air and brought them to the man. Humanity was designed to care for the rest of creation. The man was empowered by God to give each creature its name, but among all the animals, no suitable helpmate for the man was found. Man was himself an animal, but no animal was like the man. He had power over all the animals as evidenced by his ability to name them. Creation was incomplete until the man had another human to be his helper in carrying out his vocational and spiritual work. The human needed family to be complete.

How does the knowledge that God created humans to be helpers for one another help you understand your role in society differently?

2. Woman is Man's Helpmate (Genesis 2:21–24)

Woman is so named because she was taken from the man. For the first time in Scripture, we see the use of gendered language to describe human beings. These gendered bodies are one, as the man explains, "This is now bone of my bones, and flesh of my flesh" (from v. 23). They are both literally and figuratively one another's kin. Genesis 2 does not indicate that the woman is to be subservient to the man; rather, they are partners in the work God had assigned to him. The creation of the woman's body from the body of the man explains the motive for their sexuality. They were separated from one another, but she is part of the man. They are sexually complementary; the two physically reunite and again become one flesh. Together the man and the woman unite to form necessary and whole community. Through this positive bond, they are to bear children who, in turn, leave home and form new families fulfilling God's command to be fruitful and multiply. They should leave to cleave. In Genesis 2:24, the man and the woman are aware of the sexual differences but their sexuality is yet to be expressed.

How can men and women better honor our divinely created connection to one another?

3. Family Matters (Genesis 4:1–2)

The man and woman carry out the physical relationship that was set up for them in the Garden. The word "know" as a euphemism for sexual relations furthers the concept that there is a connection between sexuality and knowledge. For the first time in Scripture, a sexual relationship is mentioned. They have two sons.

Throughout Genesis, firstborn sons do not fare well (e.g. Ishmael, Esau). Cain and Abel are the first examples of the tension between elder sons and their younger brothers. As the firstborn son, Cain embodied the family's hope for the future. Abel's name in Hebrew means "vapor" or "nothingness." As the younger son, he was dismissed. In the New Testament, however, Abel is called a man of faith (Hebrews 11:4), and Cain is described as evil (1 John 3:12; Jude 11). Cain and Abel split the purposeful work set out in the Garden. Cain was a worker of the land, and Abel cared for the animals. The broken relationship that later develops between the brothers relates to the broken relationship that was developing between God and humanity.

How can we foster wholeness within our families?

Search the Scriptures

1. Adam observed every type of animal to see which one might make an ideal helper for him, but none of them could be the man's partner. Why do you think God made humans so different from birds, fish, and land animals?

2. What do we learn about the proper division of labor from the fact that the first two humans who were born divided the purposeful work given to the first generation of humans right down the middle?

Discuss the Meaning

1. The family is the foundation for shaping all of our relationships with one another as human beings. How our family members relate to one another from parents to siblings to children impacts how we relate to people in our extended families, communities, and beyond. How can we be more intentional about giving and receiving love and respect within our natural, adopted, chosen, and spiritual families?

2. How can we learn from negative experiences to relate well to the next generation?

Liberating Lesson

Scripture teaches that without our human family, we are incomplete. We live in a world that prioritizes independence and self-sufficiency. We are celebrated when we can do things without help. Musical artists sing about their love of "independent women" or "self-made men" and many people follow suit, proudly proclaiming that in this life all we need is ourselves. No doubt, we all must learn the importance of self-respect and self-love, but the Genesis 2 passage is clear; it is through our relationships with other human beings that we more fully appreciate our humanity. We need God and one another, too, if we desire to thrive in this life.

Application for Activation

Consider the people who are your helpers or partners in this life. Talk to them about how you can better serve one another. Pray for the people you are in a relationship with, and ask God to make you a better partner to the people you love. Do not believe the myth that all you need is yourself. If you struggle to ask for help, be open to asking for it. If you have placed undue pressure on the people who help you, consider ways that you can better support others. In the work that you do both within your household and outside of it, divide labor with respect to the gifts and abilities of each helper.

Follow the Spirit

What God wants me to do:

_____

_____

_____

_____

Remember Your Thoughts

Special insights I have learned:

_____

_____

_____

More Light on the Text

Genesis 2:18–24, 4:1–2

18 And the LORD God said, It is not good that the man should be alone; I will make him an help meet for him.

Until verse 18, God had declared everything good. The first thing that God declares as "not good" is the idea of being alone. The word "alone" is taken from the Hebrew word *bad* (**BOD**). It speaks to the fact that Adam, the first human being, needed another human being to be complete. In many African cultures, this is a revelation that a human is a communal being.

19 And out of the ground the LORD God formed every beast of the field, and every fowl of the air; and brought them unto Adam to see what he would call them: and whatsoever Adam called every living creature, that was the name thereof. 20 And Adam gave names to all cattle, and to the fowl of the air, and to every beast of the field; but for Adam there was not found an help meet for him.

Verse 19 confirms that God created the first beast from earth. We also find that God gives man responsibility for naming the beasts. This task of naming also gives human beings certain authority over all the creation. Here we also find that God respected the naming ability that He gave to man. The relationship and responsibility of man to the animal world began in the garden.

In the process of naming, Adam realized that there was no companion fit for a human being. The Hebrew word *ezer* or "help" simply means to give someone aid or uplift them. There was no one to lift up the heart of the first man Adam. There was no one like Adam and yet sufficiently different to challenge and stimulate him intellectually, emotionally, or spiritually. The knowledge that one is alone is one of the deepest realizations of human feelings. It can either lead one to seek fellowship or to despair.

21 And the LORD God caused a deep sleep to fall upon Adam and he slept: and he took one of his ribs, and closed up the flesh instead thereof; 22 And the rib, which the LORD God had taken from man, made he a woman, and brought her unto the man.

God understands the danger of loneliness. He helped Adam out of his lonely state before it resulted in problems for Adam. God sent a "deep sleep," (Heb. *tardemah,* **tar-deh-MAH***)* placing Adam in an unconscious state similar to those in trances or receiving visions (Genesis 15:12; Job 33:15).

Another key word is the Hebrew for rib. The word *tsela* (**tsay-LAH**) is an architectural term referring to a side support, usually one that has a matching support in the opposite side; in this case "rib" means from the side of a person. It was the side of Adam that God opened to form the woman, according to the text. We are told that God "brought the woman to Adam." God, therefore, formed this relationship.

23 And Adam said, This is now bone of my bones, and flesh of my flesh: she shall be called Woman, because she was taken out of Man.

Adam's response to this new relationship is to acknowledge the deep connection between himself and this other human being. The Hebrew word *'etsem* (**ET-sem**) translated as "bone," could also mean "strength," thus meaning "strength of my strength." By extension it can refer figuratively to the strong identity of an individual. Therefore, Adam could also mean to call Eve "the very substance of my being." "Flesh," of course, refers to similarity of bodily form, which must have been quite striking to Adam.

After naming all the animals, Adam names one more piece of creation. He calls her "woman" (Heb. *'ishshah,* **ee-SHAH**) because she was taken from the man (*'ish,* **EESH**). Later he would name her Eve (Genesis 3:20).

24 Therefore shall a man leave his father and his mother, and shall cleave unto his wife: and they shall be one flesh.

We see the responsibility that this new relationship calls forth for men. The Hebrew word *azab* (**ah-ZOB**) translated "leave" denotes the loosening of a bond, here the parental relationship. This permits the adult male to begin his own household. It does not imply a lack of commitment or a failure to care for one's parents, or to forsake them—denying help when necessary. The loosening of the parental relation gives way within the text for the tightening of a new relationship.

The King James Version uses the phrase "cleave unto his wife." Cleave (Heb. *dabaq,* **dah-BOK**) means to cling or adhere. By implication, it could also mean to pursue or to stick together and to follow her closely. Therefore, the man shall loosen the parental relation and take a wife. One must leave in order to cleave. They shall be "one flesh" is vital for it calls forth a deep sharing that is to characterize the marriage relation. The Hebrew word *basar* (**bah-SAR**), translated "flesh," simply refers to the human body. But it can also refer to the sharing of the whole person.

4:1 And Adam knew Eve his wife; and she conceived, and bare Cain, and said, I have gotten a man from the LORD. 2 And she again bare his brother Abel. And Abel was a keeper of sheep, but Cain was a tiller of the ground.

Adam and Eve sinned against God and are now removed from the Garden of Eden. They heeded the words of the serpent and ate from the fruit of the tree in the midst of the garden from which God forbid them to eat. As a result, sin entered the world. The perfect relationship

God had with humanity was broken. God informed Eve that bearing children would be painful and told Adam he would have difficulty tilling the ground or farm. They were cut off from the Garden and the tree of life. The whole world now feels the curse from the effect of sin.

Nevertheless the fact that sin separated Adam and Eve from God did not negate the command of God to "be fruitful and multiply, fill the earth and subdue it" (from Genesis 1:28). Adam "knew" (Heb. *yada*, **yah-DAH**) Eve, which in this case is used as a euphemism for sex but included more fully experiencing Eve. There were no sexual relations between humans until they were expelled from the Garden. Adam and Eve conceived, and Eve gave birth to her first children, Cain and Abel. Cain means "acquired" in Hebrew, and Eve said that she has acquired a son from the Lord. This speaks to the reality that all life comes from God. Eve conceived not because of simple sexual reproduction but because God willed her to have children. God gave Cain to her intentionally. The name of her second son Abel (Heb. *hebel*, **HEH-vel**) means "breath," in this case referring to vapor. His name was foreshadowing in the narrative that he would not live long, but like a breath be temporary.

Cain and Abel are described as working (v. 2:2); Cain was a tiller of the field (farmer) and Abel a keeper of the sheep (shepherd). Cain and Abel were born and began to fulfill the purpose that God had for humanity to subdue the earth, and have dominion over it by farming the land and caring for God's creation. God intentionally gave humans a purpose, which is fulfilled through living and work. The work was meant to be easy, as Adam and Eve were able to care for creation before, but the introduction of sin made it difficult. The entrance of sin into the world did not change God's purposes; it simply made it difficult for us to fulfill our God-given purpose. The work God has

called us to is a fulfillment of His purpose for our lives. Cain and Abel demonstrated this by continuing to be stewards of creation by shepherding and farming respectively.

Sources:
Butler, Trent, ed. *Holman Bible Dictionary*. Nashville, TN: Broadman & Holman Publishers, 1991. 18
Smith, William. *Smith's Bible Dictionary*. Nashville, TN: Thomas Nelson Publishers, 2004. 18, 446.

Say It Correctly

Conceive. **kuhn-SEEV**.
Abel. **AY-buhl**.

Daily Bible Readings

MONDAY
Becoming One Flesh
(Matthew 19:3–6)

TUESDAY
Married and Devoted to the Lord
(1 Corinthians 7:1–7, 32–35)

WEDNESDAY
Honor the Sanctity of Marriage
(Hebrews 13:1–6)

THURSDAY
Cultivate Deep Mutual Love
(1 Peter 1:13–16, 22–23)

FRIDAY
For the Sake of Your Prayers
(1 Peter 4:7–11)

SATURDAY
Cain Ducks Responsibility for Abel
(Genesis 4:3–12)

SUNDAY
The Family, Whole and Broken
(Genesis 2:18–24; 4:1–2)

Teaching Tips

September 30
Bible Study Guide 5

Words You Should Know

A. Enmity *'ebah* (Heb.)—Long-lasting, intense hostility.

B. Beguiled *nasha* (Heb.)- Deceived.

Teacher Preparation

Unifying Principle—Passing the Buck. Irresponsible rebellion pervades our world. Why is disregard for rules, which are necessary for ordered life, so pervasive? Although God created a perfect place for Adam and Eve, their unwillingness to trust and obey God led to the Fall, making humanity prone to disobedience.

A. Read the Bible Background and Devotional Readings.

B. Pray for your students and lesson clarity.

C. Read the lesson Scripture in multiple translations.

D. Option: Guide a time of reflection by asking the group to answer silently the following questions: When is a time you sinned against someone? What were the consequences? Who was hurt as a result? How did this affect your relationship with God? How was your relationship with God restored? Have you done all that you can to repair damaged relationships? If not, what do you need to do?

O—Open the Lesson

A. Begin the class with prayer.

B. Have the students read the Aim for Change.

C. Have the students read the In Focus story.

D. Ask students how events named in the story can weigh on their hearts and how they can view these events from a theological perspective.

P—Present the Scriptures

A. Read the Focal Verses and discuss the Background and The People, Places, and Times sections.

B. Have the class share which Scriptures stand out for them and why, with particular emphasis on today's context.

E—Explore the Meaning

A. Use In Depth or More Light on the Text to help provide more in-depth discussion of the lesson text.

B. Discuss the Liberating Lesson and Application for Activation sections.

N—Next Steps for Application

A. Summarize the value of knowing the impact of sin on our relationship with God and one another.

B. End class with a commitment to pray for repentence from sin individually and the impact it has on those close to us.

Worship Guide

For the Superintendent or Teacher
Theme: God Creates, Humans Sin
Song: "All That I Was"
Devotional Reading: Psalm 51:1–12

God Creates, Humans Sin

Bible Background • GENESIS 3
Printed Text • GENESIS 3:8–17, 20–24 | Devotional Reading • PSALM 51:1–12

—————— Aim for Change ——————

By the end of this lesson, we will: RECOGNIZE that all people experience temptation and sin; EMPATHIZE with the pain that sin creates in our lives; and CONSIDER how to heal relationships that have been hurt by sin.

—————— In Focus ——————

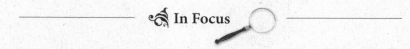

"I don't remember anything about last night. The last thing I remember is having another drink," Rodney said under his breath.

"You're lucky that woman survived," said his sister Lecretia. "Do you realize you could have killed her? Do you realize that you're going to face jail time and that we have a $20,000 fine to pay? What about your daughter? What were you thinking?!"

Rodney's felt broken and overwhelmed. His heart felt pierced. What about his daughter? He was not used to drinking a lot but had gone to a party with friends the night before and drank way more alcohol than he should. He knew he should have called for a ride. Instead, he decided to drive himself home because he lived so close to the bar.

Rodney found out later that while driving he had hit a woman crossing the street. He was at a complete loss. His decision to do what he knew was wrong had almost cost someone's life. He was grateful the woman survived, but was overwhelmed thinking about the high cost his decision would have on her family and on his own is daughter. He decided at that moment he needed to stay away from alcohol. All he could do now was pray that God would show him mercy when he had to go to court.

What goes through your mind when you encounter temptation to do what you know is wrong? What consequences can acting outside of God's will for our lives have on those closest to us?

—————— Keep in Mind ——————

"Therefore the LORD God sent him forth from the garden of Eden, to till the ground from whence he was taken" (Genesis 3:23, KJV).

"So the Lord God banished them from the Garden of Eden, and he sent Adam out to cultivate the ground from which he had been made" (Genesis 3:23, NLT).

Focal Verses

KJV **Genesis 3:8** And they heard the voice of the LORD God walking in the garden in the cool of the day: and Adam and his wife hid themselves from the presence of the LORD God amongst the trees of the garden.

9 And the LORD God called unto Adam, and said unto him, Where art thou?

10 And he said, I heard thy voice in the garden, and I was afraid, because I was naked; and I hid myself.

11 And he said, Who told thee that thou wast naked? Hast thou eaten of the tree, whereof I commanded thee that thou shouldest not eat?

12 And the man said, The woman whom thou gavest to be with me, she gave me of the tree, and I did eat.

13 And the LORD God said unto the woman, What is this that thou hast done? And the woman said, The serpent beguiled me, and I did eat.

14 And the LORD God said unto the serpent, Because thou hast done this, thou art cursed above all cattle, and above every beast of the field; upon thy belly shalt thou go, and dust shalt thou eat all the days of thy life:

15 And I will put enmity between thee and the woman, and between thy seed and her seed; it shall bruise thy head, and thou shalt bruise his heel.

16 Unto the woman he said, I will greatly multiply thy sorrow and thy conception; in sorrow thou shalt bring forth children; and thy desire shall be to thy husband, and he shall rule over thee.

17 And unto Adam he said, Because thou hast hearkened unto the voice of thy wife, and hast eaten of the tree, of which I commanded thee, saying, Thou shalt not eat of it: cursed is the ground for thy sake; in sorrow shalt thou eat of it all the days of thy life;

NLT **Genesis 3:8** When the cool evening breezes were blowing, the man and his wife heard the LORD God walking about in the garden. So they hid from the LORD God among the trees.

9 Then the LORD God called to the man, "Where are you?"

10 He replied, "I heard you walking in the garden, so I hid. I was afraid because I was naked."

11 "Who told you that you were naked?" the Lord God asked. "Have you eaten from the tree whose fruit I commanded you not to eat?"

12 The man replied, "It was the woman you gave me who gave me the fruit, and I ate it."

13 Then the LORD God asked the woman, "What have you done?" "The serpent deceived me," she replied. "That's why I ate it."

14 Then the LORD God said to the serpent, "Because you have done this, you are cursed more than all animals, domestic and wild. You will crawl on your belly, groveling in the dust as long as you live.

15 And I will cause hostility between you and the woman, and between your offspring and her offspring. He will strike your head, and you will strike his heel."

16 Then he said to the woman, "I will sharpen the pain of your pregnancy, and in pain you will give birth. And you will desire to control your husband, but he will rule over you."

17 And to the man he said, "Since you listened to your wife and ate from the tree whose fruit I commanded you not to eat, the ground is cursed because of you. All your life you will struggle to scratch a living from it.

20 Then the man—Adam—named his wife Eve, because she would be the mother of all who live.

20 And Adam called his wife's name Eve; because she was the mother of all living.

21 Unto Adam also and to his wife did the LORD God make coats of skins, and clothed them.

22 And the LORD God said, Behold, the man is become as one of us, to know good and evil: and now, lest he put forth his hand, and take also of the tree of life, and eat, and live for ever:

23 Therefore the LORD God sent him forth from the garden of Eden, to till the ground from whence he was taken.

24 So he drove out the man; and he placed at the east of the garden of Eden Cherubims, and a flaming sword which turned every way, to keep the way of the tree of life.

21 And the LORD God made clothing from animal skins for Adam and his wife.

22 Then the LORD God said, "Look, the human beings have become like us, knowing both good and evil. What if they reach out, take fruit from the tree of life, and eat it? Then they will live forever!"

23 So the LORD God banished them from the Garden of Eden, and he sent Adam out to cultivate the ground from which he had been made.

24 After sending them out, the Lord God stationed mighty cherubim to the east of the Garden of Eden. And he placed a flaming sword that flashed back and forth to guard the way to the tree of life.

The People, Places, and Times

Garden of Eden. Eden existed perhaps in East Africa or the Middle East (Genesis 2:10-14). The Pishon and Gihon rivers have been suggested to be the Blue and White Nile rivers. Cush is the land known as Ethiopia today. Yet the Tigris and Euphrates are in the Middle East, making it difficult to place Eden geographically. The name Eden is derived either from a Hebrew root word meaning "to be fruitful, plentiful" or from a Sumerian word meaning "steppe, flatland." In Eden, we learn that Satan does not honor or respect any sacred environment which God consecrates as a place of paradise and worship. Eden is a place where our original parents failed God and their posterity. It is a dismal and dreaded moment in human history that marks our distant past and mars our present and future.

Serpent. The serpent is used in the Bible to represent evil and, sometimes, the enemies of Israel (Deuteronomy 8:15; Psalm 58:4). Also in the wider ancient Near East, the serpent had great mythological and religious significance as a prominent image to explain the origin of chaos in the world.

Background

In Genesis 3, we are introduced to the complications after Creation. A snake deceived the woman, humans succumbed to sin, and God punished humanity and banished them from the Garden. Because of human sin, they endured pain in childbirth and faced mortality. The knowledge of good and evil that they gained awakened them to their shame in exile. Their exile awakened their shame and their knowledge of themselves. In some ways, the chapter shows the human passage from childhood (or being childlike) to adulthood (taking responsibility for one's actions). Genesis 3 also represents a change in the way people relate to each other socially. In the Garden, social roles and sexual expression were irrelevant as there was perfect harmony, but after the exile, social roles changed for the worse.

In Genesis 3, we also receive our first glimpse into deception about who God is and what God says. The serpent introduced the idea that obedience to the commands of God was an option rather than an expectation. In the talk between the woman and the serpent, God was referred to, but God was not a conversation partner. The woman allowed the serpent to misrepresent God, which opened her up to the possibility of disobedience. In the woman's mind, God was no longer a friend who protected humans by creating boundaries for them, but a barrier whose rules must be overcome. She and the man ate the fruit, and they became exposed to the dangers of the world. They had taken life into their own hands.

At-A-Glance

1. Nowhere to Hide from Sin (Genesis 3:8–13)
2. Consequences for Disobedience (vv. 14–17)
3. God's Punishments Have Purpose (vv. 20–24)

In Depth

1. Nowhere to Hide from Sin (Genesis 3:8–13)

God's stroll in the Garden to visit with humanity became an interrogation with two admissions of guilt. Their sin had opened Adam and Eve's eyes to the reality of their condition. They were created naked and had no shame about it, but their new eyes caused them to understand their nakedness in a new way. When they heard God approaching, they hid. But God called out to them.

The man is the first to respond to God's call. He admits his sin but blames God and the woman for it. Had God not given him the woman who gave him the fruit, he argued, he would never have eaten it. The man's response demonstrates the way that people often shift responsibility for their actions (or inactions) to

other people. The woman also confesses her sin and, like the man, refuses to take full responsibility. She tells God that the serpent had tricked her. Her use of the word "tricked" is misleading because she knew God's command as is evidenced in her ability to relay the command to the serpent. She chooses to find a way around the command. God did not give the serpent an opportunity to confess or to defend his actions.

What does God's continued conversation with humans, despite our disobedience, reveal about God's relationship with us?

2. Consequences for Disobedience (vv. 14–17)

The consequences of the disobedience are given in the reverse order of the interrogation because God is reversing the freedoms that the snake, woman, and man were given at the beginning of Creation. The snake was cursed and despised by the other animals. Snakes would crawl on their bellies; and women and their children would revile snakes. Of course, the new order of things would prevent snakes from deceiving humans again. The woman was punished with painful labor. As an added consequence, the husband and wife will now struggle for dominance over one another that neither is supposed to have. The man was punished with hard labor on the ground, which reversed the comfortable relationship he shared with the ground in Eden. All parties received their punishments without additional explanation.

What does the way the first humans received punishment teach us about how we might respond to divine punishment?

3. God's Punishments Have Purpose (vv. 20–24)

After providing the humans with garments of skin to cover their shame, God exiled them from the Garden. The humans were not expelled only for their disobedience but also because of the new eyes their disobedience provided them. The man had become "like God" and might try to eat from the tree of life to avoid mortality. Because of human disobedience, there was a wedge between the divine and humanity.

Humans were driven east of Eden. Cherubim guarded the entrance. Cherubim are heavenly creatures that have wings, faces of many creatures, and many eyes; they are closely associated with the glory of God (see Ezekiel 1 and 10). The eastern entrance, the cherubim, and the sacred trees suggest an analogy to the Jerusalem temple, which had similar architectural and iconographic features and a limitation on access (Exodus 25:18–36; 1 Kings 6:29).

How does the way God expelled humans from the Garden of Eden reveal God's compassion toward humanity?

Search the Scriptures

1. In Genesis 3:10, the man tells God that he hid from Him because his nakedness made him afraid. Why did the sudden knowledge of their nakedness terrify the humans?

2. How did the punishments for disobedience (especially those given to the humans) move humanity forward? What was the divine purpose behind the punishments?

Discuss the Meaning

1. When we sin against God it is often tempting to blame someone else instead of taking responsibility. Why do people avoid taking responsibility for their sin?

2. When we do things to hurt others, it can be easy to lash out or withdraw when confronted with their hurt. How can we begin to make things right when we sin against someone?

Liberating Lesson

Scripture teaches that God gives humanity clear commands. God gives us a vocation, a permit, and a prohibition. We are responsible for following God's commands, which exist to create healthy boundaries for us that protect us. God does not desire to cause us harm or place limitations on our freedoms.

We are currently living through politically divisive times. Many Christians want to align Jesus with their political worldview. Genesis 3 reveals that God ought not to be made a pawn in our theological or political conversations. God must be our constant partner in any conversation about God, for how can we talk about God without talking to God? It is not for humans to attempt to figure out the mind of God. It is for us to be prayerful, and to listen and obey the God who created us.

Application for Activation

Confess your sins before God. Understand that we do not serve a God of condemnation. Avoid playing the blame game. It is a sign of Christian maturity to take responsibility for your actions. Repent for the times that you have been disobedient. Do not be afraid of being honest with God. Understand that God wants to be in a relationship with humanity. God is not against us.

Consider the times when you endured punishment because of your disobedience. Was there a purpose behind the punishments you experienced?

Follow the Spirit

What God wants me to do:

_____

_____

_____

Remember Your Thoughts

Special insights I have learned:

_____

_____

_____

_____

More Light on the Text

Genesis 3:8–17, 20–24

8 And they heard the voice of the LORD God walking in the garden in the cool of the day: and Adam and his wife hid themselves from the presence of the LORD God amongst the trees of the garden. 9 And the LORD God called unto Adam, and said unto him, Where art thou?

God came down to Adam and Eve in the cool of the day, literally at "the wind of the day," or in the evening breeze. God came again to fellowship with Adam and Eve; but instead of being in the place of worship, they were hidden among the trees!

They hid among the trees in an effort to hide the outward change they had made in their appearance, covering their own nakedness with fig leaves. This change of appearance marked their inward change of thought. They knew that when they heard the Lord coming, He would want to be with them. Instead of responding in gladness, they hid in shame. What a tragic consequence sin brings.

The narrative's attention to the hiding place of Adam and Eve is significant. They hid among the trees. In Genesis 1 and 2, trees play a central role in portraying Adam and Eve's changing relationship with God. God's bountiful provision is manifested in the fruit trees. However, in chapter 3, a tree is the instrument of temptation that lures Adam and Eve

into sin and then becomes the place where the rebellious man and woman seek to hide from God. Cast out of the garden, Adam and Eve are barred from making their way back to the tree of life (v. 24). Later in Deuteronomy, a tree is described as the place of the punishment of death (Deuteronomy 21:22–23), but that is not the end of the story! The tree is also the place of the gift of life (Galatians 3:13), and as John shows in the book of Revelation, the leaves of the "tree of life" in the new heaven will be for the healing of the nations (Revelation 22:2).

God makes His first move to counter sin: He confronts the participants and demands an explanation. God is like a gentle and loving Father seeking out His own. We hear the heartfelt cry of an anguished Creator who does not come with denunciation but with disappointment. God knows where they are, but He also knows a gulf has been made between Him and humankind, a gulf that He will have to bridge. God's question is intended to prompt Adam to consider his wrongdoing. It is interesting to note that the order of interrogation is the opposite of the order of temptation. God first confronts Adam, who is responsible for watching over the garden.

10 And he said, I heard thy voice in the garden, and I was afraid, because I was naked; and I hid myself. 11 And he said, Who told thee that thou wast naked? Hast thou eaten of the tree, whereof I commanded thee that thou shouldest not eat? 12 And the man said, The woman whom thou gavest to be with me, she gave me of the tree, and I did eat.

Adam is avoiding God. Instead of saying where he was, he gives the excuse that God's voice made him afraid. The immediate consequences of sin are evident. First, sin brings alienation. God's peaceful voice and presence suddenly instill fear in Adam. Second, sin brings shame. In aiming to be like God, Adam and Eve are now in a state of the greatest wretchedness and nakedness. They are embarrassed before God. Adam and Eve know their attempt to cover themselves is a failure. Third, sin brings fear and judgment. Satan's deception exposes Adam and Eve to that death and punishment from which God promised them an exemption. The effects of sin remain the same even today. Alienation from God, shame, fear, and judgment were the first consequences of that first sin and remain so to the present time.

God begins the conversation with Adam by asking two leading questions. The first question shows that Adam doesn't need to be told of his shame because he is already experiencing guilt for his crime—a true guilt that comes from a violated conscience. With the second question, Adam's nakedness is linked to his transgression concerning the tree. The tree is no longer identified as the tree of knowledge but the tree from which God tells them not to eat (2:16–17).

God knew the answers to these questions. Together these questions explained to Adam that his sense of shame arose from his defiance of God's command. This was a sin problem and Adam's shame, fear, or self-understanding could not be addressed until the sin problem was addressed. God asked those questions and, in doing so, allowed Adam to make the best of a bad situation by repenting right then and there. Adam, however, did not own up to his sin and repent before God.

Adam was obliged to acknowledge his transgression, but he did so in such a way as to shift the blame from himself to God and the woman—"the woman whom thou gavest to be with me." Despite his culpability, the man pointed at the woman as the real offender. The immediate effect of sin was broken relationships. Broken relationship with God causes broken relationships with people. The one whom God had created Adam to be with, whom he had called flesh of his flesh, was now separate and the object of his blame for sin. Adam probably thought that since he did not pluck the fruit, he was not at fault; hence he said, "She gave me of the tree." The distance between God and humanity, and between man and woman began here; the curse of sin that was to follow was only a result of the sin itself.

So few of us genuinely confess our sin or acknowledge our guilt! In the same manner as Adam, when many people sin and experience guilt, one of their first responses is to place the blame outside of themselves rather than taking responsibility for doing wrong in their relationship with God.

13 And the LORD God said unto the woman, What is this that thou hast done? And the woman said, The serpent beguiled me, and I did eat. 14 And the LORD God said unto the serpent, Because thou hast done this, thou art cursed above all cattle, and above every beast of the field; upon thy belly shalt thou go, and dust shalt thou eat all the days of thy life: 15 And I will put enmity between thee and the woman, and between thy seed and her seed; it shall bruise thy head and thou shalt bruise his heel.

When God questioned the woman, she blamed the serpent. She said that the serpent "beguiled" her (Heb. *nasha*, **nah-SHAH**), a term often used in the context of fooling someone into a sense of false hope. Although she admitted that she was deceived (and, unlike Adam, she could rightly claim to be the victim of deception), she still passed the blame as though she had done nothing wrong.

The tempter was not asked why he deceived the woman. God only had words of condemnation for the serpent, whereas the man and woman received God's continued concern and provision in the midst of their punishment.

The serpent had no excuse; therefore, God pronounced sentence on him first. There is a clear tie between the serpent's actions and the punishment that follows.

It is important to know that God does not render judgment arbitrarily or capriciously; there always is correspondence between the crime committed and the nature of the judgment because God is the just judge. The curse upon the serpent did not necessarily suggest that the snake had previously walked with feet and legs as the other land animals. The point is rather that for the rest of its life, as a result of the curse, when the snake crawled on its belly it would "eat dust," an expression that elsewhere carries the meaning of total defeat (Isaiah 65:25).

There will not only be perpetual enmity between the woman and the serpent but also between their "seeds." The word "enmity" (Heb. 'ebah, **ay-BAH**) in this context and other passages suggests a long-lasting, intense hostility, such as is experienced among nations and that results in warfare (Numbers 35:21–22; Ezekiel 25:15, 35:5). The human race and the offspring will be forever at loggerheads. Although the same verb, "bruise," is used to describe the actions of both descendants, the location of the blow distinguishes the severity and success of the attack. The impact delivered by the offspring of the woman at the head of the serpent is mortal, while the serpent will only deliver a non-mortal blow to the heel. The Hebrew word for "seed" (Heb. zera', **ZEH-rah**), better translated as "offspring," may refer to an individual (Genesis 4:25) or to a group (Genesis 13:6).

The curse upon the serpent includes its final destruction by a descendant of the woman. The serpent was instrumental in the undoing of the woman; in turn, the woman will ultimately bring down the serpent through her offspring (the Messiah who would conquer sin and death). The relationship between the promise in verse 15 and the judgment pronounced on the woman in verse 16 is striking. Childbirth will be the means through which the serpent is defeated and by which Adam and Eve's forfeited blessing is restored. In the pain of childbirth is the reminder of the hope that lay in God's promise. Birth pangs are not merely a reminder of the futility of the Fall; they are also a sign of an impending joy. Ultimately God will destroy "that old serpent" (Revelation 12:9) for his deception of the nations (Revelation 20:2, 7–10).

16 Unto the woman he said, I will greatly multiply thy sorrow and thy conception; in sorrow thou shalt bring forth children; and thy desire shall be to thy husband, and he shall rule over thee. 17 And unto Adam he said, Because thou hast hearkened unto the voice of thy wife, and hast eaten of the tree, of which I commanded thee, saying, Thou shalt not eat of it: cursed is the ground for thy sake; in sorrow shalt thou eat of it all the days of thy life.

As part of her judgment, the wifely sorrow of Eve would be intensified, and in particular the pains of parturition multiplied. In Scripture, the pains of childbirth are symbolic of the severest anguish both of body and mind (Micah 4:9–10; John 16:21; 1 Thessalonians 5:3). The blessing of childbirth became tainted by the curse. In those moments of life's greatest blessings of marriage and children, the woman would sense most clearly the painful consequences of her disobedience to God.

As part of the judgment on the woman, her "desire shall be to [her] husband." The word "desire" (Heb. teshuqat, **te-shu-kat**) can also mean "longing." The woman was created and given to Adam as a helpmate (2:18), and her relation to the man from the first was one of interdependence. The husband was now to rule instead of being interdependent with his wife.

As a result of the Fall, the marriage vow "to love and to care" becomes "to desire and to dominate." As such, the "rule" here may refer to the harsh exploitative subjugation that, unfortunately, often characterizes the plight of women here and around the world today. The New Testament recognizes the theological significance of the broken relationship between men and women due to the Fall, Christians must actively seek healthy relationships of mutuality based on who we are in Christ (Galatians 3:28) despite our continued flaws as a result of the Fall.

Adam was last to receive his sentence: The "good land" provided by the Creator was cursed. Adam should have obeyed God's word; instead he followed his wife's word and broke God's specific command (Genesis 2:15–17). As man's judgment, Adam and his posterity could no longer "freely eat" of the produce of the land. One must note throughout chapters 2 and 3 that the theme of eating is part of man's ongoing relationship with his Creator. At first, God's blessing and provision for man are noted in the words, "Of every tree of the garden thou mayest freely eat" (2:16). Then, it was specifically over the issue of eating that the tempter raised doubts about God's goodness in His care for Adam and Eve (3:1–3). Finally, the act of disobedience is simply described as she "did eat" and "he did eat" (v. 6). It is not surprising, then, to find that the description of the judgment on the man includes eating: He is to eat in sorrow all the days of his life. From now on, the fertility of the ground would be greatly impaired. How often are all the fruits of man's toil destroyed by landslides, erosion, insects, drought, floods, and other calamities.

The earth is not what God intended. Man's sin changed everything. Anxiety and hard work would be the laboring man's portion. The earth was no longer completely good. Death had entered. Even the ground had changed.

20 And Adam called his wife's name Eve; because she was the mother of all living. 21 Unto Adam also and to his wife did the LORD God make coats of skins, and clothed them.

The word for Eve (Heb. *chavvah*, **khav-VAH**) is a derivative of the word for to breathe or to live (Heb. *chavah*, **kha-VAH**). Adam's wife is called the mother of those that live in this Scripture because she would be the first woman to give birth to a child. God intended humanity to multiply (Genesis 1:28) and that would be accomplished through natural birth. Because of the introduction of sin, this birth would be painful. But God's purpose for childbirth and procreation did not change.

God then made coats of animal skins to cover the nakedness of Adam and Eve after they ate from the tree of the knowledge of good and evil. Their disobedience to God brought them shame and awareness of their nakedness in direct contrast to their earlier innocent state: "And they were both naked, the man and his wife, and were not ashamed" (Genesis 2:25). The impact of sin was immediate and dramatic in changing their perceptions of themselves. They tried to cover themselves, but their covering of fig leaves (Genesis 3:7) was inadequate to hide their shame.

Here in verse 21 we see the first instance of God covering sin. God gives them coats of skin from animals to wear, using His creation to clothe humans. There had to be cutting and bloodshed as the first symbolic covering of sin, which sets a pattern picked up in Leviticus— that through the bloodshed of animals, sin is covered temporarily. It is ultimately through the bloodshed of Jesus Christ that sin is covered forever and we are clothed with righteousness and placed in right relationship with God by faith.

22 And the LORD God said, Behold, the man is become as one of us, to know good and evil: and now, lest he put forth his hand, and take also of the tree of life, and eat, and live for ever: 23 Therefore the LORD God sent him forth from the garden of Eden, to till the ground from whence he was taken.

God says that man has become as one of us in knowing good and evil. This knowledge was already unrighteous and skewed toward evil because it did not come from God. Knowledge of good and evil is a divine principle. But because Adam and Eve's knowledge did not come from God but rather disobedience, it was destructive rather than productive. As a result man was expelled from the Garden of Eden.

We receive a brief reminder here that there were two special trees in the garden; the tree of the knowledge of good and evil, which God told them not to eat of; and the tree of life, which they were free to eat of. God had placed before man eternal life that was free, and death that came through disobedience, even in the Garden of Eden itself. Once sin tainted humanity and all creation, they could not eat from the tree of life or they would be forever preserved in a state of sinfulness. God sent them out of the garden to till the ground or farm. They could eat fruit from the trees of the garden before sin; now Adam would have to farm the hard ground to grow his own food to live. Work was made difficult as a result of sin.

24 So he drove out the man; and he placed at the east of the garden of Eden Cherubims, and a flaming sword which turned every way, to keep the way of the tree of life.

The man is no longer in the garden and cherubim, or guardian angelic beings, are placed before the garden to protect it. They are the same beings that Ezekiel sees guarding the presence of God in his vision (Ezekiel 10). Moses was instructed to have cherubim fashioned out of gold to cover the ark of the covenant (Exodus 37:1–9). It is clear that cherubim are creatures who protect the presence of God. A flaming sword is also placed before the garden that was able to "turn every way" or move to strike as needed. All of this was intended to protect the tree of life. God would not allow humans to be forever in sin under any circumstances. Their disobedience would be kept temporary. Death would eventually end their lives in sin. Yet this was only a precedent for the atonement for sin and restoration to right relationship and eternal life with God through Jesus Christ.

Say It Correctly

Beguile. beh-**GAHYL**
Cherubim. cher-**UH**-bim.
Enmity. **EN**-mi-tee.

Daily Bible Readings

MONDAY
King David Gives in to Temptation
(2 Samuel 11:1–5)

TUESDAY
Death by Adam; Life by Christ
(Romans 5:12–19)

WEDNESDAY
Jesus Overcomes Temptation
(Matthew 4:1–11)

THURSDAY
Removing the Stumbling Blocks to
Temptation
(Mark 9:42–48)

FRIDAY
Endure Temptation, Receive Crown of Life
(James 1:12–15)

SATURDAY
The Serpent's Temptation
(Genesis 3:1–7)

SUNDAY
The Sins of the First Humans
(Genesis 3:8–17, 20–24)

Notes

_____

_____

_____

_____

Teaching Tips

Words You Should Know

A. Perfect *tamim* (Heb.)—Whole, blameless.

B. Covenant *berit* (Heb.)—An agreement between two individuals that forms a relationship, in this case an unconditional agreement between God and humankind.

Teacher Preparation

Unifying Principle—Faithful Following. Faithfulness is a needed quality of life, but it is difficult to achieve. How can persons be faithful in difficult situations? Noah is an empowering example of someone who remained faithful to what God asked him to do regardless of the opposing circumstance and consequences.

A. Read the Bible Background and Devotional Readings.

B. Pray for your students and lesson clarity.

C. Read the lesson Scripture in multiple translations.

D. Option: Ask the students to share some of their favorite hymns they like to sing to help them remain faithful and hopeful during times of difficulty.

O—Open the Lesson

A. Begin the class with prayer.

B. Have the students read the Aim for Change.

C. Have the students read the In Focus story.

D. Ask students how events named in the story can weigh on their hearts and how they can view these events from a theological perspective.

P—Present the Scriptures

A. Read the Focal Verses and discuss the Background and The People, Places, and Times sections.

B. Have the class share what Scriptures stand out for them and why, with particular emphasis on today's context.

E—Explore the Meaning

A. Use In Depth or More Light on the Text to help provide more in-depth discussion of the lesson text.

B. Discuss the Liberating Lesson and Application for Activation sections.

N—Next Steps for Application

A. Summarize the value of being faithful despite difficult circumstances.

B. End class with a commitment to pray for greater faithfulness and obedience to God.

Worship Guide

For the Superintendent or Teacher
Theme: Noah's Steadfast Faith
Song: "Who Built the Ark?"
Devotional Reading: Matthew 24:36–44

Noah's Steadfast Faith

Bible Background • GENESIS 6; 8:19
Printed Text • GENESIS 6:9b–22 | Devotional Reading • MATTHEW 24:36–44

Aim for Change

By the end of this lesson, we will: RECALL Noah's faithful obedience to God in building the ark; REPENT of the times we failed to follow God's instructions; and RESOLVE to do what God commands regardless of the challenges.

In Focus

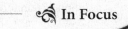

Jocelyn had been preparing for three weeks to teach her class on media and ministry at the church. She had spent hours after work making sure her slideshow presentation was beautiful and her notecards were brief. She walked into the church on Saturday morning and was shocked. Instead of being set up for her presentation, there were teenagers playing board games all around the room. She confronted the youth pastor immediately.

"Excuse me, but I'm supposed to be teaching a class on media and ministry in this room. Why are you here?" Jocelyn demanded.

"Today is our youth fellowship day," the youth pastor responded. "Did you remember to reserve the room and let the church secretary know about your class? I didn't see anything in the reservation book before I scheduled this activity with the teens."

It hit Jocelyn all at once. She had gotten so excited about her class that she had forgotten to follow through on the instructions the senior pastor had given her to set up for the class. She felt embarrassed and disappointed. She would have to follow up about her class the next week.

Not following instructions of leadership can have embarrassing and disappointing consequences. Not following the instructions of God can be even more devastating. What are some reasons people don't follow the directions of leadership? Why do people sometimes disobey the commands of God?

Keep in Mind

"Thus did Noah; according to all that God had commanded him, so did he" (Genesis 6:22, KJV).

"So Noah did everything exactly as God had commanded him" (Genesis 6:22, NLT).

Focal Verses

KJV **Genesis 6:9** These are the generations of Noah: Noah was a just man and perfect in his generations, and Noah walked with God.

10 And Noah begat three sons, Shem, Ham, and Japheth.

11 The earth also was corrupt before God, and the earth was filled with violence.

12 And God looked upon the earth, and, behold, it was corrupt; for all flesh had corrupted his way upon the earth.

13 And God said unto Noah, The end of all flesh is come before me; for the earth is filled with violence through them; and, behold, I will destroy them with the earth.

14 Make thee an ark of gopher wood; rooms shalt thou make in the ark, and shalt pitch it within and without with pitch.

15 And this is the fashion which thou shalt make it of: The length of the ark shall be three hundred cubits, the breadth of it fifty cubits, and the height of it thirty cubits.

16 A window shalt thou make to the ark, and in a cubit shalt thou finish it above; and the door of the ark shalt thou set in the side thereof; with lower, second, and third stories shalt thou make it.

17 And, behold, I, even I, do bring a flood of waters upon the earth, to destroy all flesh, wherein is the breath of life, from under heaven; and every thing that is in the earth shall die.

18 But with thee will I establish my covenant; and thou shalt come into the ark, thou, and thy sons, and thy wife, and thy sons' wives with thee.

19 And of every living thing of all flesh, two of every sort shalt thou bring into the ark, to keep them alive with thee; they shall be male and female.

NLT **Genesis 6:9** This is the account of Noah and his family. Noah was a righteous man, the only blameless person living on earth at the time, and he walked in close fellowship with God.

10 Noah was the father of three sons: Shem, Ham, and Japheth.

11 Now God saw that the earth had become corrupt and was filled with violence.

12 God observed all this corruption in the world, for everyone on earth was corrupt.

13 So God said to Noah, "I have decided to destroy all living creatures, for they have filled the earth with violence. Yes, I will wipe them all out along with the earth!

14 Build a large boat from cypress wood and waterproof it with tar, inside and out. Then construct decks and stalls throughout its interior.

15 Make the boat 450 feet long, 75 feet wide, and 45 feet high.

16 Leave an 18-inch opening below the roof all the way around the boat. Put the door on the side, and build three decks inside the boat—lower, middle, and upper.

17 Look! I am about to cover the earth with a flood that will destroy every living thing that breathes. Everything on earth will die.

18 But I will confirm my covenant with you. So enter the boat—you and your wife and your sons and their wives.

19 Bring a pair of every kind of animal—a male and a female—into the boat with you to keep them alive during the flood.

20 Pairs of every kind of bird, and every kind of animal, and every kind of small animal that scurries along the ground, will come to you to be kept alive.

21 And be sure to take on board enough food for your family and for all the animals."

20 Of fowls after their kind, and of cattle after their kind, of every creeping thing of the earth after his kind, two of every sort shall come unto thee, to keep them alive.

21 And take thou unto thee of all food that is eaten, and thou shalt gather it to thee; and it shall be for food for thee, and for them.

22 Thus did Noah; according to all that God commanded him, so did he.

22 So Noah did everything exactly as God had commanded him.

The People, Places, and Times

Noah. The son of Lamech, Noah was born into a world that had become completely corrupted. However, because Noah found favor with God, he was declared righteous. Through Noah and his family, God preserved humanity and gave to the world a new beginning. Noah can be viewed, therefore, as the second father of humankind. Many generations separated Noah and the earth's first couple.

Background

Most people are familiar with Noah as someone who built a huge boat to house his family and every species of animal during the worldwide flood. That moment in history may seem like the most memorable slice of his life, but what Noah did before this famous voyage is especially worth paying attention to. Despite being as imperfect as anyone, the Bible describes Noah as "blameless" in comparison to others in his era who lived wicked lives (Genesis 6:9). His part of God's story is primarily found in Genesis 5–9, making him one of the patriarchs of our faith—individuals with whom God established a foundational covenant in order to re-create hope for everyone else, from generation to generation.

In this case, God had to address the growing sin in the world as well as a specific evil that had infected the overall bloodline of humanity.

In his grief over this corruption yet commitment to redemption, the Lord sent a devastating flood to wash away everyone but Noah and his family. We may never fully understand the thoughts or heartache everyone who survived experienced during this time, especially since humanity was given years to turn away from its sin. What we can more practically recognize is how one household who followed God was used to redeem even the most evil of situations.

How might Noah be a very real example to us of what it means to be an imperfect person who chooses to walk with God when no one else is?

At-A-Glance

1. Righteousness Creates Faithfulness
(Genesis 6:9)
2. Faithfulness Creates Trust
(vv. 10–22)

In Depth

1. Righteousness Creates Faithfulness (Genesis 6:9)

Every relationship is fueled by one of two motives: "I have to know this person" or "I get to know this person." The same thing applies to how we view God, for some people believe we "have to" treat Him with respect or else He will makes us feel guilty (if not curse us). This actually tracks back to how we struggle to predict the consequences of our own behavior, so we just end up pinning all of the worst things in our lives on Him.

Noah saw things the other way: By living a righteous life he felt the pleasure of faithfulness (6:9). It's what happens when we do what God has asked and help re-create this world back into what He originally intended. We experience the joy He hardwired into how things were meant to be experienced. We move from "have to" to "get to" when we will faithfully protect and preserve the things we care about.

When have you experienced pleasure by doing something the way God intended for you to do versus the way others might? How did that motivate you to want to do it again the same way?

2. Faithfulness Creates Trust (vv. 10–22)

When we truly know someone, we do things more out of trust than out of the person explaining all the details. Noah was a father to three boys (v. 10), so he knew something about trying to keep them safe in a world of violence (v. 11). They had to trust his perspective as their father despite not knowing all he knew, just as Noah had to trust God's perspective and instructions. Like a father and son relationship, God and Noah had built a special kind of intimacy and trust over time as Noah lived righteously. It allowed them to form a covenant in the midst of it all (v. 18)—even if Noah didn't understand the purpose of every detail, he did it all (v. 22).

We tend to struggle with this most after experiencing great uncertainty and loss. If it feels like God has let us down in protecting our loved ones, we might let the crisis overtake our trust. Faithfulness is key for us to re-create our confidence in the Lord out of truth instead of emotion. At some point in your faith journey,

you see the harder things as a pathway to embrace the greater things.

In what ways has God demonstrated His faithfulness to you, and in what ways have you demonstrated your faithfulness to Him?

Search the Scriptures

1. Who are some people you know or have heard about whom you would describe as "righteous" and "blameless in [our] generation" (6:9)?

2. How do you feel about knowing that God wanted to destroy humanity (6:13)? How would you describe how God felt about it?

3. How did Noah's relationship with God affect his family and the future of mankind? What if Noah would have been a sinful man instead?

Discuss the Meaning

1. People can often be skeptical about the consequences of their actions or warnings of God punishing them in the future. What advice would you give the world if you could somehow get everyone to listen to you for a few moments?

2. When have you felt it to be difficult to embrace what God has called you to do despite knowing it was the right thing to do?

Liberating Lesson

Think back to a time when you made something important to you, be it a project around the house or something creative. What if you knew you had to destroy it? God knew creation would be tainted by sin yet still put His all into it. In contrast, we live in a world that makes no promises yet demands guarantees. People are generally reluctant to do even important things unless they know for sure it will be "worth it" or that something will be in it for them. God instead demonstrates what it means to give His all to what matters, just as Noah shows us how to be steadfast for God even if sometimes we stand alone. The New Testament uses salvation language to refer to Noah's experience (1 Peter 3:20; 2 Peter 2:5), suggesting the account here should be seen more as God's saving humanity from sinful self-destruction than merely as punishment for sin. We take part in this every time we stand up for the Lord, not just by saying important things before others but in right living that shows we know what's important.

Application for Activation

Missionaries, anthropologists, and ethnologists have all discovered stories about a global flood told by multiple cultures throughout history. Not all of these cultures have recognized the actual details of what happened, though. We have a habit as people of only reading the "headline" and thinking like we know the whole "story."

Gather a group together to meet with someone in authority, be it a pastor, city official, employer, teacher, or anyone else appropriate. Spend at least 10 minutes with this person asking him or her to share any current situations where a misunderstanding is having a big impact because people are only reading the "headline," not the whole "story." Perhaps people are complaining about local construction without realizing why that project is happening, or maybe a person has a great idea that has yet to be developed because others don't understand its importance. Come up with several good ways you can have a hand in helping something righteous happen by taking part in some honorable choices or communication to help sort things out. Thank God for His sovereignty in how no matter what anyone in history has done or been confused by, no one has ever been able to overtake Him or His larger plans.

Follow the Spirit

What God wants me to do:

_____

_____

_____

_____

Remember Your Thoughts

Special insights I have learned:

_____

_____

_____

_____

More Light on the Text
Genesis 6:9–22

9 These are the generations of Noah: Noah was a just man and perfect in his generations, and Noah walked with God. 10 And Noah begat three sons, Shem, Ham, and Japheth.

At Noah's birth his father Lamech gave him his name, which means comfort (Heb. *noach*, **no-AKH**). Noah is the tenth generation from Adam. He is a bridge between two worlds, the former destroyed by water and the current awaiting a destruction by fire (2 Peter 3:6–7). Noah stands out completely from his contemporaries.

Noah is described by three qualities: "just," "perfect," and "walked with God." The Hebrew word for just or righteous (*tsaddiq*, **tsad-DEEK**) portrays someone who keeps the moral law and is obedient to the will of God. The word translated "perfect" is *tamim* (**tah-MEEM**), an adjective that conveys the meaning of wholeness, perfection, and blamelessness. It was used for the sacrificial animals that

73

should have been without defect or blemish to be accepted by the Lord. The word does not convey the meaning of sinlessness but characterizes a person who abstains from iniquity or intentional gross wickedness. Lastly, Noah walked with God. This sentence places Noah on a high pedestal in the biblical record with Enoch. They are the only two people who were presented as walking with God in their time (Genesis 5:24). For all the other instances, the expression is "to walk before the Lord" (Genesis 17:1; Psalm 116:9).

The two uses of the word "generations" in this verse are actually two different Hebrew words: *toledot* (**toe-leh-DOTE**) and *dor* (**DOOR**). The *toledot* formula ("these are the generations of...") is used to introduce each of the eleven sections of the book of Genesis. "Among his generations" signifies "among his contemporaries." The generation in which Noah lived was a wicked and godless one. God depicts how the generation was so wicked that people's hearts were continually full of evil thoughts (6:5).

The uprightness of Noah shines even more in light of the conduct of his contemporaries. Living in obedience to God in such an environment was not an easy task. His generation is called "the world of the ungodly" (2 Peter 2:5). Jesus presents them as not evil in themselves, but one lacking concern for spiritual matters while too involved in temporal matters (Matthew 24:38–39).

Noah's three sons are the people the Lord used to repopulate the earth after the Flood. Shem, Ham and Japheth are therefore the ancestors of all human beings now living on earth. This suggests that irrespective of race, the post-flood population comes from the same origin. Therefore it cannot be stated that one race is superior to another. The table of nations indicates that Semitic people are descendants of Shem and Indo-European are descendants of Japheth. Africans are descendants of Ham. Some important nations of antiquity such as Egypt, a world power at one time, are African. Some are tempted to link the curse on Canaan, the son of Ham, to Africa, but this is not a responsible use of the text. The Canaanites were largely destroyed by the Israelites who inherited their land.

11 The earth also was corrupt before God, and the earth was filled with violence. 12 And God looked upon the earth, and, behold, it was corrupt; for all flesh had corrupted his way upon the earth.

The generation of Noah was marked by corruption and violence. The Hebrew word *shachath* (**shah-KHATH**) translated "corrupt" is also translated as "destroy" (v. 13), and indicates that humanity had essentially already destroyed itself before God destroyed it.

In many instances in the Bible, God decided to follow suit with the course taken by people (Romans 1:24). The Lord allows a strong delusion to those who delight in lies and unrighteousness (2 Thessalonians 2:11–12). The scale of the corruption was high and the extent was wide. The word here for violence (Heb. *chamac*, **khah-MAHK**) refers to a violence based in lawlessness. It is often a physical violence meant to disrupt society's rules, but the word is also used of non-physical oppression of the powerful over the needy.

With sorrow, God takes a look at the earth in this state. The first time God saw the earth, everything was perfect (Genesis 1:31), but then sin entered the world. This current assessment of the earth's condition is the saddest one. Corruption has overtaken its inhabitants to such an extent that nothing could be done to stop its destruction. But in the midst of this darkness, God saw a tiny light in Noah and his family who would repopulate the world after the destruction. The biblical record testifies that God is constantly involved in the condition of His creation contrary to the conception of deism. God is ever assessing the moral state of the earth both globally and individually. In search of people of integrity, the eyes of the Lord run to and fro throughout the whole earth (2 Chronicles 16:9; Zechariah 4:10).

Commentators have discussed whether the word flesh (Heb. *basar*, **bah-SAR**) concerns only human beings in this verse or if it includes animals as well. The issue is that the animal did not have moral decisions to make. Some find it difficult therefore to involve the animal kingdom in the corruption of the ways of all flesh. However, all throughout the Flood narrative, most often the phrase "all flesh" applies to both humankind and animals (v. 13). It could be an indication also of the scale and intensity of the corruption.

13 And God said unto Noah, The end of all flesh is come before me; for the earth is filled with violence through them; and, behold, I will destroy them with the earth.

Noah was privy to the confidence of God because of his right standing with the Lord. The Lord God will do nothing without revealing it to His faithful servants, the prophets, who are privileged to speak in His name (Amos 3:7). For example, Abraham got the information of the fate of Sodom and Gomorrah (Genesis 18:17–21). The righteous privilege to be in the confidence of the Lord is also a responsibility, one either to plead for God's mercy or to proclaim His righteousness by calling people to repentance. Therefore, Abraham pleaded for mercy (Genesis 18:23–33) and Noah preached to his contemporaries (2 Peter 2:5). The faithful servants are also faithful witnesses.

The word rendered "end" (Heb. *qets*, **KAY-ts**) is most often used for the end of life or a limit in a temporal sense and rarely for spatial boundaries. It is mostly encountered in the situation of divine judgment. As the world was going through a process of self-destruction, God decreed a limit to the process. All living creatures apart from those in the ark would perish because they had filled the world with violence. The expression "with the earth" does not mean the earth was to be completely destroyed as predicted for the current earth (Revelation 21:1). But the earth certainly sustained damages.

14 Make thee an ark of gopher wood; rooms shalt thou make in the ark, and shalt pitch it within and without with pitch.

After briefing Noah on the earth's moral condition and the decision to destroy it, God now gives clear instructions to Noah for building a ship. In English the word is translated ark (which comes from the Latin *arca*, meaning box) because of the box-like shape of the vessel. The Hebrew word for this vessel is *tebah* (**tay-BAH**), found twenty-eight times in the Old Testament, only in the Flood narrative and in the Exodus. It designates the vessel Noah constructed for the Flood and the box container Moses' mother made of reeds to float him down the Nile River. These should not be confused with the ark of covenant in which the Hebrew word is *'aron* (**aw-RONE**), meaning chest or box.

The wood for the construction was gopher (Heb. *gopher*, **go-FER**), the only occurrence of it in the Bible. Its meaning is unknown, therefore three translations of the word are found in the various versions of the Bible. Some maintain "gopher" wood, others translate specifically "cypress," and still others say "resinous" wood. In any case, it describes a quality wood, probably very resilient. The ark needed to be waterproof because it would float on water. So it had to be smeared with a pitch, a black, sticky tar-like substance used to waterproof roofs and boats.

The Hebrew word *qen* (**KANE**), translated "rooms," means nest, but in this context scholars suggest room or compartment. These rooms were necessary due to the various kinds of animals on board.

15 And this is the fashion which thou shalt make it of: The length of the ark shall be three hundred cubits, the breadth of it fifty cubits, and the height of it thirty cubits. 16 A window shalt thou make to the ark, and in a cubit shalt thou finish it above; and the door of the ark shalt thou set in the side thereof; with lower, second, and third stories shalt thou make it.

After the instruction to build the ark, now the details about its features are given. The dimensions of Noah's vessel are completely logical. Some scholars suggest the ark was about 95,000 square feet, yielding enough space to accommodate all the animals. The interior of the boat had to be divided into three levels and provide one entrance door. The Hebrew word for cubit (*ammah*, **am-MAH**) is a unit of measurement referring to the distance between the elbow and the tip of the middle finger of an average-sized man. It is about 18 inches. In the New Living Translation, the measurements are given as 450 feet long, 75 feet wide and 45 feet high.

The Hebrew word translated as window is *tsohar* (**tso-HAR**). It only occurs here in the Old Testament. Its meaning is not obvious, therefore scholars give two possible meanings. First, compared to words of the same root in other Semitic languages, which are rendered back or top, some scholars choose "roof" as the meaning of *tsohar*. Second, as the word is close to *tsoharaim*, which means noonday, many understood it as window. Both meanings are valid, but the first one seems likely because of the phrase that follows it. The roof of the ark could not be flat as usual, but needed to be slanted slightly down to allow the rain to drain off. In this case, the phrase "in a cubit shall thou finish it above" indicates that the middle of the roof should be raised by one cubit above the other two sides of the roof. In the case of it referring to a window, this cubit may suggest a gap of 18 inches all around the ark just below the roof, probably for airing.

The ark should have the entrance door in one of the long sides. It also should be constructed with three different levels.

17 And, behold, I, even I, do bring a flood of waters upon the earth, to destroy all flesh, wherein is the breath of life, from under heaven; and everything that is in the earth shall die.

After Noah received instructions about what to do, God informs him about the impeding destruction awaiting the earth's inhabitants by flood. The Flood narrative is encountered in various cultures all around the world. There is also a scientific debate over the scale of the biblical flood. Some suggest it was local and not global. The phrases "under heaven" and "everything that is on earth" can indicate a global scale for Noah's flood.

The Hebrew word for flood is *mabbul* (**mab-BOOL**). The term occurs only once outside the Flood narrative (Psalm 29:10). Similarly in the New Testament, only one Greek word is used to refer to Noah's flood (*kataklusmos*, **ka-ta-clues-MOSE**). In both testaments other words are used to refer to other floods. This was a one-of-a-kind event.

18 But with thee will I establish my covenant; and thou shalt come into the ark, thou, and thy sons, and thy wife, and thy sons' wives with thee.

While God decided to wipe off every living being on earth, He however chose to show His grace to Noah by establishing a covenant with him. The word for covenant in Hebrew is *berit* (**beh-REET**). This is the very first occurrence of the word in the Bible, and it is notably linked to salvation. It is a formal agreement between at least two people or between God and one or more people. There are two types of covenants. An unconditional covenant is one in which the fulfillment of God's promises is kept irrespective of the other party's involvement. A conditional covenant is one in which the fulfillment is dependent upon the involvement of the parties to the covenant. In the current case the fulfillment relies solely on God's side, therefore this is an unconditional covenant. The full content of the covenant will be revealed later after the Flood (Genesis 9:9). For now, through the covenant, Noah has the assurance of making it to a next generation with his entire family.

19 And of every living thing of all flesh, two of every sort shalt thou bring into the ark, to keep them alive with thee; they shall be male and female. 20 Of fowls after their kind, and of cattle after their kind, of every creeping thing of the earth after his kind, two of every sort shall come unto thee, to keep them alive.

For the new beginning, God's will is to preserve every species that was created in Genesis 1. One couple of every land animal had to be kept alive to maintain the survival of the species. There would be no spontaneous regeneration after the Flood, but a repopulation of the earth by every living land animal according to their kind. As the previous verse mentioned the human beings, "every living thing" here concerns only the animals.

Verse 19 states that Noah has the responsibility to bring the animals into the ark, and the last part of verse 20 states that the animals would come to Noah. The best explanation of these varying statements is that the animals on their own would come close to the ark and

Noah's task would be to take them on board. This explanation shows how the Lord holds absolute control over the animals. He would send them to Noah.

21 And take thou unto thee of all food that is eaten, and thou shalt gather it to thee; and it shall be for food for thee, and for them. 22 Thus did Noah; according to all that God commanded him, so did he.

The last command to Noah concerns the gathering of enough food for him and his family and the animals on board for the duration of the Flood. At this stage, only plants and their fruits were food for human beings and animals (Genesis 1:29–30). Noah was to gather a sufficient provision for all the animals in the ark, plus himself and his family. The Flood would start the second month of Noah's six hundredth year (Genesis 7:11), and they would come out of the ark in the second month of Noah's six hundred and first year (Genesis 8:13–14).

Noah was indeed a faithful servant. We see this in light of his integrity among his contemporaries, but even more so by his obedience to the smallest detail of God's instruction related to the building of the ark, the sampling of animals to enter the ark, and the gathering of the food for their journey. With all these, Peter mentions Noah's ministry of preaching in the years preceding the Flood to an unconcerned and unbelieving world doomed for utter destruction (2 Peter 2:5). He is therefore rightly listed among the heroes of faith in the eloquent and magnificent record of faith (Hebrews 11:7).

Sources:
Barnwell, K., and Kuhn, H. *Translator's Notes on Genesis.* Dallas, TX: SIL International, 2007.
Botterweck, J.G., and Ringgren, H. *Theological Dictionary of the Old Testament, Vol. 3.* Translated by D.E. Green. Grand Rapids, MI: William B. Eerdmans, 1978.
Botterweck, J.G., Ringgren, H., and Fabry, E.J., eds. *Theological Dictionary of the Old Testament, Vol. 8.* Translated by D.W. Stott. Grand Rapids, MI: William B. Erdmans, 1997.

Hamilton, V.P. *The New International Commentary on the Old Testament: The book of Genesis 1-17.* Grand Rapids, MI: William B. Eerdmans, 1990.

Kidner, D. *Tyndale Old Testament Commentaries: Genesis.* Edited by D. Wiseman. Downers Grove, IL: Inter-Varsity Press, 1967.

VanGemeren, W. A. *New International Dictionary of Old Testament Theology and Exegesis (Vol. III).* Grand Rapids, MI: Zondervan, 1997.

Wenham, G. J. *Word Biblical Commentary: Genesis 1-15.* Waco, TX: Word Books, 1987.

Say It Correctly

Noah. **NO-uh.**
Jepheth. **JEY-**fith.

Daily Bible Readings

MONDAY
The Lord's Sorrow for All Creation
(Genesis 6:1–8)

TUESDAY
God Will Send a Great Flood
(Genesis 7:1–5)

WEDNESDAY
Noah's Family Enter the Ark
(Genesis 7:6–10)

THURSDAY
Wild and Domestic Animals Climb Aboard
(Genesis 7:11–16)

FRIDAY
The Flood Destroys All Earthly Life
(Genesis 7:17–24)

SATURDAY
Surviving People and Animals Disembark Ark
(Genesis 8:1–5, 13–19)

SUNDAY
The Ark of Safety and Preservation
(Genesis 6:9b–22)

Notes

Teaching Tips

Words You Should Know
A. Bless *baraq* (Heb.)—To speak well of.
B. Curse *'arar* (Heb.)—To abhor or hate.

Teacher Preparation
Unifying Principle—Constantly Working.
Many tasks seem daunting or even impossible for mere human effort. How can humans accomplish such challenging and important work? Genesis teaches that God worked over many generations from Noah to Abraham to bring blessings to the entire world.

A. Read the Bible Background and Devotional Readings.

B. Pray for your students and lesson clarity.

C. Read the lesson Scripture in multiple translations.

D. Option: What people in your community are struggling? Brainstorm ways your class could be a blessing to them. Make a plan to help in the ways you can.

O—Open the Lesson
A. Begin the class with prayer.

B. Have the students read the Aim for Change.

C. Have the students read the In Focus story.

D. Ask students how events named in the story can weigh on their hearts and how they can view these events from a theological perspective.

P—Present the Scriptures
A. Read the Focal Verses and discuss the Background and The People, Places, and Times sections.

B. Have the class share what Scriptures stand out for them and why, with particular emphasis on today's context.

E—Explore the Meaning
A. Use In Depth or More Light on the Text to help provide more in-depth discussion of the lesson text.

B. Discuss the Liberating Lesson and Application for Activation sections.

N—Next Steps for Application
A. Summarize the value of knowing God works in families through generations.

B. End class with a commitment to pray for family lineage and heritage, especially for future generations.

Worship Guide

For Superintendent or Teacher
Theme: God Is Always Working
Song: "Alive"
Devotional Reading: Hebrews 11:4–10

God Is Always Working

Bible Background • GENESIS 9–12 | Printed Text • GENESIS 10:1; 11:10, 27, 31–32; 12:1–4 | Devotional Reading • HEBREWS 11:4–10

Aim for Change

By the end of the lesson, we will: EXAMINE the significance of the genealogical record in Genesis; EXPLAIN the reality that God works through generations to accomplish His will; and CELEBRATE how God has worked in our own families to bless others.

 In Focus

Darius was frustrated. His friend Kendall had been telling him that he needed to wake up to the reality that Christianity was a religion forced on him by white oppressors. Kendall argued that Darius should follow the traditional religions of Africa as he did. Darius was unsure how to respond to Kendall, but he knew he was committed to following Jesus Christ regardless of what Kendall thought. One day he had a conversation with his great-grandmother whose grandparents were former slaves. "Granny, were your parents Christian?" he asked.

"Yes, baby. They may have not been preachers, or always been perfect, but they learned how to read from that Bible." She pointed to a bookshelf in the corner of the room. "And I remember my parents singing songs about Jesus when I was young. They believed Jesus would free them from slavery, and when they finally walked into freedom they gave praise to God for delivering them!"

Darius was in awe. If his ancestors had believed in Jesus and they were slaves of people who called themselves Christians, surely he could stand up to Kendall. On his great-grandmother's bookshelf, he saw the worn Bible and a book called *Africans Who Shaped Our Faith*. He decided he would do his own study to defend his faith to Kendall.

Why is it important to know our family history? How can we encourage children in our lives to learn about Jesus in a world where there is so much opposition to Christianity?

Keep in Mind

"And I will make of thee a great nation, and I will bless thee, and make thy name great; and thou shalt be a blessing: And I will bless them that bless thee, and curse him that curseth thee: and in thee shall all families of the earth be blessed" (Genesis 12:2–3, KJV).

" I will make you into a great nation. I will bless you and make you famous, and you will be a blessing to others. I will bless those who bless you and curse those who treat you with contempt. All the families on earth will be blessed through you." (Genesis 12:2–3, NLT)

Focal Verses

KJV **Genesis 10:1** Now these are the generations of the sons of Noah, Shem, Ham, and Japheth: and unto them were sons born after the flood.

11:10 These are the generations of Shem: Shem was an hundred years old, and begat Arphaxad two years after the flood:

27 Now these are the generations of Terah: Terah begat Abram, Nahor, and Haran; and Haran begat Lot.

31 And Terah took Abram his son, and Lot the son of Haran his son's son, and Sarai his daughter in law, his son Abram's wife; and they went forth with them from Ur of the Chaldees, to go into the land of Canaan; and they came unto Haran, and dwelt there.

32 And the days of Terah were two hundred and five years: and Terah died in Haran.

12:1 Now the LORD had said unto Abram, Get thee out of thy country, and from thy kindred, and from thy father's house, unto a land that I will shew thee:

2 And I will make of thee a great nation, and I will bless thee, and make thy name great; and thou shalt be a blessing:

3 And I will bless them that bless thee, and curse him that curseth thee: and in thee shall all families of the earth be blessed.

4 So Abram departed, as the LORD had spoken unto him; and Lot went with him: and Abram was seventy and five years old when he departed out of Haran.

NLT **Genesis 10:1** This is the account of the families of Shem, Ham, and Japheth, the three sons of Noah. Many children were born to them after the great flood.

11:10 This is the account of Shem's family. Two years after the great flood, when Shem was 100 years old, he became the father of Arphaxad.

27 This is the account of Terah's family. Terah was the father of Abram, Nahor, and Haran; and Haran was the father of Lot.

31 One day Terah took his son Abram, his daughter-in-law Sarai (his son Abram's wife), and his grandson Lot (his son Haran's child) and moved away from Ur of the Chaldeans. He was headed for the land of Canaan, but they stopped at Haran and settled there.

32 Terah lived for 205 years and died while still in Haran.

12:1 The LORD had said to Abram, "Leave your native country, your relatives, and your father's family, and go to the land that I will show you.

2 I will make you into a great nation. I will bless you and make you famous, and you will be a blessing to others.

3 I will bless those who bless you and curse those who treat you with contempt. All the families on earth will be blessed through you."

4 So Abram departed as the LORD had instructed, and Lot went with him. Abram was seventy-five years old when he left Haran.

The People, Places, and Times

Abram. The significance of God's call for a nation through Abram was that up to this point no distinction existed between people and races in the manner that we think of today. After the Flood, the people were dispersed at the Tower of Babel (Genesis 11:1–9). The Bible depicts a detailed review of the descendants of Shem, Noah's eldest son. Out of Shem's lineage, through Abram, God would call out a people unto Himself to be witnesses throughout the earth of His greatness. They would receive the blessing for serving the one true and living God in the midst of idolatry around them. Ultimately, Abram's seed through forty-two generations would bring forth the Messiah who would reconcile the world back to God (Matthew 1:1–17). Abram exemplifies the faith necessary to obtain righteousness and access to the promises of God through Jesus Christ.

The Land of Canaan. In Hebrew "Canaan" (*kena'an*, **keh-NAH-an**) means low region or lowland. It refers to the country west of the Jordan and the Dead Sea, between the waters on the eastern shore of the Mediterranean Sea. Named after Ham's son, the land was given by God to Abram's posterity, the Children of Israel, as promised. In modern geography, Canaan is now Palestine and the West Bank.

Background

Genesis 6–9 provides the account of the Flood that God sent as judgment for wickedness throughout the earth. Only eight people were spared: Noah, his wife, their three sons and their wives. From these eight people, the whole earth was repopulated (Genesis 9:19).

Genesis 10 begins with a table of nations presenting the known tribes of that time. This table gave the "horizontal" genealogy of Noah's three oldest sons—Shem, Ham, and Japheth— and serves as a precursor to the scattering that will later occur at the Tower of Babel in Genesis 11. Not only will the tribes and clans be identified by their geological location, but also by their languages (Genesis 10:31).

This genealogy differs from the one provided later in chapter 11, in that the intention here is not to prove ancestry, but show affiliations and allegiances among tribes. Ancient readers would have been able to tell from its arrangement which tribes fell under God's blessing, and which were cursed (see Genesis 9:20–27; 12:1–3)—and they associated

accordingly, providing the backdrop for future conflicts and wars.

Although Shem is listed first, his genealogy is provided last, indicating that his story and descendants will be the focal point.

What does this section imply about the connections of all of the people groups of the world? How could this knowledge affect one's relationships and interactions?

At-A-Glance

1. Noah to Shem (Genesis 10:1)
2. Shem to Abram (Genesis 11:10, 27, 31–32)
3. Abram's Call (Genesis 12:1–4)

In Depth

1. Noah to Shem (Genesis 10:1)

Genesis 10:1 introduces what is called the "Table of Nations" by listing Noah's three sons, mentioning in passing that he and his wife had other sons after the Flood. Nothing else is said about those sons. However, as the sons' descendants are listed later in the chapter, one sees the ethnic, political, and geographical development of future tribes and people groups.

Shem is the father of Semitic language groups, including the Jews or Hebrews. The name "Hebrew" is believed to be derived from Eber, Shem's great-grandson; the name "Jew" is derived from Israel's son Judah. From Ham would come a variety of people groups; Cush would be modern-day Ethiopia and Sudan, and Mizraim was also called Egypt. Japheth's descendants would comprise the Indo-European language groups in the north. Since they would eventually settle far away from the Israelites, they are not major factors in Israel's history. Ham's descendants, however, are constantly intertwined in the story of the Israelites, as both antagonists and allies. For example, Canaanites, Ethiopians, and Egyptians are descendants of Ham. However, there have been intermarriages and blending of cultures that make these distinctions hard to apply in our modern era.

As you consider later conflicts in the Bible how does this genealogy provide insight?

2. Shem to Abram (Genesis 11:10, 27, 31–32)

In Genesis 11, there is a break from the genealogical record for an explanation of how people came to scatter throughout the earth at the Tower of Babel.

The genealogies continue by providing more details on Shem's line, introducing people who are pertinent to the unfolding story: Abram, Sarai, and Lot.

Genealogies recorded in the Bible often reveal God's faithfulness in keeping His promises. "Vertical" genealogies, such as this one, were also used to prove a person or tribe's claim to a kingdom or dynasty. After God blessed Shem, that blessing would be extended to future generations. Showing that Abram was in the line of Shem (nine generations removed) authenticates the promise of blessing that he would receive in chapter 12.

Consider your own genealogy. Write down your ancestors as far back as you can. What can you learn about yourself based upon stories of your ancestors?

3. Abram's Call (Genesis 12:1–4)

There are several things to note about Abram's call.

God's call to Abram required sacrifice. Abram had to leave his land, his family, and his father's house. In the ancient world, inheritance, land, and family (heirs and legacy) were extremely important. Since this call came after his father's death, Abram would be forfeiting the financial security (both present and future) found in owning his father's property

and his inheritance. He would also be walking away from responsibility as the heir who was expected to fill the role of head of household.

God's call was conditional. He promised to make Abram a great nation, bless him, make his name great, protect him through blessing and cursing others, and bless the world through him. However, these blessings were contingent upon Abram obeying the command, "Go."

Obeying God's call required a considerable amount of faith. Abram and his family were pagans who worshiped idol gods (Joshua 24:2). Therefore, he had no relationship yet with the one true God. He was given a command and promise by a God he did not know to leave all that he had ever known, at seventy-five years old, to go to a place that was yet to be determined. Abram was trusting that God's inheritance would be greater than the one he left behind.

Verse 4 begins "So Abram departed," a testament to why it would eventually be said Abraham "believed in the LORD; and he counted it to him for righteousness" (from Genesis 15:6).

Consider people in your life who have exhibited this amount of faith. How does it affect your view of and relationship with God?

Search the Scriptures

1. Read Matthew 1:1-17 (for more details, read the entire passage). What does this passage detail? Compare and contrast the passage with Genesis 11.

2. Reread Genesis 12:1–3. How does the above passage in Matthew relate to it? Describe the ultimate manifestation of "in thee shall all families of the earth be blessed" (v. 3).

3. Count the generations that passed on from Abraham to Christ. Consider that it is believed that Abraham lived between 2000 and 1500 BC. What does this teach you about

God's character? What about the level of faith of ancient followers of God?

Discuss the Meaning

1. God did not give Abram any information about where he was going. Name some qualities Abram must have possessed in order to follow God's call and leave without question or reservation.

2. Abraham built an altar wherever he went as a sign of faith, discipleship, and thanksgiving. These altars were reminders of God's faithfulness for generations. Though building altars in modern times is not practical for us, what steps can we take in order to "mark" our journey with the Lord as Abraham did?

Liberating Lesson

Racial tensions and immigration issues stand to destroy communities, as people continue to fail to treat those seen as "other" equally—with humanity, dignity, and respect.

Many of the tensions of the world can be traced back to Noah's lineage. Self-fulfilling prophesies of sorts have come to pass, when one people group believes falsehoods about another, and acts in accordance with lies and misinterpretations of Scripture.

There is an enlightening video where individuals are interviewed about their ethnic background. They claim, "I'm 100% this...", or "I can't stand this group of people." Then they take DNA tests and are astonished by the results, discovering they are more connected and related than they imagined.

Ironically, the process of healing could begin from recognizing one truth. When God started over, He started with one man and his offspring. We have the same origin.

Application for Activation

Consider what could have happened to Abram's legacy if he chose comfort and security over faith. Would there have been the miracle of Isaac's birth? The twelve tribes of Israel? David? Would his name have been in the line that would include Jesus?

Abram had no idea that his departure would have such an impact. He obeyed a God that he did not know. Yet, we struggle, even in having the benefit of hindsight.

Is there something that you feel called to do that you have not done? Are you walking in disobedience in a particular area? Why? Fear? Comfort? Desire for stability? Laziness? Distraction? Consider the potential consequences of such disobedience.

This week, ask God to bring to your remembrance God-given calls and dreams that have fallen by the wayside. Ask that He will grant you Abram-like faith to obey Him.

Follow the Spirit

What God wants me to do:

_____

_____

_____

_____

Remember Your Thoughts

Special insights I have learned:

_____

_____

_____

_____

More Light on the Text

Genesis 10:1; 11:10, 27, 31–32; 12:1–4

10:1 Now these are the generations of the sons of Noah, Shem, Ham, and Japheth: and unto them were sons born after the flood.

11:10 These are the generations of Shem: Shem was an hundred years old, and begat Arphaxad two years after the flood:

27 Now these are the generations of Terah: Terah begat Abram, Nahor, and Haran; and Haran begat Lot.

These verses from Genesis 10 and 11 highlight the lineage connecting Noah to Abram. God made promises to Noah and would also continue to have a special relationship with Abram who had an inheritance of faith and promises from God through Noah. This section is also important to show the growth and repopulation of the earth after the Flood; although God had flooded the earth, His purpose and promise for humanity would continue through the generations.

11:31 And Terah took Abram his son, and Lot the son of Haran his son's son, and Sarai his daughter in law, his son Abram's wife; and they went forth with them from Ur of the Chaldees, to go into the land of Canaan; and they came unto Haran, and dwelt there. 32 And the days of Terah were two hundred and five years: and Terah died in Haran.

Genesis 11 introduces the narrative about Abram, whose life forms the basis of three major religions: Judaism, Christianity, and Islam.

First we meet his father, Terah, who was the father of three sons, Haran, Nahor and Abram. The descendants of two, Nahor and Abram, combined to form the line of Israel, for all the wives of Isaac and Jacob came from the line of Nahor.

Terah took his family and left Chaldea. His name seems to mean a wanderer or a pilgrim.

The Old Testament does not tell us why Terah decided to move his family. His aim was to go the land of Canaan. Though this passage does not state so explicitly, something seemed to have happened to this man. Here we find grace working in the heart of the one whose children were to inherit the land of promise and serve as instruments of God, bringing the promised seed into the world.

Haran, the father of Lot, died before his father (Genesis 11:28). When Terah left Ur, he took his extended family with him, including Lot. This is vital to people of African descent, for we have always been people who value the extended family. In the past grandparents took in their grandchildren if their children died before them.

The city of Haran was a halfway mark that fell short of their goal to reach Canaan. They were not far from the Promised Land, yet they never proceeded to it. Terah left Ur to go to Canaan but settled in Haran instead, where he stayed until his death.

Just as we do not know why Terah set out, we do not know why he stopped before reaching his goal. Though scholars have some conjectures, it is important only to note that they stopped short. They found employment and proceeded to enter into relationships with the people of the place. It took a tragedy for Abram to leave Haran and head where God directed him (Acts 7:4).

The death of his father did not change Abram's calling. While it is good that Abram respected his father, often children must take their parents' vision further. Abram's respect for his father was not to stand in the way of God's command.

12:1 Now the LORD had said unto Abram, Get thee out of thy country, and from thy kindred, and from thy father's house, unto a land that I will shew thee:

This verse relates the first recorded time God spoke to a person since Noah. After a long silence, God begins His direct work with His creation, beginning a family that would eventually bring the Savior. We have no indication that Abram was seeking God. Purely out of His grace, God chooses to bless Abram. He appoints a place for him, then challenges and charges him. This call is full of implication for the relationship that will develop between Abram and the Lord. God will have regard and respect for Abram, making a special people out of him.

God's words were "get thee out." This was directed to three important levels of Abram's life, progressing from the remote to the personal. The first was directed to the sentiment of national attachment. The Hebrew literally reads "from thy land." Ancients defined themselves by a radical connection to their own parcel of earth. Relating to this attachment to earth or land may be hard for people in America today, but for people of the indigenous world, this was once considered the ultimate attachment. This was Abram's world. Owning a parcel of land meant stability and provision. Your own land was necessary for providing food and goods for your family. Another idea that this command may call up in the minds of ancient people is abandoning their god. For many ancients, their god was tied to their land, so if you moved too far away, your god had no power in your new land. God was asking Abram to do something radical.

Secondly, the "get thee out" was toward Abram's extended family connections. The Hebrew term *moledeth* (**mo-LEH-deth**) speaks to the lineage of Abram, both direct ancestors and cousins. Staying at Haran would have given them a sense of being among their own people.

The third direction of the "get thee out" was toward his father's house. Again the phrase "out of thine father's house" can mean a variety of things as it especially relates to one's immediate family. It can also refer to the social status of one's mother as the daughter of someone of high standing.

However, after these negatives, God tells Abram how the "get thee out" has a positive direction. God said "Get thee … unto a land that I will show thee." There was a constructive formation being proposed by God. God was indicating that He was moving toward something great and wanted Abram to be more than a quiet spectator.

God was going to show Abram a land. If Abram would obey, then it would appear to him what God was doing. The Hebrew for "shew" (*ra'ah*, **rah-AH**) here can refer to physically looking at or experiencing something. For example, God showed Moses the plans for the tabernacle (Exodus 26:9), and He shows mercy to the psalmist (Psalm 85:7). The meanings can blend here. God promises Abram will both see the land with his eyes and experience it as he lives there.

2 And I will make of thee a great nation, and I will bless thee, and make thy name great; and thou shalt be a blessing: 3 And I will bless them that bless thee, and curse him that curseth thee: and in thee shall all of the earth be blessed.

In verse 2 we see God's promises to Abram. Here God is clear that He will bestow greatness and blessing upon Abram. God will bring forth that which He has charged and committed to Abram. God was ready to deal with any displeasing hindrance and execute the promise. This promise is in seven parts, which is important because seven is the number of completion or perfection in Hebrew thought. This means the blessing from God to Abram is a perfect promise, not just words but a divine oath. By speaking seven times God was indeed swearing an oath by Himself to Abram.

The first part is a promise directed to Abram's posterity. God says, "I will make thee a great nation." The word "make" is taken from the Hebrew word *asah* (**asaw'**). Other uses of this specific grammatical construction deal with fashioning objects out of copper or wood (Exodus 27:3; Isaiah 44:17). Here, the image is that similarly, God will fashion a nation out of Abram. More than just fashioning a nation, God will fulfill His purpose for that nation and furnish her with all that she needs to be God's nation. God will bring this about through Abram's obedience. In order to keep this promise, God will embark on a journey, keeping and laboring to maintain what He has "made," showing us divine sacrifice and service. What was God going to make? God says, "a great nation." The word great is from the Hebrew *gadol* (**gaw-DOLE**), which means great in all ways. God was going to make a high and noble people, a big (numerous) people.

The second promise reads, "I will bless (Heb. *baraq*, **bah-ROCK**) thee." God knows that human beings need immediate blessing. God understands that as much as Abram loves to have a great posterity, he also desires to be blessed in his lifetime. Abram will be a man who benefits from his relationship with God. The abundance of God's blessing was now promised to Abram. This blessing was completely based on the character of God. God will personally affirm Abram for whatever Abram does for God's sake. Abram has no reason to look for his self-affirmation from any other source than the God whom he came to know. Abram was going to receive blessing from God, not from a human being.

The third part of this promise is directed to Abram's name: "I will... make thy name great." The idea here is that Abram will occupy a definite and conspicuous position in the history of humankind. Abram's name will be recognized wherever it is named. Having a great name means Abram will be a man of honor and authority. It also refers to his nobility of character. His renowned name will be reported throughout history.

The fourth part is where God adds "thou shall be a blessing." Instead of using the future tense, as the English translates, the Hebrew verb here is an imperative, which makes this a command that implies Abram should uphold or live out this blessing. Many of us know people who are blessed but fail to bless others. We also may have met people who are renowned, but whose presence has not been a blessing. In fact, there are some whose memories make us curse the day we met them. Just because someone is great does not mean that he or she will bless others. Our history as people of African descent is full of people who were famous in their lands not because they were a blessing, but a curse to us.

The fifth promise speaks to what God will do for those who bless Abram (v. 3). To keep the rhythm of the text and the process of oath-taking, which was common among the ancients and some traditional African people, this should be read, "I will make them a blessing that bless you." God will prepare a blessing for those who bless Abram. This could mean that God will say thanks to those who reach out to Abram and to his children. Another reading could be that God is the one who leads those who bless Abram to bless him. They would not bless Abram if God's Spirit does not move within their hearts. This promise is very important, particularly given the fact that Abram will live out his life as a stranger in a strange land. The unwritten rule of the ancient world and in traditional African cultures is that those who minister to strangers or pilgrims were in fact ministering to God and shall be blessed by Him.

The sixth promise from God to Abram is related to people's treatment of Abram and Sarai in their pilgrimage. The King James Version reads, "and curse them that curseth thee." Other versions are clearer in their reading as it relates the ancient rite of promise-making and oath-taking. The New Living Translation does a better job portraying that two different Hebrew words were translated "curse" in the KJV. The first "curse" (Heb. 'arar, aw-RAR) tells us what God will do. The word is from a primitive root that means to abhor or to hate. God then will hate and attack those who curse Abraham. The second Hebrew word translated curse is the word qalal (kaw-LOL; NLT: treat with contempt), from a root word meaning to make light of someone so that they become a joke. It also means to make something or someone feel small. As Abram was a stranger in the land to which God called him, he was an easy target. People could trifle with him and revile him because his family was not great and no great warriors were around to defend him. This was a warning to those who may feel great in themselves and thus be led to trample upon Abram's human rights because he was a stranger.

The seventh part in the King James Version reads, "in thee shall all the families of the earth be blessed." God's final promise to Abram was a universal promise. This blessing includes all human beings. The Hebrew mishpakhah (mish-pah-KHAW) is often translated "families" as it is here, but the way it is used here can also refer to all classes of people. It can refer to the whole race or humanity as a species. In the final word, Abram's call is for the blessing of all tribes, people, and kindred.

4 So Abram departed, as the Lord had spoken unto him; and Lot went with him: and Abram was seventy and five years old when he departed out of Haran.

Here, Abram begins his second journey to Canaan. Abram brought out the various properties that he had acquired in Haran. He was now assured that God will bear him out. His departure from Haran was in obedience to God's Word.

We are told that Abram was seventy-five years old when he left Haran. One is never too old to strike out on a new venture for the Lord. As an older man of seventy-five, Abram followed the commandment to shoot forth into a new area and spread his wings. Though it may have been the winter of age in human eyes, God's command caused Abram to spring up and stand out for God and for the blessing of humanity. Any time is a good time to obey the Lord; any age is a good age. Abram ran with the promise.

Sources:
Global Study Bible, English Standard Version. Wheaton, IL: Crossway Publishers, 2012. 48-53.
Keener, Craig S. The IVP Bible Background Commentary: Old Testament. Downers Grove, IL: Intervarsity Press, 2000. 647-650, 40-43.),
Radmacher, Earl D., ed. Nelson Study Bible, New King James Version. Nashville, TN: Thomas Nelson Publishers, 1997. 21-25.
Unger, Merrill F. The New Unger's Bible Dictionary. Chicago, IL: Moody Press, 1988. 462-463. 372, 644.
Walvoord, John F., and Roy B. Zuck, eds. The Bible Knowledge Commentary: Old Testament. USA: Victor Books, SP Publications, Inc., 1985. 41-47.

Say It Correctly

Chaldean. kal-**DEE**-uhn.
Arphaxad . **ARE**-fax-ahd.
Haran. **HAIR**-en.

Daily Bible Readings

MONDAY
Noah's Mandate: Fill the Earth
(Genesis 9:1–7)

TUESDAY
God's Covenant with Noah and Animals
(Genesis 9:8–17)

WEDNESDAY
Families and Nations Descended from Noah
(Genesis 9:18–19; 10:1–4, 6–8, 21–23)

THURSDAY
The Lord Scatters the People
(Genesis 11:1–9)

FRIDAY
Abram, Sarai, and Lot in Canaan
(Genesis 12:5–9)

SATURDAY
Noah to Abraham, Faith in Action
(Hebrews 11:4–10)

SUNDAY
God's Blessings from Noah to Abraham
(Genesis 10:1; 11:10, 27, 31–32; 12:1–4)

Notes

Teaching Tips

Words You Should Know

A. Circumcision *mul* (Heb.)—Removal of the foreskin on a baby boy.

B. Isaac *Yitschaq* (Heb.)—Laughter.

Teacher Preparation

Unifying Principle—Promises Give Hope. Because of past promises that were not fulfilled, we find it hard to trust future promises. What can help us have faith and confidence to depend on important promises that shape our lives? Although Abraham and Sarah had to wait a long time for God's promise of a son to be born to them to shape all people of the earth, God showed them that this promise was trustworthy.

A. Read the Bible Background and Devotional Readings.

B. Pray for your students and lesson clarity.

C. Read the lesson Scripture in multiple translations.

D. Option: Lead the students in singing a hymn that speaks of the importance of faith (some possibilities: "Standing on the Promises of God," "It Is Well with My Soul," "Living by Faith").

O—Open the Lesson

A. Begin the class with prayer.

B. Have the students read the Aim for Change.

C. Have the students read the In Focus story.

D. Ask students how events named in the story can weigh on their hearts and how they can view these events from a theological perspective.

P—Present the Scriptures

A. Read the Focal Verses and discuss the Background and The People, Places, and Times sections.

B. Have the class share what Scriptures stand out for them and why, with particular emphasis on today's context.

E—Explore the Meaning

A. Use In Depth or More Light on the Text to help provide more in-depth discussion of the lesson text.

B. Discuss the Liberating Lesson and Application for Activation sections.

N—Next Steps for Application

A. Summarize the value of knowing God as a promise keeper.

B. End class with a commitment to pray for our elders, our children, and those waiting on God's promises to show up in their lives.

Worship Guide

For the Superintendent or Teacher
Theme: Abraham and Sarah Trust God's Promise
Song: "Lord Jesus, Think On Me"
Devotional Reading: Luke 1:26–38

Abraham and Sarah Trust God's Promise

Bible Background • GENESIS 18:9–15; 21:1–7
Printed Text • GENESIS 18:9–15; 21:1–7 | Devotional Reading • LUKE 1:26–38

Aim for Change

By the end of the lesson, we will: REMEMBER to trust the promises of God; APPRECIATE the value of patience for God's promises; and CELEBRATE that God keeps promises in unexpected ways by grace.

In Focus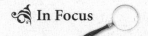

Cassandra had been waiting on God to send her the husband God wanted for her. She felt strongly that God had called her to be married, and despite some bad dating experiences and heartbreak, she still felt God intended her for marriage.

"It's like impossible for us to find good men these days," her friend Gina told her. "And it's even more unlikely that men want to commit to marriage. With so many people getting divorced, it's easy to get what you want when you want it. So many people are doing their own thing—it's just unrealistic, girl. You might as well find someone you like to chill with and leave it at that like the rest of us."

"Girl, I hear you, it's hard out here, but I believe in what God has for me," Cassandra responded. That was three years ago. As Cassandra stared at her fiancé John, she was glad she had trusted God. He wasn't what she thought she wanted, but he was everything she needed in a husband. God had been faithful to her and given her the desire of her heart.

"I'm glad God brought us together in His timing. I was out here acting crazy just before I met you," John said. "I am so grateful, I don't know what to say, honey."

All Cassandra could do was laugh. John had no idea how much of an answered prayer he was.

How does it feel when you finally receive something you have been waiting on for a long time? Did it come at a time you expected, or did it surprise you?

Keep in Mind

"And the LORD visited Sarah as he had said, and the LORD did unto Sarah as he had spoken" (Genesis 21:1, KJV).

"The Lord kept his word and did for Sarah exactly what he had promised"
(Genesis 21:1, NLT).

Focal Verses

KJV **Genesis 18:9** And they said unto him, Where is Sarah thy wife? And he said, Behold, in the tent.

10 And he said, I will certainly return unto thee according to the time of life; and, lo, Sarah thy wife shall have a son. And Sarah heard it in the tent door, which was behind him.

11 Now Abraham and Sarah were old and well stricken in age; and it ceased to be with Sarah after the manner of women.

12 Therefore Sarah laughed within herself, saying, After I am waxed old shall I have pleasure, my lord being old also?

13 And the LORD said unto Abraham, Wherefore did Sarah laugh, saying, Shall I of a surety bear a child, which am old?

14 Is any thing too hard for the LORD? At the time appointed I will return unto thee, according to the time of life, and Sarah shall have a son.

15 Then Sarah denied, saying, I laughed not; for she was afraid. And he said, Nay; but thou didst laugh.

21:1 And the LORD visited Sarah as he had said, and the LORD did unto Sarah as he had spoken.

2 For Sarah conceived, and bare Abraham a son in his old age, at the set time of which God had spoken to him.

3 And Abraham called the name of his son that was born unto him, whom Sarah bare to him, Isaac.

4 And Abraham circumcised his son Isaac being eight days old, as God had commanded him.

5 And Abraham was an hundred years old, when his son Isaac was born unto him.

6 And Sarah said, God hath made me to laugh, so that all that hear will laugh with me.

7 And she said, Who would have said unto Abraham, that Sarah should have given

NLT **Genesis 18:9** "Where is Sarah, your wife?" the visitors asked. "She's inside the tent," Abraham replied.

10 Then one of them said, "I will return to you about this time next year, and your wife, Sarah, will have a son!" Sarah was listening to this conversation from the tent.

11 Abraham and Sarah were both very old by this time, and Sarah was long past the age of having children.

12 So she laughed silently to herself and said, "How could a worn-out woman like me enjoy such pleasure, especially when my master—my husband—is also so old?"

13 Then the LORD said to Abraham, "Why did Sarah laugh? Why did she say, 'Can an old woman like me have a baby?'

14 Is anything too hard for the LORD? I will return about this time next year, and Sarah will have a son."

15 Sarah was afraid, so she denied it, saying, "I didn't laugh." But the LORD said, "No, you did laugh."

21:1 The LORD kept his word and did for Sarah exactly what he had promised.

2 She became pregnant, and she gave birth to a son for Abraham in his old age. This happened at just the time God had said it would.

3 And Abraham named their son Isaac.

4 Eight days after Isaac was born, Abraham circumcised him as God had commanded.

5 Abraham was 100 years old when Isaac was born.

6 And Sarah declared, "God has brought me laughter. All who hear about this will laugh with me.

7 Who would have said to Abraham that Sarah would nurse a baby? Yet I have given Abraham a son in his old age!"

children suck? for I have born him a son in his old age.

The People, Places, and Times

The Wilderness of Paran. Paran is a desert area located in the northeastern Sinai Peninsula, with the Arabah on the east and the wilderness of Shur on the west. The region experiences very little rainfall (less than 10 inches per year). The Wilderness of Paran or Desert of Paran is thought to be the place where the Israelites spent part of their forty years of wandering. The Wilderness of Paran is the spot that Ishmael settles near and where this conversation between the Lord, Abraham, and Sarah occurs. It was from Kadesh, in Paran, that the twelve scouts were sent into the Promised Land to gather information for the Israelites, a little more than two years after the Exodus from Egypt (Numbers 10:11; 13:1–3). King David spent some time in the Wilderness of Paran after Samuel died (1 Samuel 25:1). This region is part of modern-day Egypt and Saudi Arabia.

Background

Our text for this lesson is a small snapshot of a much larger narrative surrounding God, Abraham, and Sarah. Amid concerns about having no son to whom to leave his vast estate upon his death, Abraham (then known as Abram) receives a promise from God in Genesis 15 that he would not have to leave his inheritance to a servant in his home, but to an heir of his own flesh and blood. Though Abram was well into his eighties when God promises him a son, God's track record with Abram stabilized his faith for God to do the seemingly unthinkable; the Bible reveals Abram believed the Lord for an heir to be born. As time continues, Sarah (or Sarai at the time) seeks to help God, assuming she is too old to produce the son of the promise that Abram anticipates. Sarai gives her servant Hagar to Abram to become his mate and the future mother of Abram's firstborn, Ishmael, at the ripe old age of eighty-six. It is not long before tension arises between the two women of the house. Sarai deals harshly with her servant Hagar and regrets allowing her to bear Abram's son.

The narrative shifts in Genesis 17 when God reveals Himself once again to the now ninety-nine-year-old Abram. In this visitation, God changes Abram's name to Abraham and Sarai's name to Sarah, promising Abraham he would become "a father of many nations" (Genesis 17:5) and confirming Sarah's birthing of a son called Isaac in a year's time. Shortly after God renews His covenant with Abraham and clarifies Sarah's role in the process, the Bible says the Lord meets Abraham as he rests under a mamre tree at the beginning of Genesis 18. Abraham looks up and sees three travelers or visitors whom he goes out of his way to accommodate. As Sarah and the household servants make preparations for the guests within the tents, Abraham engages in a transformative conversation with the visitors outside—presumably unaware of Sarah quietly listening from inside of the tent.

At-A-Glance

1. Dealing with Our Doubts (Genesis 18:9–15)
2. Faithfulness in the Face of the Fantastic (Genesis 21:1–7)

In Depth

1. Dealing with Our Doubts (Genesis 18:9–15)

As Sarah listens to Abraham and the visitors discuss the miracle that will occur through her womb, she is tickled by the prospect. It has been about thirteen years since the birth of Ishmael. Sarah has been barren her entire life and is now approaching ninety years old. How crazy must this visitor be to believe Sarah would give birth to a child a year from now? Afraid to blow her cover, Sarah laughs silently to herself, "How could a worn-out woman like me enjoy such pleasure, especially when my master—my husband—is also so old?" (v. 12, NLT). For Sarah, a feat like this is doubtful and her statement presents at least two sources of doubt. The first is her perceived internal barriers to the possibility. The text identifies Sarah as very old, far beyond child-bearing years, and she even sees herself as "a worn-out woman." She has not had any success in bearing children in the past eighty-nine years, so what would change this now? Certainly, child-bearing was a young woman's game, not the work of one well into her eighties. In short, if it could have happened through her, Sarah surmises it would have already occurred.

Moreover, Sarah also doubts the external resources she has to get the job done—namely her ninety-nine-year-old husband Abraham! In Sarah's mind, this idea of childbirth is especially laughable "when my master—my husband—is also so old." Yet, her statement gives us a clue that the idea—though unlikely—is a favorable one for her, as she would like to bear a child but just does not know if it is possible.

What are some of your doubts as it relates to what you hear God speaking to you in this season of life?

2. Faithfulness in the Face of the Fantastic (Genesis 21:1–7)

When we pick up on the story again in Genesis 21:1–7, we find a temporary, yet appropriate bookend for the narrative around Abraham, Sarah, and the birth of their son Isaac. God is faithful to the promise He makes to Abraham (Genesis 15 and 17), and Sarah "gave birth to a son for Abraham in his old age. This happened at just the time God had said it would" (Genesis 21:2). This is a fantastic feat, one that leaves both Abraham and Sarah grateful and relieved. Appropriately, in the face of God's faithfulness, Abraham is moved to obedience and has Isaac circumcised on the eighth day, "as God had commanded" (v. 4). Abraham is grateful for the faithfulness of God, one who keeps even the most fantastic of promises. As a result, Abraham is committed to being faithful and obedient to God in return, handling the blessing and promise in the way God had instructed him.

How do you show appreciation to God in the face of answered prayer?

Search the Scriptures

1. Sarah is not the only biblical figure to laugh at the prospect of one of God's promises. Can you identify any other biblical figures who laughed at God's vision for them? What were their reasons?

2. The visitors who meet Abraham and Sarah at their tents seemingly repeat to Abraham what God has spoken to him in the previous chapter. Why do you think God would send these visitors shortly after speaking to Abraham? What might this say about Abraham? What might this teach us about God?

Discuss the Meaning

1. Why is it important to wait on the promises of God instead of trying to get to the promises in our own strength?

2. How does God's display of faithfulness affect your desire to be faithful to God and others?

Liberating Lesson

When God proposes doing the fantastic in our lives, it is natural to have doubts. Sometimes we are doubtful because of perceived deficits in us and other times we are doubtful because we do not believe we have adequate resources to complete the task. It can also be frustrating to trust God when we feel we have missed the window to do some of the things He has told us to do, such as returning to school, engaging in a new romantic relationship, or starting a business. While some of what God speaks to us may seem laughable, it is not impossible. This text reminds us of God's nature to keep His promises. Be mindful and watchful for God to confirm what He has spoken to you. When God makes good on His promises to us, it is important to show our appreciation by handling the blessing in the way God has instructed us. In many ways, obedience is the best "thank you" we can provide to God when He does the fantastic in our lives.

Application for Activation

Take a moment to write down some of the things you believe God is speaking to you about your future. Under each of these items, identify the doubts that you have about the part you will play in seeing the vision actualized. In a different color, identify the doubts you have about the resources you will need and currently possess for the vision to come to fruition. Take a moment to pray for God to give you the faith to trust Him in spite of your doubts and to perform even the most laughable of tasks. Then, take another moment to reflect on the vision and how God desires to use it for His glory. What are God's instructions to you about how to handle this vision? Whom should

it benefit? How can you be faithful to God once you're walking in His promise for you?

Follow the Spirit

What God wants me to do:

_____

_____

_____

_____

Remember Your Thoughts

Special insights I have learned:

_____

_____

_____

_____

More Light on the Text
Genesis 18:9–15; 21:1–7

9 And they said unto him, where is Sarah thy wife? And he said, Behold, in the tent.

In 18:1–8, Abraham receives visitors whose identity is unknown to him. He, however, welcomes them with a good meal before the conversation could start. This is an example of how important expressing hospitality was in Abraham's culture. In Africa, hospitality is also a key issue today in rural areas; unless a visitor is properly welcomed, the formal greetings cannot take place. The book of Hebrews—perhaps referring to this event—urges believers to exercise hospitality because in doing so some accommodate angels unknowingly (13:2). Though Abraham does not know the visitors, the narrator of Genesis states their identity:

the Lord (18:1). The visitors throughout chapters 18 and 19 are sometimes called men (18:2; 19:10, 12), or three men (18:2), and in other instances two angels (19:1). Some suggest therefore that this is the angel of the Lord in the company of two other angels. These are the visitors who inquire about Sarah. The event happens at Mamre where there were oak trees, a place believed to be Hebron (23:19; 35:27).

The visitors' question is rhetorical. They know Sarah's whereabouts. The same type of question was addressed to Adam after the Fall and to Cain after the murder of Abel. These visitors also know Abraham's marital status and even his wife's name. The Lord is omniscient and knows everything. The question is to direct Abraham's thoughts toward who is behind the scenes, namely Sarah. Abraham had already received what the Lord is about to say (Genesis 17:15–16, 19).

10 And he said, I will certainly return unto thee according to the time of life; and, lo, Sarah thy wife shall have a son. And Sarah heard it in the tent door, which was behind him.

One of the three men will now lead the conversation. Sarah, though the key target in this conversation, is indoors separate from the action. It is possible that it was not customarily good for her to actively take part in the conversation. However, from where she was, she could hear the conversation. Abraham from that moment may have known the real identity of the one speaking to him because earlier he had been privileged to get the same information.

Now, though, there is more precision about the date of birth of the awaited child. When the Lord mentioned that He would "return" (Heb. *shub*, **SHOOVE**), the idea is to show favor. The verb used is found elsewhere portraying God's gracious intervention (Zechariah 1:3; Psalm 80:14). The period of the return is mentioned as "the time of life" (KJV) or "about this time next year" (NLT). The same Hebrew phrase is also found in 2 Kings 4:16, when Elisha promises a woman that she will have a child the following year.

The Lord's patience in building one's faith can be perceived here. After many years of waiting for a child, the barren Sarah had given up and suggested God intended the promised child to come from another woman (Genesis 16:1–3). Prior to this Abraham had been reassured that he will have a biological son as his heir (Genesis 15:1–4) and not an adopted one. After lifting Abraham's faith in Genesis 17 in revealing the name of the son, now it was Sarah's turn to be strengthened in her faith.

11 Now Abraham and Sarah were old and well stricken in age; and it ceased to be with Sarah after the manner of women. 12 Therefore Sarah laughed within herself, saying, after I am waxed old shall I have pleasure, my lord being old also?

Though Abraham was old (around ninety-nine) at the time of this encounter, his age was not such a great obstacle compared to the Sarah's situation. Later on, Abraham will have children from Keturah at an even older age (Genesis 25:1–2). But for Sarah, not only was she barren when she was still young (11:30), now she is too old. The phrase "the manner of women" (KJV) is a reference to menses. She was beyond menopause. The might of the Lord is displayed here. Nothing stops the manifestation of divine will, not even barrenness or menopause.

The prospect of conceiving a child in such conditions is unbelievable for Sarah. She laughs at the possibility of bearing a child. This was not an open laughter but a soft inner laughter that will go unnoticed before humans but not in front of the Lord. Her laughter comes after her husband's laughter earlier concerning the same prediction. The occasion surrounding the child birth issue is full of laughter. Abraham laughs in joy and disbelief at the assurance of a son (Genesis 17:17), and Sarah laughs in unbelief at the prospect of a son (18:12). The name Isaac (Heb. *Yitschaq*, **yits-KHAWK**, laughter) was already given when Abraham first laughed at God's promise (Genesis 17:19). However, other scholars suggest that Sarah's laughter of unbelief is a result of hopelessness and not pride, which explains a self-restraint in expressing too openly her doubt.

13 And the LORD said unto Abraham, Wherefore did Sarah laugh, saying, Shall I of a surety bear a child, which am old? 14 Is anything too hard for the LORD? At the time appointed I will return unto thee, according to the time of life, and Sarah shall have a son.

The Lord's omniscience is displayed here again. Sarah's inner laughter and thought does not go unnoticed. The Lord's inquiry about the reasons for her laughter is a rebuke of her unbelief. Abraham had laughed when he first heard the news but he was not rebuked (Genesis 17), although he had bowed before laughing signifying his willingness to follow God. If Sarah had been briefed previously about Abraham's earlier encounter with the Lord, she would have been less surprised by the announcement.

With all these human conditions making the fulfillment of the promise humanly impossible, the Lord asks a question to shift Abraham and Sarah's thinking from their own limitations to God's limitless power. As the angel assured Mary, nothing is impossible for the Lord (Luke 1:37). This passage not only displays God's omniscience, but also His omnipotence. The fact that He could read Sarah's inner thought should assure her and Abraham of God's ability to fulfill what He has promised.

The Lord then reiterates what He said earlier in verse 10. Therefore the phrase "at the time appointed" is added to the "time of life" earlier used in verse 10. Sarah's unbelief will not affect the fulfillment of the promise at the appropriate time. The repetition of the promise of the visit reinforces its certainty. Here we see further evidence of God's omnipotence even over time. He will fulfill His promise in His time, and we know that He makes everything beautiful in His time (Ecclesiastes 3:11). The Lord controls time and circumstances in life.

15 Then Sarah denied, saying, I laughed not; for she was afraid. And he said, Nay; but thou didst laugh.

Fear motivated Sarah's denial of her laughter. Fear leads people to do irrational things. It leads Sarah to commit a second sin of lying after the first of unbelief. It was the factor underlying Abraham's deception of the Egyptians about his wife (Genesis 12:11–13). In Jesus' parables of the talents, the servant with only one talent hid it because he was afraid of investment (Matthew 25:24–25).

The Lord maintained His rebuke. He knows everything and we cannot deceive Him about what we do. The best thing to do when confronted by the Lord is to accept and repent, so that in His gracious love He will forgive us.

21:1 And the LORD visited Sarah as he had said, and the LORD did unto Sarah as he had spoken. 2 For Sarah conceived, and bare Abraham a son in his old age, at the set time of which God had spoken to him.

As should be expected, the Lord fulfills the promise and visits Sarah. The word used for "visit" (Heb. *paqad*, **paw-KAHD**) is used in many ways throughout the Bible. When God is the subject of this verb, it indicates His special interest in an individual, whether for judgment or blessing. The closest parallel to its use here is in the story of Hannah (1 Samuel 2:21). In both places, God shows His special interest in these women by bestowing His merciful blessing to alleviate the hardship and stigma of barrenness. The fulfillment of the promise is affirmed in verse 1.

At last, Sarah was able to conceive and give birth through the might of the Lord. The human limitation of their "old age" is again mentioned to demonstrate the power of God to overcome any human hindrance. This happened "at the set time" as forecast in Genesis 17:21 and 18:14. The Lord is always faithful to His promises. As nothing prevents Him from doing His will, believers should live with the firm assurance that He will do what He promises to do. Not even human doubt can prevent Him from fulfilling a promise.

At last, the promise God made to Abraham in Genesis 12 and reiterated many times is fulfilled in Isaac's birth. Isaac is the promised son, not Ishmael, who is the result of Sarah's doubt.

3 And Abraham called the name of his son that was born unto him, whom Sarah bare to him, Isaac. 4 And Abraham circumcised his son Isaac being eight days old, as God had commanded him.

The son is named Isaac, a name already given by God to Abraham (Genesis 17:19). God promises the birth of several children in the Bible and gives their names even before conception; John the Baptist and Jesus are two examples in the New Testament. This is a warning for our generation when people play with the lives of the unborn. Even though many promote abortion on the basis that what is in the womb is not yet a baby (so not a human being), and therefore can be disposed of without any problem, God has human beings in His mind even before conception. God is the only sovereign over human life in each stage of its development, and even the youngest life is sacred.

The rite of circumcision on the eighth day was given to Abraham and his descendants to set them apart from other nations. Abraham and every male in his household went through circumcision as a sign of the covenant between the Lord and Abraham, and his descendants (Genesis 17:11). Those who were circumcised at this occasion were older. Isaac was the first to be circumcised as required at eight days old. During the years in the wilderness, the rite was not observed, so when the people reached Gilgal at the entrance of the Promised Land, circumcision was performed (Joshua 5:5–7). As a Jewish child Jesus was circumcised (Luke 2:21), which is evidence of His humanity and entitled Him to all the duties and prerogatives of a Jew.

5 And Abraham was an hundred years old, when his son Isaac was born unto him. 6 And Sarah said, God hath made me to laugh, so that all that hear will laugh with me.

Abraham's age at the birth of Isaac is significant because of the time spent between his departure from his homeland—after the Lord's promise to bless his descendants—and the actual birth of a son. The significance of his ability to father a child is beside the point here because in later years, he will have other children with no apparent divine intervention (Genesis 25:1–2). From his departure from Haran, twenty-five years have passed since the first encounter with God. But finally the promised son has come. Isaac is called as such because Ishmael does not share in the promise.

Sarah's previous laughter in unbelief is the source of more laughter in unison with those who will hear the news of the birth. Some scholars think the term can be understood to mean "to laugh at" rather than "to laugh with." But even in the case of some teasing her, when the news goes public, everyone rejoices with her in amazement for what the Lord has done.

7 And she said, who would have said unto Abraham, that Sarah should have given children suck? For I have born him a son in his old age.

Indeed no one would have believed Sarah could have a child at her age. First, she was a barren woman; second, she was very aged and beyond the possibility of childbearing because she was post-menopause. To her question resounds the other question in Genesis 18:14, "Is any thing too hard for the Lord?" What was beyond human capability and imagination had been accomplished by the mighty power of the Lord and Creator of the universe.

Sources:

Botterweck, J. G. *Theological Dictionary of the Old Testament.* Revised Edition, Vol. 2. Translated by J.T. Willis. Grand Rapids, MI: William B. Eerdmans, 1977.

Gaebelein, F.E. *The Expositor's Bible Commentary: Genesis,* Vol. 5. Grand Rapids, MI: Zondervan, 1990.

Hamilton, V.P. The *New International Commentary on the Old Testament: The book of Genesis 18-50.* Grand Rapids, MI: William B. Eerdmans, 1995.

Kidner, D. *Tyndale Old Testament Commentaries. Genesis: An Introduction and Commentary.* Downers Grove, IL: Inter-Varsity Press, 1967.

Levine, B.A. *The Jews Publication Society.* Edited by N.M. Sarna. Philadelphia: The Jews Publication Society, 1989.

VanGemeren, W.A. *New International Dictionary of Old Testament Theology and Exegesis,* Vol. 3. Grand Rapids, MI: Zondervan., 1997.

Packer, J. I., and M.C. Tenney, eds. *Illustrated Manners and Customs of the Bible.* Nashville, TN: Thomas Nelson, 1997.

Wenham, G.J. *Word Biblical Commentary: Genesis 16-50,* Vol. 2. Waco, TX: Word Books, 1994.

Daily Bible Readings

MONDAY
God Honors Covenants with Abraham
(Psalm 105:1–11)

TUESDAY
Hagar Births Abraham's Son, Ishmael
(Genesis 16:7–11, 15–16)

WEDNESDAY
Gentiles Share in Abraham's Promise
(Galatians 3:6–9, 13–14)

THURSDAY
Abram Believes God
(Genesis 15:1–6)

FRIDAY
God's Covenant Extended through Isaac
(Genesis 17:15–22)

SATURDAY
Abraham Hosts God's Messengers
(Genesis 18:1–8)

SUNDAY
Child of Faith and Laughter
(Genesis 18:9–15; 21:1–7)

Say It Correctly

Abraham. **A**-bra-ham.
Issac. **I**-zek.
Sarah. **SAIR**- a.

Teaching Tips

Words You Should Know

A. Kindness *chesed* (Heb.)—Goodness, mercy of God.

B. Damsels na'arah (Heb.)—Girls, young maidens.

Teacher Preparation

Unifying Principle—Make a Decision. People often must face decisions that will change their lives forever. How can we make the most of the opportunities life gives us? Rebekah took initiative in answering the call to become the wife of Isaac and to play an important role in the unfolding of God's promises.

A. Read the Bible Background and Devotional Readings.

B. Pray for your students and lesson clarity.

C. Read the lesson Scripture in multiple translations.

D. Option: Ask the students to explain what this lesson teaches about God's faithfulness to God's people.

O—Open the Lesson

A. Begin the class with prayer.

B. Have the students read the Aim for Change.

C. Have the students read the In Focus story.

D. Ask students how events named in the story can weigh on their hearts and how they can view these events from a theological perspective.

P—Present the Scriptures

A. Read the Focal Verses and discuss the Background and The People, Places, and Times sections.

B. Have the class share what Scriptures stand out for them and why, with particular emphasis on today's context.

E—Explore the Meaning

A. Use In Depth or More Light on the Text to help provide more in-depth discussion of the lesson text.

B. Discuss the Liberating Lesson and Application for Activation sections.

N—Next Steps for Application

A. Summarize the value of knowing God as sovereign Creator.

B. End class with a commitment to pray for new opportunities, healthy relationships, and direction from God for our decisions.

Worship Guide

For the Superintendent or Teacher
Theme: Isaac and Rebekah Continue the Legacy
Song: "God Will Provide"
Devotional Reading: Ephesians 5:21–33

Isaac and Rebekah Continue the Legacy

Bible Background • GENESIS 24
Printed Text • GENESIS 24:12–21, 61–67 | Devotional Reading • EPHESIANS 5:21–33

—————————— Aim for Change ——————————

By the end of the lesson we will IDENTIFY the opportunity God gave to Rebekah; RECALL the opportunities God has given us; and RESOLVE to say yes when God gives us new opportunities.

—————————— 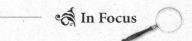 In Focus ——————————

Rashad had been looking for work for over a year, but was finally feeling hopeful after his friend from church told him about a job fair coming up in his area. He put on his best suit, went to the library to print out twenty copies of his resume, and made sure to wear the cross necklace his mom had given him as a teenager under his shirt. As he walked around the crowded fair he felt a bit overwhelmed with the long lines and professional-looking job-seekers. He stopped by the door and thought to himself. A woman came in dressed fairly casually dragging a big suitcase with her arms clearly full.

"Hey, do you need some help?" Rashad offered.

"Yes, please, thanks a lot. My name is Georgia and you are?" the woman replied.

"My name is Rashad, nice to meet you. Where do you need this?" Rashad responded.

"Oh, that booth down there, thank you again. I've been walking for about a block and no one has offered to help me. I'm glad you stopped to care. I'm a recruiter from a Fortune 500 company, I figure someone would have offered to help, but they didn't. What brings you here?"

Sometimes having the heart of a servant is the doorway to God's opportunities for us. Have you ever had an unexpected opportunity or experience because you were willing to be helpful?

—————————— Keep in Mind ——————————

"And Rebekah arose, and her damsels, and they rode upon the camels, and followed the man: and the servant took Rebekah, and went his way" (Genesis 24:61, KJV).

"Then Rebekah and her servant girls mounted the camels and followed the man. So Abraham's servant took Rebekah and went on his way" (Genesis 24:61, NLT).

Focal Verses

KJV **Genesis 24:12** And he said O LORD God of my master Abraham, I pray thee, send me good speed this day, and shew kindness unto my master Abraham.

13 Behold, I stand here by the well of water; and the daughters of the men of the city come out to draw water:

14 And let it come to pass, that the damsel to whom I shall say, Let down thy pitcher, I pray thee, that I may drink; and she shall say, Drink, and I will give thy camels drink also: let the same be she that thou hast appointed for thy servant Isaac; and thereby shall I know that thou hast shewed kindness unto my master.

15 And it came to pass, before he had done speaking, that, behold, Rebekah came out, who was born to Bethuel, son of Milcah, the wife of Nahor, Abraham's brother, with her pitcher upon her shoulder.

16 And the damsel was very fair to look upon, a virgin, neither had any man known her: and she went down to the well, and filled her pitcher, and came up.

17 And the servant ran to meet her, and said, Let me, I pray thee, drink a little water of thy pitcher.

18 And she said, Drink, my lord: and she hasted, and let down her pitcher upon her hand, and gave him drink.

19 And when she had done giving him drink, she said, I will draw water for thy camels also, until they have done drinking.

20 And she hasted, and emptied her pitcher into the trough, and ran again unto the well to draw water, and drew for all his camels.

21 And the man wondering at her held his peace, to wit whether the LORD had made his journey prosperous or not.

61 And Rebekah arose, and her damsels, and they rode upon the camels, and followed

NLT **Genesis 24:12** "O LORD, God of my master, Abraham," he prayed. "Please give me success today, and show unfailing love to my master, Abraham.

13 See, I am standing here beside this spring, and the young women of the town are coming out to draw water.

14 This is my request. I will ask one of them, 'Please give me a drink from your jug.' If she says, 'Yes, have a drink, and I will water your camels, too!'—let her be the one you have selected as Isaac's wife. This is how I will know that you have shown unfailing love to my master."

15 Before he had finished praying, he saw a young woman named Rebekah coming out with her water jug on her shoulder. She was the daughter of Bethuel, who was the son of Abraham's brother Nahor and his wife, Milcah.

16 Rebekah was very beautiful and old enough to be married, but she was still a virgin. She went down to the spring, filled her jug, and came up again.

17 Running over to her, the servant said, "Please give me a little drink of water from your jug."

18 "Yes, my lord," she answered, "have a drink." And she quickly lowered her jug from her shoulder and gave him a drink.

19 When she had given him a drink, she said, "I'll draw water for your camels, too, until they have had enough to drink."

20 So she quickly emptied her jug into the watering trough and ran back to the well to draw water for all his camels.

21 The servant watched her in silence, wondering whether or not the LORD had given him success in his mission.

61 Then Rebekah and her servant girls mounted the camels and followed the man. So the man: and the servant took Rebekah, and went his way.

62 And Isaac came from the way of the well Lahairoi; for he dwelt in the south country.

63 And Isaac went out to meditate in the field at the eventide: and he lifted up his eyes, and saw, and, behold, the camels were coming.

64 And Rebekah lifted up her eyes, and when she saw Isaac, she lighted off the camel.

65 For she had said unto the servant, What man is this that walketh in the field to meet us? And the servant had said, It is my master: therefore she took a veil, and covered herself.

66 And the servant told Isaac all things that he had done.

67 And Isaac brought her into his mother Sarah's tent, and took Rebekah, and she became his wife; and he loved her: and Isaac was comforted after his mother's death.

Abraham's servant took Rebekah and went on his way.

62 Meanwhile, Isaac, whose home was in the Negev, had returned from Beer-lahai-roi.

63 One evening as he was walking and meditating in the fields, he looked up and saw the camels coming.

64 When Rebekah looked up and saw Isaac, she quickly dismounted from her camel.

65 "Who is that man walking through the fields to meet us?" she asked the servant. And he replied, "It is my master." So Rebekah covered her face with her veil.

66 Then the servant told Isaac everything he had done.

67 And Isaac brought Rebekah into his mother Sarah's tent, and she became his wife. He loved her deeply, and she was a special comfort to him after the death of his mother.

The People, Places, and Times

Rebekah. Like Sarah, Rebekah, too, was barren (Genesis 25:21). In biblical times barrenness was more than a physical or social problem; it was thought to be the result of disobeying God (Deuteronomy 7:14). However Isaac prayed to God and Rebekah conceived, thus carrying two male children in her womb.

Background

In today's text, Abraham and his family are in the midst of some major transitions. In Genesis 23, Abraham experiences the death of his wife Sarah, who lives to be a hundred and twenty-seven years old. Abraham spends time weeping and mourning his wife in Canaan. Despite being offered land among the Hittites to bury Sarah without charge, Abraham strikes a deal with the Hittites and is deeded Ephron's

field in a place called Machpelah, which housed the cave where Abraham ultimately buries her in the land of Canaan (Genesis 23:17).

At the beginning of Genesis 24, after securing the deed for his family burial ground in Canaan and laying his wife to rest, Abraham is now very old and has been blessed "in every way" (Genesis 24:1, NLT). The final order of business for Abraham is to ensure the continuation of his family legacy through his son Isaac. Abraham summons his oldest servant and sends him on an assignment to bring Isaac a wife from among the people in Abraham's homeland. Abraham's instructions are specific and tactical, and Abraham makes his servant swear by oath to bring Isaac a wife from among his people, but never to take Isaac to the land of his father.

At-A-Glance

1. The Retention of Culture (Genesis
24:12–14)
2. A Reliance on Confirmation (vv. 15–21)
3. A Reward of Special Comfort (vv. 61–67)

In Depth

1. The Retention of Culture (Genesis 24:12–14)

The text opens in verse 12 with Abraham's oldest servant asking God for success in finding and bringing back a wife for Isaac from among Abraham's family. For Abraham, it is critical that Isaac not marry a woman from the Canaanites, among whom they currently live. As Abraham's bargaining session with Ephron and the Hittites in the previous chapter reveals, Abraham is revered as a "mighty prince" (Genesis 23:6) in the land and it is likely that Isaac would have had very little trouble finding a wife among the Canaanites. But Abraham knew that the customs, practices, and god of the Canaanites were not consistent with those of his own people. For Abraham, Isaac needed to live out the covenant that was made between him and the Lord with a wife who shared his culture, beliefs, and love for the true and living God.

How important is it for you to be in covenant relationship with people of common culture and beliefs?

2. A Reliance on Confirmation (vv. 15–21)

In the midst of the servant's prayer before meeting Rebekah, the servant sets up a "test" to confirm the success of his mission and God's unfailing love to Abraham in selecting a wife for Isaac. In verse 14, the servant prays, "This is my request. I will ask one of them, 'Please give me a drink from your jug.' If she says, 'Yes, have a drink, and I will water your camels, too!'—let her be the one you have selected as Isaac's wife. This is how I will know that you have shown unfailing love to my master." The servant's test is brilliant on two levels. First, asking God to confirm His presence in the selection process speaks to the servant's love for Abraham and trust in his God. It was not enough for the servant to come home with a good choice; he desired God's choice. Moreover, the servant's test is one that has nothing to do with the young woman's external beauty. A woman who would offer to relieve both the servant and his camels would be displaying a great deal of compassion, kindness, and a willingness to serve. A reliance on God for confirmation in this way ensured that the woman who the servant brought back to Canaan would be one favored by God and who possessed a holistic beauty.

How can we be sure that the choices we make are consistent with God's best for us?

3. A Reward of Special Comfort (vv. 61–67)

Verses 61–67 reveal the faithfulness of God in a dynamic way. As Isaac is meditating after a trip from Beer-lahai-roi, he looks up to see Rebekah and her servants coming toward him in the distance. When Rebekah sees Isaac, she confirms his identity with the servant first and proceeds to symbolically indicate to Isaac that she is his bride. She dismounts her camel as a sign of honor and submission, ceremoniously veils her face, and soon enters into Sarah's tent and becomes Isaac's wife.

It is interesting that this scene plays out following Isaac's trip to Beer-lahai-roi, which was the place of Hagar's well (Genesis 16:14). Beer-lahai-roi stood as a reminder to Isaac (and his father Abraham) of the loss of relationship he experienced with his older brother Ishmael earlier in his life—and he comes from that place during the season in which he is also mourning the loss of his mother Sarah. Yet the Bible records that Rebekah was "a special comfort to him after the death of his mother" (v. 67, NLT). It is a beautiful reminder of the faithfulness of God! While Abraham orchestrates the mission to find Rebekah for the role she would play in carrying out the future of the covenant, and because the servant seeks confirmation of God's choice, God divinely provides Isaac a wife who could be a special comfort and source of strength to endure his present pain.

Can you identify a time when following God's choice came with additional benefits you did not anticipate?

Search the Scriptures

1. Abraham makes his servant swear by oath to bring a wife for Isaac from among his homeland but never to take Isaac there. What are Abraham's motivations for this? What are the risks for Isaac in returning to his father's homeland?

2. Isaac takes Rebekah as his wife with seemingly no pushback and very little conversation with Rebekah. Why do you think the story plays out this way?

Discuss the Meaning

1. Why is it important for followers of Jesus to be available to serve and help others?

2. Should we wait until we have all of our needs met before helping others as followers of Jesus Christ? Why or why not?

Liberating Lesson

Today, Blacks in America live in a world that is increasingly being labeled as a post-racial society. While the many disparities in the criminal industrial complex and educational system suggest race is still very much a driving factor in the way systems are sustained in this country, it is also true that racial and cultural lines are increasingly blurring together. Millennials are the most racially and culturally diverse generation in American history as flavors of this nation's "melting pot" continue to mix together through interracial marriages, cultural adaptation, and childbirth. The mixing of cultures, races, and even philosophies is not inherently bad, but this text informs us of the importance of retaining some cultural and spiritual standards and boundaries. As it relates to our families and legacies, the text reminds us that though we may have plenty of options from among "enemy territory," our families and deepest relationships must be built with people who serve the same covenant-keeping God as we do.

Application for Activation

Take some time to survey the ministries and offerings in your community of faith. Are there any that are committed to building and celebrating the cultural identity of people of African descent? If so, identify ways to enhance these programs. If not, brainstorm with your classmates two or three ways to create spaces that enhance cultural awareness in your faith community. How can we provide space for young people to remain connected to their cultural heritage? What resources exist within our local community that can assist us in exposing the next generation to their cultural heritage in exciting and meaningful ways?

Follow the Spirit

What God wants me to do:

_____

_____

_____

_____

Remember Your Thoughts

Special insights I have learned:

_____

_____

_____

_____

More Light on the Text

Genesis 24:12–21, 61–67

Genesis 24 is unique in a number of ways. It is unique not only because it is the longest chapter in the book of Genesis (sixty-seven verses), but because of the importance of the topic it covers: the institution of marriage. The author narrates in detail Abraham's final words and his wishes for his son on this most important institution in a man's life and how it was fulfilled. The chapter is also significant because it recounts how God uses yielding hearts to fulfill and perpetuate His purposes, plans, and promises. It tells the story of how God directs and answers the prayer of those who put their trust in Him, and how "The steps of a good man are ordered by the LORD: and he delighteth in his way" (Psalm 37:23). In this narrative, we discover that God's sovereignty does not nullify or opposes human freewill, nor does it force man to do God's will. Rather God uses the one who willingly yields to Him as an instrument to accomplish His sovereign will.

12 And he said, O LORD God of my master Abraham, I pray thee, send me good speed this day, and shew kindness unto my master Abraham.

Abraham is now advanced in age (v. 1), about one hundred and forty years old (cf. Genesis 21:5; 25:20), and is living in the land of Canaan among pagans. His greatest concern is to find a wife for his son Isaac before he dies. He then commissions the "oldest servant" in his house, probably Eliezer (15:2) who must be very old by now, to go down to his homeland Haran (not Ur of the Chaldeans, cf. Genesis 11:31) to find Isaac a wife. This is to fulfill God's covenant promise to bless Abraham with many offspring and give them Canaan for their inheritance (Genesis 12:1–3; 13:14–17; 15:18; 21:12). Abraham wanted Isaac to live in Canaan, but didn't want him to marry one of the local girls. So Abraham made his servant take an oath on three things. First, he must not take a wife for Isaac from among the Canaanite women. Second, he must choose a wife from among Abraham's own relatives (v. 3); and third, he must not, under any circumstances, take Isaac back to Abraham's country of origin (vv. 5–6). Based on his personal experience, Abraham reassures his servant of the Lord's leading and guidance in the venture (vv. 7–9).

Armed with this assurance and in a faithful obedience to his master's request, the servant sets out to fulfill his master's bidding. It was customary in those days for parents to choose a wife for their son. The servant takes with him ten camels and other goods as dowry, which was the custom in ancient Near Eastern countries. He journeys to Mesopotamia, to the city of Nahor, and reaches the outskirts of the village. He and his camels set down to rest near a well in the evening when the women usually came to draw water (vv. 10–11). There, Abraham's servant prays to God for success and guidance in his mission.

He acknowledges that he can do nothing without God. As the "oldest servant" (v. 1) in Abraham's household, he had experienced God at work in his master's life. Moreover, Abraham had already assured his servant that God would send His angel to guide him (v. 7). Based on his personal witness and Abraham's encouragement, the unnamed servant calls on the Lord for guidance, using a combination of God's names "Lord God" (Heb. *Yahweh 'elohim*, **YAH-weh el-oh-HEEM**). The Hebrew, Jehovah or Yahweh, "the self-existent One" or "Eternal," from "I AM," is the Jewish proper and personal name for the supreme and only true God. *'Elohim* is from the common word for a god (Heb. *el*, **ELL**), but plural to show God's majesty. By combining both names and associating them with "my master Abraham" is a display of confidence and faith. The servant is confident that the same God who had been faithful to his master will lead him. Unlike the nonexistent gods whom the Canaanites worshiped, this God is living and active.

At the well, the servant makes a cause-and-effect prayer. If God would answer his prayer, it will be tantamount to showing kindness to his master. The phrase "send me good speed this day" simply asks that God grant him success in his undertaking. His success would mean a show of God's *chesed* (**KHEH-sed**; kindness, goodness, or mercy) to his master Abraham. *Chesed* can also be translated as "faithfulness," and so could refer to God's faithfulness in fulfilling His covenant promises with Abraham.

13 Behold, I stand here by the well of water; and the daughters of the men of the city come out to draw water: 14 And let it come to pass, that the damsel to whom I shall say, Let down thy pitcher, I pray thee, that I may drink; and she shall say, Drink, and I will give thy camels drink also: let the same be she that thou hast appointed for thy servant Isaac; and thereby shall I know that thou hast shewed kindness unto my master.

Sitting by the well, believing in the promises of God and trusting in His providence to guide him, the servant continues his prayer. He proposes a specific sign to assure him of the right woman the Lord would send his way. It would not be unusual for women to offer water

to weary travelers; the culture and hospitality of the day demanded such service. Jesus asked the woman at the well for drinking water (John 4:7). However, the servant's request here is unique: It lies not on whether the young woman would offer him water to drink, but that she would also offer water to his camels (v. 14). The phrase "And let it come to pass" is the Hebrew *hayah* (**haw-YAW**), which means "let it be" or "let it happen," a future proposal or wish. The servant is specific in his prayer to the Lord. He is not looking for just any woman for his master, rather he wants the one whom God would choose. The specificity of the request doesn't mean he lacked confidence in the Lord; he is not giving God a condition or dictating to Him, but is demonstrating his total trust in the Lord's ability to work wonders.

Many young women usually came to the well at this time of the day. But to avoid making the wrong choice by sheer sentiment, and to be sure of God's leading in the matter, the servant makes an unusual request: the offer to give water to his camels. Moreover, he wanted a woman with an attitude of service for his master, one willing to go the extra mile. This woman would be a kind, industrious, and virtuous—a prudent woman from the Lord (Proverbs 19:14; 31). He needed a woman with the right heart, so he asked for God's help because seeing hearts is His specialty (1 Samuel 16:7). Again, the answer to this unusual request would confirm that God has shown kindness (*chesed*) to Abraham (v. 14).

15 And it came to pass, before he had done speaking, that, behold, Rebekah came out, who was born to Bethuel, son of Milcah, the wife of Nahor, Abraham's brother, with her pitcher upon her shoulder. 16 And the damsel was very fair to look upon, a virgin, neither had any man known her: and she

went down to the well, and filled her pitcher, and came up.

As he was speaking and had scarcely finished praying, the Lord had providentially already answered his prayer. Verse 15 starts with the same Hebrew verb (*hayah*, **haw-YAW**) as in verse 14, now in past tense, as a narrative answer to all that the servant had asked in the previous verse. This sets the tone, urgency, and speed with which God answered his prayer. The idea here is that while he is still praying, God has already answered his request, which is consistent with God's character and promise. This is a concrete example of what He promised the prophet, "while they are yet speaking, I will hear" (from Isaiah 65:24). Everything the servant asked for, the Lord answered and even better. Of all the ladies who would come to the well that evening, the Lord's choice for Isaac was the first, with every detailed specification Abraham had ordered (vv. 1–5) and precisely what the servant had prayed. By divine providence, Rebekah, "who was born to Bethuel, son of Milcah, the wife of Nahor, Abraham's brother," shows up.

Often God answers our prayer even beyond our expectation. Paul says that God "is able to do exceeding abundantly above all that we ask or think" (Ephesians 3:20). Although the servant never asked for a physically beautiful young lady for his master, God went beyond his request. He brought to him a woman who was physically, as well as morally, beautiful.

Although she is old enough to marry, Rebekah has kept her purity. Her chastity is emphasized twice: She is "a virgin" and "neither had any man known her." ("Known" is a euphemism for "had sex with.") She was not promiscuous, which probably was a common practice among her peers. In ancient times, virginity was a thing of pride to both the family and their daughters; it was a highly sought after quality in Jewish culture. There were

laws guarding its violation (Exodus 22:16–17; Deuteronomy 22:13–29). Families looked for young women with such moral upbringing for a wife.

Just as the servant had requested, a damsel arrives, carrying a water pitcher on her shoulder. Immediately, without taking notice of the man at the well, she goes down and fills her pitcher with water. Carrying her water-filled pitcher, the girl comes up to go home, as she routinely must have done for years. But today, unbeknownst to her, her life is about to change for good. God's purpose for her is about to unfold.

17 And the servant ran to meet her, and said, Let me, I pray thee, drink a little water of thy pitcher. 18 And she said, Drink, my lord: and she hasted, and let down her pitcher upon her hand, and gave him drink. 19 And when she had done giving him drink, she said, I will draw water for thy camels also, until they have done drinking.

As she returns with her water-filled jar, the servant runs to meet her and asks for a drink of water. Without hesitation Rebekah grants his request. After he had finished drinking, the young woman also offers to "draw water for thy camels also until they have done drinking," exactly the sign the servant had proposed to God. It is not an easy task to quench the thirst of a dehydrated camel, much less ten camels. Camels often feed and drink water to last them for over a week's journey. A thirsty camel would drink almost forty gallons at a time. It would take more than 400 gallons of water and many trips up and down to satisfy the camels' thirst. Water jars were usually large and heavy; the servant definitely is aware of how tedious and almost impossible this task would be when he asked for the sign from God. Fulfilling this unusual and difficult sign would unequivocally assure the servant of God's will. Years later,

Gideon would use a similar method to ascertain God's will for the task the Lord set before him to do (Judges 6:36–40).

20 And she hasted, and emptied her pitcher into the trough, and ran again unto the well to draw water, and drew for all his camels. 21 And the man wondering at her held his peace, to wit whether the Lord had made his journey prosperous or not.

Rebekah now goes to work. The phrase "And she hasted" is to say she quickly went to work. She would need to go several times to draw water to fill the trough until all the camels had enough to drink. This is hospitality to the highest degree—caring for a stranger and his animals, and doing it freely and cheerfully is the wonder of it all. Without knowing, Rebekah was by providence not only the instrument by which God fulfilled the servant's proposed sign, she was indeed the answer to his prayer and the desire of his master. She gives him drink and offers her services for his camels—the very sign the servant proposed. Rebekah has no idea that she is positioning herself to become the mother of Jacob and grandmother of the twelve tribes of Israel. She is humbly setting herself up for great honor as part of the lineage of God's chosen people. The writer of Hebrews says, "Be not forgetful to entertain strangers: for thereby some have entertained angels unawares" (Hebrew 13:2).

Meanwhile, the servant watches with keen interest as Rebekah goes several times up and down from the well drawing water for the thirsty animals. Apparently she is accustomed to this type of work. Although they appear naturally simple and humble, such duties in ancient times were not regarded as degrading (Genesis 29:9; Exodus 2:16–17). "To wit" in modern language is "to know." The servant still needs to know if this is the right woman. Even after this show of hospitality, the servant has to make sure Abraham's terms had been fulfilled. He wants "to know whether the LORD had made his journey successful or not" (v. 21b). He probably wanted to be definitely sure that Rebekah was the person God has chosen.

In the next verses (vv. 22–60), the servant hears Rebekah's lineage and gives her many expensive gifts: "a golden earring of half a shekel weight, and two bracelets for her hands of ten shekels weight of gold" (v. 22). He asks whether there is room for him and his entourage at her home. Rebekah welcomes him and takes him to her family. The servant narrates fully how his master, Abraham, had requested him to go back to his roots to find a wife for his son. He also relates in great detail how the Lord providentially guided him to their house. He asks for Rebekah's hand in marriage for his master's son, Isaac. The family obliges, nonetheless Rebekah makes the final decision.

61 And Rebekah arose, and her damsels, and they rode upon the camels, and followed the man: and the servant took Rebekah, and went his way. 62 And Isaac came from the way of the well Lahai-roi; for he dwelt in the south country.

With the family's blessings (v. 60), Rebekah and her maids and the servant with his entourage left Mesopotamia for Hebron. It was a journey of about 450 miles on camels' backs and about a month's journey. The word "damsels" comes from the Hebrew *na'arah* (**nah-ah-RAW**), which means "girl" or "young maiden." Here it is in the plural, indicating Rebekah had more than one serving attendant. Rebekah's going to draw water, then, is a display of humility and service. Her position did not stop her from attending to her family's chores. Indeed she seemed to delight in serving.

With the conjunction "And" the narrator indicates verses 61 and 62 occur simultaneously. That is to say that while Rebekah and her group with the servant were en route, Isaac came up from the south country along the way of the well Lahai-roi. At this time Isaac was living on his own, in the southern region of Hebron separate from his parents, anticipating the return of the servant with good news to establish his own family. The mention of the well Lahai-roi is significant to Isaac because of its meaning: "well of the Living One who sees me" (Genesis 16:14, NLT). The well got this name when God miraculously provided for and blessed the pregnant Hagar when she fled from Sarai's bitterness (Genesis 16:1–16). God had protected and provided for Hagar and Ishmael even though he was not the son of promise; how much more would God provide for Isaac who had the blessing? Yahweh is the Living God. He knows and sees everything about us; He plans all things for the good of His children and for His glory.

63 And Isaac went out to meditate in the field at the eventide: and he lifted up his eyes, and saw, and, behold, the camels were coming. 64 And Rebekah lifted up her eyes, and when she saw Isaac, she lighted off the camel. 65 For she had said unto the servant, What man is this that walketh in the field to meet us? And the servant had said, It is my master: therefore she took a veil, and covered herself.

Like his father Abraham, Isaac is a man of prayer. Both must have been in prayer awaiting the return of the servant with good news: a wife. It was evening time; Isaac went to the field via the well Lahai-roi to meditate. He appears to know the value of meditation (Psalm 1:2). As he was about to settle down for his meditation, he saw the camels coming. The use of the article "the camels" indicates this was a familiar group of camels—he was able to recognize them from afar. Almost simultaneously Rebekah lifted her eyes and saw Isaac coming toward them. She inquired who was approaching the caravan. After learning from the servant that it was Isaac, she quickly dismounted from the camel to meet him. As an act of respect and submission, she took a veil and covered herself as was the custom when a bride meets her bridegroom. The covering of the face with a veil has continued in many cultures today and in most church weddings.

When she met Isaac and realized who he was, Rebekah was gentle and humble. She didn't complain about the tedious journey or the difficulty of leaving her family to come to a strange place. Realizing God's providence at work, she cheerfully accepted her new relations.

66 And the servant told Isaac all things that he had done. 67 And Isaac brought her into his mother Sarah's tent, and took Rebekah, and she became his wife; and he loved her: and Isaac was comforted after his mother's death.

After introducing the couple, the servant then recounted the journey in detail to Isaac. Isaac then took Rebekah into his late mother's house. They became husband and wife. He loved her and she became a consolation to him for the death of his mother.

Sources:
Biblesoft's New Exhaustive Strong's Numbers and Concordance with Expanded Greek-Hebrew Dictionary. Copyright © 1994, 2003, 2006, Biblesoft, Inc. and International Bible Translators, Inc.
Interlinear Transliterated Bible. Copyright © 1994, 2003, 2006 by Biblesoft, Inc. All rights reserved.
Jamieson, Fausset, and Brown Commentary, Electronic Database. Copyright © 1997, 2003, 2005, 2006 by Biblesoft, Inc. All rights reserved.
Keil & Delitzsch Commentary on the Old Testament: New Updated Edition, Electronic Database. Copyright © 1996 by Hendrickson Publishers, Inc. All rights reserved.
Life Application Study Bible NIV, Carol Stream, IL: Tyndale House Publishers, Inc., and Grand Rapids, MI: Zondervan.
Wiersbe, Warren W. *The Bible Exposition Commentary: Old Testament* © 2001-2004 by Warren W. Wiersbe. All rights reserved.
Butler, Trent C., gen. ed. *Holman Bible Dictionary.* Nashville, TN: Broadman & Holman Publishers, 1991.
Packer, J.I., and Tenney, M.C., eds. *Illustrated Manners and Customs of the Bible.* Nashville, TN: Thomas Nelson Publishers, 1980.

Say It Correctly

Rebekah. Re-**BEK**-ah.
Abraham. **A**-bra-ham.
Bethuel. **BETH**-u-el.

Daily Bible Readings

MONDAY
Mutual Love of Wives and Husbands
(Ephesians 5:21–33)

TUESDAY
Inherit the Blessings of Marriage
(1 Peter 3:1–9)

WEDNESDAY
Jacob Meets Rachel at the Well
(Genesis 29:1–14)

THURSDAY
Searching for a Wife for Isaac
(Genesis 24:1–14)

FRIDAY
Rebekah Becomes Isaac's Wife
(Genesis 24:45–51)

SATURDAY
Rebekah Blessed for Her Commitment
(Genesis 24:54b–61)

SUNDAY
Isaac and Rebekah Joined in Love
(Genesis 24:12–21, 61–67)

Notes

Teaching Tips

Words You Should Know

A. Sod Pottage *nazid* (Heb.)—Lentil stew.

B. Birthright *bekorah* (Heb.)—Certain privileges within a family, in this case an inheritance.

Teacher Preparation

Unifying Principle—Sibling Rivalry. We are often discouraged when our lives do not go smoothly but are disrupted by human conflict and struggle. How can our efforts amount to anything worthwhile when riddled with human frailty and error? God was present in the lives of Esau and Jacob, in spite of their selfish actions.

A. Read the Bible Background and Devotional Readings.

B. Pray for your students and lesson clarity.

C. Read the lesson Scripture in multiple translations.

D. Option: Write or have the students develop in class a modern-day skit about sibling rivalry that resolves with forgiveness between family members.

O—Open the Lesson

A. Begin the class with prayer.

B. Have the students read the Aim for Change.

C. Have the students read the In Focus story.

D. Ask students how events named in the story can weigh on their hearts and how they can view these events from a theological perspective.

P—Present the Scriptures

A. Read the Focal Verses and discuss the Background and The People, Places, and Times sections.

B. Have the class share what Scriptures stand out for them and why, with particular emphasis on today's context.

E—Explore the Meaning

A. Use In Depth or More Light on the Text to help provide more in-depth discussion of the lesson text.

B. Discuss the Liberating Lesson and Application for Activation sections.

N—Next Steps for Application

A. Summarize the value of reconciling with family members.

B. End class with a commitment to pray for families and forgiveness.

Worship Guide

For the Superintendent or Teacher
Theme: A Troubled Birth
Song: "Family"
Devotional Reading: Matthew 16:13–20

A Troubled Birth

Bible Background • GENESIS 25:19–34
Printed Text • GENESIS 25:19–34 | Devotional Reading • MATTHEW 16:13–20

Aim for Change

By the end of the lesson, we will: CONTRAST the carelessness of Esau with the planning of Jacob; APPRECIATE relationships where selfishness is not the driver; and CONSIDER opportunities to bridge broken relationships with family members.

In Focus

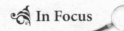

Jasmine was very close to her mother; they spoke every day and spent time together at least once a week. Erica, the eldest daughter, was a bit of a "wild child." Erica was never quite sure what she wanted to do, and seemingly only contacted her mother to ask for things. Jasmine decided for her mother's 70th birthday that they should all go on a cruise. Her father, mother, and younger brother all got ready for the trip. Erica emailed, texted, and talked about how excited she was to go, too. However, when time for the trip finally came, Erica had not purchased her plane ticket. She was frantic because she wanted to go and asked Jasmine for help. "I can't lend you money for a plane ticket right now," Jasmine replied. "The airfare is really high and we've been planning for months."

"So you would just leave me here?" Erica stammered.

"You are leaving yourself. Mom will be celebrating with me and the rest of the family. Who knows if you'll even be here when we get back!"

Erica was heartbroken. She walked out of the room and did not look back. Jasmine felt emotional and began to think about what she had said. She did not know if there was any way to help the situation, and it wasn't her fault Erica was unprepared. But she knew she would miss having her sister on the trip. She knew the first thing she had to do was pray.

Oftentimes family members can bring the greatest joys and challenges in our lives. Why is it sometimes more difficult to give to our families than our friends?

Keep in Mind

"And the Lord said unto her, Two nations are in thy womb, and two manner of people shall be separated from thy bowels; and the one people shall be stronger than the other people; and the elder shall serve the younger" (Genesis 25:23, KJV).

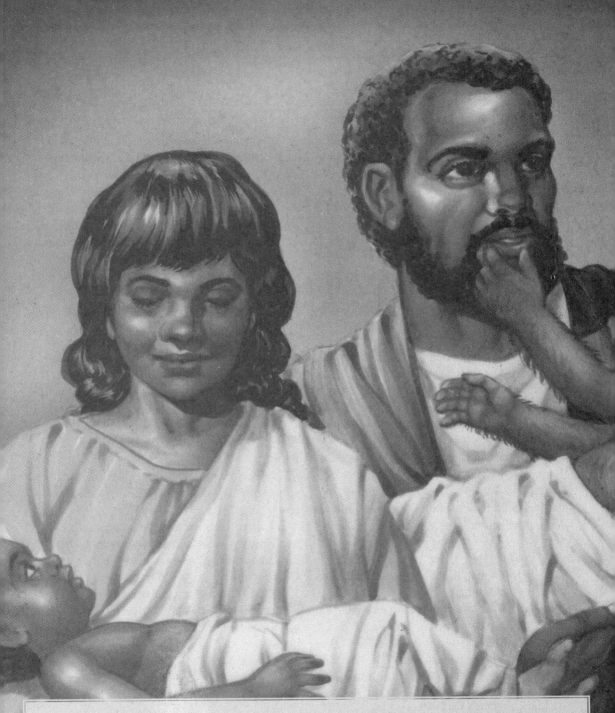

"And the Lord told her, "The sons in your womb will become two nations. From the very beginning, the two nations will be rivals. One nation will be stronger than the other; and your older son will serve your younger son" (Genesis 25:23, NLT).

Focal Verses

KJV Genesis 25:19 And these are the generations of Isaac, Abraham's son: Abraham begat Isaac:

20 And Isaac was forty years old when he took Rebekah to wife, the daughter of Bethuel the Syrian of Padanaram, the sister to Laban the Syrian.

21 And Isaac intreated the LORD for his wife, because she was barren: and the LORD was intreated of him, and Rebekah his wife conceived.

22 And the children struggled together within her; and she said, If it be so, why am I thus? And she went to enquire of the LORD.

23 And the LORD said unto her, Two nations are in thy womb, and two manner of people shall be separated from thy bowels; and the one people shall be stronger than the other people; and the elder shall serve the younger.

24 And when her days to be delivered were fulfilled, behold, there were twins in her womb.

25 And the first came out red, all over like an hairy garment; and they called his name Esau.

26 And after that came his brother out, and his hand took hold on Esau's heel; and his name was called Jacob: and Isaac was threescore years old when she bare them.

27 And the boys grew: and Esau was a cunning hunter, a man of the field; and Jacob was a plain man, dwelling in tents.

28 And Isaac loved Esau, because he did eat of his venison: but Rebekah loved Jacob.

29 And Jacob sod pottage: and Esau came from the field, and he was faint:

30 And Esau said to Jacob, Feed me, I pray thee, with that same red pottage; for I am faint: therefore was his name called Edom.

31 And Jacob said, Sell me this day thy birthright.

NLT Genesis 25:19 This is the account of the family of Isaac, the son of Abraham.

20 When Isaac was forty years old, he married Rebekah, the daughter of Bethuel the Aramean from Paddan-aram and the sister of Laban the Aramean.

21 Isaac pleaded with the LORD on behalf of his wife, because she was unable to have children. The LORD answered Isaac's prayer, and Rebekah became pregnant with twins.

22 But the two children struggled with each other in her womb. So she went to ask the LORD about it. "Why is this happening to me?" she asked.

23 And the LORD told her, "The sons in your womb will become two nations. From the very beginning, the two nations will be rivals. One nation will be stronger than the other; and your older son will serve your younger son."

24 And when the time came to give birth, Rebekah discovered that she did indeed have twins!

25 The first one was very red at birth and covered with thick hair like a fur coat. So they named him Esau.

26 Then the other twin was born with his hand grasping Esau's heel. So they named him Jacob. Isaac was sixty years old when the twins were born.

27 As the boys grew up, Esau became a skillful hunter. He was an outdoorsman, but Jacob had a quiet temperament, preferring to stay at home.

28 Isaac loved Esau because he enjoyed eating the wild game Esau brought home, but Rebekah loved Jacob.

29 One day when Jacob was cooking some stew, Esau arrived home from the wilderness exhausted and hungry.

32 And Esau said, Behold, I am at the point to die: and what profit shall this birthright do to me?

33 And Jacob said, Swear to me this day; and he sware unto him: and he sold his birthright unto Jacob.

34 Then Jacob gave Esau bread and pottage of lentiles; and he did eat and drink, and rose up, and went his way: thus Esau despised his birthright.

30 Esau said to Jacob, "I'm starved! Give me some of that red stew!" (This is how Esau got his other name, Edom, which means "red.")

31 "All right," Jacob replied, "but trade me your rights as the firstborn son."

32 "Look, I'm dying of starvation!" said Esau. "What good is my birthright to me now?"

33 But Jacob said, "First you must swear that your birthright is mine." So Esau swore an oath, thereby selling all his rights as the firstborn to his brother, Jacob.

34 Then Jacob gave Esau some bread and lentil stew. Esau ate the meal, then got up and left. He showed contempt for his rights as the firstborn.

The People, Places, and Times

Jacob. He was the younger son of Isaac and Rebekah, and Esau's twin brother. God changed his name from Jacob to Israel (which means "God prevails") after Jacob proved his perseverance by wrestling with an angel (Genesis 32:22–32).

Esau. He was the eldest son of Isaac and Rebekah, and the twin brother of Jacob. A rugged outdoorsman, Esau was favored by his father. Eventually, Esau went to live in a mountainous region south of Moab along the Dead Sea. The area came to be known as Edom, which means "red" or "ruddy," characterized by the red sandstone that covers much of the terrain, as well as Esau's red hair and complexion.

Background

Isaac married Rebekah, a woman from his father's family, in keeping with Abraham's wishes (she is the granddaughter of Milcah, who was introduced in Genesis 11:29). He had survived the tension created by Abraham fathering a child (Ishmael) by Hagar, the result of Abraham and Sarah's feeble attempt to help God fulfill His promise of an heir.

Ishmael was conceived in accordance with tradition of the time, when a handmaiden could be used to birth an heir in the case of a barren wife.

In ancient Middle East, the firstborn would be the intended heir to receive a double portion of the inheritance (land, livestock), the greater covenantal blessing, and headship of the tribe. Typically, the inheritance would be divided by the number of sons, plus one. Isaac's estate would have been divided into thirds, with Esau intended to receive two-thirds of the estate upon Isaac's death. Esau failed to value its importance in the present, because he would not receive it until the unforeseen future.

Both Isaac and Jacob would deviate from tradition, by God's supernatural intervention, in birth and blessing. Interestingly, Jacob would also follow in his grandfather's footsteps by taking spiritual matters into his own hands to secure a promise made by God, creating strife that would last for generations.

Jealousy and sibling rivalry is not new—Cain and Abel, Rachel and Leah, Joseph and his brothers. How has sibling/familial rivalry impacted your family, either your family of origin or in your own home?

At-A-Glance

1. Jacob and Esau's Birth (Genesis 25:19–26)
2. Esau Sells His Birthright (vv. 27–34)

In Depth

1. Jacob and Esau's Birth (Genesis 25:19–26)

Isaac's wife, Rebekah, was barren (like Isaac's mother), which seemingly endangered the Lord's promise to make Abraham into "a great nation" (Genesis 12:2). Isaac sought God, perhaps learning from Abraham's experience, and pleaded with Him. As with Abraham, it would be two decades before God answered.

Rebekah's pregnancy was tumultuous, which prompted her to "inquire of the Lord" to find out what was wrong with her baby. God responded with an oracle, telling her that she was carrying the fathers of two nations who would be at odds with one another.

It is interesting that God says that they will "be separated"—a prediction of what will later occur as a result of Jacob and Rebekah's deception.

Naming children during those times was a weighty task, as many believed it could control a person's destiny. A name could pronounce blessings or hope for the future. Other times it was a way to honor or connect with ancestors. Sometimes it was a way to mark something significant about the birth or events surrounding it.

The names given to Jacob and Esau were wordplays on other Hebrew words. Esau's name sounded like the Hebrew word for "hairy." Jacob's name sounded like the word for "heel-catcher," a meaning which can be fleshed out as "may God be at his heel (protect)" or "he who catches the heel (tricks)." In God's sovereignty, their conception and births would be a foreshadowing of their futures.

Do you know what your name means? Is it true to who you are? What about your child or children?

2. Esau Sells His Birthright (vv. 27–34)

The differences between the twins were evident from birth and time would reveal more. Esau, the more rugged one, was the hunter and outdoorsman who was favored by his father. Jacob, described as plain and quiet, had tasks that allowed him to stay near the tents and spend more time with his mother, making him her favorite. The favoritism shown by both parents would later be the undoing of their family.

Narratives indicate that Esau is impulsive and short-sighted. Here, he allows his immediate need and hunger to overshadow wisdom and future provision ("I am at the point to die: and what profit shall this birthright do to me?"). Later, he marries an Ishmaelite woman (Genesis 28:9), strengthening the family ties between the two sons who did not receive God's blessing, Ishamel and Esau.

Because he sold his birthright for red lentil stew, Esau receives the name "Edom," which means "red" in Hebrew. It was also the name of an area known for its red sandstone, where he would eventually settle. His descendants would be the Edomites, and that nation would struggle with Jacob's descendants, the Israelites, throughout history.

Perhaps knowing about the prediction that he would be the stronger nation, Jacob seizes an opportunity to help bring it to fruition. He willingly takes advantage of his brother's weakness to secure a better future for himself. Both brothers neglected to count the cost their decisions would have on future generations.

Consider a time when you were short-sighted or impulsive, perhaps even taking advantage of someone. What was the outcome?

Search the Scriptures

1. What did Jacob and Rebekah do when they faced difficult situations (Genesis 25:21–22)?

2. What does the name "Edom" refer to (vv. 25, 30)?

Discuss the Meaning

1. How does this story of sibling rivalry or family strife that impacted a family for generations make you think about your own family or families around you?

2. God had already revealed the destiny of the twins Esau and Jacob (Genesis 25:23). Why did Jacob then resort to deceit and trickery instead of prayer and trust in God for the outcome?

Liberating Lesson

Our society has become woefully individualistic, expressed in mottos such as, "Pull yourself up by your own bootstraps" and "It's a dog eat dog world." It is completely contrary to Scripture and to many African cultures (and African American communities) that embrace proverbs like, "If you want to go quickly, go alone. If you want to go far, go together." Many of our communities are struggling because of Jacob and Esau mentalities—focusing only on self and the present. The abolishment of slavery and the civil rights movement succeeded because people came together with a focus on making life better not just for themselves, but for future generations.

Application for Activation

Paul warns the church, "Don't be selfish; don't try to impress others. Be humble, thinking of others as better than yourselves. Don't look out only for your own interests, but take an interest in others, too" (Philippians 2:3–4). We see how Jacob and Esau failed to apply this verse. How have you been affected by others looking out for themselves more than you? How did it impact the relationship? Search your heart and see if you need to forgive someone.

What have you pursued, or what are you pursuing out of selfish ambition? How well do you apply the Philippians verses to your daily life—work, home, school and church? Ask God to bring to mind those you have offended. Seek forgiveness from Him and them.

Follow the Spirit

What God wants me to do:

_____

_____

_____

_____

Remember Your Thoughts

Special insights I have learned:

_____

_____

_____

_____

More Light on the Text
Genesis 25:19–34

The section introduces the whole cycle of Jacob and Esau and offers glimpses of three episodes in their early years that both determine and illustrate the subsequent course of their careers. In these sixteen verses, we have their future lives in a nutshell.

19 And these are the generations of Isaac, Abraham's son: Abraham begat Isaac: 20 And Isaac was forty years old when he took Rebekah to wife, the daughter of Bethuel the Syrian of Padanaram, the sister to Laban the Syrian. 21 And Isaac intreated the Lord for his wife, because she was barren: and the Lord was intreated of him, and Rebekah his wife conceived.

The opening, "These are the generations of Isaac" is one of the ten headings marking a new division within Genesis (see Genesis 2:4; 5:1; 6:9; 11:27; 25:12). The introduction here is designed specifically to connect Isaac's offspring with Abraham. Isaac's sons are the central characters and the reader's attention is on them.

The story begins by summarizing Isaac's marriage to Rebekah. It looks forward to Jacob's future journey to Paddan-Aram and his dealings with his uncle, Laban (Genesis 29–31).

The word "intreated" (Heb. *'athar*, **aw-THAR**) is not commonly used for prayer in the Old Testament. It occurs often when specifically praying that God remove some bad thing, whether plague (Exodus 8:8–9, 28–30; 9:28; 10:17–18), curse (2 Samuel 21:14), or as here barrenness. Its usage also suggests the earnestness with which Isaac sought the Lord for the fulfillment of His promise. There is an important lesson: Though God had already promised to multiply his family, Isaac prayed for it. It is also significant that although Isaac prayed for many years and his request seemed to go unnoticed, he did not stop praying or believing God for an answer. The fulfillment of God's promise is always sure, even though it may appear to be slow.

22 And the children struggled together within her; and she said, If it be so, why am I thus? And she went to enquire of the LORD. 23 And the LORD said unto her, Two nations are in thy womb, and two manner of people shall be separated from thy bowels; and the one people shall be stronger than the other people; and the elder shall serve the younger. 24 And when her days to be delivered were fulfilled, behold, there were twins in her womb. 25 And the first came out red, all over like an hairy garment; and they called his name Esau. 26 And after that came his brother out, and his hand took hold on Esau's heel; and his name was called Jacob: and Isaac was threescore years old when she bare them.

Rebekah's happiness was soon clouded by the agonies of the twins that she carried, as the children struggled within her. The words "struggled together" (Heb. *ratsats*, **rawts-ATS**) elsewhere refers to political oppression and shattering objects into pieces. The children in her womb dashed against or bruised each other, suggesting a violent agitation occurring inside her, so much so that she was apprehensive about her own safety and for the safety of her unborn children.

Concerned about the situation, Rebekah went to inquire of the Lord. Note the uniqueness of the conflict here. The prenatal fight between twins rages so vehemently that their mother is driven to despair. "Why am I thus?" Rebekah wonders in despair. Even in the womb there didn't appear to be enough room for Esau and Jacob. Their mother's womb became their first battlefield, an ominous sign of what was to follow among their descendants.

How the Lord communicated with Rebekah is not explicitly stated. More important was the message: The "two nations" inside her womb were struggling with each other. The word "nations" (Heb. *goy*, **GO-ee**), as used here, generally refers to "a people, tribe, or nation at large" (cf. Genesis 10:5). Rebekah had not one but two manner of "people" (Heb. *le'om*, **leh-OME**) struggling inside her. The use of the Hebrew word *le'om* has a particular significance. At its root, *le'om* implies togetherness or a cohesive unit, and indicates an ethnic or cultural bond. God was letting Rebekah know that the struggle between her unborn sons had implications far beyond mere sibling rivalry. The two were embarking upon a journey that would last throughout their lives and the lives of their descendants. Jacob is the father of the Israelites. His older brother is the father of the Edomites.

Next we find the power that biblical people placed in names. Esau was the firstborn: "And the first came out red." The word "red" (Heb. *admoni*, **ad-mo-NEE**) means of a reddish color. They called him Esau, the hairy one. This simply means that he was covered with red hair. The name Esau has a loose connection with a place called Seir, the early name for Edom to the southeast of the Dead Sea, where Esau later settled (Genesis 32:3; 36:8). At birth Jacob did not simply follow close upon the heels of Esau, but seized Esau's heel, as if he would trip him up. He had his brother's heel by the hand while in his mother's womb; the name Jacob means "heel-catcher." Esau interprets his brother's name to mean "supplanter" (Genesis 27:36). As with Esau, so, too, Jacob's name would take on a meaning later in life as his deceptive nature became evident. From the very beginning, the twins' birth had great significance for later events in their lives. Twins were considered by some ancient people to be a blessing from God.

27 And the boys grew: and Esau was a cunning hunter, a man of the field; and Jacob was a plain man, dwelling in tents. 28 And Isaac loved Esau, because he did eat of his venison: but Rebekah loved Jacob.

As the boys grew up, their different personalities began to emerge. Esau, the rough and hairy child, became the great hunter and sportsman. On the other hand, Jacob is described as a "plain man," that is, someone who dwells in tents. This word usually has the moral connotation of uprightness or perfection (Genesis 6:9; Job 1:1, 8; 2:3), which used here may mean Jacob was a blameless or plain nice man.

We also see here the parental attachment to one child in preference over another. Isaac loved Esau, and Rebekah loved Jacob. Parents must carefully guard against such partiality and realize it as both sinful and dangerous. The reason for Rachel's special love for Jacob is not stated. Nevertheless, whatever her motives, the scene is now set for Rebekah to use her husband's appetite to acquire the blessing for the son she admired most (Genesis 27). The brothers are already moving inexorably toward realizing the prophetic announcement of their division. The conduct of both parents was less than commendable. Their favoritism led to the strife that existed between the two brothers. While siblings can exhibit vastly different personalities, no one child should be slighted, neglected, or preferred by their parents.

29 And Jacob sod pottage: and Esau came from the field, and he was faint: 30 And Esau said to Jacob, Feed me, I pray thee, with that same red pottage; for I am faint: therefore was his name called Edom.

When Esau returned from hunting, he was "faint." That he was faint (Heb. *'ayeph*, **aw-YAFE**) simply means that he was worn out. It is a type of hunger combined with parched throat that results in total weariness. Jacob had food. The Hebrew word *nazid* (**nah-ZEED**), translated "pottage" refers to soup. The phrase then in a modern translation might say Jacob boiled (sod) soup (pottage). The writer sets the story by pointing out that Esau got into trouble, trying to show not so much Jacob's deceitfulness but Esau's lack of self-control.

Esau asked Jacob to feed him. The Hebrew word *la'at* (**law-AHT**), which Esau uses, comes from the root that means to swallow greedily. Simply speaking it means gluttony. It looked good, and Esau had to have some. This moment of greed followed him through generations. His greed not only affected him, it affected his posterity.

31 And Jacob said, Sell me this day thy birthright.

Jacob knew that he had his brother where he wanted him. Jacob knew that Esau was not thinking straight. Jacob made him an offer he could have refused. Jacob's words were "sell me." To a speaker of the English language the impact of this word is not obvious. But in the Hebrew language the word *makar* (**maw-KAR**) could imply slavery in this context. What Jacob was saying is for Esau to turn over his life to him on account of food. In the African culture it was immoral to use food as punishment or as a means of blackmail. Jacob did blackmail Esau.

In biblical times to have a birthright (Heb. *bekorah*, **beh-ko-RAH**) meant that one had certain privileges. These privileges usually belonged to the firstborn male child in a family. In the Old Testament, the privileges of the firstborn were clearly defined. They included the official authority of the father, a double portion of the father's property, the functions of the domestic priesthood, and authority and superiority over the rest of the family (Genesis 27:27–29; 49:3; Numbers 8:14–17; Deuteronomy 21:17). Included in the birthright was a double portion of whatever inheritance the parents may have to give. Sometimes deceit and intrigue developed—even murder

—as each family member sought to be the one to inherit double portion.

Another aspect of the birthright was the spiritual blessing that the father, and in some cases the mother, usually bestowed. At stake for Esau and Jacob was not just their father's material possessions but also the spiritual legacy of their grandfather, Abraham. When Jacob asked for Esau's birthright, he was positioning himself to be the direct spiritual heir of the Abrahamic covenant. In African cultural terms Jacob was inverting the natural order of the family. He was saying to his brother, "Make me your senior."

32 And Esau said, Behold, I am at the point to die: and what profit shall this birthright do to me?

Esau insisted that he was barely alive. The Hebrew for "at the point to die" could be translated "walking toward death." In his own eyes his hunger meant that he was continually in conversation with death. Here we find the amazing power that uncontrolled desire exercises over the self. He did not understand that the spiritual blessing that was his was the only security he had over the power of death. Esau saw eating Jacob's food as the only cure for his death. Esau then adds the clincher: "What profit shall this birthright do to me?" Esau's not knowing how the birthright would benefit him leads one to consider that he did not deserve it.

33 And Jacob said, Swear to me this day; and he sware unto him: and he sold his birthright unto Jacob.

Jacob saw his brother's weakness. He wanted the birthright. It was serious to him. He was not going to take a mere promise. The only thing he knew that could bind Esau to his word in the presence of God and in community was an oath. Jacob calls him to swear an oath.

In the Old Testament oaths were sacred appeals to God to make sure that promises would be kept. African societies have oral laws that surrounded the enforcement of oaths. It was also believed that God paid attention to the spoken word of an individual. In the Old Testament, word is power. One's word was intricately bound with one's life. So the oath that Jacob asked his brother Esau to swear was binding. Breaking it would lead to serious consequences, though these are not specifically stipulated in the text.

The Hebrew words for swear (*shaba*, **shaw-VAH**) and for the number seven (*sheba*, **SHEH-va**) might be related (cf. Genesis 21:30–31). Seven is often regarded as the biblical number of completion, such as in creation. There is an old Igbo custom in which a promise is made seven times in order to put it into effect.

34 Then Jacob gave Esau bread and pottage of lentiles; and he did eat and drink, and rose up, and went his way: thus Esau despised his birthright.

After the oath-taking, Jacob gives Esau the simple meal. Then the narrative lists four verbs in a matter-of-fact list, as Esau completes these simple, straightforward actions with as little thought as he gave up his birthright. He "ate" (Heb. *akal*, **aw-KAL**). Figuratively speaking, he burnt up the food. He satisfied his lust. Having been consumed and devoured by his lust, he freely fed his lust.

He also drank. The word *shathah* (**shaw-THAW**) means to drink or feast. He had himself a banquet. This speaks more to the inner character of Esau as one who was controlled by his appetite. Then, he simply got up and left. Amazingly, he had just lost his birthright over a pot of stew, and he just arose and went away.

The writer concludes the story by saying "thus Esau despised his birthright." The word despise is quite important. It is translated from *bazah* (Heb. **baw-ZAW**), which has the root idea of treating something more lightly than it should be treated, without reverence to the importance of the matter. Esau, by being so flippant, despised his spiritual and cultural heritage. By ignoring his own spiritual heritage, which was tied to his birthright, Esau became a person of scorn and subject to the judgment of God.

Sources:
Global Study Bible, English Standard Version. Wheaton, IL: Crossway Publishers, 2012. 67-70.
Keener, Craig S., *The IVP Bible Background Commentary: Old Testament*. Downers Grove, IL: Intervarsity Press, 2000. 647-650, 56-58.
Radmacher, Earl D., ed. *Nelson Study Bible*, New King James Version. Nashville, TN: Thomas Nelson Publishers, 1997. 48-52.
Unger, Merrill F., *The New Unger's Bible Dictionary*. Chicago, IL: Moody Press, 1988. 372, 644.
Walvoord, John F., and Roy B. Zuck, eds. *The Bible Knowledge Commentary: Old Testament*. USA: Victor Books, SP Publications, Inc., 1985. 67-70.

Say It Correctly

Padanaram. pad-em **AIR**-em.
Esau. **EE**-saw.

Daily Bible Readings

MONDAY
Water Issue Resolved Peacefully, Peoples
Blessed
(Genesis 26:6–22)

TUESDAY
Jacob and Esau Reconcile, Families Blessed
(Genesis 33:4–11)

WEDNESDAY
Too Late for Repentance
(Hebrews 12:14–17)

THURSDAY
Commit to God's Love and Justice
(Hosea 12:2–6)

FRIDAY
Differences Settled Peacefully
(Genesis 26:28–33)

SATURDAY
God Blesses Ishmael and His Descendants
(Genesis 21:8–13; 25:17–18)

SUNDAY
Different Traits Rooted in Conception
(Genesis 25:19–34)

Notes

_____

_____

_____

_____

Teaching Tips

Words You Should Know

A. Firstborn *bekor* (Heb.)—First in rank or chief as well as first born.

B. Raiment *malbush* (Heb.)—Clothing.

Teacher Preparation

Unifying Principle—Deception in the Family. Deceiving others is a way that people get what they want. Does human deception erase the worth of human accomplishment? Even though the deception used by Rebekah and Jacob disrupted their family, God still worked through their situation to accomplish the planned and promised divine redemption of fallen humanity.

A. Read the Bible Background and Devotional Readings.

B. Pray for your students and lesson clarity.

C. Read the lesson Scripture in multiple translations.

D. Option: As a class, compare and contrast the methods of people who seek help from others in honest ways with those that are manipulative. Discuss strategies for healthy communication of our needs to one another.

O—Open the Lesson

A. Begin the class with prayer.

B. Have the students read the Aim for Change.

C. Have the students read the In Focus story.

D. Ask students how events named in the story can weigh on their hearts and how they can view these events from a theological perspective.

P—Present the Scriptures

A. Read the Focal Verses and discuss the Background and The People, Places, and Times sections.

B. Have the class share what Scriptures stand out for them and why, with particular emphasis on today's context.

E—Explore the Meaning

A. Use In Depth or More Light on the Text to help provide more in-depth discussion of the lesson text.

B. Discuss the Liberating Lesson and Application for Activation sections.

N—Next Steps for Application

A. Summarize the value of knowing God as the one who blesses us.

B. End class with a commitment to pray for forgiveness, honesty, and reconciliation in families.

Worship Guide

For the Superintendent or Teacher
Theme: Jacob Receives Isaac's Blessing
Song: "Sweet Hour of Prayer"
Devotional Reading: Psalm 24:1–6

Jacob Receives Isaac's Blessing

Bible Background • GENESIS 27:1–28:5
Printed Text • GENESIS 27:5–10, 18–19, 21–29 | Devotional Reading • PSALM 24:1–6

Aim for Change

By the end of the lesson, we will: IDENTIFY how Jacob and Rebekah used deception with Isaac; REPENT of the times we have deceived others; and COMMIT to finding ways to express our needs and desires to others in honest and loving ways.

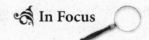 In Focus

Sibling rivalry is bad enough without the parents also choosing sides, but that's the way it was with Maurice and Darren. They argued with and competed against each other their whole lives. As the firstborn, Darren was Dad's favorite—the one Dad played sports with, taught boxing, and took on hunting trips. On the other hand, Mom made it to every one of Maurice's school events; Dad just offered apologies to him for not being there. Dad threw a party for Darren when he won a football scholarship, but was out of town on business for Maurice's college graduation. Mom gave Maurice a car for a graduation gift, and Darren was jealous. Throughout their lives, Dad paid Darren's bills because he "needed it more," but didn't do the same for Maurice.

One day, Mom suggested a way for Maurice to get some of Dad's assets. He wondered why he had agreed to the scheme; he could have—should have—said no, but he didn't.

The fraud was exposed, and Maurice went to prison. But what hurt the most was the look in his grandfather's eyes at the trial. At the sentencing hearing, his grandfather said to Maurice, "You never had to do it. Everything was going to be yours. All you had to do was wait." Now, as the cell door closed behind him, Maurice whispered a prayer, asking for forgiveness.

Can we trust that what God has provided now is enough, and that He has more abundance in store for us?

Keep in Mind

"And he discerned him not, because his hands were hairy, as his brother Esau's hands: so he blessed him" (Genesis 27:23, KJV).

"But he did not recognize Jacob, because Jacob's hands felt hairy just like Esau's. So Isaac prepared to bless Jacob" (Genesis 27:23, NLT).

Focal Verses

KJV **Genesis 27:5** And Rebekah heard when Isaac spake to Esau his son. And Esau went to the field to hunt for venison, and to bring it.

6 And Rebekah spake unto Jacob her son, saying, Behold, I heard thy father speak unto Esau thy brother, saying,

7 Bring me venison, and make me savoury meat, that I may eat, and bless thee before the LORD before my death.

8 Now therefore, my son, obey my voice according to that which I command thee.

9 Go now to the flock, and fetch me from thence two good kids of the goats; and I will make them savoury meat for thy father, such as he loveth:

10 And thou shalt bring it to thy father, that he may eat, and that he may bless thee before his death.

18 And he came unto his father, and said, My father: and he said, Here am I; who art thou, my son?

19 And Jacob said unto his father, I am Esau thy first born; I have done according as thou badest me: arise, I pray thee, sit and eat of my venison, that thy soul may bless me.

21 And Isaac said unto Jacob, Come near, I pray thee, that I may feel thee, my son, whether thou be my very son Esau or not.

22 And Jacob went near unto Isaac his father; and he felt him, and said, The voice is Jacob's voice, but the hands are the hands of Esau.

23 And he discerned him not, because his hands were hairy, as his brother Esau's hands: so he blessed him.

24 And he said, Art thou my very son Esau? And he said, I am.

25 And he said, Bring it near to me, and I will eat of my son's venison, that my soul may bless thee. And he brought it near to him, and

NLT **Genesis 27:5** But Rebekah overheard what Isaac had said to his son Esau. So when Esau left to hunt for the wild game,

6 she said to her son Jacob, "Listen. I overheard your father say to Esau,

7 'Bring me some wild game and prepare me a delicious meal. Then I will bless you in the LORD's presence before I die.'

8 Now, my son, listen to me. Do exactly as I tell you.

9 Go out to the flocks, and bring me two fine young goats. I'll use them to prepare your father's favorite dish.

10 Then take the food to your father so he can eat it and bless you before he dies."

18 So Jacob took the food to his father. "My father?" he said. "Yes, my son," Isaac answered. "Who are you—Esau or Jacob?"

19 Jacob replied, "It's Esau, your firstborn son. I've done as you told me. Here is the wild game. Now sit up and eat it so you can give me your blessing."

21 Then Isaac said to Jacob, "Come closer so I can touch you and make sure that you really are Esau."

22 So Jacob went closer to his father, and Isaac touched him. "The voice is Jacob's, but the hands are Esau's," Isaac said.

23 But he did not recognize Jacob, because Jacob's hands felt hairy just like Esau's. So Isaac prepared to bless Jacob.

24 "But are you really my son Esau?" he asked. "Yes, I am," Jacob replied.

25 Then Isaac said, "Now, my son, bring me the wild game. Let me eat it, and then I will give you my blessing." So Jacob took the food to his father, and Isaac ate it. He also drank the wine that Jacob served him.

26 Then Isaac said to Jacob, "Please come a little closer and kiss me, my son."

he did eat: and he brought him wine and he drank.

26 And his father Isaac said unto him, Come near now, and kiss me, my son.

27 And he came near, and kissed him: and he smelled the smell of his raiment, and blessed him, and said, See, the smell of my son is as the smell of a field which the LORD hath blessed:

28 Therefore God give thee of the dew of heaven, and the fatness of the earth, and plenty of corn and wine:

29 Let people serve thee, and nations bow down to thee: be lord over thy brethren, and let thy mother's sons bow down to thee: cursed be every one that curseth thee, and blessed be he that blesseth thee.

27 So Jacob went over and kissed him. And when Isaac caught the smell of his clothes, he was finally convinced, and he blessed his son. He said, "Ah! The smell of my son is like the smell of the outdoors, which the LORD has blessed!

28 "From the dew of heaven and the richness of the earth, may God always give you abundant harvests of grain and bountiful new wine.

29 May many nations become your servants, and may they bow down to you. May you be the master over your brothers, and may your mother's sons bow down to you. All who curse you will be cursed, and all who bless you will be blessed."

The People, Places, and Times

Birthright. In the previous lesson, we saw how Jacob bartered with Esau to gain his birthright, or inheritance. While Jacob's actions gave him access to the financial blessings reserved for the eldest, he did not automatically receive the spiritual and covenantal blessing. Isaac, aging and blind, decided it was time to bestow his blessing upon Esau.

Background

In ancient Middle Eastern culture, blessings (and sometimes curses) were pronounced by the patriarch of the family, often when aging or on his deathbed. These blessings were used to get his affairs in order, assuring not only that his estate would be cared for, but his legacy preserved. Various blessings could be bestowed upon different members of the family (usually sons), with the eldest son receiving the greater blessing and authority. These blessings and curses often invoked the assistance of a deity to make it come to pass. Similar to the naming of children after birth, these blessings were often seen as prophetic, securing the future of those being blessed or cursed. Such pronouncements were binding—what was said could not be "unsaid," regardless of error, or as we will see, if gained by deception.

It is important to note that deception seemed to be a family trait, particularly when it was believed that one's life or livelihood was at stake. Abraham lied when he was asked about Sarah being his wife. Isaac did the same when the men of Gerar inquired about Rebekah when they relocated during a famine. In this lesson, we see that Jacob and Rebekah work together to deceive Isaac and cheat Esau. Later in Genesis, Jacob will be deceived by his uncle.

What character traits—positive or negative—can you identify that have been passed down through generations in your family? How have they affected you personally? Your family (dynamics, legacy, relationships)?

At-A-Glance

1. Rebekah Plots (Genesis 27:5–10)
2. Jacob Lies (vv. 18–19)
3. Scheme Executed (vv. 21–27)
4. Isaac Blesses (vv. 27–29)

In Depth

1. Rebekah Plots (Genesis 27:5–10)

In verses 1–4, Isaac, supposing that his death is near (he would, however, go on to live for several more decades), gives Esau instructions to prepare a meal so that he can pronounce his blessing over him. Rebekah overhears this conversation. Perhaps remembering the oracle predicting that Jacob would be the greater twin, she devises a scheme to trick Isaac into blessing Jacob. Like Abraham and Sarah before her, Rebekah decides to "help" God, taking advantage of Isaac's blindness and creating a plan that manipulates his other senses—taste, smell, and touch.

Rebekah then commands Jacob to join her. While he does protest, it is not because he believes the plan is evil, but because he fears being caught and cursed. She responds, "Let your curse be on me, my son; only obey me" (v. 13). While God would still bless Jacob, their actions would negatively affect them both. After Jacob flees from Esau, Rebekah and Jacob would never see one another again.

What is the difference between guilt and conviction? Why does differentiating between the two matter?

2. Jacob Lies (vv. 18–19)

Jacob executes his mother's plan. As instructed, he uses goatskins to appear hairy like Esau. He wears Esau's clothes that Rebekah gave him. He presented the meal to Isaac that she prepared. While she orchestrated this entire process, Jacob had the opportunity to choose righteousness, and failed. When asked, "Who are you, my son?" he lied, "I am Esau, your firstborn." It is then evident that he had taken full ownership of the scheme. He would go on to lie again, attributing his supposed quick success in hunting and cooking to God.

What impact have lies—either told to you or by you—had on your life?

3. Scheme Executed (vv. 21–27)

At multiple points, there are glimpses that Isaac was suspicious of Jacob, and aware he could be deceived. However, similar to other experiences—his own, Abraham's and even Rebekah's—he trusts himself and his own senses instead of seeking God.

He uses logic, inquiring about the speed in which Jacob returned from hunting. He uses touch, requesting to feel Jacob to see if his arms were hairy. He uses hearing, acknowledging that the voice sounded like Jacob's and not Esau. Still suspicious, he asks again if Jacob was really Esau (and Jacob lied for the third time). In a final act of confirmation, he uses smell, asking Jacob to come near to be kissed, as was typical in a blessing. As Isaac kisses him, he smells Esau's scent on the clothing. Satisfied by his senses, Isaac blesses Jacob. Rebekah and Jacob's scheme is successful, but would come at a price.

Consider a time when you made a major decision because it appealed to your "senses" (e.g., logic, emotions) instead of asking God for direction. What was the outcome?

4. Isaac Blesses (vv. 27–29)

Isaac ironically begins his blessing over Jacob by focusing on a trait that belonged to Esau—"the smell of a field." He asks God to make him prosperous (ample dew, rich land, and abundant crops), grant him dominion over other nations, and for favor and protection (curses and blessings). The mercy of God would bring these things to pass, despite Jacob's guilt.

Reflect on a situation where God blessed you in spite of your actions.

Search the Scriptures

1. Read Genesis 12:1–3. In what ways is Isaac's blessing similar to Abram's call? In what ways is it different?

2. Read Genesis 48:13–14. What simple action did Jacob (Israel) perform to give the greater blessing to the younger son? What does this say about God's sovereignty?

Discuss the Meaning

1. How can you love your family even when they don't treat you fairly?

2. Is it worth it to deceive people to make an expected result happen?

Liberating Lesson

Our country has a lengthy dismal relationship with deception. Native Americans stripped of their lands in deceptive deals. African Americans prevented from obtaining freedom, civil rights and fair treatment because of dishonest practices. Politicians campaign on promises left unfulfilled once in office.

But deception is not new. Centuries ago, David wrote, "Help, LORD; for the godly man ceaseth; for the faithful fail from among the children of men. They speak vanity every one with his neighbour: with flattering lips and with a double heart do they speak" (Psalm 12:1–2).

How do we respond? Write? Debate? Protest? Tweet? At appropriate times, absolutely. But ultimately, we must do the hardest thing of all—seek God—who responded to David with, "For the oppression of the poor, for the sighing of the needy, now will I arise, saith the LORD; I will set him in safety from him that puffeth at him" (Psalm 12:5).

Application for Activation

Social media. Taxes. Work projects. Simple conversations. There are daily opportunities to lie and deceive. It is imperative that we realize that "the heart is deceitful above all things, and desperately wicked: who can know it?" (Jeremiah 17:9). Recognizing this can keep us humble and alert.

In what ways have you recently been tempted to lie or deceive? What motivated you? Did you give in to the temptation? What can you do to safeguard against such temptation in the future?

Follow the Spirit

What God wants me to do:

_____

_____

_____

_____

Remember Your Thoughts

Special insights I have learned:

_____

_____

_____

_____

More Light on the Text
Genesis 27:5–10, 18–19, 21–29

When parents play favorites with their children, the family becomes dysfunctional. It will be characterized with deception, division, and manipulation. This is doubly so when one either through human wisdom or selfish desire tries to change God's plan or help Him accomplish it. This can be said of Isaac and Rebekah's family. God has promised to channel His blessing through Jacob, the younger twin brother (Genesis 25:23). Rebekah is aware of this. Consequently, Jacob not only became her favorite, she planned to ensure that Jacob would overshadow his older twin brother, Esau. Meanwhile, Isaac is aware of God's plan, but he preferred Esau, his firstborn (Genesis 25:28). Apparently, this created a rift in the family. While Isaac attempted to alter God's plan by trying to bestow the blessing on Esau, Rebekah through manipulation and deception tried to help fulfill God's plan.

Genesis 27 begins with a description of Isaac's physical condition. He has greatly aged (now probably about one hundred thirty-seven years old). As a result he could no longer see. It is common for people to lose their sight as they age, especially in biblical times (Genesis 48:10; 1 Samuel 4:15). However, Isaac's other sensory organs, including his appetite, hearing, and feeling/touch, remain intact. He knows that his death is at hand. Since he doesn't know when, he wants to perform his last patriarchal duties before he dies: bestowing of blessings on the firstborn. He therefore invites Esau to a private meeting. Esau is "a skilled hunter" known for making sumptuous and tasty dishes from his games (Genesis 25:27–28). Isaac asks him to go out to the field and hunt some game and "make me savoury meat, such as I love, and bring it to me, that I may eat; that my soul may bless thee before I die" (Genesis 27:4). Isaac is aware of God's plan that the younger son was to receive the covenant blessing (25:19–23), yet he intends to give the blessing to Esau. Moreover, he is aware that Esau had despised his birthright and sold it to Jacob, thereby relinquishing his rights (Genesis 25:29–34). In addition, Isaac couldn't have forgotten that

Esau had disqualified himself when he married Canaanite women (Genesis 26:34–35).

5 And Rebekah heard when Isaac spake to Esau his son. And Esau went to the field to hunt for venison, and to bring it. 6 And Rebekah spake unto Jacob her son, saying, Behold, I heard thy father speak unto Esau thy brother, saying, 7 Bring me venison, and make me savoury meat, that I may eat, and bless thee before the Lord before my death.

As Isaac hatches his plan to bless Esau, Rebekah is eavesdropping. The word "heard" is the Hebrew *shama'* (**shaw-MAH**), that is "to hear with attention or interest," "to listen attentively" or "to hear intelligently." That means Rebekah didn't just happen to hear their discussion on passing; she purposefully paid attention with keen interest to the conversation. Equipped with the knowledge of the ancient Near Eastern tradition and the importance of an aging man's last words, Rebekah monitors Isaac's every movement. It isn't that she just stumbles into Isaac's conversation with Esau. Oral statements, including deathbed bequests and blessings, had legal force in ancient Near Eastern law (Genesis 49:28–32). This is also consistent with African tradition and culture. Rebekah must have intentionally watched out for the day Isaac would plan to bless his preferred son. As she listens, Rebekah overhears Isaac's plan to bless Esau.

Scarcely has Esau left to hunt for the venison for his father when Rebekah calls Jacob's attention to Isaac and Esau's conversation. She reveals Isaac's plot.

8 Now therefore, my son, obey my voice according to that which I command thee.

Rebekah makes her own plan to secure the blessing for Jacob. As earlier noted, God has already informed her that Jacob would become the family head (25:23–26). But Rebekah takes matters into her own hands to ensure her own favorite son receives that promised blessing. She resorts to doing something to bring about what God has already said would happen. Rebekah decides to control Jacob and deceive her husband.

To stress the seriousness of the matter, Rebekah uses the conjunction "therefore" (Heb. *'attah*, **at-TAW**). In other words, based on the information, action must be taken. The parental favoritism is about to bear its toxic and deceptive fruit (Genesis 25:28). In the context of this endearing and personal phrase "my son" is the notion of preferential treatment by Rebekah. Rebekah calls on him to obey every instruction she is about give him. The word "obey" is the same Hebrew for to "hear" or "listen" (*shama'*, **shaw-MAH**) as found in verse 5 (Deuteronomy 4:4). Here, listen is synonymous with obedience. When we tell children to "listen to your parents," it is more than paying attention; it is to listen with the intent of obeying or following an instruction. With the clause, "obey my voice according to that which I command thee" Rebekah leaves no room for Jacob not to obey.

9 Go now to the flock, and fetch me from thence two good kids of the goats; and I will make them savoury meat for thy father, such as he loveth: 10 And thou shalt bring it to thy father, that he may eat, and that he may bless thee before his death.

Rebekah outlines her plan, one so quick and detailed that it could be assumed she thought it through well in advance. She instructs Jacob to go to their family flock and choose two young goats; she volunteers to cook them for Jacob just the way Isaac likes them. Some people will do anything to accomplish whatever they devise in their hearts, even deceitful things. Having lived with her husband Isaac these many years, Rebekah knows quite well the type of food he craves. However, to pull off this scheme—turning goat meat to taste like venison—will take extraordinary skill.

Verse 10 reiterates the purpose for the deception—for Jacob to gain Isaac's blessing. For Rebekah, the end justifies the means. No matter how good our intensions, we should not attempt to accomplish them by doing what is wrong. God doesn't need our help to fulfill His plan. Judas didn't have to betray Jesus for God to accomplish His salvation plan for mankind (see Matthew 26:24–25). He could have done it in spite of man's help. However, Rebekah proved to be as deceitful as her son, Jacob, whose name signifies deceit (v. 36; 25:26).

18 And he came unto his father, and said, My father: and he said, Here am I; who art thou, my son? 19 And Jacob said unto his father, I am Esau thy firstborn; I have done according as thou badest me: arise, I pray thee, sit and eat of my venison, that thy soul may bless me.

Verses 11–17 detail the dialogue between Jacob and his mother. He objects and gives excuses why the plot could fail. His objections are not based on the moral dilemma, but rather on being caught and its consequences—a curse rather than blessing. Jacob is not concerned about his mother's immoral device to deceive his old and vulnerable father. Instead he is concerned how it would affect him if the plot fails. Morality has disappeared in this family. While Jacob hesitates and questions his mother's plan, although for the wrong reason, Rebekah is fully wrapped up in it. She prepares the food and hands it over to Jacob to present to Isaac, his blind father.

As a grown man of forty years (26:34), Jacob could have resisted and refused to connive with his mother's deception. But instead he conforms to it and takes the food to his unsuspecting father. Here begins a series of Jacob's lies in order to obtain what God has already promised him. The first falsehood is when he claims to be who he is not. It is tragic enough to lie, but to lie to someone you call "my father" is even worse; worse still is when one takes advantage of another's disability. Nevertheless, Jacob uses the endearing phrase "my father" to evoke trust. Although Isaac has lost his sight, he has not lost his hearing. Suspicious of the voice, Isaac asks, "Who art thou, my son?" Jacob answers, "I am Esau thy firstborn." The Hebrew for "firstborn" is *bekor* (**beh-KORE**) with the idea of "firstborn" in rank, hence, "chief." Although, Esau sold his birthright to Jacob (25:31–34), he did not sell his name. His claim to be Esau only deepens Jacob and his mother's deception.

Jacob's second series of falsehoods is when he lies about the food and the Lord (vv. 19–20). He claims to have complied with his father's wishes and calls the goat meat "my venison." He says, "I have done just as you told me; please arise, sit and eat of my game, that your soul may bless me." Jacob's absolute goal is the blessing; it doesn't matter the method he uses to achieve it or the lies he tells. The Hebrew for "to bless" is *barak* (**baw-RAK**), which in some contexts means "to kneel," but in other uses, such as when people "bless" God, it can mean "to bless (as act of adoration)." When the object of this verb is a person, *barak* is to invoke God's blessing or benefits, so that God would cause the person to prosper. Surprised how quickly the food is brought, Isaac asks how this was possible. Jacob falsely gives credit to the Lord for achieving his goal. People often use the name of the Lord falsely to obtain what they want. Unfortunately this is found within Christian circles and churches today. This is dangerous and blasphemous—it is using the name of the Lord in vain.

21 And Isaac said unto Jacob, Come near, I pray thee, that I may feel thee, my son, whether thou be my very son Esau or not. 22 And Jacob went near unto Isaac his father; and he felt him, and said, The voice is Jacob's voice, but the hands are the hands of Esau. 23 And he discerned him not, because his hands were hairy, as his brother Esau's hands: so he blessed him.

The next series of lies Jacob tells has to do with his identity and his love for his father. Still suspicious and unwilling to rely on his ears, Isaac asks Jacob to approach so he can feel if this is the right son. Remember that Esau was born with what was "like a hairy garment all over" (Genesis 25:25). Mindful that this could have resulted in failure to their deceitful plot, Jacob gave this very objection to his mother Rebekah (27:11–12). However, to cover this loophole, Rebekah uses "the skin of the young goats" to cover Jacob's "arms and the smooth part of his neck" (27:16). The sense of touch is one of the faculties Isaac has not lost. Jacob approaches his father. After feeling Jacob's hands, Isaac says, "The voice is Jacob's, but the hands are Esau's" (from v. 22). Tricked by Jacob, Isaac mistook the goatskin for human hair. He could not "discern" whether it was Jacob or Esau. The verb "discerned" the narrator uses here is the Hebrew *nakar* (**naw-KAR**), which means "to recognize or acknowledge." That is to say, Isaac was confused and uncertain as to who it was. Nonetheless, he decides to bless him, thinking that it was Esau.

The family's state of dysfunction caused by favoritism is apparent throughout this narrative. God has said in his oracle to Rebekah that the "elder shall serve the younger" (Genesis 25:23). Esau sold his birthright to Jacob for a pot of stew (v. 34). There is no reason to assume these two events were not common knowledge among the family. Therefore, Isaac is aware that God has planned to extend the blessing He promised to Abraham through Jacob, not Esau. Nevertheless, he thought he could alter God's plan.

24 And he said, Art thou my very son Esau? And he said, I am. 25 And he said, Bring it near to me, and I will eat of my son's venison, that my soul may bless thee. And he brought it near to him, and he did eat: and he brought him wine, and he drank.

Isaac is still not fully convinced it is not Jacob he is about to bless. Therefore to be certain the blessing goes to the rightful person in his mind, Isaac asks again if the son before him is really Esau. Jacob lies again and says he is. Then Isaac asks him to bring the food closer so that he can eat and bless him. Jacob brings the food and Isaac eats; he also brings the wine to Isaac and he drinks. After eating and drinking, Isaac prepares to bless Jacob, supposing it is Esau.

26 And his father Isaac said unto him, Come near now, and kiss me, my son. 27 And he came near, and kissed him: and he smelled the smell of his raiment, and blessed him, and said, See, the smell of my son is as the smell of a field which the LORD hath blessed:

After eating the meal, Isaac asks Jacob to come and kiss him as yet another test. Jacob commits another fraud and kisses his father. A kiss in every culture is a symbol of love. Jacob's kiss is hypocritical, a kiss of betrayal—the type Judas gave to Christ (Luke 22:48). As Jacob kisses his father, Isaac smells the odor of his garment. Rebekah had thought ahead and took care to provide for this particular test. She gave Jacob some of Esau's clothes to wear (v. 15). The smell finally convinced him that it is Esau because it smells like the field and so sets the stage for giving of the blessing.

28 Therefore God give thee of the dew of heaven, and the fatness of the earth, and plenty of corn and wine: 29 Let people serve thee, and nations bow down to thee:

be lord over thy brethren, and let thy mother's sons bow down to thee: cursed be every one that curseth thee, and blessed be he that blesseth thee.

Finally convinced, thinking that it is really his son Esau, Isaac pours blessings on Jacob. As the spiritual head of the family, Isaac has the right to pass on blessing as related to the covenant of Abraham. It must be noted that in the ancient Near Eastern culture any blessing once bestowed would never be rescinded. This is the case here as would be confirmed later in the chapter (vv. 35–40). Isaac blesses Jacob in two major areas of life: prosperity and authority.

Firstly, Jacob will be blessed with natural and material wealth—comprising agricultural prosperity. The produce of the land and animals measured wealth in their culture. Isaac blesses Jacob with dew to water his crops, and with abundant grain and wine, the staples of their diet. These are common elements of blessings (Deuteronomy 33:13, 28). Secondly, Isaac adds political authority with reference to his own people and other nations. Other nations will bow before him, and his own brethren will bow and serve him. Here Isaac reaffirms God's prophecy regarding the two boys: "The sons in your womb will become two nations. From the very beginning, the two nations will be rivals. One nation will be stronger than the other; and your older son will serve your younger son" (25:23, NLT). By using the plural "brethren" Isaac looks beyond Jacob and Esau's day to the future when Abraham's seed would multiply.

In addition to these blessings, Isaac also assures Jacob of the Lord's protection. Here he quotes the Lord's original promise of protection to Abraham (Genesis 12:3). In spite of man's flaws and his attempt to falter or alter God's purposes, God's promises and plan will always prevail. It is not the bestowal of these words by Isaac upon Jacob that made him blessed. Rather, Jacob was blessed because God chose him, long before Isaac pronounced the blessing (Genesis 25:23).

We need to understand through this account that God's attributes of constancy, grace, and justice are made plain. In spite of Jacob and his mother Rebekah's dubious method to obtain the blessing promised, God never changed His plan to bless Jacob. The Lord remained faithful to His word. Although He did not approve of the deceptive method they used to achieve their goal, God did not withhold His blessing on Jacob. This is grace in action. His attribute of justice is displayed in the consequences that followed Jacob's life: (1) Jacob was exiled from his family for many years; (2) Jacob never saw his mother again; (3) his brother wanted to kill him (27:41–42); (4) he was deceived by his uncle, Laban; (5) his family became torn with strife; (6) Esau became the founder of an enemy nation. Jacob would have received the birthright and blessing anyway without his and Rebekah's assistance (25:23).

Sources:
Global Study Bible, English Standard Version. Wheaton, IL: Crossway Publishers, 2012. 71-73.
Keener, Craig S., *The IVP Bible Background Commentary: Old Testament*. Downers Grove, IL: Intervarsity Press, 2000. 59-60.
Radmacher, Earl D., ed. *Nelson Study Bible*, New King James Version. Nashville, TN: Thomas Nelson Publishers, 1997. 54-56.
Unger, Merrill F., *The New Unger's Bible Dictionary*. Chicago, IL: Moody Press, 1988. 173, 174.
Walvoord, John F., and Roy B. Zuck, eds. *The Bible Knowledge Commentary: Old Testament*. USA: Victor Books, SP Publications, Inc., 1985. 72-74.
The Bible Exposition Commentary: Old Testament. Copyright © 2001-2004 by Warren W. Wiersbe. All rights reserved.
Biblesoft's New Exhaustive Strong's Numbers and Concordance with Expanded Greek-Hebrew Dictionary. Copyright © 1994, 2003, 2006 Biblesoft, Inc. and International Bible Translators, Inc.
Blue Letter Bible, OT, Online.
Guzik, David, Study Guide for Genesis 27, *Blue Letter Bible*, OT, Online
Holy Bible, New Living Translation, Copyright © 1996, 2004 by Tyndale Charitable Trust. Used by permission of Tyndale House Publishers. All rights reserved.
Interlinear Transliterated Bible. Copyright © 1994, 2003, 2006 by Biblesoft, Inc. All rights reserved. [For more detail see the full copyright page.]
Life Application Study Bible NIV. Carol Stream, IL: Tyndale House Publishers, Inc., and Grand Rapids, MI: Zondervan.
Zondervan NIV Study Bible, Copyright © 1973, 1995, 2002, 2008. Grand Rapids, MI: Zondervan.

Say It Correctly

Isaac. i-**ZEK**.
Esau. **EE**-saw.
Jacob. **JAY**-cob.
Rebekah. Re-**BEK**-ah.

Daily Bible Readings

MONDAY
Reject Deceit, Seek God's Face
(Psalm 24:1–6)

TUESDAY
Live Openly and Honestly
(1 Peter 2:18–25)

WEDNESDAY
Isaac Prepares to Bless Esau
(Genesis 27:1–4)

THURSDAY
Rebekah Diverts Isaac to Bless Jacob
(Genesis 27:5–17)

FRIDAY
Esau Loses Blessing; Exiled
(Genesis 27:30–40)

SATURDAY
Jacob Charged to Marry Cousin
(Genesis 27:46–28:5)

SUNDAY
Jacob Received Isaac's Blessing
through Deceit
(Genesis 27:5–10,18–19, 21–29)

Teaching Tips

Words You Should Know

A. Haran (Heb.)—A city in Mesopotamia near the Euphrates River.

B. Vow *neder* (Heb.)—A solemn oath or promise.

Teacher Preparation

Unifying Principle—Finding Strength. In the midst of human turmoil, we grow weary and can lose sight of the purpose for our lives. How can we escape the confusion to refresh and reorient ourselves to get back on track? God created an opportunity for the weary Jacob to reconnect with his spiritual mission and resources for him to begin his life's journey with renewed vigor.

A. Read the Bible Background and Devotional Readings.

B. Pray for your students and lesson clarity.

C. Read the lesson Scripture in multiple translations.

D. Option: Invite students to share about a time when they might have said, "Surely the LORD is in this place—and I did not know it!" (Genesis 28:16). What is it like to realize that God has been with us all along? How can that realization change the course of our lives?

O—Open the Lesson

A. Begin the class with prayer.

B. Have the students read the Aim for Change.

C. Have the students read the In Focus story.

D. Ask students how events named in the story can weigh on their hearts and how they can view these events from a theological perspective.

P—Present the Scriptures

A. Read the Focal Verses and discuss the Background and The People, Places, and Times sections.

B. Have the class share what Scriptures stand out for them and why, with particular emphasis on today's context.

E—Explore the Meaning

A. Use In Depth or More Light on the Text to help provide more in-depth discussion of the lesson text.

B. Discuss the Liberating Lesson and Application for Activation sections.

N—Next Steps for Application

A. Summarize the value of retreating and resting in God.

B. End class with a commitment to pray for rest, restoration, and refreshing in the presence of the Lord.

Worship Guide

For the Superintendent or Teacher
Theme: Jacob Forms a Relationship with God
Song: "We Are Climbing Jacob's Ladder"
Devotional Reading: Psalm 42:1–5

Jacob Forms a Relationship with God

Bible Background • GENESIS 28:10–22
Printed Text • GENESIS 28:10–22 | Devotional Reading • PSALM 42:1–5

—— Aim for Change ——

By the end of the lesson, we will: SYMPATHIZE with Jacob's feeling weak and vulnerable; AFFIRM that God's strength meets us in our human weakness; and RESOLVE to make time for God to refresh us when we feel weak.

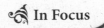 In Focus

Pastor Reed had been the full-time senior pastor at his church for fifteen years. He preached two services every Sunday, made it a point to be at Sunday School, plus a church ministry meeting every day of the week. Then he also faithfully fulfilled all of his administrative, pastoral care, and sermon preparation work.

One Sunday he found out that his younger brother had died in a car accident. Then his mother was diagnosed with breast cancer. One of his associate ministers told him a former deacon was spreading rumors about him mismanaging money. On top of this, Pastor Reed had preached through illness three times already this year. He decided in the midst of all he was going through, something had to be done.

His associate pastor said, "Pastor Reed, the congregation needs you healthy, and we need new vision for the next year. I think it may be time for you to take a sabbatical. At least a month to take care of you and your family. The church will be OK while you're away. God can give you restoration and fresh revelation, but you have to take time with God away from the church to listen again." Pastor Reed looked down. He knew his associate minister was right. He needed God to meet him with strength during his time of weakness.

Why do people wait until they are overwhelmed to seek God for restoration? Have you had a time when you needed God to restore you, but were afraid to take time to care for yourself amid other responsibilities?

—— Keep in Mind ——

"And, behold, I am with thee, and will keep thee in all places whither thou goest, and will bring thee again into this land; for I will not leave thee, until I have done that which I have spoken to thee of" (Genesis 28:15, KJV).

"What's more, I am with you, and I will protect you wherever you go. One day I will bring you back to this land. I will not leave you until I have finished giving you everything I have promised you" (Genesis 28:15, NLT).

Focal Verses

KJV **Genesis 28:10** And Jacob went out from Beersheba, and went toward Haran.

11 And he lighted upon a certain place, and tarried there all night, because the sun was set; and he took of the stones of that place, and put them for his pillows, and lay down in that place to sleep.

12 And he dreamed, and behold a ladder set up on the earth, and the top of it reached to heaven: and behold the angels of God ascending and descending on it.

13 And, behold, the LORD stood above it, and said, I am the LORD God of Abraham thy father, and the God of Isaac: the land whereon thou liest, to thee will I give it, and to thy seed;

14 And thy seed shall be as the dust of the earth, and thou shalt spread abroad to the west, and to the east, and to the north, and to the south: and in thee and in thy seed shall all the families of the earth be blessed.

15 And, behold, I am with thee, and will keep thee in all places whither thou goest, and will bring thee again into this land; for I will not leave thee, until I have done that which I have spoken to thee of.

16 And Jacob awaked out of his sleep, and he said, Surely the LORD is in this place; and I knew it not.

17 And he was afraid, and said, How dreadful is this place! this is none other but the house of God, and this is the gate of heaven.

18 And Jacob rose up early in the morning, and took the stone that he had put for his pillows, and set it up for a pillar, and poured oil upon the top of it.

19 And he called the name of that place Bethel: but the name of that city was called Luz at the first.

20 And Jacob vowed a vow, saying, If God will be with me, and will keep me in this way

NLT **Genesis 28:10** Meanwhile, Jacob left Beersheba and traveled toward Haran.

11 At sundown he arrived at a good place to set up camp and stopped there for the night. Jacob found a stone to rest his head against and lay down to sleep.

12 As he slept, he dreamed of a stairway that reached from the earth up to heaven. And he saw the angels of God going up and down the stairway.

13 At the top of the stairway stood the LORD, and he said, "I am the LORD, the God of your grandfather Abraham, and the God of your father, Isaac. The ground you are lying on belongs to you. I am giving it to you and your descendants.

14 Your descendants will be as numerous as the dust of the earth! They will spread out in all directions—to the west and the east, to the north and the south. And all the families of the earth will be blessed through you and your descendants.

15 What's more, I am with you, and I will protect you wherever you go. One day I will bring you back to this land. I will not leave you until I have finished giving you everything I have promised you."

16 Then Jacob awoke from his sleep and said, "Surely the LORD is in this place, and I wasn't even aware of it!"

17 But he was also afraid and said, "What an awesome place this is! It is none other than the house of God, the very gateway to heaven!"

18 The next morning Jacob got up very early. He took the stone he had rested his head against, and he set it upright as a memorial pillar. Then he poured olive oil over it.

19 He named that place Bethel (which means "house of God"), although it was previously called Luz.

that I go, and will give me bread to eat, and raiment to put on,

21 So that I come again to my father's house in peace; then shall the LORD be my God:

22 And this stone, which I have set for a pillar, shall be God's house: and of all that thou shalt give me I will surely give the tenth unto thee.

20 Then Jacob made this vow: "If God will indeed be with me and protect me on this journey, and if he will provide me with food and clothing,

21 and if I return safely to my father's home, then the LORD will certainly be my God.

22 And this memorial pillar I have set up will become a place for worshiping God, and I will present to God a tenth of everything he gives me."

The People, Places, and Times

Bethel. Located about 12 miles north of Jerusalem and west of the Jordan River, Bethel has many significant connections to Old Testament events. Bethel was originally called Luz and belonged to the Canaanites. Upon his entry into Canaan, Abraham set up camp between Bethel and Ai (Genesis 12:8). It is here that Abraham worshiped God when he returned from Egypt (13:3–4). When Jacob fled from Beersheba to Haran, he spent the night here and dreamed of a ladder reaching to heaven with angels climbing up and down (28:11–12). This prompted Jacob to rename the city from Luz to Bethel, which means "house of God" (v. 19).

During times of trouble, the people of Israel went to Bethel to seek counsel of God (Judges 20:18; 21:2). It was also at Bethel that the Ark of the Covenant was entrusted to the care of Aaron's grandson, Phinehas (20:27–28). After the nation was divided, Bethel was included in the northern kingdom of Israel and became the official center of worship. Under King Jeroboam, Bethel became a site of idol worship (1 Kings 12:28–33) and was not purged of its idols until the reign of King Josiah of Judah (2 Kings 23:15).

Background

Jacob had stolen the blessing and birthright of his brother Esau by tricking him and his father Isaac. Isaac was nearing death in his old age and was concerned about his descendants inheriting the promise of God. Jacob's mother Rebekah knew that Esau would try to kill Jacob to get revenge once Isaac had died, so she decided to send him to live with his uncle Laban in Haran until Esau calmed down. Rebekah also knew that Jacob could find a wife from her own family in her hometown instead of marrying a local girl where they lived in Canaan. Neither Isaac nor Rebekah wanted their children to marry Canaanite women who worshiped different gods and would have allowed unrelated descendants to inherit the promise.

Isaac reaffirms to Jacob, his inherited son of promise, that God would bless him, multiply him, and be with him in the same way He had been with Isaac and Abraham before him. The promise to Abraham, Isaac, and now Jacob was similar yet more specific than the blessing God had given Adam and Eve in the garden. Esau learns of the prohibition on marrying Canaanite women and decides to marry into his uncle Ishmael's family, again reinforcing the contrast between the son of promise and the one who forfeited the promise. Isaac sends his son Jacob to the same place his father Abraham told him his wife would be found, the house of Betheuel and Laban in Haran. Jacob is weary after his long journey from Beersheba to Haran to find a wife and decides to rest in the wilderness near Luz, where our Scripture takes place.

At-A-Glance

1. Resting in Promise (Genesis 28:10–12)
2. Renewing the Promise (vv. 13–17)
3. Remembering the Promise (vv. 18–22)

In Depth

1. Resting in Promise (Genesis 28:10–12)

Jacob is traveling from the house of his father Isaac in Beersheba in Canaan to the house of his uncle Laban in Haran. During his journey, he stops at sunset near the city of Luz. Jacob embodies obedience to his parents in making the journey to find a wife from his own family line. This is a welcome change from the Jacob who had been a selfish trickster concerning his brother Esau's blessing and birthright. As a result, Isaac kept his word of blessing, but sent Jacob to travel alone in the wilderness with no servants, resources, or protection. His sin against his brother did not negate the promise of God, but it did have the consequence of losing his father Isaac's provision and protection for his journey. Jacob now walks through the wilderness alone because he tricked his brother. His deceit leaves him confused about his purpose, in danger at home, and weary on his trip.

Too tired to continue alone in the night, Jacob sets up camp and decides to rest his head on a rock as he sleeps. When he falls to sleep, he dreams about a stairway reaching from earth up to heaven and angels going up and down it. Jacob discovers as he dreams that there is a connection between earth and heaven in that place. Jacob has the revelation that God was present while he slept undistracted by his journey and danger at home. God was present for Jacob even while he was alone in the wilderness.

2. Renewing the Promise (vv. 13–17)

God identifies Himself as "the LORD God of Abraham thy father, and the God of Isaac" (Genesis 28:13). There is to be no mistake. Jacob is in the presence of the God honored and revered by his father and his grandfather.

At this point God confirms His covenant blessings that He had promised to both Abraham and Isaac of land, numerous descendants, protection, and God's presence. Jacob had not experienced the blessing of God until his arrival in the place that God had promised to bless.

We would do well to remember that for some of us, our blessings will not happen until we get to the place where God wants to bless us. Here Jacob was a fugitive, fleeing from the wrath of his brother. He was certainly not a likely candidate to be selected by God. Jacob's actions toward his father and brother clearly indicated he was a thief and a deceiver. Yet God had chosen him to be the steward of the great covenant.

When Jacob awakens from his dream, he is astonished. He has encountered God for himself. Jacob does not have to rely on the testimony of his father or grandfather; he now knows without a doubt, "Surely the LORD is in this place" (Genesis 28:16). Now he recognizes that God is right there on the spot he is standing on! Not only is God present, but God has promised him the very blessings he had unsuccessfully tried to steal. No longer is Jacob alone or running away from his past. He now has God's promise: "I will not leave thee, until I have done that which I have spoken to thee of" (v. 15). Rather than escape his past, Jacob now has the hope of a future that is rightfully his.

Jacob goes from alone with nothing on his journey to renewed in purpose and in the presence of the Lord who will provide everything he needs. Knowing that Jacob now has divine assurance that God will never leave him, we can now understand Jacob's description of this place as "dreadful." The use of the word "dreadful" implies a reverential awe at what Jacob had experienced. Jacob understood, perhaps for the first time in his life, how awesome and powerful God was and how weak and ineffective he was.

3. Remembering the Promise (vv. 18–22)

Here in the desert, outside of this Canaanite city, God had chosen to reveal His presence. It is no wonder that Jacob wants to preserve the memory of this awesome experience and erect a memorial. He does not have the necessary materials to build a proper altar, so he uses the materials at hand: stones. This act is reminiscent of Jacob's grandfather Abraham, who similarly constructed an altar in the place God had appeared to him (Genesis 13:18).

What a wonderful reminder to Christian parents, grandparents, and caregivers. Our children are always watching us. We must model godly behavior, and provide them with models of godly worship and thanksgiving. Our praise, worship, and acts of thanksgiving are not private matters but ought to be demonstrated daily. God's presence in our lives has to be shown to them. If they see us build altars to God, they will know to build altars. If they see us recognize and worship God—even after mistakes, setbacks, and wilderness experiences—they will know God can meet them in their wilderness as well. In memorializing the spot where he had discovered God, Jacob also swore to adopt his grandfather's practice

in dedicating to God a tenth of all he received (Genesis 14:20).

Search the Scriptures

1. What does Bethel mean (Genesis 28:19)?

2. What does God promise Jacob (vv. 13–15)? What does Jacob promise God (vv. 21–22)?

Discuss the Meaning

1. When Jacob found himself tired from running, God made him rest and spoke to him. Are there times where God has made you rest or slowed you down to speak to you? Explain.

2. Jacob received a great blessing from God at a time when his actions made him the least deserving. Discuss a time when you were certain that God had confirmed His promises to you when you felt undeserving or weak.

Liberating Lesson

It can be very difficult for people to find resources, opportunities, and renewed purpose in society after wandering in the wilderness because of their own sinful choices. Whether it be recovering addicts, newly released prison inmates, or political refugees from violent wars, many people find themselves feeling isolated with limited resources on their way to renewed promise. How can we show mercy and build places of rest and renewal in our congregations for those who are trying to change and find purpose after bad choices or circumstances leave them in the wilderness? How can we create an environment where people can encounter God's presence and promise when they are trying to rejoin communities?

Application for Activation

Our involvement in our careers and families make it difficult for many of us to spend "quiet time" with the Lord. Yet, if we are to hear Him, we have to make time. Determine to find time early in the morning, late in the evening, or another time that is just for you and God. Close yourself away from others, and turn off your TV and phone. Begin by praying, and then read the Scriptures. Allow God to speak to you through His Word.

Follow the Spirit

What God wants me to do:

_____

_____

_____

_____

Remember Your Thoughts

Special insights I have learned:

_____

_____

_____

_____

More Light on the Text

Genesis 28:10–22

10 And Jacob went out from Beersheba, and went toward Haran. 11 And he lighted upon a certain place, and tarried there all night, because the sun was set; and he took of the stones of that place, and put them for his pillows, and lay down in that place to sleep.

In obedience to his father's command to seek a wife (v. 2) but also in compliance with his mother's counsel to evade the wrath of Esau, Jacob set out on his journey toward Haran. As Jacob traveled from Beersheba to Haran, he came to a place where he was obliged to stop all night because the sun had set. Jacob might have intended to reach Luz, but because the sun had set, he opted to stop and rest for the night. Using the verb "lighted upon" (Heb. *paga'*, **paw-GAH**) suggests that the stop was not anticipated, and to Jacob's mind seemed like chance. Rather, the stop was divinely appointed; the place where he stopped had already been consecrated by one of Abraham's altars (12:8, 13:4). Jacob took some of the stones and made them his pillow. Hard headrests were common pillows in those days, rather than today's soft cushions.

12 And he dreamed, and behold a ladder set up on the earth, and the top of it reached to heaven: and behold the angels of God ascending and descending on it.

Jacob fell asleep and had a dream where he saw a "ladder" (Heb. *sullam*, **sool-LAWM**) resting upon the earth with the top reaching to heaven and upon it angels of God going up and down. Although the etymology of the Hebrew word for ladder is not entirely certain, its meaning and symbolism are without doubt. It was a visible symbol of the real and uninterrupted fellowship between God in heaven and God's people upon Earth. The presence of the angels, God's messengers, served to support the notion that God wanted to communicate with Jacob. Also dreams often served as instruments of divine revelation in the Old Testament. As Jacob slept, he had a powerful dream that gave him insight into the realm of God's power. In ancient days gods were thought to be confined by certain physical boundaries, but also having special places where heaven touched earth. As Jacob saw the ladder stretched from heaven to earth, God revealed to Jacob that He was available and accessible.

What a much-needed, refreshing, and inspiring experience for Jacob! God showed up for him at the right time. Jacob was tired, lonely, and forlorn when he arrived at Bethel. He had no company to travel with, no place but the ground for a bed, and no pillow but a stone for his head, but he experienced God in a personal and unusual way. The doors at home, to his family, and to Beersheba were shut, but the window of heaven was wide open to him. God showed a ladder of hope to a hopeless Jacob who was caught up with a problem of his own making. For a short while, God made His presence, promise, and providence accessible to Jacob. God never ceases to seek relationship with humanity and He continues to communicate with humanity in unexpected ways.

13 And, behold, the LORD stood above it, and said, I am the LORD God of Abraham thy father, and the God of Isaac: the land whereon thou liest, to thee will I give it, and to thy seed.

The vision was not just about angels. The Lord "stood" (Heb. *natsab*, **naw-TSAB**) above the ladder; this is a personal revelation of Jehovah to Jacob. In proclaiming Himself to Jacob as the God of his fathers, God not only confirmed to him all the promises made to Abraham and the blessing for which Isaac had prayed (Genesis 28:3–4) in their fullest extent, but God also assured Jacob of protection on his dangerous journey and a safe return to his home (v. 14). God revealed Himself as God who keeps promises through generations. He reinforces the promise of this land that will continue to be central throughout the Old Testament.

14 And thy seed shall be as the dust of the earth, and thou shalt spread abroad to the west, and to the east, and to the north, and to the south: and in thee and in thy seed
shall all the families of the earth be blessed. **15 And, behold, I am with thee, and will keep thee in all places whither thou goest, and will bring thee again into this land; for I will not leave thee, until I have done that which I have spoken to thee of.**

Jacob seems to have left home with a heavy heart. Through this dream, God reiterated His promises to Abraham (Genesis 12:1–3; 13:14–17; 15:1–5, 18–20 17:1–8; 22:16–18) and Isaac (Genesis 26:3–4, 24), relayed to Jacob the prosperity of his descendants, and reassured the fearful patriarch of His presence during this dangerous journey. The Hebrew used in His promise of presence, not to leave (*'azab*, **aw-ZAHV**), is also translated forsake or abandon; its common use between God and His people makes it a covenantal word.

The promise to make Jacob's children "as the dust of the earth" is a direct quote from a previous promise to Abraham (Genesis 13:14–16). There, God clearly uses this simile to emphasize the multitude of descendants. Here, with the next phrase "they shalt spread abroad," God seems to include a sense of ubiquity of influence, too. There is no place on Earth where there is not dust. Similarly, there will be no place on Earth where Jacob's descendants are not found.

God showed him the communication that exists between heaven and Earth—the guard of angels—and His ever watchful eye looking down on him, whether awake or asleep. God confirmed Jacob's destiny as the heir of God's promise to his forefathers and to the world. Jacob then has nothing to fear. No evil would happen to him while God was his guardian and strong defense. The Lord, in this dream, completely dispelled Jacob's fears by confirming the covenant and promises He had made to Abraham and renewed with Isaac.

16 And Jacob awaked out of his sleep, and he said, Surely the Lord is in this place; and I knew it not.

When Jacob wakes from the dream, he knows God had made this place His peculiar residence. In that moment Jacob realized that God had been with him even when he did not know it. Jacob had fallen asleep fearful, helpless, alone, sorrowful, and anxious, without any thought that he was especially cared for or watched by Abraham's God. He thought he had been exiled from the presence of the Lord because he had cooperated in deceiving his brother Esau. Instead, God offered him promise, not condemnation. The Lord gave Jacob the promise of future generations and of God's continued presence with them.

17 And he was afraid, and said, How dreadful is this place! This is none other but the house of God, and this is the gate of heaven.

Jacob seems to wake up in two stages. As he awakened, a feeling of awe came upon him. He voices how special this place is. "House of God" (Heb. *bet elohim*; **BATE eh-lo-HEEM**) anticipates the name Jacob was about to give to the place, "Bethel" (v. 19). "Gate of heaven" occurs only here in the Old Testament, but the concept that heaven, the divine abode, has one or more entrances is a familiar idea in ancient thought.

The dream had, no doubt, left an impression so strong that Jacob declared, "How dreadful is this place!" Here the word "dreadful" comes from the Hebrew *yare'* (**yaw-RAY**) and means both "to be afraid" and "to stand in awe or godly fear." This particular form is used variously to refer to the dangerous wilderness (Deuteronomy 8:15), shining crystal (Ezekiel 1:22), or more often God's awesome miracles (2 Samuel 7:23; Psalm 66:3). It describes things (whether good or bad) that make you stop and consider them. As Jacob continued on his journey, he was to carry with him a holy awe of the gracious presence of God.

18 And Jacob rose up early in the morning, and took the stone that he had put for his pillows, and set it up for a pillar, and poured oil upon the top of it. 19 And he called the name of that place Bethel: but the name of that city was called Luz at the first.

The appearance of the ladder, the Lord standing at its top, and the movement of the angels left Jacob with a true sense of God's commitment to keep His covenant with Jacob's forefathers. Consequently, when he arose, he solemnly dedicated one of the stones and vowed to follow God himself and bring his tithes to the God who dwelt in this place (vv. 18–22).

The next morning Jacob turned the pillow into a pillar. He erected the stones upon which he had laid his head as a monument of the extraordinary vision he had in this place. The word "pillar" here (Heb. *natsab*, **naw-TSAB**) derives from the same word used for the Lord standing in verse 13. It could mean a heap of stones that is piled up for a memorial, hence the word monument. The pillow stones served to mark the place of his restoration. Jacob's experience moved him to worship and praise the Lord. He poured oil upon the top to consecrate it as a memorial of the mercy that had been shown him there.

Jacob named the place Bethel, "house of God" (Heb. *Bethel*, **bate-ALE**); the town had been called Luz. It appears that Jacob gave the name not to the place where the pillar was set up, but to the town in the surrounding neighborhood where he had received this divine revelation. He would renew this name on his return from Mesopotamia (35:15).

20 And Jacob vowed a vow, saying, If God will be with me, and will keep me in this way

that I go, and will give me bread to eat, and raiment to put on, 21 So that I come again to my father's house in peace; then shall the LORD be my God: 22 And this stone, which I have set for a pillar, shall be God's house: and of all that thou shalt give me I will surely give the tenth unto thee.

Jacob made a vow (Heb. *neder*, **NEH-der**). This was no ordinary vow, but a grand and solemn expression of Jacob's complete acceptance of the Lord to be his God, the significance of which is underscored by its mention again at key points in Jacob's journey (Genesis 31:13; 35:1–3, 7). Typically, in the Old Testament, vows were made in situations of distress. Jacob's vow was no exception. He was in a distressed state. He was running away from home and the threat of death. But now he has received an unexpected revelation announcing his return to his country and guaranteeing him safety on the journey. Here God showed Jacob the future and confirmed to him the covenant promise.

God had already made an unconditional promise to Jacob to watch over him and bring him back to this land (v. 15). Jacob did not need to do anything in return, but still, he offered to God an altar, a tithe, and a commitment. One thing is certainly clear from this episode: Jacob was gradually coming to the end of himself. Instead of relying on his abilities, he was to stop being the "trickster," as his name implies, and to rely on God to supply His needs and protect him.

Yet Jacob seems to establish some conditions for this relationship, so he offered to mark the Lord's sacred space and to tithe as a sign of his commitment. The "if" in Jacob's vow is the progression of Jacob taking God at His word: "If God is going to do so much for me, then I will do something for Him." Jacob's character as a bargainer did not change instantly as he sought to know God's character as sovereign and faithful. Although Jacob waits until much later in life to rid his house of idols once God has demonstrated more of the promise (Genesis 35), he makes the commitment to God here in Genesis 28. In other words, if God were willing to fulfill His covenant promise, then Jacob would acknowledge and worship Him as his God, both by building an altar and tithing all his possessions. Jacob did not yet know that God was sovereign and ever faithful, but we can have faith in God's character and do not need to bargain with Him for what He has already promised.

Sources:

BibleGateway.com. *The Holy Bible, New Living Translation*. Wheaton, Illinois: Tyndale House, 2007. (accessed August 1, 2012).

Bible Study Tools. www.BibleStudyTools.com. "Old Testament Hebrew Lexicon—King James Version." (accessed August 4, 2012).

HarperCollins Study Bible (NRSV). New York: Harper Collins Publishers, 2006. 35–55.

Henry, Matthew. "Genesis." *Matthew Henry's Commentary on the Whole Bible*, Vol. 1 (Genesis to Deuteronomy). Genesis 29. http://www.ccel.org/ccel/henry/mhc1.Gen.xxix.html. (accessed August 1, 2012).

Strong, James. Free Bible Study Tools. *Strong's Concordance with Greek and Hebrew*. http://www.tgm.org/bible.htm (accessed August 5, 2012).

Unger, Merrill F., R.K. Harrison, Howard Vos, and Cyril Barber. *The New Unger's Bible Dictionary*. Chicago: Moody Publishers, 1988. 635, 644–646.

Say It Correctly

Bethel. **BETH**-uhl.
Beersheba. beer-**SHE**-buh.

Daily Bible Readings

MONDAY
Samuel Hears the Voice of God
(1 Samuel 3:1–9)

TUESDAY
Elijah Meets God's Angel
(1 Kings 19:4–9)

WEDNESDAY
The Lord Renews the Weary
(Isaiah 40:27–31)

THURSDAY
A Great Priest for the People
(Hebrews 10:19–25)

FRIDAY
Tithe to Support Levites and Community
(Deuteronomy 14:22–29)

SATURDAY
Nathanael Will See Greater Things
(John 1:47–51)

SUNDAY
Transformed by God's Visitation
(Genesis 28:10–22)

Notes

_____

_____

_____

_____

Teaching Tips

Words You Should Know

A. Supplant *aqab* (Heb.)—Take the place of another.

B. Reproach *cherpah* (Heb.)—It also means shame, scorn, or disgrace.

Teacher Preparation

Unifying Principle—Amassing Wealth. Obstacles and loss often block our efforts to accomplish something worthwhile. How can we overcome these setbacks in order to live lives that count for good? God intervened to help Jacob overcome seeming defeat by not only gaining many possessions but also escaping the wrath of a selfish and deceptive father-in-law.

A. Read the Bible Background and Devotional Readings.

B. Pray for your students and lesson clarity.

C. Read the lesson Scripture in multiple translations.

D. Option: Ask students to write on a piece of paper difficult situations they are facing and put these papers into a basket. Have a time of prayer to seek God's intervention and blessing over these situations.

O—Open the Lesson

A. Begin the class with prayer.

B. Have the students read the Aim for Change.

C. Have the students read the In Focus story.

D. Ask students how events named in the story can weigh on their hearts and how they can view these events from a theological perspective.

P—Present the Scriptures

A. Read the Focal Verses and discuss the Background and The People, Places, and Times sections.

B. Have the class share what Scriptures stand out for them and why, with particular emphasis on today's context.

E—Explore the Meaning

A. Use In Depth or More Light on the Text to help provide more in-depth discussion of the lesson text.

B. Discuss the Liberating Lesson and Application for Activation sections.

N—Next Steps for Application

A. Summarize the value of knowing God as provider and miracle worker.

B. End class with a commitment to pray for provision, peace, and fruitfulness from God.

Worship Guide

For the Superintendent or Teacher
Theme: God Blesses Jacob and His Family
Song: "Way Maker"
Devotional Reading: Psalm 46

God Blesses Jacob and His Family

Bible Background • GENESIS 30
Printed Text • GENESIS 30:22–32, 43| Devotional Reading • PSALM 46

——— Aim for Change ———

By the end of the lesson, we will: ANALYZE how God provided for Jacob and his family; IDENTIFY with Jacob's difficult family relationships; and PRAY for God's intervention in our own times of crisis.

——— In Focus ———

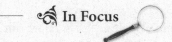

Judith was a lawyer who handled mergers and acquisitions litigation for an international firm. Eventually, the firm transferred her to the Brussels office, initially for three years. There was no promise of partnership, but there was the unspoken understanding that she wouldn't get on the track if she turned the transfer down.

She and the firm prospered in that time. But she felt a calling to do social justice work, one that had grown with every return visit to see her family and hometown. Judith felt now that she had done enough for the firm, and that it was time to go home, for good.

Mr. Kanigher, the senior partner, tried to dissuade her. "It's been wonderful having you here, Judith," he said. "I wish you wouldn't go. You've grown this office from a handful of people to millions in annual billables. It wouldn't have happened without you. What can I do to get you to stay? There's got to be something I can give you. Name it."

Judith thought for a moment. "I'll tell you what," she said. "You commit to having each associate do pro bono cases for international legal aid groups, and give me the time to work any such case of my choosing."

Mr. Kanigher agreed! Judith returned to her office, sank back in her chair, and sighed. Now she could focus on her future.

Our service to others can take many forms. Are we using our talents as God would have us?

——— Keep in Mind ———

"And God remembered Rachel, and God hearkened to her, and opened her womb" (Genesis 30:22, KJV).

"Then God remembered Rachel's plight and answered her prayers by enabling her to have children" (Genesis 30:22, NLT).

Focal Verses

KJV **Genesis 30:22** And God remembered Rachel, and God hearkened to her, and opened her womb.

23 And she conceived, and bare a son; and said, God hath taken away my reproach:

24 And she called his name Joseph; and said, The LORD shall add to me another son.

25 And it came to pass, when Rachel had born Joseph, that Jacob said unto Laban, Send me away, that I may go unto mine own place, and to my country.

26 Give me my wives and my children, for whom I have served thee, and let me go: for thou knowest my service which I have done thee.

27 And Laban said unto him, I pray thee, if I have found favour in thine eyes, tarry: for I have learned by experience that the LORD hath blessed me for thy sake.

28 And he said, Appoint me thy wages, and I will give it.

29 And he said unto him, Thou knowest how I have served thee, and how thy cattle was with me.

30 For it was little which thou hadst before I came, and it is now increased unto a multitude; and the LORD hath blessed thee since my coming: and now when shall I provide for mine own house also?

31 And he said, What shall I give thee? And Jacob said, Thou shalt not give me any thing: if thou wilt do this thing for me, I will again feed and keep thy flock.

32 I will pass through all thy flock to day, removing from thence all the speckled and spotted cattle, and all the brown cattle among the sheep, and the spotted and speckled among the goats: and of such shall be my hire.

43 And the man increased exceedingly, and had much cattle, and maidservants, and menservants, and camels, and asses.

NLT **Genesis 30:22** Then God remembered Rachel's plight and answered her prayers by enabling her to have children.

23 She became pregnant and gave birth to a son. "God has removed my disgrace," she said.

24 And she named him Joseph, for she said, "May the LORD add yet another son to my family."

25 Soon after Rachel had given birth to Joseph, Jacob said to Laban, "Please release me so I can go home to my own country.

26 Let me take my wives and children, for I have earned them by serving you, and let me be on my way. You certainly know how hard I have worked for you."

27 "Please listen to me," Laban replied. "I have become wealthy, for the LORD has blessed me because of you.

28 Tell me how much I owe you. Whatever it is, I'll pay it."

29 Jacob replied, "You know how hard I've worked for you, and how your flocks and herds have grown under my care.

30 You had little indeed before I came, but your wealth has increased enormously. The LORD has blessed you through everything I've done. But now, what about me? When can I start providing for my own family?"

31 "What wages do you want?" Laban asked again. Jacob replied, "Don't give me anything. Just do this one thing, and I'll continue to tend and watch over your flocks.

32 Let me inspect your flocks today and remove all the sheep and goats that are speckled or spotted, along with all the black sheep. Give these to me as my wages.

43 As a result, Jacob became very wealthy, with large flocks of sheep and goats, female and male servants, and many camels and donkeys.

The People, Places, and Times

Padan Aram. This is the region of Mesopotamia from south of the Amanus Mountains (in eastern Turkey) around the northern branches of the Euphrates River. This region comprised part of what is known as the Fertile Crescent, which stretches from the Persian Gulf to the Amanus Mountains back down the coast to Egypt.

Laban. He was the son of Bethuel, brother of Rebekah, and father of Leah and Rachel. Laban was a member of the segment of the family of Terah that remained in Haran when Abraham and Lot migrated to Canaan.

Background

After fleeing from Esau, Jacob would become well acquainted with God's discipline, at the hand of his uncle Laban. Laban repeatedly deceived Jacob. Ironically, Jacob, the "trickster" who supplanted custom by stealing the blessing and birthright from the firstborn, was fooled into marrying Leah, Laban's firstborn daughter, because of custom. Marrying Leah and Rachel, the daughter he loved, would cost Jacob fourteen years of labor—seven for which he volunteered to serve in exchange for Rachel's hand in marriage, and the other seven he was swindled into working.

However, an unintended outcome of Laban's deception was that it led to tension, envy, and competition between his daughters. Rachel was barren, but Leah was fruitful. Leah would personally bear six sons because "the Lord saw she was unloved, [and] He opened her womb" (29:31). In response to His grace, Leah would give her sons names that reflected her hope in and gratitude toward the Lord.

Rachel "envied her sister" (Genesis 30:1), using a Hebrew word here to describe an overwhelming sense of rage. After first demanding that Jacob "Give me children, or else I die!" she resorted to what was customary during ancient Middle Eastern times. Rachel gave her slave, Bilhah, to Jacob as a surrogate, hoping she would produce an heir. She did. However, Leah responded by doing the same, giving over her slave, Zilpah. This competition would continue for years, with ten sons and one daughter being born by three women, before Rachel ever conceived her first child.

In what ways have you seen parents—your own or others—create sibling rivalry? How does it affect the entire family?

In Depth

1. Rachel Finally Conceives (Genesis 30:22–24)

After years of agonizingly watching Leah, Bilhah, and Zilpah give birth, God finally "remembered" and "listened to" Rachel, answering her years-long prayers by opening her womb. Rachel recognizes that her conception was a gift from God and names her son Joseph, which means "may He add," and sounds similar to the Hebrew word meaning, "take away." While she celebrated that God took away her disgrace by the birth of this son, she also boldly asked—by prayer and his naming—that God would grant her another son.

Joseph's birth did not simply remove Rachel's shame, but it firmly established her status in Jacob's family. A barren wife, if not protected by her relatives, would often be shunned and discarded by her husband. Now that she had produced an heir, her relatives would have less cause for concern, which now provided Jacob with the freedom to move back to his homeland.

Many times, God does not answer our prayers immediately. In the midst of waiting for current ones, we forget what He has done in the past. What long-term prayers have you seen God answer in the past?

2. Jacob's Increase (vv. 25–32, 43)

After years of shepherding Laban's flocks and beginning his own family, Jacob was ready to establish his household and legacy. It was time to return to his homeland. His request to move on was met with resistance. Both Laban and Jacob recognized that Laban's wealth increased as a result of God's favor upon Jacob. Perhaps to add credibility, Laban claimed to have received this information through divination, which would later be recognized as a sin in Deuteronomy. Regardless of how he obtained the information, it is apparent that God revealed it.

Laban knew it was in his best interest to persuade Jacob to remain, so he selfishly sets out to negotiate wages with Jacob. It was customary for shepherds to receive 10 to 20 percent of livestock born in the flocks they cared for. Jacob requested the spotted, speckled and dark sheep, goats, and lambs, which were rare and less valuable than unblemished ones. His proposal would have given him fewer flocks, and made it obvious which animals belonged to him.

While this arrangement seems fair and appropriate and Laban agrees to the terms, the following passages reveal that Laban deceives Jacob (again). He removes those animals, decreasing the chances that more with those characteristics would be produced. But God would still bless Jacob. As time progressed, Jacob's flocks were stronger and more plentiful. As promised, he became a rich man. The time to return to his home would soon come.

How have you seen God's hand or blessing in your life in the face of opposition or challenges?

(Note: Remember that God's blessings are not only financial.)

Search the Scriptures

1. Read Genesis 29:15 and 30:28. Why would Laban's promise in the second verse have made Jacob cautious or distrustful?

2. In what ways do you see similar stories in the lives of the women in this family—Sarah, Rebekah, Rachel? How is Leah different?

Discuss the Meaning

1. Laban prospered because of the work Jacob did for him, but had to be told by an outside party that it was because of God's favor. How are we blind to the ways God blesses us?

2. Rachel struggled with infertility which impacts many women today and can be a very difficult experience. How can we value women around us who cannot give birth? How can we affirm God's faithfulness in the midst of such difficult situations?

Liberating Lesson

Sometimes it seems that regardless of what a person or community does, they simply cannot get ahead. Opposition is ever present. The oppressed seem to never be able to rise above the oppression. But God tells a different story.

Jacob's story reminds us that it is impossible to thwart God's plan. Neither Jacob nor Laban's deception were capable of doing so. Yes, there were negative consequences, but God prevailed. Laban hid flocks, and Jacob used ingenuity to produce more. Jacob was tricked after seven years of labor, but worked seven more to get the wife he loved. And even the wife he was tricked into marrying would be the one to birth the leader of the tribe who brought us Jesus. God is firmly in control.

Application for Activation

"Now faith is the assurance of things hoped for, the conviction of things not seen" (Hebrews 11:1).

A hallmark of the lives of these early patriarchs was that sooner or later they (and their wives) had to demonstrate faith—the belief that the God of the universe would keep His promises to make them into great nations, and bless them and others through them. Their faith informed their prayers.

What things are you trusting God for that have yet to come to pass?

Are there prayers that you have stopped praying because of disappointment or frustration?

In what ways has your faith waned because of unanswered prayers?

Meditate on Hebrews 11:1 and revisit those prayers, asking God to help your unbelief when you struggle.

Follow the Spirit

What God wants me to do:

_____

_____

_____

_____

Remember Your Thoughts

Special insights I have learned:

_____

_____

_____

_____

More Light on the Text

Genesis 30:22–32, 43

Jacob had connived with his mother Rebekah to steal his father's blessing that traditionally belonged to his elder twin brother, Esau (Genesis 27:21–29). Esau is furious and plans to kill him. Aware of the plot, Rebekah advises Jacob to flee to her brother, Laban, in Haran until Esau's anger subsides. Furthermore, she did want Jacob to marry from the Canaanite women like his brother, making the flight even more crucial. Rebekah therefore convinces their father, Isaac, to send Jacob off to his uncle Laban's house. With a father's blessing and the specific instruction to take a wife from the daughters of Laban, Isaac sends Jacob to his uncle in Haran (Genesis 27:41–28:5).

Chapter 29 recounts what happened next. Jacob arrives in Haran and meets Rachel, his uncle's younger daughter, at the same well where the servant Eliezer met Jacob's mother, Rebekah, some years before (Genesis 24:15ff). Rachel introduces Jacob to her father (Jacob's uncle), Laban. Laban is excited and receives Jacob into his home. The older daughter is Leah. A month after Jacob arrived at his home, Laban asks Jacob to name his wages for his services. Because Jacob loves Rachel more than Leah, Jacob offers to serve his uncle seven years in order to marry Rachel. After the seven years, Laban tricks Jacob and gives Leah as his wife. But Jacob does not love Leah. So he decides to work seven more years for Rachel. After serving him for a week, Laban also gives Rachel in marriage to Jacob. Leah would have four children quickly after marriage, while Rachel had none.

Genesis 30:1–21 recounts how Rachel out of envy tries to manipulate the hand of God by giving Jacob her maid to have children for her. Leah does the same. Both maids had two sons each for their mistresses. Later Leah had two more sons and a daughter, Dinah. However,

Rachel was still childless. Being a mother carried a high degree of honor in their culture, and barrenness carried dishonor. That is why Rachel said to Jacob, "Give me children, or else I die." At this, Jacob's anger was aroused against Rachel, and he said, "Am I in God's stead, who hath withheld from thee the fruit of the womb?" (from Genesis 30:1–2).

22 And God remembered Rachel, and God hearkened to her, and opened her womb. 23 And she conceived, and bare a son; and said, God hath taken away my reproach: 24 And she called his name Joseph; and said, The Lord shall add to me another son.

After all her human efforts to have her own children are exhausted, God remembers Rachel and hears her. It appears after Rachel could not get what she wanted because of her jealousy, anger, and manipulation (30:1–8), she then turns to prayer. She seems to have finally realized that children are a blessing that only God can give; it is to be received only by prayer through faith in God (e.g., Genesis 25:21; 1 Samuel 1:11). The Hebrew word *zakar* (**zaw-KAR**) means more than just "remember" as in "to bring to mind again"; it is also "to meditate on" and "to be mindful of or care for." By implication here and earlier in the text (Genesis 29:31), God has shut Rachel's womb (cf. 1 Samuel 1:6). The biblical use of the word "remember" is often used not just to recall a person, but to do so with concern and compassion. When God "remembers" his sons and daughters, it is with favor and care (Nehemiah 5:19; 13:31). Now God remembered Rachel and "hearkened to her" prayer.

The word "hearken" is the Hebrew *shama'* (**shaw-MAH**), that is "to hear with attention or interest," "to listen attentively" or "to hear intelligently." In other words, God listened with interest to Rachel or paid attention to her with the intent to answer her petition.

Consequently God "opened her womb." The word "open" translates the Hebrew *pathach* (**paw-THAKH**), which paints a picture of something being untied. But here it appears God purposely shut her womb. Oftentimes, God uses a temporal infertility to demonstrate His sovereign authority over the affairs of His people (See Sarah, Genesis 16; Rebekah, 25; Hannah, 1 Samuel 1; Elizabeth, Luke 1:7). However, we cannot say for certain why God shut Rachel's womb.

After God allows Rachel to conceive and bare a child, she says that God has removed her reproach. The word "reproach" comes from the Hebrew *cherpah* (**kher-PAW**); it also means shame, scorn, or disgrace. That indicates that God's giving her a child has removed the social stigma that barrenness had placed on her. Therefore she calls the son Joseph, (Heb. *Yoseph*, **yo-SAFE**), which means "may he add" from *yasaph* (**yaw-SAHF**), "to add." There is a play on words here, as this verb and *'asaph* (Heb. **aw-SAHF**, take away) in the preceding clause (v. 23) sound so similar. The name presents the birth of this son in a two-fold light: removing the reproach of sterility and hoping for another son. While Rachel rejoices that God has removed the shame, she also prays, "May the LORD add yet another son to my family" (v. 24, NLT). This prayer was answered with the birth of Benjamin ("son of my right hand"). However, his delivery led to Rachel's death (Genesis 35:16–20).

25 And it came to pass, when Rachel had born Joseph, that Jacob said unto Laban, Send me away, that I may go unto mine own place, and to my country. 26 Give me my wives and my children, for whom I have served thee, and let me go: for thou knowest my service which I have done thee.

The birth of Joseph seems to mark the beginning of a new era in the life of Jacob and his family. Jacob's agreement of fourteen years of service with Laban (his uncle and father in-law) has been completed at the birth of his eleventh son, Joseph. His family has grown from one lone man who fled for his life from his brother (27:14–45) to a large family of two wives, two concubines, eleven sons, and a daughter (30:21). Although we don't have record of his age at this time, Jacob is no longer a young man. Some have placed him at ninety-one years old at this time. But the most probable age would be seventy-four years (assuming he fled to Padan Aram at sixty years and served Laban for fourteen years). Whatever the age, Jacob felt it was time to return home to start a new life with his family in the country God promised him, Canaan.

Jacob approaches Laban after Joseph's birth to ask for permission to move back to his people and country. The verse begins with the typical Hebrew word *wayehi* (**wah-yeh-HEE**), which is often translated "and it came to pass" (v. 25). This word connects the previous narrative with the next and signals its importance in the life story of this patriarch. It also gives the time frame of the events that follow. In other words, after Rachel had given birth to Joseph, Jacob asks to go back to his own land and country, Canaan, where God's promises to Abraham and his father Isaac as revealed to him would be fulfilled (Genesis 28:10–15).

Jacob had never regarded Haran as home. The Hebrew word Jacob used for "my own place" is *maqom* (**maw-KOME**); it means a standing place or place of abode. He wants to stand on his own and build his own home, not in Haran, but in the land where he was born and raised, Canaan. Until now he has been serving his father-in-law Laban. He now wants to branch out on his own and go home.

It is customary in Jewish and other cultures that after one has served for a number of years, his master will let him go with his blessings (Deuteronomy 15:12–18; Leviticus 25:39–55). Based on the cultural norms of the time, it appears Jacob is aware of his rights as an apprentice or servant. Therefore he asks Laban to allow him with his family "for whom I have served you" to leave. Jacob served Laban fourteen years, fulfilling his own part of the agreement with Laban, so it was time for him to leave with all his wives and children.

According to their tradition, the Jews regard Canaan as home regardless where they live. They always return to their homeland. Jacob requested that at death he should be taken back to Canaan and buried there, not in Egypt (Genesis 49:29–33). Joseph made a similar request from his brothers (Genesis 50:25). The Igbo of Nigeria have similar tradition. They always maintain connection with homeland and prefer to be carried home at death. Rarely would an Igbo regard a foreign land his "home"—they would use the cliché "home away from home" to describe their foreign place of abode. A similar idea is behind Jacob's approach to Laban for permission to return to his country, and appropriately so because of the Lord's covenant promise to Abraham (Genesis 12:7).

27 And Laban said unto him, I pray thee, if I have found favour in thine eyes, tarry: for I have learned by experience that the Lord hath blessed me for thy sake. 28 And he said, Appoint me thy wages, and I will give it.

Laban is reluctant to allow Jacob and his family to go, though, not because he so much cares for them or would miss them. Rather it is because of what he can gain further from Jacob's services and his God, Jehovah. He knows that the Lord God has blessed him and his flock because of Jacob. Laban is certainly aware of God's promises to Abraham and his descendants (Genesis 12:3). So he asks Jacob to stay and serve him. He says to Jacob, "I pray thee, if I have found favour in thine eyes, tarry," an appeal so strong that it would be difficult for Jacob to refuse.

Moreover, he tells Jacob that he had "learned by experience" that God blessed him because of Jacob. The word translated "learned by experience" here is the Hebrew *nachash* (**naw-KHASH**). It means to practice divination, observe signs or omens, or practice fortune-telling. All these are an abomination before the Lord and are strictly forbidden because it reflects pagan worship (Deuteronomy 18:10, 14). We can infer from this that Laban is not interested in the Lord God of Abraham, Isaac and Jacob; he is interested in God's blessings only. He worshiped idols (Genesis 31:19, 34–35). Nonetheless, Laban realized that it was because of Jacob that God blessed him. God will later use Joseph the same way in Egypt (Genesis 39:2–5). To make Jacob stay, Laban asks him to name his price and promises to pay it.

It is amazing how common it is that people would acknowledge the truth about God but still worship idols. It is equally interesting how the Lord could, because of one righteous man, bless other people. For example, He said if He could find ten righteous men in Sodom, He would not destroy the city (Genesis 18:32). It is also important to understand that the Lord often blesses people not because they are good or righteous, but because of who He is.

29 And he said unto him, Thou knowest how I have served thee, and how thy cattle was with me. 30 For it was little which thou hadst before I came, and it is now increased unto a multitude; and the Lord hath blessed thee since my coming: and now when shall I provide for mine own house also?

Jacob reminds Laban how faithful he had been to him and how his small flock has greatly increased since Jacob started serving

him fourteen years ago. Reiterating Laban's earlier assertion, Jacob says, "and the Lord hath blessed thee since my coming." Jacob continues and rhetorically asks, "and now when shall I provide for mine own house also?" That is to say, "Isn't it time for me to find my way and build up my own family?" Notice while Laban attributes his blessing to the Lord using the practice of divination, Jacob credits it to the Lord through divine revelation (Genesis 28:13–15).

31 And he said, What shall I give thee? And Jacob said, Thou shalt not give me any thing: if thou wilt do this thing for me, I will again feed and keep thy flock: 32 I will pass through all thy flock to day, removing from thence all the speckled and spotted cattle, and all the brown cattle among the sheep, and the spotted and speckled among the goats: and of such shall be my hire.

Desperate to get a direct answer, Laban repeats his question, "What shall I give thee?" He is prepared to give anything for Jacob to stay and continue serving him, so that the Lord would keep blessing him through Jacob. Laban is thinking only about himself. He wants Jacob to serve him in perpetuity so that he would be richer. The longer Jacob stays, the richer he would become because of God's blessing coming through Jacob. Only very few employers would like to see their good workers progress and let them go to stand on their own. Most would like to have their underlings in absolute servitude with no freedom, provided they themselves are enriched. They are afraid if they did, it would affect their business. They only think of the good they can get from their workers, and not the good of the workers. Here Laban epitomizes the selfish attitude of many rich employers and businesspeople toward their employees.

Although Laban always strives to get the upper hand, Jacob knows to be wary of him. It is because of Laban's trickery in breaking his initial deal with Jacob that his family is consumed with jealousy and rivalry. Jacob begins his reply saying, "Thou shalt not give me any thing." In that culture with strong family ties, the more Jacob accepts from Laban—even in the form of wages—the more indebted he will be to him. Hopefully, Jacob also realizes that just as the Lord blessed Laban since Jacob began to work for him, even so the Lord will continue to bless Jacob when he leaves Laban, even if Laban swindles him again. He is confident that the Lord is the one who will bless him, not Laban.

Jacob offers to continue to tend to Laban's flock on one condition. The kind of sheep that Jacob has been herding are normally all white and goats all black. The number of speckled and spotted animals would usually be few. Jacob offers to take only the speckled and spotted animals as his wages, while all the solid white sheep and solid black goats, which are greater in number, would belong to Laban. This way Jacob makes sure that Laban will accept his terms that seem generous, trusting in his own ingenuity and in the Lord to prosper him.

Laban accepts Jacob's proposal. He separates the animals accordingly. Laban hands over Jacob's animals to his own children; they took them to a three-day journey away from Jacob.

43 And the man increased exceedingly, and had much cattle, and maidservants, and menservants, and camels, and asses.

The narrator explains (vv. 33–42) how through wisdom and providence the Lord altered the course of nature in Jacob's favor. Jacob's flock greatly multiplies more than Laban's to the envy of his children. Laban would repeatedly from time to time try to change the agreement, but each time Jacob's flocks grew in number (Genesis 31:7). In the meantime, Jacob "increased exceedingly." The verb "increased" is the Hebrew *parats* (**paw-ROTS**), which means to break out or to burst out. The adverb "exceedingly" comes from the Hebrew *me'od* (**meh-ODE**). It appears in double form in Hebrew here as *me'od me'od*, literally meaning "exceedingly, exceedingly," to express how prosperous Jacob became. It expresses the intensity of Jacob's wealth—he burst out exceedingly in exceeding wealth, not only in sheep and goats, but also in male and female servants, camels, and asses. As a result, he incurred the envy and anger of Laban and his family. But God was with Jacob and his family.

Sources:

Global Study Bible, English Standard Version. Wheaton, IL: Crossway Publishers, 2012. 73-77.

Keener, Craig S., *The IVP Bible Background Commentary: Old Testament*. Downers Grove, IL: Intervarsity Press, 2000. 61-63.

Radmacher, Earl D., ed. *Nelson Study Bible, New King James Version*. Nashville, TN: Thomas Nelson Publishers, 1997. 58-61.

Unger, Merrill F., *The New Unger's Bible Dictionary*. Chicago, IL: Moody Press, 1988. 710.

Walvoord, John F., and Roy B. Zuck, eds. *The Bible Knowledge Commentary: Old Testament*. USA: Victor Books, SP Publications, Inc., 1985. 74-78.

Biblesoft's New Exhaustive Strong's Numbers and Concordance with Expanded Greek-Hebrew Dictionary. Copyright © 1994, 2003, 2006 Biblesoft, Inc. and International Bible Translators, Inc.

Blue Letter Bible

Holy Bible, New Living Translation. Copyright © 1996, 2004 by Tyndale Charitable Trust. Used by permission of Tyndale House Publishers. All rights reserved.

The Bible Exposition Commentary: Old Testament. Copyright © 2001-2004 by Warren W. Wiersbe. All rights reserved.

Packer, J. I., and M. C. Tenney, eds. *Illustrated Manners and Customs of the Bible*. Nashville, Tenn.: Thomas Nelson Publishers, 1980. 433.

"JBF": Jamieson, Fausset, and Brown Commentary, Electronic Database. Copyright © 1997, 2003, 2005, 2006 by Biblesoft, Inc. All rights reserved.

Keil and Delitzsch Commentary on the Old Testament: New Updated Edition, Electronic Database. Copyright © 1996 by Hendrickson Publishers, Inc. All rights reserved.

Say It Correctly

Laban. **LAY**-ban.
Rachel. **RAY**-chel.

Daily Bible Readings

MONDAY
Jacob Marries Leah and Rachel
(Genesis 29:15–30)

TUESDAY
Leah Gives Birth to Four Sons
(Genesis 29:31–35)

WEDNESDAY
The God of Jacob Brings Victory
(Psalm 20)

THURSDAY
Jacob Steals His Family from Laban
(Genesis 31:1–9)

FRIDAY
Jacob and Laban Make Peace
(Genesis 31:43–50)

SATURDAY
Rachel Gives Birth to Two Sons
(Genesis 30:22–24; 35:16–21)

SUNDAY
Jacob Prospers at Laban's Expense
(Genesis 30:22–32, 43)

Notes

_____

_____

_____

_____

Our Love For God

This quarter's study begins with God's demands for our complete and undivided love as shown in passages from Deuteronomy and Psalms. It proceeds with our response to God's love in the advent of Christ, and the epistles' interpretations of the nature and extent of our responses to God's love in Christ. It concludes with passages from three of the psalms expressing glorification of God.

UNIT 1 • God Commands Our Love, Respect, and Obedience

The Deuteronomy passage contains a presentation of God's demand for total love and devotion. The session from Joshua contains his faithful statement of love and reverence for a liberating God. In Psalm 103, David expresses love and glorification of God for God's creative, sustaining, and protective actions. Luke portrays the advent of Christ and human response to God's act of fulfillment of God's promise. We are challenged in Matthew to love God through compassionate works.

Lesson 1: December 2, 2018
Love and Devotion
Deuteronomy 6:1–9

In the midst of life's challenges and uncertainties, people search for a foundation on which to make decisions. What is that foundation? God instructed the Israelites that the basis for meeting all of life's circumstances is to love God absolutely, and Matthew records that Jesus repeated those instructions.

Lesson 2: December 9, 2018
Choose to Love and Serve God
Joshua 24:1–3, 13–15, 21–24

At critical junctures in life, people are forced to make life-changing decisions. How do they decide which path to take? When challenged by Joshua to serve God or other gods, the Israelites definitively chose to love and serve God.

Lesson 3: December 16, 2018
Love and Worship God
Psalm 103:1–17, 21–22

People feel anxiety and confusion when they remember their personal failures and as they continually face life's trials. What consolation is there? The psalmist lists the many reasons God's steadfast love inspires enthusiastic thanksgiving rather than dismay.

Lesson 4: December 23, 2018
(Christmas Lesson)
Jesus: God's Loving Promise
Luke 1:26–31; 2:22, 25–35

Some people wait a long time for a promise to be kept. What assurance do we have that God's promise about salvation will be kept? God's angel spoke to Mary, and the Holy Spirit spoke through Simeon, to declare that in Jesus God was sending a Savior and keeping the promise.

Lesson 5: December 30, 2018
Modeling God's Love
Matthew 25:31–46

Responsible people are pulled in a multitude of directions in trying to take care of themselves and their families. Why then would one extend effort beyond self and family? Jesus teaches His disciples that loving acts to the forsaken and needy are really demonstrations of love to Him.

UNIT 2 • Loving God by Trusting Christ

Matthew continues to inspire trust in God for all things, while James encourages total submission to God in love. In his letter to the

Philippians, Paul gives an interpretation of human devotion to God in Christ; promotes selfless devotion through exemplification of Christ's total submission to God in love; and encourages giving up everything for the sake of one's love for Christ.

Lesson 6: January 6 , 2019
Hold Fast to God's Love
2 Thessalonians 2:13–3:5; 2 John 4–11

Effective personal relationships are often thwarted by destructive forces. What can counteract these forces? Paul and John instruct the believers to walk steadfastly in the love of God by loving one another and following God's commandments.

Lesson 7: January 13, 2019
Submit to God in Love
James 4:1–10

Destructive thoughts and desires lead to further destructive behavior. What can be done to break this cruel cycle? James asserts that loving and obeying God opens the door to God's blessings and frees us from conflicts and disputes.

Lesson 8: January 20, 2019
Submit to God in Christ
Philippians 1:12–21

It is easy to become demoralized by difficult circumstances and adversaries. How can people maintain their joy? Paul willingly submits to God's will and rejoices that his sufferings have led to further proclamation of the Gospel.

Lesson 9: January 27, 2019
Devote All to Christ
Philippians 2:1–11

Personal interests and selfish ambitions can lead to controversies that threaten our relationships. How can people overcome their divisiveness? Paul commends the example of Christ, who humbly emptied Himself in order to serve God and others through His sacrifice.

Lesson 10: February 3, 2019
Renounce Everything for Christ
Philippians 3:7–14

People strive to enhance their standing before others by calling attention to their abilities and honors. What is the proper attitude toward our accomplishments? Paul tells the Philippians that he willingly suffered the loss of his accomplishments for the greater goal of gaining and being found in Christ.

UNIT 3 • Love Songs That Glorify God

The quarter ends with Psalm 48, which focuses on a song of adoration for God's steadfast love; Psalm 66 focuses on part of a love song of praise to God for all God's mighty works of goodness; and Psalm 91 closes this unit with a praise song to God for assurance of protection and comfort for those who love God

Lesson 11: February 10, 2019
Pondering God's Steadfast Love
Psalm 48:1–3, 9–14

In a world of constant change, nothing seems permanent or of abiding worth. What abides when everything else seems to be in flux? The psalmist ponders the steadfast, everlasting, and all-inclusive love of God while worshiping God in the Temple.

Lesson 12: February 17 , 2019
Praising God's Mighty Works
Psalm 66:1–9, 16–20

People marvel at the legacies of those whose powerful influence has changed the world. What is the true measure of might? The psalmist praises the mighty works of God, the Creator of the universe and the Savior of God's people.

Lesson 13: February 24 , 2019
Living with God's Loving Assurance
Psalm 91:1–8, 11–16

People often live in fear that misfortune will befall them. Where can we find protection from danger? The psalmist looks to God for protection in the midst of life's calamities.

Our Love for God

by Allen Reynolds

We love God because God first loved us. There is no greater love than the love of God shown in its most perfect form through the life, death, and resurrection of Jesus Christ. In response to our holy and loving God who has acted to deliver us from the bondage of sin, we show our love for God. When God delivered the Children of Israel of out Egypt, God showed His love for His people. God offered them a covenant—an agreement to a new relationship with new boundaries. The response God requested in the covenant with Israel was for the people to love God with all of their heart, mind, soul, and strength and to love their neighbors as themselves. This is the summation of all the Law and the prophets Jesus says when asked what is the greatest commandment (Matthew 22:37-40). Yet heeding this command seems to be the hard for us as human beings. Love is a verb; it is something we do. Love is the simple command of God and the deep need of humanity. But it is the most difficult thing in the world for us to get right consistently. Let us investigate some of the ways that Scripture teaches us to love God.

and multiply, and replenish the earth, and subdue it" (from Genesis 1:28) and "but of the tree of the knowledge of good and evil, thou shalt not eat of it" (from Genesis 2:17). Yet humans do not show love for God because they disobey His commands. Then God creates a covenant with the nation of Israel after delivering them from 400 years of slavery in Egypt. The first lesson of this quarter, from Deuteronomy 6:1-9, known as the Shema, gives a brief summary of that covenant and the commandments that Israel is to obey. The commands include recognizing that the Lord God is God and our only God; not worshiping idols or false gods; taking time to rest and acknowledge God as God; honoring our parents; not murdering; not stealing; not coveting what belongs to our neighbors; not lying about our neighbors; and not committing adultery. These are also known as the Ten Commandments. When we keep these commandments as well as the others in Scripture, we show love for God. Joshua reiterates this love in Joshua 24 by noting he will serve God and only God as his Lord as well as remember and keep God's commandments.

Love for God through Obedience

Love for God looks first like obedience to God because of the new relationship we with have with God. Obedience simply means to do what God has told us to do. The Bible is full of commands that God gives people to obey. Some of the first commands were "be fruitful,

Love for God through Worship

Love for God looks like worshiping God in spirit and in truth (John 4:24). Worship is taking time to acknowledge God as God. This is one way to perform the act of the first commandment. We often think of worship as singing; praising with our mouths; dancing for God; bowing before God; lifting our hands; and shouting about who God is and what God has done. However, worship includes showing honor to God and sharing intimacy with God with our entire being. Giving is an act of worship. Quiet meditation is an act of worship. Partaking in communion or Eucharist is an act of worship. Serving others is an act of worship. Serving at church is an act of worship. Rest is an act of worship. Crying to God is an act of worship. Celebrating holidays is an act of worship. God's intention as seen in Exodus, Leviticus, and Deuteronomy was never to have worship confined to the Temple. The very lives of God's people in everything we do is meant to be worship—acknowledging God and our special relationship with God. The Psalms are excellent examples of capturing the revelation of loving God through our worship in every way, in every circumstance, and at all times.

Love for God through Serving Others

Love for God looks like serving others. When we care for God's people and God's creation, we are showing our love for God. When we give a treat to the child of a friend or help someone with work around their house, that person feels love. God loves and delights in seeing us love one another. We are called to care for the least and the last; the lonely and the lost; the widow, the orphan, and the stranger. We are called to make room at the table for those who have disabilities, those who are immigrants, and those who are homeless. We are called to visit people who are ill, incarcerated, and overlooked (Matthew 25:44-45). We are called to advocate for justice on behalf of the oppressed, mistreated, and marginalized. We show we love God by feeding God's children, caring for them, and loving them. We show we love God by feeding, clothing, and helping people meet their basic needs.

Love for God through Sacrifice

Most of all, we show we love God by sacrifice and surrender to God. Jesus tells us there is no greater love than to lay down one's life for a friend. Jesus is our faithful friend. He calls us to take up our crosses and follow Him daily. Jesus calls us to give up doing things our way, trying to save ourselves, trying to fix ourselves, and trying to make people conform to us. Following Jesus requires sacrifice. It means rejection by those who reject Him. It means being misunderstood sometimes. It means putting God first in our decisions and giving more than we receive from others. It means not saying what is most popular but instead saying what is right. It means hoping in our suffering and holding joy in our trials.

Loving God means choosing God's will instead of our will. It means doing what brings God glory instead of what brings us comfort. It means loving ourselves enough to trust that God made us on purpose—and not trying to be something we see, but choosing to be what He says. Loving God through sacrifice looks like forgiving those who have hurt us and those who don't like us. It means showing mercy to those who don't deserve it. Loving God means recognizing what is natural, and choosing to be more than that even if it isn't easy. It means recognizing Jesus as Lord, seeking His glory in all we do.

Jesus has shown us perfect love. Jesus made the ultimate sacrifice by dying on the Cross for our sins and resurrecting for our hope. And Jesus invites us to die to ourselves daily so that we can live the resurrected life with Him. The Gospels, Paul's letters, and the other New Testament epistles show us this great love that we can follow to show our love for God.

Allen Reynolds is the Editor of Adult & Customized Content at UMI.

That Great Love

by Kimberly Baker, M.S.

The love of God is the greatest love that we will ever know. Throughout the Bible, there are many expressions and examples of God's love. The greatest expression of it that we will ever experience is the sacrificing of His Son. John 3:16 tells us: "For God so loved the world that He gave His only begotten Son, that whosoever believeth in Him shall not perish, but have everlasting life." As a result of this selfless act, we know that God loves us. He is our Father and wants us to know the love of a father. In this quarter, we will examine what it means to love God unconditionally. Our students need to see how God demonstrates His love in the Bible and what that love means for us today.

Love is a part of God's nature. The Bible tells us that God is love (1 John 4:8), and love is a key theme. In the beginning, God's love for man compels Him to create a helpmeet for him in the form of woman. God sets Adam and Eve in the Garden and gives them all of the advantages of being His children. They were given direction and guidance, as a father gives his children. When they did wrong, He did not destroy them. He just deprived them of the privileges of being His children. They were forced to fend for themselves, experiencing some pain and suffering along the way. But He promised them that their children would get an opportunity to return to Him—by way of His Son, who was going to come to earth and reconcile them back to God. That was all part of the plan, to demonstrate the love that God had for them and for us.

God gives the Israelites clear instruction: "And you must love the LORD your God with all your heart, all your soul, and all your strength" (Deuteronomy 6:5, NLT). This is the greatest commandment of the Old Testament. The Israelites were instructed to love God with their all. God prepared them in the wilderness to go into the Promised Land. He reminded them that He chose them just because: "The LORD did not set his heart on you and choose you because you were more numerous than other nations, for you were the smallest of all nations! Rather, it was simply that the LORD loves you" (from Deuteronomy 7:7-8, NLT). It was that simple. The love of God was demonstrated in that He saved them from a life of slavery and death. They were delivered and brought into the land of promise, which had been given first to Abraham and now to his children. God was fulfilling His promise.

He gave the Israelites the Law by which they were to be governed, but these laws were to be summed up in terms of love: Love God, and love our neighbor (Matthew 22:34-40, NLT). Who is our neighbor? Anyone who gives us an opportunity to show God's love (Luke 10:29-37). Love is to be shown as a response to a need. We are even commanded to love our enemies (Luke 6:27-36).

As teachers of the Word of God, we would be remiss if we did not look at Jesus Christ as the perfect example of God's love for us. Throughout the Old Testament, we see God's love demonstrated in the promise of the Savior:

"For a child is born to us,
　a son is given to us.
The government will rest on his shoulders.
　And he will be called:
Wonderful Counselor, Mighty God,
　Everlasting Father, Prince of Peace.
His government and its peace
　will never end.
He will rule with fairness and justice from the throne of his ancestor David
　for all eternity.
The passionate commitment of the LORD of Heaven's Armies
　will make this happen!" (Isaiah 9:6-7, NLT).

Jesus was promised from the beginning, in the Garden of Eden when Adam and Eve sinned before God: "And I will cause hostility between you and the woman, and between your offspring and her offspring. He will strike your head, and you will strike his heel" (Genesis 3:15, NLT). Jesus had to come and die so that man could be reconciled with God. Relationship was restored with the coming of Jesus Christ. God sent His Son because of His great love for us.

The love of God also helps us to understand what love really means. Throughout the Bible, we see agape love demonstrated. In its more formal sense, *agapao* is often used as "the love of God." We understand it as the unconditional, divine love of God. This is the love that God shows us and the love that we show mankind. We cannot do anything to gain or receive this love; it is given because of who we are and whose we are. When we love our brother, we

are showing the love of God. When we make sacrifices for one another, thinking of others before ourselves, we are doing what He would have us to do. Our students must understand that God's love is for everyone and we are to share it. The best way we can show this love is to share the Gospel with those who may not be aware. We are motivated to share that love with others because "Christ's love controls us. Since we believe that Christ died for all, we also believe that we have all died to our old life" (from 2 Corinthians 5:14, NLT). Accepting Jesus is an act of sacrifice, exemplifying the love of God. Romans 10:9 (NLT) states: "If you openly declare that Jesus is Lord and believe in your heart that God raised him from the dead, you will be saved." When we believe in our heart, we are internalizing the fact that God loves us and we desire to do what pleases God.

"The message is very close at hand; it is on your lips and in your heart so that you can obey it" (from Deuteronomy 30:14, NLT). Our heart is the center of our thoughts and actions. Where our heart is, that is where we are, "For whatever is in your heart determines what you say" (from Matthew 12:34).

We must recognize that God is the source of love. Just as we are recipients of His love, we must also be conduits for it. Others must see the love of Christ in both action and deed. Believers must be determined to share what God has already shared with us, His Son. Throughout His life on earth, Jesus Christ exemplified the love of the Father. He taught that God is love. He healed through the love of God. He corrected in the love of God. Everywhere He went, He was prepared to do the will of the Father, for He declared that He must do the works of the one who sent Him while it is day; "the night is coming and then no one can work" (from John 9:4, NLT). And we must do the same.

We are also commanded to exemplify the love of God through our acts of service to one another. In Paul's instruction to the Corinthians about spiritual gifts, he says that we must operate in love (1 Corinthians 13). In the church, we must be prepared to receive those who are in despair, looking for the light that resides in us. We are encouraged to keep ourselves in the love of God (Jude 21). What better way to do this than by the fruit of the Spirit:

"But the Holy Spirit produces this kind of fruit in our lives: love, joy, peace, patience, kindness, goodness, faithfulness, gentleness, and self-control. There is no law against these things! Those who belong to Christ Jesus have nailed the passions and desires of their sinful nature to his cross and crucified them there" (Galatians 5:22-24, NLT).

These are principles that we can use in our daily walk, where we demonstrate our character. Our character should never come into question as long as we live by the love of the Lord. And if we love God the way we say we do, there should be no incident. Everything we do, should be done to please the Father. What better way to do this than to show love to our fellow man as God requires us.

We must be prepared to teach our students that God is love. Through examples in the Bible, we can demonstrate that love must be the reality of everything that we do, both in word and deed. Throughout the biblical text, we have examples of how to live a life of love. We understand it to be a selfless act. Jesus Christ is the greatest example we can ever have, in that He loved us enough to provide the ultimate example: Himself.

Kimberly Baker, M.S., is a Christian educator from Chicago, IL who has served churches for over 20 years. She is a contributing writer for *Precepts for Living®*.

Who Doesn't Love Great Benefits?

by Mwikali Munyao

We live in a world where everyone is wondering what they will get out of life. Every moment sometimes is reduced to a transaction, and every thought can sometimes feel like you are standing in a bargaining court. It is all about getting the best, being the first to attain and maintain it. That is the reason why people will line up on a cold day to buy the latest gadget. The concept of winning and being first is etched on their mind. The biggest motivation for this is love. Looking for what you love, wanting to be loved, doing something you love, or being around people who genuinely love you.

God has created humanity to win in love and life. It is a reality that is so often diluted and minimized by Christians when the world has embraced this concept. Winning at all costs is different all together, but the idea of embracing yourself as a winner seems rather foreign to many Christians, yet is one of the most reasonable expectations God has for us. He expects us to win, and win big. He wants us to love and be loved well. The biggest example He gave us is through His love for us. The ultimate sacrifice He gave of His only Son is proof that He withholds nothing from us, and wants us to succeed in this life because we are victorious in Him.

Psalm 103 is very inspiring depending on your viewpoint. If you only look at this Scripture as verses for inspiration, the revelation will be limited to that capacity. However, taking the limits off, and looking at it with the eyes of a great and loving God, changes your perspective about life, loving God, and worshiping Him.

1. God believes in assurance and insurance.

If you own a car and intend to drive it, you legally need to have proof of insurance. The money you pay monthly or biannually to the insurance company does not make you jump with joy each time you look at your bank account. However, you have a sense of confidence when you have that insurance card in your glove compartment. Why? Because purchasing car insurance is a way to prove that you are a law-abiding citizen, and that you care about your life and the lives of other motorists.

Psalm 103:2 is God's assurance to us that, as His children, He has us covered.

"Bless the LORD, O my soul and forget not all His benefits."

2. God has benefits lined up for us.

Different times, different seasons, there are benefits to make us navigate through life with grace, strength, and peace that God thought about us and ensured we had the best. He assures us He is always in control. The best insurance for a Christian is God. Settle that in your spirit and receive all the benefits He has scheduled for your life.

3. God loves recycling and upgrading.

Many Christians, including myself, struggle with the "what if's" in our lives. We say things like, "Maybe if I had done this, then that would not have happened." You can get in a boxing match and punch your self-esteem to shambles with this question to no avail—until Psalm 103:4 gets an opportunity to minister to you.

"Who redeemeth thy life from destruction; who crowneth thee with lovingkindness and tender mercies."

God knows the mistakes you have made. It does not help Him or yourself to throw a pity party and waste so many tissues crying over things you cannot change. The reality is, God wants to comfort you. He wants to let you know that if you will only surrender and believe, whatever was sent to destroy you, He will and can redeem—not once, not twice, but consistently—and save your life from destruction. Why? Because sometimes it's patterns we have learned that have to be continually broken.

It may be cycles you have created in your life to attract destruction. So daily, as you are willing, God is able to redeem your life from destruction. I call that the best recycling heaven can offer. God is able to take my worst and make it so amazing. He can turn all things to work for my good, but I have to let Him.

To be bestowed a crown, one has to have the posture to receive. If God is going to redeem

our lives and crown us with love and tender mercies, it will come down to one act from us: our ability to receive. Nothing is as hurtful as a shunned gift. Especially if you have put so much effort into getting, wrapping, and delivering it. How many times daily, weekly, monthly do we shun God because we do not understand His love?

Let me phrase it this way: How many times do we prefer to cuddle rejection and have dinner with abandonment because that is what we are accustomed to? Why do we do that instead of taking a leap of faith to walk with Jesus who loves us so much?

For redemption to happen in our lives, we will need to surrender all. Your good, bad, and ugly. As you do, reciprocate your brokenness by receiving the love from God, who does not judge you, but sees your tender heart and extends His mercy. That is true worship.

4. Grant God the permission to be a Father to you.

The concept of having a Father you cannot see is so foreign and sometimes the subject is so touchy that many ministers tend to leave it alone. I prefer to dive into this subject and not ignore it, because God keeps speaking it in His Word. Look at Psalm 103:13.

"Like as a father pitieth his children, so the LORD pitieth them that fear Him."

There was a particular incident in my life that I remember so well (I have had a few of these may I add). I was very hurt and went to pray about some things that had happened to me. I did not know what to tell God because no words would come out of my mouth. The pain was so excruciating that tears just welled up in my eyes. As I tried to gather my thoughts to at least tell God I was there (as though He did not know), I heard God's voice tenderly and audibly tell me, "My daughter, your tears have a voice. Let them talk to me, let them flow."

Since that day, I regularly schedule crying days (please don't judge), especially for times when I do not know what to do and it seems that God is far away. Of course I cannot manipulate God, and it would be wrong to think our tears do that, but it changed how I viewed crying before the Lord.

When I see people kneeling at the altar and all they can do is cry, letting the deep wail from their soul come out as they express to God what they feel inside, I always think about what God told me that day. Our tears have a voice.

God does not want to pity us because it is a sign of weakness, but sometimes you want to know you have a God you can run to and share your fears, frustrations, secrets, pains, and hurts with Him. Even if it is in tears. This Scripture assures you of the benefit of comfort from a loving Father who empathizes in those moments you feel alone and hopeless.

Loving and worshiping God go hand in hand. It comes down to perspective. It's looking at your life and seeing the hand of God, what He has done, what He is capable of doing. Releasing control, surrendering all, knowing that God is not keeping a large black book on you, but desires for you to excel in life. It changes you. All of a sudden, the Word of God becomes the handbook for life. You first go to it as a manual for study, to understand the benefits you qualify for in your daily life.

As you start your week, remember, the love of God is a two-way street. We show God true worship and love by receiving Him and allowing His love to permeate our lives. He already showed us His ultimate love by sending His only Son to die for us. Now we have the opportunity to reciprocate this love by living for Him in total surrender and submission.

Remember this week to bless God and know great benefits are waiting to manifest in your life. But you have to discover them, and let them flow because they are free to those who receive by faith.

Dear God,

Thank you for the consistent reminder of your love, care, and thoughtfulness. I am not just an existing figure or a statistic; I am your child. You have great things for me, and I want to experience them. I surrender my life. I surrender the control I have had over the perspective of my life, how things should be, where I should go, whom I should end up with, and what career I should aspire to have.

All the worries and concerns that seem to cloud my mind daily, I surrender to you and receive the benefit of this beautiful day. You are here with me, and that alone is a great benefit. I pour out my heart to you, and receive your comfort and confidence that you have tomorrow covered.

When I wake up tomorrow, the benefits will be right there, waiting for me. Only a loving Father like you can think so strategically about everything. I am truly special in your eyes. And for that, I say thank you.

Amen.

Mwikali Munyao is a contributing writer to *Urban Faith* and *Precepts for Living®* from Chicago, IL by way of Kenya.

The Adult Learner Enjoys Small Groups

by La Verne Tolbert, Ph.D.

Teachers sometimes worry about the number of students in their classes because for many, this is the measure of successful teaching. However, Jesus ended His ministry with a small group of disciples—eleven to be exact plus the women. Their ministry became so dynamic that they "turned the world upside down" (Acts 17:6). The wise adult teacher never counts numbers as an indication of successful teaching.

Adult learners thrive in small group settings! Here they find a safe place to ask questions about the Bible that they may hesitate to ask in a larger setting. More important, adults are more likely to be vulnerable and share about their challenges and struggles as they apply biblical principles to their lives. Some may share details about their marriage and family. Others may reveal their frustrations with caring for aging parents. And still others may need reassurance that God cares for them in their singleness, joblessness, or homelessness. The teacher who is sensitive to the exciting possibilities of teaching adults in small groups will value this time together. Three to twelve students constitute a small group.

A Safe Place

Begin each class with the reminder that here is a "safe place" for sharing. Tell students that whatever is discussed during class time is considered to be confidential. Anyone who shares information about someone in the group will not be allowed to return. Add this disclaimer: Information about sexual or physical abuse of a child must be reported. Teachers are mandated reporters, meaning that they are held legally responsible for alerting authorities about sexual or physical abuse of children.

Initially, it may take as many as four weeks for learners to relax and feel comfortable in the small group setting, especially if they are meeting others for the first time. It's important for teachers to be sensitive to each student and not allow one talkative person to dominate the entire class session. Allow even the quiet ones a space to share and to respond.

Appoint a timekeeper so that the class session ends on time. If you are allotting 35 minutes for the lesson and 25 minutes for discussion, for example, a timekeeper will encourage you stick to the timeframe. Beginning on time

honors those students who make the effort to arrive on time. Ending on time signals that everyone's busy schedule is respected. When you start and stop on time, this provides incentive for students to return again and again, week after week.

Too Large for Small Group?

There may be a time when the small group is no longer a small group. New attendees may expand your class beyond the twelve recommended students. When this happens consistently, it's time to split the class and form another small group. As uncomfortable as this may seem, students will actually appreciate this protection of an intimate setting, which ensures that everyone gets a chance to be heard.

The leader for this new group may emerge from current students, or it may be a new teacher. If it's the latter, invite the new teacher to sit in your class for a couple of sessions and help you lead it. This way, students are more accepting when it's time to separate.

Enjoy your small group! Remember, students may grow more when the class doesn't grow larger.

La Verne Tolbert, Ph.D., is author of *Teaching Like Jesus: A Practical Guide to Christian Education in Your Church* (Zondervan).

REV. THOMAS A. DORSEY
(1900–1993)

During the first week of January 2006, billowing flames gutted, ravaged, and razed the Pilgrim Baptist Church, a historic landmark on Chicago's South Side. Parishioners and other onlookers were devastated by the magnitude of the destruction to the more than 100-year-old edifice. At one time the church had boasted a membership of 10,000 and been the church home of the famous American arranger, pianist, and composer, Thomas A. Dorsey. Not only was the versatile and prolific Dorsey known as the "Father of Gospel Music," he was also considered to be one of the most influential figures ever to impact the gospel music genre.

While the fire reduced all but the shell of the Pilgrim Baptist Church to rubble, it did not destroy the community spirit of the congregation. It also could not diminish the legacy of Rev. Dorsey, who had written more than 1,000 songs in his lifetime, half of which were published.

From 1932 into the 1970s, Reverend Dorsey organized and directed the choir at Pilgrim Baptist Church. Legendary gospel icons—including Mahalia Jackson, Sallie Martin, and Rosetta Tharpe—began their music careers singing his songs of praise and adoration to the living God.

Considered one of the most revered figures in spiritual music, Rev. Thomas A. Dorsey was born in Villa Rica, Georgia. A child prodigy, Dorsey taught himself how to play a wide range of instruments. He learned shape-note singing (a style of unaccompanied singing and sight reading) and emotional, moaning spiritual songs while attending church with his parents. His musical talents were so widely recognized that a gospel tune was called "a Dorsey" until Dorsey himself coined the name "gospel." Then his music was known as "gospel" or " gospel blues."

After moving to Chicago in 1916, Dorsey continued his musical training at the Chicago School of Composition and Arranging. He published his first composition in 1920, and to earn money, he worked as a composer and arranger for the Chicago Music Publishing Company.

In 1921, after he heard William M. Nix's inspirational singing at the National Baptist Convention, Dorsey decided to begin composing sacred music. He registered his first composition in 1922. After becoming the director of music at New Hope Baptist Church, he combined his sacred music with his blues technique. This collective effort made him one of the progenitors of gospel blues. Dorsey began battling ongoing, incapacitating depression in 1926. In 1928, he made Jesus Christ his personal Savior. However, for financial reasons he continued to compose and play his unusual blend of blues in secular music venues.

In 1932, Dorsey's wife, Nettie Harper, died in childbirth and his newborn son died soon after. Distraught and stricken with grief, Dorsey renounced blues music and consecrated his life to doing the will of the Lord. He even made his living through selling sheet music rather than going back to the blues circuit.

One day as he consoled himself at his piano, he composed a song that has blessed and comforted countless hurting hearts down through the ages: "Take My Hand, Precious Lord." This song incorporates elements from his blues background, African American spirituals, and Christian hymns, and it has been translated into 32 languages. In fact, Mahalia Jackson (whom he worked with extensively in the 1930s and 1940s) sang it at the funeral of Dr. Martin Luther King Jr. Her work with Rev. Dorsey established Mahalia as the preeminent gospel singer and Dorsey as the dominant gospel composer of that era.

Elvis Presley's recording of Dorsey's second most popular God-inspired song, "Peace in the Valley," sold millions of copies. It is considered to be Dorsey's most widely recognized work and was a nationwide hit in both African American and white arenas. Dorsey wrote the song for Mahalia Jackson, who was his demo singer at the time. However, it had its greatest success in the white market due to Elvis Presley, Red Foley, and other white Southern gospel artists who scored hit after hit with the song. "We'll Understand It Better By and By" was another of Dorsey's greatest songs. It, too, has blessed untold millions across the United States and beyond.

In 1933, while serving as musical director of Pilgrim Baptist Church, Dorsey founded the National Convention of Gospel Choirs and Choruses and presided as its president for more than 40 years. He continued to write songs but did not record anything after 1934.

Dorsey's music ministry was not without controversy, especially in conservative Christian circles. Some felt that "his rhythmic jazz and blues-influenced style made his music unworthy to be played in churches."4 It is reported that on some occasions, when he performed what was labeled his "sacred blues," Dorsey was even thrown out of some of the best churches.

Today, Thomas A. Dorsey is lauded as a Christian, an accomplished pianist, choir director, and a prolific composer. We praise God that He saved Thomas A. Dorsey. His God-given gift still comforts us through the music that flowed through this wonderful man of God.

Sources:

Granger, Thom. "Say 'Amen,' Somebody, Thomas Dorsey remembered on 10th birthday." CCM Magazine, July 1999, 12.

Pace, Eric. "Thomas A. Dorsey Is Dead at 93; Known as Father of Gospel Music." The New York Times. January 25, 1993. http://www.nytimes.com/1993/01/25/arts/thomas-a-dorsey-is-dead-at-93-known-as-father-of-gospel-music.html.

Teaching Tips

Words You Should Know

A. Shema *shema* (Heb.)—Deuteronomy 6:4-9, which form a twice daily prayer for some devout Jews, means to hear and understand.

B. Statute *choq* (Heb.)—Policies, less strict than commandments.

Teacher Preparation

Unifying Princple—Obedience. Amid life's challenges and uncertainties, people search for a foundation on which to make decisions. What is that foundation? In Deuteronomy, God instructs the Israelites that the basis for meeting all of life's circumstances is to love God absolutely. Matthew records that Jesus repeated those instructions.

A. Read the Bible Background and Devotional Readings.

B. Pray for your students and lesson clarity.

C. Read the lesson Scripture in multiple translations.

D. Option: As a class, share creative ways to keep God's commandments "on your hearts."

O—Open the Lesson

A. Begin the class with prayer.

B. Have the students read the Aim for Change

C. Have the students read the In Focus story.

D. Ask students how events named in the story can weigh on their hearts and how they can view these events from a theological perspective.

P—Present the Scriptures

A. Read the Focal Verses and discuss the Background and The People, Places, and Times sections.

B. Have the class share what Scriptures stand out for them and why, with particular emphasis on today's context.

E—Explore the Meaning

A. Use In Depth or More Light on the Text to help provide more in-depth discussion of the lesson text.

B. Discuss the Liberating Lesson and Application for Activation sections.

N—Next Steps for Application

A. Summarize the value of obedience to God

B. End class with a commitment to pray for a heart of obedience and surrender to God's will.

Worship Guide

For the Superintendent or Teacher
Theme: Love and Devotion
Song: "Yes"
Devotional Reading: Mark 12:28–34

Love and Devotion

Bible Background • DEUTERONOMY 6:1–9
Printed Text • DEUTERONOMY 6:1–9 | Devotional Reading • MARK 12:28–34

—————————— Aim for Change ——————————

By the end of the lesson, we will: AFFIRM that loving God requires obeying God's word; EMBRACE the commandment to love God with all of ourselves; and DISCUSS ways to share God's love with the next generation.

————————— 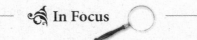 In Focus —————————

Grandma Mabel was the matriarch of her family. She was a strong Christian woman, who upon the death of her husband of twelve years had raised their two sons and daughter in a middle-income neighborhood in a declining city. She raised them with convictions and let them know that in spite of their great loss, they were going to be all right—they were going to make it; God would see to it. Grandma Mabel taught them Christian values and lived those values before her children. On her nurse's salary and the insurance that her husband left them, they were able to survive and thrive. Even more, because of their father's Christian legacy and what Grandma Mabel had continued to teach and live, all three children followed Christ and shared Him by the way they lived.

Each graduated from college and found success in their chosen fields. One son was a social worker and the other an accountant. Her daughter became a teacher.

Grandma Mabel often reminded her children, their spouses, and her grandchildren how prayer and obedience to God's Word brought her through hard times. Prayer and obedience to God's commands held her family together. Prayer and obedience to God's commands helped her survive heartaches and the lonely days and nights.

In today's study, Moses teaches the wilderness generation that God still expects them to follow His commands when they go into the Promised Land.

How has seeing other people remain devoted in their faith impacted your own faith?

—————————— Keep in Mind ——————————

"And thou shalt love the LORD thy God with all thine heart, and with all thy soul, and with all thy might" (Deuteronomy 6:5, KJV).

"And you must love the LORD your God with all your heart, all your soul, and all your strength." (Deuteronomy 6:5, NLT).

Focal Verses

KJV **Deuteronomy 6:1** Now these are the commandments, the statutes, and the judgments, which the LORD your God commanded to teach you, that ye might do them in the land whither ye go to possess it:

2 That thou mightest fear the LORD thy God, to keep all his statutes and his commandments, which I command thee, thou, and thy son, and thy son's son, all the days of thy life; and that thy days may be prolonged.

3 Hear therefore, O Israel, and observe to do it; that it may be well with thee, and that ye may increase mightily, as the LORD God of thy fathers hath promised thee, in the land that floweth with milk and honey.

4 Hear, O Israel: The LORD our God is one LORD:

5 And thou shalt love the LORD thy God with all thine heart, and with all thy soul, and with all thy might.

6 And these words, which I command thee this day, shall be in thine heart:

7 And thou shalt teach them diligently unto thy children, and shalt talk of them when thou sittest in thine house, and when thou walkest by the way, and when thou liest down, and when thou risest up.

8 And thou shalt bind them for a sign upon thine hand, and they shall be as frontlets between thine eyes.

9 And thou shalt write them upon the posts of thy house, and on thy gates.

NLT **Deuteronomy 6:1** These are the commands, decrees, and regulations that the LORD your God commanded me to teach you. You must obey them in the land you are about to enter and occupy,

2 and you and your children and grandchildren must fear the LORD your God as long as you live. If you obey all his decrees and commands, you will enjoy a long life.

3 Listen closely, Israel, and be careful to obey. Then all will go well with you, and you will have many children in the land flowing with milk and honey, just as the LORD, the God of your ancestors, promised you.

4 Listen, O Israel! The LORD is our God, the LORD alone.

5 And you must love the LORD your God with all your heart, all your soul, and all your strength.

6 And you must commit yourselves wholeheartedly to these commands that I am giving you today.

7 Repeat them again and again to your children. Talk about them when you are at home and when you are on the road, when you are going to bed and when you are getting up.

8 Tie them to your hands and wear them on your forehead as reminders.

9 Write them on the doorposts of your house and on your gates.

The People, Places, and Times

Moses. He was the leader, presenter of the law, and prophet of Israel who God used to lead His people out of slavery in the land of Egypt. God gave the covenant laws, including the Ten Commandments, to Moses at Mount Sinai amid smoke and flames (Exodus 19:18).

Canaan. It is a country just to the west of the Jordan River. The name was also used in an extended sense to refer to all of Palestine west of the Jordan to the Mediterranean Sea. Thus,

Jerusalem was considered to be part of the land of Canaan.

Background

Deuteronomy is the fifth book of the Law (Pentateuch) written by Moses. The Jews called it "five-fifths of the law." The word "Deuteronomy" means "repetition of the law." The name was a mistranslation in the biblical Greek Septuagint and the Latin Vulgate of a phrase that means "copy of this law" (17:18). It was written for the new generation of Israelites who had come out of the wilderness and were looking forward to occupying the Promise Land (Canaan). It was Moses' farewell address before he transferred leadership to Joshua. He wanted to partially restate and explain the importance of the laws before he died. He emphasized the significance of obedience to God's commandments. Moses reminded the Israelites that blessings were rewards for obedience, while curses were the consequences of disobedience. He reflected on God's redemption from slavery in Egypt as well as God's punishment for their disobedience while in the wilderness. Because of what God had done, they were urged to trust, love, and obey God. In Deuteronomy 6, Moses offered an explanation of the first commandment, which should be the foundation for all we do and believe.

Why is it good to remember and reflect on our past as Christians?

At-A-Glance

1. Love God By Obeying His Word
(Deuteronomy 6:1–3)
2. Love God with Total Devotion (vv. 4–5)
3. Love God By Sharing the Word (vv. 6–9)

In Depth

1. Love God By Obeying His Word (Deuteronomy 6:1–3)

In Moses' first address to the Israelites, he gave a review of the mighty acts of God (1:1–4:43). In this second address he offers principles for godly living because we must know and act upon God's Word (4:44–29:1). Moses is concerned that the people will possess "the land that floweth with milk and honey" (v. 3) but forget who blessed them with it as well as their promise to devote themselves in obedience to God's Word. It is important to "fear" God and keep His commandments. To fear God means to honor and respect Him. If we love God, we should respect Him enough to obey His commands. If we do so, it will go well with us and future generations. Thus, it is important to teach our children, grandchildren, and younger Christians the Word of God and the importance of showing our love for Him by obeying His commands.

How can our love, obedience, and fear of God influence future generations?

2. Love God with Total Devotion (vv. 4–5)

Verses 4 through 9 are known as the Shema, which is Hebrew for "hear," the first word in the text. Devout Jews recite this prayer twice a day, in the morning and in the evening, in compliance with verse 7.

In verse 4, Moses is like a teacher calling his students to attention. He wants them to listen to his important declaration about God: "The Lord our God is one Lord!" "One" is expressing compound unity, which validates the Trinity. Moreover, this helps us understand the importance of Israel's complete devotion to God alone. We cannot serve other gods because He is a jealous God (5:9).

Jesus repeats the instructions in v. 5 and says that this is the greatest commandment combined with the command to love your neighbor

(Matthew 22:37–39). God loves us, so our love for Him must involve our whole being—not only worshipping and serving God but loving our neighbors. If we love God, we must show it by our actions toward others (1 John 3:17).

How do you demonstrate your love of God?

3. Love God By Sharing the Word (vv. 6–9)

Some Jews take these verses literally and bind phylacteries, or small leather boxes containing selected texts from the Torah, on their foreheads and arms. In addition there are some who place mezuzahs, a small box containing this text and parts of the Torah, on the right side of the doorpost. The purpose is to not only keep these commandments but to have physical reminders of the presence of God's Word in their lives. Our love for God is not about legalistic obedience but a life devoted to the living God by teaching and living out His Word daily.

God wants us to always study the Word and apply it to our daily lives so it can help and guide us in our decision-making. We will not be deceived by the enemy if we know the Word by heart and use it.

God desires for us to talk about His Word wherever we find ourselves, day or night. As we teach His Word, our children and others are listening. The Holy Spirit is able to use us to transform lives. People will see God at work in us and be encouraged to seek Him.

What is the most recent opportunity you have had to teach someone younger about the application of God's Word to daily living?

Search the Scriptures

1. Why do you think that Moses repeats the word "Hear" (vv. 3-4)?

2. Why does Moses emphasize the importance of teaching children and future generations (v. 7)?

Discuss the Meaning

1. In what ways do you need to grow in showing love for God?

2. How does the definition of love for God differ or agree with the way that society portrays love?

Liberating Lesson

Our love for God must involve our whole heart, soul, and mind. This also includes loving our neighbors. We have to teach and demonstrate for our children and future generations what love encompasses. There is a rise in hate crimes across the United States and the world. If hate is taught to children, they may grow up to hate. But if we teach love of God and others, they more than likely will grow up loving all. This love for all humanity was demonstrated during Hurricane Harvey in August 2017. Many cities were flooded by heavy rains. People of every race, religion, and culture rescued those stranded in their houses and donated food, clothing, and money. This is the love of God personified. We have to love and worship God with our whole beings.

Application for Activation

Traditionally, we show our love and devotion for God through worship, singing, and dance. But we can also worship God in other ways. As you sit in the next worship service, observe and listen for additional ways God wants you to worship Him. During quiet time at home, pray for new ways to teach your children and younger generations the Word. For example, you can hang pictures that include Scriptures, give your children Christian video games, or purchase clothing that has Christian themes printed on them. Most important, every day and night read and meditate on the Word so that it becomes a part of your daily life.

Follow the Spirit

What God wants me to do:

_____

_____

_____

_____

Remember Your Thoughts

Special insights I have learned:

_____

_____

_____

_____

More Light on the Text

Deuteronomy 6:1–9

In the preceding chapter, Moses rehearsed the Sinai law for the Children of Israel and the circumstances under which it was initially given. He urged them to always keep the law of God so that they could reap the benefit, which was long life in the land the Lord had promised them. The next nine verses define the law, how the people were to keep it, and to what extent they should keep it in order for them to reap the benefits that come with it. They were to preserve the law by teaching it to the generations to come. The portion under discussion today constitutes what practicing Jews call the Shema, which is also the basis for the Christian belief in the one eternal God.

1 Now these are the commandments, the statutes, and the judgments, which the LORD your God commanded to teach you, that ye might do them in the land whither ye go to possess it: 2 That thou mightest fear the LORD thy God, to keep all his statutes and his commandments, which I command thee, thou, and thy son, and thy son's son, all the days of thy life; and that thy days may be prolonged.

The phrase, "Now these are the commandments, the statutes, and the judgments," includes the summarized commandments Moses had just rehearsed with them in the previous chapter, and the ones that were to follow. The Lord, Moses says, had ordered him to teach them or to remind them of the Law, which they would keep when they possessed the Promised Land. He rehearsed the Law in their hearing so that they would remember to obey and fear the Lord. The fear of the Lord, which means reverence in one's heart for God, is the most powerful force for obedience.

Proverbs describes the fear of the Lord as "the beginning of wisdom" (9:10). The kind of "fear" (*yare'*, **yaw-RAY**) used here (Deuteronomy 6: 2) is not to be afraid of God as if he were a dreadful and vengeful being ready to punish them for the smallest infraction of His Law. It speaks more of respecting or revering God as the Father who deserves to be honored and heeded. When we fear God, we respect Him both as the law-giver and as a just and righteous judge, bearing in mind His justice as well as His mercy and patience.

Moses uses three Hebrew words, "commandments" (*mitsvah*, **meets-VAW**) which are the hard laws, "statutes" (*choq*, **KHOKE**) which are akin to policies, and "judgments" (*mishpat*, **meesh-PAWT**) which are the applications of the Law. These terms showed varying degrees of rigidity or functionality as the Israelites sought to set themselves apart from the surrounding cultures and be a light to the nations. These words emphasize the importance of keeping the law of God. The Law was to be perpetuated throughout the history of Israel. The reward for keeping the Law was that the Israelites, their children, and future generations would live long. To live long refers not necessarily to an individual long life, which probably was included, but rather to the long life of Israel as a nation. That is, the Israelites would possess the land for a long time; conversely, if they failed to fear the Lord and keep His commandments, they would lose the land.

Therefore, as each generation remembered to obey the commandments, they would enjoy the benefits of the land, and their days would be prolonged. The Law was intended for their well-being so that Israel could enjoy life to the fullest. For it is given "that it may be well with thee" (from v. 3; cf. 5:33; 6:18; 12:28).

However, Israel's captivity by Persia and Judah's exile to Babylon are consequences of their failure to keep the law of the Lord.

3 Hear therefore, O Israel, and observe to do it; that it may be well with thee, and that ye may increase mightily, as the LORD God of thy fathers hath promised thee, in the land that floweth with milk and honey.

"Hear therefore," or "in view of the benefits," Moses pleads with them to listen to (hear) and obey (observe) the law of the Lord. The use of these two words is notable. First, the two verbs are near homonyms in Hebrew. This rhetorical device grabs the audience's attention and helps them remember what is said. Further, the Hebrew for "hear" (*shama*, **shaw-MAH**) often means more than just to pay attention to sounds; it implies listening, understanding, and acting on that knowledge. "Obey" is within the semantic range—the word's range of meanings—of "hear." It is striking then that Moses follows up with "observe" (Heb. *shamar*, **shaw-MAR**), which is also translated as "keep" or "obey." Its meaning, therefore, overlaps with *shama's* but can further mean "guard." Thus the

Israelites are to listen to God's laws, obey them, and work to preserve them in their memory and their culture.

If they will endeavor to keep the commandments, things will go well with them; they will multiply in keeping with the promise the Lord made to their fathers (Genesis 15:5; 28:14). That promise includes living in the land that flows with milk and honey, which describes the fertility and productivity of the land. In a culture where bread and wine were the basic staples of one's diet, milk and honey are prime examples of luxuries.

4 Hear, O Israel: The LORD our God is one LORD: 5 And thou shalt love the LORD thy God with all thine heart, and with all thy soul, and with all thy might.

Verses 4–9 constitute the Shema, (similar to 11:18–21, and Numbers 15:37–41) the creed of Israel in the Hebrew liturgy, which pious Jews recite twice daily in their worship. It expresses the heart of Israel's confession of faith, and confirms first the covenant relationship between Israel ("the Lord our God") and second the unity of God ("the Lord is one"). The word translated "one" is the Hebrew *'echad* (**ekh-AWD**; Genesis 2:24; 3:22; 11:1, 6) related to *achad* which means "to unify; collect; to be united as one." Here, Moses implicitly declared the uniqueness of God of Israel, namely that Yahweh is the one God, and He is not a pantheon of many gods that are worshiped by the surrounding nations. Rather than ruling over one sphere or having one power as other gods did, Israel's God was God alone over everything, uniting all power. The phrase in verse four could also be translated "The LORD is our God, the LORD alone." This translation would emphasize that the Israelites were to worship no gods in addition to Yahweh.

Moses began this declaration by calling for the whole congregation of the people of Israel to pay attention—"Hear, O Israel" (*Shema'* *yisra'el*, **shuh-MAH yees-raw-EL**)—to this important information, namely the uniqueness of God, and their response to Him. Moses invited the people to give Yahweh their complete allegiance by loving Him with the totality of their being: "with all thine heart, and with all thy soul, and with all thy might." Yahweh was to be Israel's sole object of worship and affection, not other gods. Verse 4 has been regarded as the positive way of expressing the negative commands of the first commandments of the Decalogue (5:7–10; Exodus 20:3–6).

In the New Testament, Christ, responding to the inquiry of the young lawyer, added the phrase "with all your mind," and described these two verses (vv. 4–5) as "the first and great commandment" (Matthew 22:37–38; cf. Mark 12:29–30; Luke 10:27). Notably, Jesus also added the phrase "with all your mind" to His citation of these verses. This was necessary when speaking to the heavily Hellenized (Greek-influenced) culture of Jesus' day. Israelites at the time of Moses did not have a concept of "mind" that was distinct from "heart." Whereas the Greeks thought of the mind as the seat of intellect and the heart as the seat of emotion, the ancient Hebrews thought of the heart as holding both.

This type of love requires total surrender of the whole being to God, who has given Himself completely, without reservation, and unconditionally to love the people of Israel. He, therefore, deserves and expects them to reciprocate with the same unreserved and total love for Him. This command to love the Lord is found frequently in Deuteronomy and expresses the response God expects from His people (10:12; 11:1, 19:9; 30:6); it is also found in the covenant renewal after entering the land (Joshua 22:5; 23:11).

Scripture often links the command to love with the command to obey. God speaks to Moses and states, "But I [God] lavish unfailing love for a thousand generations on those who love me and obey my commands" (Exodus 20:6, NLT). Nehemiah prays to God recognizing the connection of love and obedience to covenant: "O LORD God of heaven, the great and terrible God, that keepeth covenant and mercy for them that love him and observe his commandments" (from Nehemiah 1:5, KJV). Jesus said to His disciples, "If ye love me, keep my commandments. … He that hath my commandments, and keepeth them, he it is that loveth me: and he that loveth me shall be loved of my Father, and I will love him, and will manifest myself to him" (John 14:15, 21). Obeying is the natural outworking of loving.

6 And these words, which I command thee this day, shall be in thine heart: 7 And thou shalt teach them diligently unto thy children, and shalt talk of them when thou sittest in thine house, and when thou walkest by the way, and when thou liest down, and when thou risest up.

"And these words, which I command thee this day," looks forward to the commands that are to follow.

These commandments were to be stored in their hearts, where nothing could touch them. The word translated "heart" is *lebab* (Heb. **lay-BAWB**) and is also used in verse 5. It refers to the seat of understanding, intellect, and intention. It is where we do our thinking, and where our character is formed. The heart represents the nucleus of the human being in which decisions and moral choices, both good and bad, are made. True love, worship, and holy principles come from within the heart, as do the evil issues of life (Mark 7:19–23). The heart is also the seat of consciousness or memory; therefore, to store the commandment in our heart is to keep it in our consciousness as long as we live.

In other words, God's commandments should become a part of our being, and we are to be conscious of them all the days of our lives. Verse 7 uses a literary device common in Hebrew called a merism, which names two extremes in order to refer to the entire spectrum. Thus "when thou sittest in thine house, and when thou walkest by the way" means not just those two extremes, but everywhere. Likewise, "when thou liest down and when thou risest up" means all the time.

This is made explicit in the command that parents teach the commandments to their children diligently. The phrase "to teach diligently" translates the Hebrew word *shanan* (**shaw-NON**), which indicates "to sharpen, or to pierce." They were to teach the children the Law constantly and systematically, formally and informally, until these words of the commandments pierce through their hearts. The commandments should be the center of their daily life, in conversation at home, or on the road. They should go to bed at night, and arise in the morning with the law of the Lord embedded in their hearts so that they would not forget it. The Israelites were to teach the commandments to their children, not only to instruct them in the ways of the Lord from an early age (Proverbs 22:6) but perhaps to help preserve the Law and their heritage for generations (Deuteronomy 6:20–25).

8 And thou shalt bind them for a sign upon thine hand, and they shall be as frontlets between thine eyes. 9 And thou shalt write them upon the posts of thy house, and on thy gates.

To make the Law a visible and permanent part of their life, the Israelites were to bind them upon their hands as a constant reminder of their allegiance to Yahweh and the Law, and post it on their forehead and on the lintels of their houses. Binding them on their hands is probably a figurative expression of how diligent their allegiance to the Law should be. The imagery is also used in the Jewish rituals of the Passover, in the sacrifice of the firstborn animals and the redemption of the firstborn sons (Exodus 13:9, 16). The same idea is expressed with similar metaphors in a number of the Proverbs, regarding mercy and truth (3:3), obedience to parental commandments (6:21), and keeping God's Law (7:3). The Jews later interpreted it literally and enclosed some written portions of the Law in small cases, called phylacteries (cf. Matthew 23:5), and bound them on their hands and foreheads. The significance of these instructions is well understood, and that is to keep them conscious of God, by a visible and constant reminder of the Law.

Sources:

Life Application Study Bible, New Revised Standard Version. Wheaton, IL: Tyndale House Publishers, Inc., 1989. 278–279.

Packer, J. I., Merrill C. Tenney, and William White Jr.. *Nelson's Illustrated Encyclopedia of Bible Facts.* Nashville, TN: Thomas Nelson Publishers, 1995.

Unger, Merrill F. *The New Unger's Bible Handbook.* Chicago, IL: Moody Press, 1984. 110–112.

Unger, Merril F. *Unger's Bible Dictionary.* Chicago, IL: Moody Press, 1985. 262–263.

Vine, W. E. *Vine's Complete Expository Dictionary of Old and New Testament Words.* Edited by Merrill F. Unger and William White Jr. Nashville, TN: Thomas Nelson Publishers, 1996.

Say It Correctly

Shema. shuh-**MAH**.

Daily Bible Readings

MONDAY
The Most Important Instruction
(Matthew 22:37–40)

TUESDAY
Treat Your Neighbors Justly
(Leviticus 19:13–18)

WEDNESDAY
Fulfilling the Royal Law
(James 2:8–13)

THURSDAY
Don't Forget the Lord
(Deuteronomy 6:10–15)

FRIDAY
Do What Is Right and Good
(Deuteronomy 6:16–19)

SATURDAY
Fear the Lord and Live Rightly
(Deuteronomy 6:20–25)

SUNDAY
The Lord Is God Alone
(Deuteronomy 6:1–9)

Notes

_____

_____

_____

_____

Teaching Tips

Words You Should Know

A. Sanctuary *miqdesh* (Heb.)—A place set apart for worship.

B. Sincerity *tamim* (Heb.)—Suggests fullness, completeness, integrity or being without blemish or spot.

Teacher Preparation

Unifying Principle—Choose to Serve God. At critical junctures in life, people are forced to make life-changing decisions. How do they decide which paths to take? When challenged by Joshua to serve God or other gods, the Israelites definitively chose to love and serve God.

A. Read the Bible Background and Devotional Readings.

B. Pray for your students and lesson clarity.

C. Read the lesson Scripture in multiple translations.

D. Option: Brainstorm strategies for putting away false gods and serving the Lord instead.

O—Open the Lesson

A. Begin the class with prayer.

B. Have students read the Aim for Change

C. Have students read the In Focus story.

D. Ask students how events named in the story can weigh on their hearts and how they can view these events from a theological perspective.

P—Present the Scriptures

A. Read the Focal Verses and discuss the Background and The People, Places, and Times sections.

B. Have the class share what Scriptures stand out for them and why, with particular emphasis on today's context.

E—Explore the Meaning

A. Use In Depth or More Light on the Text to help provide more in-depth discussion of the lesson text.

B. Discuss the Liberating Lesson and Application for Activation sections.

N—Next Steps for Application

A. Summarize the value of choosing to love and serve God as the most important thing in our lives.

B. End class with a commitment to pray for strength and resolve in choosing to serve God despite what others might be doing.

Worship Guide

For the Superintendent or Teacher
Theme: Choose to Love and Serve God
Song: "You Are God Alone"
Devotional Reading: Psalm 81

Choose to Love and Serve God

Bible Background • EXODUS 20:1–11; JOSHUA 24
Printed Text • JOSHUA 24:1–3, 13–15, 21–24 | Devotional Reading • PSALM 81

Aim for Change

By the end of the lesson, we will: DECLARE our loyalty to God and God alone; RESOLVE to put God first in all things; and OBEY His teachings and commandments.

 In Focus

Bill sighed as he saw his supervisor approaching with a stack of files. He was hoping to leave work on time; but this was the end of the fiscal year, which meant crunch time at his accounting firm. For the next four weeks, Bill knew he would be working longer-than-usual hours and wouldn't get to do what he really loved: acting.

He came alive whenever he performed on stage or before the cameras, even if he was just a face in a crowd scene or had a single line in a TV commercial. Making a living as an actor, however, required constant effort offstage: updating his demo reel and photos; finding casting notices; going to auditions; and attending acting classes when he could spare the money and the time. Work at the accounting firm was steady, but he found it harder to focus on numbers when he wanted to be in rehearsal. Once again, Bill thought about concentrating full time on acting. The fear of being broke always made him push that thought aside, but today it didn't.

He remembered the first time his mother saw him act, in a church production of *The Best Christmas Pageant Ever*. He was 12. Mom was in the front row, smiling at his every word. When it was over, she told him, "Bill, you have a gift from God. It pleases me so to see you use it." He knew she would not be happy to see him behind a desk going through the motions instead of using the talents God gave him to the fullest.

Can we do our best for God if we put our energy into things God has not called us to do?

Keep in Mind

"And if it seem evil unto you to serve the LORD, choose you this day whom ye will serve; whether the gods which your fathers served that were on the other side of the flood, or the gods of the Amorites, in whose land ye dwell: but as for me and my house, we will serve the LORD" (Joshua 24:15, KJV).

"But if you refuse to serve the LORD, then choose today whom you will serve. Would you prefer the gods your ancestors served beyond the Euphrates? Or will it be the gods of the Amorites in whose land you now live? But as for me and my family, we will serve the LORD" (Joshua 24:15, NLT).

Focal Verses

KJV **Joshua 24:1** And Joshua gathered all the tribes of Israel to Shechem, and called for the elders of Israel, and for their heads, and for their judges, and for their officers; and they presented themselves before God.

2 And Joshua said unto all the people, Thus saith the LORD God of Israel, Your fathers dwelt on the other side of the flood in old time, even Terah, the father of Abraham, and the father of Nachor: and they served other gods.

3 And I took your father Abraham from the other side of the flood, and led him throughout all the land of Canaan, and multiplied his seed, and gave him Isaac.

13 And I have given you a land for which ye did not labour, and cities which ye built not, and ye dwell in them; of the vineyards and oliveyards which ye planted not do ye eat.

14 Now therefore fear the LORD, and serve him in sincerity and in truth: and put away the gods which your fathers served on the other side of the flood, and in Egypt; and serve ye the LORD.

15 And if it seem evil unto you to serve the LORD, choose you this day whom ye will serve; whether the gods which your fathers served that were on the other side of the flood, or the gods of the Amorites, in whose land ye dwell: but as for me and my house, we will serve the LORD.

21 And the people said unto Joshua, Nay; but we will serve the LORD.

22 And Joshua said unto the people, Ye are witnesses against yourselves that ye have chosen you the LORD, to serve him. And they said, We are witnesses.

23 Now therefore put away, said he, the strange gods which are among you, and incline your heart unto the LORD God of Israel.

NLT **Joshua 24:1** Then Joshua summoned all the tribes of Israel to Shechem, including their elders, leaders, judges, and officers. So they came and presented themselves to God.

2 Joshua said to the people, "This is what the LORD, the God of Israel, says: Long ago your ancestors, including Terah, the father of Abraham and Nahor, lived beyond the Euphrates River, and they worshiped other gods.

3 But I took your ancestor Abraham from the land beyond the Euphrates and led him into the land of Canaan. I gave him many descendants through his son Isaac.

13 I gave you land you had not worked on, and I gave you towns you did not build—the towns where you are now living. I gave you vineyards and olive groves for food, though you did not plant them.

14 So fear the LORD and serve him wholeheartedly. Put away forever the idols your ancestors worshiped when they lived beyond the Euphrates River and in Egypt. Serve the LORD alone.

15 But if you refuse to serve the LORD, then choose today whom you will serve. Would you prefer the gods your ancestors served beyond the Euphrates? Or will it be the gods of the Amorites in whose land you now live? But as for me and my family, we will serve the LORD.

21 But the people answered Joshua, "No, we will serve the LORD!"

22 "You are a witness to your own decision," Joshua said. "You have chosen to serve the LORD." "Yes," they replied, "we are witnesses to what we have said."

23 "All right then," Joshua said, "destroy the idols among you, and turn your hearts to the LORD, the God of Israel."

24 And the people said unto Joshua, The LORD our God will we serve, and his voice will we obey.

24 The people said to Joshua, "We will serve the LORD our God. We will obey him alone."

The People, Places, and Times

Shechem. The name means "shoulder or back." Shechem is both a district and a city in the hill country of Ephraim in northern Palestine. Shechem was the first capital of the Northern Kingdom of Israel. Rehoboam, successor to King Solomon, went to Shechem to be crowned king over all of Israel. Samaria eventually became the permanent capital of the Northern Kingdom. It was at Shechem that Jesus visited with the Samaritan woman at Jacob's Well.

Idol. A graven image or representation of a god or goddess. In the context of the Bible, idolatry or worshiping idols is the great departure from God's will that opens the door for all other sins; it is breaking the first commandment (Exodus 20:3–4). The Israelites throughout Scripture give into temptation to worship the gods of the nations around them that represent fertility, fruitfulness, weather, power, wealth, and other natural forces. For the Christian, an idol can be anything in our lives that is given more trust and attention than God.

Background

The ancient Israelites' journey across the Jordan River into the promised land of Canaan is chronicled in the book of Joshua. As directed by God, Joshua provided guidance to the twelve tribes during this critical time in their history. Arrival in Canaan is an important moment in their history because this is the land God promised to their ancestors (Genesis, Chapters 12–50). The conquest of this land occurred after the Israelites were attacked; they had to fight for what they knew God promised them generations ago. The land was divided among the tribes, and Joshua called two national assemblies. The setting of the assembly recorded in today's passage was Shechem, the heart of the Promised Land. This historically significant city was the prime setting for Joshua to lead a covenant ceremony among the Israelites. During the ceremony, Joshua stood as a prophet reminding them of God's promise and provision. The Israelites voluntarily chose to take a vow of personal piety by turning their backs to idols and foreign gods. They made personal commitments to love and serve the God of Israel.

What are examples of modern idols or false gods we put before God?

At-A-Glance

1. Remembering God's Promise
(Joshua 24:1–3)
2. Recognizing God's Provision (vv. 13–15)
3. Reaffirming Our Piety (vv. 21–24)

In Depth

1. Remembering God's Promise (Joshua 24:1–3)

Joshua assembles the twelve tribes and their governing officials before God. Joshua has already built an altar and engaged in a covenant ceremony in Shechem (Joshua 8:30–35). Shechem functions as a sanctuary for the ancient Israelite people. The prophet prepares the Israelites to engage corporately in a vow renewal ceremony by first reminding them of God's initial promise to multiply Abraham's offspring (Genesis 12:1–3).

Abraham was worshiping idols before God revealed Himself to Abraham as the true God. Yet after this encounter the descendants of Abraham chose again to turn back to idols. This choice had a negative effect on their descendants' future. The distraction of foreign gods delayed their possession of God's promise.

Joshua reminds the people assembled in Shechem how a bad decision by their ancestors affected the history of their people.

How have distractions delayed the fulfillment of God's promises in your life?

2. Recognizing God's Provision (vv. 13–15)

We learn God's promises always come with God's provision. God not only gave the Israelites the Canaanite land as promised, but also provided already-built towns and fruit-bearing plants. God ensured their basic food and shelter needs were met in Canaan prior to their arrival.

Verse 13 shows us an example of God's unconditional love and generosity despite ourselves. God did not default on the promise, because the Israelites turned to serve other gods. The Creator's back is never turned on us. Instead, God loves us through our wrong decisions and always keeps promises. Thankfully, God does what He promises!

After recognizing God's provision, Joshua challenges the Israelites to make a necessary decision. The prophet questions to whom they will offer their sincere and faithful worship. Ultimately, this covenant renewal ceremony is an opportunity to correct the wrong decisions of their ancestors. Joshua takes a stand and

declares his household will break the family tradition and serve the Lord.

In your experience, how have you been challenged to turn away from idols and toward God?

3. Reaffirming Our Piety (vv. 21–24)

In response to God's promise and provision, the Israelites must decide if they will either continue serving idols or wholeheartedly serve God. The people respond to Joshua's challenge by publicly committing to serve the Lord. Making this public declaration with other believers is important for two reasons. First, this nation voluntarily chooses God. They are not forced to enter into relationship with God and neither are we. We must resist the temptation of idols and commit to serving God daily. Second, witnessing others reaffirm the vow creates a sense of accountability. We cannot live out our faith on our own. We ought to surround ourselves with believers, who share similar commitments. After reaffirming their vow to God, the Israelites are encouraged to repent by Joshua. They had to turn away from their idols completely. We cannot wholeheartedly serve God if our practices are to serve the world or serve ourselves. Our heart and actions must be in alignment with God when renewing our vows.

How does this covenant ceremony relate or compare to modern-day renewal ceremonies (wedding vows, the Lord's Supper)?

Search the Scriptures

1. Why do you think the Scripture reflects on the past traditions and choices of the Israelites' ancestors (Joshua 24:2, 14–15)? How might their family heritage shape the decision they must make about their faith at Shechem?

2. What do the Israelites have to do when they decide to follow God (v. 23)?

Discuss the Meaning

1. What are some examples of modern-day idols that people place before God?

2. How might reaffirming our commitment to God among others help us to stay committed?

Liberating Lesson

It might be time to renew our vow to love and serve God considering the political climate in America, the growing tensions among nations around the world, and the numerous acts of injustice faced by black and brown people daily in our communities. This is not a reference to just any God, but the God of justice, who sides with the oppressed. As we incline our ear to the heart of the Lord, we should pay close attention to how God is calling us to serve oppressed people. We are called to stand up against injustice to ensure that all of God's people have access to His promises.

Application for Activation

While work, family, hobbies, relationships, and other commitments require our time, nothing should be prioritized before God. Spending excessive amounts of time watching television, working extra hours, and traveling can turn our attention away from God. Each of these commitments can become idols. One way to indicate which distractions prevent us from loving and serving God with our whole heart is to take a personal inventory of how we use our time. Make a schedule of how your time is spent in a typical week. How much time is devoted to loving and serving God? Is your time well-balanced?

Follow the Spirit

What God wants me to do:

_____

Remember Your Thoughts

Special insights I have learned:

_____

_____

_____

_____

More Light on the Text
Joshua 24:1–3, 13–15, 21–24

Israel has conquered all the lands as the Lord promised. Israel is now settled, for "the Lord had given rest unto Israel from all their enemies round about" (from Joshua 23:1). A few years later, some suggest about 25 to 30 years after Israel entered the land, Joshua is now almost 110 years old (13:1; 24:29). He knows his life and leadership will soon end. He gathers all the tribes of Israel to address them. He reminds them of all that the Lord has done for them and charges them to maintain a good relationship with Yahweh by keeping "all that is written in the book of the law of Moses, that ye turn not aside therefrom to the right hand or to the left" (from 23:6). This is the first of two such gatherings Joshua calls before he dies.

24:1 And Joshua gathered all the tribes of Israel to Shechem, and called for the elders of Israel, and for their heads, and for their judges, and for their officers; and they presented themselves before God. 2 And Joshua said unto all the people Thus saith the LORD God of Israel, Your fathers dwelt on the other

side of the flood in old time, even Terah, the father of Abraham, and the father of Nachor: and they served other gods. 3 And I took your father Abraham from the other side of the flood, and led him throughout all the land of Canaan, and multiplied his seed, and gave him Isaac.

Some scholars suggest that the gathering in chapter 24 is a continuation of the gathering in chapter 23. While the location of the gathering of chapter 23 is not mentioned, Shechem is mentioned as the place for the gathering of chapter 24. Shechem is an appropriate place for this solemn gathering considering the patriarchal tradition. Shechem is an ancient city. Abraham built an altar at Shechem when he arrived in Canaan (Genesis 12:6–7); Jacob bought a piece of ground and built an altar for the Lord here (Genesis 33:18–20; cf. Joshua 24:32). Shechem is one of the cities consecrated as a city of refuge for anyone who mistakenly kills another (20:7–9; 21:21). For all these reasons, Shechem is a sacred place for such an important meeting.

The word for "to gather" is the Hebrew verb 'asaph (aw-SAF) and that is "to assemble, to bring together." In this case Joshua is summoning them for an important occasion. Joshua summons all the tribes of Israel with her elders, heads, judges, and officers to this sacred site. The clause, "and they presented themselves before God," seems to suggest that God initiated the assembly through a divine revelation to Joshua.

From verse 2 to 13 is Joshua's address, which details the historical redemptive acts of God for Israel. Speaking on God's behalf ("thus says the Lord," v. 2), Joshua summarizes the story of Israel from the time of Abraham to the very point of their existence, including how the Lord has been with them providentially in all situations, and how He has loved and blessed them unconditionally.

13 And I have given you a land for which ye did not labour, and cities which ye built not, and ye dwell in them; of the vineyards and oliveyards which ye planted not do ye eat.

This is the conclusion of Joshua's summary of Israel's history up to the point of the address. Joshua is making a statement about what the Israelites are about to enter. God has given the land to the Israelites and taken it from the people of Canaan because God promised it to Abraham. The people of Israel were provided for by the providence of God; they could not claim their success based on their own efforts. God was giving them land, cities, and resources, abundantly providing for the Israelites as they entered into the place that God had called them. In this case, because God gave the vision, God also supplied the provision for the people God had liberated from bondage.

It would be misguided to interpret this Scripture as God's authorization for colonialism and displacement of people in our modern world. God who was ruler of the earth itself had decided to plant Israel in the land of Canaan and therefore made complete provision for Israel in the land. A helpful rendering of this verse highlights that the Israelites were about to receive a promised land that was not built by their own work. No human being exists in autonomy or is entirely self-made, nor is any nation. We are all indebted to the peoples who have gone before us—and ultimately God who created and owns everything—for anything we receive.

14 Now therefore fear the LORD, and serve him in sincerity and in truth: and put away the gods which your fathers served on the other side of the flood, and in Egypt; and serve ye the LORD.

In verses 2–13, Joshua serves as God's prophetic spokesman, now he begins his final personal exhortation to the Children of Israel. That is, in view of the Lord's acts in history, Israel is to maintain a good and God-fearing relationship with Yahweh.

First, they are to fear the Lord—to have an attitude of reverence, respect, and honor toward God as the Hebrew word *yare'* (**yah-RAY**) implies. It is in this sense that the word "fear" is used here; in contrast to being afraid of the Lord, as if God were a terror or cruel judge waiting to pounce on His subject for any mistake or wrongdoing. The fear of the Lord is an attitude of awe produced by the majesty, love, and goodness of God shown to His people. The Bible speaks often of the fear of God (Deuteronomy 4:10; 6:13, 24; Psalm 130:4). Proverbs says that fear of the Lord is the beginning or foundation of wisdom and knowledge (1:7; 9:10).

Second, Israel is to serve the Lord in sincerity and in truth. To serve (Heb. *'abad*, **aw-VAHD**) the Lord means to worship Him. The word is elsewhere translated "to work or labor." Worshiping God is not just singing praises or listening to sermons; it is doing the work of loving our neighbors and caring for them. The word for sincerity (Heb. *tamim*, **taw-MEEM**) also suggests "fullness, complete, integrity or without blemish or spot." This is the word used to describe an acceptable offering to God. The word truth (Heb. *'emet*, **EH-met**) elsewhere means "sureness or faithfulness." To worship the Lord thus, is the only way to serve Him. It should be devoid of hypocrisy and falsehood, for God hates such flaws (Proverbs 6:17, 19). Jesus tells the woman at the well in Samaria that "true worshipers shall worship the Father in spirit and in truth" (from John 4:23). In his response to the woman's argument that their forefathers worshiped on the mountains of Samaria (John 4:20, i.e., in Shechem), Jesus alludes to what Joshua declares here to the people of Israel. Worshiping God sincerely and faithfully is an outgrowth of a heart that is in awe of Him. It is a heart the serves Him completely with no reservation.

Such sincere and unreserved service of the Lord is to be exclusive and has no room for other gods. Therefore, the people are to "put away the gods which your fathers served" (v. 2). Jacob made the same demand on his household (Genesis 35:2); Samuel also called on all of Israel to "put away the strange gods and Ashtaroth from among you, and prepare your hearts unto the LORD, and serve him only" (from 1 Samuel 7:3). The gods from whom the Israelites are to disassociate themselves include not only those beyond the Euphrates that Abraham had worshiped ("the other side of the flood"), but also the gods of Egypt.

This indicates that Israel served the gods of Egypt while they were there. Egypt is identified earlier in this chapter (vv. 2–13) as the place where the people cried out to God and were delivered, giving us a general sense that Israel was innocent while they lived in Egypt. However, this verse, with other Old Testament passages, presents a different picture of the situation. For example, later prophets recount how Israel played the harlot, a common metaphor for idolatry, while in Egypt (Ezekiel 20:7; 23:3–8). The making and worship of the molten calf in the Sinai desert is an indication that the Israelites were used to worshiping such gods, like the Egyptians' gods (Exodus 32). But Joshua calls on them to put away these other gods, and serve only the Lord.

15 And if it seem evil unto you to serve the LORD, choose you this day whom ye will serve; whether the gods which your fathers served that were on the other side of the flood, or the gods of the Amorites, in whose land ye dwell: but as for me and my house, we will serve the LORD.

Joshua now speaks to their conscience. After reviewing the redemptive acts of God in history and challenging them to do away with other gods to serve the only the Lord, Joshua leaves room for them to make their choice. "And if it seem evil unto you to serve the Lord" presses the decision. The possibilities are clear. Either they choose to worship the Lord, or serve the gods of their forefathers, or the gods of the Amorites whose land they now occupy. Choosing to serve other gods is not a real smart choice but a possible option. Joshua wants them to think for themselves and make an honest and voluntary choice. He is not offering an alternative, but is seeking a confession of faith in Yahweh from them, which he gets (vv. 16–20). Without waiting for them to reply, Joshua declares his resolve to worship the Lord with his household—"but as for me and my house, we will serve the LORD."

21 And the people said unto Joshua, Nay; but we will serve the LORD. 22 And Joshua said unto the people, Ye are witnesses against yourselves that ye have chosen you the LORD, to serve him. And they said, We are witnesses.

In spite of Joshua's words in verse 20, the people reconfirm their pledge unequivocally to serve the Lord. The picture here is that of a shout of "No!" (Heb. *lo'*, **LOW**) in unison, "We will serve the LORD!" Joshua's seeming negativity and threat of punishment for disobedience do not discourage or deter them from reaffirming their pledge to God for the second time (cf. v. 18). In his response to their reaffirmation of faith in the Lord, Joshua holds them accountable and responsible to their pledge. Using judicial language, Joshua calls them witnesses to their vow to serve the Lord. Again, in unison, they reply, "We are witnesses!"

Every covenant has to be sacred and witnessed; otherwise, there is no accountability for the parties involved. A "witness" (Heb. *'ed*, **ADE**) gives testimony or bears evidence. Not only was Joshua a witness to their choice, but the people were witnesses for each other. By acknowledging their service to the Lord, the Israelites were reconfirming their covenant with Yahweh. By their own words, they were witnesses to the covenant should they ever decide to break it again. Although we cannot and will not do it perfectly, we must demonstrate daily our faith in the God of the covenant. Most assuredly, if we do not, our own hearts are witnesses against us, in addition to the all-knowing God.

23 Now therefore put away, said he, the strange gods which are among you, and incline your heart unto the LORD God of Israel.

The people had made a choice. They had voluntarily rejected the idol gods and promised to remain faithful to the God of their forefathers. For the Israelites, the demonstration of their faith in the God of the covenant was the single, but difficult, action of putting away their idols. By putting away all idols and having no other gods before Him, we show to the Lord and to world that we belong to the Lord our God. Deep emotional attachments to and lust for the hidden idols of our hearts will destroy our lives. Believers should ask God for His grace to be faithful and keep themselves from the idols of today's world.

24 And the people said unto Joshua, The LORD our God will we serve, and his voice will we obey.

Now they have reaffirmed their choice by expressing their commitment to serve the Lord, and "obey" (Heb. *shama*, **shaw-MA**, "listen to, hear") His voice. It is said that even today sheep recognize the voice of their shepherd; they will not respond to any other voice.

When the shepherd says, "Come," they follow. This picture of devotion is why Jesus said, "My sheep hear my voice … and they follow me" (from John 10:27). Like the people of Joshua's day, we must choose whom we will serve and obey. Jesus is our Good Shepherd. No matter how educated or wealthy we are, in reality, without a shepherd, we are just like sheep that are prone to self-destruction. The Christian today has the voice of God revealed to him in God's Word from Genesis to Revelation. We are called to hear, believe, and obey. Are you listening? Are you hearing His voice? Renew your commitment to serve God and obey His Word. God is still looking for covenant keepers today.

Sources:
Butler, Trent, ed. *Holman Bible Dictionary*. Nashville, TN: Holman Bible Publishers, 1991. 1258-1259, 1334.

Daily Bible Readings

MONDAY
Rules on People Relating to God
(Exodus 20:1–11)

TUESDAY
Rules on People Relating to People
(Exodus 20:12–17)

WEDNESDAY
Keep the Faith and Live
(Joshua 23:2–6, 14–16)

THURSDAY
Rescued from Egypt, Settled in Canaan
(Joshua 24:4–12)

FRIDAY
We Promise to Serve God
(Joshua 24:16–21)

SATURDAY
Covenant with God Confirmed
(Joshua 24:25–28)

SUNDAY
Choose to Love and Serve God
(Joshua 24:1–3, 13–15, 21–24)

Notes

Teaching Tips

December 16
Bible Study Guide 3

Words You Should Know

A. Iniquity *avon* (Heb.)—Sin.

B. Hosts *sabaoth* (Heb.)—Angel armies.

Teacher Preparation

Unifying Principle—Look to God. People feel anxious and confused when they remember their personal failures and continue to face life's trials. What consolation is there? The psalmist lists many reasons that God's steadfast love should inspire enthusiastic thanksgiving rather than dismay.

A. Read the Bible Background and Devotional Readings.

B. Pray for your students and lesson clarity.

C. Read the lesson Scripture in multiple translations.

D. Option: Have the class identify distractions that sometimes prevent wholehearted worship. Discuss strategies for overcoming these distractions.

O—Open the Lesson

A. Open class with prayer.

B. Ask students to read the Aim for Change

C. Have students read the In Focus story.

D. Ask students how events named in the story can weigh on their hearts and how they can view these events from a theological perspective.

P—Present the Scriptures

A. Read the Focal Verses and discuss the Background and The People, Places, and Times sections.

B. Have the class share what Scriptures stand out for them and why, with particular emphasis on today's context.

E—Explore the Meaning

A. Use In Depth or More Light on the Text to help provide deeper discussion of the lesson text.

B. Discuss the Liberating Lesson and Application for Activation sections.

N—Next Steps for Application

A. Summarize the value of worshiping God with our whole being.

B. End class with a commitment to worship God authentically in spirit and truth.

Worship Guide

For the Superintendent or Teacher
Theme: Love and Worship God
Song: "My Heart Says Amen"
Devotional Reading: Psalm 86:1–7

Love and Worship God

Bible Background • PSALM 103:1–17, 21–22
Printed Text • PSALM 103:1–17, 21–22 | Devotional Reading • PSALM 86:1–7

—————— Aim for Change ——————

By the end of the lesson, we will: EXAMINE what it means to praise the Lord with our whole heart and mind and soul; APPRECIATE His righteousness, compassion, and grace; and give THANKS for His mercy and goodness.

————— ❧ In Focus 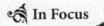 —————

As he stood at the altar waiting for Sherri to come down the aisle, Darryl's heart swelled with joy. He knew that God had brought them together from the moment he saw her across campus one Friday night and followed her into the chapel for services. Not only did he meet the one who would pledge to be by his side, Darryl heard a message that night that transformed him and opened his heart to God's goodness. Before long, Darryl and Sherri were regular attendees at chapel services.

Soon they were both volunteering for the campus food pantry and delivering bags of groceries to needy families in the community. But it was a mission trip to Appalachia, which he joined at Sherri's invitation, that really showed Darryl the spiritual rewards of steadfast faith. During that week, Darryl met people in poor health who lived in grinding poverty and had little but the certainty that God was with them through their struggles.

On the ride back to campus, Darryl prayed. He gave thanks to God for giving him the opportunity to be in college, and for the reminder that things are different for many people. That night, Darryl proposed and Sherri said yes to marrying him. Now, in the chapel before family and friends and God, Darryl said another prayer of thanks that their lives would forever be bound.

Are we grateful for how God has blessed us, including all the ways He has shown us mercy and forgiven our sins?

—————— Keep in Mind ——————

"As far as the east is from the west, so far hath he removed our transgressions from us" (Psalm 103:12, KJV).

"He has removed our sins as far from us as the east is from the west" (Psalm 103:12, NLT).

Focal Verses

KJV **Psalm 103:1** Bless the LORD, O my soul: and all that is within me, bless his holy name.

2 Bless the LORD, O my soul, and forget not all his benefits:

3 Who forgiveth all thine iniquities; who healeth all thy diseases;

4 Who redeemeth thy life from destruction; who crowneth thee with lovingkindness and tender mercies;

5 Who satisfieth thy mouth with good things; so that thy youth is renewed like the eagle's.

6 The LORD executeth righteousness and judgment for all that are oppressed.

7 He made known his ways unto Moses, his acts unto the children of Israel.

8 The LORD is merciful and gracious, slow to anger, and plenteous in mercy.

9 He will not always chide: neither will he keep his anger for ever.

10 He hath not dealt with us after our sins; nor rewarded us according to our iniquities.

11 For as the heaven is high above the earth, so great is his mercy toward them that fear him.

12 As far as the east is from the west, so far hath he removed our transgressions from us.

13 Like as a father pitieth his children, so the LORD pitieth them that fear him.

14 For he knoweth our frame; he remembereth that we are dust.

15 As for man, his days are as grass: as a flower of the field, so he flourisheth.

16 For the wind passeth over it, and it is gone; and the place thereof shall know it no more.

17 But the mercy of the LORD is from everlasting to everlasting upon them that fear him, and his righteousness unto children's children.

NLT **Psalm 103:1** Let all that I am praise the LORD; with my whole heart, I will praise his holy name.

2 Let all that I am praise the LORD; may I never forget the good things he does for me.

3 He forgives all my sins and heals all my diseases.

4 He redeems me from death and crowns me with love and tender mercies.

5 He fills my life with good things. My youth is renewed like the eagle's!

6 The LORD gives righteousness and justice to all who are treated unfairly.

7 He revealed his character to Moses and his deeds to the people of Israel.

8 The LORD is compassionate and merciful, slow to get angry and filled with unfailing love.

9 He will not constantly accuse us, nor remain angry forever.

10 He does not punish us for all our sins; he does not deal harshly with us, as we deserve.

11 For his unfailing love toward those who fear him is as great as the height of the heavens above the earth.

12 He has removed our sins as far from us as the east is from the west.

13 The LORD is like a father to his children, tender and compassionate to those who fear him.

14 For he knows how weak we are; he remembers we are only dust.

15 Our days on earth are like grass; like wildflowers, we bloom and die.

16 The wind blows, and we are gone— as though we had never been here.

17 But the love of the LORD remains forever with those who fear him. His salvation extends to the children's children

21 Yes, praise the LORD, you armies of angels who serve him and do his will!

21 Bless ye the LORD, all ye his hosts; ye ministers of his, that do his pleasure.

22 Bless the LORD, all his works in all places of his dominion: bless the LORD, O my soul.

22 Praise the LORD, everything he has created, everything in all his kingdom. Let all that I am praise the LORD.

The People, Places, and Times

Psalms. The name of the book that is a collection of poems, prayers, and praises directed to the God of Israel by various individuals. The book begins with "Blessed is the man," or, as some may have it, "Blessed be the man," and ends with "Praise the Lord." Thus, it begins with a blessing directed toward human beings and ends with praise directed toward God. The Hebrew Bible places this book in part of a section called Ketuvim, or "the Writings." At least 20 of the psalms deal directly and solely with praise. The psalms are grouped into five books: Book 1: Psalms 1—41, Book 2: Psalms 42—72, Book 3: Psalms 73—89, Book 4: Psalms 90—106, and Book 5: Psalms 107—150. Some psalms are imprecatory (calling God to punish His people's enemies) while others are an exclamation of praise. The psalms have served throughout the ages as devotionals.

Background

The book of Psalms is often referred to as a collection of prayers or songs, which creatively express and recount ancient Israel's experiences with God. There are multiple psalm types evidenced within each of the five books in Psalms, including prayers for help (laments), songs of thanksgiving, psalms of trust, and hymns. Psalm 103 is a hymn of praise, which exhorts us to praise God individually and collectively in all circumstances. The psalmist David begins by admonishing himself to bless (praise) God with the totality of his being as he recalls the blessings God bestows upon individual believers. The mere thought of such blessings calls the psalmist to give God praise. The scope of this hymn broadens from an individual perspective to one that includes a reflection on God's action on behalf of the ancient Israelite people. God's action is not reserved for individual believers but extends to the corporate body of believers, most notably the oppressed. The dynamic nature of God's character is shown through the Creator's merciful, gracious, loving, compassionate, and forgiving actions toward those who revere God. The psalmist ends by calling even the angels and other universal beings to bless the Lord, because God reigns over us all. God has dominion over all of the universe; therefore, all that has been created ought to give praise to God for His goodness.

Is there a time in your personal life, throughout the history of African Americans, or within your congregation where God's care was evident and caused you to respond with worship and devotion?

At-A-Glance

1. Bless the Lord Individually (Psalm 103:1–5)
2. Bless the Lord Corporately (vv. 6–17)
3. Bless the Lord Universally (vv. 21–22)

In Depth

1. Bless the Lord Individually (Psalm 103:1–5)

"Bless the Lord," means to acknowledge God with praise and thanksgiving. It means to speak well of God, to declare God's goodness. The fullness of our gratitude is shown when every aspect of our being is completely engaged and devoted to worshipping God. We offer God our whole self when giving praise because God cares for each part of us. We bless the Lord as individuals for two reasons. First, we offer God praise simply for who He is in our lives. We revere God as the Holy One. Out of our own might and actions we cannot be holy because of sin. We need God to work on our behalf, so that we may become holy. Second, we offer God thanksgiving in response to all He has done. The psalmist reminds us of six benefits God shares with us, including physical healing (v. 3). God heals our physical bodies from sickness and disease. God also heals our heart and soul from sin. We give God praise because of all the benefits we receive from Him.

How have you benefited from God's healing power in some aspect of your life?

2. Bless the Lord Corporately (vv. 6–17)

When offering praise and thanksgiving unto God, we must remember God's activity in the world around us. We cannot become consumed with our individual relationship with God, because we experience God's goodness, care and comfort corporately, too. The opportunity to go through life with others is a gift, especially as trouble arises. God is a refuge for us collectively in times of trouble. The ancient Israelites sought God's comfort during their captivity in Egypt. God was a liberator in freeing the oppressed. The ancient Israelites saw God's character as He extended mercy and grace to them in spite of their iniquities.

God's love abounds even when we show our worst sinful selves. He does not remain angry when we sin but instead shows compassion by moving those transgressions from us (v. 12). Our humanity is marked by its temporal nature. We all enter and will leave this world on dates determined before we were formed in our mothers' wombs. God's love extends beyond our lifespan, from the beginning to the end of time. It is comforting to know that God knew we would sin before the Creation. Yet He still loves us. This is another reason we should offer praise and thanksgiving unto God.

What are the benefits of praising God corporately during times of trouble?

3. Bless the Lord Universally (vv. 21–22)

God is the Creator of all existence, including the divine assembly. Angels, mighty ones, ministers, and the heavenly hosts exist within the realm of the Lord's kingdom. No one is excused from blessing the Lord. The psalmist reminds us even the angels must offer praise and thanksgiving unto the Lord and obey His spoken Word. In essence, all of creation is called to worship the Lord universally.

Why do you think the psalmist ends with "bless the Lord, O my soul?"

Search the Scriptures

1. Why do you think the psalmist emphasizes the importance of and reasons for individual, corporate and universal offerings of praise to God?

2. How does the metaphor in verse 13 help us better understand how God views and treats our transgressions?

Discuss the Meaning

1. Psalm 103:21 calls for blessings on all those servants of God who carry out His will. How does working with others bring greater glory to the Lord?

2. The psalmist declares that the Lord has removed our sins as far as the east is from the west. Share how knowing we are forgiven through Jesus Christ causes you to feel about God.

Liberating Lesson

Unfortunately, we live in perilous times. Black and brown people are violently killed by state-sanctioned violence; incarceration rates for minorities are disproportionately high; and poor people are systemically oppressed. It often seems like people and systems in our society are not held accountable for the actions, decisions, policies, and laws that negatively affect oppressed people. Where is the justice?

Fortunately, the text reminds us of God's activity, character, and nature. God sides with and seeks justice for the oppressed. As many of us protest the injustices on this earth, we should not forget to praise God for all the Lord has done in the past.

Application for Activation

As God gifts us with life each day, we must give credit where credit is due. Offering praise through worship and devotion is the least we can do to express our gratitude for all God has done, is doing, and will do in our future. Suggested below are two ways we can respond to the Psalmist's exhortation.

• Start a gratitude journal or list. Record what God does in your life daily and why you are grateful.

• In your local congregation, start a "Wall of Gratitude" so people can publicly give God praise for God's activity in the world.

Follow the Spirit

What God wants me to do:

_____

_____

_____

_____

Remember Your Thoughts

Special insights I have learned:

_____

_____

_____

_____

More Light on the Text
Psalm 103:1–17, 21–22

The inscription on this psalm of praise is attributed to King David. However, the time and the occasion for the composition of this song is unknown. Several scholars suggest that David wrote this psalm toward the end of his life. The psalm is one of the four that conclude Book Four of the book of Psalms (90-106). Each psalm emphasizes the praise of the Lord for different reasons. Psalm 103 praises the Lord for His benefits to His people; Psalm 104 talks about God's care for His creation; Psalm 105 praises the Lord for His wonderful acts on behalf of Israel; and Psalm 106 praises Him for His longsuffering with Israel's rebelliousness.

As we study Psalm 103, we discover that there is no petition or plea for anything, only praise. We are reminded that God's blessings to Israel are dependent on their obedience to God's covenant (vv. 17–18). Believers today, although under grace, likewise should understand that to enjoy God's best requires obedience to His will. It appears that the psalmist is soliloquizing as he reflects on the goodness of the Lord to him and to Israel. Overwhelmed with the Lord's benevolence, he bursts into praise and worship. David begins the psalm with personal praise (vv. 1–5), moves to national praise (vv. 6–19), and concludes with a call to public or universal praise (vv. 20–22).

1 Bless the LORD, O my soul: and all that is within me bless his holy name. 2 Bless the LORD, O my soul, and forget not all his benefits:

David begins this psalm with a summon to his "soul" to "bless the Lord." The word "bless" is the Hebrew *barak* (**baw-RAK**), which can also be translated "praise." To praise or bless is to speak good of something or somebody. When applied to God, "bless" means praise as an expression of our gratitude, worship, and adoration for who He is and for what He has done or does. When it is applied to humans, it means a prayer that they be blessed or happy. The phrase "God bless you" is a common greeting among Christians. In churches, we often conclude services by giving a blessing to the congregation (cf. Numbers 6:23–27).

The word "soul" is a translation of the Hebrew *nephesh* (**NEH-fesh**), which refers to the total person, life, or mind. The psalmist summons the entire makeup of his person to bless God. This means heart, soul, mind, and all his faculties and intellect are to be focused on praising the Lord. This calls for a total commitment to God and worship of Him. Unless everything within us is engaged in praising the Lord, our worship is a mere religious ritual. Praise must come from our whole being.

David repeats the call for his soul to bless the Lord, emphasizing its importance, and adds "forget not His benefits." In other words, remember all the good things God has done. As humans, we often tend to focus more on our problems and needs instead of on what God has done in our lives. Moses knew how prone people are to forgetting their blessings, so he reminded Israel to endeavor to remember and never forget all that Lord did for them (Deuteronomy 6:12; 8:11). David reminds us, too.

3 Who forgiveth all thine iniquities; who healeth all thy diseases 4 Who redeemeth thy life from destruction; who crowneth thee with lovingkindness and tender mercies; 5 Who satisfieth thy mouth with good things; so that thy youth is renewed like the eagle's.

David now lists six benefits (blessings) he received from the Lord: forgiveness, healing, redemption, love and mercies, satisfaction, and renewal. The verbs used here to describe these blessings are in the present continuous tense; they are continuous actions that never stop. God's blessings and dealings with His people are a continuous process. They portray God's mercy and love to His people.

Of chief importance to David is that the Lord "forgives all… iniquities." There is no limit to God's mercy, and there is no type or degree of sin God cannot forgive. Elsewhere David prays, "Hide your face from my sins and blot out all my iniquity" (Psalm 51:9). David's sins found in Scripture are great. He orders Uriah's murder so that he can sleep with Bathsheba. He ignores the sexual assault on his daughter. He isolates his son Absalom. Yet God still loves David and could forgive his sins.

The second blessing mentioned here is God's power to heal. The word "disease" is the Hebrew *tachalu'* (**tah-khah-LOO**), which means "sickness" (Deuteronomy 29:22) or disease (2 Chronicles 29:22). Some believe that this phrase is a parallelism to the previous clause, that is forgiving iniquities is like healing diseases. Sin is often regarded as a disease of the soul or spiritual sickness. Although this is true, it is equally probable that David is referring to healing of physical ailment.

The Lord promised to heal Israel's diseases (Exodus 15:26); Christ healed people who were spiritually sick (Luke 5:31), physically sick, or a combination of both (Matthew 9:2, 6). No matter how healing is effected (through a doctor, medication, prayer, or miracle), all healing is of God.

The next blessing in David's list is redemption. The word redeem (Heb. *ga'al*, **gaw-AHL**) means "to deliver, to save or to ransom from danger or bondage." The word "destruction" (Heb. *shachath*, **SHAH-khath**) is also rendered corruption, pit, or grave (Psalm 6:5; 16:10; 28:1). It depicts God rescuing someone from the pit of death or grave (Psalm 56:13). Here David recalls several times God delivered him from the hands of his enemies: from King Saul (1 Samuel 19) and from his own son Absalom (2 Samuel 15). This is also a reminder to the children of Israel of the Lord's act of deliverance from their bondage in Egypt.

Included in this catalogue of blessings is God's "lovingkindness and tender mercies" for humanity, described here as a crown. Among its other uses in the Old Testament, a crown symbolizes a bestowing of honor (Psalm 8:5; cf. 2 Kings 11:12; Psalm 65:11). Here David experiences God's love and compassion as an honor. The word for crowneth (Heb. *'atar*, **aw-TAR**) in other contexts means "to surround." The picture comes to mind of God surrounding us, honoring us, and beautifying us with His abundant lovingkindness and mercies.

Another reason David's soul ought to bless the Lord is because the Lord "satisfieth [his] mouth with good things; so that [his] youth is renewed like the eagle's." Here David refers to physical or tangible things. When one has enough, the degree of stress is reduced. Nothing weakens the body and ages one more than poverty and stress. As king, David was usually not short of worldly goods (2 Samuel 12:8; Psalm 23:1). The final clause refers to the Lord's act of strengthening and maintaining believers' youthfulness even in old age so they are able to soar like the eagle (Isaiah 40:31; cf. Psalm 92:12–14; 2 Corinthians 4:16–18).

6 The LORD executeth righteousness and judgment for all that are oppressed. 7 He made known his ways unto Moses, his acts unto the children of Israel.

After reflecting on his personal blessings and his praise to the Lord, David turns to communal or national praise (vv. 6–19). He recalls God's blessings and merciful dealings with His people, Israel. As a righteous and just God, the Lord executes "righteousness" (*tsedaqah*, **tsed-aw-KAW**), and "judgment" or justice (*mishpat*, **meesh-PAWT**) for the oppressed. He sees that the oppressed receive fair judgment from their oppressors. Israel was delivered from slavery in Egypt and experienced justice on several occasions on battlefields as the Lord rescued them from the hands of their oppressors.

African Americans were enslaved in the United States for almost two and a half centuries. However, injustice against African Americans is still alive and ongoing in many places today. A day is coming when God will complete His work of liberation and execute righteousness and judgment on our behalf.

Verse 7 recalls God's dealings with Israel. He manifested Himself to His People by His acts and His ways. He spoke to Moses directly and revealed His plans and the reasons for His actions (Exodus 33:13–14). As the Lord used Moses to rescue Israel from its oppressors, He uses Christ to liberate those who believe in Him from the bondage of sin and Satan. Christ shall finally deliver us on His return.

8 The LORD is merciful and gracious, slow to anger, and plenteous in mercy. 9 He will not always chide: neither will he keep his anger for ever. 10 He hath not dealt with us after our sins; nor rewarded us according to our iniquities. 11 For as the heaven is high above the earth, so great is his mercy toward them that fear him.

Verses 8–11 capture the essence of God's character of grace, mercy, and unfailing love toward humanity, the crown of His creation.

207

The Hebrew for the word "merciful" is *rachum* (**rah-KHOOM**), which means compassionate. The Hebrew translation for "gracious" is *channun* (**khan-NOON**), which comes from a root that means "to bend or stoop in kindness to an inferior; to favor." The Lord is full of all these traits. He is patient with His people; He restrains His anger. He does not always rebuke or chastise us (cf. Isaiah 57:16), nor does He pay us back according to our sins (Psalm 78:38–39). If He did, there would be no hope for sinful humanity. The psalmist presents us with a glimpse of the greatness of God's mercy. He compares it with the height of the heavens (cf. Psalm 57:10). Just as the distance between the heavens and the earth is great beyond our thoughts, so great and limitless is God's mercy toward His people—those who fear (love or reverence) Him. In spite of how sinful we are, God's forgiveness and mercy toward those who love Him is limitless and eternal.

12 As far as the east is from the west, So far has He removed our transgressions from us. 13 Like as a father pitieth his children, so the LORD pitieth them that fear him.

God's mercy is demonstrated in His forgiveness of our sins. In this psalm, David uses a directional metaphor to describe the extent of God's forgiveness—the distance between east and west. They are opposites, the implication is that our sin is the complete opposite of our place in God. That's how far our sins have been removed. There is no end to His forgiveness; it never ends.

Using a parental metaphor, David demonstrates God's love, grace, and compassion for His people, playing on the affection a father has for his child. In the Bible, God is often compared with a father or a parent, a portrait that excellently depicts the concept of God's character. Teaching His disciples to pray, Jesus refers to God as "Our Father" (from Matthew 6:9), and again He compares how God cares for His people to the way a father cares for his son (7:9–11). A father is always ready to care for the child's needs and willing to forgive when the child does wrong or commits an offense.

This is a perfect portrait of God's love and compassion for us, His children. The father's response to the prodigal son accurately depicts the Lord's fatherly response to those who repentantly come to Him (Luke 15:22–24). No matter how sinful we are, God's grace never wears out; nothing we do can alter God's loving grace and mercy for those who fear Him. This is the kind of God we worship and who should be praised.

14 For he knoweth our frame; he remembereth that we are dust. 15 As for man, his days are as grass: as a flower of the field, so he flourisheth. 16 For the wind passeth over it, and it is gone; and the place thereof shall know it no more. 17 But the mercy of the LORD is from everlasting to everlasting upon them that fear him, and his righteousness unto children's children.

The Lord shows us mercy because of our relationship with Him and because of our weak and feeble makeup. David declares, "For He knoweth our frame..." The word "frame" is the Hebrew *yetser* (**YAY-tsehr**), from its verb *yatsar* (**yaw-TSAR**), which means to shape or work into a form, and is used several times in pottery analogies. God is often portrayed as the potter and humanity as the clay (Isaiah 45:9; 64:8; Jeremiah 18:6). As our Creator, the Lord knows us well: He knows what we are made of because He made us. As our designer, the Lord remembers and does not forget our framework. He created us out the dust (Genesis 2:7; 3:19). He knows how frail we are and how easily we can crumble and disintegrate.

The psalmist applies agrarian and horticultural motifs to describe the brevity of our lifespan and the temporal nature of humanity on earth. David compares us to the grass or the flower that quickly grows up and blossoms but easily fades and is blown away by the wind and is gone (cf. Psalm 90:5–9; Isaiah 40:6–8). Because God is aware of our makeup, our weak and feeble nature, and the shortness of our lives, He deals gently with us, and extends His love, mercy, and compassion to us.

David says that God's mercy is "from everlasting to everlasting." That means that God's love, His mercy and grace toward humanity, have their foundation in eternity—even before the foundation of the earth and lasting beyond the end of the earth. God's mercy has no beginning and it has no ending—it has ever been and will ever be. These blessings, the psalmist says, are for those who fear Him and for their posterity; from generation to generation (see Exodus 20:6; Acts 2:39).

21 Bless ye the LORD, all ye his hosts; ye ministers of his, that do his pleasure. 22 Bless the LORD, all his works in all places of his dominion: bless the LORD, O my soul.

David begins this psalm with a personal call to praise the Lord. He recounts the benefits he has received that make it imperative for him to bless the Lord. He then stirs up a national praise and urges the entire world, especially the nation of Israel, to praise. He instructs all created beings to join in the praise of the Lord. All the powerful and obedient angels who listen and obey the Lord (v. 20), the heavenly armies, and all the ministers that serve the Lord and do His will (v. 21) should join in praising the Lord. That means all angels in all their ranks and duties should continue to praise the Lord.

The psalmist concludes with a call to all God's creation everywhere to praise and bless the Lord. No creation, animate or inanimate, is exempt from praising the Lord (cf. Psalm 148). Finally, David ends the psalm the way he started by calling on his soul to praise the Lord. As part of God's creation, the psalmist again reminds himself to join other creatures in singing praises in worship to the Lord.

When we remember who God is, we will have no reason not to praise the Lord. Try to grasp the magnitude of what He has done and does for us: His love, compassion, mercy and grace, forgiveness, and salvation. Everything we have would not even be enough to praise Him. We need to heed the psalmist's call here to show our love to God by praising and giving Him thanks with all that is within us at all times and in all circumstances.

Sources:
Clarke, Adam. *Commentary on the Bible by Adam Clarke: Psalms: Psalms Chapter 103.* Internet Sacred Text Archive Home, http://www.sacred-texts.com/bib/cmt/clarke/psa103.htm
Barnes, Albert. *Notes on the Old Testament: Psalms.* Baker Book House, 2005
Jamieson, Fausset, and Brown. *Commentary Critical and Explanatory on the Whole Bible.* Public Domain. London, England, 1871.
Wiersbe, Warren W. *The Bible Exposition Commentary: Old Testament (The Pentateuch).* Colorado Springs, CO: Cook Communications Ministries International, 2004.
Kohlenberger, John R. III, *NIV Exhaustive Bible Concordance, Third Edition - a Better Strongs Bible Concordance.* Grand Rapids, MI: Zondervan Publishing House, 2005.

Daily Bible Readings

MONDAY
Nothing Separates us from
God's Love
(Romans 8:31–39)

TUESDAY
An Answer in Time of
Trouble
(Psalm 86:1–7)

WEDNESDAY
Let Me Walk in Your Truth
(Psalm 86:8–13)

THURSDAY
Acts of God's Steadfast Love
(Nehemiah 9:16–21)

FRIDAY
God Abounds in Steadfast
Love
(Exodus 34:1–7)

SATURDAY
God Forgives and Loves
People
(Numbers 14:13–20)

SUNDAY
The People Bless the Lord
(Psalm 103:1–17, 21–22)

Notes

_____

_____

_____

_____

_____

_____

_____

_____

_____

Teaching Tips

Words You Should Know

A. Espoused *mnesteuo* (Gk.)—Engaged or promised to marriage.

B. Consolation *paraklesis* (Gk.)—Comfort and encouragement.

Teacher Preparation

Unifying Princple—God is a Promise Keeper. Some people wait a long time for a promise to be kept. What assurance do we have that God's promise of salvation will be kept? God's angel spoke to Mary, and the Holy Spirit spoke through Simeon, to declare that in Jesus God was sending a Savior and keeping the promise.

A. Read the Bible Background and Devotional Readings.

B. Pray for your students and lesson clarity.

C. Read the lesson Scripture in multiple translations.

D. Option: Let students share testimonies about the significance of Christ's birth to their faith.

O—Open the Lesson

A. Begin the class with prayer.

B. Have the students read the Aim for Change

C. Have the students read the In Focus story.

D. Ask students how events named in the story can weigh on their hearts and how they can view these events from a theological perspective.

P—Present the Scriptures

A. Read the Focal Verses and discuss the Background and The People, Places, and Times sections.

B. Have the class share what Scriptures stand out for them and why, with particular emphasis on today's context.

E—Explore the Meaning

A. Use In Depth or More Light on the Text to help provide deeper discussion of the lesson text.

B. Discuss the Liberating Lesson and Application for Activation sections.

N—Next Steps for Application

A. Summarize the value of knowing that God has kept His promise to bring salvation through Jesus Christ.

B. End class with a commitment to remember salvation and other promises God has kept to us through Jesus Christ.

Worship Guide

For the Superintendent or Teacher
Theme: Jesus: God's Loving Promise
Song: "O Come, O Come, Emmanuel"
Devotional Reading: Isaiah 49:1–7

Jesus: God's Loving Promise

Bible Background • LUKE 1:26–31; 2:21–35
Printed Text • LUKE 1:26–31; 2:22, 25–35 | Devotional Reading • ISAIAH 49:1–7

Aim for Change

By the end of the lesson, we will: REMEMBER God's words of affirmation and comfort to Mary; CONSIDER the love and sovereignty of God revealed in Jesus' birth; and SHARE testimonies of how Christ's birth impacts our faith.

In Focus

Grandpa James beamed as his grandson Reggie strode up the walkway. No, it's Reginald these days, he reminded himself. "Reggie" was the little kid he took to the circus, not the grown man before him wearing the uniform of the U.S. Marine Corps—complete with a chestful of medals and ribbons, and a major's gold leaf on his shoulders.

Reginald called, "Grandpa!" and matched his grandfather's wide smile with a happy grin of his own. Right behind him were his mother Regina and father Dwayne.

"I never thought I'd see the day when you came back to us," Grandpa James said. Reginald's postings during his years in service had taken him all over the globe, from South Carolina to Afghanistan, and more. But after 10 years in, Reginald was back home. Over lunch, the family discussed the circumstances that had prompted Reginald to retire in order to run the family business: Grandpa James' stroke and limited recovery. "I have to caution you: It won't be easy," James said.

"I can handle it, Grandpa," Reginald said.

"I know that, boy, but I'm worried about them," James said, pointing at Dwayne and Regina. "They're going to be anxious about you, because you're young; and people will criticize, complain, and try to undermine you. But I have faith in God you'll do well."

Have you ever had someone in your life who believed you would succeed and supported you unconditionally?

Keep in Mind

"For mine eyes have seen thy salvation, Which thou hast prepared before the face of all people" (Luke 2:30–31, KJV).

"I have seen your salvation, which you have prepared for all people" (Luke 2:30–31, NLT).

Focal Verses

KJV **Luke 1:26** And in the sixth month the angel Gabriel was sent from God unto a city of Galilee, named Nazareth,

27 To a virgin espoused to a man whose name was Joseph, of the house of David; and the virgin's name was Mary.

28 And the angel came in unto her, and said, Hail, thou that art highly favoured, the Lord is with thee: blessed art thou among women.

29 And when she saw him, she was troubled at his saying, and cast in her mind what manner of salutation this should be.

30 And the angel said unto her, Fear not, Mary: for thou hast found favour with God.

31 And, behold, thou shalt conceive in thy womb, and bring forth a son, and shalt call his name JESUS.

2:22 And when the days of her purification according to the law of Moses were accomplished, they brought him to Jerusalem, to present him to the Lord;

25 And, behold, there was a man in Jerusalem, whose name was Simeon; and the same man was just and devout, waiting for the consolation of Israel: and the Holy Ghost was upon him.

26 And it was revealed unto him by the Holy Ghost, that he should not see death, before he had seen the Lord's Christ.

27 And he came by the Spirit into the temple: and when the parents brought in the child Jesus, to do for him after the custom of the law,

28 Then took he him up in his arms, and blessed God, and said,

29 Lord, now lettest thou thy servant depart in peace, according to thy word:

30 For mine eyes have seen thy salvation,

31 Which thou hast prepared before the face of all people;

32 A light to lighten the Gentiles, and the glory of thy people Israel.

NLT **Luke 1:26** In the sixth month of Elizabeth's pregnancy, God sent the angel Gabriel to Nazareth, a village in Galilee,

27 to a virgin named Mary. She was engaged to be married to a man named Joseph, a descendant of King David.

28 Gabriel appeared to her and said, "Greetings, favored woman! The Lord is with you!"

29 Confused and disturbed, Mary tried to think what the angel could mean.

30 "Don't be afraid, Mary," the angel told her, "for you have found favor with God!

31 You will conceive and give birth to a son, and you will name him Jesus.

2:22 Then it was time for their purification offering, as required by the law of Moses after the birth of a child; so his parents took him to Jerusalem to present him to the Lord.

25 At that time there was a man in Jerusalem named Simeon. He was righteous and devout and was eagerly waiting for the Messiah to come and rescue Israel. The Holy Spirit was upon him

26 and had revealed to him that he would not die until he had seen the Lord's Messiah.

27 That day the Spirit led him to the Temple. So when Mary and Joseph came to present the baby Jesus to the Lord as the law required,

28 Simeon was there. He took the child in his arms and praised God, saying,

29 "Sovereign Lord, now let your servant die in peace, as you have promised.

30 I have seen your salvation,

31 which you have prepared for all people.

32 He is a light to reveal God to the nations, and he is the glory of your people Israel!"

33 Jesus' parents were amazed at what was being said about him.

34 Then Simeon blessed them, and he said to Mary, the baby's mother, "This child is

33 And Joseph and his mother marvelled at those things which were spoken of him.

34 And Simeon blessed them, and said unto Mary his mother, Behold, this child is set for the fall and rising again of many in Israel; and for a sign which shall be spoken against;

35 (Yea, a sword shall pierce through thy own soul also,) that the thoughts of many hearts may be revealed.

destined to cause many in Israel to fall, and many others to rise. He has been sent as a sign from God, but many will oppose him.

35 As a result, the deepest thoughts of many hearts will be revealed. And a sword will pierce your very soul."

The People, Places, and Times

Nazareth. The name of a city meaning "branch." Nazareth only gained prominence after the ministry of Jesus. Located in lower Galilee, it lies halfway between the Sea of Galilee and the Mediterranean Sea. In Jesus' day, Nazareth was a small village with only one spring to supply fresh water to residents. Today that spring is known as Mary's well. Nazareth did not have a good reputation in Jesus' day, as reflected in Nathanael's question, "Can there any good thing come out of Nazareth?" (from John 1:46). Jesus was rejected by His townspeople and thrown out of the synagogue there (Luke 4:16–30; Matthew 13:54–58; Mark 6:1–6).

Firstborn. Jewish families had to adhere to strict ceremonies after the birth of a child. If the child was a male, he had to be circumcised and named on the eighth day. God made a covenant with Abraham and commanded that, as a sign of the covenant, every male should be circumcised (Genesis 17:10–14). This included slaves and foreigners before they could become Jewish citizens or take part in Passover. Moses clarified that circumcision was a legal requirement (Leviticus 12:3).

Firstborn children had to be redeemed when they turned one month old. In memory of the death of Egypt's firstborn and the preservation of the firstborn of Israel, all the firstborn of

Israel belonged to God (Exodus 13:2, 11–16). An offering of five shekels was given to the priest to redeem the child from God (Numbers 18:15–16).

Background

Luke strongly affirmed that Jesus was Israel's long-awaited Messiah, King and Deliverer. Christ was the fulfillment of God's promise to His people to send a Savior. The first part of Luke's Gospel is devoted to divinely orchestrated events that lead to the birth of the Messiah. Previous verses in Luke 1 tell how the angel Gabriel spoke to Zacharias and told him that his wife was going to bear him a son; the son would became known as John the Baptist. In the sixth month of Elizabeth's pregnancy, Gabriel appeared to her relative, Mary. Mary and Joseph were faithful Jews who adhered to the requirements of the Law. They had Jesus circumcised on the same day that he was named, as John the Baptist's parents had done (1:59). They followed the angel's instructions and named the child Jesus (v. 31). Luke described Mary in such a way as to elevate two ideas: first, that she was still a virgin; second, that she was espoused, or engaged, to Joseph. Engagement in those days was a much more serious affair than it has become. According to the type of engagement Joseph and Mary had, she was already considered his legal wife.

A period of time normally elapsed between the espousal and the actual celebration of the marriage, when the couple would begin to live together.

At-A-Glance

1. Testimony of God's Favor
(Luke 1:26–31)
2. Testimony of God's Faithfulness
(Luke 2:22, 25–28)
3. Testimony of God's Fulfillment
(vv. 29–32)
4. Testimony of Prophecy (vv. 33–35)

In Depth

1. Testimony of God's Favor (Luke 1:26–31)

Gabriel addressed Mary as "thou that are highly favored," indicating that the Lord had a special purpose for her. Understandably, the sight of Gabriel and the words he was saying were a lot for a young woman to absorb. Mary was trying to figure out what Gabriel was talking about. As much as being afraid, she was probably overwhelmed.

Sensing Mary's fear, Gabriel assured her not to be afraid. She was not in trouble with the Lord. On the contrary, she had found favor with God. She was about to conceive and give birth to a son. Gabriel even told her the son's name would be Jesus. The name Jesus is the Greek equivalent of the Hebrew word "Joshua," meaning "the Lord is salvation." The boy to whom Mary would give birth would bring salvation to the world. Undoubtedly, every mother believes she has given birth to a wonderful person. Gabriel wanted Mary to understand the full extent of what she was about to experience. Her son would be called many names, including Son of the Highest.

What importance has your given or adopted name had in your life?

2. Testimony of God's Faithfulness (Luke 2:22, 25–28)

Joseph and Mary took Jesus to the Temple in Jerusalem to be ceremonially dedicated to the Lord as was required for all firstborn sons in Israel according to Jewish Law. Joseph and Mary's encounter with Simeon did not happen by accident. God fulfilled His promise to Simeon by allowing him to be in the Temple at just the right moment. He was able to gaze upon the consolation of Israel: the Messiah. Rabbis commonly used the phrase "consolation of Israel" to mean the fulfillment of Jewish messianic hopes. Like Zacharias and Elisabeth, Simeon was devout in morality and faith. The Holy Ghost had revealed to him that he would not die until he had seen the Messiah. Simeon's desire was to witness the fulfillment of God's promise for His people.

There was also a law requiring the redemption of the firstborn child (Exodus 13:2, 12–16). Because God had spared the firstborn of Israel during the tenth plague in Egypt (Exodus 12:12–13), He required that Israel's firstborn be dedicated to Him. Later the Lord allowed the tribe of Levi to become a substitute for the firstborn (Numbers 3:11–13). Joseph and Mary's observance of this ritual at the time of Jesus' birth symbolized their commitment to the Lord. Keeping the ritual was an act of worship in obedience to God, recognizing that children, like everything else, come from God and belong to Him. The redemption price for male children was five shekels of silver (Numbers 18:16). This requirement was to be fulfilled when the child was a month old. Apparently, Joseph and Mary fulfilled the two requirements at the same time.

Exactly where Simeon met them in the Temple is not known. Since Mary was present, they were either in the Court of Gentiles or the Court of Women. It must have been the most magnificent feeling Simeon had ever known, to hold the baby Jesus in his arms. Simeon identified Jesus as the embodiment of God's salvation. Seeing the promise of the Lord as a living being and holding the babe of promise in his arms moved Simeon to bless God before singing a song of praise.

How does Simeon's role in the Gospel demonstrate the sovereignty of God?

3. Testimony of God's Fulfillment (Luke 2:29–32)

The song of Simeon's praise begins in verse 29. This song is now known as the "Nunc Dimittis," which are the first two words of the Latin translation. Simeon was now ready to die, having witnessed the fulfillment of God's promise, knowing that the salvation of his people had come to earth. He was faithful to God's Word and to the law of Judaism. His song contained not only praise but a prophetic aspect. By recognizing that Jesus was the fulfillment of God's promise, Simeon then took on the attitude that would have been fitting for all of Israel. While Jesus was yet a babe in his arms, the Jewish prophet foresaw that salvation was intended for all of humanity.

Two thousand years ago, Simeon prophesied that Jesus was sufficient for all—Jew and Gentile alike. The Gospel is not reserved for a select few, as some would have it. Simeon and those who lived during Jesus' day had the privilege of seeing salvation in the flesh. Today we see salvation through the eyes of faith as we invite others to join us. Even though He is no longer with us in the flesh, we too can marvel at the hope that lies in Him, just as Simeon did that day in the Temple.

How do you respond when you finally receive something you have long awaited?

4. Testimony of Prophecy (vv. 33–35)

Understandably Joseph and Mary were amazed at what was said about Jesus.

Simeon foretold the great and powerful effect Mary's Son would have upon the world. The presence of her Son would divide the nation. Those who rejected Him would fall, but those who received Him would be lifted up. The Messiah would do away with the proud and lift up the downtrodden and oppressed.

The baby, who was totally dependent on them at that moment, had the future of the world in His hands. Joseph and Mary would have to continue to trust in Him to lead and guide them as they raised and nurtured the child who already held the name Savior.

How does the birth of Jesus push us to make a choice between acknowledging or rejecting God?

Search the Scriptures

1. How did Mary react to Gabriel's words (Luke 1:29)?

2. What words did Simeon say to indicate that Jesus was the Savior for all people (2:32)?

3. What difficult prophecy did Simeon give Mary concerning her own fate (v. 35)?

Discuss the Meaning

1. Mary was troubled and confused when the angel Gabriel visited her until he assured her that she was favored by God. How can such assurance give you the confidence to fulfill God's will?

2. Simeon faithfully waited to meet the Messiah before he died, not knowing how the wait would be. Can we be so patient?

Liberating Lesson

It can be easy to take for granted the tremendous blessings we have compared to our elders and ancestors. Much of what we now enjoy in our lives are things for which our parents, grandparents, and ancestors hoped, dreamed, prayed, and worked. How can we share the gifts, accomplishments, and blessings we have with those in the generation before us who have long waited to see what we have ever day? How can we share those blessings with the generation that comes after us, allowing them to enjoy the things for which we prayed and worked?

Application for Activation

It seems like we wait a long time to see some of God's promises in our lives. When they arrive, it can be challenging to give back to God or accept the responsibility that comes with the promised thing. Whether a promotion, a relationship, a home, a healing, or a breakthrough, how can we make sure to give it back to God for God's glory? Take some time to write down what you have asked for and received from God and how it is being used to bring Him glory. What are you waiting on from God now? Ask God for wisdom to use your blessings to glorify Him and love others.

Follow the Spirit

What God wants me to do:

_____

_____

_____

_____

Remember Your Thoughts

Special insights I have learned:

_____

_____

_____

_____

More Light on the Text

Luke 1:26–31; 2:22, 25–35

Luke, the physician, begins the book that bears his name with a preface stating the purpose of his writing and to whom he is writing the Gospel (1:1–4). He begins the historical narration with the story of John the Baptist's birth—from the angel's announcement to his father, Zacharias, until the sixth month of Elizabeth's pregnancy (1:5–25). Luke then turns to the angel Gabriel's announcement to Mary of the conception and consequent incarnation of Christ, and Mary's reaction to this unusual news (vv. 26–38).

1:26 And in the sixth month the angel Gabriel was sent from God unto a city of Galilee, named Nazareth, 27 To a virgin espoused to a man whose name was Joseph, of the house of David; and the virgin's name was Mary.

It has been six months since Gabriel told Zacharias he would have a son. The angel's mission is to announce the coming birth of yet another son.

Gabriel, which means "my warrior is God," is one of the chief angels. He is sent "to a virgin espoused to a man." The word translated "espoused" (Gk. *mnesteuo*, **muh-nace-TEW-oh**) means to be promised in marriage or to be betrothed. Betrothing in the Jewish custom was the most important part of marriage. It was as legal as the actual marriage; and could not be broken off except by a bill of divorce. Although the couple was regarded as husband and wife, they did not engage sexually until the actual marriage took place according to the custom. Girls were usually espoused only a few years after the age of puberty, i.e., in their early teens. Usually the parents of the adolescent chose the spouse for their child.

This Jewish custom is comparable with many African marriages, where not only do the parents arrange or negotiate for their sons or daughters' marriages, they also arrange for their betrothal at infancy. Traditionally, in most communities in the Igbo land of Nigeria, families betroth their children at birth. When a boy is born, the father starts planning for his wife to be. He looks for a good family, preferably among family friends, in which a girl is born. He places a token (engagement present) into the cup of the newborn girl. This signifies a promise of marriage between the two.

This act is usually binding and honored by the two families. The children are introduced to each other at a very young age and told they have been betrothed to marry. Although they are regarded as husband and wife, they cannot have sex until they are officially married. They are to keep themselves pure and reserved for each other. The girl lives with her parents until after the actual marriage ceremonies are completed. She then goes and lives with the husband. This is the idea expressed here by Luke.

The angel goes to the village of Nazareth, and approaches a virgin engaged to a man named Joseph. The virgin's name is Mary. Luke refers to Joseph as "of the house of David," and Matthew's genealogical account traces Joseph's lineage also to King David. This is in fulfillment of the messianic prophecy that the Messiah will be from the lineage of David (Psalm 132:11, 17; Isaiah 9:6–7, 16:5; cf. Luke 1:32).

28 And the angel came in unto her, and said, Hail, thou that art highly favoured, the Lord is with thee: blessed art thou among women.

"Hail" here is the Greek *chairo* (**KIE-ro**) a common form of greeting, used in various ways and on various occasions. "Highly favoured" is derived from the noun *charis*, which means grace, usually interpreted as unmerited favor from God. *Charis*, "grace" with "peace" (Gk. **eye-REE-nee**) was a form of Jewish greeting,

and was used also in ancient correspondence. Here the angel says both *chairo* and *charis*, probably to reflect both the Jewish and Greek culture of the time.

Next the angel adds "the Lord is with you." Mary is not only endued with divine grace or God's favor; the angel assures her of the Lord's presence with her. Finally, the angel adds, "Blessed art thou among women." The idea here is that above all women, Mary was the most "blessed" (Gk. *eulogeo*, **ew-lo-GEH-oh**). The word means to praise, to speak well of, or to invoke a benediction upon someone. It also has the idea of making happy or bestowing blessings. Because of what God is going to accomplish through her, Mary would either be the most well spoken of among all women, the most blessed, or both.

29 And when she saw him, she was troubled at his saying, and cast in her mind what manner of salutation this should be. 30 And the angel said unto her, Fear not, Mary: for thou hast found favour with God.

The word "troubled" (Gk. *diatarasso*, **dee-ah-ta-RASS-so**) means to disturb wholly or to be greatly agitated or alarmed. She was gripped with fear. Earlier, when Zacharias saw the angel, "he was troubled," (Gk. *tarasso*, **ta-RASS-so**), which means the same as *diatarasso* but to a lesser extent (v. 12). Both of these imply inner commotion.

Mary was more perplexed at the angel's greeting than the angel's appearance. She "cast in her mind," (Gk. *dialogizomai*, **dee-ah-low-GEED-zow-my**), simply means that she pondered the type of greeting it was. She was more afraid and agitated than surprised at the strange greeting. That's why the angel calms her and tells her not to fear, assuring her that she has found favor with God.

31 And, behold, thou shalt conceive in thy womb, and bring forth a son, and shalt call his name JESUS.

The angel goes on to explain why and how she has found favor with God, that she has been chosen by God to bear a son: Jesus. Mary is to be the agent through whom God fulfills His divine plan. Notice the wording here is identical to the virgin birth passage of Isaiah (7:14), and reminiscent of the Lord's assurance to Hagar (Genesis 16:11). She would "bring forth" (bear) a son whom they would name Jesus. The name Jesus (*Iesous*, **ee-ay-SOOCE**) is the Greek equivalent of the Hebrew Joshua (*Yehoshua*), which means "Yahweh is salvation." It is the earthly name of God's Son. It describes the purpose of His birth—to deliver and save the people of God from their sins (Matthew 1:21). The name also means "deliverer." The name Jesus/Joshua, was common among the Jews, perhaps because they yearned for their son to be the promised Messiah, or at least a great leader like Joshua of the Old Testament.

This practice is common among Africans. In many cases, names reflect the parents' wishes for the children. However, choosing the name "Jesus" for Mary's son was a direct command from God, and it described distinctly the purpose of Christ as the real Redeemer, the one Israel had been expecting.

2:22 And when the days of her purification according to the law of Moses were accomplished, they brought him to Jerusalem, to present him to the Lord.

25 And, behold, there was a man in Jerusalem, whose name was Simeon; and the same man was just and devout, waiting for the consolation of Israel: and the Holy Ghost was upon him. 26 And it was revealed unto him by the Holy Ghost, that he should not see death, before he had seen the Lord's Christ.

Luke 2:21–38 is a narrative of the purification ceremony of Mary and Jesus according to the Jewish custom. Luke explains an extraordinary event, which is unique to Jesus—the confirmation of the mission of Christ through prophecy. Here Luke introduces us to Simeon whom he describes as "just and devout," a man "waiting for the consolation of Israel." We know nothing about Simeon outside of this brief narrative. However, he must be a devout Jew who is expecting the coming of the Messiah.

At the time of Christ' birth, religion in Israel was at a low point. Yet in the midst of the religious vacuum was a man Luke describes as "just and devout," a man who "the Holy Ghost was upon." The word "just" (Gk. *dikaios*, **DEE-kie-oce**) is equivalent to righteous. He not only observed the divine law but conformed to the will of God. Hence he is described as "devout" (Gk. *eulabes*, **ew-lah-BASE**), a pious man, one who is devoted to and who reveres God (see Luke 1:6; cf. Philippians 3:6).

Simeon was among the few pious men expecting the coming of the Lord Jesus, which Luke called the "consolation of Israel." The noun "consolation," (Gk. *paraklesis*, **pah-RAH-klay-seese**)—comfort, exhortation, or encouragement—describes the coming ministry of Christ. *Paraklesis* is related to the word Comforter (*parakletos*) applied to the Holy Spirit especially in John's Gospel (John 14:16, 26; 15:26; 16:7). Here, the coming of Christ was to be a comfort for the people of Israel, who at this time were under the rule of the Roman Empire. Israel had been promised a deliverer and a counselor, one who would restore to Israel the Davidic kingdom (Isaiah 9:6–7). The word "waiting" (Gk. *prosdechomai*, **pros-DEH-kho-my**) implies doing so patiently and with confidence. Simeon was waiting confidently and patiently for the fulfillment of the Lord's

220

promise of the Messiah. His confidence lay in his relationship with God and in his trust in the God of Israel who is faithful in keeping His promises.

Moreover, the Holy Spirit had assured him that he would not die until he saw the Lord's Christ (Messiah). The word "revealed" (Gk. *chrematizo*, **khray-mah-TEED-zo**) used here is often used for divine communication. Here Simeon had been told through the Holy Spirit that he would see the Messiah in his lifetime.

Luke does not give details about Simeon's age, status, or background except to say he was full of the Holy Spirit. If he were a priest, Luke likely would have made that clear in his narrative as in the case of Zacharias (cf. 1:5). Unlike the prophetess Anna, whose age is hinted at (vv. 36–38), Luke does not share Simeon's age.

27 And he came by the Spirit into the temple: and when the parents brought in the child Jesus, to do for him after the custom of the law, 28 Then took he him up in his arms, and blessed God, and said,

It was a requirement for Jewish worshipers to routinely go into the Temple to pray. As a devout Jew, Simeon, therefore, must have formed the habit. On this special occasion, however, "he came by the Spirit into the temple" and met with Mary and Joseph with Jesus as they came to fulfill their Jewish rites. The language here seems to indicate that the meeting was neither prearranged nor was it a coincidence. Rather it was divinely planned with providential timing. He came by the Spirit, which means that he was led by the Holy Spirit into the Temple in order to fulfill the promise of verse 26. One function of the Holy Spirit is to lead God's people.

While Simeon was in the Temple, Mary and Joseph brought Jesus to perform the Jewish ritual of dedicating the firstborn. Through divine revelation, Simeon was informed that this child was the long-awaited Messiah.

Simeon takes Jesus "up in his arms"—a common practice in the Jewish tradition (Mark 10:13–16)—and blesses God. We transliterate the Greek word *eulogeo* to the English word eulogy or to eulogize. During funerals, when we speak well of, or praise, people for what they have done for others or achieved in life, we eulogize them. Here Simeon is praising God, which includes a thanksgiving for God's faithfulness in fulfilling His promise not only to Israel but to him personally.

29 Lord, now lettest thou thy servant depart in peace, according to thy word: 30 For mine eyes have seen thy salvation,

Simeon begins his eulogy to God by expressing his gratitude for being allowed to see the Messiah in fulfillment of God's promise (v. 26). The underlying tone here is of satisfaction for a task accomplished. Now that the Messiah has arrived, Simeon seems to say that the Lord should let him go. With Jesus in his arms, Simeon has seen the promised "Star out of Jacob" (Numbers 24:17), the "Sun of righteousness" (Malachi 4:2). He has beheld the redemption of God in the person of Christ Jesus. Now the watch is over. He is now to be discharged according to God's word. Note the contrast between God the "Lord" and Simeon "the servant." The word "peace" (Gk. *eirene*, **eye-REE-nee**) used here has the sense of tranquility or rest and contentment.

After seeing God's promised salvation, Simeon is ready to depart peacefully into God's presence. Simeon does not say that he has seen the Messiah (although it is implied), but that he has seen God's salvation personified and embodied in Christ Jesus—the Messiah. To see Jesus is to see salvation, a theme Luke repeatedly emphasizes in his book (1:69, 71, 77; 19:9).

31 Which thou hast prepared before the face of all people; 32 A light to lighten the Gentiles, and the glory of thy people Israel.

Contrary to the expectation and belief of the Jewish religion that the Messiah was to come only for the people of Israel, salvation is universal in scope. The phrase "before the face of all people" supports this fact. God's plan of salvation is not only available to the few pious people, or to the nation of Israel, but to all people of the earth because His love is universal (John 3:16). Verse 31 echoes the prophecy of Isaiah (52:10) and the psalmist's song which says "all the ends of the earth have seen the salvation of our God" (from Psalm 98:3).

There are dual functions of this salvation. First, it will dissipate the spiritual darkness that has enveloped the Gentiles for centuries. The darkness represents ignorance, sin, and misery; it is a symbol of death and disobedience. In place of the darkness, redemption will bring light—a symbol of life, growth, knowledge, and obedience—to the nations.

Second, salvation will bring glory to the nation of Israel. That means nations will realize the glorious special privilege Israel has enjoyed in its relationship with God through the ages, a privilege now consummated and perfected in the birth and person of Christ Jesus. Here, we see that the same light that brings revelation to the Gentiles (Isaiah 42:6; 49:6)—those who sit in darkness and in the shadow of death (Luke 1:79)—also brings salvation to Israel, God's people (1:77).

33 And Joseph and his mother marveled at those things which were spoken of him. 34 And Simeon blessed them, and said unto Mary his mother, Behold, this child is set for the fall and rising again of many in Israel; and for a sign which shall be spoken against;

Mary and Joseph knew through the announcement of the angel Gabriel (1:26–38; Matthew 1:20–21), that their child was the Christ—the expected Messiah. This destiny was confirmed by the supernatural conception, by the words of Elizabeth (1:41–45), and by the words of the shepherds (2:15–19). Still they could not fully comprehend the significance of it all. They were amazed and overwhelmed at the words of Simeon. The word "marveled" (Gk. *thaumazo*, **thou-MAD-zo**) used here is not expressing doubt but excitement. It means "to admire, to have in admiration, or to wonder."

After that, Simeon blessed them all. Simeon then addressed Mary, predicting the effect Christ's birth will have on the nation of Israel, and on her. Notice that Simeon now addresses Mary alone. The reason is clear. Joseph did not father Jesus in the natural sense of the word. Joseph can be described as a stepfather. It is apparent that Simeon is aware of this unique situation. Apart from this meeting with Simeon, the visit to the Temple when Jesus was twelve (vv. 42–48), and in the genealogy of Christ (3:23), there is only one other mention of Joseph in the rest of Luke (Luke 4:22).

Luke uses the emphatic Greek word *idou* (**ee-DOO**), translated "behold" here, to call attention to important information. Simeon informs Mary that the "Child is set for the fall and rising of many in Israel." Simply stated, this means the presence of Christ will be a curse for those who reject Him but a blessing for those who accept Him. The prophet Isaiah says, concerning the Messiah, "And he shall be for a sanctuary; but for a stone of stumbling and for a rock of offence to both the houses of Israel, for a gin and for a snare to the inhabitants of Jerusalem. And many among them shall stumble, and fall, and be broken, and be snared, and be taken." (Isaiah 8:14–15; cf., Matthew 21:42–44; Acts 4:11; Romans 9:33; 1 Corinthians 1:23). Simeon says that Jesus, on the one hand, will be a stone on which some will trip, fall, and perish; on the other hand, He will be a stepping-stone that will enable others to arise and be saved.

Not only that. Christ will also be a means by which those who have fallen will be able rise "again." The idea here is that He will be the means of salvation for sinners, or those who first reject Him and later repent. They would rise again into new life; their relationship with God would be restored. The phrase also speaks of those who fall because of Him "rising again," referring to the resurrection of the saints—the raising of the dead in Christ into eternal life. Either one is theologically sound. There is no neutrality, Simeon seems to point out. Either He is rejected, which results in a downfall, or He is received, which results in a rising again.

Simeon adds that Jesus is also set "for a sign, which shall be spoken against." The birth, death, and the person of Christ have been the basis for untold controversies among many throughout the generations. Christ always has been the object of hostility among unbelievers. He was rejected to the point of crucifixion. From the beginning, many rejected and persecuted Him, and many have spoken against Him, rejecting God's salvation.

35 (Yea, a sword shall pierce through thy own soul also,) that the thoughts of many hearts may be revealed.

Simeon foretells the anguish that Mary will experience because of the Christ. It will be a heart-piercing sorrow—as sharp and painful as the sword. He describes the extreme anguish Mary will undergo seeing her Son suffer. This was fulfilled at the Cross when she stood watching her son die (John 19:26).

Through Christ, His life, death, and resurrection, "the thoughts of many hearts will be revealed." The Gospel brings light to the inner being of all humanity and exposes their character and attitude toward God and His Christ. The Gospel of John describes Jesus as a light that shines in the darkness (1:5) and gives light to everyone in the world (1:9). Later in the same Gospel, Jesus calls Himself the "light of the world" (8:12; 9:5; 12:35).

Sources:
Butler, Trent, ed. *Holman Bible Dictionary*. Nashville, TN: Broadman & Holman Publishers, 1991. 1010–1011.

Daily Bible Readings

MONDAY
The Birth of John Promised
(Luke 1:11–16)

TUESDAY
The Lord Was with John
(Luke 1:57–66)

WEDNESDAY
Let It Be According to Your
Word
(Luke 1:32–38)

THURSDAY
Joseph Obeys the Lord
(Matthew 1:18–25)

FRIDAY
Anna Speaks of Child Jesus
(Luke 2:36–38)

SATURDAY
Angels Announce Good
News to Shepherds
(Luke 2:8–14)

SUNDAY
Testimonies to the
Promised Savior
(Luke 1:26–31; 2:22, 25–35)

Teaching Tips

Words You Should Know

A. Brethren *adelphoi* (Gk.)—Brothers and sisters, family members.

B. Possess *kleronomeo* (Gk.)—To inherit or take authority over.

Teacher Preparation

Unifying Principle—Care for the Least of These. Responsible people are pulled in many directions in trying to take care of themselves and their families. Why then would one extend that effort to even more people? Jesus teaches His disciples that loving acts to the forsaken and needy are really demonstrations of love to Him.

A. Read the Bible Background and Devotional Readings.

B. Pray for your students and lesson clarity.

C. Read the lesson Scripture in multiple translations.

D. Option: Have the class act out a scene in which a believer helps a poor unbeliever who is unreceptive when the Gospel is shared. Pose these questions after the role-play is concluded: Do we help the poor because they need help, or do we help them only as a means of sharing Christ with them? Is there a third alternative?

O—Open the Lesson

A. Begin the class with prayer.

B. Have the students read the Aim for Change.

C. Have the students read the In Focus story.

D. Ask students how events named in the story can weigh on their hearts and how they can view these events from a theological perspective.

P—Present the Scriptures

A. Read the Focal Verses and discuss the Background and The People, Places, and Times sections.

B. Have the class share what Scriptures stand out for them and why, with particular emphasis on today's context.

E—Explore the Meaning

A. Use In Depth or More Light on the Text to help provide deeper discussion of the lesson text.

B. Discuss the Liberating Lesson and Application for Activation sections.

N—Next Steps for Application

A. Summarize the value of knowing we must care for those in need as part of loving Jesus Christ.

B. End class with a commitment to pray for the hungry, the thirsty, the sick, the imprisoned, and the lonely.

Worship Guide

For the Superintendent or Teacher
Theme: Modeling God's Love
Song: "We Must Go"
Devotional Reading: James 2:14-26

Modeling God's Love

Bible Background • MATTHEW 25:31–46
Printed Text • MATTHEW 25:31–46 | Devotional Reading • JAMES 2:14–26

————————— Aim for Change —————————

By the end of the lesson, we will: ANALYZE the parable of the sheep and the goats; AFFIRM the call to treat those in need as we would treat Christ; and ASSESS how to care for the poor and outcast in our own lives.

————————— 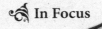 In Focus —————————

Mr. Whitelow and his son were doing their routine shopping. At checkout, they noticed an older gentleman and his son putting some items back because they didn't seem to have enough money to pay for them. Mr. Whitelow went over and discreetly told the cashier he would pay for their groceries. The cashier informed the gentleman that his groceries had been paid for and he didn't have to put anything back.

As Mr. Whitelow and his son were packing their groceries in the car, the older gentleman and his son came over and expressed their extreme appreciation for what they had done. The Whitelow's reply was simply, "Praise God! Praise God!"

Unbeknownst to the Whitelow's, their neighbor Greg had been watching. Greg came over after work the next day and asked Mr. Whitelow about what he had seen. He wanted to know if he knew the older gentleman and his son.

Mr. Whitelow told Greg that he didn't know them but that it was his responsibility, but, as a Christian, to help those in need.

Greg confessed that he had never helped a stranger, especially not one who had not asked for help. He said he felt guilty because he had never even considered helping someone in that way. Mr. Whitelow shared that helping others was an opportunity to serve Jesus.

In today's lesson, believers see positive consequences of merciful behavior and negative consequences of failing to live a righteous life. When have you helped the poor?

————————— **Keep in Mind** —————————

"And the King shall answer and say unto them, Verily I say unto you, Inasmuch as ye have done it unto one of the least of these my brethren, ye have done it unto me" (Matthew 25:40, KJV).

"And the King will say, 'I tell you the truth, when you did it to one of the least of these my brothers and sisters, you were doing it to me!'" (Matthew 25:40, NLT)

Focal Verses

KJV **Matthew 25:31** When the Son of man shall come in his glory, and all the holy angels with him, then shall he sit upon the throne of his glory:

32 And before him shall be gathered all nations: and he shall separate them one from another, as a shepherd divideth his sheep from the goats:

33 And he shall set the sheep on his right hand, but the goats on the left.

34 Then shall the King say unto them on his right hand, Come, ye blessed of my Father, inherit the kingdom prepared for you from the foundation of the world:

35 For I was an hungred, and ye gave me meat: I was thirsty, and ye gave me drink: I was a stranger, and ye took me in:

36 Naked, and ye clothed me: I was sick, and ye visited me: I was in prison, and ye came unto me.

37 Then shall the righteous answer him, saying, Lord, when saw we thee an hungred, and fed thee? or thirsty, and gave thee drink?

38 When saw we thee a stranger, and took thee in? or naked, and clothed thee?

39 Or when saw we thee sick, or in prison, and came unto thee?

40 And the King shall answer and say unto them, Verily I say unto you, Inasmuch as ye have done it unto one of the least of these my brethren, ye have done it unto me.

41 Then shall he say also unto them on the left hand, Depart from me, ye cursed, into everlasting fire, prepared for the devil and his angels:

42 For I was an hungred, and ye gave me no meat: I was thirsty, and ye gave me no drink:

43 I was a stranger, and ye took me not in: naked, and ye clothed me not: sick, and in prison, and ye visited me not.

NLT **Matthew 25:31** "But when the Son of Man comes in his glory, and all the angels with him, then he will sit upon his glorious throne.

32 All the nations will be gathered in his presence, and he will separate the people as a shepherd separates the sheep from the goats.

33 He will place the sheep at his right hand and the goats at his left.

34 Then the King will say to those on his right, 'Come, you who are blessed by my Father, inherit the Kingdom prepared for you from the creation of the world.

35 For I was hungry, and you fed me. I was thirsty, and you gave me a drink. I was a stranger, and you invited me into your home.

36 I was naked, and you gave me clothing. I was sick, and you cared for me. I was in prison, and you visited me.'

37 Then these righteous ones will reply, 'Lord, when did we ever see you hungry and feed you? Or thirsty and give you something to drink?

38 Or a stranger and show you hospitality? Or naked and give you clothing? **39** When did we ever see you sick or in prison and visit you?'

40 And the King will say, 'I tell you the truth, when you did it to one of the least of these my brothers and sisters, you were doing it to me!'

41 Then the King will turn to those on the left and say, 'Away with you, you cursed ones, into the eternal fire prepared for the devil and his demons.

42 For I was hungry, and you didn't feed me. I was thirsty, and you didn't give me a drink.

43 I was a stranger, and you didn't invite me into your home. I was naked, and you didn't give me clothing. I was sick and in prison, and you didn't visit me.'

44 Then shall they also answer him, saying, Lord, when saw we thee an hungred, or athirst, or a stranger, or naked, or sick, or in prison, and did not minister unto thee?

45 Then shall he answer them, saying, Verily I say unto you, Inasmuch as ye did it not to one of the least of these, ye did it not to me.

46 And these shall go away into everlasting punishment: but the righteous into life eternal.

44 Then they will reply, 'Lord, when did we ever see you hungry or thirsty or a stranger or naked or sick or in prison, and not help you?'

45 And he will answer, 'I tell you the truth, when you refused to help the least of these my brothers and sisters, you were refusing to help me.'

46 And they will go away into eternal punishment, but the righteous will go into eternal life."

The People, Places, and Times

Sheep and Goats. God's judgment on the nations (Matthew 25:32) was a standard part of Jewish expectations for the future. God would ultimately separate the "sheep" and the "goats." Several distinctions are made between the two. For instance, while sheep and goats grazed together, they were separated at night by shepherds in Palestine. Goats needed to be kept in a warm place; sheep preferred the outdoors. Goats were considered less valuable than sheep. Finally, in some instances sheep represented good and goats represented trouble. Thus, the comparison in Matthew 25:33. With these examples in mind, we can understand why Jesus used sheep and goats in His parable about separation and judgment.

Helping the Poor. In the Bible, God judged people on how they treated the poor (vv. 34–45). Specifically, Jesus says that if a person treats the poor unfavorably, then that person can expect no different treatment for himself. Jesus lists righteous deeds found in Jewish ethics and includes visiting the incarcerated (vv. 35–36). Devotion to Jewish religion included visiting the sick, helping the poor, and welcoming strangers in one's home. Doing such deeds was like treating Christ in the same manner.

Background

There are four key participants in this parable, all of whom play a role in the Last Judgment: the Son of Man who appears with all His angels (v. 31); the nations, or Gentiles, who are divided into those who have and those who have not joined with God (v. 32); the King (Jesus) (v. 34); and brethren, or those who were once judged by man and now judge those who judged them (v. 40). The King is sitting on the throne, and the Gentiles (nations) are standing before the Judge.

The judgment of the sheep and goats occurs at the conclusion of the Great Tribulation to determine who may enter the kingdom of God. The basis of the judgment is the relationship of men to Christ as demonstrated by their treatment of those in need (Matthew 25:34–36). Those who are saved (sheep) enter the kingdom prepared for them (v. 34), while the lost (goats) go away into eternal punishment (v. 46). In the end, the kingdom consists only of the saved.

At-A-Glance

1. The Great Appearing (Matthew 25:31)
2. The Great Division (vv. 32–40)
3. The Great Condemnation (vv. 41–46)

In Depth

1. The Great Appearing (Matthew 25:31)

Jesus is coming back. Jesus uses His Second Coming as the basis for teaching His disciples how to act.

Several things come to the forefront in this passage. First, the Son of Man will return. Although we do not know when, the time has been set. Next, the Second Coming will be "in his glory." Jesus came the first time clothing His glory in a body of flesh. Instead of being wrapped in light riding upon the chariots of the sun (2 Samuel 23:3–5), He was wrapped in swaddling clothes and sleeping in a manger. But this time His glory will be splendidly displayed to the furthest parts of the universe.

Finally, all the holy angels, tens of thousands of them, are with Him and at His command. What a glorious sight! This time—unlike His first coming, when He chose not to call the angels to help Him—He will not hesitate to use the power at His disposal. This time He is not coming to serve but to receive the service due to Him. The text tells us that "then shall he sit upon the throne of glory," reminding us of His royalty. The throne clearly indicates His Lordship. Though He is coming in glory, He is not agitated. He is at rest in His display of power. He sits upon the throne. Only Christ can come with such power yet remain seated. At Jesus' first coming, very few came to worship Him (only shepherds and wise men). In this appearing, all the nations shall be gathered before Him. We are not told who gathers them, but nonetheless we are gathered in the presence of the One who sits on the throne.

2. The Great Division (vv. 32–40)

When Jesus appears, there will be a great division. Jesus enters the parable, dividing sheep and goats. Rather than address them as He is separating evil men from good men, or people of faith from unbelievers, he addresses them as He is separating His sheep from the goats. An indication of possession already sets us up to know that though all are His, only the sheep enter into His rest. The people of all nations, whether powerful or powerless, will stand before His throne to be judged.

This judgment will not be based on earthly possessions or racial superiority but rather on whether they belong to Him. The "goats," as the Son of Man says in the text, are not His. By their very nature, they remain outside of His nature. They are also separated by their manifest character, that is, what they did or did not do. Many people claim to be born of God but do not act accordingly. When people who do not know God do evil, it is expected. But when those who profess to know God do evil, it raises questions about their relationship with Christ.

Jesus does not ask the sheep what they did because He already knows. Instead, He states exactly what separates them from the goats. First, He invites them with the words, "Come, you blessed of my father." The invitation affirms them as His kin and blood relation. They are not strangers. Then He tells them to "inherit the kingdom prepared for you from the foundation of the world." This inheritance reminds us of why God created humanity and of His generous offer to Adam as the ruler of all that God made. The group which He metaphorically calls sheep is now to inherit what God prepared from the beginning.

3. The Great Condemnation (vv. 41–46)

Compare verse 34 with verse 41. He will say to those on the left, which are referred to as goats, "depart from me." This command to the group that first rejected Him has a ring of finality to it. When he came near to them, they chased Him away. Now He will chase them away. Those who refuse to participate in His nature, who will not become related to Him, will hear "depart from me."

Those who the King pronounces as blessed are defined by their actions of outreach. Some were so caught up with their own survival that they did not give to others. But we place ourselves under divine judgment when we excuse ourselves from feeding the hungry because we claim not to have enough for ourselves. When we hoard resources and call it being thrifty while others suffer, we are not showing the character of Jesus.

What distinguishes people who have the nature of Jesus from the world is their propensity to care for others. The "sheep" and the "goats" are separated by their attitude of caring. No doubt the goats would have cared for those around them if it was clear that those in need were indeed Christ clothed as the beggar. But the basic difference is this: Those who had Jesus' nature were naturally drawn to caring for others, even without knowing it was Jesus whom they were serving. The key here is that we must treat everyone in need as we would treat the Lord. What will separate us from those who are perishing is not how much we love the lovely, but how we treat the undesirable.

This is a warning to us as we walk in the Lord. Jesus comes to us in ways that we do not readily recognize Him. We are called to care for the least of these. Jesus is very clear that He represents them and that our treatment of them reflects our treatment of Him. Our giving and our caring must grow out of the fact that we are His sheep. His sheep will reflect the nature of the caring Jesus. He shows in this parable that service to the poor is service to Him. To reach out is to be blessed and have the honor of entering Christ's rest; but to be selfish and create discord is to be put on His left and to go away into eternal punishment (vv. 45–46).

Search the Scriptures

1. What is the distinction between the sheep and the goats (Matthew 25:40, 45)?

2. What is the significance of this judgment happening when King Jesus appears in glory with His angels (v. 31)?

Discuss the Meaning

1. Have you ever been approached by someone in the street asking for food and ignored the request? Why did you decide to give or not give them food or money?

2. For Thanksgiving or Christmas, have you ever volunteered to serve food or spend time with people who do not have a home or family? Have you ever volunteered any time when there was no holiday?

3. Have you ever visited anyone you knew was in prison or in the hospital? Did you go to see them because you felt obligated or because you really cared about them?

Liberating Lesson

There are people in our communities who need our help, but we don't see them because we view them as part of the landscape. We wish they would go away, but Jesus taught us that "Inasmuch as you did it not to one of the least of these, you did it not to me" (from Matthew 25:45). The way we treat those in need is how we treat our Father in heaven. If we have no regard for others, we have no regard for our Father in heaven.

Christ did not say, "Let me check your references, your resume, and your ability to pay me back." He said, "Come unto me, all ye that labour and are heavy laden, and I will give you rest" (Matthew 11:28). Jesus opens His heart for us to pour in all our pain and despair; and He promises us joy, peace, and relief. We make and set conditions, but God pardons us when we fail to glorify Him. If we really trusted in God, we would not set conditions before we care for others. God loves and takes care of us unconditionally and blesses us continually. God expects us to show His love and care to the poor, outcasts, widows, orphans, the incarcerated, the sick, and the least of these in our midst.

Application for Activation

All of us have the opportunity to donate clothes, feed the hungry, assist at a shelter, get involved in a prison ministry, or visit the hospitalized. We often leave these duties to the deacons and missionaries of the church; however, we are all disciples of Christ and share in the same responsibility. If you are not already part of a ministry that helps meet these needs, join one. If your church does not have this type of outreach, start one. It's up to you. Are you a sheep or a goat?

Follow the Spirit

What God wants me to do:

_____

_____

_____

_____

Remember Your Thoughts

Special insights I have learned:

_____

_____

_____

_____

More Light on the Text

Mathew 25:31–46

31 When the Son of man shall come in his glory, and all the holy angels with him, then shall he sit upon the throne of his glory:

This passage of Scripture is not so much a parable as it is prophecy. It does, however, have some parabolic traits in that it details the shepherd, sheep, and goats. The point here is to describe the events of Jesus' Second Coming. When Christ returns, He will come in His full glory, the same glory that clothed Him before He descended from heaven. His angels will accompany Him and will help gather all the people together at the same time.

32 And before him shall be gathered all nations; and he shall separate them one from another, as a shepherd divideth his sheep from the goats: 33 and he shall set the sheep on his right hand, but the goats on the left. 34 Then shall the King say unto them on his right hand, Come, ye blessed of my Father, inherit the kingdom prepared for you from the foundation of the world:

Jews and Gentiles will not assemble in two different groups but stand together before the judgment of the King. Once more, Jesus teaches in a context with which the Jews are familiar. Sheep and goats typically graze together in the daytime but are separated at night. In this passage, the sheep go one way and the goats go another. The right side symbolizes blessing, honor, and favor; the left side symbolizes worthlessness and condemnation.

Jesus refers to Himself as "King" (Gk. *basileus*, **bah-see-LEWS**). In this case the King is not just King of the Jews, but King of kings who has all power and holds eternal judgment. Elsewhere, He calls Himself by other titles, and in so doing uses the first person, e.g., "I am the good shepherd" (John 10:11). In this verse, He uses the third person to maintain the narrative of a parable, although he clearly identifies Himself as the subject in following verses. Once the sheep and goats are separated, Jesus will address the sheep, inviting them into God's kingdom. The word translated here as "come" is the Greek *deute* (**DEW-tay**), which Matthew significantly used when Jesus called His disciples to follow Him (4:19), and in another illustration of welcoming His followers (22:4).

Matthew uses the Greek word *kleronomeo* (**klay-ro-no-MEH-oh**), meaning "to possess," and signals the sheep to inherit or take possession of the kingdom. This speaks of the kingdom of God, the place where God is acknowledged as sovereign and His presence brings wholeness and holiness. This idea extends from the Promised Land of Genesis and Exodus, where there is peace, prosperity, and fruitfulness in God's presence, to ultimately of possessing the kingdom of God on earth. Jesus calls the sheep blessed, not because of the grace they received but how they used it. He adds that this place has been prepared specifically for them from the beginning of the world. Here in this prophetic parable Jesus marries two important themes of the Gospel of Matthew: stewardship and judgment. Judgment is eternal and based on how the sheep and goats steward the grace of God that they are given and use it to care for others.

35 For I was an hungred, and ye gave me meat: I was thirsty, and ye gave me drink: I was a stranger, and ye took me in: 36 naked, and ye clothed me: I was sick, and ye visited me: I was in prison, and ye came unto me.

Jesus lists some acts of compassion that the sheep performed. The Bible is replete with such acts that His audience might recall. Rebekah giving water to the servant of Jacob. Ruth and Naomi receiving provision in Boaz's field. Abraham and Sarai providing shelter for the three angelic beings in the wilderness. The prophet Elisha visiting the widow woman and her son. These stories all serve as narrative testimonies of righteous people performing the law of God in the Torah to care for the needy of society (Deuteronomy 10:18–19, 24:19–22).

Jesus here reminds people of something they already knew: the command to keep the law of God. But He adds the weight that to keep the law and care for God's people is to care for the Son of God Himself. The need for compassion still exists today, and many people feed the hungry, satisfy the thirsty, house the homeless, clothe the destitute, and visit the sick and imprisoned. But the service is just as crucial as the motivation behind it. Some people get involved because of tax benefits, a guilty conscience, or obligations within a group or organization.

37 Then shall the righteous answer him, saying, Lord, when saw we thee an hungred, and fed thee? or thirsty, and gave thee drink? 38 When saw we thee a stranger, and took thee in? or naked, and clothed thee? 39 Or when saw we thee sick, or in prison, and came unto thee?

Few people have seen Jesus with unmistakable certainty. But the righteous unknowingly served Him by ministering to others. Christ was never hungry, thirsty, a stranger, naked, sick, or imprisoned. Thus, confusion filled their minds. Yet the implication is clear: Jesus is found with people at society's margins. When we care for those who are in need, we are pleasing God. Evidently, the righteous sacrificed themselves to attend to someone else, and their unselfishness pleased God. It is remarkable that they show authenticity in intention and action; they did not do what they did because they knew they were serving Jesus directly, they did it because they had compassion. The honesty of their confusion in response to the King's words reveals their pure hearts.

40 And the King shall answer and say unto them, Verily I say unto you, Inasmuch as ye have done it unto one of the least of these my brethren, ye have done it unto me.

Jesus calms the sheep by reminding them to their merciful deeds born of God's love for them. The brethren of Christ are all who share a bond with Him through His sufferings and afflictions. He identifies with them, making their pain, sorrow, and tribulation His own. Jesus points to the least of His brethren, highlighting the humility exercised by the righteous in serving those thought unworthy of service. The Greek word used for brethren is *adelphos* (**ah-del-FOCE**), meaning brothers or sisters and signifying the kinship of immediate family. This use is in contrast to using brethren as in fellow countrymen or simply a fellow Jew. Jesus was saying that those who serve the least of these are His family.

41 Then shall he say also unto them on the left hand, Depart from me, ye cursed, into everlasting fire, prepared for the devil and his angels: 42 for I was an hungred, and ye gave me no meat: I was thirsty, and ye gave me no drink: 43 I was a stranger, and ye took me not in: naked, and ye clothed me not: sick, and in prison, and ye visited me not.

The Lord uses the same standards for both groups and parallels them to each other. Whereas Jesus invites those on the right to come, He commands those on the left to depart (Gk. *poreuo*, **po-REW-oh**). The Greek here connotes "going one's way." Christ recognizes that the goats have not been following Him, and invites them to continue along the path that they have chosen. Because the goats have chosen not to serve those in need, they are condemned to death.

Just as God made the kingdom of heaven ready for the righteous, He made the everlasting fire ready for the unrighteous (Revelation 20:11–15). Originally, the fire was designated for Satan and his followers (Revelation 12:9). But since sin and death entered the world, humanity was destined to join Satan in this judgment. God did not prepare this place for us because He is "not willing that any should perish" (2 Peter 3:9). But since God is just, our disobedience demanded that we be punished unless proper atonement was made. Christ made that atonement, so humanity must live through the One who paid our debt. Otherwise, we must suffer God's judgment.

44 Then shall they also answer him, saying, Lord, when saw we thee an hungred, or athirst, or a stranger, or naked, or sick, or in prison, and did not minister unto thee? 45 Then shall he answer them, saying, Verily I say unto you, Inasmuch as ye did it not to one of the least of these, ye did it not to me. 46 And these shall go away into everlasting punishment: but the righteous into life eternal.

Neither the sheep nor the goats appear puzzled by their destination but seem bewildered by the reason for going there. None of them expected to live or die based on how they treated Jesus because they did not think they ever had the opportunity. But because the goats chose not to serve those in need, they were condemned to death.

A similar circumstance exists today. Many people are not aware of the good they do through the Holy Spirit, and many don't recognize the chance to love as Christ loved and to serve Him by serving others. Furthermore, some people believe they are sheep, when God sees them as goats. Jesus reiterates that the service done unto others is also done unto Him. If anyone masks a deed of goodwill behind an expectation of selfish gain, it carries no spiritual value. If we do "spiritual" works and perform "religious" rituals but neglect the needs of people in our communities, we have missed the mark of our call in Christ. Our service to our fellow man is not just leftover charity for those who are destitute but an act of service to Christ Himself.

Sources:

Hebrew-Greek Key Word Study Bible, King James Version. Chattanooga, TN: AMG Publishers, Inc., 1991.

Keener, Craig S. *The IVP Bible Background Commentary: New Testament.* Downers Grove, IL: Intervarsity Press, 1993. 118–119.

Radmacher, Earl D., ed. *Nelson Study Bible, New King James Version.* Nashville, TN: Thomas Nelson Publishers, 1997. 1620–1625.

Ryrie, Charles C. *Ryrie Study Bible, New International Version.* Chicago, IL: Moody Press, 1986. 1358.

Unger, Merrill F. *The New Unger's Bible Dictionary.* Chicago, IL: Moody Press, 1988. 72, 940–994, 1211.

Walvoord, John F., and Roy B. Zuck, eds. *The Bible Knowledge Commentary: New Testament.* Wheaton, IL: Victor Books, SP Publications, Inc., 1983. 80–81.

Exell, Joseph S., and Henry Donald Maurice Spence-Jones, eds. *The Pulpit Commentary.* Vol. 15. Grand Rapids, MI: Eerdmans Publishing Company. 484.

Daily Bible Readings

MONDAY
Live by Faith
(Habakkuk 1:2–4; 2:1–4)

TUESDAY
Rewards for Hospitality
(Matthew 10:40–42)

WEDNESDAY
Welcoming Children
(Mark 9:33–37)

THURSDAY
Wait, The Lord Will Come
(1 Thessalonians 4:13–18)

FRIDAY
Keep Awake and Ready
(Matthew 25:1–13)

SATURDAY
Multiply God's Gifts
(Matthew 25:14–30)

SUNDAY
Inherit the Kingdom
(Matthew 25:31–46)

Notes

Teaching Tips

Words You Should Know

A. Doctrine *didache* (Gk.)—Principle teaching of Christian faith.

B. Deceiver *planos* (Gk.)—Impostor, or corrupter; one who wanders, leads astray, or seduces.

Teacher Preparation

Unifying Principle—Steadfastness. Effective personal relationships are often thwarted by destructive forces. What can counteract these forces? Paul and John instruct the believers to walk steadfastly in the love of God by loving one another and following God's commandments.

A. Read the Bible Background and Devotional Readings.

B. Pray for your students and lesson clarity.

C. Read the lesson Scripture in multiple translations.

D. Option: Ask a class to describe current issues or false teachings that are becoming more prevalent in our culture today. Discuss ways to encourage believers to walk in the truth.

O—Open the Lesson

A. Begin the class with prayer.

B. Have the students read the Aim for Change.

C. Have the students read the In Focus story.

D. Ask students how events named in the story can weigh on their hearts and how they can view these events from a theological perspective.

P—Present the Scriptures

A. Read the Focal Verses and discuss the Background and The People, Places, and Times sections.

B. Have the class share what Scriptures stand out for them and why, with particular emphasis on today's context.

E—Explore the Meaning

A. Use In Depth or More Light on the Text to help provide more in-depth discussion of the lesson text.

B. Discuss the Liberating Lesson and Application for Activation sections.

N—Next Steps for Application

A. List reasons for the importance of loving God by loving others.

B. End class with a commitment to pray for those in need in our communities.

Worship Guide

For the Superintendent or Teacher
Theme: Hold Fast to God's Love
Song: "On Christ the Solid Rock I Stand"
Devotional Reading: John 15:12–17

Hold Fast to God's Love

**Bible Background • 2 THESSALONIANS 2:13–3:5; 2 John 4–11
Printed Text • 2 THESSALONIANS 3:1–5; 2 JOHN 4–11 | Devotional Reading • JOHN 15:12–17**

—————— Aim for Change ——————

By the end of the lesson, we will: IDENTIFY Paul and John's command to hold on to God's love; EMBRACE the command that we show love for God by loving others; and DECIDE to love Jesus by obeying His commandments.

—————— In Focus ——————

The phone had not rung with his voice on the other end for years. Ruby clasped her fingers and prayed fervently for her son, Will, who was serving a life sentence in prison. "Lord," she whispered through tears, "teach him your ways. Show him your unfailing love."

Morning by morning, she prayed for exactly the same things and was careful to live God's way on purpose so she could approach God with a clear conscience. She attended church regularly, tithed, served at the local food pantry, forgave others quickly, and asked for forgiveness even quicker. Ruby knew how to walk in her faith. Like David of the Bible, she was an imperfect woman who chased passionately after God's own heart.

Unfortunately, Will had walked away from God to a life of crime years ago. Many told Ruby to give up on him and to stop praying for his salvation. But Ruby still vividly remembered the promises she and her husband made the day Will was dedicated in their church decades earlier. Through her steadfast prayers, she begged God to save him. Even though he would likely die behind bars, he could still accept Christ as his Savior and experience a different kind of liberation. As she said Amen, the phone rang.

"Mama, it's me. I've got something to tell you," the voice said. "I've been reading the Bible you gave me. Can you answer some questions?" Will asked.

How can walking in God's commandments bless you and your family even when it seems fruitless?

—————— Keep in Mind ——————

"And this is love, that we walk after his commandments. This is the commandment, That, as ye have heard from the beginning, ye should walk in it" (2 John 6, KJV).

"Love means doing what God has commanded us, and he has commanded us to love one another, just as you heard from the beginning" (2 John 6, NLT).

Focal Verses

KJV 2 Thessalonians 3:1 Finally, brethren, pray for us, that the word of the Lord may have free course, and be glorified, even as it is with you:

2 And that we may be delivered from unreasonable and wicked men: for all men have not faith.

3 But the Lord is faithful, who shall stablish you, and keep you from evil.

4 And we have confidence in the Lord touching you, that ye both do and will do the things which we command you.

5 And the Lord direct your hearts into the love of God, and into the patient waiting for Christ.

2 John 4 I rejoiced greatly that I found of thy children walking in truth, as we have received a commandment from the Father.

5 And now I beseech thee, lady, not as though I wrote a new commandment unto thee, but that which we had from the beginning, that we love one another.

6 And this is love, that we walk after his commandments. This is the commandment, That, as ye have heard from the beginning, ye should walk in it.

7 For many deceivers are entered into the world, who confess not that Jesus Christ is come in the flesh. This is a deceiver and an antichrist.

8 Look to yourselves, that we lose not those things which we have wrought, but that we receive a full reward.

9 Whosoever transgresseth, and abideth not in the doctrine of Christ, hath not God. He that abideth in the doctrine of Christ, he hath both the Father and the Son.

10 If there come any unto you, and bring not this doctrine, receive him not into your house, neither bid him God speed:

NLT 2 Thessalonians 3:1 Finally, dear brothers and sisters, we ask you to pray for us. Pray that the Lord's message will spread rapidly and be honored wherever it goes, just as when it came to you.

2 Pray, too, that we will be rescued from wicked and evil people, for not everyone is a believer.

3 But the Lord is faithful; he will strengthen you and guard you from the evil one.

4 And we are confident in the Lord that you are doing and will continue to do the things we commanded you.

5 May the Lord lead your hearts into a full understanding and expression of the love of God and the patient endurance that comes from Christ.

2 John 4 How happy I was to meet some of your children and find them living according to the truth, just as the Father commanded.

5 I am writing to remind you, dear friends, that we should love one another. This is not a new commandment, but one we have had from the beginning.

6 Love means doing what God has commanded us, and he has commanded us to love one another, just as you heard from the beginning.

7 I say this because many deceivers have gone out into the world. They deny that Jesus Christ came in a real body. Such a person is a deceiver and an antichrist.

8 Watch out that you do not lose what we have worked so hard to achieve. Be diligent so that you receive your full reward.

9 Anyone who wanders away from this teaching has no relationship with God. But anyone who remains in the teaching of Christ has a relationship with both the Father and the Son.

11 For he that biddeth him God speed is partaker of his evil deeds.

10 If anyone comes to your meeting and does not teach the truth about Christ, don't invite that person into your home or give any kind of encouragement.

11 Anyone who encourages such people becomes a partner in their evil work.

The People, Places, and Times

Paul. The apostle Paul, a Roman citizen born in Tarsus, was converted after encountering God on the road to Damascus. He was transformed from persecuting believers in Christ to being a preacher of the Gospel (Acts 9:1–31). He traveled on three missionary journeys spreading the Gospel. Paul visited Thessalonica, preached in the city's synagogue, and established the church during his second missionary journey (Acts 17:1–4). After less than a month, he encountered violent harassment so he was sent away for his own safety (17:5–9). He wrote 1 Thessalonians from Corinth around AD 51. About six months later, he wrote this second letter.

John the Apostle. John was the son of Zebedee and the brother of James. Along with James, John was called by Jesus to become one of the twelve disciples while they were fishing (see Matthew 4:21–22). His name appears in each of the apostolic lists. Jesus gave John and James the nickname "Boanerges," meaning sons of thunder (Mark 3:17). Their prominence among the Twelve is indicated by their presence along with Peter at the raising of Jairus' daughter by Jesus (Luke 8:51) and at the transfiguration of Jesus (Matthew 17:1; Mark 9:2). Paul attests to John's prominence by referring to him as one of the "pillars" of the Jerusalem church (Galatians 2:6–10). According to some traditions, John survived until AD 100 in Ephesus, but it is also possible that he was martyred much earlier along with his brother James.

Background

The letter to the church at Thessalonica was written by the Apostle Paul, who established the church community there during his second missionary journey. This letter was written when Timothy returned from Thessalonica bringing Paul a report that the church was standing strong in faith. They stood firm in the face of the persecution that had precipitated Paul's departure. The letter of 2 Thessalonians was most likely written from Corinth within three or four months of 1 Thessalonians and focuses on the second coming of Christ.

John the apostle wrote 2 John most likely from Ephesus. This letter was written to a congregation of believers for encouragement and instruction. He warns the church about deceivers, and urges the believers to love one another and remain grounded in sound teaching.

At-A-Glance

1. Hold onto God's Love
(2 Thessalonians 3:1–5)
2. Express God's Love (2 John 4–6)
3. Be Watchful in God's Love (vv. 7–11)

In Depth

1. Hold onto God's Love (2 Thessalonians 3:1–5)

Paul begins by asking for prayer. He had shared the message of Christ and His love at Thessalonica and was preparing to share it with others. He prays for his deliverance as well as that of other believers. Paul encourages the Thessalonians to continue in the things he taught and commanded them. Paul prays that the believers at Thessalonica will be led into a full understanding of God's love and its expression, which will enable them to stand firm in the truth. Paul doesn't just pray that they will experience God's love themselves; he prays that they will enter into the expression of that love toward God and others. As the church at Thessalonica was likely facing pressure and persecution, Paul wanted them to fully experience "the patient endurance that comes from Christ" and fully express God's love for them (v. 5).

When are you most aware of God's love for you?

2. Express God's Love (2 John 4–6)

God loves us, and when we love one another, we imitate the love of God. Loving others is also a way we can express our love for God. God loves His children, and we can demonstrate love for the Father by showing genuine love to His children.

John notes that the command to love one another is not new. Believers are to be characterized by love for each other, as Jesus taught (John 13:34–35).

As God demonstrated His love for us in a sacrificial manner, we are to sacrificially love others. We are to submit to one another in humility (1 Peter 5:5). We are to be patient and gentle with each other, and to forgive, comfort, and encourage one another. We are to pray for one another and love each other "in deed and in truth" (from 1 John 3:18).

Love for God is reflected by obedience to His commandments. This mirrors Jesus' teaching that loving Him meant following His commandments (John 14:15). We show love for God by humbly submitting to His will in obedience, knowing that His commands are not burdensome (1 John 5:3).

As children demonstrate their love for their parents through obedience, we demonstrate our love for God through obedience. To love is to obey. Obedience is a response that is prompted by love—not simply by duty. A person who does not love will not obey, so obedience can be used as an indication of a person's true love for God.

Does your level of obedience to God reflect great love for Him, or does it reflect very little?

3. Be Watchful in God's Love (vv. 7–11)

John warns the church of those who present a false message of Christ. Specifically, some were teaching that Jesus did not come in a physical body. John describes anyone spreading this teaching as a deceiver and an antichrist. John urges the church to continue in the truth they were taught. They are not to welcome false teachers or participate in their evil work.

Instead, John instructs the church to continue in the truth about Christ, noting that whoever abides in the truth of Christ the Son has God the Father as well. Continuing in the truth will enable the church to receive a full reward.

In an age of a variety of teachings about the person, mission, and message of Christ, how do you ensure that you remain grounded in sound teaching?

Search the Scriptures

1. Paul highlights the Lord's faithfulness and expresses his confidence in the Lord

that the Thessalonians will continue in his teaching (2 Thessalonians 3:3–4). Why is Paul's confidence in the Lord, rather than the Thessalonians such an important distinction?

2. What is the importance of clinging to sound teaching (2 John 9)? What are the consequences of wandering away from the truth?

Discuss the Meaning

1. In a society where it is customary for everyone to create (and break) his or her own rules, how can we improve our understanding of and adherence to God's commandments?

2. From your perspective, describe what walking according to God's laws should look like in your life. Which commandments do you need to work harder on following? Why?

3. How can you successfully identify false prophets and deceivers using the Word of God? How should you respond to them and their messages?

Liberating Lesson

In such difficult times, marked by division and strife, we are called to love one another. We often do well loving people who are similar to us, but God does not call us to only love people like us. He calls us to love one another. This includes people who may hold different traditions and those with differing political views. This includes the poor, the sick, and the immigrants. We are to extend God's love to this broken, dying world.

At the same time, we must ensure that we hold fast to sound teaching and continue in the things we have been commanded. We must also walk in integrity and work to earn our living. Finally, we must be committed to the spread of the love of God and message of the Gospel.

Application for Activation

Think of ways to show your love for God. How can you show love for those in your home, school, workplace, or neighborhood? Look for ways to express God's love to others.

Also, examine your demonstration of love for God through obedience. Are there additional ways that you can offer your obedience in humble submission? Finally, how are you participating in spreading the message of Christ? Pray for opportunities to spread the Gospel and for others who are sharing the message of Christ.

Follow the Spirit

What God wants me to do:

_____

_____

_____

_____

Remember Your Thoughts

Special insights I have learned:

_____

_____

_____

_____

More Light on the Text

2 Thessalonians 3:1–5; 2 John 4–11

1 Finally, brethren, pray for us, that the word of the Lord may have free course, and be glorified, even as it is with you.

Before closing this letter, the Apostle Paul asked the Thessalonians to earnestly pray for

241

him and his companions, as they had faithfully done for the converts. Biblical history shows that Paul and the other apostles often suffered persecution for the Gospel's sake (Acts 19:23; 2 Corinthians 1:8–9; 11:23–28), and Paul recognized that they needed the saints to pray for them. Paul could witness to the Thessalonians in their times of troubles because he had experienced a great deal himself. Thus, he needed and asked for their prayers.

In addition, the Thessalonians were to pray so "that the word of the Lord may have free course, and be glorified"—that it would spread rapidly and be honored wherever it went. Paul recognized that Satan was always trying to hinder God's Word and His work. In the spirit world, the fight between good and evil is very real, but an all-powerful God can meet any of Satan's challenges.

2 And that we may be delivered from unreasonable and wicked men: for all men have not faith. 3 But the Lord is faithful, who shall stablish you, and keep you from evil.

There was no doubt in Paul's mind that many false teachers and others were enemies to the preaching of the Gospel—they were being used by Satan to impede the spreading of the Good News, but they were no match for the power of God. The saints, therefore, can pray to be delivered from false ministers, who bring more harm than good to the preaching of the Gospel. Paul wanted the Thessalonians and us to pray to be delivered from those who have neither conscience nor honor when it comes to preaching God's Word—they are influenced by Satan. In other words, they have their own agendas. Paul wanted us to not only pray together, but we are to pray for one another as well.

There was no doubt in Paul's mind that these false teachers and preachers were "unreasonable and wicked men" who did not have faith in Christ. In Greek, "unreasonable" is *atopos*

(**AH-to-poce**) and means "improper, wicked, unrighteous, harmful." Paul, however, knew God to be faithful to His children. Therefore, he explained to the Thessalonians that this same faithful God would "stablish" them and also "keep you [the believers] from evil." In other words, God would help them build their hope on the firm foundation, which is Jesus Christ. God, through His Holy Spirit, keeps them from the evil ones both inside and outside the church. In addition to establishing them, He would preserve ("keep") them (v. 3). John explained this "keeping" in his Gospel: "My sheep hear my voice, and I know them, and they follow me: And I give unto them eternal life; and they shall never perish, neither shall any man pluck them out of my hand" (John 10:27–28). In other words, they would be kept, as in protected and led away from evil. Indeed, in spite of their trials and tribulations, the Thessalonians had grounds to hope in the Lord, who is a faithful God. We also have reason to hope and not give up on God in our struggles.

4 And we have confidence in the Lord touching you, that ye both do and will do the things which we command you.

Paul and his fellow laborers had "confidence" (Gk. *peitho*, **PAY-tho**), which means "belief in, faith in, trust in," that the Thessalonians were doing all of the things that they had commanded them to do to stay on the right track in their walk with the Lord. Paul and his companions' confidence in the Thessalonians was based on their assurance or belief in the Lord, who is faithful. God would empower these struggling new believers by His Spirit, so that they would be able to comply and do what was right. With God's help, the Thessalonians would be a positive, fruitful witness for Him. Others would come to know Jesus through their witness.

5 And the Lord direct your hearts into the love of God, and into the patient waiting for Christ.

Paul made a short prayer for the Thessalonians, praying that God would direct their hearts. The word "direct" in Greek is *kateuthuno* (**ka-tew-THOO-no**) and means "to guide, to remove hindrances." In essence, Paul prayed that, through the Holy Spirit, their hearts would be guided into the love of God. He knew that the Thessalonians, as it is with us, on their own could neither keep themselves or their hearts pure. The Holy Spirit had to work in them and guide them into God's truths.

Our love for God, with the help of the Holy Spirit, drives us to want to obey His commands. If we lean on and depend on Him, He will come into our dire situations and help us be overcomers, too. We need only to follow God's love and Christ's patient waiting (Gk. *hupomone*, **hoo-pow-MOW-nay**, patience or endurance). While simple to say, these ideas are life-changing when fully understood and applied. God shows us what love looks like. We see Him providing good things for His people and keeping them from harm. We also see Him freely sacrificing His own Son as the price to redeem His people. Likewise, Christ shows us what patience or endurance looks like. Jesus patiently taught His disciples over several years, explaining truths from the Scriptures and showing how He fulfilled prophecy. Jesus also endured the cruel torture of crucifixion when He could have stopped it at any time. This is the love and patience Paul prays the Thessalonians will be guided in living out.

2 John 4–11

The important themes of belief, obedience, and love treated in the first letter of John are also central to his second and third letters. John manifests concern for the inner life of the church and for the doctrinal danger that threatens it externally. He urges his readers to be watchful and walk in the truth.

4 I rejoiced greatly that I found of thy children walking in truth, as we have received a commandment from the Father.

John's heart was highly elated at the consistent Christian life that members of the congregation practiced, as they are "walking in truth." The Greek word *peripateo* (**peh-ree-pah-TEH-oh**), which literally means to walk around, is figuratively used to signify the whole round of activities of the individual life. The use of the word "truth" (*aletheia*, **ah-LAY-thay-ah**) includes its doctrinal and ethical denotations. To walk in the truth involves belief and behavior. Walking in the truth conveys the imagery of a path along which one walks and keeps on course without deviating. The tense of the verb indicates this healthy spiritual life is a continued pattern. The truth that John talks about did not originate with humankind, not even with the apostles themselves, who originally received it. The truth originated in divine revelation. And so does the command to obey it. In John's epistle both the truth and the commandments are synonymous (cf. vv. 5–6).

5 And now I beseech thee, lady, not as though I wrote a new commandment unto thee, but that which we heard from the beginning, that we love one another.

John proceeds from commendation to exhortation, based on personal request (Gk. *erotao*, **air-oh-TAH-oh**; to ask, beg, appeal, or entreat). The commandment he affirms and urges on his readers was not new; it was as old as the Gospel (John 13:34–35). Here, John ties the command to believe to the command to love. To believe in the full humanity and divinity of Christ and His redemptive mission, and to demonstrate brotherly love is proof of the new birth (1 John 4:7; 5:1).

6 And this is love, that we walk after his commandments. This is the commandment, That, as ye have heard from the beginning, ye should walk in it.

John pursues the line of argument of his Gospel and first letter—that Christian love is more than mere emotion; it is action or demonstration. Love for God and for Christ is expressed in practical obedience (John 14:15, 21; 15:10; 1 John 5:2–3). Jesus summarized the whole Law in the greatest commandment: love (Matthew 22:34–40). Here, John urges a continual walk in love.

7 For many deceivers are entered into the world, who confess not that Jesus Christ is come in the flesh. This is a deceiver and an antichrist.

In the second part of this message (vv. 7–11), John draws the church's attention to the threat from without: false teaching. He describes the heretics, identifies their error, and warns not to be deceived or give any encouragement to them. John commands watchfulness. He urges the believers to remain loyal not only in love, but also to the teaching of Christ.

John affirms the appearance of false teachers in the world. The Greek word *exelthon* (**eks-AIL-thahn**; entered) means to go out, rendering the sentence "deceivers have gone out into the world." The errors of the heretic are both moral and doctrinal; the latter is in focus here. The Greek word *homologeo* (**ho-mo-lo-GEH-oh**), translated as "confess," also means to acknowledge, admit, or affirm. These heretics deny the incarnation of Christ as fully man and God in the flesh. Anyone who denies that Jesus Christ is God in the flesh is considered in the spirit of antichrist. This biblical truth is very important for every Christian. During John's life, many who believed in Christ were influenced by philosophical schools and mystery cults that ignored or ascribed evil to the body, which John likely was addressing in these verses. The early church remained committed to Jesus Christ's incarnation as core to the faith, showing God willed to redeem fallen humanity rather than simply discard it and start over. The spirit of antichrist tries to lead people away from the truth that Jesus is God in the flesh. John describes any false teacher as a "deceiver" and "antichrist." The Greek word *planos* (**PLAH-noce**), translated as "deceiver," implies an impostor, or corrupter, one who wanders, leads astray, or seduces. This is a repeat of his earlier warning against "deceivers" and "many antichrists" (1 John 2:18, 26; 4:1–3). An antichrist is literally someone who is against the Messiah. This is not a separate category of people from the deceivers, but instead those who deceive concerning Christ's nature are opposed to Christ, and are described with both of these terms.

8 Look to yourselves, that we lose not those things which we have wrought, but that we receive a full reward.

This is the first command of the letter: a warning to be on guard. The Greek word *blepete* (**BLEH-peh-teh**), written in present tense, implies continual watchfulness to prevent disaster. John commands readers to reject the enticement of error for two reasons: to prevent the ruin of what both they and John had worked for, and to ensure that they would be paid their reward in full. The rewards would likely include their new freedom from the bondage of sin, the legalism of the law, the tyranny of evil, and the limitations of themselves. John would also be concerned with the eternal glory they would receive at the resurrection. This is one place to consider heavenly rewards in light of obedience to God beyond salvation itself. Jesus' parables of the pounds and talents seem to point to the promise of heavenly rewards and we see that reality of heavenly rewards throughout the New Testament (Matthew 6:1, 1 Peter 1:17, Luke 6:23). As Peter points out, these rewards are not salvation which is by grace, but heavenly rewards given for obedience.

9 Whosoever transgresseth, and abideth not in the doctrine of Christ, hath not God. He that abideth in the doctrine of Christ, he hath both the Father and the Son.

Two contradictory consequences of heterodoxy (or false doctrine) and orthodoxy are stated. The negative is mentioned first. The false teachers were trying to change the core doctrine the Christians had received, but he who fails to abide (to stay, or to remain) by the doctrine cannot have Christ and His salvation. The opposite is also true. To remain continually in the doctrine (Gk. *didache*, **dee-dah-KAY**) or teaching of Christ (in belief in and in obedience to Him) is proof of the believer's personal relationship to both the Father and the Son.

10 If there come any unto you, and bring not this doctrine, receive him not into your house, neither bid him God speed: 11 For he that biddeth him God speed is partaker of his evil deeds.

John adds a practical note after warning about deceivers. He says that the church is not to receive these deceivers into their houses. He then goes even further to say that they should not even bid them "God speed" (Gk. *chairo*, **KHEYE-roh**). This is the word for "rejoice" or "be glad." It was a common greeting that essentially meant "Be well." By receiving false teachers into your home or wishing them well, you partake (Gk. *koinoneo*, **koy-noh-NEH-oh**) in the false teachers' evil deeds. This is a key to the idea of this sacred community: The church is responsible to be light in the community. We are the body of Christ in the world. If the church or believers see people violating the livelihood of others or see someone suffering and do not show love, but rather give a stamp of approval, it is a bad reflection on the church and Christ. We become like the Levites and Pharisees who see the man on the side of the road and walk by, instead of the good Samaritan who stops to show God's love which is the core of John's message to followers of Jesus (Luke 10:29–37, 2 John 5).

Sources:
Achtemeier, Paul C. gen. ed. *Harper's Bible Dictionary*. San Francisco, CA: Harper and Row Publishers, 1985. 498–601.
Comfort, Philip W., and Walter A. Elwell, eds. *Tyndale Bible Dictionary*. Wheaton, IL: Tyndale House Publishers, Inc., 2001. 719–28.
Crosby, Terence Peter. *Opening Up 2 & 3 John*. Opening Up Commentary. Leominster, UK: Day One Publications, 2006.
Douglas, James D., ed. *New Bible Dictionary*. 2nd ed. Downers Grove, IL: InterVarsity Press, 1982. 269.
Henry, Matthew. *Matthew Henry's Commentary on the Whole Bible: Complete and Unabridged in One Volume*. Peabody, MA: Hendrickson, 1994.
Key Word Study Bible. New International Version. Grand Rapids, MI: Zondervan Bible Publishers, 1996. 1442.
Life Application Study Bible. New International Version. Wheaton, IL: Tyndale House Publishers, Inc., 1991. 1909, 2285–87.
McNaughton, Ian. *Opening Up 2 Thessalonians*. Opening Up Commentary. Leominster, UK: Day One Publications, 2008.
Wright, N.T. *Surprised by Hope: Rethinking Heaven, the Resurrection, and the Mission of the Church*. New York: HarperOne, 2008.
The New Oxford Annotated Bible. New Revised Standard Version. New York: Oxford University Press, Inc., 2001. 395–400.
Rainbow Study Bible. New International Version, Grand Rapids, MI: Zondervan Bible Publishers, 1992. 1381.
Richards, Lawrence O. *The Bible Reader's Companion*. Electronic ed. Wheaton, IL: Victor Books, 1991.
Unger, Merrill F. *The New Unger's Bible Handbook*. Chicago, IL: Moody Press, 1998. 249, 640, 831.
Walvoord, John F., and Roy B. Zuck. *The Bible Knowledge Commentary: An Exposition of the Scriptures*. Wheaton, IL: Victor Books, 1985.

Say It Correctly

Ephesus. **EF**-uh-suhs.
Galatians. guh-**LAY**-shehnz.

Daily Bible Readings

MONDAY
Love as I Have Loved You
(John 15:12–17)

TUESDAY
Live in Love and Light
(1 John 2:7–11)

WEDNESDAY
Live by the Truth
(1 John 2:20–27)

THURSDAY
Support Coworkers
(3 John 2–8)

FRIDAY
Stand Firm in the Faith
(2 Thessalonians 2:13–17)

SATURDAY
Do What Is Right
(2 Thessalonians 3:6–13)

SUNDAY
Love God and One Another
(2 Thessalonians 3:1–5; 2 John 4–11)

Notes

_____

_____

_____

_____

Teaching Tips

Words You Should Know

A. Lust *hedone* (Gk.)—Passion or desire for pleasure.

B. Submit *hupotasso* (Gk.)—Obey God in humility.

Teacher Preparation

Unifying Principle—Submit to God. Destructive thoughts and desires lead to further destructive behavior. What can be done to break this cruel cycle? James asserts that loving and obeying God opens the door to God's blessings and frees us from conflicts and disputes.

A. Read the Bible Background and Devotional Readings.

B. Pray for your students and lesson clarity.

C. Read the lesson Scripture in multiple translations.

D. Option: Role-play a church fight in which two people are arguing over budget priorities. As the two squabble, have someone play the part of Satan, who reacts with delight and eggs them on. When the squabble ends, ask, "Who won, and why?"

O—Open the Lesson

A. Begin the class with prayer.

B. Have the students read the Aim for Change.

C. Have the students read the In Focus story.

D. Ask students how events named in the story can weigh on their hearts and how they can view these events from a theological perspective.

P—Present the Scriptures

A. Read the Focal Verses and discuss the Background and The People, Places, and Times sections.

B. Have the class share what Scriptures stand out for them and why, with particular emphasis on today's context.

E—Explore the Meaning

A. Use In Depth or More Light on the Text to help provide more in-depth discussion of the lesson text.

B. Discuss the Liberating Lesson and Application for Activation sections.

N—Next Steps for Application

A. Summarize the value of knowing God as sovereign Creator.

B. End class with a commitment to pray for families, natural resources, and scientists.

Worship Guide

For the Superintendent or Teacher
Theme: God Created the Heavens and Earth
Song: "No Gray"
Devotional Reading: Proverbs 3:27-35

Submit to God in Love

Bible Background • JAMES 4:1–10
Printed Text • JAMES 4:1–10 | Devotional Reading • PROVERBS 3:27–35

—————— Aim for Change ——————

By the end of the lesson, we will: RECOGNIZE how worldly desires create conflicts; REPENT of the ways we caused unnecessary conflict with others; and DEVELOP ways to seek God in humble submission.

——————  In Focus ——————

When her mother opened the door to her bedroom, six-year-old Sarah waved her glittery wand and demanded, "Bow down to me, peasant! You are beneath me!"

Her mother, Pam, gently responded, "Sarah, we don't talk like that in this house."

"I know, Mommy, but it looks so cool on *Spell Sisters*! I just had to try it," she explained.

Her mother's face fell with even more disappointment. Immediately, the little girl realized that without thinking she had confessed her huge secret to her mother. She had been secretly watching a forbidden TV show during her tablet time.

Pam had forbade Sarah to watch *Spell Sisters*, a show for teenagers that she feared would lead to inappropriate actions like this. Her daughter was too young and impressionable. She wanted to protect her from bad things and people.

Pam patiently explained to Sarah that thoughts and words have power so we have to watch what we allow to influence us. "That's one of the reasons we read the Bible, and attend church every week," Pam said carefully. "These are activities that help us think about God's will and help us stop doing or saying things we shouldn't."

Sarah understood. As a consequence of her disobedience, Sarah was not allowed tablet time until trust was restored.

Sarah was influenced by the TV show to say and do things that she shouldn't. How can we use God's Word to refresh our thoughts, words, and actions?

—————— Keep in Mind ——————

"Draw nigh to God, and he will draw nigh to you. Cleanse your hands, ye sinners; and purify your hearts, ye double minded" (James 4:8, KJV).

"Come close to God, and God will come close to you. Wash your hands, you sinners; purify your hearts, for your loyalty is divided between God and the world" (James 4:8, NLT).

Focal Verses

KJV **James 4:1** From whence come wars and fightings among you? come they not hence, even of your lusts that war in your members?

2 Ye lust, and have not: ye kill, and desire to have, and cannot obtain: ye fight and war, yet ye have not, because ye ask not.

3 Ye ask, and receive not, because ye ask amiss, that ye may consume it upon your lusts.

4 Ye adulterers and adulteresses, know ye not that the friendship of the world is enmity with God? whosoever therefore will be a friend of the world is the enemy of God.

5 Do ye think that the scripture saith in vain, The spirit that dwelleth in us lusteth to envy?

6 But he giveth more grace. Wherefore he saith, God resisteth the proud, but giveth grace unto the humble.

7 Submit yourselves therefore to God. Resist the devil, and he will flee from you.

8 Draw nigh to God, and he will draw nigh to you. Cleanse your hands, ye sinners; and purify your hearts, ye double minded.

9 Be afflicted, and mourn, and weep: let your laughter be turned to mourning, and your joy to heaviness.

10 Humble yourselves in the sight of the Lord, and he shall lift you up.

NLT **James 4:1** What is causing the quarrels and fights among you? Don't they come from the evil desires at war within you?

2 You want what you don't have, so you scheme and kill to get it. You are jealous of what others have, but you can't get it, so you fight and wage war to take it away from them. Yet you don't have what you want because you don't ask God for it.

3 And even when you ask, you don't get it because your motives are all wrong—you want only what will give you pleasure.

4 You adulterers! Don't you realize that friendship with the world makes you an enemy of God? I say it again: If you want to be a friend of the world, you make yourself an enemy of God.

5 Do you think the Scriptures have no meaning? They say that God is passionate that the spirit he has placed within us should be faithful to him.

6 And he gives grace generously. As the Scriptures say, "God opposes the proud but gives grace to the humble."

7 So humble yourselves before God. Resist the devil, and he will flee from you.

8 Come close to God, and God will come close to you. Wash your hands, you sinners; purify your hearts, for your loyalty is divided between God and the world.

9 Let there be tears for what you have done. Let there be sorrow and deep grief. Let there be sadness instead of laughter, and gloom instead of joy.

10 Humble yourselves before the Lord, and he will lift you up in honor.

The People, Places, and Times

Desire. Often the word is used to express dangerous passions growing out of one's erroneous evaluation of the world and its pleasures. Scripture reveals that the desires that drive human beings are deeply rooted in our sinful human nature. Speaking of our days before we decided to follow Christ, Paul says we were "following the passionate desires and inclinations of our sinful nature," which made us "subject to God's anger" (from Ephesians 2:3, NLT). He also encouraged believers, "Do not let sin control the way you live; do not give in to sinful desires." (Romans 6:12, NLT). Driven by these passions, people easily fall into sin.

Background

The book of James is written by James, the brother of Jesus and leader of the church in Jerusalem. It was most likely written to Jewish Christians meeting in house churches outside of Palestine. James writes his letter with a focus on the faith of the believer and instructs believers on how to live out that faith. This faith should be expressed in one's lifestyle. The message of the book of James is that once individuals come to faith in Jesus, their lives, their thoughts, and their desires should all be oriented toward what pleases the Lord. Faith and right action should complement one another in the life of the believer.

At-A-Glance

1. Destructive Desire (James 4:1–3)
2. Faithful Fulfillment (vv. 4–5)
3. Pure Pursuit (vv. 6–10)

In Depth

1. Destructive Desire (James 4:1–3)

While Christians should be characterized by brotherly love, James is addressing a church that was hostile and divided. He begins by considering the cause of the wars and disputes that had arisen. The hostility had arisen from the evil desires within, specifically, desires for one's own pleasure.

The people turned to fighting and waging war to satisfy their own desires and ambitions. They did not turn to God to ask for what they desired. They sought to obtain their desires by their own means. Any petition to God was rooted in hedonism and a desire for pleasure or position.

How can you ensure that your interactions with others arise from pure motives?

2. Faithful Fulfillment (vv. 4–5)

After coming to faith, believers should abandon their old worldview. We should let go of the negative values, beliefs, and ways of thinking we held before becoming followers of Christ. We cannot hold on to both. When we accept Christ, we should allow Him to reshape us. To resist this process is to remain friends with the world. James notes that whoever is a friend of the world is an enemy of God.

God does not want to compete with the world for our affections. God has put His Spirit within us, and He wants us to be faithful to Him alone. God's Spirit "yearns jealously" for our full attention and affection. We cannot give faithful service to God and the world. God demands that we are faithful to Him first and foremost.

Reflect on the areas where you invest your time, talent, and treasure. Do they reflect love for God or for the world?

3. Pure Pursuit (vv. 6–10)

James offers the solution for the hostility and hedonism that plagued the church: submission to God. We are to humbly and purely submit our desires and ourselves to God. Submission to God should be the believer's first priority. We must submit to His wishes and standards.

When we draw near to God in humble submission, God draws near to us. God's love for us is immeasurable. When we recognize our need for Him and draw closer to Him, God draws near to us.

Humble submission is what God desires (Micah 6:8). James urges readers to humble themselves before the Lord and to "cleanse your hands," which refers to the ceremonial purification worship rites of priests in the Old Testament (James 4:8). It was symbolic of turning from sin. He also urges readers to purify their hearts, symbolizing an inward purification as well. James instructs readers to show genuine sorrow and remorse for sinful lifestyles.

Believers must submit themselves to God. The act of submitting yourself to God is paired with resisting the devil. When we do so, the enemy flees from us and we triumph over temptation.

James writes that God opposes the proud, but exalts those who humble themselves before Him. What have you done to draw near to God recently?

Search the Scriptures

1. James writes that to be friends with the world is to be an enemy of God. What does it mean to engage the world but not love worldliness?

2. James encourages us to humble ourselves before the Lord. In times past, people frequently did this by fasting, often with sackcloth and ashes. What does humbling ourselves before the Lord look like today?

Discuss the Meaning

1. Tell of a time when your media- or social media-influenced thoughts or words led you to a compromising situation. What does Scripture say about the importance of those thoughts and actions?

2. Give both a biblical and modern example of submission to God. How does God reward true submission throughout the Bible? Give examples.

Liberating Lesson

When we look at the conflicts in our world, whether disputes among our neighbors or wars between nations, the motive is often meeting selfish desires at the expense of others. As believers we must be attentive to not satisfy ourselves in ways that marginalize, take advantage of, or harm others. We must remain wholly committed to God, yet also engage the broken world around us. God cares for the lost and He expects us to show His love to the world. This has a direct impact on how we treat others—believers and unbelievers. Let the love of God lead you as you interact with others. Guard against conflict arising from inner desires and ambitions. However, we must take care to make sure that God remains the center of our affection. We cannot allow worldly pleasures and desires to draw us away from God or cause conflict with one another. We must resist the devil, draw near to God, and submit to God every day of our lives, choosing to reflect Christ in intentions and actions.

Application for Activation

One of the most important things a believer can do is draw close to God. Set aside some time in the next seven days to spend with God. Pour your heart out to Him and listen for what He has for you. God also expects us to be loyal to Him alone. While we must interact with the world, we must also remain wholly faithful to the Lord. We must remain in constant contact with Him through His Word and prayer. As you pray, examine the motives behind your desires and be sure that they align with the heart of

God. Finally, submit yourself to God. Submit your thoughts and your ways to Him. Let your interactions with others be motivated with the pure motive of God's love.

Follow the Spirit

What God wants me to do:

_____

_____

_____

_____

Remember Your Thoughts

Special insights I have learned:

_____

_____

_____

_____

More Light on the Text

James 4:1–10

4:1 From whence come wars and fightings among you? come they not hence, even of your lusts that war in your members?

In this passage, James is addressing the community as a whole, not individuals. This is a more detailed explanation of the principle mentioned previously that confusion and disorder result from envy and strife (3:16). He asks the believers to identify the origin of wars (*polemos*, **POH-leh-moce**) and fightings (*mache*, **MAH-khay**) among them. These words can be used to describe conflict between both individuals and between nations. The phrase "wars and fightings" can mean heated verbal arguments and serious armed struggle. Paul told Titus, to "avoid…strivings [*mache*] about the law; for they are unprofitable and vain" (Titus 3:9). Certainly some things are worth fighting for, or at least defending. However, the struggle must be done in a God-honoring way.

Unrighteous attitudes come from lust (*hedone*, **hay-doh-NAY**), which can be translated as "passion." This word is not necessarily negative because it can also be translated as "pleasure." But in the New Testament it is always used negatively (Luke 8:14; Titus 2:3; 2 Peter 2:13). James continues the military image to suggest that lusts or passions are waging wars within individuals. There is a battle, for example, between the desires of the body and the desires of the spirit. Peter alludes to this type of conflict: "Abstain from fleshly lusts, which war against the soul" (from 1 Peter 2:11). Paul also is plagued with this type of internal conflict: "But I see another law in my members, warring against the law of my mind, and bringing me into captivity to the law of sin which is in my members" (Romans 7:23).

2 Ye lust, and have not: ye kill, and desire to have, and cannot obtain: ye fight and war yet ye have not, because ye ask not. 3 Ye ask, and receive not, because ye ask amiss, that ye may consume it upon your lusts.

The first part of this verse explains the implications of frustrated desire. James says the source of these conflicts is lust or desire for something. When such desires are unfulfilled, people commit murder. Again, when a person desires something and cannot get it, fighting and war could result. This pattern of unfulfilled and unchecked desires is present in the New Testament. Envy led certain Jewish leaders to arrest Jesus, and Pilate knew this (Mark 15:10). In the case of Jesus, it led to His death. James was warning the believers that if they continued in this manner, their unfulfilled desires could lead to killings. His question already tells us that there have been wars and fighting among them (v. 1). Even today, envy and unfulfilled desires are behind many personal conflicts and national war.

James gives two reasons why the believers do not have what they want. The first is simple: They do not have because they do not ask. The second reason is connected to the first; when they ask, they do not receive because they ask wrongly. James then explains what it means to ask wrongly: They ask in order to satisfy their lusts. These believers are still operating within the realm that created their problems in the first place, namely, their lusts. To ask only to satisfy one's selfish desire is just as much of a problem as not asking at all; both are feeding our lust and causing conflict. James contrasts their behavior with the principle that Jesus used in prayer, "Ask, and it shall be given you" (from Matthew 7:7). If what we ask is within God's will, we can be confident that He listens to us (1 John 5:14).

4 Ye adulterers and adulteresses, know ye not that the friendship of the world is enmity with God? Whosoever therefore will be a friend of the world is the enemy of God.

The phrase "ye adulterers and adulteresses" is one word in Greek, *moichalides* (**moy-kah-LIH-dess**), which means adulteresses, not adulterers. Why does James use this feminine term to describe the believers? In the following verses, James quotes heavily from the Old Testament. His use of the term "adulteresses" picks up the imagery of the relationship between God and Israel in the Old Testament. The relationship between God and Israel is sometimes referred to as a marriage (Isaiah 54:4–6; Jeremiah 2:2). Israel's disobedience is considered "spiritual adultery." The prophet Hosea uses this language profusely (Hosea

2:5, 7, 16, 20). Jesus also used this terminology to describe the Israelites when He calls them "an evil and adulterous generation" (Matthew 12:39). James is justified to call the believers adulteresses because they were developing intimacy with the world.

James reiterates a point that we cannot serve God and the world at the same time. James' strong language and position are based on his conviction that the believers' confession must match their lifestyle. They cannot be double-minded. James is making the point that to be intimate with the world is a betrayal of God. We cannot authentically proclaim that God is the only one who satisfies us and then seek satisfaction from the world.

5 Do ye think that the scripture saith in vain, The spirit that dwelleth in us lusteth to envy?

The "spirit" (Gk. *pneuma*, **puh-NEW-mah**) that dwells in us could be a reference to the Holy Spirit who dwells in born-again believers (cf. 1 Corinthians 3:16). It could also be a reference to the breath of God that is in all human beings right from creation, which is the human spirit. Thus, James could be appealing to the believers that God owns them either by virtue of creation or by virtue of their new life in Christ. The implication is that the Spirit dwelling in believers in Jesus Christ should not be united to the world, but be faithful to Christ.

6 But he giveth more grace. Wherefore he saith, God resisteth the proud, but giveth grace unto the humble.

The first part of verse 6 is a quotation of Proverbs 4:34, and the second part is similar to 1 Peter 5:5–9. In fact, a comparison of James 4:6–9 and 1 Peter 5:5–9 shows that the two passages share many exhortations. It seems that the suggestion here is not new to the believers. James is reinforcing the idea that he is not giving a new commandment, but standing in the tradition of giving wisdom to interpret what the Scripture already said. God is gracious to His children, and He gives them grace to live for Him when they recognize they need God and submit to His will rather than their own.

However, God resists the proud who live in sin by earthly wisdom. Those who believe they are self-sufficient and do not need God or are "self-made" are proud in their own eyes. This is a common theme in the Old Testament (Psalm 18:27; Zephaniah 3:11–12).

7 Submit yourselves therefore to God. Resist the devil, and he will flee from you. 8 Draw nigh to God, and he will draw nigh to you. Cleanse your hands, ye sinners; and purify your hearts, ye double minded. 9 Be afflicted, and mourn, and weep: let your laughter be turned to mourning, and your joy to heaviness.

Verses 7–10 are a series of commands. These commands call believers to discard the habits of the old life and to practice these new ones. James recognizes the danger of the devil and calls for the believers to resist him. Resisting the devil is crucial because his primary purpose is to do everything he can to ruin believers' lives. This resistance is paired in the following verse with drawing close to God.

These verses describe the procedure of drawing near to God. The first step is repentance. This is signified by the cleansing of hands (an external action) and the purification of hearts (an internal action). James calls the people who need cleansing double-minded. Previously James had called these people unstable (1:8), but it also carries the image of these believers who want to be a friend of God and a friend of the world, too (4:4). This theme of drawing near to God in worship with clean hands and hearts is an Old Testament concept.

King David said clean hands and a pure heart were necessary for those who would minister before the Lord (Psalm 24:3–4).

James also calls the believers to be remorseful and mourn over their sins. This is similar to the prophetic language of calling the Israelites back to God. The Lord called the Children of Israel back to Himself through the prophet Joel because the Day of the Lord was near. He says, "Turn ye even to me with all your heart, and with fasting, and with weeping, and with mourning: And rend your heart, and not your garments" (from Joel 2:12–13). Deep sorrow and repentance over our sins is the appropriate response to sinning. Believers can sometimes fall into carelessness about sin, taking it lightly because of Christ's forgiveness. This forgetfulness, however, is not the real joy and peace God wants His children to have. True joy comes from genuine repentance before God and knowledge of having peace with God through Jesus Christ.

10 Humble yourselves in the sight of the Lord, and he shall lift you up.

This is the last in a series of commands that James gives. Humility before God is to recognize our true state as human beings. God is God; we are not. We are poor, wretched, and needy compared to God's holiness. Many preachers have said, "True humility isn't to think less of yourself, but to think of yourself less." It is living with the mindset that puts God at the center of your life in thought and action. It is recognizing our deep constant need for God regardless of what we have. This state of humility is best exemplified in the parable Jesus told of the two people who came to pray in the Temple (Luke 18:10–14). One was a Pharisee and the other was a tax collector. The tax collector recognized his spiritual poverty before God and asked for mercy. Jesus concluded, "everyone that exalteth himself shall be abased [humbled]; and he that humbleth himself shall be exalted" (from v. 14). Deep humility in the Christian life is synonymous with total dependence on God.

Sources:

Keener, Craig S. *The IVP Bible Background Commentary New Testament*. Downers Grove, IL: InterVarsity Press, 1993.

Richards, Larry, and Lawrence O. Richards. *The Teacher's Commentary*. Wheaton, IL: Victor Books, 1987.

Utley, Robert James. *Jesus' Half-Brothers Speak: James and Jude*. Vol. 11. Study Guide Commentary Series. Marshall, TX: Bible Lessons International, 2000.

Walvoord, John F., and Roy B. Zuck. *The Bible Knowledge Commentary: An Exposition of the Scriptures*. Wheaton, IL: Victor Books, 1985.

Daily Bible Readings

MONDAY
One Teacher, Many Students
(Matthew 23:1–11)

TUESDAY
Members Depend on Each Other
(1 Corinthians 12:19–26)

WEDNESDAY
Solve Conflicts One to One
(Matthew 5:21–26)

THURSDAY
Longing for God's Help
(Psalm 42)

FRIDAY
Walk in Newness of Life
(Romans 6:1–14)

SATURDAY
Boasting an Insult to God
(James 4:13–7)

SUNDAY
Godly Approach to Worldliness
(James 4:1–10)

Notes

_____

_____

_____

_____

Teaching Tips

Words You Should Know

A. Magnified *megaluno* (Gk.)—Increased, made great, enlarged.

B. Pretense *prophasis* (Gk.)—An attempt to make something appear true, doing something for show.

Teacher Preparation

Unifying Principle—Submit to God. It is easy to become demoralized by difficult circumstances and adversaries. How can people maintain their joy? Paul willingly submits to God's will and rejoices that his sufferings have led to further proclamation of the Gospel.

A. Read the Bible Background and Devotional Readings.

B. Pray for your students and lesson clarity.

C. Read the lesson Scripture in multiple translations.

D. Option: Present information to the class regarding Christians who are persecuted for their faith today (see opendoors.org, persecution.com, and others). Brainstorm how to pray for and assist in tangible ways those who are persecuted.

O—Open the Lesson

A. Begin the class with prayer.

B. Have the students read the Aim for Change.

C. Have the students read the In Focus story.

D. Ask students how events named in the story can weigh on their hearts and how they can view these events from a theological perspective.

P—Present the Scriptures

A. Read the Focal Verses and discuss the Background and The People, Places, and Times sections.

B. Have the class share what Scriptures stand out for them and why, with particular emphasis on today's context.

E—Explore the Meaning

A. Use In Depth or More Light on the Text to help provide more in-depth discussion of the lesson text.

B. Discuss the Liberating Lesson and Application for Activation sections.

N—Next Steps for Application

A. Summarize the value of submitting to God despite our circumstances.

B. End class with a commitment to pray for incarcerated persons and those who are persecuted for their faith.

Worship Guide

For the Superintendent or Teacher
Theme: Submit to God in Christ
Song: "The Name of the Lord"
Devotional Reading: 1 Peter 4:12–19

Submit to God in Christ

Bible Background • PHILIPPIANS 1:12–21
Printed Text • PHILIPPIANS 1:12–21 | Devotional Reading • 1 PETER 4:12–19

—————— Aim for Change ——————

By the end of this lesson, we will: ANALYZE Paul's circumstances spreading the Gospel despite others' responses; DECIDE to be faithful and forgive others; and REJOICE in opportunities to do God's work in the world through Jesus Christ.

—————— In Focus ——————

When the year started, Brenda had been vice principal of a high school, managing 1,600 teenagers through SATs, state-mandated exams, and parental expectations. City council members pushed for better test scores, criticizing the principals and school administrators for poor results—without acknowledging those administrators worked with limited resources and money. The school board responded with greater pressure on all the schools to show changes each quarter. Brenda worked with her teachers, trying to help them keep the balance between test preparation and teaching the things tests don't measure, such as kindness, cooperation, and judgment.

There were improvements at Brenda's high school, but the numbers were deemed insufficient. Brenda was reassigned to a middle school as an English and social studies teacher.

"It's not fair," her friend Moravia said. "I can't believe you're not mad."

"I'm in the classroom," Brenda said. "I'm helping kids learn. I'm teaching what they need to know so they can know how to think, how to figure out the world around them. I think that's a good thing, for them and for me. God has put me where He wants me to be."

Some who teach the Gospel preach from envy and rivalry, but the Word of God is stronger than the motives of the people who spread it. Can we discern the message no matter who is the messenger?

—————— Keep in Mind ——————

"But I would ye should understand, brethren, that the things which happened unto me have fallen out rather unto the furtherance of the gospel" (Philippians 1:12).

"And I want you to know, my dear brothers and sisters, that everything that has happened to me here has helped to spread the Good News" (Philippians 1:12, NLT).

Focal Verses

KJV **Philippians 1:12** But I would ye should understand, brethren, that the things which happened unto me have fallen out rather unto the furtherance of the gospel;

13 So that my bonds in Christ are manifest in all the palace, and in all other places;

14 And many of the brethren in the Lord, waxing confident by my bonds, are much more bold to speak the word without fear.

15 Some indeed preach Christ even of envy and strife; and some also of good will:

16 The one preach Christ of contention, not sincerely, supposing to add affliction to my bonds:

17 But the other of love, knowing that I am set for the defence of the gospel.

18 What then? notwithstanding, every way, whether in pretence, or in truth, Christ is preached; and I therein do rejoice, yea, and will rejoice.

19 For I know that this shall turn to my salvation through your prayer, and the supply of the Spirit of Jesus Christ,

20 According to my earnest expectation and my hope, that in nothing I shall be ashamed, but that with all boldness, as always, so now also Christ shall be magnified in my body, whether it be by life, or by death.

21 For to me to live is Christ, and to die is gain.

NLT **Philippians 1:12** And I want you to know, my dear brothers and sisters, that everything that has happened to me here has helped to spread the Good News.

13 For everyone here, including the whole palace guard, knows that I am in chains because of Christ.

14 And because of my imprisonment, most of the believers here have gained confidence and boldly speak God's message without fear.

15 It's true that some are preaching out of jealousy and rivalry. But others preach about Christ with pure motives.

16 They preach because they love me, for they know I have been appointed to defend the Good News.

17 Those others do not have pure motives as they preach about Christ. They preach with selfish ambition, not sincerely, intending to make my chains more painful to me.

18 But that doesn't matter. Whether their motives are false or genuine, the message about Christ is being preached either way, so I rejoice. And I will continue to rejoice.

19 For I know that as you pray for me and the Spirit of Jesus Christ helps me, this will lead to my deliverance.

20 For I fully expect and hope that I will never be ashamed, but that I will continue to be bold for Christ, as I have been in the past. And I trust that my life will bring honor to Christ, whether I live or die.

21 For to me, living means living for Christ, and dying is even better.

The People, Places, and Times

Prison. Imprisonment during Paul's time could take a variety of forms. At Philippi, Paul was imprisoned in the town jail under the charge of a keeper, where there was an inner, perhaps underground, chamber containing stocks (Acts 16:24). Stocks had several holes, allowing a prisoner's legs to be forced wide apart to ensure greater security and greater pain. In Caesarea, Paul was imprisoned in

Herod's praetorium, a high-level judicial building (23:35), but when a prisoner at Rome, he was allowed to stay in his own lodging with a soldier always chained to him (28:16, 30).

Background

Philippians is a letter written by Paul during a time of imprisonment. While scholars debate the exact time and location of Paul's writing, lessons from his imprisonment about how the Philippian community should appropriately respond to persecution and adversity in light of the Gospel is clear. In Philippians 1, we read Paul's opening words that are surprisingly full of joy and gratitude, something one would not typically expect from an inmate. Paul grounds his unusual response to his situation in his life's mission—the advancement of the Gospel. Imprisonment has assured Paul of this mission as he has found greater zeal to proclaim Christ. He has used his situation as an opportunity to showcase the power of the Gospel as he preaches to his fellow prisoners and even to the imperial guard! In jail chains, Paul comes to the conclusion that no matter what is happening in his life, the Gospel of Jesus Christ can be proclaimed with power and efficacy. Paul emerges with joy, from proclaiming Christ despite his circumstances, and with gratitude, for the prayers of the Philippian saints and the help of the Holy Spirit empowering him to preach with perseverance.

Describe a time when your perspective changed in a bad situation, and it made all the difference.

At-A-Glance

1. Prison Can't Stop the Gospel
(Philippians 1:12–14)
2. People Can't Stop the Gospel (vv. 15–18)
3. The Gospel Goes Forth by Prayer
(vv. 19–21)

In Depth

1. Prison Can't Stop the Gospel (Philippians 1:12–14)

While the location and timing of Paul's imprisonment is not clear, its purpose is. Instances of Paul's incarceration elsewhere in Scripture (Acts 16:29–34; 21:10–14; 23:10–11; 26:21–22; 28:30–31), and from Paul's own pen here in Philippians, express his imprisonment is explicitly for the "furtherance of the gospel" (1:12). Through Paul's life, we see even the chains of imprisonment could not stop the Gospel from being spread through the life of a believer. The Gospel can be shared even in the most oppressive and adverse situations in life. The Gospel is not limited to a physical place, like a church, but can be effective wherever there are convicted believers and open hearts. Paul discovered that no situation could hinder the mission of his life so that he was "waxing confident…without fear" (1:14) in a situation that would suggest the opposite.

How can you spread the Gospel in your life now?

2. People Can't Stop the Gospel (vv. 15–18)

Paul discovered nothing could stop the spread of the Gospel—not prison, and not other people with bad motives. As Paul had gained "greater boldness without fear" (1:14), so had other preachers, some of whom preached "of envy and strife" (v. 15). This group of preachers added to Paul's suffering, but through their preaching, they also added new believers to the church. Although these preachers' motives were bad, the results were good. There were other preachers who preached from "goodwill" (1:15), and like their counterparts, also added new believers to the Church. Instead of focusing on motives, Paul chose to focus on mission. He trusted that God would work out His plan of salvation regardless of how it was preached or who preached. What truly mattered to Paul was that the Gospel was preached and that new believers were brought into the church.

What really matters to you such that you do not have to participate in it to fully support it?

3. The Gospel Goes Forth by Prayer (vv. 19–21)

Paul acknowledged the difficulty of maintaining his joyful perspective. He realized it was only through the Philippians' prayers and the help of the Spirit that he could rejoice at the Gospel's spread despite his imprisonment and other preachers' bad motives. These things not only emboldened his preaching, but also emboldened his hope for his life. While Paul desired release from prison, he trusted that the result of the legal proceedings associated with his incarceration, whether free or chained, would result in the glory of God. He had the confidence of being in Christ. Paul came to the conclusion that living in Christ does not free one from problems, difficulties, persecution, or adversity, but Christ is the totality of the believer's life. He was assured that his life was guaranteed in Christ and that his experiences had a greater purpose.

How does knowing "Christ is life" affect how a Christian should live?

Search the Scriptures

1. What were some positive outcomes of Paul's imprisonment (Philippians 1:13–14)?

2. What did Paul plan to do about the people who preached Christ from envy, strife, and contention (v. 18)?

Discuss the Meaning

1. How do you find the strength to keep working when people are against you?

2. How can facing challenge or opposition sometimes help us accomplish a goal?

Liberating Lesson

Paul makes it clear that his imprisonment is purposeful. His suffering advances the spread of the Gospel, even reaching those who inflicted suffering upon him (the imperial guard). The liberating Gospel can and must be preached even when the preacher is in chains. From police brutality, to disproportionate rates of unemployment and underemployment, to many other forms and expressions of racial injustice, suffering seems to mark the everyday existence of African American life in the United States. As these injustices are sinful and cause much suffering, like Paul, we are to preach the liberating Gospel even while suffering in chains. We can resist through our suffering with the joy that comes from prayer and the Holy Spirit. We can find our hope for living through suffering with purpose because Christ has guaranteed us eternal life.

Application for Activation

Think about your life. Consider your suffering. Consider the suffering of others in your family, at your job, in your community, and in the world. Consider the suffering and imprisonment of persecuted Christians across the world. Consider how you will respond to suffering—not with a passive joy, but with a resistant joy like Paul.

What is your initial reaction to suffering in your life? What is your perspective on what you face in life and in society? Where do you see God at work in adversity? How can you glorify God in your suffering? How do you rejoice in suffering?

Follow the Spirit

What God wants me to do:

_____

_____

Remember Your Thoughts
Special insights I have learned:

_____

_____

_____

_____

More Light on the Text
Philippians 1:12–21
12 But I would ye should understand, brethren, that the things which happened unto me have fallen out rather unto the furtherance of the gospel; 13 So that my bonds in Christ are manifest in all the palace, and in all other places; 14 And many of the brethren in the Lord, waxing confident by my bonds, are much more bold to speak the word without fear.

Paul's imprisonment has yielded positive results: a) the Gospel is being made known all over the region including the official residence of the governor; b) many of the brothers are now preaching the Good News with boldness. Paul's imprisonment for preaching the Gospel was intended to stop its spread in the region, however God was using his situation to reach not only the very people who kept him in prison, but also to encourage preachers all over the region to be passionate about preaching the Gospel. Paul's testimony that he was preaching in spite of being in chains was a catalyst for free believers to be even more bold about proclaiming the name of Jesus Christ. However, Paul separates these preachers into two groups according to their motives.

15 Some indeed preach Christ even of envy and strife; and some also of good will: 16 The one preach Christ of contention, not sincerely, supposing to add affliction to my bonds: 17 But the other of love, knowing that I am set for the defense of the gospel.

The first group, Paul says, preaches out of a wrong motive "of envy and strife." This group is prompted by "envy" (Gk. *phthonos*, **fuh-THO-noce**), meaning jealousy or ill will, and "strife" (Gk. *eris*, **EH-reece**), meaning rivalry, discord, or contention. They are preaching to out-preach each other, build themselves a platform, and criticize those they dislike. Paul goes on to illustrate how this group's preaching is motivated by evil (v. 16). They preach Christ out of contention, not sincerely; and not with a clean motive, but with an ulterior motive: "to add affliction to my bonds." The word "contention" is a translation of the Greek *eritheia* (**eh-ree-THAY-ah**), which means, in simple terms, selfishness or a desire to put oneself forward in a partisan way.

Who were these men who were preaching out of jealousy and selfish ambition with the intention of adding to Paul's burden? Paul does not seem as much concerned with these people and their evil plans as he is about the positive result of their preaching (v. 18). He does not intend to occupy himself or concern his audience's mind with much negativity. He leaves us with no answer. However, scholars have advanced a number of proposals as to who these people were. Certain preachers in Rome had attained some prominence before Paul's arrival. His presence in Rome and the spreading of his fame and the Gospel throughout the region were beginning to affect their prestige (vv. 13–14). The preachers' names seem to have been relegated to the background—not mentioned as often as before the apostle's arrival. They became envious and contentious; thus, their motive for preaching the Gospel was affected. Later in this letter, Paul exhorts the Philippians to be one in the mind of Christ, not putting oneself forward or being selfish (2:3). Similarly, James denounces selfishness or self-promoting "in your hearts" (James 3:14).

The second group to which Paul refers preached out of pure motive—"of good will" (1:15) and "love" (v. 17). They are also motivated by the fact that Paul has been "set for the defence of the gospel" (v. 17). "Set" (Gk. *keimai*, **KAY-my**) here can also mean destined or appointed. The word also carries the image of a law being immutably set down. This refers either to the immediate trial he is about to face for the sake of the Gospel or his overall mission of sharing the Gospel's "defence" (Gk. *apologia*, **ah-poe-low-GEE-ah**; where we get the word "apologetics"). This group was motivated out of "good will" prompted by love for Paul and the Gospel he proclaimed.

These people did not feel indignant about Paul because his fame was spreading around the region. Unlike the former group, their focus was not on themselves. They heralded Christ out of love for Him and the Gospel, and out of concern for Paul and his tribulation—a love that Paul prayed for: "And this I pray, that your love may abound still more and more in knowledge and all discernment" (1:9).

18 What then? Notwithstanding, every way, whether in pretence, or in truth, Christ is preached; and I therein do rejoice, yea, and will rejoice.

Rather than moan about the selfishly motivated preaching of the first group or dwelling in self-pity and attracting sympathy for such un-Christian behavior toward him, Paul focused on the result of their preaching. Here he says, "What then?" or "That doesn't matter" (NLT). It is another way of saying that what matters is the outcome of their preaching, which turned out to be positive. Whether

they were preaching to hurt him is not the main concern. The most important concern is advancing the Gospel. What matters to Paul is not what the people are doing to him but rather what they are doing for the Gospel.

From here, we can learn one truth: The Lord will work out His desired purpose through the Gospel regardless of how it is preached or the motive of the preachers. To Paul, it did not matter. What mattered is that in "every way"— whether in pretense, as by those with selfish motives, or "in truth," as by those who preach with sincere hearts to glorify the Lord—"Christ is preached." This is true today, too. "Pretense" (Gk. *prophasis*, **PRO-fah-seece**), is the same word used to describe the prayers of the scribes (Mark 12:40; John 15:22): an outward show, cloak, or pretext. It is the opposite of sincerity. Regardless of others' insincere showing in preaching, Paul expresses the great joy he finds in the accompanying furtherance of the Gospel: "I therein do rejoice, yea, and will rejoice." He rejoices currently and will continue to rejoice because only the goal of spreading the Gospel is in mind.

19 For I know that this shall turn to my salvation through your prayer, and the supply of the Spirit of Jesus Christ.

In this section, Paul expresses his confidence in the prayer of the brethren and optimism that he would be set free. This also makes him rejoice. The Greek preposition "for" (Gk. *gar*, **GAR**) connects the preceding statement with the assurance of his deliverance. Paul's use of *eido* (**EYE-do**) means to know, to see, to perceive with the eyes or by any of the senses. It has the sense of certainty and confidence that all will turn out well for him in the end (cf. Romans 8:28). The result will be his "salvation," or deliverance. Paul's expressed knowledge here does not mean he had information of his possible deliverance but rather that he had personal conviction that, through the prayers of the people and the work of the Holy Spirit, he would be set free from prison. In the previous verses, Paul was rejoicing because in the present he was in chains and his imprisonment brought him opportunities to share the Gospel with the entire palace guard. But Paul continued to rejoice because of his hope for the future (v. 18).

The word "salvation" or *soteria* in the Greek (**so-tay-REE-ah**) has two meanings. It can refer to salvation in a spiritual sense or it can refer to Paul's deliverance from prison, which he expected and did happen. Trusting the faithfulness of God, coupled with the prayers of the saints and the working of the Holy Spirit, Paul is persuaded that he would be set free. Paul spoke of his release from prison through the prayers of the Philippians, indicating that Paul viewed the Christian life not as a solitary discipline but as life in community with other believers in which all were bound together. Paul exemplifies that we all need the prayers of one another.

20 According to my earnest expectation and my hope, that in nothing I shall be ashamed, but that with all boldness, as always, so now also Christ shall be magnified in my body, whether it be by life, or by death.

Paul's confidence in Christ is the basis for his "earnest expectation and my hope." He has two convictions. The first is that whatever happens, he would not be ashamed. The Spirit will not let him down. This whole passage exudes confidence in the Lord. The Greek words for "earnest expectation" and "hope" are nearly identical in meaning. *Apokaradokia* (**ah-poe-kah-rah-doe-KEE-ah**) has a sense of intense anticipation, and *elpis* (**el-PEECE**) means "to expect with great confidence and faith." Paul was looking forward to his trial, which was sure to result in glorification of the Lord. Paul stated that he was not ashamed of being in prison. He was not worried about his personal reputation. In fact, he was feeling very bold. The only true shame would be if he were not trusting in God and not living in obedience to Him.

The second conviction is that he would wax bold in proclaiming the Gospel, as he had always done, but more so now. Paul was looking forward to his trial with great confidence. The end goal is clear: "Christ shall be magnified" in Paul—literally, in Paul's "body" (Gk. *soma*, **SO-mah**), in this case whether he is a survivor or martyr, which he becomes years later. The Greek word for "magnified" is *megaluno* (**meh-ga-LOO-no**), which means increased, made great, or enlarged. This was Paul's goal for his trial—to increase the greatness of the reputation of our Lord, as has always been his goal in everything he did after his encounter on the Damascus road. When he spoke of his body, he was thinking of what might be the outcome of the trial. Although Paul expected to be released, he began meditating on the other possibility—death. His body might experience physical life or bodily death, but his goal was that in either situation he would magnify the Lord. What a great testimony!

In either circumstance, he would remain faithful to the end so that Christ's name would be lifted. This is a show of courage, deeply resolute conviction, and resignation to the service of the Lord Jesus. In our lives we, too, should always seek to glorify Christ. And when troubles come our way we can trust in the Lord, knowing that if our lives have glorified Him, we can have great confidence and not be ashamed.

21 For to me to live is Christ, and to die is gain.

Paul's conviction and courage are demonstrated in his total resignation to whatever comes his way. The use of the phrase "for to me" is purposely put at the beginning of the sentence for emphasis to draw our attention to Paul's personal conviction regarding life and death. Paul gives new meaning to both "life" and "death." To him "living is Christ," which means, among other interpretations, "life means Christ." Paul's very existence is in Christ—whatever he does is inspired through his resolute relationship with Christ and for Him. To Paul, life would be meaningless and not worth living without Christ, to whom Paul owes his existence (Romans 14:7–9). He dedicates his whole being to Christ and His cause, to love and obey Him in everything and at all times, and to trust Him in all circumstances.

His resolution to live for Christ does not mean a life free from problems and difficulties. On the contrary, it means living for Christ and preaching the Gospel in spite of problems and difficulties: imprisonment (Philippians 1:7, 13), afflictions (4:14), suffering (1:29; 3:10), struggles (1:30), and all types of tribulation, both physical and emotional (2 Corinthians 11:23–27). Paul's life and ministry were not easy. They were characterized by unimaginable problems and sufferings, as we can see from these and other accounts of his life. On the one hand, for Paul to go on living means leading a dedicated and fruitful life for Christ; on the other hand, for Paul "to die is gain." He knows that death means an immediate experience of the presence of Christ. Paul is so engrossed in the Gospel and in the reality of eternity that living means working and living for Christ, and dying is even more profitable since he would be with his Lord forever. This is the hope of every believer.

Here, Paul is reiterating his total resignation to the Lord. Whatever comes his way, whether death or life or release from prison, he has turned over his life and will to that of the Lord Jesus Christ. The apostle's relationship to Christ was so close that he would only experience more joy, more closeness to Christ, and more fullness of praise when he went to be with Him. Yet, even here on Earth, he was living so in tune with Christ that his life was all about the Lord. The more time we spend in fellowship with Christ, reading His Word, answering it in praise and acts of obedience, the more heaven tugs at our hearts as well.

Sources:

Abate, Eshetu. "Philippians." In *Africa Bible Commentary.* Tokunboh Adeyemo, ed. Grand Rapids, MI: Zondervan, 2006.

BibleGateway.com. Online Bible Study tools. Grand Rapids, MI: Zondervan.

Fee, Gordon. *Paul's Letter to the Philippians.* Grand Rapids, MI: W.B. Eerdmans, 1995.

Jewell, Elizabeth F. and Frank Abate, eds. *New Oxford American Dictionary.* New York: Oxford University Press, 2001.

Oxford Universal Dictionary on Historical Principles. 3rd ed. New York: Oxford University Press, 1955.

Daily Bible Readings

MONDAY
God Sent Me to Preserve You
(Genesis 45:1–8)

TUESDAY
The Spirit Rested on the
Elders
(Numbers 11:24–30)

WEDNESDAY
Apostles Are Fools for Christ
(1 Corinthians 4:8–13)

THURSDAY
Sharing Life in Christ Now
(Philippians 1:22–26)

FRIDAY
Believing in and Suffering
for Christ
(Philippians 1:27–30)

SATURDAY
Sharing God's Grace
(Philippians 1:3–11)

SUNDAY
Telling the Good News
(Philippians 1:12–21)

Notes

_____

_____

_____

_____

_____

_____

_____

_____

_____

Teaching Tips

Words You Should Know

A. Exalt *upsoo* (Gk.)—To uplift or place higher.

B. Confess *exomologeo* (Gk.)—To openly acknowledge or speak forth.

Teacher Preparation

Unifying Principle—Humility and Sacrifice. Personal interests and selfish ambitions can lead to controversies that threaten our relationships. How can people overcome their divisiveness? Paul commends the example of Christ, who humbly emptied Himself in order to serve God and others through His sacrifice.

A. Read the Bible Background and Devotional Readings.

B. Pray for your students and lesson clarity.

C. Read the lesson Scripture in multiple translations.

D. Option: Do one or more case studies on people who left great wealth or comfort to serve with those in poverty or persecution.

O—Open the Lesson

A. Begin the class with prayer.

B. Have the students read the Aim for Change.

C. Have the students read the In Focus story.

D. Ask students how events named in the story can weigh on their hearts and how they can view these events from a theological perspective.

P—Present the Scriptures

A. Read the Focal Verses and discuss the Background and The People, Places, and Times sections.

B. Have the class share what Scriptures stand out for them and why, with particular emphasis on today's context.

E—Explore the Meaning

A. Use In Depth or More Light on the Text to help provide more in-depth discussion of the lesson text.

B. Discuss the Liberating Lesson and Application for Activation sections.

N—Next Steps for Application

A. Summarize the value of devoting ourselves to God in humility.

B. End class with a commitment to pray for humility and willingness to sacrifice.

Worship Guide

For the Superintendent or Teacher
Theme: Devote All to Christ
Song: "What A Beautiful Name"
Devotional Reading: Psalm 119:65–72

Devote All to Christ

Bible Background • PHILIPPIANS 2:1–11
Printed Text • PHILIPPIANS 2:1–11 | Devotional Reading • PSALM 119:65–72

—— Aim for Change ——

By the end of this lesson, we will: ANALYZE the work of Christ in Philippians 2:1–11; FOLLOW Christ's example of humility and sacrifice; and GROW in our ability to place the needs of others before our own.

—— 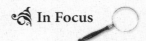 In Focus ——

Coach Jefferies walked around the ballpark looking for Rodney. He found him in the batting cages, patiently taking swing after swing. Jefferies smiled. Rodney had been at the Triple-A level in the organization a little too long, and Jefferies knew his prospects for getting a permanent spot on the big league roster were shrinking with each passing week. Rodney must have known it too, but he never complained.

Rodney was an OK batter and a decent centerfielder, competent but not exceptional. It was off the field where Rodney stood out. He never passed up a chance to help a rookie with his batting stance, or give a fielder a tip about where to position himself to get that grounder, even as they passed by him in the organization. Jefferies respected that, and thought Rodney would be pleased by the news he had for him. "Hey, Rodney—come on in the locker room when you're done, OK?"

When Rodney entered the locker room, all the players and coaches greeted him with big smiles. "What's all this?" he asked.

"We took a vote," Jefferies said, "and we're making it official: You're our team captain."

Rodney tried to demur. "There's nothing special about what I do," Rodney said. "We're a team, right? When one of us does well, we all do well."

Success is about more than just getting a higher number of points than the other team. How can we learn to be humble from Jesus Christ's example?

—— Keep in Mind ——

"Let nothing be done through strife or vainglory; but in lowliness of mind let each esteem other better than themselves" (Philippians 2:3, KJV).

269

"Don't be selfish; don't try to impress others. Be humble, thinking of others as better than yourselves" (Philippians 2:3, NLT).

Focal Verses

KJV **Philippians 2:1** If there be therefore any consolation in Christ, if any comfort of love, if any fellowship of the Spirit, if any bowels and mercies,

2 Fulfil ye my joy, that ye be likeminded, having the same love, being of one accord, of one mind.

3 Let nothing be done through strife or vainglory; but in lowliness of mind let each esteem other better than themselves.

4 Look not every man on his own things, but every man also on the things of others.

5 Let this mind be in you, which was also in Christ Jesus:

6 Who, being in the form of God, thought it not robbery to be equal with God:

7 But made himself of no reputation, and took upon him the form of a servant, and was made in the likeness of men:

8 And being found in fashion as a man, he humbled himself, and became obedient unto death, even the death of the cross.

9 Wherefore God also hath highly exalted him, and given him a name which is above every name:

10 That at the name of Jesus every knee should bow, of things in heaven, and things in earth, and things under the earth;

11 And that every tongue should confess that Jesus Christ is Lord, to the glory of God the Father.

NLT **Philippians 2:1** Is there any encouragement from belonging to Christ? Any comfort from his love? Any fellowship together in the Spirit? Are your hearts tender and compassionate?

2 Then make me truly happy by agreeing wholeheartedly with each other, loving one another, and working together with one mind and purpose.

3 Don't be selfish; don't try to impress others. Be humble, thinking of others as better than yourselves.

4 Don't look out only for your own interests, but take an interest in others, too.

5 You must have the same attitude that Christ Jesus had.

6 Though he was God, he did not think of equality with God as something to cling to.

7 Instead, he gave up his divine privileges; he took the humble position of a slave and was born as a human being. When he appeared in human form,

8 he humbled himself in obedience to God and died a criminal's death on a cross.

9 Therefore, God elevated him to the place of highest honor and gave him the name above all other names,

10 that at the name of Jesus every knee should bow, in heaven and on earth and under the earth,

11 and every tongue declare that Jesus Christ is Lord, to the glory of God the Father.

The People, Places, and Times

Philippi. It was a Roman colony in Macedonia. The people of Philippi were proud of their status as Roman citizens, promoting Latin as their official language and taking advantage of their tax-free status. Many of the social and governmental institutions of Philippi were modeled after those in Rome. The apostle Paul preached the Gospel to the city of Philippi on his second missionary journey. One of Paul's first converts in the area was a prominent Philippian businesswoman named

Lydia. She welcomed Paul and his entourage into her home, which was one of the first house churches in Philippi.

What places or cultures do we see as models in our community building?

Background

While Philippians 2 begins a new section in Paul's letter, Paul continues to expound upon themes considered in his opening. Paul turns his attention to issues affecting the Philippian community: their unity and humility. As Philippians 1 ends with a confession of what God accomplished through Christ for believers resulting in a charge to suffer joyfully like the imprisoned Paul, Philippians 2 explains how the Philippians should do this. Paul reminds them of what they have entered into as a Christian community and what they have received because of Christ's sacrifice. Delivering what scholars consider "the Philippian hymn," Paul lifts up the example of Jesus, drawing on the Christological doctrines of Christ's pre-existence, His divinity and humanity, His subjection and obedience to the Father, His suffering on the Cross, and His resurrection to accomplish salvation for all humankind. Paul uses Christ's humility as exhibited in His earthly ministry as a model for believers to embrace and embody as individuals for the benefit and unity of the entire community.

How does knowing what Christ did for the church affect how we act in the church?

At-A-Glance

1. Community is Created Through Humility
(Philippians 2:1–4)
2. Christ is the Model of Humility (vv. 5-11)

In Depth

1. Community is Created Through Humility (Philippians 2:1–4)

Paul begins his call to unity through humility by reminding the Philippians of what they have received in Christ. He lists four characteristics of the Christian community: "encouragement in Christ;" "consolation in love;" "fellowship in the Spirit;" and "compassion and tenderness" (2:1, NLT). Paul affirms these characteristics as the foundation of the Philippian community and exhorts them to maintain these to achieve unification. He encourages them to "agree wholeheartedly with each other," by "loving one another," and "working together with one mind and one purpose" (2:2, NLT).

In order to fulfill these commands, the community must exhibit the virtue of humility by considering others "better than themselves" (2:3). While Paul is calling the Philippians to unity, he is not calling for uniformity. Paul values the variety of ideas and opinions within the community, but recognizes that diversity can cause division. Paul calls for unity in diversity by way of humility. Individuals can and should maintain their individuality and diversity of thought, but must be careful to avoid selfishness and personal pride that will destroy unity. Paul encourages them to place the interests of others above individual self-interests within the community. Through this type of demonstrated humility on a personal level, unity will be achieved among the Philippians on the communal level.

What does humility look like in diversity?

2. Christ is the Model of Humility (vv. 5-11)

Paul urges the Philippians to follow the example of humility found in Christ's ministry. Through "the Philippian hymn" (vv. 5–11), Paul highlights Christ's humility by drawing specific attention to His servant's nature.

He did not use His divine status for His own personal gain or for special privileges, but to benefit others. While Christ never gave up His divine nature, He "emptied himself," or laid it aside, becoming human so that He could reach humans. Christ's humility went to the depths of the human experience by accepting and subjecting Himself to the most degrading form of capital punishment during the time of His earthly ministry—Roman crucifixion.

As Christ was willing to go to the depths of human humiliation for the benefit of others, the Philippians are called do to the same. Paul urged them to the same type of radical obedience and self-sacrifice that Christ modeled for the world by abandoning self-interest, identifying with the needs of others, and embracing the depths of human suffering for the benefit of others. Christ's incarnation—suffering, crucifixion, and resurrection—is the ultimate example of humility and is the standard for living in Christian community among the Philippians.

How can you "empty yourself" like Christ did?

Search the Scriptures

1. How did Paul ask the Philippians to help make him happy (Philippians 2:2)?

2. Why do you think Paul uses a hymn to call the Philippians to humility (vv. 5–11)? What role do hymns play in other New Testament passages?

Discuss the Meaning

1. What responsibility do you have to share your talents with other people?

2. Philippians is known as the "joy letter." What role does joy play in humility?

Liberating Lesson

While Paul uses the language of "slave" and "servant" to describe the humility that Christ modeled for believers to embody, this has the potential to take on different meanings in light of the African and African-American experiences. Modern-day believers should avoid harmful interpretations of this text that would suggest we are called to purposeless suffering that does not affirm or benefit humanity. Humility's end is to lift others out of sin and suffering, not to humiliate them or ourselves needlessly. Through humility, we are to look for those who are suffering and place their needs and interests above ours. When we do this, we fulfill the Christian mandate of humility by serving others and lifting ourselves together to God through Christ.

Application for Activation

Reflect on your relationships with God, yourself, your faith community, and your larger community. Write in your journal about your experiences to see how you already exhibit Christ's humility and how you can embody humility more fully. Ask a trusted friend where he or she sees humility at work in your life. Ask God to show you where you can serve more deeply and purposefully. What aspects of humility do you need to develop? Where is God calling for your service in your family, faith community, and greater community? How can you deepen and expand your service in the world?

Follow the Spirit

What God wants me to do:

_____

_____

_____

_____

Remember Your Thoughts

Special insights I have learned:

_____

_____

_____

_____

More Light on the Text

Philippians 2:1–11

Although chapter 2 begins a new section, it is definitely connected to and a continuation of the preceding thought in the closing section of chapter 1. There Paul exhorts and wishes that the Philippians "stand fast in one spirit, with one mind striving together for the faith of the gospel" (v. 27), that they be resolutely united in their faith even in the face of suffering from their adversaries (vv. 28–29). This indicates that the Philippian church was going through persecution. In the present section, Paul reiterates the necessity for unity and appeals for individual humility, which is the quality that will foster true oneness. The first four verses deal with Paul's appeal to them by various considerations, to live in unity and in the spirit of the Gospel, loving one another, and each preferring another to oneself. The latter seven verses speak to what the mindset of Christ is and its results.

2:1 If there be therefore any consolation in Christ, if any comfort of love, if any fellowship of the Spirit, if any bowels and mercies,

Paul starts with a cluster of clauses each introduced with the particle "if," which generally expresses conditional clauses. However, here Paul's use of "if" is rhetorical to remind the Philippians there is no doubt that Christ supplies consolation, comfort, and the rest abundantly. The phrase "fellowship of the Spirit" refers to the fellowship that comes through the indwelling presence of the Holy Spirit in both the church and individual lives of the members. In the final clause, Paul uses two words, "bowels," and "mercies." The first word translated, "bowels," is the Greek noun *splagchnon* (**SPLANGKH-non**), which means intestines and innards. In the Greek culture, bowels were regarded as the seat of the more violent passions, such as anger, anxiety, and love. To the Hebrews, bowels were the seat of only the more tender affections, especially kindness, benevolence, and compassion. Paul uses it figuratively to express an inward or deep affection, pity or sympathy (1:8; cf. Colossians 3:12; Philemon 7, 12, 20). The second word used here by Paul is *oiktirmos* (Gk. **oik-tier-MOCE**), translated "mercies." Unlike the more common word for mercy (Gk. *eleos*, **eh-LEH-oce**), *oiktirmos* appears only five times in the New Testament and is synonymous in meaning with "bowels." It is almost exclusively used by Paul and describes such feelings as pity, compassion, and kindness. It is most probable that Paul has in mind here God's affection and compassion toward the Philippians. Therefore, it seems Paul is setting up to say, "If you have experienced the tender mercies and compassion of the Lord, then respond accordingly, and demonstrate it by living it out in your lives."

2 Fulfil ye my joy, that ye be likeminded, having the same love, being of one accord, of one mind.

What would make Paul's joy complete is if the Philippians were united in love and in mind with humility, without selfishness, but caring for one another. Earlier in chapter 1 (vv. 4–5) Paul expressed the joy the Philippians had brought to him, in spite of his affliction, through their "fellowship in the gospel from the first day." "That ye be likeminded" and "of one mind" are identical in meaning, and emphasize Paul's main concern for the Philippian church, which is unity of mind. Paul's frequent use of the word *phroneo* (Gk. **fro-NEH-oh**, to think) and its derivatives in this book reflects his concern for proper Christian attitude, singleness of purpose and mental concentration, which is a catalyst for spiritual growth and holiness. It does not mean everyone should have or agree on the same thing all the time without individual or independent opinion. Rather Paul's choice of the verb *phroneo* seems to convey the idea of spiritual unity or oneness, an inward attitude of mind submitted to the authority of the Holy Spirit, which overrides personal or individual and selfish desires or opinions. The second and third clauses, "having the same love" and "being of one accord" seem to reinforce his concern expressed by the two clauses as explained above. Love is the cord that binds friends, families, fellowships, and churches together. Quite simply, any group that lacks love lacks unity. Therefore, mutual love, such as demonstrated by Christ's sacrificial death for the church, should pervade every Christian community (cf. 2 Thessalonians 1:3; 1 John 3:16).

3 Let nothing be done through strife or vainglory; but in lowliness of mind let each esteem other better than themselves. 4 Look not every man on his own things, but every man also on the things of others.

Verses 3 and 4 expand upon the central thought in the previous verses the exhortation for unity and oneness through humility. Paul says imperatively, "Let nothing be done through strife or vainglory," meaning do not oppose one another by acting selfishly for personal gain. With the word *eritheia* (Gk. **eh-ree-THAY-ah**, strife), Paul is probably alluding to his earlier description of those who preach the Gospel out of selfish and impure motives

(1:16). Paul points out that humility is the key to unity, while pride breeds strife and contention. The overarching concern here is selfishness or lack of concern for the affairs of other people, which would show an absence of the love that Paul spoke just before (v. 2).

5 Let this mind be in you, which was also in Christ Jesus:

The poetic structure and pattern of the passage have compelled many scholars to say that it was an early Christian hymn about Christ Jesus. Whether or not Paul was the composer is not as important as the message Paul tries to convey to the Philippians through it: humility. Paul begins by urging the Philippians to be of the same type of mind as Christ Jesus. The attitude that Paul has been explaining and hoping the Philippians to have (vv. 2–4) corresponds with the attitude displayed by Christ (vv. 6–9). Elsewhere in his epistles, Paul uses the life and death of Christ as a pattern for Christians to follow (Romans 15:1–7; 1 Corinthians 10:31–11:1; 2 Corinthians 8:6–9). While we cannot copy Christ's work of salvation, we can copy the spirit basic to these acts: His love, humility, and servitude to others. These are the attitudes or disposition "which was also in Christ Jesus."

6 Who, being in the form of God, thought it not robbery to be equal with God:

After the transition (v. 5), the main body of the "Christ-hymn" begins. The pronoun "who" links and identifies this historical Jesus (v. 5) with the preexistent Christ before His incarnation. The use of this relative pronoun is consistent with the beginning of other hymn-like passages in the New Testament (cf. Colossians 1:15; Hebrews 1:3).

In eternity, Christ was "in the form of God." The word *morphe* (Gk. **more-FAY**, form) has the idea of external appearance, an outward form that strikes the vision. Saying that Christ existed in the form of God is probably a subtle way of affirming the divine nature of Christ, that He possessed the very nature of God, without saying plainly that Christ was God.

The next clause, "thought it not robbery to be equal with God," seems to corroborate the above interpretation. The word "robbery" (Gk. *harpagmos*, **har-pog-MOCE**) means plundering or seizing. Here it is best interpreted that although He was equal with God in His divine nature, Jesus did not think this equality as something to be seized upon or to be held fast or held on to. That means that Christ possessed the divine nature and was by all accounts equal with God and had the right to hold tight to it and use it to His own advantage. To be in the form of God or possessing the divine nature—and for that matter being equal with God—is a position of honor, respect, and pride with many advantages, a position no mere human would ever want to give up. Contrary to this human evaluation, Christ did not view His equality with the Father as a position to greedily and selfishly hold on to, but used it for the benefit of others. This is made clearer in the following verses.

7 But made himself of no reputation, and took upon him the form of a servant, and was made in the likeness of men:

Paul clearly states that rather than holding tight to His divine nature and equality with God, Christ voluntarily "made himself of no reputation" (Gk. *kenoo,* **keh-NO-oh**), i.e., "to empty out, or to drain." While on earth, although He was and is and ever remains God, the Son laid aside all these things (while retaining His divine nature) and functioned as a human as He assumed human form. An illustration or two will suffice. One is not a pastor just because he preaches every Sunday, neither is one an accountant because she deals with figures, or a doctor because he prescribes

medicines and heals people. One is a pastor, an accountant, or a doctor by training or qualification, although they may not function in that capacity at a given time. One can function as a janitor and still be a pastor by ordination or qualification. A qualified doctor who has no job in her field of training is still a doctor by profession, but not by employment. Employment can be temporary. With Christ, He was never divested of His divine nature in His incarnation, but He "poured out himself," laying aside all the divine attributes and functioned as a human in order to reach the world.

When He "took upon" (Gk. *lambano*, **lom-BAH-no**) Himself the form of a "servant" (Gk. *doulos*, **DOO-loce**) means that He adopted or accepted the disposition, characteristics, and attributes of a slave or bond-man. Thus Paul's designation of Christ as *doulos* emphasizes that in the incarnation, Christ entered the stream of human life as a slave—a person without advantage, with no rights or privileges of his own for the express purpose of placing himself completely at the service of humanity. In serving people, He was serving God, and in taking the role of a slave, He was acting in obedience to God's will. The idea here is that Christ in all respects, both in appearance and vulnerability, was like other human beings. He was genuinely human. The use and meaning of "form" or "likeness" in this passage cannot be understood as meaning Christ took on only the shape or appearance of a man but remained some other form in reality. Such an understanding would diminish or contradict the reality of Christ's humanness in His incarnation on earth, for His human nature was as real as other human beings, except that it was not sinful as ours.

8 And being found in fashion as a man, he humbled himself, and became obedient unto death, even the death of the cross.

Paul continues to describe the thought of Christ's humility as shown not only by His assuming human form and the role of a servant, but by humbling Himself to such a degree of acceptance and subjecting Himself to the most humiliating type of death: crucifixion. This, Paul seems to convey, is the lowest step of humility. His obedience has no limits, the statement implies.

Death by crucifixion is said to have come from the Persians and developed by the Romans. It was the most humiliating and cruel form of capital punishment, reserved only for the worst criminals, such as robbers, murderers, and sometimes slaves. Both Jews and Romans were disgusted by this type of death. For the Jew, death by crucifixion not only brought shame and pain, it was considered accursed by God (see Deuteronomy 21:22–23; 1 Corinthians 1:23; Galatians 3:13). It was a humiliating public execution. The underlying thought is that if Christ humbled Himself and went so low as to die, the Philippians, and indeed all believers, should constantly endeavor to follow their master's example of humility, and strive to achieve the spirit of oneness among themselves (vv. 5–8).

9 Wherefore God also hath highly exalted him, and given him a name which is above every name:

While the foregoing section dealt with total debasement of Christ to the lowest depth of humiliation, this section (vv. 9–11) deals with His unprecedented exaltation to highest point of honor. He humbled Himself, therefore He was exalted, which follows the natural and divine order of things as taught by Christ Himself. The same rule that He laid down for others is applicable to Him and to the Philippians, and indeed to Christians of all times. The Greek word used for Christ's exaltation and usually translated as "highly exalted" is *huperupsoo*

(**hoo-pair-oop-SO-oh**). It is found only here in the New Testament. It means to exalt to the highest rank and power, as in the military or highest office, to be elevated to the highest position, to super-exalt. Here Christ is exalted beyond measure, to a point after which nothing is higher.

He is also granted or bestowed the greatest name that surpasses every thinkable name. In the ancient and modern Jewish tradition, name-giving is more than merely a means of identity, label, or distinguishing one person from another. To them, a name usually carries a relational, spiritual or historical significance; it also, in many instances, reflects the person's character, inner being, God's activity in a life, and the true nature of the individual. For example, God changed Abram's name to Abraham because He was about to make Abraham "father of many nations," which is the meaning of the new name (Genesis 17:5–8).

10 That at the name of Jesus every knee should bow, of things in heaven, and things in earth, and things under the earth;

Paul gives us a two-part purpose for Christ's exaltation and bestowal of the highest name. The name is now bestowed to the historical Jesus, who humbled Himself to the lowest depth, took up the role of a slave, and became human in time and space. He, who was obedient even to death, is to be obeyed and worshiped. The bowing of the knee is almost universally used as a sign of reverence to someone of higher authority, such as kings and chiefs, a way of paying homage or respect to the one in authority. Bending of the knee is also a symbol of worship and such worship is reserved for God only (Exodus 20:5, Isaiah 45:23). Here this honor is now applied to Jesus. Therefore, everything and everyone in the universe must fall on their knees before Christ in worship.

Paul uses this example to again reiterate that Jesus Christ is God.

11 And that every tongue should confess that Jesus Christ is Lord, to the glory of God the Father.

Now Paul reveals the second of God's two-part purpose in exalting Christ and giving Him the highest name above every other name. Here the writer reaches the climax of the hymn and gives us the name that is above other names: "Lord." It is notable that the term *kurios* (Gk. **KOO-ree-oce**) is used in Greek translation of the Old Testament (call the Septuagint, or LXX) to translate the personal name of God, Yahweh, the self-existent One. After His resurrection Jesus declared, "All power is given unto me in heaven and in earth" (Matthew 28:18; cf. Ephesians 1:20–21). He possesses the sovereign authority and rules over the entire universe.

The verb "confess" is the Greek *exomologeo* (**ex-oh-mo-lo-GEH-oh**), which is to acknowledge openly and joyfully, the Lordship of Christ. The idea here is to affirm and celebrate Jesus as Lord, to praise and honor Him. Paul says every "tongue" (Gk. *glossa*, **GLOCE-sah**) will praise Him, which can mean language or organ of speech, but used here as a metonymy for people groups that use different languages. Therefore, this confession is not limited to the church, but includes every being that speaks within the sphere of God's creation. They will all admit that Jesus is Lord, which is an allusion to Isaiah 45:23.

Paul concludes this hymn by saying that the acknowledgment of Jesus as Lord is "to the glory of God the Father." The exaltation of Christ to the utmost heights, giving Him the highest name ever imaginable, and proclaiming Christ as Lord by all peoples, has one ultimate goal—the glory of the Father. Thus, when the Son is glorified, the Father is also glorified (John 13:31–32; 14:13; 17:1).

Paul calls the Philippians to follow the example of Christ and His humility, for that is the true road to personal exaltation and the glory of God.

Sources:
Butler, Trent, gen. ed. *Holman Bible Dictionary*. Nashville, TN: Broadman & Holman Publishers, 1991. 1105, 1106.

Daily Bible Readings

MONDAY
The Suffering Servant
(Isaiah 52:13–53:9)

TUESDAY
Learning Godly Ways in Humility
(Psalm 119:65–72)

WEDNESDAY
Message of the Good News
(1 Corinthians 15:1–11)

THURSDAY
Learning Obedience Through Suffering
(Hebrews 5:1–10)

FRIDAY
Serve and Work for God's Pleasure
(Philippians 2:12–18)

SATURDAY
Envoys of Ministry in Christ's Mission
(Philippians 2:19–30)

SUNDAY
Your Call to Unity and Humility
(Philippians 2:1–11)

Teaching Tips

Words You Should Know

A. **Conform** *summorphidzomai* (Gk.)—To have the same form, shape, or likeness.

B. **Attained** *lambano* (Gk.)—To obtain, receive, or possess as a prize or reached goal.

Teacher Preparation

Unifying Principle—Humility Over Pride. People strive to enhance their standing before others by calling attention to their abilities and honors. What is the proper attitude toward our accomplishments? Paul tells the Philippians that he willingly suffered the loss of his accomplishments for the greater goal of gaining and being found in Christ.

A. Read the Bible Background and Devotional Readings.

B. Pray for your students and lesson clarity.

C. Read the lesson Scripture in multiple translations.

D. Option: As a class discuss the kinds of accomplishments people include on their résumés. Based on this text, what might be God's opinion of these achievements and honors? How can we practice humble detachment with respect to these accomplishments?

O—Open the Lesson

A. Begin the class with prayer.

B. Have the students read the Aim for Change.

C. Have the students read the In Focus story.

D. Ask students how events named in the story can weigh on their hearts and how they can view these events from a theological perspective.

P—Present the Scriptures

A. Read the Focal Verses and discuss the Background and The People, Places, and Times sections.

B. Have the class share what Scriptures stand out for them and why, with particular emphasis on today's context.

E—Explore the Meaning

A. Use In Depth or More Light on the Text to help provide more in-depth discussion of the lesson text.

B. Discuss the Liberating Lesson and Application for Activation sections.

N—Next Steps for Application

A. Summarize the value of sacrificing our own recognition and achievements for God's glory.

B. End class with a commitment to pray for perspective on the greatness of God that results in authentic humility.

Worship Guide

For the Superintendent or Teacher
Theme: Renounce Everything for Christ
Song: "I Give Myself Away"
Devotional Reading: 1 Corinthians 15:50–58

Renounce Everything for Christ

Bible Background • PHILIPPIANS 3:1–16
Printed Text • PHILIPPIANS 3:7–14 | Devotional Reading • 1 CORINTHIANS 15:50–58

—————————— Aim for Change ——————————

By the end of the lesson, we will: IDENTIFY the reason Paul did not take pride in his accomplishments; CONSIDER the value of our relationship with Jesus Christ; and DISCOVER ways to practice humility in our lives.

————————— 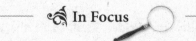 In Focus —————————

Gabrielle was finally graduating with her doctorate degree. Her friends thought it would be nice to surprise her with a celebration. Many of her friends witnessed her graduate with her bachelor's degree, get married and stay married for 29-plus years, raise three children, remain actively involved in her grandchild's life, maintain a career as a teacher, operate her own salad business, and now graduate as Dr. Gabrielle! They were extremely proud of her success.

Graduation day was here! Of course, Gabrielle was prepared but she had no idea about the huge celebration that had been planned for her. As she walked through the door, tears of joy began to flow. She was surprised and grateful.

When it was time for Gabrielle to express her thanks, some were surprised at her response. She said, "I am so grateful! Thank you for this celebration! There were so many times I wanted to give up, but God saw me through. I love my family, I love my career, and I appreciate the business God allows me to operate. But the thing I am most grateful for is my salvation. I thank God for the relationship I share with Him. My pursuit is that of God's plan, purpose, and prize. There is still so much more work to do."

In today's lesson, Paul describes what he previously viewed as great assets to what he came to realize were of relatively less value. Are you resisting the appeal of anything that prevents you from knowing and gaining Christ?

—————————— Keep in Mind ——————————

"Brethren, I count not myself to have apprehended: but this one thing I do, forgetting those things which are behind, and reaching forth unto those things which are before, I press toward the mark for the prize of the high calling of God in Christ Jesus" (Philippians 3:13–14, KJV).

"No, dear brothers and sisters, I have not achieved it, but I focus on this one thing: Forgetting the past and looking forward to what lies ahead. I press on to reach the end of the race and receive the heavenly prize for which God, through Christ Jesus, is calling us" (Philippians 3:13–14, NLT).

Focal Verses

KJV **Philippians 3:7** But what things were gain to me, those I counted loss for Christ.

8 Yea doubtless, and I count all things but loss for the excellency of the knowledge of Christ Jesus my Lord: for whom I have suffered the loss of all things, and do count them but dung, that I may win Christ,

9 And be found in him, not having mine own righteousness, which is of the law, but that which is through the faith of Christ, the righteousness which is of God by faith:

10 That I may know him, and the power of his resurrection, and the fellowship of his sufferings, being made conformable unto his death;

11 If by any means I might attain unto the resurrection of the dead.

12 Not as though I had already attained, either were already perfect: but I follow after, if that I may apprehend that for which also I am apprehended of Christ Jesus.

13 Brethren, I count not myself to have apprehended: but this one thing I do, forgetting those things which are behind, and reaching forth unto those things which are before,

14 I press toward the mark for the prize of the high calling of God in Christ Jesus.

NLT **Philippians 3:7** I once thought these things were valuable, but now I consider them worthless because of what Christ has done.

8 Yes, everything else is worthless when compared with the infinite value of knowing Christ Jesus my Lord. For his sake I have discarded everything else, counting it all as garbage, so that I could gain Christ

9 and become one with him. I no longer count on my own righteousness through obeying the law; rather, I become righteous through faith in Christ. For God's way of making us right with himself depends on faith.

10 I want to know Christ and experience the mighty power that raised him from the dead. I want to suffer with him, sharing in his death,

11 so that one way or another I will experience the resurrection from the dead!

12 I don't mean to say that I have already achieved these things or that I have already reached perfection. But I press on to possess that perfection for which Christ Jesus first possessed me.

13 No, dear brothers and sisters, I have not achieved it, but I focus on this one thing: Forgetting the past and looking forward to what lies ahead,

14 I press on to reach the end of the race and receive the heavenly prize for which God, through Christ Jesus, is calling us.

The People, Places, and Times

Libertine. These people, who were a part of the early Christian church, believed they were essentially a soul or spirit. The body was only a temporary house, having no long-term value or significance. They held a dual view of life: spiritual matter as good and physical matter as worthless. The beliefs of the libertines were countered by the ascetics, who believed that the body was evil and tried to suppress it. Conversely, the libertines believed that the body was insignificant, therefore claiming the freedom to do with it as they pleased. Paul was contending against both of these groups as he wrote to the Philippians to keep the good doctrines they were taught.

Benjamin. The tribe of Benjamin occupies the smallest territory of any of the twelve Hebrew tribes. In spite of its size, however, the tribe played a significant role in Israel's history. Saul, the first ruler of Israel, was a Benjamite, as was the Apostle Paul.

How can we guard against overvaluing or undervaluing our physical bodies and genealogy?

Background

In Philippians 3, Paul warned the church about the dangers of a distorted religion. He railed against the problem of having confidence in the flesh, versus the knowledge of Christ. With fatherly concern for the congregation, Paul warned them about people who could lead them astray. He was concerned about people who trusted more in themselves and their accomplishments. None, however, had reason to boast, according to Paul. For he himself had as much reason as anyone else, if not more. Paul had a background that was impressive by any standard, but especially by Hebrew standards. He understood from personal experience what it meant to have all the prized religious values, virtues, and achievements, only to discover that it was not the end all and be all of life. Paul was born out of the tribe of Benjamin, and was circumcised on the eighth day, according to the Law. Paul was a Hebrew born of Hebrews. (Philippians 3:5–6). He was from the tribe that had remained loyal to the Davidic line during the reign of Rehoboam (1 Kings 12:23). He was trained and educated as a Pharisee and he used that knowledge to persecute the church. If anyone had reason to place confidence in their own ability and knowledge, it was Paul.

What accomplishments or attributes do people often grow prideful about?

At-A-Glance

1. All Gain Is Through Christ
(Philippians 3:7–11)
2. Warning Against False Perfection
(vv. 12-14)

In Depth

1. All Gain Is Through Christ (Philippians 3:7–11)

If ever a person had reason to have confidence in himself and his intellectual abilities, it was Paul. Yet, even though Paul had impeccable credentials that gave him standing in the Jewish hierarchy, he gave it all up when he encountered the Master. Paul was able to speak with authority concerning the worthlessness of something that he once valued highly. He told the Philippians about his own heritage and accomplishments (vv. 5–6). So devoted was he to his way of life that he gladly and eagerly persecuted those in the church. Obviously a man of great intellectual ability, Paul came to realize that no legalistic training or adherence could save anyone. He willingly walked away from a treasured lifestyle, held in high esteem by his family and community. What he now counted as loss was not a former state of wickedness, but of goodness. Yet whatever advantages Paul had in his former life were nothing in light of the salvation he was now granted through the saving knowledge of Christ Jesus. However, Paul did not understand freedom from legalism to translate to lawlessness. As it was when he was a Pharisee, righteousness remained his consuming goal. But now he pursued righteousness from God, found through faith in Christ, not the self-righteousness of his previous life.

Therefore, our righteousness can only come through our faith in Christ. Paul wanted to know Christ and the power of His resurrection.

In order to live with Christ, we must die with Him. We cannot go back to the cross of Golgotha; however, the Christ who was victorious there can come to us and allow us to be conformed to Him and His ways.

What are some ways we see believers act self-righteously today?

2. Warning Against False Perfection (vv. 12–14)

After warning them about placing confidence in the self, Paul proceeded to warn the Philippians about the dangers of perfectionism. Although Paul strove with all that he had to attain this righteousness, he made no claim to having already achieved it. He emphatically rejected any claim to perfection. He knew from personal experience the dangers of legalism and its tendency to produce a false sense of righteousness. Apparently some at the Philippian church had deluded themselves with the notion that they were perfect. Paul emphasized that resurrection from the dead was not the only goal ahead. Even the goal that may be achieved in this life still lay ahead. Paul's goal is to attain the goal that Christ has set for him. Though unattained, perfection (completion) is his goal. He has begun the race, and is committed to finishing the course. In the meantime, he is concerned with avoiding the illusion of having actually attained the *goal*.

Since Christ grasped or took hold of Paul, he, in turn, wanted to grab hold of the perfection (completeness) that is Christ's goal for him. Conversion itself represents the beginning, not the completion of the goal. Salvation has both a beginning and a goal; it is a process, and a lifetime achievement. The King James translation to the word "perfect" in verse 15 appears to contradict Paul's insistence that he is not perfect. But what Paul meant here was that the mental attitude described in the previous sentences is the perfect attitude willing to admit shortcomings, open to correction, and willing to be re-created in Christ Jesus.

Paul advocates for completeness (perfection) in Christ, or ultimate fulfillment to put it another way. The Philippians were admonished to remain true to this point of view so that they could make further progress. They must neither forget the goal, nor suffer under the illusion that they have already attained it. Just as there was a danger in assuming perfection had been attained, Paul was well aware and equally concerned about those who treated the goal with total disregard.

How can we be committed to pursuing right living without falling into harmful perfectionism?

Search the Scriptures

1. Why did Paul now count the things of his former life as loss (Philippians 3:8)?

2. What was Paul committed to doing, even though he had not yet attained the goal (v. 13)?

Discuss the Meaning

1. How can we keep ourselves from placing our value in our personal achievements over God's grace?

2. Is it possible to be content with where God has us in life and also trying to "press toward the mark" consistently? What does that look like?

Liberating Lesson

Far too often in our society, the goal of pursuing righteousness gets pushed aside. The pursuit of careers, homes, cars, and other material goods begin to consume us, often without conscious consent. Our capitalist society conditions us to prioritize money and material success over all else and can cause us to ignore our relationships with God and one another. The system itself is not concerned with justice or just relationships and conditions, but productivity. Jesus cautioned us not to put up our treasures in places where moths eat and thieves break in and steal (Matthew 6:19–20). The material things of this world are under the control of the world's whims and are temporary and unfulfilling. Instead of our quest for things, a pursuit for Christ and His will in our lives and communities can yield true abundance in this life and the life to come.

Application for Activation

In what ways have you pushed your heavenly goal aside, giving way to earthly or material pursuits? If your life has gotten out of balance in terms of where you have placed your priorities, list some steps you can take to shift the balance correctly. List, in ranking order, the priorities your life should have, according to what pleases God.

Follow the Spirit

What God wants me to do:

_____

_____

_____

Remember Your Thoughts

Special insights I have learned:

_____

_____

_____

_____

More Light on the Text

Philippians 3:7–14

With the use of "finally," Paul seems to indicate that he was coming to the end of his letter to the Philippians (3:1). However, in content, Paul is focusing on a different aspect of the Philippians' situation, and now he addresses it. Here, he warns them against Judaizers, who he says put much "confidence in the flesh" rather than in Christ (v. 3). He gives himself as an example of one who had by all measures reached the height of fame in Judaism and was more qualified both through birth and religious rites and tradition than any other. As to preserving the Law and tradition, he was zealous about persecuting the very church that he is now preserving and building with his suffering. But that was the old Paul, as he explains in the following verses (vv. 7–14).

7 But what things were gain to me, those I counted loss for Christ. 8 Yea doubtless, and I count all things but loss for the excellency of the knowledge of Christ Jesus my Lord: for whom I have suffered the loss of all things, and do count them but dung, that I may win Christ,

The Pharisees were a sect of zealous Jews, who held steadfast to the letter of their interpretation of the law and their own traditions. To reach that height, one must definitely be born a Jew, not a proselyte, "free born," an ardent keeper of the Law, and "blameless" in all aspects of the religion (Acts 22:28; Philippians 3:6). To attain the position of a Pharisee, therefore, is a very rigorous undertaking, which requires much learning and knowledge of the Law. The position also comes with great advantages and privileges. Paul had reached that high echelon. Indeed, when it came to meeting every requirement of Judaism, being of pure stock and demonstrating fanatical zeal, he had no equal (Galatians 1:13–14). All the things to his advantage, including honor and respect, which he possessed as a Pharisee, he "counted loss for Christ" (v. 7).

Here, Paul is saying that all the positions and aspirations—that every Jewish young man dreamed of and were thought to be "gain" (Gk. *kerdos*, **KER-dos**, financial benefit) and what he has already achieved—are now *zemia* (Gk. **dzay-MEE-ah**), a "loss," worthless, or valueless to him. *Zemia* here has the idea of loss as related to a trade or business enterprise where one incurs a material or financial loss. The loss is voluntary, where for the sake of something better and bigger, one purposely decides to take on forfeiture. Paul applies the language of business and considers all the things of his past—things gained before the Damascus encounter—as losses.

Paul considered everything lost "for Christ." "For Christ" should be understood as for the purpose of gaining Christ, rather than "for Christ" as though Christ were to benefit from the loss. Paul's encounter with the living Christ on the Damascus road altered his perspective and mindset in life. He reassessed his priorities in considering access to all the worldly glory and position while being ignorant in the riches of knowing Christ on one hand, and knowing Christ as Lord then gaining eternal life on the other hand. The word "excellency" is the Greek *huperecho* (**hoo-pair-EH-kho**), which has the idea of superiority or supremacy. Paul evaluates his past—his privilege, family, religious heritage, his achievements, rise to fame as a Pharisee, power, position—and finds it worthless compared with his new privilege of knowing Christ.

The Greek noun *gnosis* (**guh-NO-seece**) for "knowledge" in this instance is more than an acquisition of facts or an intellectual awareness, but rather experiential knowledge. It is more than intellectual cognizance of the truth about Jesus Christ, but a personal and intimate relationship with Jesus. In order that he might "win" (Gk. *kerdaino*, **ker-DIE-no**, gain or acquire) Christ, Paul says, all things he had before have become dung to him, things that are worthless and useless.

9 And be found in him, not having mine own righteousness, which is of the law, but that which is through the faith of Christ, the righteousness which is of God by faith:

Another reason for counting all things "dung" is that he might be found as righteous in Christ. Prior to his conversion, Paul attained high position by personal achievement of keeping the Law, which is the standard for righteousness in Judaism. This type of self-righteousness gave rise to and is characterized by pride and arrogance (Romans 10:1–3) and contradicts the work of Christ. Instead of depending on his own righteousness based on personal merit, Paul relies now on the righteousness based on the finished work of Christ (John 17:4) received by faith alone.

Righteousness (Gk. *dikaiosune*, **dee-kie-oh-SOO-nay**) or justification were used in both Jewish and Greek communities as judicial terms, whereby a judge would either justify or condemn someone. To justify is to vindicate or to declare one right. The only criterion for righteousness before God is faith in Christ. Faith here simply means "trust," having confidence in, and accepting God's work of grace through the life and death of Christ. It is not Paul's faithfulness but Christ's faithfulness and loyalty to the Father. Therefore, Paul's desire is that his approval before God be dependent on his relationship with God through faith in Christ.

10 That I may know him, and the power of his resurrection, and the fellowship of his sufferings, being made conformable unto his death;

Paul's further goal here is that of an ongoing relationship with Christ—not a onetime knowledge of Him, but to develop a deeper relationship with the living Christ. The only obstacle was his past glory and personal advantages. Paul qualifies this intimate knowledge of Christ with a cluster of other phrases. The first is "and the power of his resurrection." He wishes to experience the transforming, life-changing power that Christ has been endowed with through His resurrection power, by which we are accepted as righteous in God's sight. The second phrase is "the fellowship of his sufferings." Paul wishes to experience Christ by sharing in His sufferings. Just as to know Christ and the power of His resurrection is an inward spiritual experience, to know Christ in the fellowship of His suffering is equally a spiritual experience expressed in terms of dying with Him (Romans 6:8; Galatians 2:19–20). It means dying to sin (Romans 6:11), and dying to self, of which Jesus Himself spoke (Mark 8:34–35). The last in this cluster of phrases, "being made conformable unto his death," tends to confirm Paul's longing for holiness. This Greek word translated "conform" is *summorphizomai* (**soom-mor-FEED-zo-my**). It is to grant or invest in the same form, to share the likeness of, or to take on the same form—in this context an actual crucifixion. Paul expects to be martyred for the faith, which he later is, but by beheading. Yet for his audience this union with Christ is participation in the unique attributes of Christ, which include His humility, His unselfish love for all, which led to His sacrificial death, and His righteousness, which through His death has been imparted to all believers.

11 If by any means I might attain unto the resurrection of the dead.

Paul is not doubting the eschatological resurrection of all believers in this verse. He is certain of the resurrection. He is rather saying that he endeavors to lead a life that conforms to the life, death, and resurrection of Christ with the goal of attaining the resurrection of the dead. The use of this conditional clause, "if by any means" (Gk. *ei pos*, **EY poce**, if somehow), is Paul's humble way of saying that salvation is not by good deeds, but depends totally on God's gracious gift from beginning and to end. This humility emphasizes that salvation is not a consequence of our good works, or personal efforts, or our attempt to live holy. That is, the future resurrection cannot be presumed based on personal efforts, neither is God's mercy to be assumed or taken for granted because we are Christian. However, there is no room for complacency. Paul recognizes this and looks forward, with great expectation, hope, and enduring faith, to the future bodily resurrection of the dead.

12 Not as though I had already attained, either were already perfect: but I follow after, if that I may apprehend that for which also I am apprehended of Christ Jesus.

Now Paul makes it clear that the attainment of the resurrection is in the future, something he sets his eyes on but has not achieved yet. It tends to expel the notion that the resurrection of all believers is only spiritual, totally and completely achieved the moment one receives Christ as Lord. It also goes on to confirm that realization of the resurrection is not what we assume we own, regardless of the life we live. Rather, the attainment of the resurrection is something to be maintained and to strive for after receiving Christ. Paul says that he has not yet "attained" (Gk. *lambano*, **lam-BAN-oh**), that is, laid hold of, taken, or received this prize. The prize is the resurrection from the dead that is still to come.

He has not yet reached his goal; neither is he "already perfect." The word translated "perfect" is the Greek *teleioo* (**teh-lay-OH-oh**) and is also translated to mean "fulfill" (Luke 2:43; John 19:28) and "finish" (John 4:34; 5:36; Acts 20:24). It has the idea of completing a given task. It has been suggested that in Philippi, some thought they had reached the goal of Christian perfection. Therefore, Paul wants to let them know that he neither thinks of himself as having "arrived"—reached his goal—nor does he see himself as "perfect," or sinless. This does not imply that Paul was lacking in spiritual experience, was deficient morally, or still cleaving to his old nature. It is another demonstration of his humility, whereby he acknowledges that in all his life, God's grace is still working.

It means also that the task is not yet complete. The race is not over. There is still a course to finish to reach the set goal. To "follow after" (Gk. *dioko*, **dee-OH-ko**) means to run swiftly to catch a person or thing. It is also translated to press on—figuratively used of one that runs swiftly in a race as in the Olympics—in order to reach the goal and win a prize. He does it so that he could "apprehend" that for which by Christ he was "apprehended" (Gk. *katalambano*, **ka-ta-lam-BAN-oh**)—or to obtain, attain, lay hold of. This is an intensified form of *lambano*, and has the sense of being seized or taking possession of. Paul implies that Christ had a definite purpose for taking possession of him.

13 Brethren, I count not myself to have apprehended: but this one thing I do, forgetting those things which are behind and reaching forth unto those things which are before, 14 I press toward the mark for the prize of the high calling of God in Christ Jesus.

These verses add emphasis, pointing to the seriousness and the importance of the matter with loving emotion. It seems that Paul,

by adding "brethren" (Gk. *adelphos*, **ah-del-FOCE**), a word of endearment, is invoking his close relationship with the church and showing deep concern that they understand the truth he is writing. The use of the word shows he is deeply moved; he is speaking the truth and would not lie to them. They are to listen and take his word for it rather than listen to those who probably claim that they have already reached perfection. Although he has totally given up everything for the cause of Christ, renounced his Pharisaic opportunities and advantages, and has identified himself with Christ both in His suffering and death, Paul does not claim that he has reached perfection. Paul is focused on the race ahead of him and avoiding any distraction from his past to impede his focus on the prize.

Here are the three things Paul does:

1. He forgets the past—the ground he has covered, or the hurdles he has scaled in the race. Good athletes do not look back when running. Otherwise, they would lose speed, direction and, more often than not, the race itself (1 Corinthians 9:24–27).

2. He "reaches forth" (Gk. *epekteinomai*, **eh-peek-TAY-no-my**), meaning he stretches himself, sparing no energy while using every ounce of his strength to reach the set goal. This is the attitude of every good competitive athlete.

3. He presses on toward the mark—the finish line, the focus of every athlete's eyes and mind from start to finish. The sense here is that the ultimate prize motivates him to persevere. Paul refers to that prize as "the high calling of God in Christ Jesus" (v. 14). Paul shares all of this to encourage believers to pursue Christ with the same zeal and focus.

Sources:
Allen, Clifford J., gen. ed. *The Broadman Bible Commentary.* Vol. 11. Nashville, TN: Broadman Press, 1971. 210.
Butler, Trent, gen. ed. *Holman Bible Dictionary.* Nashville, TN: Broadman & Holman Publishers, 1991. 165.

Say It Correctly

Apprehend. ap-ri-**HEND**.
Conformable. kuhn-**FOR**-muh-buhl.

Daily Bible Readings

MONDAY
A Matter of the Heart
(Romans 2:25–29)

TUESDAY
Persistent Faith
(Mark 7:24–30)

WEDNESDAY
Paul's Solid Credentials for Ministry
(2 Corinthians 11:21–30)

THURSDAY
Boast in Christ Jesus
(Philippians 3:1–6)

FRIDAY
Live as Heavenly Citizens
(Philippians 3:17–4:1)

SATURDAY
Guard Your Heart and Mind
(Philippians 4:2–9)

SUNDAY
Be of the Same Mind
(Philippians 3:7–14)

Notes

_____

_____

_____

_____

Teaching Tips

Words You Should Know

A. Bulwarks *chelah* (Heb.)—Fortified walls.

B. Righteousness *tsedeq* (Heb.)—Justice or right judgment.

Teacher Preparation

Unifying Principle—Steadfast Love. In a world of constant change, nothing seems permanent or of abiding worth. What abides when everything else seems to be in flux? The psalmist ponders the steadfast, everlasting, and all-inclusive love of God while worshiping God in the Temple.

A. Read the Bible Background and Devotional Readings.

B. Pray for your students and lesson clarity.

C. Read the lesson Scripture in multiple translations.

D. Option: Invite students to describe a worship setting in which they experienced God's love in a special way: a church sanctuary, a retreat center, a childhood church, and others. Discuss how we can hold such places in esteem while recognizing God's presence is what made the place special.

O—Open the Lesson

A. Begin the class with prayer.

B. Have the students read the Aim for Change.

C. Have the students read the In Focus story.

D. Ask students how events named in the story can weigh on their hearts and how they can view these events from a theological perspective.

P—Present the Scriptures

A. Read the Focal Verses and discuss the Background and The People, Places, and Times sections.

B. Have the class share what Scriptures stand out for them and why, with particular emphasis on today's context.

E—Explore the Meaning

A. Use In Depth or More Light on the Text to help provide more in-depth discussion of the lesson text.

B. Discuss the Liberating Lesson and Application for Activation sections.

N—Next Steps for Application

A. Summarize the value of knowing God's love for us is enduring and unconditional.

B. End class with a commitment to worship God individually and with other believers.

Worship Guide

For the Superintendent or Teacher
Theme: Pondering God's Steadfast Love
Song: "In The Sanctuary"
Devotional Reading: Psalm 93

Pondering God's Steadfast Love

Bible Background • PSALM 48:1–3, 9–14
Printed Text • PSALM 48:1–3, 9–14 | Devotional Reading • PSALM 93

——————— Aim for Change ———————

By the end of the lesson, we will: DISCOVER the value of worshiping God in the Temple; CONSIDER how God's steadfast love is present in our lives; and DISCUSS ways to celebrate God's love in worship individually and collectively.

——————— In Focus ———————

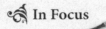

The congregation had just completed a revival last month at their church. Now the pastor was asking the church to accompany him as he did a revival at another church. The previous month had been extremely busy with the "Back to School Rally," the revival, the community parade, and the neighborhood witnessing.

When the pastor mentioned to the congregation he would preach the annual revival at a friend's church, there were cheers! A visitor asked why all the excitement when they had just finished doing all the extra activities the month before.

The member sitting next to him responded, "We have learned coming together to worship is a blessing and a privilege. We know it is important to worship privately but we also recognize the importance of worshiping together as a family. We see in the news people who are killed for exercising their right to worship when and where they want. In our country, we don't have to worry about that. So whenever we get an opportunity to gather and worship, we take it!"

The visitor seemed enlightened and appreciative of the reflection. When the pastor asked if he could see a show of hands of those who would join him at the revival church, the visitor raised his hand—and he wasn't even a member yet.

In today's lesson, believers testify to the many ways God's steadfast love has touched their lives. Do you celebrate God's love through both private and corporate worship?

——————— Keep in Mind ———————

"For this God is our God for ever and ever: he will be our guide even unto death" (Psalm 48:14, KJV).

"For that is what God is like. He is our God forever and ever, and he will guide us until we die" (Psalm 48:14, NLT).

Focal Verses

KJV **Psalm 48:1** Great is the Lord, and greatly to be praised in the city of our God, in the mountain of his holiness.

2 Beautiful for situation, the joy of the whole earth, is mount Zion, on the sides of the north, the city of the great King.

3 God is known in her palaces for a refuge.

9 We have thought of thy lovingkindness, O God, in the midst of thy temple.

10 According to thy name, O God, so is thy praise unto the ends of the earth: thy right hand is full of righteousness.

11 Let mount Zion rejoice, let the daughters of Judah be glad, because of thy judgments.

12 Walk about Zion, and go round about her: tell the towers thereof.

13 Mark ye well her bulwarks, consider her palaces; that ye may tell it to the generation following.

14 For this God is our God for ever and ever: he will be our guide even unto death.

NLT **Psalm 48:1** How great is the Lord, how deserving of praise, in the city of our God, which sits on his holy mountain!

2 It is high and magnificent; the whole earth rejoices to see it! Mount Zion, the holy mountain, is the city of the great King!

3 God himself is in Jerusalem's towers, revealing himself as its defender.

9 O God, we meditate on your unfailing love as we worship in your Temple.

10 As your name deserves, O God, you will be praised to the ends of the earth. Your strong right hand is filled with victory.

11 Let the people on Mount Zion rejoice. Let all the towns of Judah be glad because of your justice.

12 Go, inspect the city of Jerusalem. Walk around and count the many towers.

13 Take note of the fortified walls, and tour all the citadels, that you may describe them to future generations.

14 For that is what God is like. He is our God forever and ever, and he will guide us until we die.

The People, Places, and Times

Sons of Korah. Korah, a Levite, was a jealous cousin of Moses and Aaron and led an uprising against them (Numbers 16:1–33). Consequently, Korah and his congregation were destroyed, but future generations survived and became ministers of music during the time of King David and after as royal musicians (1 Chronicles 6:31–37), penning this timeless anthem to the Lord.

Do you know of any families that seem to have a heritage of music or worship?

Background

This song to the Lord is one of adoration and praise to our great King who is strong, loving, and everlasting. He is the only one deserving of such accolades. The tone of Psalm 48 is one of celebration, highlighting God's power and security that is a by-product of trusting in Him. It is similar to Psalms 46 and 47, which emphasize God's triumph over His enemies. Judah is the recipient of this victory. Psalm 48 is attributed to the Sons of Korah, who wrote ten other psalms. Some examples of other places in Scripture this psalm's sentiment is evident (46–48) were the miraculous victory the Lord granted King Jehoshaphat and Judah from the hands of their enemies (2 Chronicles 20) through praise, and King Hezekiah's miraculous protection from Assyrian invasion (2 Kings 19:35-36).

Have you ever been excited to praise God after God protected or kept you from trouble?

At-A-Glance

1. Our Great God (Psalm 48:1–3)
2. Our Righteous God (vv. 8–11)
3. Our Eternal God (vv. 12–14)

In Depth

1. Our Great God (Psalm 48:1–3)

In some Roman Jewish circles, "great" is a noble title denoting a prominent leader or one whose teaching is worth following. These verses also display where God is to be honored and praised: in His city with His people, on Mount Zion. His city is made up of those who have acknowledged His authority over creation, His immutable characteristics like His mercy, grace, love, and His judgment. Here, the city is likened to a lady, a frequent way to personalize cities in the Old Testament. Zaphon was the revered mountain of the Canaanites. Zion was an ancient fortress or mountain of Jebusite origins, but later conquered by David so that it was called "the city of David" (1 Chronicles 11:5). God is indwelling this space, a safe place for His people to worship, praise, and find comfort in Him from the outside world of temptation, defeat, and powerlessness. Verses 4–8 give more details of how God protects Israel in battle.

What is your definition of great as it relates to God? Is He great in every area of your life? Can you recall a time when you felt the safety of God's presence?

2. Our Righteous God (vv. 9–11)

God's power is evident in His actions toward His people. While worship and praise can be expressed anywhere in creation, the Temple is the place where God said that His name would dwell perpetually (2 Chronicles 7:16, 1 Kings 9:3). Here the writer compares God's praise to His name—it knows no bounds and is limitless. God is qualified to be the recipient of our praise because He is flawless, perfect, and without sin. The Bible refers to God's right hand on several occasions, in this case stating it holds righteousness or victory (Isaiah 41:10). The right hand is the hand of blessing in ancient Jewish thought, and the author notes here that God has extended the blessing of victory and safety. God exudes purity and worthiness beyond all human comprehension. God's people understand that His corrective decrees are indicative of His love.

How has God spoken to you? What have you witnessed as evidence of God's power?

3. Our Eternal God (vv. 12–14)

The writers stress the importance of looking for and focusing on what God has done, where He is working, and the coming victory so that future generations may be in awe of God's greatness and magnitude. The writers state a final declaration in this passage noting that our God's name is eternal and that He will be with us forevermore, similar to Jesus' Great Commission promise (Matthew 28:20).

What have your grandparents or elders shared about the glory of God? What will you tell your children?

Search the Scriptures

1. How did God keep Israel from physical harm (Psalm 48:3, 12–14)?

2. What characteristics of God are magnified in this psalm (vv. 1, 9–11)?

Discuss the Meaning

1. Are there any special places or memories that remind you of God's provision and protection in your life?

2. Why is it important to worship God in private and in public? Is there a difference in how we worship in either setting?

Liberating Lesson

There is a clear distinction between God-centered worship and self-centered worship. What differences are most telling? How might we accidentally fall into self-centered worship?

Our culture now has the option of staying at home to worship online or watching a service on TV. There is a consensus among some that church membership and attendance are not needed, and social media spiritual quotes and theology have become "Scripture" for many. What are the weaknesses of this kind of worship?

With the knowledge that God has taken great care in creating the world, we have the mission to convey to the lost that same love. This same love is a force to challenge the violence in our streets and the hopelessness in many of our youth. In this crucial time the church has the honorable privilege of changing the world's view of it. What is our witness in the world as it relates to today's text? What is the church's role in ensuring that the collective voice of worship stays strong?

Application for Activation

• In order to fully appreciate all that God desires for us, we must recognize His power and trust His promises. This can best take place through a daily quiet time of worship, confession, supplication, and obedience. When this happens, we can share testimonies of God's faithfulness with a hungry and thirsty world. When we become contagious Christians, our communities will change and God will be pleased. Authentic corporate worship comes from a heart of private worship as we begin to cultivate a heart and space for worship in our daily schedule (Psalm 132:3–5).

• Challenge yourself to match every insecurity or doubt with the truth of God's Word that specifically speaks to His love for you.

• Pray for safety for your family, church family, city, and world. Organize a town hall meeting at your church to pray about violence and open a dialogue on the relationships between your community, the church, and the police force.

• Plan a church clean-up day; take your family along with some cleaning supplies and spend the day preparing the sanctuary for Sunday worship. Then ask your children to reflect on what they learned and why it is important to reverence God's house.

• Write your own love song to God. Include examples of His greatness, grace, and love in your life.

Follow the Spirit

What God wants me to do:

_____

_____

_____

_____

Remember Your Thoughts

Special insights I have learned:

_____

_____

_____

_____

More Light on the Text

Psalm 48:1–3, 9–14

Jehoshaphat is one example of a king in Judah who organized his people and set up a choir of musicians with loud praise in front. The Lord set an ambush and confusion in the enemies' camp; they slaughtered one another, but granted Jerusalem victory without fighting at all. Only praise! How effectual corporate praise can be! These three psalms (46-48) focus on exalting the Lord, however, the emphasis of Psalm 48 is praise of Jerusalem, which is protected by God. The psalm begins with the praise of the Lord's greatness (v. 1); it concludes with praises of God and His goodness and assurance of His guidance for His people forever (v. 14).

1 Great is the Lord, and greatly to be praised in the city of our God, in the mountain of his holiness.

The psalm begins with an emphatic and indisputable affirmation of the greatness of the Lord. His greatness is inconceivable, but it is demonstrable in His various acts and dealings with His people, like the deliverances of His people. His greatness is apparent in the minds of those delivered as they praise the Lord. The word "great" is the Hebrew *gadol* (**gaw-DOLE**); it speaks of being "large" in magnitude, size or scale; standing out in magnitude, or degree or effectiveness. Unlike the idols other nations worship, the God of Israel is able to fight and defend His people. In the historical context of this psalm, the Lord displayed His great power in overthrowing the mighty forces that gathered to besiege His holy city, Jerusalem, where His name dwells (2 Chronicle 20; see 2 Kings 18 and 19).

African Americans reflected God's greatness during slavery in the 1800s through their spirituals. They looked to God for hope, strength and comfort, trusting that God would one day liberate them. "Swing Low Sweet Chariot" is a song of hope, liberation, and action. Because the Lord is great, He then is to be praised greatly. That means He is most worthy of praise. "Praise" is the Hebrew *halal* (**haw-LAL**) from which we have "hallelujah." The word appears more than 165 times in its different forms and uses in the Bible, mostly in praise of the Lord. Just as it was in the time of this psalm, so it is today: When we look and consider all the attributes of God, we marvel and are compelled to praise Him greatly.

This great praise is exceptional and unique for the psalmist because of its location: "in the city of our God." This refers to Jerusalem where God chose to establish His name; it is also where the Temple was located. Also known as Mount Zion, it is the dwelling place for God's name and worship center for the God of the universe. Consequently, both the city and Temple are referred to as the "mountain of his holiness," a sacred place of worship. The city is pictured as the place where all believers would gather in the last day in worship (Isaiah 2:2–5).

2 Beautiful for situation, the joy of the whole earth, is mount Zion, on the sides of the north, the city of the great King. 3 God is known in her palaces for a refuge.

The psalmist explains the aesthetic and positional components of the city and the effect it has on the people. Apart from the fact that this city is spiritually the city of God—where God dwells—it is a beautiful and elevated city. The word "situation" is the Hebrew *noph* (**NOFE**), meaning elevation or height. Therefore, the phrase "beautiful for situation" refers to the geographically elevated position of the city upon which the architecturally magnificent Temple was built. Jerusalem was built on an elevation of about 2,500 feet above sea level, hence writers talk of "going up" to Jerusalem or the mountain (Psalm 122:4; Isaiah 2:3; Micah 4:2). Josephus, the Jewish historian, writes about Jerusalem as built on two hills. Mount Zion, the Temple location is the northern part; the psalmist refers to it here as "on the sides of the north."

Opinions differ on what sense Mount Zion or the Temple could be "the joy of the whole earth." It all depends on if the Hebrew *'erets* (**EH-rets**), is rendered the "earth" or the "land." There is no evidence indicating that either the city or the Temple ever was the joy of the world globally. In reality, both were the envy of the nations, thus they endeavored to destroy them. Therefore *'erets* cannot be "earth" as in the world. But if *'erets* means "land" as in a country, territory district, or region, then it makes sense for the Temple to be the crown jewel of Judea.

Jerusalem with its Temple was a joy to the people, not only because of its geographical location and beauty, but because it was also "the city of the great King"—God's chosen city. Yahweh chose it for His residence and His worship. Therefore, worshiping God was limited to Jews in Jerusalem until Jesus came and effected a change. Jerusalem (a geographical city) is no longer the only place for the most intimate worship. The church (not a building, but a body) is now where true worship of God takes place. God is Spirit and He is everywhere; He is not physically restricted to a location. His worship takes place anywhere and in any setting (Matthew 18:20).

This great King is now identified as God. He is known in Jerusalem, His fortified city of refuge, where He reigns as King. "Palace" refers to a fortress, castle, or a fortified and an elevated place, a royal residence for a king. Not the walls, but God Himself was Zion's defense and refuge (cf. Psalm 46:1, 7, 11). For believers, God is our refuge and protection; He dwells among us and in us.

9 We have thought of thy loving kindness, O God, in the midst of thy temple.

After the brief review of God's victorious act on behalf of the people and the city (vv. 4–8), the psalmist now reflects on God's love. The word translated "thought" here is the Hebrew *damah* (**daw-MAW**), and means "to compare, to liken, resemble or to think." It is used often in the sense of reflecting on or meditating on something. The author proclaims that they had heard of Jerusalem's glory, but now they had seen it themselves (v. 8). That means they had compared in their minds what they had just experienced with what others—perhaps their predecessors—had told them about God. As they contemplate on the present act of God's love toward them, it reminds and confirms to them the Lord's past love to their fathers (Psalm 44:1–2). The phrase "in the midst of thy temple" indicates that this was a corporate reflective act of celebration among God's people. We honor God when we individually or corporately contemplate and appreciate His love. We praise God not because of what we can benefit from Him, rather we must honor and worship Him regardless. He deserves all our praises simply for who He is.

10 According to thy name, O God, so is thy praise unto the ends of the earth: thy right hand is full of righteousness.

God has established and made known His name throughout the whole world, therefore

His praise also reaches to the ends of the earth. The Hebrew translated "name" here is *shem* (**SHAME**); it can also refer to someone's reputation or fame. Throughout the Scriptures and in history, God's name is universally made known through His acts: in creation, deliverance, and protection of His people. We know many other nations had heard of the power of God (cf. Joshua 2:8–11; 1 Samuel 4:8). God's right hand, metaphorically speaking, is the instrument with which the Lord has wrought His work. God's right hand is filled with *tsedeq* (**TSEH-dek**) "justice" or "righteousness." Righteousness here refers to God's execution of justice or right judgment on those who want to attack Judah. The Lord is a righteous and just God (Exodus 9:27; Job 37:23). His name is Jehovah Tsidkenu (**SED-kay-new**), "The Lord Our Righteousness" (Jeremiah 23:6; 33:16), and He "is righteous in all his ways" (Psalm 145:17).

11 Let mount Zion rejoice, let the daughters of Judah be glad, because of thy judgments.

Using a parallelism (Mount Zion paired with daughters of Judah), the whole nation with its inhabitants is summoned to rejoice for the Lord's righteous act and justice on their behalf over their enemies. Here "Mount Zion" refers to or stands for all the inhabitants of Jerusalem, probably including the priests, the Levites, and those that attend the Temple; all are called upon to rejoice. "The daughters of Judah" probably refers to the other towns and cities of Judah that surround Jerusalem. Cities are often referred to as daughters in Scripture (Isaiah 1:8), but another interpretation of the phrase refers to women themselves rejoicing in the victory of God. This was God's righteous judgment and it called for a celebration of joy and gladness.

12 Walk about Zion, and go round about her: tell the towers thereof. 13 Mark ye well her bulwarks, consider her palaces; that ye may tell it to the generation following.

This call for celebration is continued in verses 12 and 13. Instead of being limited within the Temple (v. 9), the celebrative praise and worship should be extended within and around the citadel—around the fortified walls that surround Jerusalem. "Walk about Zion, and go round about her" is another parallelism, the second reinforcing and emphasizing the first phrase. The entire nation of Judah is to gladly and joyfully march around the holy city praising God. They should inspect the city and take note of their findings. As they go round they have to "tell" (Heb. *saphar*, **saw-FAR**) its towers; that is they have to "count, number or take account" of the towers. Towers or observation posts are usually erected on fortified walls surrounding the cities, from where the approaching forces can be detected (see 2 Chronicles 26:9–10; Isaiah 2:12–15). Such towers, though usually stronger than other parts of the castle, are the first to be attacked. The idea here is that as the people march around they must count the towers and palaces and bulwarks or structures to realize that they are still standing and intact. None of them is damaged.

As they observe and take note of these edifices and fortresses, they should imagine the disaster and the extent of damage had God not acted on their behalf. Taking notes and keeping record of these happenings is for posterity and preservation purposes, so that they "may tell it to the generation following." They pass it on to their children so they know how prosperous their God made them. The poetry of the verses supports the understanding of the passage. The Hebrew root for "tell" in verses 12 and 13 is the same, but in different verbal forms so that they have a slightly different meaning. The word *saphar* in verse 12 means "to tell, count," but the word *saphar* in verse 13 means "to retell."

14 For this God is our God forever and ever: he will be our guide even unto death.

The reason for preserving the record and passing it on to the next generation is to remind and assure them that "this God" who performed such acts "is our God ever and ever." Our God is unchangeable and consistent in His love. His love remains forever. He is, and will ever be, the covenant-keeping God of Israel and the church forever. He is not only the God of the past; He is also the God of the present. What He did in the past, He will do today and for eternity. Because He "is our God forever, He will be our guide even unto death," the psalmist concluded. As pilgrims on earth, it is consoling to know and be assured that the God who lived in the midst of His people, led the Children of Israel through the wilderness and won their battles, is the same God who is with us "even unto death" today. That's how great and awesome our God is, and He deserves to be greatly praised by His people forever.

Daily Bible Readings

MONDAY
Son of the Living God
(Matthew 16:13–20)

TUESDAY
I Am the Lord
(Ezekiel 39:7–10)

WEDNESDAY
Grow into a Precious Spiritual House
(1 Peter 2:1–8)

THURSDAY
Majesty of God's Rule
(Psalm 93)

FRIDAY
Rulers Astounded with City of God
(Psalm 48:4–8)

SATURDAY
Build Up Each Other in Worship
(1 Corinthians 14:26–33)

SUNDAY
Praise God's Steadfast Love in Worship
(Psalm 48:1–3, 9–14)

Sources:
Global Study Bible, English Standard Version. Wheaton, IL: Crossway Publishers, 2012. 71-73.
"Great." Merriam-Webster.com. Merriam-Webster, 2017. Web. December 4, 2017.
Keener, Craig S., *The IVP Bible Background Commentary: Old Testament*. Downers Grove, IL: Intervarsity Press, 2000. 59-60.
Radmacher, Earl D., ed. *Nelson Study Bible*, New King James Version. Nashville, TN: Thomas Nelson Publishers, 1997. 54-56.
Unger, Merrill F., *The New Unger's Bible Dictionary*. Chicago, IL: Moody Press, 1988. 173, 174.
Walvoord, John F., and Roy B. Zuck, eds. *The Bible Knowledge Commentary: Old Testament*. Wheaton, IL: Victor Books, SP Publications, Inc., 1985. 72-74.

Teaching Tips

Words You Should Know

A. Terrible *yare'* (Heb.)—To be feared.

B. Glorious *kabod* (Heb.)—Weighty or heavy; honorable or impressive when describing a person.

Teacher Preparation

Unifying Principle—Testimony of God's Works. People marvel at the legacies of those whose powerful influence has changed the world. What is the true measure of might? The psalmist praises the mighty works of God, the Creator of the universe and the Savior of God's people.

A. Read the Bible Background and Devotional Readings.

B. Pray for your students and lesson clarity.

C. Read the lesson Scripture in multiple translations.

D. Option: Search for hymns or songs that might serve as a response to the invitation "Come and see what God has done" (verse 5). What awesome deeds of God do these songs describe? Sing one of these songs together with the class as an act of worship.

O—Open the Lesson

A. Begin the class with prayer.

B. Have the students read the Aim for Change.

C. Have the students read the In Focus story.

D. Ask students how events named in the story can weigh on their hearts and how they can view these events from a theological perspective.

P—Present the Scriptures

A. Read the Focal Verses and discuss the Background and The People, Places, and Times sections.

B. Have the class share what Scriptures stand out for them and why, with particular emphasis on today's context.

E—Explore the Meaning

A. Use In Depth or More Light on the Text to help provide more in-depth discussion of the lesson text.

B. Discuss the Liberating Lesson and Application for Activation sections.

N—Next Steps for Application

A. Summarize the value of sharing about God's wonderful works.

B. End class with a commitment to share about God's works in our lives with others.

Worship Guide

For the Superintendent or Teacher
Theme: Praising God's Mighty Works
Song: "Praise Is What I Do"
Devotional Reading: Psalm 114

Praising God's Mighty Works

Bible Background • PSALM 66
Printed Text • PSALM 66:1–9, 16–20 | Devotional Reading • PSALM 114

—————— Aim for Change ——————

By the end of the lesson, we will: IDENTIFY the mighty works for which the psalmist praises God; EXPERIENCE awe in contemplating God's works; and REJOICE in the privilege of serving a mighty and powerful God.

———— In Focus ————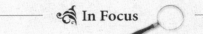

Katrina stood in the ballpark clubhouse doing her vocal warm-ups. This would be the biggest audience before which she had ever performed.

It had been a long shot several months ago when she sent her audition package to the team with a DVD of her singing the national anthem. Katrina knew the team got more than 200 submissions each year for the eighty home games, and she wasn't a professional singer. Katrina sang for the joy of it, ever since she was a little girl singing solos for Sunday services at her small home church, accompanied by the music minister on piano and a drummer.

Katrina felt well prepared, thanks to the lessons she learned from Miss Grace, the choir director. Miss Grace was better than any vocal coach, teaching the choir members all about technique, phrasing, breath control, and, most of all, presentation. Remember to smile, Miss Grace always said; the smile would change your attitude and posture and come through in your voice. "You're praising God," she told them. "You ought to be smiling."

It was time. Katrina followed the team representative through the clubhouse and into the home team dugout, and went up onto the field. Looking up at the thousands of seats in the baseball stadium, filled with cheering people that bright Sunday afternoon, Katrina couldn't help but smile.

Psalm 66 tells us to make a joyful noise to God. Without the joy, is it just noise?

—————— Keep in Mind ——————

"Make a joyful noise unto God, all ye lands" (Psalm 66:1, KJV).

"Shout joyful praises to God, all the earth!" (Psalm 66:1, NLT)

Focal Verses

KJV **Psalm 66:1** Make a joyful noise unto God, all ye lands:

2 Sing forth the honour of his name: make his praise glorious.

3 Say unto God, How terrible art thou in thy works! through the greatness of thy power shall thine enemies submit themselves unto thee.

4 All the earth shall worship thee, and shall sing unto thee; they shall sing to thy name. Selah.

5 Come and see the works of God: he is terrible in his doing toward the children of men.

6 He turned the sea into dry land: they went through the flood on foot: there did we rejoice in him.

7 He ruleth by his power for ever; his eyes behold the nations: let not the rebellious exalt themselves. Selah.

8 O bless our God, ye people, and make the voice of his praise to be heard:

9 Which holdeth our soul in life, and suffereth not our feet to be moved.

16 Come and hear, all ye that fear God, and I will declare what he hath done for my soul.

17 I cried unto him with my mouth, and he was extolled with my tongue.

18 If I regard iniquity in my heart, the Lord will not hear me:

19 But verily God hath heard me; he hath attended to the voice of my prayer.

20 Blessed be God, which hath not turned away my prayer, nor his mercy from me.

NLT **Psalm 66:1** Shout joyful praises to God, all the earth!

2 Sing about the glory of his name! Tell the world how glorious he is.

3 Say to God, "How awesome are your deeds! Your enemies cringe before your mighty power.

4 Everything on earth will worship you; they will sing your praises, shouting your name in glorious songs." Interlude

5 Come and see what our God has done, what awesome miracles he performs for people!

6 He made a dry path through the Red Sea, and his people went across on foot. There we rejoiced in him.

7 For by his great power he rules forever. He watches every movement of the nations; let no rebel rise in defiance. Interlude

8 Let the whole world bless our God and loudly sing his praises.

9 Our lives are in his hands, and he keeps our feet from stumbling.

16 Come and listen, all you who fear God, and I will tell you what he did for me.

17 For I cried out to him for help, praising him as I spoke.

18 If I had not confessed the sin in my heart, the Lord would not have listened.

19 But God did listen! He paid attention to my prayer.

20 Praise God, who did not ignore my prayer or withdraw his unfailing love from me.

The People, Places, and Times

Selah. This Hebrew expression (SEH-lah) is found most frequently in the book of Psalms. There it is used some seventy-three times. It also appears in Habakkuk 3:3, 9, and 13. The meaning of the word is widely debated by biblical scholars. On one hand, many feel that it is a technical term for music or recitation. Some believe that "Selah" denotes a pause or a suspension in singing of the psalm or recitation, and the insertion of an instrumental musical interlude. That is how the Greek

Septuagint renders the word. The psalms were sung and sometimes accompanied by instruments. In Psalm 9:16, "Selah" is paired with the Hebrew word *Higgaion* (**hig-gaw-YONE**), indicating an association with a harp or some other soft musical instrument.

Why are pauses an important part of music or speeches?

Background

Two of the most repeated commands throughout the Bible are for us to "sing" and "worship." Psalm 66 reveals that the two concepts can overlap, as singing can be a form of worship if we acknowledge God's presence and lift Him up. Worship is really about more than music, though. Worship involves surrender—all of who we are for all of who God is. To limit that to singing misses out on the transformational opportunity we have to put God first in all things all of the time. Thankfully, the Scriptures also show how God intervenes to show us the value of valuing Him by revealing how He values us. Psalm 66 walks us through this verse by verse, affirming why we should "Make a joyful noise unto God, all ye lands" (66:1). This is not merely a call for the people who get it to worship the Lord, but for all people (including those who don't yet know Him) to discover by recognizing how He created the world and is re-creating it as we respond to Him.

How have different kinds of music allowed the message of God to be spread to people who would not normally hear about God?

At-A-Glance

1. Worship is Truth-Telling (Psalm 66:1–9)
2. Worship is Story-Sharing (vv. 16–20)

In Depth

1. Worship is Truth-Telling (Psalm 66:1–9)

There may not be a shortage of opinions about God, but only the truth matters. The psalmist makes this distinction clear in that when we recognize who God has revealed Himself to be, it overtakes who we guess He is. The glory of God's name speaks to the knowledge of God's identity and works (v. 2). Glory ascribed to kings or military leaders would be related to their exploits in battle or prosperity of their land. The glory of God is the tangible knowledge of God's character and great deeds in the earth. The earth itself submits to Him, so why shouldn't we (v. 4)? In other words, worship begins with truth-telling (both personally and in community) as we declare with a mighty shout the existence of a creative power beyond our own.

God's power is devastating and should inspire us to fear Him (vv. 5–9). He has proven Himself to be good and caring with that power on our behalf which invites us to trust in Him. Unfortunately, many people never experience the best of the Lord because they demand He act as they want or expect Him to and abandon their faith when God does not. By instead identifying the mighty works God has done, experiencing awe as we contemplate His creation, and rejoicing in our redemption, we let God be God. Truth-telling blesses us and makes "the voice of His praise to be heard" (v. 8). We join in the re-creation process by acknowledging that there is a moral absolute in the world through a Creator who helps us look at broken situations and know there is a better way.

What can you praise God for no matter your circumstances?

2. Worship is Story-Sharing (vv. 16–20)

Psalm 66:16 beckons, "Come and hear, all ye that fear God, and I will declare what he hath done for my soul." The psalmist here is proclaiming the transformative experience of sharing a testimony in the midst of a congregation. God had not only heard, but answered the psalmist's prayer for help. There was an admission by the psalmist of his sin. He recognized that God was not answering his prayer because of his own imperfection in keeping the Law, but received God's mercy when he confessed his sin. God already knows what we have thought, felt, and done against His will; but He desires for us seek Him in spite of our shortcomings.

There is an important reminder here to be honest and authentic with God and others about our humanity, our sin, and unworthiness of God's mercy. We get to do this by gathering together regularly with other believers as a church, because worship is story-sharing. When we keep what God has done in our lives to ourselves, we quiet what He wants to say to others. Speaking up and telling others about our journey helps them as they wonder if the fortunate coincidences they experience might be evidence of God at work, inspiring us all to be overcomers in light of adversity.

How has God been merciful to you in spite of yourself?

Search the Scriptures

1. What exactly is a "joyful noise?" (Psalm 66:1)

2. What role does confession of sin play in the psalmist's worship (v. 18)?

Discuss the Meaning

1. When people say they love God, what do you think they typically mean?

2. Whose spiritual journey has helped you hear what God could do for your soul (66:16)? Why do you think they shared it out loud with you? Who else might benefit from hearing you share your spiritual journey out loud?

Liberating Lesson

People are often stirred by others who have used their might to change the world. The question is: What is the true measure of might? Is it not God and the mighty works He has done as the Creator of the universe and the Savior of His people?

We see it in how worship pushes us beyond ourselves and encourages us to think past the moment we are in. When we would rather stay stuck in our worry, make life about getting something else, hide our real feelings, or showcase our opinions and our pride, worship refocuses us on God. Worship sees God on the throne, thereby dethroning whatever we have put on it instead—ourselves, a loved one, the problems of life, or a fear of our enemies.

True worship is done in spirit and in truth. When we become wholeheartedly engaged with a true view of God, we realize how He is wholeheartedly engaged with a true view of us. If you are not at peace, perhaps you are at war with the idea of worshiping God.

Application for Activation

All around us, people are afraid to hope out of fear of being let down. It would be easy for us to give them a noble speech or challenge, but it is more meaningful to offer empathy first. We can nurture our fellow believers by gathering to talk about when we have felt afraid to hope. What were the circumstances? How did you work through the emotions? In what form did any kind of rescue or perspective come? How did God act on your behalf, perhaps without you realizing it?

Next, read Psalm 66 together and look for any common themes with what you shared. Instead of trying to force any insight, simply be aware of God's presence with you in this passage and moment. Encourage everyone in the group to thank Him out loud for who He is or what He has done in their lives. Let this be a prayer time when you invite Him to speak peace into you over anything making you nervous or stressed. Ask Him to guide the next 24 hours with this perspective as you intentionally keep looking for His presence. Pray for anyone you might meet who would benefit from hearing about your journey.

Follow the Spirit

What God wants me to do:

_____

_____

_____

_____

Remember Your Thoughts

Special insights I have learned:

_____

_____

_____

_____

More Light on the Text

Psalm 66:1–9, 16–20

1 Make a joyful noise unto God, all ye lands: 2 Sing forth the honour of his name: make his praise glorious.

The first four verses open the psalm by calling the entire earth to worship God.

"Make a joyful noise" (Heb. *rua'*, **roo-AH**) is a single-word command in Hebrew that means "shout." *Rua'* may refer to a variety of different shouts, but the context is clearly one of worship and celebration. "All ye lands" is literally "all the earth" in Hebrew (*'erets*, **EH-rets**). As

Creator of the entire world, the Lord deserves to receive praise from people everywhere. The praise that is offered to God should reflect the truth of who He is. The "honour" (KJV; Heb. *kabod*, **kaw-BODE**) of His name is also translated "glory" (NLT). "Glorious" (v. 2) is the same word in the Hebrew text. *Kabod* literally means "weighty, heavy." When used of a person, it means "impressive, honorable, worthy of respect."

3 Say unto God, How terrible art thou in thy works! through the greatness of thy power shall thine enemies submit themselves unto thee.

"Terrible" (KJV; Heb. *yare'*, **yaw-RAY**) literally means "to be feared." The New Living Translation translated the word as "awesome." A sober contemplation of all that God has done should create a healthy respect for Him and give pause to anyone who is hostile toward God. He called the universe into existence, creating everything that exists with the power of His Word. He holds the power of life and death in His hand. No one should think he or she can prevail against the Lord of the universe.

The verb translated "submit" (Heb. *kachash*, **kaw-KHASH**) often means "to deceive" (v. 3), but here is used to mean "cower or cringe in fear" (cf. Deuteronomy 33:29; 2 Samuel 22:45; Psalm 81:15). The enemies of God will be cut down to size when they face His holy judgment. Christ's death and resurrection means that He has defeated all of His and our enemies (Colossians 2:15). Those who align themselves with the enemies of God will share in their defeat.

4 All the earth shall worship thee, and shall sing unto thee; they shall sing to thy name. Selah.

"Worship" (Heb. *shachah*, **shaw-KHAW**) means to "bow down deeply, show obeisance."

Worship is central to the purpose for which God created humankind, and God has ordained that we must worship Him. There is a sense in which all the earth already does worship—there are worshipers of the true God all over the world from an incredible variety of ethnic and linguistic groups.

However, the worship of the whole earth is not yet what it will be one day. Isaiah foretells a day in which "every knee shall bow" (45:23). Paul applies this prediction to Christ—He will receive the praises of all people (Philippians 2:10). Psalm 2:9 paints a graphic picture: "Thou shalt break (or rule) them with a rod of iron." In Psalm 66:4, the repetition of the word "sing" (Heb. *zamar*, **zaw-MAR**) makes it clear that this worship of God will be a genuinely joyful time for the people of God. Isaiah 2:2–4 describes this joyful day: All of God's people will gather in Zion, and peace and justice will reign.

5 Come and see the works of God: He is terrible in his doing toward the children of men.

"Come and see" invites the audience in; the psalmist is serving as our tour guide. He will point out the items of significance and help us understand them. We see first a characterization of God as "terrible" or awesome in His works. Verse 3 called us to confess the awesome, fear-inspiring nature of God's works. Now we are to consider them by examining them closely in our mind's eye.

The precise meaning of the phrase "toward the children of men" is unclear. Some English translations use the same approach as the Septuagint and take the preposition "toward" to mean "on behalf of; for." The phrase may also emphasize that God's greatness overwhelms anything that human beings can do or comprehend, expressing a thought similar to that

of Paul's: "For who hath known the mind of the Lord?" (from Romans 11:34).

6 He turned the sea into dry land: they went through the flood on foot: there did we rejoice in him.

This psalm recalls the time the Lord sent a strong wind that pushed back the waters of the Red Sea, creating a stretch of dry land with walls of water on both sides (Exodus 14:21–22). The people of Israel passed through, and the pursuing Egyptians followed them. But the Lord caused the Egyptian chariots to bog down in the middle of the Red Sea, and before they could escape, the Red Sea returned to its place, wiping out the entire chariot force of the Egyptian army.

Here, the Hebrew word "flood" is literally "river" (*nahar*, **naw-HAWR**), so it may be a reference to another story in which Israel passed through a body of water: the parting of the Jordan River, which enabled the Israelites to cross over into the Promised Land (Joshua 3). However, *nahar* may refer to bodies of water other than rivers (Jonah 2:3), so the exclusive reference is not certain. "There did we rejoice" (Psalm 66:6) is actually an exhortation in the Hebrew.

7 He ruleth by His power for ever; His eyes behold the nations: let not the rebellious exalt themselves. Selah.

"His eyes" is an example of anthropomorphism, a figure of speech in which human characteristics are attributed to a nonhuman—in this instance, God. We know that, being a Spirit, the Lord does not literally have eyes. However, He is fully aware of all that is happening. Nothing is hidden from Him. The people of God can live in confidence because He is always watching. To the righteous, the eyes of the Lord are a source of comfort and assurance.

He watches in order to support those who fear Him (2 Chronicles 16:9).

But to the wicked, the eyes of the Lord are menacing reminders of certain judgment. The word "rebellious" as used here is a form of the Hebrew verb *sarar* (**saw-RAR**), which means both "to be stubborn" and "to be rebellious." The rebellious are those who refuse to listen and resist those who are in authority over them. "Exalt" (Heb. *rum*, **ROOM**) means "to raise up." The rebellious are being warned not to think too highly of themselves. They will be humbled when they stand before the Lord. Though they are proud now, they will one day regret their attitude and actions.

8 O bless our God, ye people, and make the voice of his praise to be heard:

The theme of the psalm now shifts to praising God for His faithfulness to His people. Although the people of Israel have been the direct beneficiaries of His goodness, the invitation to bless the Lord goes out to all people (see Deuteronomy 32:43). Most English versions translate "people" (Heb. *am*, **AHM**) as "peoples." The New Living Translation goes even further: "Let the whole world bless our God."

9 Which holdeth our soul in life, and suffereth not our feet to be moved.

We see here that God has preserved His people. "Holdeth our soul in life" simply means that He has kept us alive. "Suffereth not our feet to be moved" means that He has not permitted our feet to slip. Psalm 121:3 is a parallel passage: "He will not suffer thy foot to be moved: he that keepeth thee will not slumber." These passages remind us that the righteous are distinguished by their willingness to entrust themselves fully to God's care.

16 Come and hear, all ye that fear God, and I will declare what he hath done for my soul.

The psalmist issues an invitation to hear his testimony, and shifts again from general praise to God to personal proclamation of God's work in his own life. The invitation is given specifically to those that hear God, for there is a connection between reverence for the Lord and being able to hear and appreciate the testimony of God's work in the life of someone else. The Lord has done a work for the soul, or total person of the psalmist.

In verses 10–15 not printed, the psalmist speaks of trials that the nation of Israel has endured, particularly in warfare. The warfare and the destruction it caused are viewed as divine judgment on the people; that is, God was allowing destruction to come upon the people for disobedience so they might be tried and made faithful again. Yet after the trials, the psalmist speaks of bringing offerings to the house of the Lord and recognizes that God has spared him. The psalmist will not only give offerings, but keep the vows he made to God. He understands that both sacrifices and obedience belong to God, who has not simply allowed him to survive, but has made him prosper again. The psalmist's testimony declares that in the midst of the trial he cried out to God, and God answered his prayer and showed mercy toward him.

17 I cried unto him with my mouth, and he was extolled with my tongue. 18 If I regard iniquity in my heart, the Lord will not hear me:

These verses reinforce that both prayer and praise proceed from the psalmist. God is to be praised always; our cry in prayer should not be separated from declaring the praise of who God is and what God has already done. The psalmist further remarks that we cannot hold iniquity or immoral intentions in our hearts and expect the Lord to hear our prayers. God knows and searches the hearts of men and women. We cannot say we need God's help, but then want to disobey the Lord or cause harm to our neighbor and expect God to honor our requests.

19 But verily God hath heard me; he hath attended to the voice of my prayer. 20 Blessed be God, which hath not turned away my prayer, nor his mercy from me.

The psalm ends with a triumphant conclusion; God has heard and answered the prayer of the psalmist. God should be praised at all times, and God is certainly glorified when He answers long-awaited prayers. These verses remind us that God not only hears our prayers, but He also cares about what we pray. God desires to be close to us, to be in relationship with us, to have us communicate with Him in prayer, and to rejoice when He answers our prayers. The psalmist is grateful to God for showing mercy and answering his prayer. We can praise God when we receive healing, a breakthrough, understanding, wisdom, direction, and mercy. We give praise and thanks to our Lord who hears and answers prayer!

Say It Correctly

Selah. **SEL**-uh.
Extol. **IK**-stohl.

Daily Bible Readings

MONDAY
In God I Trust
(Psalm 56:1–8)

TUESDAY
God Listens to the Humble
(Luke 18:9–14)

WEDNESDAY
Faith Tested by Fire
(1 Peter 1:3–7)

THURSDAY
The Lord Is Near in Suffering
(James 5:7–12)

FRIDAY
Crossing the Jordan on Dry Land
(Joshua 4:19–24)

SATURDAY
God's Grace for Hard Testing
(Psalm 66:10–15)

SUNDAY
Praise God for His Mighty Works
(Psalm 66:1–9, 16–20)

Notes

_____

_____

_____

_____

Teaching Tips

Words You Should Know

A. **Pestilence** *deber* (Heb.)—Plague or disease.

B. **Refuge** *machaceh* (Heb.)—Shelter from outside elements such as rain, storm or danger.

Teacher Preparation

Unifying Principle—God Our Protector. People often live in fear that misfortune will befall them. Where can we find protection from danger? The psalmist looks to God for protection in the midst of life's calamities.

A. Read the Bible Background and Devotional Readings.

B. Pray for your students and lesson clarity.

C. Read the lesson Scripture in multiple translations.

D. Option: Have the class catalogue the various sorts of danger described in this psalm: pestilence, night terrors, arrows, destruction, wild animals, and so on. Have them rewrite the psalm (or portions of it) to reflect the sorts of dangers or threats they face in life.

O—Open the Lesson

A. Begin the class with prayer.

B. Have the students read the Aim for Change.

C. Have the students read the In Focus story.

D. Ask students how events named in the story can weigh on their hearts and how they can view these events from a theological perspective.

P—Present the Scriptures

A. Read the Focal Verses and discuss the Background and The People, Places, and Times sections.

B. Have the class share what Scriptures stand out for them and why, with particular emphasis on today's context.

E—Explore the Meaning

A. Use In Depth or More Light on the Text to help provide more in-depth discussion of the lesson text.

B. Discuss the Liberating Lesson and Application for Activation sections.

N—Next Steps for Application

A. Summarize the value of knowing God as our protector.

B. End class with a commitment to pray to God for safety, shelter, and protection.

Worship Guide

For the Superintendent or Teacher
Theme: Living with God's Loving Assurance
Song: "Psalm 91"
Devotional Reading: Romans 8:31–39

Living with God's Loving Assurance

Bible Background • PSALM 91:1–16
Printed Text • PSALM 91:1–8, 11–16 | Devotional Reading • ROMANS 8:31–39

Aim for Change

By the end of the lesson, we will: RECOGNIZE the many ways God protects us; RELATE to the psalmist in gratefulness declaring God's power of protection; and PROCLAIM our trust in God as our protector in the future.

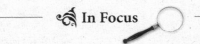 **In Focus**

Lydia, a newlywed, had recently been scheduled to have surgery to remove an ovarian mass that was causing extreme pain and was possibly cancerous. She was concerned, but not shaken. She had witnessed God's power in the life of her mother, a four-time cancer and heart attack survivor. She began to meditate on Psalms 27 and 91, and Isaiah 26:3–5, as suggested by her mother.

A week later, Lydia was involved in a fender bender caused by two very apologetic young men whom she had the opportunity to invite to church. Also, her car was perfectly fine. She was reminded of Psalm 91:11: "For he shall give his angels charge over thee, to keep thee in all thy ways." Additionally, the accident was a distraction from her current medical situation.

With prayerful tears, Lydia and her husband went through the surgery preparation while she earnestly tried her hardest to focus on the promises of the Scriptures. She fearlessly endured the surgery, recovery, and received the news that the mass was cancerous—but the cancer was not found anywhere else! Once again, the Lord's voice rang out, "With long life will I satisfy him." Lydia was grateful for God's strength and covering over her; she was honored that her life was a testimony of His promises in His Word.

How has God's Word sustained you in times of crisis?

Keep in Mind

"He shall call upon me, and I will answer him: I will be with him in trouble; I will deliver him, and honour him" (Psalm 91:15, KJV).

"When they call on me, I will answer; I will be with them in trouble. I will rescue and honor them" (Psalm 91:15, NLT).

Focal Verses

KJV **Psalm 91:1** He that dwelleth in the secret place of the most High shall abide under the shadow of the Almighty.

2 I will say of the LORD, He is my refuge and my fortress: my God; in him will I trust.

3 Surely he shall deliver thee from the snare of the fowler, and from the noisome pestilence.

4 He shall cover thee with his feathers, and under his wings shalt thou trust: his truth shall be thy shield and buckler.

5 Thou shalt not be afraid for the terror by night; nor for the arrow that flieth by day;

6 Nor for the pestilence that walketh in darkness; nor for the destruction that wasteth at noonday.

7 A thousand shall fall at thy side, and ten thousand at thy right hand; but it shall not come nigh thee.

8 Only with thine eyes shalt thou behold and see the reward of the wicked.

11 For he shall give his angels charge over thee, to keep thee in all thy ways.

12 They shall bear thee up in their hands, lest thou dash thy foot against a stone.

13 Thou shalt tread upon the lion and adder: the young lion and the dragon shalt thou trample under feet.

14 Because he hath set his love upon me, therefore will I deliver him: I will set him on high, because he hath known my name.

15 He shall call upon me, and I will answer him: I will be with him in trouble; I will deliver him, and honour him.

16 With long life will I satisfy him, and shew him my salvation.

NLT **Psalm 91:1** Those who live in the shelter of the Most High will find rest in the shadow of the Almighty.

2 This I declare about the LORD: He alone is my refuge, my place of safety; he is my God, and I trust him.

3 For he will rescue you from every trap and protect you from deadly disease.

4 He will cover you with his feathers. He will shelter you with his wings. His faithful promises are your armor and protection.

5 Do not be afraid of the terrors of the night, nor the arrow that flies in the day.

6 Do not dread the disease that stalks in darkness, nor the disaster that strikes at midday.

7 Though a thousand fall at your side, though ten thousand are dying around you, these evils will not touch you.

8 Just open your eyes, and see how the wicked are punished.

11 For he will order his angels to protect you wherever you go.

12 They will hold you up with their hands so you won't even hurt your foot on a stone.

13 You will trample upon lions and cobras; you will crush fierce lions and serpents under your feet!

14 The LORD says, "I will rescue those who love me. I will protect those who trust in my name.

15 When they call on me, I will answer; I will be with them in trouble. I will rescue and honor them.

16 I will reward them with a long life and give them my salvation."

The People, Places, and Times

Poetic Imagery in Psalms. Imagery is present throughout the Bible; however, it is very prevalent in the poetic sections of Scripture. It uses a wide variety of literary devices, including three that we encounter quite frequently in Psalms: simile, metaphor, and personification. With simile, the psalmist helps us see some truth by explicitly comparing it to something else, using the words "like" or "as." An example of simile is found in the opening verse of Psalm 42. Here, the simile compares a thirsty deer looking for water with the psalmist's own search for satisfaction in the Lord. Conversely, a metaphor makes more direct comparisons. These comparisons are made without the use of the words "like" or "as." For instance, in Psalm 23:1, we read: "The LORD is my shepherd; I shall not want." Here, the comparison of the Lord to a shepherd is made directly. Personification is the technique of ascribing human qualities to something that is non-human. We are seeing personification when we read, "What's wrong, Red Sea, that made you hurry out of their way? What happened, Jordan River, that you turned away?" (Psalm 114:5, NLT).

How does poetic language help you understand or hear a message differently?

Background

Psalm 91, known as a Psalm of Protection, is a mystery in that its authorship is unknown and it is without a title. It has been given a Latin title, "Qui habitat," derived from the first verse. In Jewish culture, it is recited before bed and seven times during a burial ceremony. For some Christians, it is recited on the first Sunday of Lent. In the Medieval Western church, the psalm is included in Good Friday readings. An additional mystery is the psalm's date of writing. Jewish schools of thought suggest that a nameless psalm be credited to the author of the preceding psalm. If this theory holds true, Moses is the author of Psalm 91. Other times a psalm's author can be discovered later in Scripture. For instance, early believers quote verses from Psalm 2, an unnamed psalm,

attributing it to David (Acts 4:25). Other key scholars have speculated that David is the author of Psalm 91, but the events of David's reign do not parallel the themes in this psalm. Aside from conjecture about its authorship, we can all conclude that Psalm 91 is a celebratory song about God's faithfulness, His power, and our response as His children.

How do you remember God's faithfulness? In what ways have you witnessed God's protection?

At-A-Glance

1. God Our Shelter (Psalm 91:1–8)
2. God Our Protector (vv. 11–13)
3. God Our Answer (vv. 14–16)

In Depth

1. God, Our Shelter (Psalm 91:1–8)

God's invitation goes out to anyone who seeks Him; He is non-discriminatory and inclusive. Dwell is to remain in a place for a time. Because God wants us but does not need us, His arms are always open when we come to this realization. To be in His shadow means that His presence is over us for our protection. The name Almighty in Hebrew is *El-Shaddai* (v. 1). The writer then expresses what the proper response is once we agree with God about who He is and how He sustains and protects us. He is ultimately the one we can wholeheartedly trust.

Furthermore, the writer showcases how God's protection is illustrated. Any plague, spiritual attack, or perceived enemy cannot withstand the power of the Lord. His comfort is unlike any other. Here the author explains how God's faithfulness will be our safe place and protective barrier, or rampart. He goes on to explain how our lives will inevitably change due to God's safe keeping. We will no longer become consumed by whatever we face, whether it is darkness, wicked imaginations, armies, tragedies, or more. You will see the downfall of those who meant to harm you, but you will remain unscathed.

How confident are you in these promises of God's protection?

2. God, Our Protector (vv. 11–13)

This passage begins with a promise that is ours if we submit to God's shelter and presence. He will perform the miracle of dispatching His messengers to surround us with His covering in every facet of our lives. The fact that we will not dash our feet against stones speaks to the surety of the angels' grasps on us when we fall. These guardian angels will do their job to keep us from the dangers of physical life and spiritual advances of the enemy and his demons. Verse 13 speaks of trampling upon lions and cobras as well as fierce lions and serpents. In other words the psalmist expects not only protection from but triumph over natural and spiritual enemies regardless of whether they are common or unique, weak or fierce.

Do you think that the role of angels has been misinterpreted in today's culture?

3. God, Our Answer (vv. 14–16)

Yet another promise is given in this passage that is conditional: God rescues those who know that they need Him, and He protects those who acknowledge His unmatched power. We will not have to wonder where He is and if He will appear. He is never tardy and He will answer with joy; He will never make us feel like a burden to Him. In fact, He is waiting on us to call Him! No trouble that we face, no turmoil that we find ourselves in is too hard for Him. Even in those messes that we have caused, He is there to clean us up as a father does with a toddler who stains his clothes. Finally, He promises to grant us a long life, not merely

existing but thriving in Him, and guarantees eternal security.

Are you distressed by areas in your life where you have not acknowledged God's ability to heal and deliver?

Search the Scriptures

1. Why does the psalmist need God to be shelter for them (Psalm 91:3–6)?

2. How does the psalmist say God responds to those who acknowledge Him and seek Him in prayer (vv. 14–16)?

Discuss the Meaning

1. Psalm 91 is one of the most iconic and memorable psalms in the Scriptures. Does Psalm 91 have any special significance for you or your family? Why or why not?

2. Think of a time when God allowed certain fears to overtake you or when He seemed distant in your time of trouble. How did you recover? What did you learn about God's response?

Liberating Lesson

The most appropriate way to "dwell" in God's shelter is prayer: listening and talking to Him. Sadly, many Christians use prayer as a last resort. Bullying at school and online is commonplace particularly with our youth. Many of us have seen the horrors of hurricanes and other natural disasters. The church can help alleviate the fears of unbelievers and new Christians in the face of medical diagnoses and wars by modeling the faith of the author of Psalm 91. The passage does not insinuate that challenge and calamity will not come, but that the Lord, our Savior is always victorious. There is power in prayer and trust in God, and when believers show faith in God for protection despite their circumstances, we testify to the hope our world so deeply needs.

Application for Activation

• The church must exhibit fearlessness and dependence on God's faithfulness even when there are elements of risk and dangerous threats, either perceived or real.

• Organize a neighborhood watch at your church. Pray for your church neighborhood. Invite local police officers and ask them to share any helpful precautions; pray for them and thank them for their service.

• Conduct an evangelistic, free lunch with prepared prayer warriors. Invite unchurched friends to share their fears and concerns about their children, life circumstances, crime, and more. In prayer circles of two or three people, pray for them based on Psalm 91 and share the Gospel of Jesus Christ. Be sure to get follow up information for those interested in knowing more about Jesus.

• How are your children conquering their fears? Pray with your family every morning and encourage them to pray for bus and playground safety, work-bound parents, and sports activities. These are also valuable talking points for family dinner conversations and carpool rides. Have them recall times when God kept them safe.

Follow the Spirit

What God wants me to do:

_____

_____

_____

_____

Remember Your Thoughts

Special insights I have learned:

_____

More Light on the Text

Psalm 91:1–8, 11–16

1 He that dwelleth in the secret place of the most High shall abide under the shadow of the Almighty. 2 I will say of the LORD, He is my refuge and my fortress: my God; in him will I trust.

The Hebrew word for "dwelleth" (*yashab*, **yaw-SHAB**), means to inhabit or remain. In this text, *yashab* describes the importance of remaining "in the secret place." While *yashab* can also be translated as merely to sit, this context makes it obvious that the subject of this psalm habitually stays in God's secret place. The Hebrew word for "in the secret" is *sether* (**SAY-thair**), which can refer to a shelter or hiding place. The phrase "of God's protection" conveys the idea of returning to God's abode, staying constantly in His presence, getting completely acquainted or connected with Him, and resting permanently in Him. The "secret place" is a refuge, a place of safety, and a covering from all forms of destructive elements that seek to attack or destroy the children of God, and to prevent us from experiencing the fullness of God's blessings and peace, and His divine providence. At least once in Scripture, God's "secret place" is in the Tabernacle (Psalm 27:5).

The word translated "Almighty" here is in Hebrew *shaddai* (**shad-DIE**). It represents an ancient title of God's protective character, and it was greatly feared by the enemies of God's people. In other words, God's children must make the Lord their refuge and habitation. In the Hebrew, the word "refuge" (*machaceh*, **makh-as-EH**) means "shelter from rain or storm, from danger." Therefore, the Lord has delegated His angels and given us the power of the Holy Spirit to build a solid spiritual wall of defense around His people to keep them from destruction.

3 Surely he shall deliver thee from the snare of the fowler, and from the noisome pestilence. 4 He shall cover thee with his feathers, and under his wings shalt thou trust; his truth shall be thy shield and buckler.

The psalmist deliberately establishes a connection between forces of opposition and God's sovereign protection. For instance, on the one hand, words such as "snare of the fowler" in Hebrew are *yaqush* (**yaw-KOOSH**), meaning "trapper" or "bait-layer" for game or fish. This phrase seems to imply human-made threats that intend to unleash havoc in people's lives, rather than mere natural disasters. The poetry builds out different sorts of troubles and attacks that can harm the writer, and the faith in the Lord's protection of His people in light of trouble. The word "pestilence" in Hebrew is *deber* (**DEH-ber**), which means "plague" or "disease." This part of Psalm 91 conveys how natural and man-made forces of evil can work against people and their communities to bring about death and destruction.

There are two metaphors used for God's protection in verse 4, those of wings and of a shield and buckler. The picture is of God protecting His faithful servant as a mother bird protects her children, shielding them from the elements or as armor protects a soldier going into battle, images that are illuminated in other memorable Scriptures (Matthew 23:37; Ephesians 6:10–19). Feathers are ascribed to God only one other place (Deuteronomy 32:11), a verse which also happens to use the same Hebrew for "hover" that described the Spirit of God hovering over Creation in the beginning (Genesis

1:2). God's metaphorical feathers of protection are reaching far and powerfully. The word "shield" (Heb. *tsinnah*, **tseen-NAH**) refers to a large shield that covered the entire body, while the Hebrew word translated "buckler," which is used only here in all Scripture, refers to something that surrounds a person. Here God's truth protects us from whatever the enemy throws at us. His truth leads us to understand absolute right and wrong, which God's Word reveals to us. If we surround ourselves in His truth, we have a safe starting point.

5 Thou shalt not be afraid for the terror by night; nor for the arrow that flieth by day; 6 Nor for the pestilence that walketh in darkness, nor for the destruction that wasteth at noonday.

Fear is an enemy with the power to create torment and disruptive behavior. Fear also has the power to neutralize a person's deep faith and absolute trust in the power and wisdom of God (cf. 2 Timothy 1:7; 1 John 4:18). When the children of God believe in the faithfulness of God and the unchanging power of His promise to protect, lead, and provide for them, it lays a strong foundation for exercising absolute confidence in His ability to provide for their spiritual salvation, too.

When a child of God dwells in His secret place, there is no reason to be frozen because of the "terror [that comes] by night" or "the arrow that flieth by day" (v. 5). The Hebrew word *qeteb* (**KEH-teb**) translated as "destruction" in the text refers to pestilential epidemics. There are pestilences that strike at night that are so pervasive that they do not clear up before noon. But God will protect us from these. The attacks in verses 5–6 also give us a picture of different time periods, but the Lord's faithful protection is consistent. The guardianship of the Lord is active throughout the entire day, indeed for all time for the one hiding in

His presence. The Lord is ever ready, in His love and power, to defend and protect us from challenges that the enemy has designed to destroy our initiatives or efforts as we desire to make progress according to God's plan for our lives.

7 A thousand shall fall at thy side, and ten thousand at thy right hand; but it shall not come nigh thee. 8 Only with thine eyes shalt thou behold and see the reward of the wicked.

Although plagues and problems impact the masses, they do not touch the person dwelling in the secret place of God's presence. This example of divine protection is a reminder that through plagues and warfare, the Lord's protection can preserve us. The preserved one becomes a survivor in the midst of the tragedy. Because the preserved one sees the "reward of the wicked," we can infer that what is being described is an act of divine justice against the wicked. While those who rebel against God and mistreat their neighbors are receiving punishment that destroys many, those who remain faithful and obedient, trusting God for their protection, will be safe.

11 For he shall give his angels charge over thee, to keep thee in all thy ways. 12 They shall bear thee up in their hands, lest thou dash thy foot against a stone. 13 Thou shalt tread upon the lion and adder: the young lion and the dragon shalt thou trample under thy feet.

In verses 9–10, the psalmist promises that since the one who dwells in the God's secret place made such a habitation, no evil or plague will affect him. The concept of divine protection in this discussion is built on the premise that the people of God must be dependent and obedient to the basic conditions or principles laid down in the Word of God in order to enjoy the fullness of God's blessings of protection, deliverance, and security.

Verses 11–12 are used by Satan when he tempts Jesus at the beginning of His ministry. Satan asks Jesus to throw Himself off the Temple, because based on these verses Jesus would not suffer harm from it. Jesus knows this is not the true meaning of these verses. The point is not that God's followers will never suffer so much as a stubbed toe; any brief look at Scripture would discount that. The point is to trust that God is always watching over us, willing to deploy even such powerful creatures as angels to keep us from falling. When He does not, we must trust, too, that it is for the best. Since we know God does not like to let us suffer and could prevent all suffering, we must trust that all suffering serves a purpose for Him, if only to make us long for heaven. Sometimes, the image of a lion is used in the Scriptures to represent Jesus Christ, the Lion of the tribe of Judah, as a symbol of His kingship and conquering power (Revelation 5:1–5). A lion is also used to refer to the devil: destructive, seeking to attack the people of God (1 Peter 5:8–9). In this particular context the psalmist could be using "lion" to represent Israel's predatory enemies. The psalmist also employed the image of the adder to symbolize actual and potential dangers posed by demonic and physical enemies of the people of God (Genesis 3:1–15; Mark 16:15–18).

14 Because he hath set his love upon me, therefore will I deliver him: I will set him on high, because he hath known my name. 15 He shall call upon me, and I will answer him: I will be with him in trouble; I will deliver him, and honour him. 16 With long life will I satisfy him, and show him my salvation.

In verse 14 God responds to the prayers and poetry of the psalmist. There is a progression from the faith for God's protection to God delivering the psalmist because of His grace. God delivers us, but He doesn't leave us just the way He found us. He exalts us, lifts us up on high, just for knowing His name and trying to worship. God searches for the heart we have for Him and offers His deliverance from trouble for those who trust Him.

Verses 15–16 give promises from God to those who trust in Him. God will hear their prayers and answer them, which can be contrasted with those who trust in idols or in themselves. It is important to note again that even when we find ourselves in trouble, God is able to be with us in the midst of it. Often we have an impulse to rush past the "in the midst" on to the deliverance, but the psalmist reminds us that God is with us in our trouble while it is still happening. God promises here that those who put their faith in Him will receive deliverance, honor, long life, and salvation. In the midst of our difficult seasons we can hold on to God's promise that although our suffering may not end today or even next week, God is with us. Our ultimate end is to see the salvation of God in this life in Jesus Christ and the life to come.

Daily Bible Readings

MONDAY
God Sustains and Cares for Jacob
(Deuteronomy 32:10–14)

TUESDAY
Trust God, No Need to Fear
(Psalm 121)

WEDNESDAY
The Lord Will Help You
(Isaiah 41:8–13)

THURSDAY
God Overpowers Adversaries
(Nahum 1:2–8)

FRIDAY
God's Protection through Oneness
(John 17:11–15)

SATURDAY
Deliverance from Violent People
(Psalm 140:1–8)

SUNDAY
Assurance of God's Protection
(Psalm 91:1–8, 11–16)

Notes

Discipleship and Mission

This quarter surveys several calls to ministry and the expectations of those called. Calls to service, as recorded in the Gospels of Mark and Luke, are highlighted. We explore Paul's call to ministry, with special attention to the Roman church. On Easter Sunday, we examine Matthew's account of the Resurrection.

UNIT 1 • Call to Discipleship

This unit has four sessions and highlights several aspects of what it means to be called by Jesus as a disciple. They include hospitality, counting the cost, reaching the lost, and salvation for all people.

Lesson 1: March 3, 2019
Called to Humility and Hospitality
Luke 14:7–14

People crave recognition and status, but are never satisfied and always want more. How does one find true fulfillment in relationship with others? Jesus taught that demonstrating humility and extending unselfish hospitality bring fulfillment in this life and the life to come.

Lesson 2: March 10, 2019
A Costly Call
Mark 1:16–20; Luke 14:25–33

People are always faced with choices between the comfortable, easy way and the more helpful but challenging way. How do we make the right choice? Jesus challenged His hearers to count the cost and recognize the consequences of discipleship.

Lesson 3: March 17, 2019
Calling the Lost
Luke 15:11–24

In our world it is easy for people to lose their way. What is our responsibility to those who go astray? Jesus taught that those who are lost are loved by God and are to be valued, searched for, and welcomed back when they return.

Lesson 4: March 24, 2019
Calling to Salvation
Luke 19:1–10

Some people can be considered unacceptable, either because of their actions or because of stereotypes held by others. How does one find acceptance? Jesus recognized Zacchaeus' interest and honored him despite the grumbling of the crowd; Zacchaeus responded with overwhelming repentance.

UNIT 2 • Call to Ministry

This unit has five sessions. It explores the diverse ways in which Jesus' disciples were challenged to exercise their call to ministry: by witnessing to the Gospel message, acting with loving-kindness, sharing the Resurrection story, and making new disciples through preaching, teaching, and baptism.

Lesson 5: March 31, 2019
Called to Discipleship
Matthew 4:12–22

People can be settled in their ways but destined for greater purposes. How do people discover and respond to that higher calling? When Jesus called His first disciples, they responded by leaving their routine work to follow Him.

Lesson 6: April 7, 2019
Call and Mission
Matthew 10:1–15

When people have discovered a greater purpose in life, they may be uncertain of what to do with that discovery. Where can persons find directions for implementing that greater purpose to benefit others? Jesus gave the first disciples direction to heal and witness to the "lost" persons of their shared community.

Lesson 7: April 14, 2019
Called to Remember
Matthew 26:1–13

People often long remember bad deeds done to them and forget good ones. Will the evil that is done to harm always outweigh the good? The woman with the alabaster jar performed an act of kindness to Jesus that will be remembered wherever the Good News is told.

Lesson 8: April 21, 2019
Called to Proclaim the Resurrection
Matthew 28:1–15

Many people live with despair and hopelessness. What is the source of genuine hope, and who can offer that hope? Jesus called and continues to call disciples to share and celebrate the Good News of His resurrection and the hope it offers to the world.

Lesson 9: April 28, 2019
Call and Commissioning
Matthew 28:16–20; Acts 1:6–8

When there have been dramatic changes in circumstances and in the roles of leadership, people are uncertain of their own roles and responsibilities. Where can they find direction and authority to act? The risen Lord commissioned the disciples, giving them authority and responsibility to continue and extend His mission and ministry throughout the world.

UNIT 3 • The Spread of the Gospel

This unit has four sessions. It begins with Paul's introduction of himself to the Jewish and Gentile Christians living in Rome. Paul affirms that the call to salvation is to Israel and to Gentiles. This call to salvation is a call to a life in the Spirit and involves a new life in Christ.

Lesson 10: May 5, 2019
Called to Righteousness
Romans 3:21–31

People sense that evil actions negatively impact their lives. Who can make amends for evil behavior? Paul told the Romans that the blood of Christ atones for all our sin.

Lesson 11: May 12, 2019
Called to Life in the Spirit
Romans 8:1–14

Consequences of past actions, the reality of impending death, and a sense that we cannot undo past mistakes weigh heavily on the human spirit. Where does one find relief from these pressures? Paul assures us that those who are in Christ Jesus have life in the Spirit and are free from condemnation.

Lesson 12: May 19, 2019
The Call of the Gentiles
Romans 11:11–24

Privileged people often feel superior to others. What is the corrective to such feelings of superiority? Paul warns the Gentile believers that their acceptance into grace must not make them feel superior to their Jewish brothers and sisters.

Lesson 13: May 26, 2019
Called to New Life in Christ
Romans 12:1–8

People often engage in a me-first way of thinking, which results in conflict and makes cooperation difficult. How do people learn to work together? Paul compares the church to a body and encourages believers to see themselves as individual members that work in sync with all the other members.

Discipleship and Mission

by Harvey Kwiyani, Ph.D.

What is Discipleship?

Discipleship is a rather strange concept in our 21st century North American context. Apart from its common use among Christians and in church settings, the word "disciple" (or "discipleship"—the process of making disciples) does not have a direct equivalent in the wider society. For instance, we do not talk about people being disciples of their managers at work, nor do we talk about football players being disciples of their coaches. The word itself is not in common parlance outside the church and other religious traditions.

Mentorship and apprenticeship come close but there is still a big difference between both of them and discipleship. While a disciple is a student attached to a master, a rabbi, or a guru for the purposes of learning the master's teachings and life, both mentorship and apprenticeship are generally focused on the student's ability to learn a trade or perform certain desirable tasks.

Being a disciple is similar to subscribing to a school of thought and sitting under the tutelage of its leaders in order to fully understand what it is about and its implications on the follower's life, and then to be able to represent it well to others who want to learn of it. Being a disciple is like a group of students surrounding a respected professor in their field of interest for a few years to learn its intricacies after which they can accurately explain their professor's ideology, show how it affects the followers' lives, and represent their institution's good name to the world.

Disciples are, thus, people who are influenced by, or follow the teachings of, or whose lives are shaped according to some thought leader. For instance, we talk about the disciples of Ayn Rand, or Desmond Tutu, and Mahatma Gandhi as people who believe in and follow the teachings of these leaders. In this sense, discipleship means studentship but, of course, the word "studentship" is not in our common vocabulary as well. Hence, in many of our Western languages and individualistic cultures, we often lack the mental models to help us conceptualize what discipleship really looks like.

Discipleship in African Contexts

Other cultures around the world are not so disadvantaged. In most African cultures, for instance, discipleship is not a foreign concept (of course, they understand it differently from what we see in Western Christianity, both in the West and in its exported forms around the world). Among many African peoples, sages and wise elders (not necessarily old people) still serve as societies' teachers, showing younger generations the wisdom that has helped their communities survive and overcome many difficulties. In their oral traditions, they pass on this great wisdom in proverbs, folk stories, and songs, repeating them as much as needed to make sure that their children have internalized the philosophies that give them identity and learned how to behave in a way that brings honor to their families and communities. In some places in Africa, for instance, initiation rites continue to serve as the entry point to a long journey of discipleship through which children became adults via the teachings of the elders. Those lessons are shaped to help them understand who they are on their own and in relation to their communities and what this means for the way they relate with the community and the wider world. This journey of learning—both the "theory" of why we do what we do as a community and the "praxis" of how to do it well—is discipleship.

I have heard many African leaders wonder why they cannot practice this kind of discipleship in their churches because, in their words, "the discipleship of head-knowledge that came with the missionaries is not helping us at all." I used to be bothered when I heard many American Christians say the African church is one mile wide and one inch deep until I had a chance to see American Christians in their communities. They are not any different from the African church—one mile wide, one inch deep, only with a little touch of arrogance that says, "we are the best."

New Ways of Thinking about Discipleship

Any form of Christianity that does not take discipleship seriously will be powerless. Indeed, discipleship is not simply a passing on of the correct doctrine. Yes, knowledge transference is an important part of the process, but it is not and can never be all that discipleship is about. Discipleship is, at least, both the sharing of a master's teaching and a real-life modeling of the demands of those teachings on followers. The Gospels seem to suggest this is what Jesus had in mind when He called His disciples

to "go and make disciples of all nations." Of course, Jesus was using a well-known term in his context—it was common for first-century rabbis to have disciples. Even John the Baptist, who was not a rabbi, had some. When the disciples heard Jesus command them to "go and make disciples," they knew what He was talking about. They were to go and do as He had done with them for three and a half years. He had modeled for them how to disciple others.

Call to Christian Discipleship

One critical aspect of the mission of Jesus was the formation of a fellowship of disciples that could be His partners in spreading the Good News and healing the world, starting in Jerusalem, Judea, Samaria and to the uttermost parts of the earth. For such a huge mission, the making of disciples would be both the methodology and the strategy. He would start with discipling a small group of twelve men while showing them how to do the same to others. These, then, would multiply to seventy, one hundred and twenty, then add three thousand more, and many more afterwards.

This fellowship of disciples of Jesus, later called the *ekklesia*, would spread from Jerusalem to the Mediterranean world—and today, two thousand years later, to every nation on earth. It is to this ministry that all followers of Christ are called, to disciple new followers of Jesus in the teachings of Christ and show them how to live those teachings out in a sick and unjust world like ours. The mission that Jesus left for us is this: to make disciples for Him of all peoples in the world. He is the Master, and we are His disciples who have been drafted into a disciple-making movement. We are disciples called to make other disciples by teaching them everything Jesus taught us and demonstrating for them how to live according to His teachings. Often though, we make church members and not disciples. This focus on membership

and church sizes usually leads us to prioritize and measure wrong variables like how many people came to church on a Sunday and not whether their lives are being transformed according to the teaching of our Master.

In the command to go and make disciples of all nations, Jesus sent us to make new disciples by teaching them until they have learned everything we learned from Him, until their lives reflect the influence of this teaching and bear witness to their status as disciples of Jesus. Such intense and intentional reshaping of life goes beyond Sunday morning or Wednesday evening services. It takes more than just memorizing a catechism. It is only possible through a long-term commitment to learning and letting our lives be shaped by the teachings of Jesus—to let His light shine through us to those whom we disciple.

Discipleship, when understood in this manner, challenges us to a different way of doing church, of talking about God and God's mission in the world, and of understanding our role in it. For instance, this type of discipleship is relational and entails community. For discipleship to happen, there must be at least a teacher and a student (who also later becomes a teacher and takes on a student). As the student receives and grows in the faith, he/she must have students as well who will be receiving and growing out of his or her ministry. And so the chain of disciples-making-other-disciples grows. Thus, true discipleship trumps individualism, which is still a challenge to American Christianity.

Disciples Follow Christ

This kind of discipleship wants to help people hear God's voice on their own so that they can grow in their faith and disciple others. Matthew 16 is pivotal in the telling of the story of the ministry of Jesus discipling the twelve. In a nutshell, He asked the disciples who the people said He was. Peter was able to give the correct answer but not because he was of a sharp mind. He got the answer right because he was able to hear the voice of the Father. Jesus declared, "flesh and blood has not revealed this to you, but My Father who is in heaven" (from Matthew 16:17, NKJV). This was after three years of discipleship, and finally, one of the disciples could hear the Spirit's voice. It must have felt like mission accomplished for Jesus. Immediately after this, Jesus started to speak about the Cross—well aware that His ministry was coming to an end. In this event, we see exactly what discipleship is about: teaching people to build their own relationships with God (so they can hear God's voice). This voice of the Spirit draws us together (saving us from the clutch of individualism) and empowers us to be countercultural and to speak the truth in the face of adversity.

Discipleship also means that sometimes quality supersedes quantity. Jesus chose to work with only twelve disciples for three and a half years, spending almost every waking hour with them—teaching them how to hear the voice of God, pray, preach, heal the sick, and many other ministries that would be needed as the church grew and their numbers multiplied. By the time He went to the Cross, He had formed very deep relationships with these men, such that even though they still really did not understand His mission, Jesus was confident that the mission was in safe hands. This may be the best way to continue in God's mission in the world: for every follower of Christ to invest themselves in a few people in a deep way, teaching and showing them what following Christ means. Unfortunately, we live in an age when the size of our churches seems to be the most important statistic about them, and the bigger the church the better we are doing. By those standards, Jesus was a failure—He had at most one hundred and twenty known disciples, most of them remained distant and clueless about what Jesus' mission was about,

and yet, through their follow-ship, Jesus continues to transform the world today. While there are some among us who have been called to mega-church ministry, all of us have been commissioned to make disciples. We must have a few discipleship relationships around us. The world needs it. It will take a great deal of time and energy, but the fruit that comes out when they begin to disciple others will be worth every effort.

Finally, discipleship is key to growth. It is true that people who embrace discipleship and invest time and energy teaching others show signs of spiritual maturity earlier than those who do not. Indeed, discipleship is not just good for the people being discipled, it is also good for the people doing the discipling. I saw a network of congregations in the Midwest get serious about discipleship. When I asked them what was their greatest lesson from discipleship, their answer was, "We have learned that the quality of our discipleship relationships has a direct impact on everything else we do as a church." Indeed, when they got better at relational discipleship, they got better at everything else. As they focused on discipleship, they saw a great deal of unity and empathy among their followers, and this made it easier for them to engage in God's mission in their cities. Disciples became leaders, and soon they had enough leaders who engaged in missions in their cities in many ways. One of their leaders finished by saying, "If you ask the secret to our growth, the answer is that we believe that without relational discipleship, we will not be able to engage in God's mission in our cities."

Harvey Kwiyani, Ph.D., is a professor of African Christianity and Theology at Liverpool Hope University in the United Kingdom.

We've Come This Far by Sharing Our Faith

by Beverly Moore

Which comes first: mission or discipleship? My question is a provocative and relevant one given today's culture and climate. Religion and faith have been marred by politics, the racial divide, and questionable actions of people professing the name of Christ coupled with an increased influence of secularism. The result is the loss of a societal moral compass. People don't know who to believe anymore, and the one institution that has been the bearer of truth at times has also fallen short. There is a need to reclaim our place in order to bring God's kingdom here on earth as it is in heaven.

As Christians, we have a mandate to "go and make disciples," according to Matthew 28:19-20. We "the body of Christ," "the church," carry on what Jesus proclaimed in Luke 4:18-19: "The Spirit of the Lord is upon me, for he has anointed me to bring Good News to the poor. He has sent me to proclaim that captives will be released, that the blind will see, that the oppressed will be set free, and that the time of the Lord's favor has come." But what does that mean in modernity? What it means is that we have not received salvation through Jesus Christ to hide it under a bushel and await His return. Our focus is to share the Good News of God's love and mercy as demonstrated through the birth, life, death, burial, and resurrection of Jesus Christ, and build communities of faith that help others along their journey of spiritual formation. In short, we are to partner with the Triune God in the process of proclamation, witness, conversion, and discipleship. It is therefore our collective mission to make disciples and build community. In many respects the church has lost sight of how to build community or what theologian Dietrich Bonhoeffer called a "visible community." The very foundation of authentic church growth is missions and discipleship.

Mission and discipleship need to move beyond the numbers game where leaders measure units of giving, to a true heart to see people free. We want to invite people to come into the grace and knowledge of God and reproduce others who receive God's love. Missions should include the heart to uplift and build up the down-trodden followed by discipleship in the spiritual disciplines. Missions should partner with the Holy Spirit to reveal who disciples are in Christ, as empowered by God to live a fruitful life. Therefore, mission outreaches are more than offerings of charity but should include social action to improve the quality of life of those impacted by systemic injustice in any form.

According to data captured by Pew Center Research in its Religious Landscape study, 79% of Black respondents claimed the Christian faith. However, in a not so recent report from another source called out that only 1% of missionaries engaged in foreign countries are African Americans, and those from one of the largest denominations. We see ministry outreaches that promote their work in helping to feed hungry children, provide clean water or help free children and women from sex trafficking. But the images reflected remind one of colonialism where good-hearted White people have come to save the day. Yet as a whole, African American/Black churches have a missionary foundation. In fact, throughout our history in this country, there have been notable church leaders who have made their mark by sharing the Christian faith on foreign and domestic soil. For example, people like George Liele, a former slave turned pastor who brought the Gospel to Jamaica in 1782, is considered one of the first American missionaries, or Betsy Stockton, recognized as the first single woman missionary in modern history who served in Hawaii. African American/Black missionaries took responsibility in carrying the Gospel message to set others free as they had been set free. This trend continues according to data from another study. The Barna Group looked at perspectives on evangelism by race and found that Black Christians were more likely versus other race/ethnic groups to feel a personal responsibility to share their religious beliefs with other people who might believe differently.

There are churches and non-governmental organizations led by African Americans that have a heart for missions, domestic or foreign, where the net is cast wide through outreach as the vehicle to introduce Christ. But we are all called to do ministry. Believers should actively engage in their individual call to reach people within their sphere of influence. We each have a responsibility to ensure that anyone we encounter, whether casually or within our inner circle, has heard the truth of the Gospel of Jesus Christ. With that said, Christians need to be equipped to engage in conversation with the culture, answer questions, and able to defend what they believe without offense. Far too often unbelievers are put off when they ask questions and are met with resistance or hostility from Christians. It is in the questions and patience with those questions where the greatest opportunity to plant and water seed resides. Therefore do not get pigeonholed into thinking that missions are relegated to remote and far off places. The greatest mission field is right where we live, work, and play.

There are those who contend that once we catch the fish it is the Holy Spirit's responsibility to clean them. But as the body of Christ, we are to bear one another's burdens and therefore discipleship undergirds spiritual formation. Healthy Christians do not become so in isolation or by never confronting the pangs of transformation; the process of progressive sanctification happens in community. Discipleship in its purest form is not meant as a "gotcha" or opportunistic self-righteousness but a chance to walk alongside people in the newness of life. Paul, after giving instructions for godly living, exhorted the readers of the epistle in Titus 2:11-13 (NLT): "For the grace of God has been revealed, bringing salvation to all people. And we are instructed to turn from godless living and sinful pleasures. We should live in this evil world with wisdom, righteousness, and devotion to God, while we look forward with hope to that wonderful day when the glory of our great God and Savior, Jesus Christ, will be revealed." Discipleship is training and practice of godly living by being accountable to your community for none of us lives unto ourselves.

In another study, the Barna Group took a look at "Racial Divides in Spiritual Practices" and found that among survey respondents White believers are more likely to refer to discipleship as a "process of learning to follow Jesus Christ as Savior and Lord, seeking to observe all that Jesus commanded, by the power of the

Holy Spirit and to his glory." Black Christians instead commonly refer to discipleship as "the process of transformation that changes us to be increasingly more like Christ through the Word, the Spirit, and circumstance." For Black Christians, spiritual progress tends to focus more on life experience rather than achieving goals, about maturing into a Christ-like character as they weather life's storm. The study also reported that 85% of Black Christians were more likely to say "deepening one's faith through education and fellowship" is a goal of discipleship. For many Black Christians, because of our historic lens, sharing the faith is about bearing witness to God's greatness and is thus more experiential than focused on doctrine.

William J. Abraham in his book *The Logic of Evangelism*, took a critical look at evangelism in today's context and argues that methods of evangelism do not do enough to truly root people into Christian life because of the focus on church growth. He says that evangelism should serve as the primary initiation into the kingdom of God and that churches must engage with members in ongoing learning, nurturing, and spiritual development that sustains a commitment to Christ. Abraham goes on to share throughout his book that true evangelism and discipleship should catapult the receiver into a personal and involved partnership with the Holy Spirit to ensure true conversion and transformation.

Conclusion

Mission and discipleship are deeply rooted in the foundation of the African American/ Black church as a means of passing on our heritage of faith in the God of our weary years. I had asked earlier, "Which comes first: mission or discipleship?" The answer was and still is both/and. The output of mission work through evangelism should immediately follow with discipleship that reproduces a heart with responsibility to reach others. Missions, evangelism and discipleship must also include the meaningful engagement with available technology and communication platforms to help churches and members stay connected especially to millennials and the generation behind them. Therefore, churches that are intentional in conducting mission, evangelism and discipleship initiatives that reach across the generations will reap the blessing of building and enacting God's kingdom.

Sources:
Abraham, William J. *The Logic of Evangelism*. Grand Rapids, MI: William B. Eerdmans Publishing Company, 1989. 104-108
Barna Group, "Racial Divides in Spiritual Practice: Research Releases in Culture & Media," January 12, 2017. https://www.barna.com/research/racial-divides-spiritual-practice/.
Barna Group, "Ethnic Groups Differ Substantially On Matters of Faith: Research Releases in Culture & Media," August 10, 2004. https://www.barna.com/research/ethnic-groups-differ-substantially-on-matters-of-faith/.
Eekhoff Zylstra, Sarah. "Black Churches' Missing Missionaries," April 2, 2013. http://www.christianitytoday.com/ct/2013/april/missing-missionaries.html.
Pew Center Research Religion and Public Life, "Religious Landscape Study: Religious Composition of Blacks." http://www.pewforum.org/religious-landscape-study/racial-and-ethnic-composition/black/.
Traveling Team, "History or Mission: African-American Mission. "http://www.thetravelingteam.org/articles/african-american-missions.

Beverly Moore is a Christian educator and longtime contributing writer to *Precepts for Living*.

Christian Discipleship is Not 'Business As Usual'

by Rev. Dr. Patricia Carroll

As 21st-century Christian educators, we must respond to the commandment of Jesus as recorded in Matthew 28:18-20:

18 Jesus came and told his disciples, "I have been given all authority in heaven and on earth. 19 Therefore, go and make disciples of all the nations, baptizing them in the name of the Father and the Son and the Holy Spirit. 20 Teach these new disciples to obey all the commands I have given you. And be sure of this: I am with you always, even to the end of the age." (NLT)

This is not a newly discovered command from Jesus, Rabbi, master, teacher. Hence, the Christian church has shown herself to be quite diligent in the pursuit of fulfilling the Great Commission, particularly in the area of teaching in the pulpit and in Sunday School classrooms.

One does not have to look very far to realize that church attendance appears to be on the decline in the United States. Believers do not seem to be excited about seeking discipleship opportunities that involve subjection to anything more than "feel good" messages or perhaps responding to missionary Sunday offerings.

As a short-term missionary from 1988 to 2000, I had the privilege of traveling to many countries, including Hong Kong, the Philippines, Kenya, and Nigeria. I found it amazing that believers in third-world countries were so hungry for the preaching and teaching of the Gospel that great sacrifices were made in order to attend our leadership and evangelistic meetings. We made at least seven trips to Italy to partner with Christ Is The Answer Ministry headquartered there.

In 2003, Middlesex Institute of Theology & Technology was birthed. I was asked to serve as Dean of Student Affairs and also to conduct sound, biblically based classes. The school, geographically situated in the middle of the state of Connecticut, attracted students from the north and south to attend our classes.

But you will receive power when the Holy Spirit comes upon you. And you will be my witnesses, telling people about me everywhere—in Jerusalem, throughout Judea, in Samaria, and to the ends of the earth (Acts 1:8, NLT).

We were serving the body of Christ—in Jerusalem and Judea. But what about that hunger for truth and liberating Gospel teachings in

Samaria and the outermost ends of the earth? What about that hunger that I witnessed during my missionary season when I traveled to France and England? How are we to respond to Acts 1:8? It is not a suggestion, but a command.

How then, shall we accomplish this great task? Boundless, but within the stretch of a Holy Ghost imagination, the information highway uses digital technology as the vehicle to facilitate the outreach to all nations for the purpose of making disciples. Opportunistically, I had enjoyed a thirty-three-year secular career as an Information Highway Technologist. I saw this as God's direction to now employ the training and passion for technology as I had been commanded.

Realistically, one must be more specific when traveling on the information highway or risk confusion. Of the multitude of exits, I chose videoconferencing. Videoconferencing technology empowers the body of Christ to actualize or fulfill the Great Commission with the pure, unadulterated Gospel of Jesus Christ, our Lord and Savior.

In just a few years, the Internet has evolved into a powerful platform changing forever the way we communicate. The Internet allows us to realize this dictum from John Wesley, who said "Do all the good you can. By all the means you can. In all the ways you can. In all the places you can. At all the times you can. To all the people you can. As long as ever you can."

The 21st-century church must make a commitment to obey 1 Peter 3:15: "But in your hearts revere Christ as Lord. Always be prepared to give an answer to everyone who asks you to give the reason for the hope that you have. But do this with gentleness and respect."

It was not my plan to teach a class on Christian apologetics. That was a subject above my pay grade. Only the pastor should be the one to teach such an in-depth subject. But God ... I was given the opportunity to discover (or uncover) that it is the goal of Christian apologetics to remove the hindrances that stand between a person and the cross of Christ. It is the goal of the law of God to help us understand life. Belief in Jesus is an extremely invasive heart procedure that brings people to life.

Believers and non-believers alike are asking legitimate questions: Does God exist? Who was this Jesus? Discipleship training must be positioned to present Gospel truths on all levels to all who hunger and thirst for righteousness. No longer is it acceptable to regard church as just another event in our routine lives, as long as it does not inconvenience us or require any extra effort on our part. It has been said that those whom God calls, He equips. Digital technology is a powerful tool to use for building up the kingdom, not just for social media activity or gaming sickness.

Concluding with this Word from the great Rabbi:

17 He saith unto him the third time, Simon, son of Jonas, lovest thou me? Peter was grieved because he said unto him the third time, Lovest thou me? And he said unto him, Lord, thou knowest all things; thou knowest that I love thee. Jesus saith unto him, Feed my sheep. (John 21:17, KJV).

Rev. Patricia A. Carroll, DTS, Dean of Middlesex Institute of Theology & Technology, Middletown, Connecticut.

The Adult Learner's Learning Styles

by La Verne Tolbert, Ph.D.

As is the case with all students, the wise teacher remembers that adults are visual, audio, and kinesthetic learners. These different ways of learning—called learning channels—are effective because this is how students prefer to acquire information. Jesus taught memorable lessons that students could see (miracles), hear (parables and teachings), and do (actions). Likewise, teachers of adults help students remember when lessons are designed with learning channels in mind.

First, it's important that teachers are aware of their own learning channels. Why? Teachers usually teach the way they prefer to learn. But classes are comprised of students who learn through all of the learning channels. Teachers can be certain that adult learners are being taught effectively when they use methods that are visual, audio, and kinesthetic. Think eyes, ears, and hands or movement.

Visual Learners

These learners appreciate seeing methods. PowerPoint, handouts, reading, writing, and media are examples of methods that address visual learners. Some methods involve two learning channels. Writing, for example, is both visual and kinesthetic. Learners see what they are writing, which is visual. And, learners

are writing, which is kinesthetic. Media, if it involves sound, is both visual and auditory.

Auditory Learners

These learners appreciate hearing methods. Music, media, discussion, reports, and debate are just a few examples of methods that address auditory learners. These are also the learners who are probably the most talkative, because they also learn by hearing their own voice. Again, some of these methods target two learning styles, but hearing is the main focus.

Kinesthetic Learners

Although they may be the fewest number in the class, these learners are important, too. They appreciate doing methods. Arts and crafts or any activity that involves movement such as writing, works for these learners. And, drawing images and building objects are not just activities for younger students. The recent popularity of adult coloring books reminds us that adults are kinesthetic learners, too.

Planning Takes Time

Here's the challenge! Planning and designing lessons that address each of the learning channels takes time. Saturday night prep for a Sunday morning lesson may not allow enough

time to creatively address the learning channels. Teachers who take time to pray about their lessons and for their students are most likely to teach effectively.

Begin Monday! Take ten minutes to quickly glance over next week's lesson. Begin praying that God will illumine points to you that should be emphasized in your class. Also pray that God will prepare the students to learn what the Holy Spirit wants them to learn. Be alert to examples or activities that may work in your class as you go throughout your week.

On Wednesday, spend an hour or two thoroughly reviewing and planning the lesson.

Note where you may need an activity. You have the rest of the week to respond to God as He brings that method across your path.

Saturday, review . . . and rest. Getting a good night's sleep is probably every teacher's best gift to the class!

La Verne Tolbert, Ph.D., is author of *Teaching Like Jesus: A Practical Guide to Christian Education in Your Church* (Zondervan).

WILLIAM HENRY SHEPPARD

(1865-1927)

African American Missionary to the Congo

When we think of great missionaries, the image we usually get is of a Caucasian man in a pith hat stomping through Africa. William Henry Sheppard defies this image. Sheppard became the first African American missionary for the Presbyterian denomination in the 1890s and established an all African American Presbyterian mission station in the Congo. He also revealed the atrocities committed against the Congolese by King Leopold II of Belgium. These achievements, along with his exquisite collection of African art and his embracement of Congolese culture and language, made Sheppard a missionary of the highest caliber.

At the age of twelve, Sheppard became a stable boy and later worked as a waiter to put himself through the then newly founded Hampton Institute. He later enrolled at the Tuscaloosa Theological Institute, where he first gained a desire to preach in Africa. That desire was put on hold for two years while he served as pastor of a church in Atlanta, Georgia. During that time, Sheppard wrote letters to the mission board of the Presbyterian church asking to open a mission in Africa. His letters were met with vague answers of rejection. Seeking to understand why, Sheppard traveled to the church office in Baltimore, Maryland. The board admitted it would not send an African American without a White man in authority over him.

This did not stop Sheppard, who teamed up with Samuel Lapsley. Lapsley challenged the system by demanding equal rights for all mission workers,

no matter their race. The two set sail for London and gained entrance into the Congo through an American ally who was a friend of Lapsley's father. Sheppard started off with stereotypical views of the Congolese as ignorant and savage but, while there, his views started to change. He began to see the Congolese as graceful, courageous, and honest. Sheppard appreciated their rich, beautiful culture, and especially admired their weaving, embroidery, woodwork, and blacksmithing. While Lapsley left to visit another missionary, Sheppard learned the native language and hunting techniques. He also helped the Congolese people avoid a famine by hunting thirty-six hippopotamuses.

Sheppard became an outspoken critic of Leopold II's regime in the Congo. He investigated reports of violence and cruelty by the administration and the rubber companies that had set up shop there. The investigation became international news when he and another Presbyterian missionary were sued by the Kasai Rubber Company for libel. They were later acquitted. Eventually, Sheppard led an all African American missionary team, which included his wife, to the Congo. This was a first-of-its-kind achievement and was supported by a predominately White denomination. Sheppard was truly an African American trailblazer.

Sources:
Jacobs, Sylvia M., ed. *Black Americans and the Missionary Movement in Africa.* Westport, CT: Praeger Publishers, 1982.
Kennedy, Pagan. *Black Livingstone: A True Tale of Adventure in the Nineteenth-Century Congo.* New York: Viking Adult, 2002.

Teaching Tips

Words You Should Know
A. Bidden *kaleo* (Gk.)—To call specifically.
B. Feast *doche* (Gk.)—An elaborate meal, banquet where people are invited.

Teacher Preparation
Unifying Principle—Humility and Hospitality. People crave recognition and status, but are never satisfied and always want more. How does one find true fulfillment in relationship to others? Jesus taught that demonstrating humility and extending unselfish hospitality brings fulfillment in this life and the life to come.

A. Read the Bible Background and Devotional Readings.
B. Pray for your students and lesson clarity.
C. Read the lesson Scripture in multiple translations.
D. Option: Have students discuss the meaning of genuine humility and contrast it with the false kind that is merely pretentious. What constitutes genuine and false humility?

O—Open the Lesson
A. Begin the class with prayer.
B. Have the students read the Aim for Change.
C. Have the students read the In Focus story.
D. Ask students how events named in the story can weigh on their hearts and how they can view these events from a theological perspective.

P—Present the Scriptures
A. Read the Focal Verses and discuss the Background and The People, Places, and Times sections.
B. Have the class share what Scriptures stand out for them and why, with particular emphasis on today's context.

E—Explore the Meaning
A. Use In Depth or More Light on the Text to help provide deeper discussion of the lesson text.
B. Discuss the Liberating Lesson and Application for Activation sections.

N—Next Steps for Application
A. Summarize the value of being humble and hospitable.
B. End class with a commitment to pray for those who feel left out of church, community, or society.

Worship Guide
For the Superintendent or Teacher
Theme: Called to Humility and Hospitality
Song: "Jesus Has a Table Spread"
Devotional Reading: Luke 14:15–24

Called to Humility and Hospitality

Bible Background • Luke 14:7–14
Printed Text • Luke 14:7–14 | Devotional Reading • Luke 14:15–24

—————————— Aim for Change ——————————

In this lesson, we will: EXAMINE the teachings of Jesus regarding humility and hospitality; REFLECT on selfish personal tendencies; and IDENTIFY ways to respect those who are considered unworthy.

—————————— 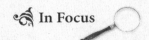 In Focus ——————————

Jill was a trustee at her church and an attention seeker. For example, she always sat up front during worship on Sunday and demanded that the ushers save her seat. She even sat next to Pastor Jones toward the head of the table at the trustee meetings.

At one meeting, Jill arrived a few moments early to mark her usual seat next to Pastor Jones. She left her belongings and went to the restroom. Upon her return, she discovered that her belongings had been moved. Sitting in the seat was a new member, Stacey, whom Pastor Jones had brought to the meeting. Jill was angry and said, "Excuse me, this is my seat. I am the only one who sits next to Pastor Jones in these meetings. And why are you even here? These are not open meetings. You just joined the church, and the bylaws say that you must be a member for at least a year before taking a leadership position."

Pastor Jones intervened, "Stacey is my guest. She is coming on board to help us with feeding the homeless on Saturday. Stacey was once homeless and used to sleep at the shelter. Her wisdom is needed because of her experience. I thought that it would be best for her to sit between the two of us as we bring her up to speed on the mission." Stunned, Jill took a new seat.

How could we be more hospitable toward those who we are unfamiliar with? How could we do better in practicing humility when asked to do something that is out of our normal routine?

—————————— **Keep in Mind** ——————————

"For whosoever exalteth himself shall be abased; and he that humbleth himself shall be exalted" (Luke 14:11, KJV).

"For those who exalt themselves will be humbled, and those who humble themselves will be exalted" (Luke 14:11, NLT).

Focal Verses

KJV **Luke 14:7** And he put forth a parable to those which were bidden, when he marked how they chose out the chief rooms; saying unto them.

8 When thou art bidden of any man to a wedding, sit not down in the highest room; lest a more honourable man than thou be bidden of him;

9 And he that bade thee and him come and say to thee, Give this man place; and thou begin with shame to take the lowest room.

10 But when thou art bidden, go and sit down in the lowest room; that when he that bade thee cometh, he may say unto thee, Friend, go up higher: then shalt thou have worship in the presence of them that sit at meat with thee.

11 For whosoever exalteth himself shall be abased; and he that humbleth himself shall be exalted.

12 Then said he also to him that bade him, When thou makest a dinner or a supper, call not thy friends, nor thy brethren, neither thy kinsmen, nor thy rich neighbours; lest they also bid thee again, and a recompence be made thee.

13 But when thou makest a feast, call the poor, the maimed, the lame, the blind:

14 And thou shalt be blessed; for they cannot recompense thee: for thou shalt be recompensed at the resurrection of the just.

NLT **Luke 14:7** When Jesus noticed that all who had come to the dinner were trying to sit in the seats of honor near the head of the table, he gave them this advice:

8 "When you are invited to a wedding feast, don't sit in the seat of honor. What if someone who is more distinguished than you has also been invited?

9 The host will come and say, 'Give this person your seat.' Then you will be embarrassed, and you will have to take whatever seat is left at the foot of the table!

10 Instead, take the lowest place at the foot of the table. Then when your host sees you, he will come and say, 'Friend, we have a better place for you!' Then you will be honored in front of all the other guests.

11 For those who exalt themselves will be humbled, and those who humble themselves will be exalted."

12 Then he turned to his host. "When you put on a luncheon or a banquet," he said, "don't invite your friends, brothers, relatives, and rich neighbors. For they will invite you back, and that will be your only reward.

13 Instead, invite the poor, the crippled, the lame, and the blind.

14 Then at the resurrection of the righteous, God will reward you for inviting those who could not repay you."

The People, Places, and Times

Pharisees. A major religious party in Jesus' time, the Pharisees were known for their strict observance of the Law of Moses and reliance on tradition. Portrayed as Jesus' adversaries in all four Gospels, the Pharisees often were outraged at Jesus' teachings and actions that portrayed a loving God who offered grace, while commanding salvation by faith (not works) alone.

Lawyers. This professional group was charged with studying, interpreting, and applying the Law of Moses. In many ways, their work mirrored that of the scribes who were originally priests, but whose roles included these same responsibilities, as well as copying the Law and writing documents.

Background

In Luke's Gospel, Christ has been heading toward Jerusalem—and the Cross—since Luke 9:51. With every step, the tension builds, and Luke 13 only adds fuel to the fire. As He has done on previous occasions, to the dismay of the Jewish leaders, Jesus heals on the Sabbath. But Jesus doesn't stop there. He calls His followers for a commitment to a kingdom where humble beginnings produce something of enormous and lasting value (cf. 13:18–21). As Jesus says, the door to this kingdom is narrow. The point is not how many can come in, or how many can come in at one time. The narrow door refers to the conditions necessary for admittance.

The warning "depart from me, all ye workers of iniquity" must have been, and should be, piercing to the soul (from vv. 26–27). Religious activity and ritual for ritual's sake can numb us to what God is doing and saying and, even worse, can separate us from God.

Luke then presents Christ's way of using a lesson on humility and the attitudes of the heart by exposing how superficial the actions of some in His audience are at common social events such as a wedding, a breakfast, a dinner, or a banquet.

How can stories like this parable help us teach and learn valuable life lessons in a different way?

At-A-Glance

1. Humility is Not Self-Gratifying
(Luke 14:7–9)
2. Humility Waits for Recognition
(vv. 10–11)
3. Humility Seeks Out Humility
(vv. 12–14)

In Depth

1. Humility is Not Self-Gratifying (Luke 14:7–9)

Jesus saw the guests pick high places of honor so that they could be seen. In response, He taught a valuable lesson through a parable. Jesus often used parables to bring about not only spiritual but cultural change in the audience's behavior.

In the parable Jesus refers to a wedding and guests who are invited (v. 8). A wedding at that time was not a simple one-day event shared between two new families; it was a celebration that lasted several days and constituted an already established or planned relationship. Family members and townspeople could be invited. Even Jesus did not go into such a setting and assume that He would be the center of attention (John 2:1–11). It was not His celebration! The place of honor would be set for the bride and bridegroom, not those in attendance.

Too often, we try to make ourselves feel important by gaining admirers or "likes" because that is culturally acceptable. Jesus is teaching us that by assuming we should be in the spotlight, we miss the purpose of being invited and humiliate ourselves in the process. Our purpose is to focus on the one being celebrated, not proclaim our position.

Does the word "humiliate" have a new meaning to you because of this parable?

2. Humility Waits for Recognition (vv. 10–11)

Jesus uses this parable to teach us that humility is an intentional action. As Christians, we should always consider others before thinking of ourselves. When the host sees that a person with whom they have a relationship has taken the lowest place, they will invite that guest to move to a higher level. Recognition, in this sense, is not just physical—for sake of reward—but it is also relational and spiritual.

Jesus teaches that those who are humble in their actions will soon receive recognition from those who can offer a greater reward.

Have you ever worked hard simply for the recognition, and did not receive it? Why do you think that happened?

3. Humility Seeks Out Humility (vv. 12–14)

Jesus was born in humble circumstances (Luke 2:7) to a family that did not have much social standing yet was spiritually the most important in any society. Through the parable, Jesus teaches that even the host of the banquet must join in creating a social hierarchy that is the reverse of what is expected. It is expected that we praise and invite those with higher social status to our celebrations, but in Jesus' parable the least, last and outcast are to be the guests of honor. Jesus is challenging the societal expectations of His audience while affirming what the Law of God said; to care for those on the margins of society such as the poor, the widow, the orphan, the foreigner, and those with disabilities (Deuteronomy 14:28–29). The poor have no ability to repay the host financially so God promises to repay the host in blessings (Deuteronomy 15:7–11).

Why is it difficult at times for us to invite those who are not like us to Jesus?

Search the Scriptures

1 What consequences of sitting in the seat of honor does Jesus warn about (Luke 14:9)?

2. When might a host be repaid for inviting people to a banquet (vv. 12, 14)?

Discuss the Meaning

1. Thinking about your own behaviors, in what ways have you come up short on showing hospitality? How could you improve? How have you excelled in your displays of hospitality? How could you go further?

2. Tell of a moment when your Christian character matured because of a humbling experience. What would you share with a new disciple about humility?

Liberating Lesson

In our world, social status seems like it means everything. Even in the virtual world, we can create a status via social media that usually does not tell the full truth about who we are. We change profile pictures and statuses often to show others who we are at the moment. But at that moment we are offering only a sample of who God has created us to be. Christian discipleship does not typically justify our desire to be important and famous. Christian discipleship requires us to take low places of recognition, which do not always offer immediate reward. Christian discipleship speaks truth to power and offers those who are least likely to be socially important an opportunity to gain recognition.

Application for Activation

During this week, gauge how important other people are to you. Is your day filled with thoughts about yourself, such as what you can gain and what you wish to satisfy in your own life? God is a selfless God and yet He would have no other gods take His place in our lives. God offers love freely to all out of His selflessness. Ask yourself whether you can honestly fulfill your purpose in life by only thinking of yourself. Is your walk with Christ about making personal gains? The choice to be a disciple is simple in the beginning, but as time goes on we must understand that our choice to follow Jesus is a choice to be selfless. We can offer the love of God to those He has allowed us to come into contact with by considering their needs first.

Follow the Spirit

What God wants me to do:

_____

_____

_____

_____

Remember Your Thoughts

Special insights I have learned:

_____

_____

_____

_____

More Light on the Text

Luke 14:7–14

7 And he put forth a parable to those which were bidden, when he marked how they chose out the chief rooms; saying unto them.

Jesus is challenging the accepted wisdom of the day with a parable critiquing expected norms of His society and presenting a spiritual truth. Luke says Christ put forth a parable. Parables in the Gospels have spiritual implications (see Mark 4:13; 7:17; Luke 8: 9–11; 18:1). Even before reporting Christ's words, Luke prepares his audience for what is to come. The word bidden is a translation of a passive form of the word *kaleo* (Gk., **kah-LEH-oh**), meaning "to call, specifically by name." Each guest received a personal invitation to attend the event. Just as the guest list was determined by the host, so were the seating arrangements. The decision of who sat at the best seats, the seats of honor (Gk. *protoklisia*, **pro-to-klee-SEE-ah**; "first seats"), was at the discretion of the host. The KJV translates this word as "rooms," although the word simply means space or place, in this case a seat at the table.

Humility begins by being thankful to have received an invitation, which is a much different attitude than "Now that I am here, who can see me?" It can be safely assumed that even for this meal, the invited guests took concerted efforts to select for themselves seats of honor, places where others might assume they were important and had a special relationship to the host and his special guest Jesus. This practical lesson has significant spiritual overtones. Where we think we ought to stand in relation to others is in all likelihood an indication of where we think we stand before God. Christ decided to use this particular social gathering as an opportunity to give a spiritual lesson on humility toward God and people.

8 When thou art bidden of any man to a wedding, sit not down in the highest room; lest a more honourable man than thou be bidden of him;

The custom in antiquity was that the most distinguished (Gk. *entimos*, **EN-teemos**, "with honor") guests at a dinner or feast arrived late and reclined (Gk. *kataklino*, **ka-ta-KLEE-no**, "lie down") in the space at the table closest to the host. Jesus admonished the disciples not to be like the other guests vying to sit in the places of honor before all the other guests arrived because someone of higher social status might still come. Jesus' choice of a wedding banquet is also a metaphor for the kingdom of God (Revelation 22:2). On another occasion, Jesus taught a parable about a king who held a wedding reception for his son as an image of the heavenly feast (Matthew 22:1–14).

9 And he that bade thee and him come and say to thee, Give this man place; and thou begin with shame to take the lowest room.

Verse 9 reinforces the idea that the host decides who should take the seats of honor. There is nothing said about the rank or stature of those invited, but it can be reasoned that the listeners understood the parable's situation. The chief seats were normally elevated and positioned in the center of the room. Being publicly asked by the host to step down and go to the back of the room, however discreetly, would leave the other guests second-guessing not the intentions of the hosts but the worthiness of that guest. Honor has a positive value for men in the society, and "shame" (Gk. *aischune*, **ice-KHOO-nay**) in this case would be the opposite of it. The man forced to move from the privileged seat at the head of the table down to the lowest end in front of all the other guests would be shamed by being relocated. Peter later writes, "Humble yourselves therefore under the mighty hand of God, that he may exalt you in due time" (1 Peter 5:6). When we strive to achieve or acquire recognition for ourselves, we are on our own. Godly humility is our best defense and remedy against the scarring emotional pains of public humiliation.

10 But when thou art bidden, go and sit down in the lowest room; that when he that bade thee cometh, he may say unto thee, Friend, go up higher: then shalt thou have worship in the presence of them that sit at meat with thee.

The word "but" in this sentence is a translation of a powerful Greek conjunction, *alla* (**al-LAH**), establishing a strong contrast to what has just preceded. *Alla* in this context sets up the contrast: Instead of exalting yourself, there is another way—live in such a way that is recognized by Jesus, the only one who really matters. Jesus commanded the disciples not to follow the example of the other guests but to do the unexpected and show humility by sitting at the farthest end of the banquet table. The expectation was that the host would seat the honored guests who arrived late at the front of the table near himself. However, it is the host's prerogative to seat guests wherever he chooses and he may invite the guest with the lowest social status to move up to the higher place of honor. This part of the verse implies God's goal to exalt us as we see in the phrase, "Friend, go up higher."

The Greek word for "worship" is *doxa* (**DOKE-sah**) and also means "glory and honor." It is a term usually reserved for God today. However, in the cultural context of Luke's day, it can refer to the enhancement of one's reputation or social status. It is the opposite of shame. The act of seating the guest of more modest status at the higher end would signal that this person was now worthy of honor. Humility is not contrary to knowing our position in Christ. Exhibiting humility, however, may be contrary to maintaining our position in the world.

11 For whosoever exalteth himself shall be abased; and he that humbleth himself shall be exalted.

Note these conjunctions. Luke introduces verse 11 with the conjunction "for" (Gk. *hoti*, **HOE-tee**). This conjunction is used to suggest that what is about to be said explains what preceded, or it provides the logical reasoning behind the previous statement. Can Christ make it any plainer? The person who does not humble himself or herself will invite public humiliation. The word "whosoever" is a translation of the word *pas* (Gk. **POSS**) meaning "all." This biblical principle applies to everyone. People who lift themselves up *hupsoo* (Gk., **hoop-SO-oh**) suffer the inevitable fate of humiliation. The Greek word for "abased" is *tapeinoo* (**tah-pay-NO-oh**) and can mean to be geographically at a low point, or in human terms, a loss of esteem or status. It is the passive form of the same word used for Jesus humbling Himself to the point of the Cross in Philippians 2. Essentially the contrast is either you choose to humble yourself or you will be humbled. These words continue the spatial metaphor used in this entire passage (near, far, low, high) both at the banquet and in relationship with the host.

In a culture where honor is such a coveted designation, a loss of honor would be a significant blow to one's standing in the community. In contrast, those who humble themselves shall have their status elevated. The real lesson Jesus is trying to impart to the disciples is that in God's kingdom, God will bring about a reversal of human social constructs. The ones considered among the lowest socially will be exalted or lifted up, and those who have enjoyed the highest social position, either as a result of the family they were born into or wealth acquired legitimately or through trickery, will be lowered.

12 Then said he also to him that bade him, When thou makest a dinner or a supper, call not thy friends, nor thy brethren, neither thy kinsmen, nor thy rich neighbours; lest they also bid thee again, and a recompence be made thee.

Jesus next turns His attention to the host. Some scholars note that the host, like the guests, is more concerned with social status than the needs of those lower on the social rung. Jesus addresses this by advising him that when he prepares dinner, he should not exclusively invite his friends, siblings, extended family members, or neighbors who have material wealth and will be obligated (and able to fulfill the obligation) to invite him to dinner in kind. The Greek word for "recompence"

(*antapodoma*, **an-ta-PO-do-mah**) means repayment. In the ancient world, gift giving was reciprocal and built relationships between the giver and receiver. However, a poor person could not repay a rich person's invitation to dine, a fact that would have been obvious to the host. This is Jesus playing out Deuteronomy 15:7-11: Don't just give to the poor, but invite them to the table to glorify God!

13 But when thou makest a feast, call the poor, the maimed, the lame, the blind:

Notice the types of gatherings Christ uses to make His point. In verse 12 it was a dinner or supper, where the focus is the meal itself. Here in verse 13 Christ refers to a feast (Gk. *doche*, **dow-KHAY**). A feast is more than a common meal, it is a gathering of people, a banquet called by the host to celebrate a particular event in a grand way. These were usually important gatherings, where those attending were often the most important people in the local community or region.

In a reversal of societal expectations, Jesus commands the host to instead invite the poor and physically disabled. The poor, maimed, lame, and blind were members of society who were dependent on public generosity for their welfare and did not have the financial resources to repay their host. Jesus counsels the host to invite society's outcasts. Jesus was very concerned with those pushed to the margins of society because of their economic disadvantage, uncleanness, or physical disability. Luke is passionate about sharing that concern.

14 And thou shalt be blessed; for they cannot recompense thee: for thou shalt be recompensed at the resurrection of the just.

Humility receives a reward in this parable. The Greek word for "blessed" is *makarios* (**ma-KAH-ree-oce**). This is the same word Christ uses in His Sermon on the Mount to describe those who will inherit the kingdom (see Matthew 5). Those who humble themselves in their thoughts and actions are blessed because they are not looking for temporal rewards. Rather, their focus is on Him who rewards His faithful followers for all eternity. Jesus tells the host if he invites the outcasts to his home for dinner, he will be blessed. Jesus' message is that performing such acts of kindness without the expectation of reward will not only bless the individual here on earth. (Luke 18:29–30) He or she will also receive a heavenly reward at the resurrection of the just (cf. Daniel 12:2–3).

Sources:
Life Application Study Bible, New Revised Standard Version. Wheaton, IL: Tyndale House Publishers, Inc. 1989. 278–279.
The NIV Study Bible (Tenth Anniversary Edition). Grand Rapids, MI: Zondervan Publishing House. 1995. 240–241, 250-251.
Manser, Martin H. "Room." *I Never Knew That Was in the Bible.* Nashville, TN: Thomas Nelson, 1999.
Unger, Merrill F. *Unger's Bible Dictionary.* Chicago, IL: Moody Press. 1985. 262-263.
Unger, Merrill F. *The New Unger's Bible Handbook.* Chicago, IL: Moody Press. 1984. 110-112.

Say It Correctly

Recompence. **REK**-uhm-pens.

Daily Bible Readings

MONDAY
Wait to Enter the King's Presence
(Proverbs 25:2–7a)

TUESDAY
Treat the Poor and Rich Impartially
(James 2:1–7)

WEDNESDAY
Love and Pray for the Persecutor
(Matthew 5:43–48)

THURSDAY
A Life Worthy of God's Call
(Ephesians 4:1–7)

FRIDAY
Serving With Love on the Sabbath
(Luke 14:1–6)

SATURDAY
The Great Dinner for All Peoples
(Luke 14:15–24)

SUNDAY
Humility, the Right Path for Believers
(Luke 14:7–14)

Notes

_____

_____

_____

_____

Teaching Tips

Words You Should Know

A. Cross *stauros* (Gk.)—An instrument of capital punishment, usually wooden.

B. Follow *akoloutheo* (Gk.)—To accompany, specifically as a disciple.

Teacher Preparation

Unifying Principle—Cost of Discipleship. We often face a choice between the comfortable, easy way and the more helpful but challenging way. How can we make the right choice? Jesus challenges His hearers to count the cost and recognize the consequences of discipleship.

A. Read the Bible Background and Devotional Readings.

B. Pray for your students and lesson clarity.

C. Read the lesson Scripture in multiple translations.

D. Option: Discuss the following questions with the class: What do you treasure? What would you give up for the sake of Christ? What might happen if we gave up our cell phones for a day and prayed instead?

O—Open the Lesson

A. Begin the class with prayer.

B. Have the students read the Aim for Change.

C. Have the students read the In Focus story.

D. Ask students how events named in the story can weigh on their hearts and how they can view these events from a theological perspective.

P—Present the Scriptures

A. Read the Focal Verses and discuss the Background and The People, Places, and Times sections.

B. Have the class share what Scriptures stand out for them and why, with particular emphasis on today's context.

E—Explore the Meaning

A. Use In Depth or More Light on the Text to help provide deeper discussion of the lesson text.

B. Discuss the Liberating Lesson and Application for Activation sections.

N—Next Steps for Application

A. Summarize the value of surrending our will and way to follow Jesus Christ.

B. End class with a commitment to pray for followers of Jesus everywhere.

Worship Guide

For the Superintendent or Teacher
Theme: A Costly Call
Song: "I Surrender All"
Devotional Reading: Philippians 3:7–16

A Costly Call

Bible Background • MARK 1:16–20; LUKE 14:25–33
Printed Text • MARK 1:16–20; LUKE 14:25–33 | Devotional Reading • PHILIPPIANS 3:7–16

Aim for Change

In today's lesson we will: UNDERSTAND the cost of being Jesus' disciple; AFFIRM the call to be disciples who make disciples and face hard choices; and RECOGNIZE our need give up things to follow Jesus as members of His church.

In Focus

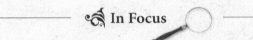

Sampson and his grandfather Lee sat on the porch talking about Sampson's decision to join the military after college. Lee was proud that Sampson would make the commitment, like he had, to serve their country. Sampson asked, "Grandpa, why did you join the military? Why did you go?"

Lee thought a moment and answered, "Well, in my day, young men were getting drafted into the Army for the war. But by the time I came of age, the draft was over. I decided to enlist, though, because I knew I should serve my country even if there was no war. I don't think we should wait on a war to help; we should serve because it is the right thing to do. But no one told me the cost of serving."

Sampson asked, "What do you mean?"

Lee replied, "I had to leave home immediately. I missed the birth of your mother and didn't get to spend Thanksgiving and Christmas with the family. It was an honor, don't get me wrong. But when you serve, your service becomes the priority."

Sampson said, "That's what Mom says about the church. She has made it her priority to make sure God's people are cared for. She has missed soccer games and dinners. But I know that she is serving for a purpose bigger than herself and that comes at a cost."

How has serving the mission of the church cost you? Have you ever had to make some sacrifices and miss out on events? What has been the reward?

Keep in Mind

"And whosoever doth not bear his cross, and come after me, cannot be my disciple" (Luke 14:27, KJV).

"And if you do not carry your own cross and follow me, you cannot be my disciple"
(Luke 14:27, NLT).

Focal Verses

KJV **Mark 1:16** Now as he walked by the sea of Galilee, he saw Simon and Andrew his brother casting a net into the sea: for they were fishers.

17 And Jesus said unto them, Come ye after me, and I will make you to become fishers of men.

18 And straightway they forsook their nets, and followed him.

19 And when he had gone a little farther thence, he saw James the son of Zebedee, and John his brother, who also were in the ship mending their nets.

20 And straightway he called them: and they left their father Zebedee in the ship with the hired servants, and went after him.

Luke 14:25 And there went great multitudes with him: and he turned, and said unto them,

26 If any man come to me, and hate not his father, and mother, and wife, and children, and brethren, and sisters, yea, and his own life also, he cannot be my disciple.

27 And whosoever doth not bear his cross, and come after me, cannot be my disciple.

28 For which of you, intending to build a tower, sitteth not down first, and counteth the cost, whether he have sufficient to finish it?

29 Lest haply, after he hath laid the foundation, and is not able to finish it, all that behold it begin to mock him,

30 Saying, This man began to build, and was not able to finish.

31 Or what king, going to make war against another king, sitteth not down first, and consulteth whether he be able with ten thousand to meet him that cometh against him with twenty thousand?

32 Or else, while the other is yet a great way off, he sendeth an ambassage, and desireth conditions of peace.

NLT **Mark 1:16** One day as Jesus was walking along the shore of the Sea of Galilee, he saw Simon and his brother Andrew throwing a net into the water, for they fished for a living.

17 Jesus called out to them, "Come, follow me, and I will show you how to fish for people!"

18 And they left their nets at once and followed him.

19 A little farther up the shore Jesus saw Zebedee's sons, James and John, in a boat repairing their nets.

20 He called them at once, and they also followed him, leaving their father, Zebedee, in the boat with the hired men.

Luke 14:25 A large crowd was following Jesus. He turned around and said to them,

26 "If you want to be my disciple, you must, by comparison, hate everyone else— your father and mother, wife and children, brothers and sisters—yes, even your own life. Otherwise, you cannot be my disciple.

27 And if you do not carry your own cross and follow me, you cannot be my disciple.

28 But don't begin until you count the cost. For who would begin construction of a building without first calculating the cost to see if there is enough money to finish it?

29 Otherwise, you might complete only the foundation before running out of money, and then everyone would laugh at you.

30 They would say, 'There's the person who started that building and couldn't afford to finish it!'

31 Or what king would go to war against another king without first sitting down with his counselors to discuss whether his army of 10,000 could defeat the 20,000 soldiers marching against him?

33 So likewise, whosoever he be of you that forsaketh not all that he hath, he cannot be my disciple.

32 And if he can't, he will send a delegation to discuss terms of peace while the enemy is still far away.

33 So you cannot become my disciple without giving up everything you own.

The People, Places, and Times

John the Baptist. Little is known about the early years of the son of Zacharias and Elisabeth. The prophets declared that John would precede the Messiah and that his purpose was to call the Jews to repentance and prepare them to receive the Messiah (Isaiah 40:1–8; Malachi 4:5–6). He was a prophet held in high regard who led a revival in Judea that prepared the people to receive Jesus' message. The Gospel of Luke records that John the Baptist was Jesus' cousin. John was a holy and righteous man who was wrongly executed by the state. His life was characterized by self-denial, humility, and holy courage. In his humility, he declined the honors that an admiring crowd wanted to confer upon him and declared himself to be no one, merely a voice calling people to repent because the kingdom of God was near.

Capernaum. This was the residence of Jesus and His apostles and the scene of many miracles and discourses, including His first sermon. Jesus spent His childhood at Nazareth, but Capernaum was His ministry headquarters. This city was located in Galilee, one of three provinces in Palestine, along with Judea and Samaria.

What have you avoided in order to follow Christ more fully?

Background

The Gospel according to Mark is a powerful, yet brief, account of the life of Jesus Christ. The beginning of Mark's Gospel differs from Matthew and Luke, as it does not have a detailed birth narrative. It begins with the story of John the Baptist, who prepares the way for Jesus. When Jesus enters the narrative, He initiates His ministry by calling in reinforcements. Jesus understands that ministry is not meant to be a solitary mission in search of understanding. Ministry is a fellowship of those who share a common goal and purpose of doing God's will and serving God's people. It is important to follow this procedure so that we, as believers, can imitate and produce those greater works that Jesus talked about (John 14:12). In these few verses we must be intentional about exploring Jesus' plan, pathway, and process for enlisting more disciples into the fold of Christianity.

Have you ever shared the Gospel of Jesus with someone who was following a different plan? What did you realize about yourself when you started the process of sharing the Good News with another person?

At-A-Glance

1. Jesus Had a Plan (Mark 1:16; Luke 14:25–27)
2. Jesus Created a Pathway (Mark 1:17–18; Luke 14:28–30)
3. Jesus Had a Process (Mark 1:19–20; Luke 14:31–33)

In Depth

1. Jesus Had a Plan (Mark 1:16; Luke 14:25–27)

Notice the context in which Jesus approaches His soon-to-be disciples. Jesus meets them in a place where they are already working toward a pre-planned purpose. They are fishing as they have always done, and Jesus calls them in the midst of their work. The Sea of Galilee is the stage for many of Jesus' acts in ministry; but at the start, Jesus finds His first disciples there.

The reality is that most of us do not have a plan when we invite people to our faith. We "go" as instructed in Matthew 28:19 but sometimes have little idea of what to share, or do not have correct information. We can wrongly assume that those we are sharing the Gospel with have had no experience with hearing it, but that is usually not the case these days. Anyone can Google what we are talking about and challenge what we claim to be truth. Therefore we must follow the plan set by Jesus.

But there is a cost to following that plan. In Luke's Gospel, Jesus tells the crowd that possessions and family can keep them from ultimately following the path marked for discipleship. As disciples we must earnestly pursue God, but at what cost will we follow Jesus Christ? Many adults admit they might lose friends and family members when they make the decision for Christ. But others sell their discipleship and morals short to gain notoriety and worldly possessions.

Being a disciple of Christ is easier said than done. Once we choose to be a disciple of Christ, we choose to be subject to God's specific will for our lives even in those good and bad, wanted and unwanted, favorable and unfavorable days and moments in life. But the outcome will be far greater than the sacrifice made in our discipleship.

Has Jesus ever interrupted your normal operations and plans and used you to complete a new task?

2. Jesus Created a Pathway (Mark 1:17–18; Luke 14:28–30)

Upon greeting the brothers Peter and Andrew, Jesus says, "Come ye after me, and I will make you to become fishers of men." Jesus makes an intriguing call for the brothers to follow Him, and they could only assume that the man calling them had a plan. Jesus made it clear that once we follow, He will send us out to fish. Jesus' pathway is made clear when He implies that He has the way to fill our discipleship nets with more people. Anyone who fishes knows that fishing can be time-consuming. There is a right way and a wrong way to catch fish. You must be patient, have the right bait, and realize that there is more than one spot to find what you are looking for.

In one sentence Jesus gives the pathway to executing the task He gives us. First, we must come. We must take up our necessary bait, i.e., fellowshipping with Jesus ourselves while also leaving behind some things that are not needed for the trip. Second, we must follow Jesus. There were probably many other fishermen out on the sea that day, but none presented a new place and purpose for the brothers. To follow Jesus requires a devoted sense of call.

Jesus uses the imagery of a builder looking to build a tower in Luke's Gospel. This desire to build is not for personal gain or glory but it is for others to see and marvel. Jesus says we must count all costs of loss and labor as they are necessary to completing the work. No major construction can be done without first itemizing the cost of labor and supplies. We, as the disciples, must also recognize that there is a cost to our labor. We will sometimes become discouraged, especially if we are looking at other towers being built around us, while trying to erect our own. Furthermore, there will be a cost for use of supplies. Our supplies as disciples will be the blood, sweat, and tears of maintaining our personal relationship with God while living in a world that is not so friendly to our proclamation.

When you came to know Jesus, what things did you leave behind—or try to—so that you could follow Him wholeheartedly?

3. Jesus Had a Process (Mark 1:19–20; Luke 14:31–33)

Jesus did not stop at the two brothers when fishing for people. He kept walking and saw James and John who also were preparing to begin their daily work. "Without delay he called them" (from v. 20). The sense of immediacy shows us that this was Jesus' plan from the beginning. The slightest hesitation could have caused the disciples to miss their assignment. When Jesus calls, we should not hesitate to answer. There is no reason for us to delay the work of God; souls are ready to encounter Christ now. It is our job to call more people into fellowship with Jesus so that they can go forward with their new lives.

Realizing that the work of discipleship cannot be done alone, Jesus draws on the imagery of a king contemplating war and utilizing his military personnel to devise a strategy. Jesus shares with us through this illustration that calling in reinforcements to aid in the battle plan is a wise idea. While it may seem easier to go alone, it is not wise because the enemy of our souls seeks to devour the weak and isolated. We need to pray for, build up, and encourage one another to ensure that we are fulfilling God's complete work for our lives.

What keeps you from being called into fellowship with other believers? What do you believe is your main distraction from following Jesus' call?

Search the Scriptures

1. Jesus' ministry began in a simple fashion. He even called simple working people to get His ministry started. Why did Jesus call these working-class citizens to major ministry jobs?

2. The Scriptures do not show Jesus being forceful when calling His followers. Why do many Christians now take power-driven approaches to gaining disciples? Do you think this is what causes many to ignore our faith?

Discuss the Meaning

1. What has being a disciple of Jesus cost you? What have you had to give up for the sake of service to the kingdom?

2. What sacrifices did Jesus make in service to the kingdom while He was on earth? How do we find comfort in the sacrifice of Christ as we move to make our own?

Liberating Lesson

Some believe God only calls those who are of a certain social status. But it is clear in these selected verses that Jesus calls anyone who is willing to come and follow.

What would the world be like if more people were willing to humble themselves and follow the teachings of a carpenter's son? How would our communities change if more people knew that Jesus came from Nazareth, the poverty stricken area that did not produce royalty by society's standards? Jesus called other unlikely people to participate in His work of sharing the Good News of God's salvation and resisting injustice. It is liberating to know that God does not play favorites but is looking for those willing to follow Jesus.

Application for Activation

The Bible is clear in its theme of fellowship. The South African philosophy "ubuntu," meaning "I am because we are," teaches us the same principle that Jesus taught His followers. We are not to be Christians only for the sake of being saved ourselves. We are called to bring others to the saving power of Jesus, sharing that there is a better life awaiting us all. Far too often Christians individualize faith, forgetting about the many others who Jesus is also calling to relationship. After accepting our relationship with Jesus, we often pursue the things that God can provide—forgetting that we must reach back for those who could also benefit from God's love. We should never limit God to being solely ours to know because God is too big for any of us to contain. The Bible teaches us that God's thoughts are not our thoughts, nor are His ways our ways (Isaiah 55:8). Some Christians act as though they alone are chosen by God. But we cannot and should not limit God to only wanting us and no one else. All are welcome in the kingdom of God, and it is up to us to help them get there with our speech and behavior.

Follow the Spirit

What God wants me to do:

_____

_____

_____

_____

Remember Your Thoughts

Special insights I have learned:

_____

_____

_____

_____

More Light on the Text

Mark 1:16–20

16 Now as he walked by the sea of Galilee, he saw Simon and Andrew his brother casting a net into the sea: for they were fishers. 17 And Jesus said unto them, Come ye after me, and I will make you to become fishers of men. 18 And straightway they forsook their nets, and followed him.

As Jesus passes along the shores of the Sea of Galilee, He sees two brothers, Simon and Andrew, fishing. Mark does not tell us whether these brothers had any encounters with Jesus prior to this time (see John 1:35–42); he does not tell us how big their fishing business is. The only information Mark relays is that, seeing these brothers casting their net, Jesus invites them to follow Him. Fishing was common in the region because fish were plentiful. Without hesitation, Simon and his brother abandon their nets and follow Jesus. In His invitation, Jesus tells them that they will be fishing for people, rather than fish. Mark uses the adverb "straightway" again (cf. v. 10) to describe how quickly the two brothers accepted the invitation. That means when Jesus asks them to follow Him, they at once left their nets and followed Jesus. The word "follow" is the Greek word *akoloutheo* (**ah-koe-loo-THEH-oh**), which means to accompany, specifically as a disciple.

19 And when he had gone a little farther thence, he saw James the son of Zebedee, and John his brother, who also were in the ship mending their nets. 20 And straightway he called them: and they left their father Zebedee in the ship with the hired servants, and went after him.

As He walks a little farther, Jesus sees brothers James and John fishing with their father and their servants. Jesus extends the same invitation to them. James and John respond immediately, leaving their father and their servants and follow Jesus. The mention of the "hired servants" suggests that Zebedee's fishing business might be a big one, but how big is not indicated. Mark also seems to indicate that the brothers are not leaving their father alone to run the business by himself. However, the main point here is the immediate response the brothers give to Jesus' call, just as in the case of Simon and Andrew. This call also demonstrates

351

the cost of discipleship, which includes not only abandoning everything to follow Jesus, including material wealth from their father, but also breaking the family ties.

Luke 14:25–33

25 And there went great multitudes with him: and he turned, and said unto them,

There were those even among the elite who were willing to accept the challenge to be humble; after all, how difficult could it be to honor others and temporarily refrain from being the center of attention? As for the masses, is there any doubt that they joyously and hopefully responded to Christ when He concluded His parable? (Read Luke 14:21–24.) Allegiance to Christ is about being a disciple, and becoming a disciple of Christ is like the melting ice in a glass of water. Slowly the form of the ice is lost and the ice takes on the properties of the water in which it was placed. This is our calling.

26 If any man come to me, and hate not his father, and mother, and wife, and children, and brethren, and sisters, yea, and his own life also, he cannot be my disciple.

Grammatically speaking, these are conditional sentences. That should not lead us to conclude, however, that discipleship is optional for the Christian. There are two words used to introduce conditional sentences in the Greek. If (Gk. *ean*, **eh-AN**) you do this or if this is true, this MIGHT happen or be true, or if (Gk. *ei*, **AY**) you do this or if this is true… this WILL happen or these are the facts. There is the "if" of probability, and the "if" of certainty. Christ completely understands the soul-stirring statement He is about to make.

Christ says if you choose, if you make a decision to follow, to enter into a relationship with Him, then these are the conditions: If you do not hate your father, mother, wife, children, brethren, sisters and even own life, you cannot

be His disciple. This is not a verse inviting us to hate our families or ourselves. God is love and desires that we love ourselves, our families and our neighbors as God loves us (Luke 10:27, Matthew 19:19.) However, this is a verse that prioritizes our relationship with Jesus as most important in our lives, the relationship that takes preeminence over everything else. As far as Christ is concerned, the only response they should have to saving grace is to define their reason for living not by their relationships with others or even their own sense self but by their relationship to Him.

27 And whosoever doth not bear his cross, and come after me, cannot be my disciple.

There are some who suggest this saying is just a parabolic phrase that eludes to Christ's listeners and many in the church today. However, to "bear" means to endure and carry, and here it suggests a necessary unity between the load being carried and the burden bearer (cf. Luke 22:10; Acts 9:15; Galatians 6:2). Moreover, only in a few occasions outside the Bible does the word cross (Gk. *stauros*, **stow-ROCE**) mean anything other than the instrument of capital punishment—most often a wooden stake used to torture and inflict unimaginable pain. When Christ says that we must bear our cross, He is saying, without qualification, that disciples must carry the thing that tells the world that they are ready to die to all that does not come from Him.

The "his" in "his cross" is a reflexive pronoun (Gk. *heauto*, **heh-ow-TOE**) that conveys a relationship of mutual possession; in this case between the would-be disciple and the cross. Using contemporary language, the one who refuses to bear the cross assigned by God cannot be His disciple. This is a difficult undertaking and maybe the reason Paul said, "I die daily" (from 1 Corinthians 15:31). Taking up our cross is a daily and persistent calling and a mark of being His disciple. It is not finished at conversion with the stopping of a few bad habits and personal agendas. The word for "bear" is a present active verb. We never stop bearing the cross of pain and suffering this side of heaven when we are Jesus' disciples. We may make light of these words, but Jesus' audience probably did not. Some surely would have seen and heard the cries and pain of someone bearing a cross.

28 For which of you, intending to build a tower, sitteth not down first, and counteth the cost, whether he have sufficient to finish it?

Just as one should not begin the construction of a building without knowing what it will take to finish, so Jesus instructs the crowd not to begin the disciple's journey without reflecting on what it will take to finish.

The word for "count" used here suggests counting with the intent of fully understanding the consequences, good or bad (cf. Revelation 13:18). Not being a disciple is to have no other option but to depend on other fallible human beings for acceptance and guidance. To be a disciple is to have the assurance that the One who knows all has covered all the bases and always has the greatest good properly in focus. Yet it comes at a high price of sacrificing comfort, convenience, gains, pleasures, and position in the world to follow God's will. That is not to say we are called to be poor or lacking but that whatever we have is subject to Christ instead of our own desires. The world would say, "Count what you have in your hand." Christ would say, "Count what I have in My hand." The decision you make will change your life and where you spend eternity. Be sure to calculate carefully.

29 Lest haply, after he hath laid the foundation, and is not able to finish it, all that behold it begin to mock him, 30 Saying,

This man began to build, and was not able to finish.

We should not think the church makes coming to Jesus too easy. Redemption is free. There is no price to pay, no work to do. God did it all. Our salvation is by grace and that through faith; it is a gift of God (see Ephesians 2:8). Christ has not stated that this is what you must do to become His disciple. He has said if you follow Him, this is what it means to be His disciple. "Faith without works is dead" (from James 2:20). Pretending to have a relationship with Christ where none exists only leads to public ridicule. The Holy Spirit enables us to be disciples as we yield to God's will, because any discipleship we try to do on our own we do not have the ability to complete.

31 Or what king, going to make war against another king, sitteth not down first, and consulteth whether he be able with ten thousand to meet him that cometh against him with twenty thousand? 32 Or else, while the other is yet a great way off, he sendeth an ambassage, and desireth conditions of peace.

At first glance, these few verses in our lesson appear to be a restatement of all that has been said before. Using the phase "cannot be my disciple" (v. 27) to structure our exposition at this juncture helps demonstrate that these verses are not just thrown in. Rather, Christ has moved us from one level of understanding of the call of the disciple to another. In verse 26 Christ addresses the issue of what it means to be a disciple. In verses 27–30 Christ discusses a need to reflect on the costs of being a disciple. In these last few verses, Christ challenges us in our mission as disciples.

Using contemporary language to paraphrase verse 31, we could say that when we are on the job and there are more against us than for us, are we willing to go all the way for Jesus? If God calls us to a ministry in a drug-infested community, are we willing to hang in there regardless? Do we see opportunities for manifestations of God and His glory when the enemies of our minds, hearts, and souls surround us? Christ rhetorically answers these questions in these verses. We should not quickly jump on the discipleship bandwagon unless we have a clear idea of what the cost entails.

The phrase "going to make," as translated by the King James Version, may state the king's actions as being more aggressive than the Greek warrants. The word for "going to make" is *poreuomai* (Gk. **poe-REW-oh-my**), which could be translated as becoming involved. Disciples are at war with the world. The world is at war with Christ (see John 15:18). The question is "Do we want in?" Jesus was clearly aware that resisting Roman oppression as Jews and later Christians would cost many disciples their comfort or their lives. One could follow Him at that cost, or compromise with the Roman Empire and fall with it. A good parallel for this passage is the parable of the unjust steward in Luke 16: Either we do what is right and follow Christ despite the battles to come, or we make friends with the world and accept the defeats and fate of the world. We cannot be lukewarm or bystanders in discipleship.

The Greek word *bouleuo* (**boo-LEW-oh**) means "to consider, to converse, or debate," and *kathizo* (Gk. **kah-THEED-zo**) means "to sit down." The sitting down comes before the consulting. Christ is saying that accepting the call to be a disciple is a matter of careful thought and unhurried reflection, in order to fully digest all that is at stake. There are many barriers in life to being a disciple. Some barriers are relational (cf. v. 26) and some are circumstantial (cf. vv. 28–32).

Christ's followers should be fully aware that becoming a disciple is a costly endeavor and not to be entered into lightly. Being a disciple changes us and affects everything around us.

Notice well that Christ has moved from illustrations directed at families, to full communities, and on to a significantly larger group.

Those who ignore the mandates of discipleship put themselves and everybody around them in a position to be hurt. While the enemy is a long way off, a wise king will "ask" (Gk. *erotao*, **eh-ro-TAH-oh**), or literally request or beg, for peace.

33 So likewise, whosoever he be of you that forsaketh not all that he hath, he cannot be my disciple.

When Jesus wraps up His discourse with "so likewise," He may very well be referring to all that has been said in chapter 14. What a wonderful and gracious term Luke uses to cite the Lord's statement here in verse 33 and in the following phrase. The Greek word *apotassomai* (**ah-poe-TASS-so-my**) is used six times in the New Testament and means to say "goodbye" before a significant separation. Are we willing to say goodbye to everything for the sake of the King and His kingdom? Christ's disciples are to say goodbye to all means not provided by God to attain and maintain a personal sense of worth and purpose in this world. Whether it is a job, a person, a ministry, or self (cf. v. 26), we cannot experience the fullness of what it means to be Christ's disciple without sacrifice. Those who are not willing to view relationships from Christ's vantage point—who do not carry their own cross, who do not consider the cost, and who are not willing to lay down their lives so that Christ might give them life more abundantly—cannot fully be His disciples.

Sources:
"Following God." The African American Lectionary: Sermon Illustrations. http://www.theafricanamericanlectionary.org/sermon.asp.

Daily Bible Readings

MONDAY
Answering the Lord's Call of
Discipleship
(Mark 4:10–20)

TUESDAY
It's Hard to Enter the
Kingdom
(Mark 10:23–31)

WEDNESDAY
The Lord's Call and Family
Conflict
(Matthew 10:34–39)

THURSDAY
The Father Honors Those
Who Follow
(John 12:20–26)

FRIDAY
Suffering and Knowing
Christ Jesus
(Philippians 3:7–16)

SATURDAY
Faithful Witness Through
Suffering
(2 Corinthians 6:1–10)

SUNDAY
Counting the Cost,
Answering the Call
(Mark 1:16–20; Luke
14:25–33)

Notes

_____

_____

_____

_____

_____

_____

_____

Teaching Tips

March 17
Bible Study Guide 3

Words You Should Know

A. Riotous *asotos* (Gk.)—Extravagant, prodigal, wasteful.

B. Hired Servant *misthos* (Gk.)—A paid hired hand.

Teacher Preparation

Unifying Principle—God Welcomes the Lost. In our world it is easy for people to lose their way. What is our responsibility to those who go astray? Jesus taught that those who are lost are loved by God and are to be valued, sought, and welcomed back when they return.

A. Read the Bible Background and Devotional Readings.

B. Pray for your students and lesson clarity.

C. Read the lesson Scripture in multiple translations.

D. Option: Use a video presentation or artists' depictions of this story to introduce the Scripture.

O—Open the Lesson

A. Begin the class with prayer.

B. Have the students read the Aim for Change.

C. Have the students read the In Focus story.

D. Ask students how events named in the story can weigh on their hearts and how they can view these events from a theological perspective.

P—Present the Scriptures

A. Read the Focal Verses and discuss the Background and The People, Places, and Times sections.

B. Have the class share what Scriptures stand out for them and why, with particular emphasis on today's context.

E—Explore the Meaning

A. Use In Depth or More Light on the Text to help provide deeper discussion of the lesson text.

B. Discuss the Liberating Lesson and Application for Activation sections.

N—Next Steps for Application

A. Summarize the value of knowing that God welcomes home those who have left and returned to Him.

B. End class with a commitment to pray for those who are lost or have walked away to return to God.

Worship Guide

For the Superintendent or Teacher
Theme: Calling the Lost
Song: "Amazing Grace"
Devotional Reading: Ezekiel 34:11-16

Calling the Lost

Bible Background • LUKE 15
Printed Text • LUKE 15:11–24 | Devotional Reading • EZEKIEL 34:11–16

—————— Aim for Change ——————

In today's lesson, we will: IDENTIFY with the characters in Jesus' parable; SENSE God's grief over His lost children; and SUGGEST culturally appropriate ways to rejoice with new believers.

—————— 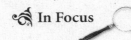 In Focus ——————

Instead of attending college after graduation, Jackson decided to move to New York to pursue a music career. His older brother Jason had finished college and decided to stay home in Chicago to help their father, Ray, run the family company. Before moving to New York, Jackson asked his father for his inheritance of $500,000. Ray gave Jackson the money, although he did not think it was the best idea. Jackson spent five months in New York partying, drinking, and spending his money. Jackson was eventually evicted from his apartment due to his reckless behavior and found himself on the couches of strangers. Instead of calling home for help, he refused in his pride. After one night of sleeping outside, he came to his senses and realized that he had hit rock bottom. It was time to return home. Jackson used the last of his money to ride the bus back to Chicago.

Ray had hoped and prayed that Jackson was well because he had not heard from him in months. When he saw him get off the bus, rather than asking questions, Ray embraced Jackson with the love that only a father could give. Holding Jackson tightly, Ray said, "Welcome home, son." Jackson hugged his father back, knowing that he was genuinely happy to see him. Ray then made arrangements for a welcome party, with food, music, and a new suit for Jackson. He was thrilled to have him home. Jason looked on as he saw the party preparations, and said nothing to his brother.

Who in this narrative do you identify with the most? How so?

—————— Keep in Mind ——————

"But the father said to his servants, Bring forth the best robe, and put it on him; and put a ring on his hand, and shoes on his feet…For this my son was dead, and is alive again; he was lost, and is found. And they began to be merry" (Luke 15:22, 24, KJV).

"But his father said to the servants, 'Quick! Bring the finest robe in the house and put it on him. Get a ring for his finger and sandals for his feet...for this son of mine was dead and has now returned to life. He was lost, but now he is found.' So the party began" (Luke 15:22, 24, NLT).

Focal Verses

KJV **Luke 15:11** And he said, A certain man had two sons:

12 And the younger of them said to his father, Father, give me the portion of goods that falleth to me. And he divided unto them his living.

13 And not many days after the younger son gathered all together, and took his journey into a far country, and there wasted his substance with riotous living.

14 And when he had spent all, there arose a mighty famine in that land; and he began to be in want.

15 And he went and joined himself to a citizen of that country; and he sent him into his fields to feed swine.

16 And he would fain have filled his belly with the husks that the swine did eat: and no man gave unto him.

17 And when he came to himself, he said, How many hired servants of my father's have bread enough and to spare, and I perish with hunger!

18 I will arise and go to my father, and will say unto him, Father, I have sinned against heaven, and before thee,

19 And am no more worthy to be called thy son: make me as one of thy hired servants.

20 And he arose, and came to his father. But when he was yet a great way off, his father saw him, and had compassion, and ran, and fell on his neck, and kissed him.

21 And the son said unto him, Father, I have sinned against heaven, and in thy sight, and am no more worthy to be called thy son.

22 But the father said to his servants, Bring forth the best robe, and put it on him; and put a ring on his hand, and shoes on his feet:

23 And bring hither the fatted calf, and kill it; and let us eat, and be merry:

NLT **Luke 15:11** To illustrate the point further, Jesus told them this story: "A man had two sons.

12 The younger son told his father, 'I want my share of your estate now before you die.' So his father agreed to divide his wealth between his sons.

13 A few days later this younger son packed all his belongings and moved to a distant land, and there he wasted all his money in wild living.

14 About the time his money ran out, a great famine swept over the land, and he began to starve.

15 He persuaded a local farmer to hire him, and the man sent him into his fields to feed the pigs.

16 The young man became so hungry that even the pods he was feeding the pigs looked good to him. But no one gave him anything.

17 When he finally came to his senses, he said to himself, 'At home even the hired servants have food enough to spare, and here I am dying of hunger!

18 I will go home to my father and say, "Father, I have sinned against both heaven and you,

19 and I am no longer worthy of being called your son. Please take me on as a hired servant."'

20 So he returned home to his father. And while he was still a long way off, his father saw him coming. Filled with love and compassion, he ran to his son, embraced him, and kissed him.

21 His son said to him, 'Father, I have sinned against both heaven and you, and I am no longer worthy of being called your son.'

22 But his father said to the servants, 'Quick! Bring the finest robe in the house and put it on

24 For this my son was dead, and is alive again; he was lost, and is found. And they began to be merry.

him. Get a ring for his finger and sandals for his feet.

23 And kill the calf we have been fattening. We must celebrate with a feast,

24 for this son of mine was dead and has now returned to life. He was lost, but now he is found.' So the party began."

The People, Places, and Times

Fatted Animals. In ancient times, a young animal was set aside to be fattened before it was slaughtered. In the Old Testament, the fatted, or choice, animals were sometimes associated with prosperity (Genesis 41:2; Ezekiel 34:3, 16, 20). "Fatted animals" was also used as a general reference to the strongest or choicest among the flock. Fattened cattle were part of the menu for banquets and feasts, such as wedding celebrations. In the New Testament, James (5:5) associates the fatted animal with a day of slaughter.

Inheritance. In the ancient Hebrew tradition, the possessions of the father were passed on to his sons. Daughters could receive the father's inheritance only in the absence of sons. Before this ruling from the Lord went into effect, a man who had no sons left his inheritance to his brothers, to his father's brothers, or to his male next-of-kin (Numbers 27:1–11). The Hebrew interpretation of inheritance did not necessitate death before the disposition of property. Traditionally, the eldest son was to receive a double portion (Deuteronomy 21:17) of the father's inheritance, although this rule was not absolute. Reuben lost his place of prominence because of committing adultery with Bilhah (Genesis 35:22, 49:3–4; 1 Chronicles 5:1); Esau relinquished his birthright to Jacob (Genesis 25:29–34).

Background

Parables are illustrations Jesus uses to teach kingdom concepts, principles, or to demonstrate the nature of God using characters and settings relatable to the hearer's everyday life and customs. His aim is to make the kingdom known to His disciples and others following Him. There are three parables of Jesus in Luke 15: the lost sheep (vv. 1–7), the lost coin (vv. 8–10), and the prodigal son. Each story demonstrates God's heart in retrieving that which is lost and the great lengths to which love drives Him to recover what belongs to Him. The parable of the lost sheep is also in Matthew 18:12–14, but the lost coin and prodigal son are only told in Luke's Gospel.

The telling of parables was often prompted by Jesus' encounters with the Pharisees and scribes to answer their complaints and accusations, or confront their attempts to entrap Him. In Luke 15:1–2, their complaint was about Jesus' inclusion of sinners at the dinner table with them. The Pharisees and scribes positioned themselves in their community above the average person. Because of their knowledge of the Law, they were considered the authority on what was acceptable. But here Jesus leveled the access to God the Father because through the Son all are welcome at the dinner table—a place of communion and intimacy.

At-A-Glance

1. Life on My Own Terms (Luke 15:11–13)
2. Rock-Bottom Results (vv. 14–19)
3. Fully Restored (vv. 20–24)

In Depth

1. Life on My Own Terms (Luke 15:11–13)

Jesus, the ultimate storyteller, uses a powerful climax to this discourse to grab the hearers' attention and make a memorable point. He uses an illustration that hits home because those listening could in some way relate to the story of this family conflict with an unexpected resolution. His central characters are a father and his sons. The younger son makes what is considered an insulting and brazen request of his father: to receive his share of the inheritance before his father's death. The father grants his request and releases him to do whatever he pleases. The younger son leaves and goes far from his father's house to live as he wishes. He pursues a wild life with no inhibitions and no rules but also no protection. Jesus shows how the younger son takes for granted what it means to be in his father's house with all the rights and privileges he receives because of his connection.

2. Rock-Bottom Results (vv. 14–19)

Jesus, in this part of the story, shares with those listening the results of the younger son's decision to leave his father's protective covering and provision. The younger son has spent all of his share of his father's inheritance, which could be assumed to be a sizable amount. His sin and folly has left him broken inside and out. The younger son has plummeted into an existence that is beneath his heritage. Worse yet, a famine has hit the country.

The younger son has nothing left to support himself with during this troublesome time and has to find work in a foreign country. He is able to get a job doing something no upstanding orthodox Jew would even think to do: working in the fields feeding pigs. Pigs are considered unclean, and for the son to be around them—especially to feed them—is disgraceful. This character in Jesus' parable has hit such a low and is so famished that he desires to eat what the pigs are eating but is not allowed.

Satan always seeks to lure people into what appears attractive, exciting, and fun. As Jesus shows in this parable though, the result always leaves a person worse off than they could ever imagine.

The son in his despair realizes that there is another way out of his trouble. He comes to his senses and recognizes that he can go home and work for his father as one of his hired hands. The son decides not to die of hunger but to go back to his father. He says within himself that he will ask for forgiveness and further debase himself by acknowledging that because of his actions and behavior he is no longer worthy to be called a son but will be satisfied to be received as a hired hand.

3. Fully Restored (vv. 20–24)

The younger son moves on his decision and heads home, but while making his way toward the property, his father recognizes him from afar and runs out to meet him. His father is filled with compassion and so grateful to see him alive that he throws his arms around his son's neck and kisses him. This is not the greeting the younger son expects. The father could have been angry with him for spending his inheritance and returning home broke. He could have banished him from his property. But the father's response is the opposite.

The father loves as only a parent can: unconditionally. This parable is Jesus' most powerful depiction of the love of God as Father. This parable displays God's redemption. Humanity deserves to be cast out but because of the Father's fierce, unending love we are called back into relationship.

The repentant son wants to explain to his father how he has sinned against him and God; he truly wants to accept responsibility for his poor decisions and brazen behavior, bringing shame to himself and his family name. The younger son humbles himself before his father, believing he is no longer worthy to be his son. The father has a different response to his son's request. He calls his servants to bring out the best robe and put a ring on his son's finger and sandals on his feet. The father has fully restored the fallen son. He puts his son back in his rightful place and gives him authority as if he never left. The father then calls for a celebration with the finest of food and drink because this son who was dead is now alive again, he was lost but now has been found.

The telling of this story by Jesus must have been very jarring for the Pharisees and scribes. A son who behaved so poorly would never be accepted back into a typical Jewish household or received in such a way by a father. But Jesus shows what God the Father is really like. His nature and character is not to see His creation banished for eternity, for He longs for us to return to fellowship with Him and repent (2 Peter 3:9). As noted in Scripture, God opposes the proud but gives grace to the humble who turn away from sin (James 4:6–8; 1 Peter 5:5–6). The parable of the prodigal son gives the original hearers and believers today a display of God's great love, mercy, and grace that we can do nothing to earn.

Search the Scriptures

1. Compare and contrast the actions and responses of the son and the father at the beginning and end of the lesson text.

2. What does it mean when Jesus says that "he came to himself" (v. 17)?

Discuss the Meaning

1. How should we embrace our sisters and brothers when they come into the body of Christ? Sometimes people leave our local church for various reasons. How should we celebrate their return?

2. In what ways do we understand the love of God by the character of the father in the parable?

Liberating Lesson

The parable of the prodigal son is a timeless display of the dangers of living outside God's protective covering. No matter what distance we place between God and ourselves, He is always reaching to retrieve that which is lost. God's love is boundless; but it takes a conscious decision to receive God's love. He told this parable for those listening in His time, and the illustration carries on with us in our time to share with others the Father's redemptive, unfailing love. In response to the revelation that the Father is constantly reaching for those who are lost, we are called to seek those whom the world would deem "lost." Homeless, incarcerated, addicted, and oppressed people are the very ones God wants to give an opportunity for relationship with Jesus Christ, even if they put themselves in their negative situation. How can we be more intentional about receiving those who were "lost" when they make efforts to return to community?

Application for Activation

Take the time to reveal the Father's love by extending mercy to someone in your sphere of influence. Search your heart for someone you need to forgive or someone you may need to approach for forgiveness. We were never meant to live in the bondage of unforgiveness; we must restore and be restored.

Follow the Spirit

What God wants me to do:

_____

_____

_____

_____

Remember Your Thoughts

Special insights I have learned:

_____

_____

_____

_____

More Light on the Text

Luke 15:11–24

Luke 15 focuses on the parables of lost things: a coin (vv. 4–7), a sheep (vv. 8–10), and—in this passage—the lost son. The New Testament has many kinds of parables. This particular parable relates to human relationships, specifically a father who loses a son.

Luke 15:1–2 identifies Jesus' audience and what prompts Jesus to address these parables to them: "Then drew near unto him all the publicans and sinners for to hear him. And the Pharisees and scribes murmured, saying, This man receiveth sinners, and eateth with them."

Jesus strategically and subversively uses everyday metaphors and illustrations in parables to respond to the constant surveillance and negative reactions of the Pharisees, scribes, and Sadducees. The early Christian community is often divided over how to accept the teachings of Jesus as an itinerant preacher traveling with His disciples—especially because Jesus does not teach or abide by the traditional religious rules and regulations. When the disciples ask Jesus why He speaks in parables, Jesus explains that He means to keep things hidden from unbelievers. But He gives the disciples further instruction and shares "the mysteries of the kingdom of heaven" (Matthew 13:10–17).

11 And he said, A certain man had two sons: 12 And the younger of them said to his father, Father, give me the portion of goods that falleth to me. And he divided unto them his living.

Although most commentators focus on the lost son and his actions and relationship with the father, the story is about two sons. In Luke's Gospel we often see what might be called a juxtaposition between the haves and the have-nots, the prominent and the unnoticed, the Jews and the Gentiles. A good example of this juxtaposition is found in Luke 7 with the centurion who has a sick servant in Capernaum (vv. 1–10), and the widow in Nain who lost her only son (vv. 11–15). This parable is similar in that the two sons serve the purpose of comparison in the narrative. One son is identified as the lost or prodigal son; the other is often identified as the good or dutiful son.

The younger son makes a request of the father. Jesus' original audience would readily understand how inheritance is distributed in families and the importance of the birth order. The younger son in Jewish tradition does not receive the same inheritance as the firstborn or the eldest son. The Law states the elder son receives two-thirds of the inheritance and the younger son only one-third (Deuteronomy 21:17).

The phrase "he divided unto them his living" is interpreted as the man dividing his life savings or his estate between his two sons. Although the practice was allowed and customary, the story quickly positions the younger son as audacious enough to demand an inheritance as if it already belongs to him. The son does not treat the inheritance as the gift to be given by the father that it is. The son's arrogance is illustrated in that he not only wants his inheritance at such a young age, he feels he can manage it on his own without the assistance of the father.

13 And not many days after the younger son gathered all together, and took his journey into a far country, and there wasted his substance with riotous living. 14 And when he had spent all, there arose a mighty famine in that land; and he began to be in want.

Rather than remain in the safety and comfort of the father's house, the younger son wishes to launch out on his own. He does not see himself as needing the father's wisdom and personal instruction. By going to a "far country," this son is not only distancing himself geographically from the father; he is also distancing himself spiritually. In this far country, he then wastes everything—all that he has been given by the father. It is interesting to note that the story says he wasted his money on "riotous" or extravagant living (Gk. *asotos*, **ah-SOW-toce**), not necessarily prostitutes as his older brother later suggests. The story uses a familiar motif of famine to demonstrate that the situation has evolved into one of deep concern. As an agricultural society, Jesus' listeners would be familiar with the idea of famine and the severity of the situation, given the lack of both communal and individual resources.

15 And he went and joined himself to a citizen of that country; and he sent him into his fields to feed swine. 16 And he would fain

have filled his belly with the husks that the swine did eat: and no man gave unto him.

These verses further amplify just how lost the son is. The son—who at home had shelter, servants, and a relationship with his father—is now joined to a citizen of a foreign country. The narrative amplifies his powerlessness: no inheritance, no family, and no home. The son who demanded an inheritance and felt compelled to pursue his own freedom is now bound to a foreigner who can dictate his life decisions in the way that the son had not wanted the father to do.

More tragic is that a Jew is sent to the fields to feed swine. The act of feeding swine for a Jew of wealth demonstrates his distance not just from the father's home but also from Jewish customs. Swine is forbidden in Jewish Law and considered "unclean" (Deuteronomy 14:8, Leviticus 11:7). The son is so famished that not only would he work in a field with pigs, but he would have eaten the food of the pigs. Again, the parable illustrates that the distance is not only geographical but spiritual.

The helplessness and humiliation of the son is visible to all. The deepest level of frustration and desperation is that in these circumstances "no man gave unto him." Although he desperately needs charity, he is too far away and too far gone to receive it.

17 And when he came to himself, he said, How many hired servants of my father's have bread enough and to spare, and I perish with hunger! 18 I will arise and go to my father, and will say unto him, Father, I have sinned against heaven, and before thee, 19 And am no more worthy to be called thy son: make me as one of thy hired servants.

"When he came to himself" is an idiom that means to come to one's senses or to be aware, or to come to consciousness. A modern idiom might say he "woke up." This is an important transition in the narrative. After the humiliation and depth of his sin and loss, the son now speaks. But the conversation now is very different from his request at the beginning of the story.

The question of status reinforces the son's new awareness of his situation. The son who was privy to a large inheritance now realizes that even those with no familial relations, the hired servants (Gk. *misthos*, **mees-THOCE**; different from *doulos*, slave), have more status and are treated better. It would be better to be a hired hand in his father's house than a slave somewhere else. With this new understanding of his life situation and a full realization of his mistakes and sin, he then thinks of doing something about it.

The next statement not only shows that he acknowledges his sin; he is contrite. He no longer feels worthy to be called a son. He is in a very different posture. As an act of restitution, he will settle to live as a servant in his father's house.

20 And he arose, and came to his father. But when he was yet a great way off, his father saw him, and had compassion, and ran, and fell on his neck, and kissed him.

In the previous verses he thinks about returning. Now he decides to act on his thoughts. These two verses are very important to understanding the power dynamics in the narrative. In the beginning the son asks for the inheritance and leaves to explore the world on his own. Now in the narrative, he rises to seek out his father.

The next part of the narrative is perhaps why this story is so powerful. Similar to the other lost items—the coin (15:4–7) and the sheep (15:8–10)—when they are found there is a celebration. The compassionate father is obviously on the lookout for the lost son. Before the son reaches the house, the father is moving in his direction to reach him. More profoundly visible in the narrative are the father's actions in response to the son. The father: a) sees him; b) is filled with compassion; c) runs to him; d) throws his arms around him; e) and kisses him. Those listening to this parable would not have expected the father's actions. Surely the father would be angry, list all the sins of the son, and demand some form of punishment for wasting the inheritance. Instead, the list we get is the father's overwhelming, joyous acts of welcome for his son.

21 And the son said unto him, Father, I have sinned against heaven, and in thy sight, and am no more worthy to be called thy son.

The younger son in the parable is used to reveal a clear picture of repentance and grace. In the Christian understanding of sin, there is always the opportunity for repentance. However, it is difficult to judge whether the person repenting is truly admitting their mistakes. No one can see the heart of a sinner to determine if that person is truly repentant. But, certainly like the son in the parable, humility is always a good place to start. Moreover, a change of heart and action is evidence that a person is ready for a new beginning (vv. 17, 20).

This verse is a strong contrast to the beginning of the parable—with a boastful son demanding what he considers to be rightfully his. He humbly realizes that he has made a mistake and sinned. More important, the son now has a different understanding of his relationship with the father. Instead of taking a posture of arrogance, he now sees himself as not even worthy of his filial status and is willing to be a servant. The ancient community listening to this parable would have quickly understood the power dynamics expressed in one who is a son of wealth wanting to only be a servant.

22 But the father said to his servants, Bring forth the best robe, and put it on him; and put a ring on his hand, and shoes on his feet: 23 And bring hither the fatted calf, and kill it; and let us eat, and be merry: 24 For this my son was dead, and is alive again; he was lost, and is found. And they began to be merry.

This is the true power of the narrative. The robe, ring, sandals, and the fatted calf are all items that ordinarily would be reserved for a son. What better vision of Christianity than to remind people who have made mistakes that there is always an open door and a party for all those who wish to return home. The son who has spent all of the inheritance on riotous living is welcomed back into the father's house with a wonderful party.

It is here that the reader should notice the beauty of the narrative. Jesus is telling this story to the Pharisees and Sadducees who had many laws and restrictions (Luke 15:1–2). Here is the son who has clearly sinned. In every aspect, the son has violated the customs and laws of the Jewish people. The Pharisees would have anticipated a story where this son is now punished. However, the father in the story (who is positioned as God) does not even list all the son's infractions and sins. This would be alarming to the Pharisees that a son who has made so many mistakes could not only be embraced—but even given a party.

This parable illustrates mercy (not getting what we deserve) and gives a clear picture of grace (getting what we do not deserve). The fact that the son is not punished but can return home to a celebration is a great story that demonstrates the overwhelming, incredible, unconditional forgiveness of God. Like a compassionate father, God is always offering us an opportunity to come to ourselves and return home. By admitting our mistakes, we receive the celebrations of God's unconditional love and full restoration with all the rights and privileges of a child of God.

Sources:

Brown, Colin. Ed. *The New International Dictionary of the New Testament Theology.* Vol. 2. Grand Rapids, MI: Zondervan, 1976.

Butler, Trent. gen. ed. *Holman Bible Dictionary,* Nashville, TN: Broadman & Holman Publishers, 1991. 480, 696

Nolland, John. *Word Biblical Commentary,* Vol. 35B. Dallas, TX: Word Books, 1993.

"Prodigal." Merriam-Webster.com. Accessed August 20, 2017. https://www.merriam-webster.com/dictionary/prodigal.

Vallet, Ronald E. *Stepping Stones of the Steward: A Faith Journey through Jesus' Parables.* Grand Rapids, MI: W.B. Eerdmans Publishers, 1994.

Say It Correctly

Prodigal. **PRAH**-di-guhl.
Parable. **PAIR**-uh-buhl.
Synoptic. sih-**NAHP**-tik.

Daily Bible Readings

MONDAY
Transformed by Christ Into New Life
(Ephesians 2:1–10)

TUESDAY
God Seeks the Scattered People
(Ezekiel 34:11–16)

WEDNESDAY
God's Compassion for Straying People
(Hosea 11:1–4, 8–9)

THURSDAY
Calling Sinners to Repentance
(Luke 3:12–13; 5:27–32)

FRIDAY
Finding the Lost Sheep and Coin
(Luke 15:1–10)

SATURDAY
Plea for Understanding and Recognition
(Luke 15:25–32)

SUNDAY
Family Members, Forgiven and
Reconciled
(Luke 15:11–24)

Notes

Teaching Tips

March 24
Bible Study Guide 4

Words You Should Know

A. Publican *telones* (Gk.)—Tax collector.

B. Abide *meno* (Gk.)—To lodge as a guest.

Teacher Preparation

Unifying Principle—Calling the Unlikely. Some people can be considered unacceptable, either because of their actions or because of stereotypes held by others. How does one find acceptance? Jesus recognized Zacchaeus' interest and honored him despite the grumbling of the crowd; Zacchaeus responded with overwhelming repentance.

A. Read the Bible Background and Devotional Readings.

B. Pray for your students and lesson clarity.

C. Read the lesson Scripture in multiple translations.

D. Option: Have students list people in today's society who may be considered unacceptable in some religious or social groups, either because of their actions or because of stereotypes. Discuss how we as Christians can reach out to them in similar manner as Jesus did to Zacchaeus.

O—Open the Lesson

A. Begin the class with prayer.

B. Have the students read the Aim for Change.

C. Have the students read the In Focus story.

D. Ask students how events named in the story can weigh on their hearts and how they can view these events from a theological perspective.

P—Present the Scriptures

A. Read the Focal Verses and discuss the Background and The People, Places, and Times sections.

B. Have the class share what Scriptures stand out for them and why, with particular emphasis on today's context.

E—Explore the Meaning

A. Use In Depth or More Light on the Text to help provide more in-depth discussion of the lesson text.

B. Discuss the Liberating Lesson and Application for Activation sections.

N—Next Steps for Application

A. Summarize the value of knowing that even people others think are unacceptable are called by God.

B. End class with a commitment to pray for the wealthy, the powerful, the ignored, the poor, and the overlooked.

Worship Guide

For the Superintendent or Teacher
Theme: Calling to Salvation
Song: "Lord, I Want to Be a Christian"
Devotional Reading: 1 Chronicles 16:8–13, 23–27

Calling to Salvation

Bible Background • LUKE 19:1–10
Printed Text • LUKE 19:1–10 | Devotional Reading • 1 CHRONICLES 16:8–13, 23–27

—————————— Aim for Change ——————————

In today's lesson we will: IDENTIFY how Zacchaeus and Jesus ignored social taboos; REPENT of sinful attitudes we may have held toward certain people; and CHALLENGE the stereotypes we have of others so we can better share Christ with them.

—————————— ✎ In Focus ——————————

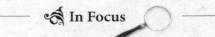

Rev. Thompson, although fairly new to the area and the Olive Hill Church, was building a community center for the children in South Central Los Angeles. Zoe, a local police officer, had a reputation for being controversial and unjust when it came to the arrest of teenagers in the community. Rev. Thompson was making arrangements to visit her at the police station on behalf of community residents. One Sunday, Rev. Thompson looked out into the congregation during offering and saw Zoe in worship. Several members were displeased with her presence. After the service, he approached Zoe about setting up a meeting. Zoe was impacted by the sermon and touched by the presentation on the church's efforts to build a community center. She was open to meeting with Rev. Thompson to discuss how she could be a resource.

Zoe said to Rev. Thompson, "Look, I am not perfect in my job. I may have been unfair in how I have served. I can admit that. However, I do want to support the efforts of the community center. Here is a check of my own money that I want to give as a donation. I want to hear about the people of South Central and how we can do a better job with police accountability and safety for our youth." Sensing a genuine change in Zoe, Rev. Thompson accepted the gift. On the following Sunday, Zoe decided to join Olive Hill. Rev. Thompson told the church to rejoice as heaven rejoices.

Do we understand that people's jobs are not always attached to who they are? What do we do when our jobs challenge us to be controversial?

—————————— Keep in Mind ——————————

"For the Son of man is come to seek and to save that which was lost" (Luke 19:10, KJV).

"For the Son of Man came to seek and save those who are lost" (Luke 19:10, NLT).

Focal Verses

KJV **Luke 19:1** And Jesus entered and passed through Jericho.

2 And, behold, there was a man named Zacchaeus, which was the chief among the publicans, and he was rich.

3 And he sought to see Jesus who he was; and could not for the press, because he was little of stature.

4 And he ran before, and climbed up into a sycomore tree to see him: for he was to pass that way.

5 And when Jesus came to the place, he looked up, and saw him, and said unto him, Zacchaeus, make haste, and come down; for to day I must abide at thy house.

6 And he made haste, and came down, and received him joyfully.

7 And when they saw it, they all murmured, saying, That he was gone to be guest with a man that is a sinner.

8 And Zacchaeus stood, and said unto the Lord: Behold, Lord, the half of my goods I give to the poor; and if I have taken any thing from any man by false accusation, I restore him fourfold.

9 And Jesus said unto him, This day is salvation come to this house, forsomuch as he also is a son of Abraham.

10 For the Son of man is come to seek and to save that which was lost.

NLT **Luke 19:1** Jesus entered Jericho and made his way through the town.

2 There was a man there named Zacchaeus. He was the chief tax collector in the region, and he had become very rich.

3 He tried to get a look at Jesus, but he was too short to see over the crowd.

4 So he ran ahead and climbed a sycamore-fig tree beside the road, for Jesus was going to pass that way.

5 When Jesus came by, he looked up at Zacchaeus and called him by name. "Zacchaeus!" he said. "Quick, come down! I must be a guest in your home today."

6 Zacchaeus quickly climbed down and took Jesus to his house in great excitement and joy.

7 But the people were displeased. "He has gone to be the guest of a notorious sinner," they grumbled.

8 Meanwhile, Zacchaeus stood before the Lord and said, "I will give half my wealth to the poor, Lord, and if I have cheated people on their taxes, I will give them back four times as much!"

9 Jesus responded, "Salvation has come to this home today, for this man has shown himself to be a true son of Abraham.

10 For the Son of Man came to seek and save those who are lost."

The People, Places, and Times

Jericho. Just 18 miles east of Jerusalem, Jericho was situated near a main road, so there were probably many publicans, or tax collectors, who collected the customs for the government as the people went in and out of the city. Jericho was a highly populated and ethnically diverse city important for commerce and culture on a major Roman road in the Judea province.

Zacchaeus. The chief publican in Jericho was already rich (probably through legal and illegal means). Publicans were despised by the people because they not only collected taxes for the hated Roman Empire, they also kept some of the proceeds for their own use. Since

Zacchaeus was chief among the publicans, he was probably very wealthy and very despised.

Background

Luke's Gospel was written to give another historical account of Jesus' life and ministry as the Son of God, this time emphasizing that Jesus brought salvation to the Jews and Gentiles. We see in Luke's writings what Jesus taught regarding love for neighbors; His inclusion of Gentiles in the definition of a neighbor; and concern for the weak, poor, marginalized, and outcast. The record of Jesus' interaction with Zacchaeus is only found in Luke's Gospel.

The encounter with the tax collector is found soon after Jesus shares a parable with some of the religious elite in answer to those who look down on others. He compares and contrasts the prayer posture of a Pharisee and a tax collector (Luke 18:9–14). In this parable, the Pharisee is proud that he follows the Law and exalts himself in self-righteous prayer. In contrast the tax collector humbly comes before God in prayer asking for mercy. Jesus ends the parable by stressing that the one who is justified is the one who humbles himself in prayer (v. 14). We see Jesus' illustration brought to life in His meeting with Zacchaeus.

At-A-Glance

1. Counted Out (Luke 19:1–5)
2. Called In (vv. 6–10)

In Depth

1. Counted Out (Luke 19:1–5)

Jesus passes through Jericho, a notable, bustling city in biblical history with a mixed population of Jewish elitists and the unsavory. Here, Jesus healed blind Bartimaeus who got His attention as He passed by—despite the crowd's efforts to stop him (Mark 10:46–52). Luke adds a different dimension to the town of Jericho by highlighting Zacchaeus. He is chief tax collector and considered a traitor to his people and a puppet of their oppressor, the Roman government, which occupied Israel. Zacchaeus profits greatly from his position and is rich. He is also a short man, which probably is a second strike against him.

Ostracized by his people, Zacchaeus is on his own in trying to find a spot to see Jesus when he hears He is coming to town. Zacchaeus maneuvers through the crowd and climbs up a sycamore tree to capture a glimpse of Jesus as He passes by. It is in that moment that Jesus recognizes him because Jesus can read hearts and perceive when someone presses their way through a crowd to get to him (Luke 8:43–48).

We should be encouraged that Zacchaeus' efforts pay off and Jesus spots him because when we seek Jesus with our heart, He will find us (Jeremiah 29:12–14). Of all the people in the crowd, of all the houses available to Him in Jericho, Jesus purposefully calls out Zacchaeus—the short tax collector perched in the sycamore tree—and asks to dine at his house. This account shows us that no one is counted out.

2. Called In (vv. 6–10)

Zacchaeus quickly comes down from the tree. The surrounding people murmur about Jesus going to the home of this notorious sinner, but Zacchaeus receives Jesus into his home with joy. Jesus' act of inclusion, mercy, and grace compel Zacchaeus to make an astounding and heartfelt gesture. He submits to Jesus as Lord and pledges to give half of what he owns to the poor; and he will repay those he has extorted four times as much as he has taken. Only a true encounter with Jesus from a heart ready to receive Him can make such a declaration.

Compare Zacchaeus' response to that of the rich young ruler (Luke 18:18–23) whom Jesus tells to sell all he has, give it to the poor, and follow Him. The rich young ruler leaves sad because, although he follows the Law and believes the Law, he is unable to trust Jesus to let go of all and follow Him. Zacchaeus, unprompted, volunteers from the heart to give what he has in response to the mercy received.

Jesus responds that Zacchaeus, as a son of Abraham, and his household have received salvation. The Son of Man, God incarnate in the earth to repair the breach, has come to seek out and save that which was lost through sin. Jesus emphasizes that Zacchaeus is a son of Abraham to restore his position as an heir of salvation—joint heir with Him by faith not by his works (Romans 8:17; Ephesians 2:8–9).

Zacchaeus' money and works did not bring salvation to him or his household; he was called in because of his repentant and humbled heart.

Search the Scriptures

1. What was the significance of Zacchaeus making the effort to see Jesus?

2. How did Jesus see Zacchaeus in the midst of the crowd? How did the crowd respond?

3. Why did Zacchaeus receive salvation as a son of Abraham?

Discuss the Meaning

1. How do Zacchaeus and Jesus ignore the social taboos? How does their boldness lead to a new life for Zacchaeus?

2. In what ways have people stereotyped you for being passionate about the Gospel of Jesus? Stereotyped you because of your career? How would that feel? Now, given that feeling, how can one move past social and cultural stereotypes to embrace people who are different from ourselves?

Liberating Lesson

Jesus ignored the taboos surrounding association with tax collectors. He was purposeful in reading Zacchaeus' heart from a sycamore tree; and from this look of mercy, salvation was given and received. What would happen in our culture if we moved beyond stereotypes and biases to truly see each other as God intended? Jesus saw Zacchaeus' heart and restored him as a son of Abraham. As the body of Christ, we are instruments in bringing restoration and healing to our broken world.

Application for Activation

In response to this lesson, examine stereotypes and biases of any kind. Search your heart and pray for God to unearth any values or beliefs that do not align with His Word. God has shown great mercy. Discuss as a class how to actively be an extension of mercy in your spheres of influence. Make the effort to go outside your comfort zone to seek out someone in need of God's love expressed through you.

Follow the Spirit

What God wants me to do:

_____

_____

_____

Remember Your Thoughts

Special insights I have learned:

_____

_____

_____

More Light on the Text
Luke 19:1–10

Luke's account of Jesus' encounter with Zacchaeus in this passage comes at the end of the long section that details Jesus' journey to Jerusalem (Luke 9:51–19:27). We find in the passage hints about various themes in the book, such as Jesus' journeying to Jerusalem (19:1, 4), concern for the poor (19:8), and the coming of the eschatological salvation (God's kingdom) into history (19:5, 9). However, the main focus of the incident involves the coming of salvation and God's kingdom to the outcasts and the proper use of money. Jesus' parabolic teaching concerning the coming of salvation to the outcasts receives concrete expression here, just as with Bartimaeus (18:35–43), in the life of Zacchaeus, who is also an outcast.

The story of Zacchaeus is in sharp contrast to that of the rich ruler (18:18–23). Both are powerful and wealthy. The rich ruler keeps the commandments and could be considered religious, but he cannot do the one thing remaining, which is hand his life to Jesus and signal his surrender by selling his possessions and giving them to the poor. On the other hand, Zacchaeus is considered a "sinner" because of his profession.

1 And Jesus entered and passed through Jericho. 2 And, behold, there was a man named Zacchaeus, which was the chief among the publicans, and he was rich.

Jericho was a rich, prosperous, and very important city. It lay in the Jordan valley on both the approach to Jerusalem and the crossings of the river, which gave access to the lands east of the Jordan. It had a great palm forest and world-famous balsam groves that perfumed the air for miles around. Its gardens of roses were known far and wide. It was known as "The City of Palms." Josephus, the Jewish historian, called it "a divine region," "the fattest in Palestine." The Romans carried its dates and balsam to worldwide trade and fame. There must have been at Jericho one of the principal custom houses because of the export of balm that grew in that oasis and was sold far and wide, and because of the considerable traffic that took place on the road. A toll was collected from travelers and traders here. Zacchaeus was head of the office.

The name Zacchaeus (ultimately from Heb. *zakak*, **zaw-KAK**) means "pure" or "innocent." But given his profession, Zacchaeus is considered anything but pure. However, as the story unfolds, he will live up to his name in this encounter with Jesus.

He is a chief among the publicans (Gk. *architelones*, **ar-khee-teh-LOW-nace**), suggesting that Zacchaeus is no ordinary tax collector but probably a commissioner over the district of Jericho, a position which he may have lobbied for or purchased from the Roman authorities. Because the local Jews hate and ostracize those who worked for Rome, Zacchaeus must have been a lonely and despised person.

Despite his wealth, Zacchaeus occupies a marginal social position. Although "he was rich," and a man of great means, he is not happy. Thus he seems to be a perfect example of a rich man's difficulty of getting into heaven (Luke 18:24–27). As an administrator for the Roman government's tax office, Zacchaeus has amassed great wealth by overtaxing the Jewish people and taking a cut from the taxes gathered by other tax collectors whose work he administers. His wealth, however, cannot provide the one thing he wants more than anything else.

3 And he sought to see Jesus who he was; and could not for the press, because he was little of stature. 4 And he ran before, and climbed up into a sycomore tree to see him: for he was to pass that way.

Zacchaeus wanted to set his eyes on Jesus and so he sought after Him. Perhaps Zacchaeus had heard that Jesus accepted people like him. He longed to see this remarkable Jesus for himself. For all his wealth and privileges, Zacchaeus recognized his own deep spiritual needs, which only Jesus could satisfy. But Zacchaeus ran into two problems. First, was the crowd that pressed on Jesus. Second, was his physical stature. His natural state gave him a disadvantage in seeking after Jesus.

Zacchaeus ran ahead and climbed a sycamore tree. This is a highly unusual act for a person of great wealth and eminent position. Because he sought Jesus so intensely, Zacchaeus threw caution to the winds and did something that many would have considered beneath the dignity of a grown, wealthy man—he climbed up a tree. The sycamore fig tree of the area was a large tree with low branches, which made it easy to climb. There was no room for pride at this point. He did not mind humiliation as the price to see Jesus up close.

Such undignified behavior indicates that more than curiosity is at play here.

5 And when Jesus came to the place, he looked up, and saw him, and said unto him, Zacchaeus, make haste, and come down; for to day I must abide at thy house. 6 And he made haste, and came down, and received him joyfully.

Jesus "looked up, and saw him." Jesus sees him in the sense of knowing about his need and reaching out to meet that need. What a great lesson we can learn from this episode. Jesus sees every person, no matter where he or she is: in the dark places of one's sin and shame, and in one's home and work and play as one seeks to know the truth. Jesus knows and sees everything about every person; but there is one person in particular whom he sees. He sees the one who is seeking Him. Zacchaeus

is an example. He is desperate to see Jesus, so he struggles against the odds and finds a place where he can. The place he chooses means humiliating himself and exposing himself to people who are bitterly opposed to him, but he is willing to suffer whatever it takes to get a look at the Savior. Because Zacchaeus seeks Jesus so diligently, Jesus sees him.

Jesus knew and called Zacchaeus by name. This was bound to strike Zacchaeus and be very meaningful to him. When anyone, especially a stranger, calls us by name, our ears perk up and our senses become more alert. Jesus knows every person's name. He says He calls His sheep by name (John 10:3). Jesus knew the importance of a person's name. He desires to address every one of us by name, but we must let Him. We have to do as Zacchaeus did: seek to find the place and vantage point where we can see Jesus, then Jesus will see us and call us by name.

Jesus told Zacchaeus to hurry and to come down because He "must abide at [his] house" that day. The word "abide" in Greek, *meno* (**MEE-no**), can mean "to lodge" as a guest. Jesus wasn't physically asking to move in with Zacchaeus. But He may be implying He would move in spiritually. Jesus was interested in having a real relationship with him, beginning with a meal and time spent together.

In some cultures, sharing a meal is one of the symbols of reconciliation and the end of hostilities between warring factions. To show the importance of the matter, Jesus used the word *dei* (Gk. **DAY**), translated "must," which has the force of compulsion or divine necessity. Jesus had a divine appointment with Zacchaeus. Zacchaeus' response is no less important. He quickly climbed down and received Jesus joyfully.

7 And when they saw it, they all murmured, saying, That he was gone to be guest with a man that is a sinner.

The reaction of the bystanders was in complete contrast to that of Zacchaeus. Instead of rejoicing with a sinner coming to the Savior, they murmured. The word "murmured" in Greek is *diagogguzo* (**dee-ah-gon-GOO-zoo**), also used in Exodus 16:2, 7-8, and is reminiscent of the ungrateful, murmuring Hebrews in the wilderness who didn't yet understand the nature of God. It was an unheard-of thing or taboo for a Jewish rabbi or any other religious leader to bring himself so low as to stay in the house of a publican. Moreover, the Jews felt that Jesus' fellowship with sinners made Him ceremonially unclean and theologically suspect. Therefore they were greatly offended at the notion of Jesus allowing Himself to be entertained in the house of Zacchaeus, a prominent member of the despised and outcasts.

8 And Zacchaeus stood, and said unto the Lord: Behold, Lord, the half of my goods I give to the poor; and if I have taken any thing from any man by false accusation, I restore him fourfold.

A mighty revolution has taken place in Zacchaeus' life as a result of his acquaintance with Jesus. He declares openly that he has decided as a spontaneous act of repentance, gratitude, and love to give half of his goods to the poor and in every case restore fourfold whatever he has taken in the past by his callous and heartless extortions when he was collecting customs. He was using the Old Testament standard as restitution for a violent robbery (Exodus 22:1; 2 Samuel 12:6). This was a much larger sum than later Levitical Law (Leviticus 6:5; Numbers 5:7), where only an added one-fifth was required as restitution. Zacchaeus' restitution was proof of a changed heart, not a means to it. This statement, combined with the previous promise, meant he was not a wealthy man anymore.

This is his public statement of confession, repentance, and restitution—a sign that a brand new relationship of love and forgiveness had been established with God through this encounter with Jesus, the Messiah. In receiving Jesus and spending just a little time with Him, Zacchaeus knew he had to repent and make restitution. First he just sought after Jesus; but in seeking Jesus he also came to seek repentance. The story of Zacchaeus is that of a transformed life, a life that literally fulfills 2 Corinthians 5:17 (NLT). "This means that anyone who belongs to Christ has become a new person. The old life is gone; a new life has begun!" There was some evidence of life-change immediately. How true it is that we come to Jesus as we are; but when we do so we do not remain as we are.

9 And Jesus said unto him, This day is salvation come to this house, forsomuch as he also is a son of Abraham.

Jesus' pronouncement shows that Zacchaeus is indeed a lost sinner, guilty and in need of redemption. The contrast of salvation coming to Zacchaeus' house with the grumbling of the critical multitude is noticeable and significant. A new relationship with God is evidenced by this man's changed attitude and actions, which impacts his household, that is, the whole family (cf. Acts 10:2; 11:14; 16:15, 31–33; 18:8).

Zacchaeus has received salvation, "forsomuch as he also is a son of Abraham," that is "because he is also a Jew" despite his occupation as a tax collector. This is a reminder to self-righteous Jews that Zacchaeus is also a descendant of Abraham. He is not cut off from Israel and the blessing that is coming from Jesus. Although he is already a racial Jew, now through faith in Jesus, he has become a true descendant of Abraham by faith (cf. Romans 2:28–29; 4:12; Galatians 6:16). Jesus' words are also an announcement that Zacchaeus has now, in a new and living way, become a son of Abraham, the father of the faithful. Through the new birth he is now a spiritual son of Abraham, and a member of the new Israel (i.e., the church). His lineage does not bring salvation, but his faith—evidenced by his public confession and restitution—surely does.

This salvation was a present reality (cf. 2 Corinthians 6:2), as well as a future consummation. Moreover, it is important to note that salvation from Jesus, although it has in view the individual man in the first instance (v. 5), is extended to Zacchaeus' house. The phrase "to this house" implies that the other members of the family and servants would be affected by Zacchaeus' conversion.

Household evangelism is seen several times in Acts (cf. 10:2; 11:14; 16:15, 31–34; 18:8). This is in contrast with Western individualism. There is clear evidence from the apostles' missionary efforts in Acts and even Jesus' ministry that the bonds of family membership provide means and ways of the faith that saves (Luke 10:5; John 4:53).

10 For the Son of man is come to seek and to save that which was lost.

Here we have Jesus' own statement of His major purpose in coming into the world. The truth of this universal statement is grounds for the assurance given to Zacchaeus in verse 9. A miracle of grace of such magnitude could take place in Zacchaeus because Jesus came precisely for that purpose: seeking and saving that which was lost. This may be an allusion to the Septuagint translation of Ezekiel 34:16, where there is an anticipation of God Himself and a messianic David coming to the rescue of the house of Israel. It certainly relates to Mary's song foretelling Jesus' mission even before His birth (Luke 1:68–79). It is similar to the emphasis of the parables in Luke 15, as well as the central summary statement of the Gospel of Mark (Mark 10:45) and Paul's affirmation to Timothy (1 Timothy 1:15). God's central message bears repeating: He came to redeem lost and hopeless humanity.

Sources:

Attridge, Harold, W. *The Harper Collins Study Bible*, New Revised Standard Version. New York, NY: Harper One, 2006. 1800.

William Barclay, *The Gospel of Luke, The New Daily Study Bible*. Louisville, KY; London: Westminster John Knox Press, 2001.

Cabal, Ted et. al., *The Apologetics Study Bible*, Holman Christian Standard, Nashville, TN: Holman Bible Publishers, 2007. 1507-1509, 1551.

Carroll, John T. *Luke*. Interpretation. Louisville, KY; London: Westminster John Knox Press, 2012.

Godet, Frédéric Louis. *A Commentary on the Gospel of St. Luke*, trans. Edward William Shalders and M. D. Cusin, Vol. 2. New York: I.K. Funk & Co., 1881.

Lenski, R. C. *The Interpretation of St. Luke's Gospel*. Minneapolis, MN: Augsburg Publishing House, 1961.

Morris, Leon. *Luke*. Tyndale New Testament commentaries. Grand Rapids, MI: Wm B. Eerdmans, 1988.

Nolland, John. Luke 18:35–24:53, *Word Biblical Commentary*, Vol. 35C. Dallas, TX: Word Inc., 1998.

Stein, Robert H. Luke, vol. 24, *The New American Commentary*. Nashville, TN: Broadman & Holman Publishers, 1992.

Van der Maas, Ed M., ed. *Halley's Bible Handbook: Deluxe Edition (25th Edition)*. Grand Rapids, MI: Zondervan, 2007. 547, 615.

Say It Correctly

Jericho. **JER**-ih-koh.
Restitution. res-tih-tyoo- **SH**uhn.
Sycamore. **SIH**-kuh-more.
Zacchaeus. za-**KEE**-uhs.

Daily Bible Readings

MONDAY
Laws of Confession and Restitution
(Exodus 22:1–3; Numbers 5:5–7)

TUESDAY
Israel's Salvation and Commitment to God
(Deuteronomy 26:16–19)

WEDNESDAY
I Must Proclaim the Good News!
(Luke 4:38–43)

THURSDAY
Let the Children Come to Me
(Luke 18:15–17)

FRIDAY
Entering the Kingdom of God
(Luke 18:18–30)

SATURDAY
Blind Man Receives Sight and Salvation
(Luke 18:35–43)

SUNDAY
Receiving Salvation, Correcting Injustice
(Luke 19:1–10)

Notes

_____

_____

_____

_____

Teaching Tips

Words You Should Know

A. Repent *metanoeo* (Gk.)—Rethink or change one's mind, meaning turn to God.

B. Straightway *eutheos* (Gk.)—Immediately.

Teacher Preparation

Unifying Principle—Discipleship. People can be settled in their ways but destined for greater purposes. How do people discover and respond to that higher calling? When Jesus called His first disciples, they responded by leaving their routine work to follow Him.

A. Read the Bible Background and Devotional Readings.

B. Pray for your students and lesson clarity.

C. Read the lesson Scripture in multiple translations.

D. Option: Invite someone who has served on mission trips or in other settings away from the usual comforts of home to discuss with your class what it was like to give up their comfortable way of life, even for a short time. Compare and contrast this sacrifice with the disciples' experience.

O—Open the Lesson

A. Begin the class with prayer.

B. Have the students read the Aim for Change.

C. Have the students read the In Focus story.

D. Ask students how events named in the story can weigh on their hearts and how they can view these events from a theological perspective.

P—Present the Scriptures

A. Read the Focal Verses and discuss the Background and The People, Places, and Times sections.

B. Have the class share what Scriptures stand out for them and why, with particular emphasis on today's context.

E—Explore the Meaning

A. Use In Depth or More Light on the Text to help provide deeper discussion of the lesson text.

B. Discuss the Liberating Lesson and Application for Activation sections.

N—Next Steps for Application

A. Summarize the value of sacrificing our routines to be disciples of Jesus.

B. End class with a commitment to pray for greater discipleship in your church.

Worship Guide

For the Superintendent or Teacher
Theme: Called to Discipleship
Song: "We Are Called"
Devotional Reading: Psalm 91

Called to Discipleship

Bible Background • MATTHEW 4:12–22
Printed Text • MATTHEW 4:12–22 | Devotional Reading • PSALM 91

——— Aim for Change ———

In today's lesson we will: RECOGNIZE how the disciples accepted Jesus' call; REFLECT on how choosing to follow Jesus transformed their lives; and WORSHIP God for the blessings in our lives that have come because we follow Jesus.

——— 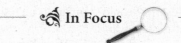 In Focus ———

Scott had built a reputation as an excellent basketball player in his town. One day, Scott decided he didn't want to play basketball alone, so he approached Bobby and his brothers at the community basketball court. Bobby had a great three-point shot and knew how to steal the ball with ease. Scott told Bobby, "Hey man. I've seen your skills; you're good. How about you join my team? You could be good just playing with your brothers, or we could all work together and show the community what a real team looks like. We could build an interstate league."

Bobby replied, "A league? That would be awesome. But how would we get enough people? And how can I just leave my home to play basketball?"

Scott said, "Don't worry about leaving home. Home will remain home, but you have a gift worth sharing. Join me! With faith and consistency, people will want to know more about us."

After three weeks of playing together at the community basketball court, Scott, Bobby, and Bobby's brothers got an invitation to play in another town. Eventually seven other young men joined them and people would follow the team to watch them play their games.

Are we invited or forced to be disciples of Christ? How has Christ invited us?

——— Keep in Mind ———

"And he saith unto them, Follow me, and I will make you fishers of men"
(Matthew 4:19, KJV).

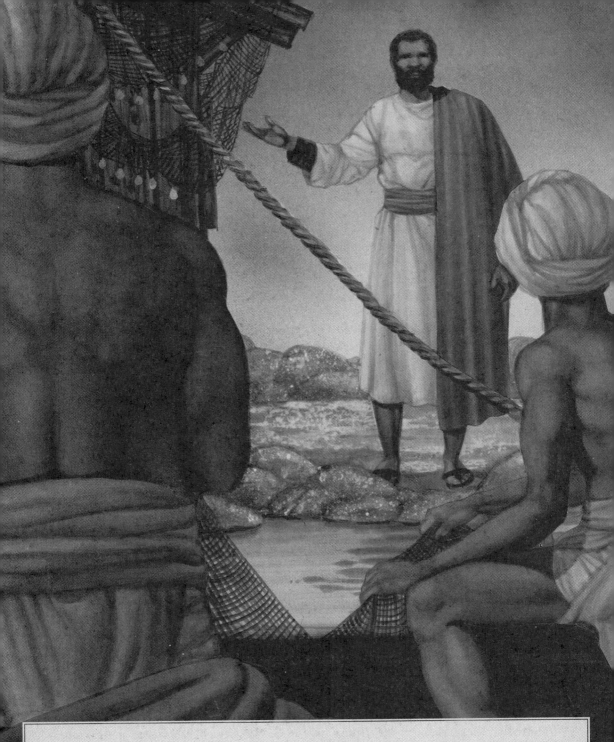

"Jesus called out to them, 'Come, follow me, and I will show you how to fish for people!'"
(Matthew 4:19, NLT).

Focal Verses

KJV **Matthew 4:12** Now when Jesus had heard that John was cast into prison, he departed into Galilee;

13 And leaving Nazareth, he came and dwelt in Capernaum, which is upon the sea coast, in the borders of Zabulon and Nephthalim:

14 That it might be fulfilled which was spoken by Esaias the prophet, saying,

15 The land of Zabulon, and the land of Nephthalim, by the way of the sea, beyond Jordan, Galilee of the Gentiles;

16 The people which sat in darkness saw great light; and to them which sat in the region and shadow of death light is sprung up.

17 From that time Jesus began to preach, and to say, Repent: for the kingdom of heaven is at hand.

18 And Jesus, walking by the sea of Galilee, saw two brethren, Simon called Peter, and Andrew his brother, casting a net into the sea: for they were fishers.

19 And he saith unto them, Follow me, and I will make you fishers of men.

20 And they straightway left their nets, and followed him.

21 And going on from thence, he saw other two brethren, James the son of Zebedee, and John his brother, in a ship with Zebedee their father, mending their nets; and he called them.

22 And they immediately left the ship and their father, and followed him.

NLT **Matthew 4:12** When Jesus heard that John had been arrested, he left Judea and returned to Galilee.

13 He went first to Nazareth, then left there and moved to Capernaum, beside the Sea of Galilee, in the region of Zebulun and Naphtali.

14 This fulfilled what God said through the prophet Isaiah:

15 "In the land of Zebulun and of Naphtali, beside the sea, beyond the Jordan River, in Galilee where so many Gentiles live,

16 the people who sat in darkness have seen a great light. And for those who lived in the land where death casts its shadow, a light has shined."

17 From then on Jesus began to preach, "Repent of your sins and turn to God, for the Kingdom of Heaven is near."

18 One day as Jesus was walking along the shore of the Sea of Galilee, he saw two brothers—Simon, also called Peter, and Andrew—throwing a net into the water, for they fished for a living.

19 Jesus called out to them, "Come, follow me, and I will show you how to fish for people!"

20 And they left their nets at once and followed him.

21 A little farther up the shore he saw two other brothers, James and John, sitting in a boat with their father, Zebedee, repairing their nets. And he called them to come, too.

22 They immediately followed him, leaving the boat and their father behind.

The People, Places, and Times

Matthew. The author of the Gospel of Matthew. His names means "gift of Jehovah," and he is also known by his priestly tribal name, Levi (Mark 2:14). Matthew wrote the genealogy of Christ and documents His claim to be Messiah. Matthew was a publican, a Jewish man employed by the conquering Romans to collect taxes. The Jewish people saw him as a traitor, and they despised him. After his conversion to Christ, Matthew's ministry was to preach mostly to the Jews. He cites Old Testament Scripture nearly 100 times in his Gospel, and he mentions the phrase "kingdom of heaven" thirty-two times (e.g., Matthew 13:1–53). He was present at the ascension of Jesus.

Background

As His earthy ministry and reputation gained prominence throughout the region—from Nazareth to Judea, Samaria, and Galilee—Jesus experienced rejection, opposition, and escalating hostility. Particularly in His hometown of Nazareth, the reaction to His ministry ranged from amazement to mistrust. However, no reaction was harsher than that of the Roman government under Herod.

Herod's familial line had been particularly violent throughout all its generations. From Herod the Great (73–4 BC), who slaughtered all of Bethlehem's males under the age of two, to Herod Antipas (c. 20 BC–AD 39), who ordered the execution of John the Baptist, they had a deep history of resisting God's purposes and rejecting God's prophets, and they used any means necessary to silence opponents.

The Romans were becoming even more hostile and violent in their rejection of Jesus. After John the Baptist was arrested, Herod Antipas took the power and presence of the kingdom of God head-on. Imprisoned for condemning Herod's incestuous relationship with his niece Herodias, John refused to be silenced (Matthew 4:12; Mark 6:17). Herod Antipas, whom Jesus called "that fox" (Luke 13:32), reacted in typical Roman fashion—he wanted John dead.

After learning of John's death, Jesus moved to Capernaum, an important seaport city located on a major trade route. More important, His actions triggered fulfillment of a centuries-old revelation that the Messiah would be the light to the land allocated by divine covenant to the tribes of Zebulon and Naphtali, where Capernaum was located.

At-A-Glance

1. Jesus Starts His Ministry (Matthew 4:12–16)
2. The Kingdom of Heaven (v. 17)
3. Called as Disciples (vv. 18–22)

In Depth

1. Jesus Starts His Ministry (Matthew 4:12–16)

Jesus commences His ministry in an unexpected place—Galilee. Galileans were considered unclean, and the region had a disproportionate number of those who were considered heathens. Referred to as "Galilee of the Gentiles," the province was populated by Phoenicians, Arabians, Syrians, and Greeks. Jewish Galileans were generally wealthy and extreme in their religious bigotry. It is in this highly diverse mosaic of people, economic statuses, occupations, cultures, beliefs, biases, and attitudes that Jesus chooses to start His ministry.

Jesus moves to Capernaum, located on the Sea of Galilee. This puts Him in the heart of a region where the weight of Roman occupation and oppression overshadows the landscape. The people have been plunged into a pervasive Roman darkness marked by taxes and death. Jesus preaches, using familiar prophecies in His message and offering a great light of deliverance to the people "living in darkness," "living in the land of the shadow of death." This was the same promise of God spoken by the prophet Isaiah. God said that the Messiah would be the light to the land of Zebulon and Naphtali and that God will make glorious "the way of the sea, beyond Jordan, in Galilee of the nations" (Isaiah 9:1).

Kingdoms under human authority are in a constant state of darkness. Jesus is still calling the nations to come out of the darkness into the kingdom of light under God's authority.

How does Jesus' arrival in Capernaum fulfill the prophecies of the coming Messiah, delivered by Isaiah? How can we use these Scriptures to give hope to those "living in darkness"?

2. The Kingdom of Heaven (v. 17)

From the beginning of His ministry, Jesus consistently expressed His concern for saving the people from sin and for establishing the presence of God in their lives. Using the same language spoken by John the Baptist, Jesus adds a sense of urgency to His message: The kingdom of heaven is near. Aiming directly at hearts that live in the darkness of sin, Jesus offers them the light of God and the keys to the kingdom by way of repentance. The kingdom of heaven is closer than the people realize.

How can we live our lives in ways that show our repentance? How will you show others how your life changed after you came out of the darkness of sin and into the light of Jesus?

3. Called as Disciples (vv. 18–22)

Jesus sees two men, Simon (called Peter), and Andrew, while He is walking by the Sea of Galilee. These brothers are fishermen engaged in their trade when Jesus challenges them to disrupt all societal norms and conventional expectations. Both men are engaged in meeting their family's living needs. Both men have as a priority meeting the fishing quotas they paid as in-kind taxes to tax collectors on behalf of Rome.

Jesus invites Simon Peter and Andrew to re-order their priorities. He offers them the opportunity to catch something much more valuable than fish. In following Jesus, they will fish for people. Fishermen had a reputation for being rough and unpolished,

and were largely despised. But when Jesus appears, their lives change. They immediately accept Jesus' transformational call, which gives them new purpose for their lives. They are experienced and well-prepared for their calling, but instead of catching food to feed the body for a short time, Simon Peter and Andrew will be casting their nets to catch people for eternal life.

How can we become better "fishers of people"? How can we extend our nets farther to draw in more people for Jesus?

Search the Scriptures

1. Why did Jesus move from Nazareth to Capernaum (Matthew 4:12–13)? Compare how Jesus was received in the two cities (See Matthew 13: 53–58).

2. What message did Jesus preach (v. 17)?

3. How did Simon and Andrew respond when Jesus called them (v. 22)?

Discuss the Meaning

1. When you first accepted the call to follow Jesus, how did you feel? Nervous? Confident? Reserved?

2. Since Jesus came into your life, how has your life changed for the better?

3. How would your life have been different had you not followed Jesus?

Liberating Lesson

Many times, we get complacent in our attitude about life. We claim: "if it ain't broke don't fix it." We remain content to stay in our lane or stick to what we know; we don't ever want to make waves. Yet, we often lament that nothing changes in our lives and that we can't ever seem to get ahead, leaving us unfulfilled and uninspired. Repeatedly doing the same thing the same way but expecting a different outcome is popularly described as "insanity." Jesus knows that living under God's authority requires making a life change. His ministry inspires this transformation.

As a prophet, He challenges people with unpopular spiritual truths. As the Son of God, He offers the kingdom of heaven to those who repent. As the Son of God, He offers forgiveness to those who rejected Him because they could not see beyond the man.

Jesus calls all kinds of people to be disciples. Simon Peter and Andrew were motivated to answer the call, and they willingly left their comfort zone for Jesus. They did not make excuses about the inconvenience of following Him. Instead, they acted immediately. Jesus calls each of us to follow Him, and to use all that we have for the kingdom of heaven. When He asks us to serve Him, we must be like the disciples. We must act immediately.

Has a reluctant spirit hindered you from responding to Jesus? Are you uncomfortable changing the way you do things, yet get frustrated when nothing changes for the better in your life? When Jesus calls, how will you answer?

Application for Activation

How is Jesus calling you to work as His disciple? We can use perspective and skills we already possess to share the Good News of salvation through Christ Jesus.

• Ask God to show you how to do more in casting your net as a "fisher of people."

• Do you have access to social media? Use this platform to reach out to others.

• Pray for those who may reject you. Pray for God to send someone from whom they will receive His truth.

• Examine your discipleship. Are you content with going along to get along? Do you need to change the way you are doing things to become a more effective disciple for Jesus?

Follow the Spirit

What God wants me to do:

_____

_____

_____

_____

Remember Your Thoughts

Special insights I have learned:

_____

_____

_____

_____

More Light on the Text

Matthew 4:12–22

12 Now when Jesus had heard that John was cast into prison, he departed into Galilee; 13 And leaving Nazareth, he came and dwelt in Capernaum, which is upon the sea coast, in the borders of Zabulon and Nephthalim:

John the Baptist was Jesus' cousin, and as we learn from the beginning of Luke (Luke 1:39–56), their families were close. John the Baptist baptized Jesus, he was the forerunner of Jesus, and he publicly acknowledged that Jesus was not just his younger cousin but the Lamb of God and the Messiah who would take away the sins of the world.

John the Baptist was widely recognized as a prophet in first century Judea after nearly 400 years of there being no prominent prophet in Israel following the death of Malachi. John proclaimed that everyone should repent and return to God's ways rather than the ways of the Roman Empire and its idolatry. Because of his influence, the religious and political leaders hesitated to kill John for fear of inciting rebellion. However, they wanted to silence him and preserve their reputations. The compromise was to place John in prison. Jesus—tested in the wilderness by Satan, and indwelled by the Holy Spirit—walked into his place as the preeminent prophet in Judea. Jesus journeys from His hometown in Nazareth to another part of the Galilean region, a city called Capernaum that becomes a second home and home base for His ministry.

14 That it might be fulfilled which was spoken by Esaias the prophet, saying, 15 The land of Zabulon, and the land of Nephthalim, by the way of the sea, beyond Jordan, Galilee of the Gentiles; 16 The people which sat in darkness saw great light; and to them which sat in the region and shadow of death light is sprung up. 17 From that time Jesus began to preach, and to say, Repent: for the kingdom of heaven is at hand.

Matthew has already referenced Jesus' fulfillment of several prophecies (1:23; 2:6, 15, 18, 23). Now he makes it clear that Jesus beginning His public ministry with the power of the Holy Spirit in Capernaum is yet another fulfillment of biblical prophecy (cf. Isaiah 9:1–2)—that the land of Zebulon and Naphtali, two tribes of Israel that were in darkness and under the judgment of God, would be made glorious because of God's mercy. Then Jesus preaches that all Israel should repent (Gk. *metanoeo*, **meh-ta-no-EH-oh**, rethink or change one's mind) and turn back to God and away from idols because the kingdom of God is "at hand" or near. Jesus' exhortation is clear: The old way of being under the bondage of sin is done; renew your minds and recommit to God because the reign of God is here!

18 And Jesus, walking by the Sea of Galilee, saw two brethren, Simon called Peter, and Andrew his brother, casting a net into the sea: for they were fishers.

In these verses, we see the power of Jesus' call and the type of obedience He desires. This passage is the only extended report, in the Gospel of Matthew, of how Jesus chose His disciples. There is a brief description of how Matthew, the tax collector, was called (Matthew 9:9). But there is no mention of the calling of the other seven disciples. Peter and Andrew, two brothers, were described as men who were making a decent living as professional fishermen. They were, no doubt, good at what they were doing and felt confident in their abilities. They were about the business of fishing, casting their nets into the sea, when Jesus appeared.

When Jesus arrives, our lives are never the same. The plans we have, the direction we think our lives are going in, can suddenly take a very dramatic turn. It's exciting and a great adventure to meet Jesus and to hear His new plans for us, but it takes courage and faith to follow Him whether we are new disciples or have walked with Him for years.

19 And He saith unto them, Follow me, and I will make you fishers of men. 20 And they straightway left their nets and followed him.

Jesus found them at their trade and indicated to them that the same abilities they used to lure and catch fish, they would be able to use to bring people into the kingdom of God. Even though they may not have been as proficient and confident in their ability to do that, He assured them He would "make" them able to do the job.

Jesus is the one who makes all of His followers able to do the good works they are called to do. He equips and prepares us. He said to fishermen, "Follow me." This is translated from the

Greek word *deute* (**DYOO-teh**), which means "come." It is a command or exhortation. Jesus clearly expected them to obey and follow Him.

They responded, the text says, "straightway," translated from the Greek word *eutheos* (**ew-THEH-oce**), which means "immediately." They left their nets and followed Him. Some Christians today are called to do exactly that, to leave their jobs and professions and follow Jesus' call into ministry. Seminaries are full of "second career" students who have left comfortable positions in law, advertising, teaching, journalism, and other careers to become fishers of people. But even those Christians who are not called to leave everything behind and start over are called to follow Jesus. We are all to be evangelists, drawing people into the kingdom, through the way we live, the way we serve, and the people we are. The type of obedience Jesus wants is just what these disciples immediately exemplify. Sometimes, our tendency is to wait or put it off until everything is right, but we should choose to follow the Lord immediately, because tomorrow might be too late.

21 And going on from thence, he saw other two brethren, James the son of Zebedee, and John his brother, in a ship with Zebedee their father, mending their nets; and he called them. 22 And they immediately left the ship and their father and followed him.

Jesus goes on to call two more disciples, James and John, who are also referred to as the Sons of Thunder (Mark 3:17). They, too, were in their boat, doing work related to their profession as fishermen alongside their father. But when Jesus called, they responded immediately and left the boat. Matthew mentions that they left their father and followed Jesus. Here is an illustration of how following Jesus can sometimes cause stress in your family.

Many scholars have struggled, trying to figure out the meaning behind Jesus' words that He "came not to send peace, but a sword… to set a man at variance against his father, and the daughter against her mother" (from Matthew 10:34–36). Or when He said that if you do not "hate" your mother and father and all your relatives, you "cannot be" His disciple (Luke 14:26). Basically, scholars have agreed that Jesus was establishing the kingdom as a priority for His followers. This priority takes precedence over these all-important family relationships. In most cultures there is great respect for elders and families, and this is a very good thing. We do want to love our families and give of ourselves to them. But nothing, and no one should stand in the way of following Jesus. The Father to whom we owe our greatest loyalty and obedience is our heavenly Father. Sometimes, like James and John, part of our call may mean leaving behind our family of origin, comfort, and familiarity to follow God's call for our lives.

Sources:

Blount, Brian K. *True to Our Native Land: An African American New Testament Commentary.* Minneapolis, MN: Fortress Press, 2007.

Coogan, Michael D. *The Oxford History of the Biblical World.* New York, NY: Oxford University Press Inc., 2001.

Ehrman, Bart D. *The New Testament: A Historical Introduction to the Early Christian Writings* (4th edition). New York, NY: Oxford University Press Inc., 2000, 2004, 2008.

Hason, K. C. *The Galilean Fishing Economy and the Jesus Tradition.* Biblical Theology Bulletin: Journal of Bible and Culture. Vol. 27, No. 3. (1997), 99-111.

Life Application Study Bible. Grand Rapids, MI: Zondervan and Tyndale House Publishers, Inc. 2011.

The New Interpreter's Study Bible. Nashville, TN: Abingdon Press, 2003.

Ryken, L.J. Wilhoit, and T. Longman III. *Dictionary of Biblical Imagery.* Downers Grove, IL: InterVarsity Press, 1998.

Say It Correctly

Naphtali(m). **NAF**-tuh-lee(m).
Zebulun. **ZEB**-yoo-luhn.
Zebedee. **ZEB**-i-dee.

Daily Bible Readings

MONDAY
Jethro Hears of the Egyptian Deliverance
(Exodus 18:1–9)

TUESDAY
Sustained by God
(Deuteronomy 8:1–11)

WEDNESDAY
God Speaks to Disciples
(Luke 9:28–36)

THURSDAY
Well Pleased
(Matthew 3:11–17)

FRIDAY
Tempted in the Wilderness
(Matthew 4:1–11)

SATURDAY
Good News and Healing
(Matthew 4:23–25)

SUNDAY
Called and Enabled for Ministry
(Matthew 4:12–22)

Notes

_____

_____

_____

_____

Teaching Tips

Words You Should Know

A. Disciple *mathetes* (Gk.)—Learner who is under a teacher.

B. Apostle *apostolos* (Gk.)—One who is sent out on a mission, an ambassador of a sender.

Teacher Preparation

Unifying Principle—Called for Purpose. When people have discovered a greater purpose in life, they may be uncertain of what to do with that discovery. Where can persons find directions for implementing that greater purpose to benefit others? Jesus gave the first disciples direction to heal and witness to the "lost" persons of their shared community.

A. Read the Bible Background and Devotional Readings.

B. Pray for your students and lesson clarity.

C. Read the lesson Scripture in multiple translations.

D. Option: Have two students play the role of missionaries in an area that is resistant to the Gospel. One of them believes it is time to "shake the dust off their feet" and go elsewhere; the other believes fruitful work can yet be done where they are. Let them discuss the pros and cons of leaving and staying.

O—Open the Lesson

A. Begin the class with prayer.

B. Have the students read the Aim for Change.

C. Have the students read the In Focus story.

D. Ask students how events named in the story can weigh on their hearts and how they can view these events from a theological perspective.

P—Present the Scriptures

A. Read the Focal Verses and discuss the Background and The People, Places, and Times sections.

B. Have the class share what Scriptures stand out for them and why, with particular emphasis on today's context.

E—Explore the Meaning

A. Use In Depth or More Light on the Text to help provide more in-depth discussion of the lesson text.

B. Discuss the Liberating Lesson and Application for Activation sections.

N—Next Steps for Application

A. Summarize the value of knowing our mission to share the kingdom of God with others.

B. End class with a commitment to pray for the sick, those in bondage, and those in need.

Worship Guide

For the Superintendent or Teacher
Theme: Call and Mission
Song: "I Love to Tell the Story"
Devotional Reading: Matthew 15:21–28

Call and Mission

Bible Background • MATTHEW 10
Printed Text • MATTHEW 10:1–15 | Devotional Reading • MATTHEW 15:21–28

—————————— Aim for Change ——————————

By the end of the lesson, we will: RECOGNIZE the disciples' mission in Matthew 10; IDENTIFY challenges that we might experience in fulfilling Christ's mission for the church; and PREPARE for greater participation in the mission of the church.

——————————  In Focus ——————————

The members of Lakeside Church called themselves congregants, but Pastor Roberts was uneasy with this language. It bothered him that people thought the church was a place for releasing personal problems as opposed to being a community where all could participate in community service, social justice, and worship.

After a few weeks of teaching discipleship, Pastor Roberts thought it would be time to put teachings into practice. "We are disciples and we are called to make more disciples and do greater works for the kingdom of God," he explained. "Church is not just a slot machine or a microwave; everyone has a role to play. Today, we aren't going to have worship as usual. We're going to have a special Evangelism Day. We are going to reach out and invite people to come worship with us. If the people want to know more, then tell them more. If not, then keep it moving. Those who have the true desire to come will."

Together, the disciples of Lakeside Church went out into the community, shared the Good News of Jesus, and invited more people to worship. Some refused to hear what they had to say, and others received them well. The following Sunday, fifty new people came to church and thirty joined.

How could you see yourself more as a disciple of Jesus Christ? Although there are challenges, what are some of the rewards in making more disciples?

—————————— Keep in Mind ——————————

"And when he had called unto him his twelve disciples, he gave them power against unclean spirits, to cast them out, and to heal all manner of sickness and all manner of disease"
(Matthew 10:1, KJV).

"Jesus called his twelve disciples together and gave them authority to cast out evil spirits and to heal every kind of disease and illness" (Matthew 10:1, NLT).

Focal Verses

KJV Matthew 10:1 And when he had called unto him his twelve disciples, he gave them power against unclean spirits, to cast them out, and to heal all manner of sickness and all manner of disease.

2 Now the names of the twelve apostles are these; The first, Simon, who is called Peter, and Andrew his brother; James the son of Zebedee, and John his brother;

3 Philip, and Bartholomew; Thomas, and Matthew the publican; James the son of Alphaeus, and Lebbaeus, whose surname was Thaddaeus;

4 Simon the Canaanite, and Judas Iscariot, who also betrayed him.

5 These twelve Jesus sent forth, and commanded them, saying, Go not into the way of the Gentiles, and into any city of the Samaritans enter ye not:

6 But go rather to the lost sheep of the house of Israel.

7 And as ye go, preach, saying, The kingdom of heaven is at hand.

8 Heal the sick, cleanse the lepers, raise the dead, cast out devils: freely ye have received, freely give.

9 Provide neither gold, nor silver, nor brass in your purses,

10 Nor scrip for your journey, neither two coats, neither shoes, nor yet staves: for the workman is worthy of his meat.

11 And into whatsoever city or town ye shall enter, enquire who in it is worthy; and there abide till ye go thence.

12 And when ye come into an house, salute it.

13 And if the house be worthy, let your peace come upon it: but if it be not worthy, let your peace return to you.

NLT Matthew 10:1 Jesus called his twelve disciples together and gave them authority to cast out evil spirits and to heal every kind of disease and illness.

2 Here are the names of the twelve apostles: first, Simon (also called Peter), then Andrew (Peter's brother), James (son of Zebedee), John (James's brother),

3 Philip, Bartholomew, Thomas, Matthew (the tax collector), James (son of Alphaeus), Thaddaeus,

4 Simon (the zealot), Judas Iscariot (who later betrayed him).

5 Jesus sent out the twelve apostles with these instructions: "Don't go to the Gentiles or the Samaritans,

6 but only to the people of Israel—God's lost sheep.

7 Go and announce to them that the Kingdom of Heaven is near.

8 Heal the sick, raise the dead, cure those with leprosy, and cast out demons. Give as freely as you have received!

9 Don't take any money in your money belts—no gold, silver, or even copper coins.

10 Don't carry a traveler's bag with a change of clothes and sandals or even a walking stick. Don't hesitate to accept hospitality, because those who work deserve to be fed.

11 Whenever you enter a city or village, search for a worthy person and stay in his home until you leave town.

12 When you enter the home, give it your blessing.

13 If it turns out to be a worthy home, let your blessing stand; if it is not, take back the blessing.

14 If any household or town refuses to welcome you or listen to your message, shake its dust from your feet as you leave.

14 And whosoever shall not receive you, nor hear your words, when ye depart out of that house or city, shake off the dust of your feet.

15 Verily I say unto you, It shall be more tolerable for the land of Sodom and Gomorrha in the day of judgment, than for that city.

15 I tell you the truth, the wicked cities of Sodom and Gomorrah will be better off than such a town on the judgment day.

The People, Places, and Times

The Disciples. The disciples in today's text are Jesus' inner circle, those who were willing to drop everything and walk with Jesus. The Gospels portray the disciples as those who were dedicated to Jesus, although they were often slow to learn and quick to retaliate—not unlike the rest of us. Since God used such unlikely people to turn the world upside down after Christ's resurrection and the advent of the Holy Spirit, we should be encouraged, especially in times when we may feel we do not merit the title of disciple. In today's lesson we see that in spite of immaturity and imperfections, the disciples had a strong desire to learn from Jesus and follow Him, and Jesus entrusted them to share His message and ministry.

Background

Jesus continued His public ministry throughout Galilee, teaching in the synagogues, proclaiming the Good News of the kingdom of heaven, and healing all types of diseases and sicknesses. His fame and reputation grew throughout the lands, drawing crowds of thousands of followers everywhere He went. Jesus' message was consistent: He came not to abolish the Law, but to fulfill it (Matthew 5:17). As Jesus' reputation grew among those oppressed and maligned, so did the number of His enemies. The religious leaders who should have recognized Jesus as the Messiah were particularly uncomfortable with His popularity, miracles, teaching, and authority. Jesus and His

five disciples were teaching that the kingdom of heaven is the fulfillment of God's promises: where justice prevails and where God favors the meek. Driven by His compassion and concern for the "sheep without a shepherd," Jesus prayed to God for more laborers to send into this plentiful harvest of souls in need of salvation (Matthew 9:36–37). God added more disciples in answer to Jesus' prayers for more workers.

At-A-Glance

1. The Disciples (Matthew 10:1–4)
2. The Mission of the Twelve (vv. 5–10)
3. Worthy of the Word (vv. 11–15)

In Depth

1. The Disciples (Matthew 10:1–4)

Jesus established His front-line mission team with twelve men from all walks of life. Among the disciples are four fishermen, a zealous political activist, and a tax collector. These were ordinary men who became extraordinary because of Jesus. They had diverse backgrounds and experiences: Some were outcasts of society, some were despised, and at least one was greedy and self-absorbed. But the one characteristic they had in common was their willingness to follow Jesus.

The men were called to be disciples—from the Greek word meaning "learner" or "follower." They were learning from Jesus how to be strong ambassadors for the kingdom of heaven; they were following Christ Jesus in the transformation of lives.

Jesus' twelve disciples had special significance to the Jewish audience. In a historical context, twelve is tied to God's covenant with His people—Israel started out as twelve tribes headed by twelve patriarchs. Now, God was bringing in a new kingdom for His people, one in which those who repented and followed Jesus would "sit upon twelve thrones, judging the twelve tribes of Israel" (Matthew 19:28).

When Christ calls you to follow Him, how do you respond?

2. The Mission of the Twelve (vv. 5–10)

Jesus charged His disciples to emulate His own ministry. He was sent to "the lost sheep of the house of Israel" (Matthew 15:24) and referred to those in the crowds who followed Him as "sheep without a shepherd" (Matthew 9:36). Remaining faithful to God's covenant with Israel, Jesus sends the disciples to go only to the Jews in this instance, although later commands them to go to the Gentiles. Centuries before, the Jews had been chosen to tell the world, including the Gentiles, about the reign of God (Isaiah 49:6; Micah 4:2; Zechariah 8:23). The disciples were to: deliver the message that the kingdom of heaven is near; perform the tasks of healing the sick, raising the dead, curing diseases, and driving out demons; and trust God, taking no money during their mission. Finally, Jesus sends them out with a principle of generosity to follow as they minister to others. He reminds them to freely bless others as God had freely blessed them.

How has God prepared you for your assignment? How will you bless others as God has blessed you?

3. Worthy of the Word (vv. 11–15)

The disciples were instructed to minister to those worthy to receive the proclaimed Word. The worthiness of a person was determined by their willingness to hear the Good News of the kingdom of God. Turning disciples away was equivalent to rejecting the Messiah.

Jesus also prepared the disciples for anticipated rejection. If they were not welcomed, Jesus told them to leave and shake the dust from their feet, a gesture that was triggered by people making the wrong choice not to receive Jesus. He told the disciples that those who rejected the Word would be worse off than Sodom and Gomorrah, cities destroyed by God for their wickedness.

Jesus offers the opportunity for salvation to all of us, and He cautions us not to ignore His call. The opportunity may not come again.

Are you receptive to the teachings from God? How do you respond when others reject your efforts to share Jesus' teachings?

Search the Scriptures

1. What authority did Jesus give to the twelve disciples (Matthew 10:1)?

2. Who were the disciples instructed to avoid on their mission (v. 5)?

3. What were the disciples to do if a home was deemed worthy of receiving God's Word (v. 13)?

4. What were the disciples to do if a home did not welcome them (v. 14)?

Discuss the Meaning

1. In the text, Jesus gives the church the mission of making more disciples. How are you contributing to the mission of the kingdom? Has anything prevented you from living out the mission and the call to make more disciples?

2. How do we make disciples in the 21st century? How do we deal with it when people reject our message today?

Liberating Lesson

Once we commit to following Jesus and walking in our purpose for Him, we must also be prepared for criticism and disapproval. Often, this negative feedback can be debilitating and cause us to doubt our call and purpose. We need to be aware that sometimes criticism and judgment against us really has nothing to do with us. Although some criticism is unavoidable and sometimes hurtful, we can encourage ourselves to remember that God is our defense and vindicator, to keep our peace, and to pray for those who unjustly criticize us. Criticism can be a blessing or a curse, depending on how we respond to it.

In today's lesson, Jesus sends the disciples out as materially poor messengers who were entirely dependent on God and the generosity of others. They would face criticism and rejection from some of those they visited even though they were truly messengers of the Master. It is important to recognize that Jesus was homeless, and the disciples who followed Him were sent with no material possessions but had access to the kingdom of God. Some would have rejected the disciples and missed the power of God showing up in their lives simply because they were fixated on how the messengers looked or bothered by sharing with strangers. We must be cautious not to write off those who appear to be materially lacking as less important or not worthy of our attention, because God could be positioning them to be His messengers and ministers of His love and power for us.

Application for Activation

Jesus called His twelve disciples. He did not draft them, or bargain for them, or even accept them as volunteers. Jesus chose them to serve Him in a very special way. He used their gifts, experience, knowledge, and obedience to transform lives and proclaim the kingdom of heaven.

Jesus calls us today, and we, too, can choose to follow Him.

• Know that God can use anyone, no matter how insignificant he or she may appear to be.

• Remember that God does not always call the qualified, but He will always qualify the called.

• Rejoice in the knowledge that God's message of salvation is for all people, regardless of race, gender, or national origin.

• Bless others. God has freely showered us with His blessings, and we should generously give of our time, love, and possessions.

Follow the Spirit

What God wants me to do:

_____

_____

_____

Remember Your Thoughts

Special insights I have learned:

_____

_____

_____

More Light on the Text

Matthew 10:1–15

1 And when he had called unto him his twelve disciples, he gave them power against unclean spirits, to cast them out, and to heal all manner of sickness and all manner of disease. 2 Now the names of the twelve

apostles are these; The first, Simon, who is called Peter, and Andrew his brother; James the son of Zebedee, and John his brother; 3 Philip, and Bartholomew; Thomas, and Matthew the publican; James the son of Alphaeus, and Lebbaeus, whose surname was Thaddaeus; 4 Simon the Canaanite, and Judas Iscariot, who also betrayed him.

As He traveled around Galilee, Jesus spoke about the need for more workers in the kingdom in light of the enormity of the harvest (Matthew 9:35–36). As an initial response to that need, Jesus empowers the twelve disciples to extend His ministry. The twelve are the beginning of a stream of workers in the church who will continue the work of proclaiming the presence and displaying the power of the kingdom of God. Matthew's first mention of "the twelve" leads parenthetically to the listing of their names prior to their instructions.

An important feature of this list is its diversity. Jesus chose His disciples from a variety of backgrounds and life experiences. It is notable that Matthew—a tax collector in the employment of Rome, and as such regarded as a traitor—was in the same group with Simon the Canaanite, elsewhere called Simon the Zealot and presumably a nationalist. Even then, as we do today, people associated based on their political leanings, and each person refused to see the other as a true believer. In the presence of Jesus, men who would otherwise have been enemies became friends willing to sacrifice for one another and live together embracing one another. Simon the Zealot and Matthew the tax collector would have been bitter enemies outside of the mission to be Jesus' disciples: Zealots were much like protesters who were open to violence against the state in remaining loyal to their Judaism, and tax collectors were seen as traitors to their people for position and money. Jesus' power and teaching should bring

people together rather than tear them apart as our religious traditions so often do.

The disciples' apparent common characteristic was that none of them was privileged or from backgrounds of high socioeconomic status. They were ordinary people with neither academic attainments nor social pedigrees and advantages, but through Jesus they would do extraordinary things. Doubtless, the Lord sees in every person, not only what that person is, but also what He can make her or him. These disciples were chosen not only for what they were, but also for what they were capable of becoming under Christ's influence and in His power. Therefore, no one can say, "I have nothing to offer." We all have something to offer to Jesus, and He can transform and use it for His glory and greatness.

The disciples were able to support, protect, and empower each other better than if each went alone. There is definitely an allusion to the Law where at least two witnesses were required for an evidence to be credible (Deuteronomy 19:15). Furthermore, by staying together in smaller rather than larger groups, the disciples were able to maximize their reach. Timeless principles for discipleship and missions appear here. We need each other, someone with whom we can be close in fellowship, ministry and accountability.

The choice of twelve disciples is symbolic particularly in the correspondence of its number to the twelve tribes of Israel (cf. 19:28) and in its suggestion as the fulfillment of the hope of Israel. That they were twelve might also suggest that Jesus pulls together a community of followers, in conscious opposition to the current leadership of Israel, as the new recipients of God's revelation and grace.

Here the Twelve are called apostles for the first and only time in Matthew with reference at once to the immediate minor mission and to the later great one. The Greek word *apostolos* (**ah-POE-stow-loce**, literally: one who is sent out) refers generally to one sent on a mission, who represents and shares the authority of the one who sends. It is used here with specific reference to the original twelve apostles. The force of the word here is "commissioned," in this case by Christ. As apostles, they are the envoys of the Lord, with profound implications for their life, ministry, and message. The disciples—who had been with Jesus for some time—had touched, talked, shared, communed, prayed, meditated, and fellowshipped with Him. They had shared and been taught the Scriptures by Him and probably had been taught how to preach and teach. They had certainly witnessed His preaching and teaching and how He went about both.

It is also noteworthy that the Twelve are called disciples in verse 1 and apostles in verse 2. This is probably to highlight or accentuate that we must first be learners before we become teachers—first taught of God, before being sent of God. Even so, we must remain as disciples regardless of our calling. Discipleship is lifelong, and not a mere three-week instructional program.

The ministry is not a profession; it is a calling and a commission from Christ. Those who choose to be ministers without a true call and commissioning of the Lord will find themselves ministering primarily in their own strength. Such people will also find their heart empty, feeling the constant pressure of having to come up with ideas and programs through human ability. Jesus not only called the Twelve to a mission, He also gave them power to do it. The same principle holds true today: Whom God calls, God equips. Christ gave His messengers power (NLT: authority). The Greek word for authority is *exousia* (**ek-soo-SEE-ah**), which involves the right to regulate or control the activities of one or more individuals. Your equipping may not be completely evident before the ministry begins,

but it will be evident along the way. The authority and power given by the Lord has nothing to do with social position, wealth, fame, or earthly dominion. The Lord's servant is given power to reach and help people. This is an important lesson for the motives and actions of God's servants, both lay and clergy. Here the authority is over "unclean spirits," a designation that is often used for demons. The Greek words *nosos* (**NO-soce**) and *malakia* (**mah-lah-KEE-ah**), translated respectively as disease and sickness, are similar; although the latter is more general, both describe illness. The point is simply that Jesus has invested the disciples with power over every kind of ailment whether physical or spiritual.

5 These twelve Jesus sent forth, and commanded them, saying, Go not into the way of the Gentiles, and into any city of the Samaritans enter ye not: 6 But go rather to the lost sheep of the house of Israel.

When Jesus "commanded" (Gk. *paragello*, **pah-ron-GHEL-low**) the Twelve, His giving them orders has important significance. Among its several usages is the idea of a military command. Obedience is not an option. The nuance of this word compared to its synonyms brings out the continuing nature of these commands. These are the things anyone who calls himself an apostle must do, not just some commands Jesus once gave to these twelve men.

Jesus now tells them where to go, and where not to. Their mission is restricted to the lost house of Israel. At first sight, limiting the mission to Israel appears to contradict or conflict with the Great Commission in 28:18–20 where the command extends to all nations and all people. There is no contradiction. As Jesus soon says, there is an anticipation of the disciples going into Gentile territory (10:18). Here it is a matter of strategy and priority. Jesus' commands fit the larger pattern of His own ministry prior to His death. They also match the missionary priority Paul maintained throughout Acts and articulated to the church of Rome (Romans 1:16). The "lost sheep" of Israel does not refer to a portion of the nation but to all the people (cf. Matthew 9:36; Jeremiah 50:6). The sending of these twelve was a conscious expansion of that work. Now the work of Jesus was being done by many more than simply Jesus. God's plan was to reach the whole world, but beginning with Israel. There was certainly enough work to do among the lost sheep of the house of Israel to keep the Twelve busy until God directly commanded them to expand their ministry. They have a clear, limited objective.

7 And as ye go, preach, saying, The kingdom of heaven is at hand. 8a Heal the sick, cleanse the lepers, raise the dead, cast out devils:

Having identified the people to be reached by the mission, Jesus now clearly spells out the mission's purpose. The fundamental objective of the mission is to proclaim the dawning of the kingdom of heaven. The disciples were not to go to entertain; they were to proclaim the nearness of the kingdom. The verb for preach (Gk. *kerusso*, **kay-ROO-so**) has thus far been restricted in its usage only in connection with the kingdom (Matthew 3:1–2; 4:17, 23; 9:35). The disciples both had a message to preach and a power to display. In this, they were truly followers of their Master. They must go in confidence, expecting God to work.

They are to go to the lost, the distressed and the poor. Often the poor, the needy, and the marginalized respond most readily to the Good News, while the affluent isolate themselves.

The command to proclaim the nearness of the kingdom is followed by four imperatives in verse 8. Healing of the sick, raising of the dead, cleansing of lepers, and casting out demons are part of the Good News of the kingdom—indeed, it is that which they exemplify and symbolize. Matthew has given examples of each of these from Jesus' own ministry (cf. in order: 8:15; 8:3; 9:25; 8:32). There is no indication that the commands were intended or originally understood in any other way than literally (cf. the raising of the dead in Acts 9:36–43; 20:7–12). There is also no indication that these miracles have ceased with the first disciples. No scriptural warrant exists to suggest that this authority has been permanently withdrawn. It is wise for Christians today to both believe in God's power to do such miracles through His people, while remaining careful and not too quick to believe unsubstantiated reports of such miracles.

8b freely ye have received, freely give. 9 Provide neither gold, nor silver, nor brass in your purses, 10 Nor scrip for your journey, neither two coats, neither shoes, nor yet staves: for the workman is worthy of his meat.

The blessings of discipleship come solely by grace and as such must be similarly imparted (v. 8b). Jesus charged His disciples nothing, and He expected them to minister unto others without charge. This is the foundational principle for the commands that follow. Disciples were to be dependent on God, not on their own wealth or possessions, for necessities. There is to be no charge for the proclamation or the accompanying healings. As the disciples received "freely," so they are to give freely. All the resources the disciples need—money, travel provisions, and extra clothing—will be given to them (v. 11) by those who accept their ministry (vv. 9–10). The disciples are not to profit from the Gospel, but their basic needs are to be met. Accordingly, they are not to take with them money (silver, gold, or brass) for their belts or even bother with the ordinary things a traveler takes along: a knapsack (KJV: "scrip"), an extra shirt, a pair of sandals, or a staff. They are to be totally committed to the cause and its urgency, and in that total, unrestricted commitment to rely exclusively on the provision the Lord will make through those who receive them (cf. 6:25–34). They should expect God to meet their needs, without taking undue concern for their own needs. Furthermore, they should expect that God would normally meet their needs through the inspired hospitality of others.

Matthew emphasizes the simplicity, austerity, and urgency of the mission. The point of Jesus' strictness is not to leave His disciples deprived and defenseless but dependent on others for their nourishment in every area of life. We must recognize that there are Scriptures that recognize dependence both on others' support and on one's own resources earned through a different trade (cf. 1 Corinthians 9:1–18; Philippians 4:10–19). One must not draw a line in the sand here. Decisions must be made based on what advances the Gospel in an honorable way in any given context. Doubtless, a serious danger of paid ministry is that preachers will tailor their message to suit their financiers or benefactors. Even though the Twelve could expect the people they serve to meet their needs, they should never require payment in order to meet their needs. The foundational principle was "freely you have received, freely give."

11 And into whatsoever city or town ye shall enter, enquire who in it is worthy; and there abide till ye go thence. 12 And when ye come into an house, salute it. 13 And if the house be worthy, let your peace come upon it: but if it be not worthy, let your peace return to you. 14 And whosoever shall not receive you, nor hear your words, when ye depart out of that house or city, shake off the dust of your feet. 15 Verily I say unto you, It shall be more tolerable for the land of Sodom and Gomorrha in the day of judgment, than for that city.

As they enter each new location, the disciples must look for those who are "worthy." "Worthy" in verse 11 is the same word translated "worth" in verse 10 and "deserving" in verse 13. Here, worthiness does not imply a moral quality but openness to the message and ministry of the disciples. Such "worthiness" referred to here is demonstrated by the receptivity shown to the disciples and their message. In light of verse 14, the term must refer to the response of welcoming the disciples, not to any necessary merit or virtue in the individuals. The worthy person is the one who provides hospitality to the disciples, and they are to remain with that person during the time of their ministry in that community. Such people will provide the characteristic hospitality given to friends and respected people who traveled in the ancient Roman world: good food and a bed. This hospitality proved vital, given the generally nefarious state of public lodging—hotbeds of theft and prostitution.

The apostles are to approach all communities in peaceable ways and for peaceful purposes. If they are not received, they are to withdraw. The disciples were to be prepared for a mixed response to their message. Not all would receive the Good News; indeed some would be hostile toward it. God will deal with the hard-hearted cities who refuse to come to Him, just as He will provide for those who serve Him. Shaking the dust off the feet was an established symbol of rejection among many Gentile nations whenever they returned from foreign lands. This symbolic action by the apostles is now applied to Jewish cities. Rejecting the disciples' message is seen as a serious sin, indeed, worse even than the gross rebellion of Sodom and Gomorrah in Old Testament times (cf. Genesis 18:20–19:28). The increasing culpability of such rejection probably stemmed from the fact that God's revelation in Christ was that much more clear and immediate. Jesus' strategy and attitude for dealing with those who reject His followers and their message is still appropriate for Christians today: Do not take judgments into your own hands but leave the fate of those who reject the message of Christ in the hands of God (v. 15).

Sources:

Barclay, William. *The Gospel of Matthew*, Vol. 1, The Daily Study Bible Series. Philadelphia, PA: The Westminster John Knox Press, 1976.

Blount, Brian K. *True to Our Native Land: An African American New Testament Commentary*, Minneapolis, MN: Fortress Press, 2007.

Blomberg, Craig. *Matthew*, Vol. 22, The New American Commentary. Nashville, TN: Broadman & Holman Publishers, 1992.

Clarke, Adam. *Commentary on the Bible*. G. Lane and P.P. Sandford, n.d.

Coogan, Michael D. *The Oxford History of the Biblical World*. New York, NY: Oxford University Press Inc., 2001.

Crosby, M.H. *House of Disciples: Church, Economics, and Justice in Matthew*. Maryknoll: Orbis, 1988.

Ehrman, Bart D. *The New Testament: A Historical Introduction to the Early Christian Writings*, 4th edition. New York, NY: Oxford University Press Inc., 2000, 2004, 2008.

Green, Michael. *The Message of Matthew: The Kingdom of Heaven*, The Bible Speaks Today, Leicester, England; Downers Grove, IL: InterVarsity Press, 2001.

Hagner, Donald A. *Matthew 1–13, Vol. 33A*. Word Biblical Commentary. Dallas, TX: Word, Inc., 1998.

The New Interpreter's Study Bible. Nashville TN: Abingdon Press. 2003.

Life Application Study Bible. Grand Rapids, MI: Zondervan and Tyndale House Publishers, Inc., 2011.

Ryken, Leland, James C. Wilhoit, and Tremper Longman III, eds. *Dictionary of Biblical Imagery*. Downers Grove IL, Inter Varsity Press, 1998.

Schweizer, E. *The Good News According to Matthew*. Richmond, VA: John Knox, 1975.

Daily Bible Readings

MONDAY
Jeremiah, Prophet to the Nations
(Jeremiah 1:4–10)

TUESDAY
Ananias Welcomes and Baptizes Saul
(Acts 9:10–19)

WEDNESDAY
Paul Called by a Vision
(Acts 16:6–10)

THURSDAY
Jesus Sends Out the Twelve
(Mark 6:7–13)

FRIDAY
A Great Harvest but Few Workers
(Matthew 9:35–38)

SATURDAY
Handling and Surviving Persecution
(Matthew 10:16–25)

SUNDAY
The Twelve Chosen and Commissioned
(Matthew 10:1–15)

Say It Correctly

Alphaeus. **AL**-fay-uhs.
Bartholomew. bar-**THAHL**-uh-myoo.
Canaanite. **KAY**-nuh-nait.
Gomorrah. guh-**MORE**-uh.
Lebbaeus. **LEB**-bee-uhs.
Thaddeus. **THAD-dee-uhs**.

Teaching Tips

Words You Should Know

A. Precious *barutimos* (Gk.)—Having heaviness, great value.

B. Waste *apoleia* (Gk.)—Utter destruction or ruin.

Teacher Preparation

Unifying Principle—Boldness Remembered. People often long remember bad deeds done to them and forget good ones. Will the evil that is done to harm always outweigh the good? The woman with the alabaster jar performed an act of kindness to Jesus that will be remembered wherever the Good News is told.

A. Read the Bible Background and Devotional Readings.

B. Pray for your students and lesson clarity.

C. Read the lesson Scripture in multiple translations.

D. Option: Discuss the difference between "waste" and "worth" as a class. If waste is giving too much for too little, what do the actions of the woman, the disciples—and even Caiaphas—say about what they believe Jesus is worth? What is Jesus worth to us?

O—Open the Lesson

A. Begin the class with prayer.

B. Have the students read the Aim for Change.

C. Have the students read the In Focus story.

D. Ask students how events named in the story can weigh on their hearts and how they can view these events from a theological perspective.

P—Present the Scriptures

A. Read the Focal Verses and discuss the Background and The People, Places, and Times sections.

B. Have the class share what Scriptures stand out for them and why, with particular emphasis on today's context.

E—Explore the Meaning

A. Use In Depth or More Light on the Text to help provide more in-depth discussion of the lesson text.

B. Discuss the Liberating Lesson and Application for Activation sections.

N—Next Steps for Application

A. Summarize the value of knowing God as Sovereign Creator.

B. End class with a commitment to pray for families, natural resources, and scientists.

Worship Guide

For the Superintendent or Teacher
Theme: Called to Remember
Song: "Alabaster Box"
Devotional Reading: Acts 2:29–39

Called to Remember

Bible Background • MATTHEW 26:1–13
Printed Text • MATTHEW 26:1–13 | Devotional Reading • ACTS 2:29–39

———————————— **Aim for Change** ————————————

By the end of this lesson we will: CONTRAST the deeds of the woman with the reactions of the disciples; APPRECIATE the woman's display of love for Jesus; and REMEMBER our call to share the Good News of Jesus Christ despite resistance or ridicule.

 **In Focus**

Rose was a longtime housekeeper at one of the fanciest hotels in the city. She was respected at her job and often trained the new maids. She lived in a small apartment with her husband, John, who was a mail carrier.

One day, Rose received a check for $100,000—the largest amount of money she had received in her life. According to the letter, a distant relative remembered her in a will and wanted Rose to use the funds as she wished. Rose prayed about it for a few weeks and decided to donate the money to her church's struggling capital campaign. John objected vehemently, and they argued about it several times. But her mind was made up.

Her pastor, Rev. Jamison, was so overjoyed that he called her to express his gratitude. "Mother Rose, I assure you, we will remember your sacrifice!"

Rose wasn't concerned with being remembered, but rather with doing what God had told her to do. She passed away later that year. Three years later, her church opened Rose's House, a temporary shelter for homeless young women with children on the same block as the church. Rev. Jamison invited John to the opening ceremony to tour the home and meet the women whom the church was helping. John stood on the porch and wept quietly, "I get it now, Rose. I really do."

God honors sacrifices made from a pure heart. How can remembering believers' good deeds bring others closer to Christ? Why does God call us to remember His good deeds?

———————————— **Keep in Mind** ————————————

"Verily I say unto you, Wheresoever this gospel shall be preached in the whole world, there shall also this, that this woman hath done, be told for a memorial of her" (Matthew 26:13, KJV).

"I tell you the truth, wherever the Good News is preached throughout the world, this woman's deed will be remembered and discussed" (Matthew 26:13, NLT).

Focal Verses

KJV **Matthew 26:1** And it came to pass, when Jesus had finished all these sayings, he said unto his disciples,

2 Ye know that after two days is the feast of the passover, and the Son of man is betrayed to be crucified.

3 Then assembled together the chief priests, and the scribes, and the elders of the people, unto the palace of the high priest, who was called Caiaphas,

4 And consulted that they might take Jesus by subtilty, and kill him.

5 But they said, Not on the feast day, lest there be an uproar among the people.

6 Now when Jesus was in Bethany, in the house of Simon the leper,

7 There came unto him a woman having an alabaster box of very precious ointment, and poured it on his head, as he sat at meat.

8 But when his disciples saw it, they had indignation, saying, To what purpose is this waste?

9 For this ointment might have been sold for much, and given to the poor.

10 When Jesus understood it, he said unto them, Why trouble ye the woman? for she hath wrought a good work upon me.

11 For ye have the poor always with you; but me ye have not always.

12 For in that she hath poured this ointment on my body, she did it for my burial.

13 Verily I say unto you, Wheresoever this gospel shall be preached in the whole world, there shall also this, that this woman hath done, be told for a memorial of her.

NLT **Matthew 26:1** When Jesus had finished saying all these things, he said to his disciples,

2 "As you know, Passover begins in two days, and the Son of Man will be handed over to be crucified."

3 At that same time the leading priests and elders were meeting at the residence of Caiaphas, the high priest,

4 plotting how to capture Jesus secretly and kill him.

5 "But not during the Passover celebration," they agreed, "or the people may riot."

6 Meanwhile, Jesus was in Bethany at the home of Simon, a man who had previously had leprosy.

7 While he was eating, a woman came in with a beautiful alabaster jar of expensive perfume and poured it over his head.

8 The disciples were indignant when they saw this. "What a waste!" they said.

9 "It could have been sold for a high price and the money given to the poor."

10 But Jesus, aware of this, replied, "Why criticize this woman for doing such a good thing to me?

11 You will always have the poor among you, but you will not always have me.

12 She has poured this perfume on me to prepare my body for burial.

13 I tell you the truth, wherever the Good News is preached throughout the world, this woman's deed will be remembered and discussed."

The People, Places, and Times

Bethany. It is the name of one of two cities often mentioned together in the Old Testament: Bethphage and Bethany. You would find Bethany about two miles along your way from Jerusalem to Jericho, on the southwestern side of the Mount of Olives (Mark 11:1). In

Bethany, some of the most important events of Jesus' life occurred. Martha, Mary, and Lazarus lived there, so this was where Jesus raised Lazarus from the dead (John 11). During Jesus' final week before He was crucified, He spent at least one night in Bethany (Matthew 21:17). Also, from a site near Bethany, Jesus ascended into heaven (Luke 24:50). The village of Bethany is also near the Jordan River where John the Baptist baptized people (John 1:28).

Caiaphas. He was the high priest before whom Jesus stood trial (Matthew 26:3, 57; John 18:13, 24). A member of the Sadducees and the Sanhedrin council, Caiaphas was the son-in-law and eventual successor of the high priest, Annas. He held the position from AD 18 until he was deposed by Vitellius, Pontius Pilate's successor, in AD 36–37. John records in his Gospel that Caiaphas judged it was expedient that Jesus should die for the people (John 11:49–52; 18:14).

Background

Matthew tells the account of the woman anointing Jesus with perfume just days before the Last Supper. Some scholars suggest Matthew and Mark may have chosen to relay this event before the Last Supper to contrast the complete devotion of Mary with the betrayal of Judas, the next event they recount in their Gospels. (John's Gospel also builds tension with Judas in this scene, but in a different way; see John 12:4.) Biblical scholars have concluded that this woman from Bethany who anointed Jesus was Mary, the sister of Martha and Lazarus (John 12:1–3). This event of Mary anointing Jesus soon before His death is recorded in Matthew, Mark, and John. Luke relates a similar story of Jesus being anointed with perfume by an unnamed sinful woman (Luke 7:36-50), but key details of the accounts differ, leading scholars to conclude that it was a separate event.

At-A-Glance

1. The Plot to Kill Jesus (Matthew 26:1–5)
2. The Expensive Oil Used to Bless Jesus (vv. 6–7)
3. The Disciples Did Not Understand the Blessing (vv. 8–9)
4. Jesus Explains the Blessing (vv. 10–13)

In Depth

1. The Plot to Kill Jesus (Matthew 26:1–5)

Jesus was a masterful teacher. He wanted His disciples and the people to know what would transpire during the end times, despite what the Pharisees taught (see Matthew 24–25). Jesus' teaching was so convicting and radically different from traditional laws that the religious leaders couldn't stand it any longer; they had to do something about it. They were determined to destroy Jesus at all costs, no matter what they had to do. Jesus knew that the time of His betrayal and crucifixion would come after the Feast of the Passover (Matthew 26:2). Therefore, He was determined to prepare His followers for the next phase of ministry. As Jesus spent intimate time with the disciples, His purpose was to give them hope even in the midst of confusing, troubling times.

Matthew says that the chief priests, scribes, and elders conferred together with Caiaphas, the high priest of Jerusalem, for the purpose of destroying Jesus. Matthew is seemingly pointing to the fulfillment of a prophecy attested by King David: "The kings of the earth set themselves, and the rulers take counsel together, against the Lord, and against His anointed..." (Psalm 2:2). The high priest supposedly served God and the people. But Caiaphas knew it would be expedient to get rid of Jesus if he was to maintain his position in the Jewish nation. How easy it is for people to manipulate the truth for the sake of expedience!

405

Like Caiaphas, people are often more concerned about position and prestige than they are about truth. The Pharisees were concerned about the holiday, and they intended to remain in good standing with the Jews, despite their hypocrisy (Matthew 26:5). However, the religious leaders didn't understand that God would use their actions to bring about His much higher plan in the lives of all people. Believers will face opposition; sometimes it may even come from within the body of Christ. We also know that whenever God begins to use a believer to promote His kingdom, Satan will plot to destroy that person. In spite of this, we can be encouraged because we know that God uses our enemies to bring about a much bigger plan in our lives. As the Apostle Paul affirms, everything works together for the good of people who love God and are called according to His purpose (Romans 8:28).

2. The Expensive Oil Used to Bless Jesus (vv. 6–7)

Some scholars suggest that Jesus was a guest of Simon because He had healed him of his leprosy. Although Matthew doesn't say specifically, there were likely many people at Simon's house with Jesus and His disciples, since that was how they ate meals in those days. Among Simon's guests was a woman whom God used to prepare Jesus for His burial, one of the most important events in history. Matthew doesn't give her identity, possibly because to him that is not as important as her actions. While Jesus and His disciples shared one of their last meals together, the woman must have understood the importance of this opportunity to honor Jesus (cf. John 12:1–2). She had in her possession an "alabaster box of very precious ointment" (Matthew 26:7). The word "alabaster" describes a very compact and translucent material made of hard calcium that was often used to make carved vases in which to store perfume. The vases are usually made without handles and can be easily broken to remove their contents.

Suddenly and without notice, the woman approached Jesus in the midst of supper and poured the anointing "perfume" on His head (v. 7). The woman did not ask Jesus for anything. Instead, she recognized the power of the moment and decided to give the Savior her best. How often do we come to Jesus asking Him to bless us instead of giving Him our best like this woman did? While the disciples and Simon's other guests ate their meals, the woman anointed the Lord recognizing Jesus as the Christ ("Anointed One") of Israel. Though Jesus had already shared what would happen to Him, it seems as though the disciples had no clue about what our Savior would endure—but this woman did!

3. The Disciples Did Not Understand the Blessing (vv. 8–9)

Scripture indicates that the disciples were not pleased with her actions. In fact, Matthew uses the word "indignation" (26:8) to describe their attitude, which was marked by anger, scorn, and contempt. The disciples demonstrated insensitivity to Jesus and this woman. When the disciples saw the oil being poured on Jesus, they murmured among themselves, convinced that the oil was wasted (v. 8). How foolish of them to think it was a waste to give the Lord the best! They thought that instead of being poured out on Jesus, the oil should have been sold and profits generated so they could feed and take care of the poor. John records the oil used as "about a pint of pure nard" (John 12:3), which was imported from India and worth about a year's wages. The disciples have a logical point to make, but they do not comprehend God's will.

4. Jesus Explains the Blessing (vv. 10–13)

Amid the disciples' criticism, Jesus quickly comes to the woman's defense because she was willing to share with and minister to Him. Jesus is so impressed that He uses the woman's actions as another teaching moment for the disciples. According to Moses, Israel would always have to minister to the poor and outcast (Deuteronomy 15:11), so the disciples' attitude did not carry weight with Jesus. In fact, Jesus made it clear that it was their duty to take care of the poor, whether or not the oil was sold for that purpose (Matthew 25:41–46). However, Jesus affirms that this woman recognized the moment and took time to honor Him. Jesus was about to give His life as a ransom for many; therefore, it was more important to prepare for His death than it was to sell oil. Because of this woman's sacrifice and service, Jesus declared that wherever the Gospel is preached, her example of sacrificial giving would be told in memory of her. That is, as the story is told of Jesus' death and burial, everyone would know that this woman of Bethany used her alabaster box of perfume to anoint the Lord (26:13).

Are we willing to give the Lord our best in service, worship, and obedience, or are we holding back a portion for our own needs?

Search the Scriptures

1. How did Jesus' disciples respond to the woman's anointing of Jesus (Matthew 26:8–9)?

2. What reason did Jesus give for the woman's anointing Him (v. 12)?

3. When Jesus talks about the Gospel being preached in the whole world, of what is He speaking (v. 13)?

Discuss the Meaning

1. How can we give a sacrificial offering to Jesus?

2. Are you willing to give your best to the Lord in service, worship, and obedience? Why? Why not?

Liberating Lesson

There are so many hurting people in our society—so many who need somebody to demonstrate love to them. There are many who need someone to give extravagantly out of their love for them and their love for Jesus. Jesus was the first to give extravagantly for us; He gave His life to give us life more abundantly. It is important not to misinterpret Jesus' comment about the poor being with us always, as He advises for us to give to the poor as though we are giving to Him (Matthew 25:40). One way we love Jesus extravagantly is by loving one another extravagantly, modeling His kind of love. It requires more focus on the people in front of you and honoring them than on the benefit you will receive from showing love. How can you love someone extravagantly this week? How will you share God's best with those in need?

Application for Activation

Spend time in prayer this week and ask the Lord to give you the grace to discern any objectors in your life, so you can love and forgive them. Also, ask the Lord to help you recognize people He will use to bless and minister to you in your time of need. Don't allow the fear of betrayal to destroy God-ordained friendships. Thank God every day for being in control of your life, and learn to see His hand in every situation you face.

Follow the Spirit

What God wants me to do:

_____

_____

_____

_____

Remember Your Thoughts

Special insights I have learned:

_____

_____

_____

_____

More Light on the Text

Matthew 26:1–13

1 And it came to pass, when Jesus had finished all these sayings, he said unto his disciples, 2 Ye know that after two days is the feast of the passover, and the Son of man is betrayed to be crucified.

Jesus has just finished giving the prophecy of the "Great Assize" or final judgment between the sheep and the goats. The feast of Passover that the Jews kept every year was approaching, and Jesus knew He was to be crucified during that feast. The tone of the narrative in Matthew has shifted from judgment on humanity based on their relationship with the Great King and Shepherd, to the holy Lamb of God taking on judgment on behalf of humanity. The disciples were warned numerous times that Jesus would die, which would have completely shocked them had they understood His message. Yet His disciples continued not to understand what Jesus was saying until He was betrayed and arrested.

3 Then assembled together the chief priests, and the scribes, and the elders of the people, unto the palace of the high priest, who was called Caiaphas, 4 And consulted that they might take Jesus by subtilty, and **kill him. 5 But they said, Not on the feast day, lest there be an uproar among the people.**

The assembly of the Sanhedrin, also translated "council," was made up of seventy members plus the high priest (who served as the president) and functioned as the Jewish supreme tribunal. Its jurisdiction at the time of Christ and during the Roman occupation was wide, covering civil and religious matters of Jewish Law and, to some degree, criminal matters. Capital cases, however, required the confirmation of the Roman procurator (John 18:31), though the procurator's judgment was usually in accordance with the demands of the Sanhedrin, which in Jewish Law had the power of life and death. The Sanhedrin had administrative authority and could make arrests and carry them out with its own law enforcement officers (cf. Matthew 26:47; Mark 14:43; Acts 4:1). The phrase "assembled together" (Gk. *sunechthesan*, **soon-EKH-theh-san**, "brought together") indicates that the council was summoned for an extraordinary session consisting of the chief priests, the scribes, and the elders of the people. Caiaphas was the high priest between AD 18 and 36. In that capacity and according to custom, he would preside over the session that would be summoned in his open courtyard.

The religious leaders had several obstacles to overcome before they could achieve their goal of having Jesus killed. First, Jesus was popular with the people; additionally, Roman law restricted the religious leaders' capacity to try capital cases. Their desire to eliminate Jesus necessitated that they devise a way to overcome these obstacles. The grammatical structure of the Greek word *sunebouleusanto* (**soo-neh-boo-LEW-san-toe**, which means "having planned together" and is translated as "consulted" here) conveys the meaning of pre-existing, deliberate, and consensual conspiracy to capture Jesus by subtlety (Gk. *dolos*, **DOE-loce**, guile or deception) and have Him killed. Any doubts the religious leaders might have had about Jesus' popularity among the people were powerfully erased by the events of the preceding days. The people had responded spontaneously to Jesus' triumphal entry into Jerusalem (Matthew 21:8–11), the cleansing of the Temple (vv. 15–16), and the debates with the Pharisees, Herodians, and Sadducees (22:15–46). Hence, the leaders were wary of possible mob action against them. They resolved not to arrest Jesus at the height of the Passover festivities, reasoning that to act otherwise would cause an uproar (Gk. *thorubos*, **THOW-roo-boce**, tumult or riot) among the people. Obviously, they were not acting in the people's best interests.

6 Now when Jesus was in Bethany, in the house of Simon the leper, 7 There came unto him a woman having an alabaster box of very precious ointment, and poured it on his head, as he sat at meat.

While the religious leaders of the day were busy at the high priest's palace plotting how to kill Jesus, the believers were at Bethany giving Him honor in the home of Simon the leper. New Testament scholars have worked very hard, without much agreement, to identify the particular Simon in whose home this gathering took place. It is likely that Simon was one of the many lepers Jesus cured during His earthly ministry. But what is important for us to note here is how Jesus—the King of kings—graciously relates to men of lowly position. Among the Jews, lepers were considered religiously and ceremonially unclean, and were therefore quarantined or avoided (Leviticus 13:1–46). As in many human societies even today, the social stigma that "clean" people imposed on lepers oftentimes remained even after the disease had been cured. Jesus did not just cure Simon of leprosy and keep His distance, He also broke all sociocultural and religious barriers to come near to eat with him in his own home.

The woman is not mentioned by name in this passage. But some scholars have identified her as Mary, the sister of Martha and Lazarus (John 12:3). Whoever she was, this woman brought with her some very expensive perfume encased in an equally expensive container. The term "alabaster box" actually refers to a flask or jar made of special white or yellow limestone named after Alabaster, the town in Egypt where it is chiefly found. Matthew describes the perfume as precious. The Greek word translated as "precious" is *barutimos* (**bah-ROO-tee-moce**), which means "of heavy value" (from Gk. *barus*, **bah-ROOSE**, physically weighty or heavy). The woman poured out on Jesus' head this highly expensive perfume. She may have intentionally poured the ointment on Jesus' head and also intentionally rubbed some on His feet, a conclusion one could gather from the variance in the Gospel accounts that tell the story. It is even more probable that what the Holy Spirit is communicating through the apostles is similar to the phenomenon recorded in Psalm 133:2 concerning the priestly ordination of Aaron. The anointing oil that was poured on Aaron's head dripped down through his beard, onto his garments, and down onto his feet. Whatever the case, the important fact is that this woman spared no expense in showing her devotion to her Lord. She bought a very expensive ointment and poured it on Jesus.

8 But when his disciples saw it, they had indignation, saying, To what purpose is this waste? 9 For this ointment might have been sold for much, and given to the poor.

The disciples were obviously challenged, and possibly provoked to jealousy, by this woman's act of devotion to the Lord. The phrase "had indignation" (Gk. *aganakteo*, ah-gah-nak-TEH-oh) is from the Greek for displeased, incensed, angered, or offended. In other words, they voiced outrage over what they perceived to be an act of inexcusable extravagance. The Greek word *apoleia* (**ah-POE-lee-ah**) translated as "waste" in this passage, means destruction and implies utter ruin. The disciples' focus on the realizable market value of this oil blinded them from seeing the significance of the Lord's anointing. They had placed their commercial interest ("sold for much") and social action ("given to the poor") over personal devotion to the Lord (v. 9).

Matthew does not tell us that it was indeed Judas who championed or instigated this criticism (John 12:4–6). Through John, we get a clearer understanding of the real motive behind this pseudo-piety. Judas' motivation was not concern for the "poor." Instead, as treasurer of Jesus' group and one who always stole from the purse, he needed abundant cash available to make his pilfering more difficult to detect. While venting frustration that was cloaked in the religious garb of caring for the materially poor, Judas was oblivious to the depth of his own spiritual poverty. How tragic it is when people who seem overly concerned about the material poverty of others are blinded to their own deeper spiritual poverty.

10 When Jesus understood it, he said unto them, Why trouble ye the woman? for she hath wrought a good work upon me. 11 For ye have the poor always with you; but me ye have not always.

The construction of Jesus' question here indicates the extent of the disciples' indignation at this woman for what she had done. Apparently, they did not just express their opinions and then get on with dinner. They must have continued haranguing her with their diatribe and quite possibly with gestures also. The word translated as "trouble" is from *kopos*

(**KOE-poce**), which means fatiguing work, labor, or a beating. The Lord's rebuke seems to be intended to agitate the disciples' minds and to cause them to think through their motivation for the harassment they were meting out to this woman. If they stopped to think about it, they would see the absurdity of not allowing the woman to express herself and her devotion with her own goods in the way she deemed fit. Moreover, the Lord declares she had performed "a good work" for Him (Gk. *ergon kalon*, **AIR-gohn kah-LONE**, meaning something good, noble, beautiful, or morally unobjectionable). We need discernment so that we will not call evil what the Lord calls good (see Isaiah 5:20).

"If helping beggars makes you feel good," the Lord seems to be saying in verse 11, "then you have the poor always with you." Nothing in this passage should be taken to imply that the Lord does not care for the poor or want His followers to care for the poor. Jesus understood and declared that an integral part of His ministry mandate was to preach the Gospel to the poor (cf. Luke 4:18). Throughout His earthly ministry, by His words and actions, Jesus demonstrated an overwhelming compassion and concern for those who were poor, whether materially or spiritually. The disciples' error was that they were pitting social action against devotion to the Lord. Ministry of any kind should never be conceived of as independent or in place of personal devotion to the Lord. True compassion and justice flows from a personal relationship with and devotion to Him. The Lord continues, in essence, to say, "Seek the good, but Me you will not always have." Jesus wanted the disciples to care for the poor, but to recognize that He was headed to His death on the cross and not criticize the woman for worshiping. The disciples should follow suit and honor Him while they had Him with them in the flesh.

12 For in that she hath poured this ointment on my body, she did it for my burial. 13 Verily I say unto you, Wheresoever this gospel shall be preached in the whole world, there shall also this, that this woman hath done, be told for a memorial of her.

Jesus further explained the deeper significance of the Bethany woman's action: She did it "for my burial" (Gk. *to entaphiasai me*, **TOE en-ta-fee-AD-sie may**, "to bury me"). This woman, whoever she was, understood what Jesus had been saying to His disciples about His imminent death. Jewish burial customs prescribed that dead bodies be anointed and prepared in special ways for burial. Joseph of Arimathea and Nicodemus eventually prepared Jesus' body for burial by wrapping it in linen cloths (John 19:38–40). But unlike the other disciples, who were wrapped up in their own notions of a coming political kingdom and jostling for position in the kingdom (Luke 22:24–30; Acts 1:6–8), this woman was expressing her emotions and devotion. Jesus had been teaching that He would die and be raised from the dead on the third day. Perhaps she was the only one who really understood the true significance of what He taught.

Jesus' death is a good message (Gk. *euaggelion*, **ew-ang-GHEL-ee-on**, Gospel; Matthew 26:13) because it announces the destruction of the power of sin, with all of sin's anti-life manifestations. The Gospel is to be "preached" (Gk. *kerusso*, **kay-ROO-so**, proclaim, herald, announce) to "the whole world" (Gk. *en holo to kosmo*, **en HOE-lo toe KOS-mo**, "in the entire cosmos"). Christ was talking about worldwide evangelism when He declared that wherever the Gospel is preached in the whole world, the story of what this woman did would also be told as a "memorial" (Gk. *mnemosunon*, **mnay-MOW-soo-non**, remembrance) of her. Her prophetic action would be tied to the Gospel story because the Cross of Christ is the central message of the Gospel.

Sources:
Achtemeier, Paul J., ed. *Harper's Bible Life Application Study Bible*, New Living Translation. Wheaton, IL: Tyndale House, 1996. 1463.
Youngblood, R.F., F.F. Bruce, and R.K. Harrison, eds. *Nelson's New Illustrated Bible Dictionary*. Nashville, TN: Thomas Nelson, 1995. 180.
Zodhiates, Spiros. *Complete Word Study of the New Testament with Greek Parallel*. Iowa Falls, IA: World Bible Publishers, 1992.

Say It Correctly

Caiaphas. **KAHY-uh-fuhs.**

Daily Bible Readings

MONDAY
The Original Passover Celebration
(Exodus 12:1–14)

TUESDAY
Care for the Poor
(Luke 16:19–31)

WEDNESDAY
Mary Anoints Jesus' Body for Burial
(John 12:1–8)

THURSDAY
One Must Die for the Nation
(John 11:47–53)

FRIDAY
Judas Negotiates the Handover of Jesus
(Matthew 26:14–16)

SATURDAY
Jesus Celebrates the Last Passover Meal
(Matthew 26:17–29)

SUNDAY
Jesus Defends the Woman's Beautiful Act
(Matthew 26:1–13)

Teaching Tips

Words You Should Know

A. Sepulcher *mnema* (Gk.)—A memorial or tomb.

B. He is risen *egerthe from egeiro* (Gk.)— "He is raised," to resurrect, get up, awaken.

Teacher Preparation

Unifying Principle—Resurrection Life. Many people live with despair and hopelessness. What is the source of genuine hope, and who can offer that hope? Jesus called and continues to call disciples to share and celebrate the Good News of His resurrection and the hope it offers to the world.

A. Read the Bible Background and Devotional Readings.

B. Pray for your students and lesson clarity.

C. Read the lesson Scripture in multiple translations.

D. Option: Role-play the women's report to the disciples and have them share their joy at seeing the risen Christ with your class. Debrief by having participants tell their own experience of encountering Resurrection joy.

O—Open the Lesson

A. Begin the class with prayer.

B. Have the students read the Aim for Change.

C. Have the students read the In Focus story.

D. Ask students how events named in the story can weigh on their hearts and how they can view these events from a theological perspective.

P—Present the Scriptures

A. Read the Focal Verses and discuss the Background and The People, Places, and Times sections.

B. Have the class share what Scriptures stand out for them and why, with particular emphasis on today's context.

E—Explore the Meaning

A. Use In Depth or More Light on the Text to help provide more in-depth discussion of the lesson text.

B. Discuss the Liberating Lesson and Application for Activation sections.

N—Next Steps for Application

A. Summarize the value of knowing Christ as our resurrected Savior!

B. End class with a commitment to pray for salvation for those in your family and community.

Worship Guide

For the Superintendent or Teacher
Theme: Called to Proclaim the Resurrection
Song: "He Lives"
Devotional Reading: 1 Corinthians 15:12–22

Called to Proclaim the Resurrection

Bible Background • MATTHEW 28:1–15
Printed Text • MATTHEW 28:1–15 | Devotional Reading • 1 CORINTHIANS 15:12–22

—————————— Aim for Change ——————————

By the end of the lesson we will: IDENTIFY how the women's attitude changed when they met the risen Christ; RECALL how we reacted when we first accepted Jesus Christ; and COMMIT to sharing the Good News of Jesus Christ with others.

—————————— In Focus ——————————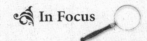

Sheila tenderly held their son in her arms. His skin was so soft and warm. He smiled happily in his sleep. "How about Robert Jr.?" she asked her husband softly through tears of joy. Robert gently hugged them both. They were speechless upon meeting the answer to their prayers for the blessing of a child.

The couple had been trying to have a baby since their Jamaican honeymoon thirteen years ago. They had waited until they were married to consummate their union. They were both young and healthy. But to their dismay, old-fashioned methods and modern medicine seemed to produce the same sad results, causing a deep-flowing discouragement in Sheila. Robert remained hopeful, though. He regularly requested prayer from their church's healing ministry. He knew God had a plan for their family, so in faith he remained patient.

Now, he couldn't believe how his sorrow had quickly turned to overwhelming, life-altering joy with God's promise finally fulfilled. "Actually, I was thinking Immanuel," he replied with a bright smile. He took his son and paced back and forth, retelling parts of the story—their story—to the sleeping baby.

Sometimes the sorrow of unanswered promises, unexpected circumstances, or death blinds us from seeing the future joy God is preparing for us through answered prayers and promises fulfilled. Which stories in your life that demonstrate God's glory have been too good to keep to yourself?

—————————— Keep in Mind ——————————

"Then said Jesus unto them, Be not afraid: go tell my brethren that they go into Galilee, and there shall they see me" (Matthew 28:10, KJV).

"Then Jesus said to them, 'Don't be afraid! Go tell my brothers to leave for Galilee, and they will see me there' " (Matthew 28:10, NLT).

Focal Verses

KJV **Matthew 28:1** In the end of the sabbath, as it began to dawn toward the first day of the week, came Mary Magdalene and the other Mary to see the sepulchre.

2 And, behold, there was a great earthquake: for the angel of the Lord descended from heaven, and came and rolled back the stone from the door, and sat upon it.

3 His countenance was like lightning, and his raiment white as snow:

4 And for fear of him the keepers did shake, and became as dead men.

5 And the angel answered and said unto the women, Fear not ye: for I know that ye seek Jesus, which was crucified.

6 He is not here: for he is risen, as he said. Come, see the place where the Lord lay.

7 And go quickly, and tell his disciples that he is risen from the dead; and, behold, he goeth before you into Galilee; there shall ye see him: lo, I have told you.

8 And they departed quickly from the sepulchre with fear and great joy; and did run to bring his disciples word.

9 And as they went to tell his disciples, behold, Jesus met them, saying, All hail. And they came and held him by the feet, and worshipped him.

10 Then said Jesus unto them, Be not afraid: go tell my brethren that they go into Galilee, and there shall they see me.

11 Now when they were going, behold, some of the watch came into the city, and shewed unto the chief priests all the things that were done.

12 And when they were assembled with the elders, and had taken counsel, they gave large money unto the soldiers,

13 Saying, Say ye, His disciples came by night, and stole him away while we slept.

NLT **Matthew 28:1** Early on Sunday morning, as the new day was dawning, Mary Magdalene and the other Mary went out to visit the tomb.

2 Suddenly there was a great earthquake! For an angel of the Lord came down from heaven, rolled aside the stone, and sat on it.

3 His face shone like lightning, and his clothing was as white as snow.

4 The guards shook with fear when they saw him, and they fell into a dead faint.

5 Then the angel spoke to the women. "Don't be afraid!" he said. "I know you are looking for Jesus, who was crucified.

6 He isn't here! He is risen from the dead, just as he said would happen. Come, see where his body was lying.

7 And now, go quickly and tell his disciples that he has risen from the dead, and he is going ahead of you to Galilee. You will see him there. Remember what I have told you."

8 The women ran quickly from the tomb. They were very frightened but also filled with great joy, and they rushed to give the disciples the angel's message.

9 And as they went, Jesus met them and greeted them. And they ran to him, grasped his feet, and worshiped him.

10 Then Jesus said to them, "Don't be afraid! Go tell my brothers to leave for Galilee, and they will see me there."

11 As the women were on their way, some of the guards went into the city and told the leading priests what had happened.

12 A meeting with the elders was called, and they decided to give the soldiers a large bribe.

13 They told the soldiers, "You must say, 'Jesus' disciples came during the night while we were sleeping, and they stole his body.'

14 If the governor hears about it, we'll stand up for you so you won't get in trouble."

14 And if this come to the governor's ears, we will persuade him, and secure you.

15 So they took the money, and did as they were taught: and this saying is commonly reported among the Jews until this day.

15 So the guards accepted the bribe and said what they were told to say. Their story spread widely among the Jews, and they still tell it today.

The People, Places, and Times

Women. Jesus paid attention to women, included them, and acknowledged their place in the kingdom. At the risk of censure from a male-oriented society, Jesus talked to women, responded to their touch, healed them, received their emotional and financial support, and used them as main characters in His stories. Luke mentions a group of women who traveled with Jesus as He journeyed from town to town (Luke 8:1–3). Among them were Mary of Magdala, Joanna, and Susanna. These women provided financial support for Jesus and the twelve apostles. Women were the first at the tomb after the Resurrection. As such, they were the first to broadcast His victory over death (Luke 23:55–24:11). Matthew, Mark, Luke, and John all called attention to the loyal women who participated in Jesus' Galilean ministry and followed Him all the way to the Cross and the grave. The New Testament brings a distinct picture of women into focus. Jesus, and later Paul, elevated the status of women so that they could be full participants in the kingdom of God. However, they (as well as each man) are urged to use their responsibility, as well as their freedom, to find their place in the body of Christ. The spirit of freedom and love in Christ belongs to women as well as men.

Background

Women witnessed Jesus' crucifixion up close. Women, who had known His healing power, gathered at Jesus' feet in His finest and final hour. Motivated by gratitude, courage, and love, these women did not run away, hide, or deny Christ. In spite of His public humiliation and grotesque execution, these women wanted to be identified with the crucified Messiah. Although they could not trade places with Him or take Him down, these women were not watching out of helplessness or coincidence. They were witnesses to His crucifixion in preparation for their purpose of delivering the message of eternal faith that the Messiah had risen!

After Jesus died, His body was taken by the disciples and entombed. However, resonating among the religious leaders was Jesus' prophecy that He would be raised in three days. To ensure that the disciples did not come back and steal the body and then fabricate a story of resurrection, a large boulder was set before the tomb and soldiers were assigned to stand guard. They did not perceive, even yet, His power.

At-A-Glance

1. Women at the Tomb (Matthew 28:1–8)
2. Jesus Appears to the Women (vv. 9–10)
3. Religious Leaders Bribe the Guards (vv. 11–15)

In Depth

1. Women at the Tomb (Matthew 28:1–8)

As Mary Magdalene and the other Mary went to Jesus' tomb, the earth quaked, an angel opened the tomb, and the guards became like dead men. It stands to reason that because there are no specifics given on the Resurrection process, the most important point made is that the tomb was, and remains, empty. While the women were on their way to the tomb, laden with spices and hoping the guards would allow them to anoint Jesus' dead body in loving grief, an earthquake occurred. But the earthquake did not deter the women. The guards, on the other hand, upon seeing the angel, were so afraid they fainted into a deep sleep, an act that would become for them a convenient alibi and lie to explain the empty tomb. But the women, instead of experiencing a teary-eyed, tragic scene at the sepulcher, were met by an angel.

The angel told the women that Jesus had been raised and instructed them to tell the disciples to meet Him in Galilee. Unlike the guards, the women's fear was not overwhelming, for they retained hope in the prophecies of a risen Messiah. Their fear was in seeing the unusual, but it was not immobilizing. Yes, they were frightened, but they were also filled with great joy. Their humanness made them afraid. Their hopefulness filled them with joy. Their fear was smothered by great joy as they listened to the angel, for their hope had been realized. The women were the first to know of the resurrected Messiah. Oh, what joy filled their souls! They were obedient and went to tell the disciples what they had seen (v. 8).

2. Jesus Appears to the Women (vv. 9–10)

Jesus first appeared to the women, not the eleven disciples. On their way to deliver the message, lest they be accused of relaying hearsay, the women were graced with the very presence of the Lord. As the women joyfully hurried to tell the disciples, Jesus met them and encouraged them to tell the disciples to go to Galilee where they would see Him. This was the Jesus they remembered, but He was now embodied in full divinity. They bowed to Jesus and grabbed His feet as a sign of ultimate reverence and submission.

Indeed, He was to be worshiped. He had fulfilled God's plan of salvation. Who could doubt that He was and is the Son of God? These women saw Him with their own eyes and believed. Even though the disciples had denied and deserted Him (all except John), Jesus forgave them. He sent the women to tell the brothers the Good News: Jesus was no longer dead (v. 10). Their relationship would now be even stronger than before. He would meet them in Galilee as He had previously told them (cf. Mark 14:28).

Sadly, the disciples were still afraid of the religious leaders and they were still hiding in Jerusalem (John 20:19). Therefore, Jesus met them first in Jerusalem (Luke 24:36), and later in Galilee (John 21).

3. Religious Leaders Bribe the Guards (vv. 11–15)

Some of the guards told the leading priests that Jesus was not in the tomb. What they feared had come to pass (v. 11). Of course, an urgent meeting had to be called to strategize. If people were excited about Jesus before the crucifixion, there would be no containing them (and Christianity) once the believers found out about Jesus' resurrection. The leaders knew they had to do something, so they decided to bribe the soldiers and get them to lie about Jesus and His resurrection (v. 12). The religious leaders were in a state of panic. Therefore, lying was not beneath their dignity. They had to stop Jesus and the Good News at all costs. In fact, these leaders were willing to support the guards in the lie that Jesus' disciples stole the body while the guards were sleeping (vv. 13–14). However, denying the Resurrection, ignoring it, or lying about it did not change the fact that Jesus had died and risen from the dead. The complete work of Jesus' coming was finished!

Search the Scriptures

1. What natural phenomena heralded the supernatural Resurrection (Matthew 28:2)?

2. Why did the angel roll the stone away (v. 6)?

3. What four messages did the angel give the women (vv. 5–7)?

4. What emotions did the women express upon receiving the call to carry the Good News of the risen Lord (v. 8)?

Discuss the Meaning

1. What does Jesus' resurrection mean for believers everywhere? For sinners everywhere? For evil and death?

2. Why is it important for believers to share the Good News of Jesus' resurrection?

Liberating Lesson

When Jesus Christ rose from the dead, it was the most important, awesome, and unexpected event in history. It was so unexpected that the women who learned of it first, as well as the disciples, the guards who kept the tomb, and the religious leaders all reacted differently to the news. The Good News as we know it—Jesus Christ had overcome sin, death, and the grave and liberated us from the power and punishment for sin—was challenging news for those who held power.

As the Gospel is preached in the early church, people respond by accepting or rejecting it at the point of the Resurrection, because the wisdom of the world rejects it and tries to cover it up to maintain position and status quo. As disciples of Jesus Christ who preach of a Savior who overcame death itself, we can expect opposition and denial from those who have something to lose by acknowledging the power of God over the principles and practices of the world. In what ways has your faith community faced opposition when trying to preach the truth of Jesus Christ's life in the face of a culture of death? How can we be bolder to share the Good News when people may question the power of God to challenge our expectations and transform our lives?

Application for Activation

Christ met unbelievers where they were. He realized what many Christians today still do not seem to understand. Cultivators have to get out in the field. According to one count, the Gospels record 132 contacts Jesus had with people. Six were in the Temple, four in the synagogues, and 122 were out with people in the mainstream of life. When was the last time you told somebody about the crucified Christ and the risen Lord? Do you feel you lack opportunity? This week make a list of ten people who you come in contact with daily. Make it a point to ask them if they know Jesus, and share the tenets of salvation with them. As the women did, run and tell somebody that Jesus, the Christ, is risen!

Follow the Spirit

What God wants me to do:

_____

_____

_____

_____

Remember Your Thoughts

Special insights I have learned:

_____

_____

More Light on the Text
Matthew 28:1–15

1 In the end of the sabbath, as it began to dawn toward the first day of the week, came Mary Magdalene and the other Mary to see the sepulcher.

When the sabbath was over, and it began to dawn toward the first day of the week, Mary Magdalene and others went out to visit the grave. Counting days in the Jewish tradition challenges the suggestion regarding Jesus being crucified on Thursday. It is worthwhile to recall that the Jewish day begins and ends at sundown or 6 p.m. rather than midnight. He died and was buried before 6 p.m. on what we call Good Friday; that's day one. Saturday at 6 p.m. is the end of day two, and early Sunday morning, day three, God raised Jesus from the dead. This knowledge accounts for the three days between Jesus' death and resurrection.

Matthew highlights the roles of women in his Gospel. The first to carry the word is Mary and the first to carry the Resurrection message are women. God chose a woman in the beginning of Matthew, and Christ sent women first, according to Matthew.

2 And, behold, there was a great earthquake: for the angel of the Lord descended from heaven, and came and rolled back the stone from the door, and sat upon it.

The word "earthquake" in Greek is *seismos* (**says-MOCE**), which is where we get our English word "seismic." Earthquakes occur several places in the Bible, including at the Cross when Jesus committed Himself into God's hands (Matthew 27:51), and on Mount Sinai when God gave Moses the Ten Commandments (Exodus 19:18). Notice the association of these two earthquakes with liberation. The Hebrews had been delivered from Pharaoh and Jesus had been delivered from death. It was certainly this phenomenal occurrence that brought the centurion to proclaim, "Truly this was the Son of God" (from Matthew 27:54). To their astonishment, the women found that a great earthquake had occurred that Sunday morning. The angel of the Lord now appears and rolls away the boulder so that the women can see that Jesus has risen.

Celestial phenomena must also be considered. At various places in our lives, God shakes our consciences to awareness and our sinful selves to repentance, and great is the Resurrection to renewed, revived, and refreshed hope in Jesus Christ.

3 His countenance was like lightning, and his raiment white as snow:

The angel's appearance was as dazzling as lightning, and his clothes were snowy white. In some churches baptismal candidates worship in white to symbolize purity. It is fitting for the angel of the Lord to wear a bright, white robe, symbolizing the fact that Jesus has come through a great tribulation and now advises His people to be of good cheer. Not only because He has overcome the world, but also because our resurrected bodies will also bear the garment of light (Revelation 7:9–15). The description of the angel of the Lord echoes Daniel 10:6.

4 And for fear of him the keepers did shake, and became as dead men.

The phrase "were shaken" (Greek *eseisthesan*, **eh-SAYS-thay-sahn**) denotes how the keepers of the tomb were shaking just as the earth had shaken. They were struck with terror and fell down as though dead. Of all the Gospel writers, only Matthew includes this detail. The appearance of the angel so terrified the guards posted at the tomb that they were rendered unconscious. The women were also in fear (vv. 5, 8; cf. Daniel 10:7–9; Revelation 1:17). According to the Gospel of Mark, the women were speechless (Mark 16:5). One can understand the women's fear in the light of the circumstances that surrounded the death of their Master.

5 And the angel answered and said unto the women, Fear not ye: for I know that ye seek Jesus, which was crucified.

The angel spoke to the women saying in his own way, "Don't be afraid. I know that you are looking for Jesus, the one who was killed on the Cross. There is reason, not for fear, but for joy, because Jesus who was crucified is risen from the dead." These women had no reason to be frightened. They were beloved by the Lord. The angel spoke to the women only. The reaction of the believing women is set in sharp contrast with the reaction of the pagan soldiers. The angel reassured them that there was no need to be afraid. A woman of that time might have experienced fear for a number of reasons. However, Jesus elevated women to their rightful position in a biased society. And, in the end, the women came to believe in God's call in their lives through Jesus Christ.

Therefore, the fears the angel addressed here have to do with the reason they cannot find Jesus in the tomb. They came to anoint Jesus' body with oil and spices, but cannot since He is gone. In the book of Mark, they raised the question, "Who will roll the stone away?" In Luke, they found the stone rolled away and went in, but did not find Jesus. In John, Mary Magdalene sees the stone rolled away and runs to tell Peter that "they" have taken Jesus' body away. It is this panic that the angel addresses. Jesus is not stolen, lost, or taken away to some unknown place. He is risen.

6 He is not here: for he is risen, as he said. Come, see the place where the Lord lay.

In both Matthew and Mark, the angel invites the women to enter the tomb and examine the place where Jesus was laid to rest. In John, the women are asked, "Why do you seek the living among the dead?" The angel graciously extends an invitation to these women to believe God's Word. Understandably, the women had been through a lot and had cause to be concerned about the body of Jesus. They had witnessed the government's abusive treatment of Jesus and watched in horror as He was beaten, tortured, and forced to carry the old rugged cross. They were at Golgotha and heard the cruel accusations hurled at Jesus. The angel is assuring these women that it was God—not the government, the culture, or the opinions of man—who had the last word and that "He is risen." The words of the angel echo throughout the Scriptures (see Matthew 28:10; Luke 2:10). They are meant to cheer the hearts of Christians in every age in the expectation of the Resurrection. They remind us that Christians have no cause for alarm, whatever may happen in the world. God does not want His servants to dwell in fear.

7 And go quickly, and tell his disciples that he is risen from the dead; and, behold, he goeth before you into Galilee; there shall ye see him: lo, I have told you.

The phrase "he is risen" is translated from the Greek word *egerthe* (**ey-GAIR-thay**), meaning "he was raised." Jesus was raised to life from the dead just as He said He would be. The tone in this verse is just as urgent as the tone Matthew uses at Jesus' triumphal entry in chapter 21, "immediately and straightway." The Greek word *tachu* (**ta-KHOO**), which means "quickly," is used here in conjunction with a past participle that means "having gone" to come together to mean "when you have gone quickly." The women were to run and tell the disciples of Jesus' resurrection.

There is no time for delay, apathy, or doubt. Jesus is not only risen, but also en route to the place where He devoted most of His earthly ministry, Galilee. It is also a major center of Judaism during the life of Jesus. There the women, the disciples, and others will see the man from Galilee, their friend and resurrected Lord.

8 And they departed quickly from the sepulchre with fear and great joy; and did run to bring his disciples word.

The "fear" Matthew refers to here is from the Greek word *phobos* (**FOE-boce**), which includes respectful, reverence, and a sense of awe in its definition. Since it is used in tandem with Matthew's reference to "great joy," it can be concluded this fear is not the same as being afraid. The fear of the women did not disappear completely, but it was overpowered with a "great joy" because of the reality of the Resurrection.

Mark's account specifically directs the women to "go tell His disciples and Peter." Luke reads more casually, "And returning from the tomb they told all this to the eleven and to all the rest." There is not the same intensity in Luke as there is in Matthew's and Mark's narration. John highlights the importance of the Gospel writer's message to Christ's disciples and Peter.

You may remember that John, identified as the disciple whom Jesus loved, outran the others to the tomb upon hearing Mary Magdalene say, "They have taken away the LORD out of the sepulchre, and we know not where they have laid him" (from John 20:2). Only John writes of the Jewish burial linen wrappings and their neatness, implying that Jesus experienced no particular anxiety or struggle in getting out of them. And such is the case with eternal things. They shall come to pass in God's time and in

God's way. The message of the Resurrection is one of trusting in God. It also indicates His body had not been stolen. John also speaks of himself as the one who saw these things and as a result, believed (John 20:8).

9 And as they went to tell his disciples, behold, Jesus met them, saying, All hail. And they came and held him by the feet, and worshipped him.

As the women obeyed the angel's instructions, Jesus appears and greets them with the common greeting of the time. The person who meets the risen Lord lives in the joy of His presence. There is no indication the women ever doubted Him, but those who did—Peter, Pharisaic Jews, and pious priests—would meet the risen Savior and either worship Him, as Peter and the others did, or bribe the keepers of the tomb, as the pious priests did.

Those who believed touched His feet. There are times when kneeling at the feet of Him, who was, is, and is to come, is the most appropriate posture to take. By this action they are showing their submission to Jesus, as practiced in their culture when a subject rendered obeisance to a sovereign prince. They prostrate themselves in adoration. This gesture is viewed as a sign of a living faith where the touch and the bended knee welcomes the Christ. It has been said the condition of the heart is more important than the position of the body while praying. Conversely, the position of the body often determines the condition of the heart. His presence will surely call forth some form of worship.

10 Then said Jesus unto them, Be not afraid: go tell my brethren that they go into Galilee, and there shall they see me.

Jesus calls the women to believe in the promise of God, share the Good News, rejoice at His appearing, and not be afraid of others' disbelief. The disciples labeled these women foolish (Luke 24:11) and refused to believe them. They were preoccupied with the sad turn of events: their denial (Peter), their loss (Judas committed suicide), their fear (abandoning Jesus), and their grief (the death of their Rabbi). And yet, they have nothing to lose by going to the place where they first met the Lord.

Jesus uses the word "brethren" (Gk. *adelphos*, **ad-el-FOS**) to refer to His disciples (John 20:17). Matthew records that Jesus had used the word "brethren" more generally and symbolically (Matthew 12:50; 25:40). Jesus also used the more familiar term "friend" before (John 15:15). If we think of their recent infidelity and cowardliness shown at the time of Jesus' suffering, to call the disciples brothers is surprising. By calling them "brethren," Jesus is not only showing them His love, He is also underlining their privileged position as co-heirs of His inheritance (Romans 8:17).

11 Now when they were going, behold, some of the watch came into the city, and shewed unto the chief priests all the things that were done. 12 And when they were assembled with the elders, and had taken counsel, they gave large money unto the soldiers,

The phrase "when they were going" is a single participle in the Greek. It suggests that even as the women were on their way, some of the soldiers who had been guarding the tomb went into Jerusalem and told the chief priests all that had happened.

The soldiers, although terrified by the earthquake, the angel, and the stone-rolling, had enough strength to go and report what had happened. It is interesting that Jesus' enemies knew about the Resurrection even before the apostles. Being incapable of refuting the evidence but not willing to accept it, the enemies

of Jesus tried to suppress it illegally. Their decision was not taken lightly. All the elders (the Sanhedrin) were involved. The translation for *sumboulion* (Gk. **soom-BOO-lee-on**) is "counsel" in this Scripture. It points to the fact that the soldiers and elders were all of like mind; they agreed in their plot to lie about Jesus.

The elders gave the soldiers a considerable sum of money in an attempt to bribe them. The betrayal of Judas cost them only thirty silver coins (Matthew 26:15). The effort to cover up their crime is going to cost them much more. The guards received enough money to bribe them to invent a lie.

13 Saying, Say ye, His disciples came by night, and stole him away while we slept. 14 And if this come to the governor's ears, we will persuade him, and secure you. 15 So they took the money, and did as they were taught: and this saying is commonly reported among the Jews until this day.

The idea is that the elders instructed the soldiers to say that the disciples had stolen Jesus' body at night, while they were asleep. The elders were not concerned with the Resurrection itself, but with its repercussions on the people. The penalty for a guard or soldier sleeping on duty was death (Acts 12:19). The elders probably hoped to corrupt Pilate also with money. He probably couldn't care less about the corpse of a Jew. The elders assured the soldiers that if the information reached the governor, they would do their best to calm him. Thus, the soldiers were to be free from all anxiety. In other words, the elders would accept responsibility if any difficulty should occur. The soldiers took the money and did as they were instructed. This lie was commonly circulated among the Jews at the time when Matthew wrote this Gospel. Yet the truth remains, Jesus is risen as He said!

Sources:
Holman's Bible Dictionary for Windows, Version 1.0, Parsons Technology, 1994.

Say It Correctly

Sepulchre. **SEP**-uhl-ker.

Daily Bible Readings

MONDAY
I Am the Resurrection and the Life
(John 11:17–27)

TUESDAY
Judas Returns Money, Hangs Himself
(Matthew 27:3–10)

WEDNESDAY
Jesus Crucified
(Matthew 27:32–44)

THURSDAY
Guards Secure the Tomb
(Matthew 27:62–66)

FRIDAY
Mary Meets Jesus Outside the Tomb
(John 20:11–18)

SATURDAY
Reigning Triumphant with Christ
(Revelation 20:1–6)

SUNDAY
"Meet Me in Galilee!"
(Matthew 28:1–15)

Notes

Teaching Tips

Words You Should Know

A. Disciple *mathetes* (Gk.)—Committed learner under a teacher.

B. Commandment *entole* (Gk.)—Firm instruction, often referring to the Law of God when used in the New Testmaent.

Teacher Preparation

Unifying Principle—Called to Make Disciples. When there have been dramatic changes in circumstances and in the roles of leadership, people are uncertain of their own roles and responsibilities. Where can they find direction and authority to act? The risen Lord commissioned the disciples, giving them authority and responsibility to continue and extend His mission and ministry throughout the world.

A. Read the Bible Background and Devotional Readings.

B. Pray for your students and lesson clarity.

C. Read the lesson Scripture in multiple translations.

D. Option: Invite students to create a basic summary of "everything that [Jesus has] commanded you" (Matthew 28:20). What items are most important for new believers to understand? Which are actions? Which are beliefs?

O—Open the Lesson

A. Begin the class with prayer.

B. Have the students read the Aim for Change.

C. Have the students read the In Focus story.

D. Ask students how events named in the story can weigh on their hearts and how they can view these events from a theological perspective.

P—Present the Scriptures

A. Read the Focal Verses and discuss the Background and The People, Places, and Times sections.

B. Have the class share what Scriptures stand out for them and why, with particular emphasis on today's context.

E—Explore the Meaning

A. Use In Depth or More Light on the Text to help provide more in-depth discussion of the lesson text.

B. Discuss the Liberating Lesson and Application for Activation sections.

N—Next Steps for Application

A. Summarize the importance of our comission to share the Gospel and make disciples.

B. End class with a commitment to pray for believers to share the Gospel and people to receive Jesus Christ.

Worship Guide

For the Superintendent or Teacher
Theme: Call and Comissioning
Song: "Send Me"
Devotional Reading: Colossians 3:12–17

Call and Commissioning

Bible Background • MATTHEW 28:16–20; ACTS 1:6–8
Printed Text • MATTHEW 28:16–20; ACTS 1:6–8 | Devotional Reading • COLOSSIANS 3:12–17

—— Aim for Change ——

By the end of the lesson we will: COMPARE Jesus' commission in Matthew to His commission in Acts; AFFIRM that Jesus is with us in our commission; and ACCEPT our commission to make disciples of all nations.

—— 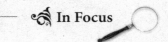 In Focus ——

Sharon came to work disappointed in the outcome of last night's gubernatorial election results. She had been hopeful her candidate would win, but was now gravely discouraged.

John was obviously thrilled because his candidate did win. He was openly excited for the outcome of the race. He came to work energetic and bubbly.

Stephen's candidate lost the race also. However, he seemed as happy and jubilant as John. Sharon was confused. She knew Stephen was a Christian like her and she thought she knew who his candidate for governor was. Sharon asked Stephen what was going on.

Stephen assured Sharon he was disappointed his candidate did not win but he trusted God. Stephen told her, "I don't know what will happen now that we have a new governor. The thought of the changes he can possibly make are frightening. So, I chose to focus my attention on God. With God, all things are possible. I make my attitude reflect His power. My disappointment could hinder my testimony. I don't want to misrepresent God."

Sharon had to agree. She, too, wanted to be a faithful witness to Christ in the power of the Holy Spirit. Her candidate lost the race, but in Christ she was still a winner.

Christians confess they don't have all the answers but this doesn't disqualify them from offering a faithful witness to Christ in the power of the Holy Spirit. In today's lesson, the disciples are taught to obey everything Jesus commanded. Are you a witness for Christ wherever you go?

—— Keep in Mind ——

"Go ye therefore, and teach all nations, baptizing them in the name of the Father, and of the Son, and of the Holy Ghost: Teaching them to observe all things whatsoever I have commanded you: and, lo, I am with you always, even unto the end of the world. Amen" (Matthew 28:19–20, KJV).

"Therefore, go and make disciples of all the nations, baptizing them in the name of the Father and the Son and the Holy Spirit. Teach these new disciples to obey all the commands I have given you. And be sure of this: I am with you always, even to the end of the age" (Matthew 28:19-20, NLT).

Focal Verses

KJV **Matthew 28:16** Then the eleven disciples went away into Galilee, into a mountain where Jesus had appointed them.

17 And when they saw him, they worshipped him: but some doubted.

18 And Jesus came and spake unto them, saying, All power is given unto me in heaven and in earth.

19 Go ye therefore, and teach all nations, baptizing them in the name of the Father, and of the Son, and of the Holy Ghost:

20 Teaching them to observe all things whatsoever I have commanded you: and, lo, I am with you always, even unto the end of the world. Amen.

Acts 1:6 When they therefore were come together, they asked of him, saying, Lord, wilt thou at this time restore again the kingdom to Israel?

7 And he said unto them, It is not for you to know the times or the seasons, which the Father hath put in his own power.

8 But ye shall receive power, after that the Holy Ghost is come upon you: and ye shall be witnesses unto me both in Jerusalem, and in all Judaea, and in Samaria, and unto the uttermost part of the earth.

NLT **Matthew 28:16** Then the eleven disciples left for Galilee, going to the mountain where Jesus had told them to go.

17 When they saw him, they worshiped him—but some of them doubted!

18 Jesus came and told his disciples, "I have been given all authority in heaven and on earth.

19 Therefore, go and make disciples of all the nations, baptizing them in the name of the Father and the Son and the Holy Spirit.

20 Teach these new disciples to obey all the commands I have given you. And be sure of this: I am with you always, even to the end of the age."

Acts 1:6 So when the apostles were with Jesus, they kept asking him, "Lord, has the time come for you to free Israel and restore our kingdom?"

7 He replied, "The Father alone has the authority to set those dates and times, and they are not for you to know.

8 But you will receive power when the Holy Spirit comes upon you. And you will be my witnesses, telling people about me everywhere—in Jerusalem, throughout Judea, in Samaria, and to the ends of the earth."

The People, Places, and Times

Jerusalem. Under Rome, Jerusalem was conquered in 63 BC by Pompey and reached its pinnacle of grandeur and strength as a result of the building program of Herod the Great, whom Rome appointed king of Judea in 40 BC. Herod strengthened the Hasmonean walls, which had been built during the second century BC. At the top of the western hill, he built a huge palace complex for himself. To strengthen this and include more of the western area of the city, Herod then built a second wall that circled from the middle of the Hasmonean wall to a fortress north of the Temple Mount called the Antonia. To further strengthen this second wall, which was open to attack from the west, a quarry was opened in front of it that served as a defense moat. A section of this was not worth quarrying and it was left standing on the mound of limestone. It was called Golgotha, or

427

the "skull" (John 19:17). This part of the quarry belonged to Joseph of Arimathaea, who cut his family tomb into the exposed hill of the quarry adjacent to Golgotha. This is now part of the Church of the Resurrection and probably was the burial place of Jesus.

Background

Matthew 28 begins very early on the Sunday morning when Jesus rose from the dead. Mary (the mother of Jesus) and Mary Magdalene came to view the tomb, only to meet the angel who informed them that the Lord has risen and has gone before them to Galilee. Later, Jesus met the two women and again instructed them to tell His disciples whom He called His brothers to meet Him in Galilee. Matthew skips the story of their journey to Jerusalem and, instead, tells of the bribing of the guards with the intention of discrediting the Resurrection by spreading the news that Jesus' body had been stolen. Before long, Matthew has the disciples meeting Jesus at a mountain to which He had directed them. This meeting in Galilee is the setting for the last five verses of the Gospel of Matthew. In these verses, Matthew records the first post-Resurrection exhortation that Jesus gave His disciples—to make disciples for Him in all nations, to teach them, and to baptize them in the name of the Father, the Son, and the Holy Spirit.

If you actually went and made disciples of all nations, what would your life look like? If this is different from how it looks now, what are the reasons and how would you correct it?

Acts 1:6–8, on the other hand, is set just a mile outside Jerusalem, at the Mount of Olives from where Jesus ascended into heaven. As Luke begins his historical narrative of the birth of the church that makes the book of Acts, he has to tell of Jesus' ascension. But before we get to the ascension, Jesus gives the disciples a farewell speech with parting instructions.

So this is the very last of Jesus' conversations with His disciples, taking place forty days after Matthew 28. Since that meeting on a hill in Galilee, we know Jesus met with His disciples both in Judea and in Galilee, but now, Jesus is ready to depart and, as we see in the book of Acts, the disciples are ready for the mission. He takes the occasion to encourage them to wait for the Spirit in Jerusalem who will empower them to be His witnesses in Jerusalem, Judea, Samaria and to the ends of the earth. The Spirit will also help them understand that He had come to establish a spiritual kingdom, not an earthly one that could liberate Israel from Roman rule.

What kind of witness can your friends see from your life? Does it testify of Jesus' kingship and love for the world?

At-A-Glance

1. Resurrection Over Doubt (Matthew 28:16–17)
2. Doubt to Disciple Nations (vv. 18–20)
3. Disciple to Witness (Acts 1:6–8)

In Depth

1. Resurrection Over Doubt (Matthew 28:16–17)

Both Matthew 28 and Acts 1 are Scriptures that record events that took place after the Resurrection. Matthew 28 is basically the first encounter between Jesus and the disciples post-Resurrection. Acts 1 is the last such encounter. They both carry the same thread of thought: how to keep the movement (later called The Way and eventually the *ekklesia* or church) going and growing. Critical to this growth of the movement was the practice of discipleship. After the traumatic event of Jesus' crucifixion and death, the disciples had to wonder what they were to do now. Jesus was dead and had not left them any instructions on how to carry on His mission and ministry. Moreover, one of His own disciples, Judas, had betrayed Him then hung himself (Matthew 27:5). So when word came for them to gather in Galilee where He would meet them, it had to be an exciting turn of events.

When they gathered at the mountain in Galilee, Jesus was there to meet them. Upon gazing at their Lord and Savior one more time, the eleven disciples began to worship Him (v. 16). This was spontaneous praise and thanksgiving for the Messiah who had transformed their lives. He was alive!

In spite of seeing Christ with their own eyes and worshiping Him, a few had doubt creep into their hearts and minds (v. 17). Sometimes the foundation of our faith can be overcome with thoughts of uncertainty. When we cannot explain the spiritual, we tend to ignore or dismiss it. But the disciples continued to worship Him in spite of their doubts. We have to continue to worship and serve Christ in the midst of our uncertainties because our faith will increase as we grow spiritually.

Do you recall a time when you struggled to worship God because you had doubts about Him? Share your experience.

2. Doubt to Disciple Nations (vv. 18–20)

Jesus tells His disciples to go and make disciples of all nations. God gave all power and authority to Jesus (v. 18). This means when God raised Him from the dead and seated Him at His right hand, He was given power and dominion over all things in heaven and on earth (Ephesians 1:20–23). The disciples were under His authority and called to make more disciples (v. 19). The disciples understood what Jesus meant by "making disciples." He had just done this with them for the past three and a half years. He was telling them to go and do

what He had done with them so that other people could also become disciples of Jesus. He told them to teach the new disciples everything He had taught them. This is how disciples are made—through teaching them what Jesus says and what it means for our daily lives. And this command to make disciples goes to every follower of Christ. Disciples have to make other disciples until the nations learn the teachings of Christ and how to live accordingly. We are to go teach any person who will listen, regardless of race or nationality, about Jesus. When they accept Him as Lord and Savior, they are to be baptized as a sign of their union and commitment to Christ. And we are to teach them to be devoted to the Word of God (vv. 19–20).

Jesus ended His Great Commission with the promise that He will always be with us (v. 20). The disciples may have been puzzled how Jesus would remain with them. But Jesus promised to send His Holy Spirit to be present with them—and us—forever (cf. John 14:16, 26).

Why is baptizing and teaching the Word to new believers so important?

3. Disciple to Witness (Acts 1:6–8)

Acts 1 continues on the same theme of discipleship, adding that the disciples would be Jesus' witnesses in the entire world. Thus, in word and deed, they would testify of the teachings and the works of Jesus to the world. Jesus spent forty days after the Resurrection with the disciples teaching them about the kingdom of God. He urged them to remain in Jerusalem to await the coming promise of the Holy Spirit. While gathered with them on one occasion, the disciples questioned Him about restoring Israel's kingdom (v. 6). Many Jews thought the Messiah's coming meant they would be freed from Roman rule and He would be their new king. But Jesus told them these events would happen according to the Father's timetable, which was a secret.

Most importantly, they needed to have the baptism of the Holy Spirit before they went forth to witness for Christ in Jerusalem, Judea, Samaria, and the other parts of the world (v. 8). Without the power of God we can do nothing. The Holy Spirit gives us direction and power to act. The word translated "witness" can also be translated "martyr." Following Christ happens at a cost. His followers are called to be witnesses and martyrs at the same time. Some will be called to obey even to the death—unto martyrdom—and that is part of the sacrifice that comes with following Christ. We are invited to lay down our lives for the sake of His kingdom, and to do this, we need the Holy Spirit's empowerment.

How is your life a witness for Christ?

Search the Scriptures

1. Where were the disciples supposed to teach about Jesus to make disciples (Matthew 28:19; Acts 1:8)?

2. What part does the Holy Spirit play in discipleship and making disciples (Matthew 28:19; Acts 1:8)?

Discuss the Meaning

1. How is making disciples connected to witnessing for Christ?

2. How does discipleship work in your church? Are you discipling anybody at the moment? Are your disciples making other disciples?

3. The disciples seemed not fully prepared for the work that Jesus had for them. They did not fully understand the kingdom and dealt with doubt. Yet, Jesus still trusted them with the mission of discipling the nations. What does this teach you about God's mission?

Liberating Lesson

As we respond to Jesus' call to follow Him, we also respond to His call for us to make disciples for Him. Embracing one without the other is not possible if we are to be true followers. As we become disciples, we must endeavor to disciple others. We are part of a disciple-making movement in which real disciples make other disciples. We disciple others not only by teaching them the words of Jesus but also by letting them see the witness of our lifestyles. What is holding you back from answering the call to be a missionary for Christ? We do not need to be fearful because God is with us. He will guide and protect His people. May our congregations spend more energy making disciples and not making members!

Application for Activation

This week take the time to pray and specifically ask God to reveal to you how He is calling you to share the Gospel. He may have you start in your home because it is often the most difficult place to be a witness when we live with unbelievers. You may also want to speak to your pastor and local missionaries in your church or those who serve overseas. They may be able to offer spiritual guidance. Answering the call does not always mean you have to leave your job.

1. Become serious about discipleship—both to be a disciple and to disciple others locally and among the nations.

2. Be very intentional about following the countercultural nature of the demands of Christ in our individualistic consumer culture.

3. Seek to stay connected to the Holy Spirit for the power that helps us make disciples and effective witnesses in the world.

Follow the Spirit

What God wants me to do:

_____

_____

_____

_____

Remember Your Thoughts
Special insights I have learned:

_____

_____

_____

_____

More Light on the Text
Matthew 28:16–20; Acts 1:6–8

In many communities a person's last words receive very special attention. Loved ones want to honor the dying person's wish as best as they can, more so if the person is a respected elder or somewhat influential in society, especially when the words prescribe what should happen in the future. Such words often concern straightforward issues like where to be buried or, at times, complex wishes like relocating an entire village to avoid conflict. In some African cultures, people revere the dying words of an influential person as though such words had come from the future, usually from the spirit world of the ancestors, to guide the community from a vulnerable and needy today to a safe and prosperous tomorrow. This belief shapes the way some people read the Bible, especially the last words of people like Moses, Joshua, David, Paul, and especially Jesus Christ.

This week's verses take place after the Resurrection and give us the climax of all Jesus' exhortations, which is foundational to the way we think about mission and evangelism.

Matthew 26:16 Then the eleven disciples went away into Galilee, to the mountain which Jesus had appointed for them.

The disciples have trekked up north from Jerusalem and were now at the agreed location in Galilee—on the mountain where Jesus would show Himself to the eleven for the first time since that fateful Friday when they abandoned Him. On this mountain, Jesus would begin His efforts to reconnect, reconcile, and recommission His disciples. Matthew points out that the disciples were no longer the band of twelve as had been the case throughout the Gospel—until just a few days ago. Now, they remain with eleven disciples. By saying, "the eleven disciples," Matthew surprises us into remembering not only that Judas had left the team (and that for a few weeks, his place would remain vacant), he also reminds us of all the events of that weekend: Peter had denied the Lord; the disciples had scattered in fear; and the disciples were still vulnerable and less-than-perfect human beings after spending three and a half years with Jesus.

The women were also most likely part of the trip to Galilee, but Matthew's focus here is on the male disciples. We do not hear a great deal about the women in general, but we know for certain that the ministry of Jesus had many women supporters and followers. The apostles went to Galilee at the instruction of the women—this simple fact affirms the ministry of the women in their community.

Galilee is important for Matthew. This encounter between the risen Jesus and the disciples is peculiar to Matthew's Gospel. This is where the disciples started their journey with Jesus, where He began His ministry and gathered most of His disciples. Many of them were Galileans—an identity that brought about Peter's denial of the Lord and put them at risk in Jerusalem (Matthew 26:73–74).

431

17 And when they saw him, they worshipped him: but some doubted.

There must have been some anticipation as they approached the mountain. What would He look like and what would He say to them? And then, they saw Him: the Jesus they had seen die on the Cross was alive. In keeping with prophecy, He had proven He was stronger than death by coming back to life three days after dying. He is indeed king over death and thus is worthy of their worship. In response, they prostrate themselves before Him. Indeed, worship is the only acceptable response to seeing Jesus, especially as in this case; they are seeing Him for the first time after the Resurrection. When the women saw Him, they, too, worshiped (Matthew 28:9), and now the disciples did the same.

And yet, some doubted. Many scholars agree that "doubt" here is better translated "indecisive" or "hesitated." The disciples were still men of little faith so, as some worshiped, others hesitated (Matthew 14:31). Matthew does not explain why they hesitated. Some scholars suggest those who hesitated were outside the eleven, which could be true if there were other disciples at the event who were not yet acknowledged in the text. Whatever the case, we see here that doubt or indecisiveness does not disqualify people from the faith. It shows again that the disciples were not perfect in their understanding of Jesus and yet they received the calling and training from the Master.

18 And Jesus came and spake unto them, saying, All power is given unto me in heaven and in earth.

It appears here that Jesus had been at a distance when they worshiped. He responded to the worship by coming close to them. This is also how God responds to worship; when praises go up, God's glory comes down (see Psalm 67). And so, Jesus comes toward them and begins to speak to them, "all authority is given to me." Jesus is letting His disciples know that their situation has changed. No longer is He simply the suffering servant, the Son of Man with nowhere to lay His head. He has become the risen Lord who has all power. Death no longer had power over Him; He had risen in glory.

19 Go ye therefore, and teach all nations, baptizing them in the name of the Father, and of the Son, and of the Holy Ghost. 20 Teaching them to observe all things whatsoever I have commanded you: and, lo, I am with you always, even unto the end of the world. Amen.

The resurrection of Jesus proves the authority that He has been given, which is greater than the authority they had seen as they journeyed with Him. It demonstrates that His words and teachings are trustworthy, He is all-powerful, and that what He says comes to pass, both in heaven and on earth. Therefore, because of this authority, the disciples were to go and make disciples for Him of all nations. Thus, Jesus' newly given authority has implications for His followers here on earth—it would change their lives.

Contrary to most English translations of verse 19, "go" is not a command in Greek; it is a past participle. A more direct translation would be "having gone." The going out is not even the issue. Jesus assumes you are already out in the mission field. The command, rather, is "teach all nations," which is lacking as a translation, too. "Teach" in verse 19 and "teaching" in verse 20 are different verbs in the Greek. "Teach" (v. 19) is *matheteuo* (**mah-thay-TEW-oh**, make disciples), which is related to the noun "disciple" (*matheter*, **mah-THAY-tace**) and rarely made into a verb. Discipleship is an intense, committed path of learning under a master. "Make disciples" is the (grammatical) core of the Great Commission.

A disciple is both a student and a follower—a student who learns the teachings of the master and a follower who imitates his lifestyle. A first-century disciple did not enroll in a school but committed himself under a teacher or rabbi. Throughout their time with Jesus, the twelve had been disciples. Here, He commanded them to do what He had done with them to others. They had to teach whatever they had learned from Jesus to others while teaching them to do the same to others until disciples of Christ could be found in every nation. Disciple-making had been Jesus' strategy, and it would also be His disciples' strategy.

The grammar of the sentence is set up to show that making disciples will be done in two parts: baptizing and teaching. Baptizing would be both the initiation rite into the kingdom of God and the fellowship of the Spirit, as well as a public signal of identification with Jesus and His kingdom. Matthew adds that the baptism was to be in the name of the Father, the Son, and the Spirit. While this may not be a full articulation of later Trinitarian theology, it certainly reflects awareness, especially as at Jesus' baptism by John, that the Father, Son, and Spirit are involved in this all-important rite. Thus, those baptized in the name of the Father, Son and the Spirit share in Jesus' baptism and His authority. Scholars clarify to be baptized into the name is to be the under the authority and into the possession of that name, like servants under a lord. Thus, by baptism, the convert becomes affiliated and therefore the protégé of the person named.

"Teaching" (Gk. *didasko*, **dee-DASS-ko**) is the other half of discipleship. The Twelve are to teach the new disciples to observe (Gk. *tereo*, **teh-REH-oh**; keep, watch, guard from harm) everything Jesus commanded them. "Commanded" is *entello* (Gk. **en-TELL-oh**), related to the noun *entole* (Gk. **en-TOE-lay**), which is most often used in the New Testament to refer to the Law of Moses. *Tereo* (observe) is often paired with *entole* (commandment) throughout the New Testament (Matthew 19:17; John 15:10). Jesus' word choice here brings to mind not just all that He taught His disciples during His incarnation, but all that they have ever learned about God from the Old Testament as well.

Jesus establishes a new way of life for His disciples and commands them to go and make disciples for Him in all nations. Earlier, Jesus had given them the limited commission in which they were only allowed to preach to the lost sheep of Israel (Matthew 10:5–6). Now, they are to make disciples in all nations, both Jews and non-Jews. Even though *ethnos* (Gk. **ETH-noce**) is generally translated "Gentiles," in this case it is rightly translated "nations" because Jesus means not just the Gentiles, but all people groups of the world, including the Jews (cf. John 11:50–52; Acts 10:22). The prophecy that in Abraham all families of the earth would be blessed comes to fulfillment in this mission (Genesis 12:3).

Jesus finished His new commandment with an assurance that He would be with them to the end of the age. Such an assurance is greatly needed to accomplish their work. There will never be a time when Jesus' disciples are not in His company as they go to make disciples in all nations, and this communion is not to be delayed. It is something that may be known here and now. He is forever Emmanuel, "God with us." As God promised Joshua when he took over the ministry from Moses, Jesus was also telling His disciples that He would never leave them or forsake them. What a comforting assurance.

Today, this call to participate in God's mission of making disciples of the nations is given to everyone, both clergy and the laity. Of course, we are called to different assignments and maybe to different parts of God's vineyard, but the truth is that every Christian is a missionary for God. The role of the career missionary may still exist, but it only supplements the missionary calling of all believers. Additionally, we are invited to engage in God's mission wherever God is at work. This will be both in our neighborhoods and in countries on the other side of the world. It will especially most likely be outside the Sunday service at church. God is engaged in mission on Monday at work or school just as much as on Sunday. In a nutshell, God's mission breaks the barriers between the clergy and the laity and also between the sacred and the secular. Jesus' disciples are called to do the same.

Acts 1:6 When they therefore were come together, they asked of him, saying, Lord, wilt thou at this time restore again the kingdom to Israel?

Here, Jesus is about to go to heaven. This is His last conversation with His disciples before returning to His Father. The ascension takes place in verse 9. Luke is clear that it has been forty days since the Resurrection. It is close to forty days since that meeting in Galilee (depending on how long it took the disciples to walk from Jerusalem). Over that period, Jesus had shown Himself to the disciples a few more times with numerous signs of His authority, proving to them that He is indeed the Son of God, the Messiah. He had also given them many instructions on what to do after He has ascended and left the mission to them. However, it seems even until His ascension, the disciples did not understand what He was about. They still expected Him to establish a kingdom that would liberate Palestine from Roman rule. As He waited to be lifted up to heaven, the disciples asked Him if now was the time to restore the temporal kingdom of Israel. They still hoped for an earthly kingdom in which Jesus would be the ruler to lead the Jews

to subdue the power of Rome and dominate the nations. They totally misunderstood the timing of the kingdom. And yet, it is to these ill-prepared men that Jesus, in His grace, gives the responsibility of world mission.

This and many other stories that we see in the Gospels and the book of Acts suggest that while participating in God's mission requires preparation, perfection is not a prerequisite. As the saying goes, "God does not call the qualified, He qualifies the called." We are all called to participate in God's mission in the world; we will learn a greater part of how to do that on the job.

7 And he said unto them, It is not for you to know the times or the seasons, which the Father hath put in his own power. 8 But ye shall receive power, after that the Holy Ghost is come upon you: and ye shall be witnesses unto me both in Jerusalem, and in all Judaea, and in Samaria, and unto the uttermost part of the earth.

Jesus corrects the disciples' misunderstanding of the kingdom by simply stating that they would not, and indeed should not, know God's timetable. Times and seasons for everything are in the Father's hands who has securely established them in His authority. He had told them earlier that the kingdom was near them (Luke 10:9), or already within them (Luke 17:21), but it was a spiritual kingdom, not the one they had anticipated. This kingdom of heaven was already with them, but not in its fullness. Above all, whatever was already there of the kingdom was already but not yet growing. The kingdom expanded through making disciples, and hence, they were all called to be His witnesses. Further, they would receive the power through the Holy Spirit to be His witnesses all around the world. Of course, implied in Jesus' words is another command. The disciples would testify about Jesus, proclaiming the reality of His death and resurrection as well as His kingdom and lordship to make disciples around the world.

The Greek word for "witness" here is *martures* (**mar-TOUR-es**), which is elsewhere translated "martyrs." Living the life of a witness of Christ would be a sacrifice only possible through the empowerment of the Spirit. Such a life would reflect the instructions, death, and resurrection of the Lord Jesus, even in the midst of persecution and death. It would essentially be a life laid down for the cause of His mission. He had told them before to pick up their crosses (Luke 9:23–24), love Him and His mission more than their lives (John 12:25), and follow Him. Essentially, witnesses would often proclaim the Good News as sheep among wolves (Luke 10:3)—their lives surrendered to God and yet always in danger.

Christ's ordering of the spread of the disciple-making church is reflected in the development of the story of Acts. The spread of the church in Jerusalem and all Judea and Samaria is explored in chapters 1 through 9. The wider spread unto the uttermost part of the earth (which some have interpreted as Rome) is in chapters 10 through 28. This instruction repeats the one given in Matthew 28—to make disciples of all nations. The kingdom of God is for all nations and not just the Jews. We see later in Acts the Spirit of God make proclaiming of the Gospel to the Gentiles possible both with the Ethiopian eunuch (Acts 8:26) and the house of Cornelius (Acts 10:1). It was not until Acts 11 when the early disciples made a decision to preach to Gentiles, but even then, it was Jewish Christians who lived outside Palestine in the diaspora who made the move. It appears that even the apostles did not properly understand this global mandate for mission until much later. However, we see God breaking through in miraculous ways to invite the Gentiles into the kingdom.

Sources:

Morris, Leon. *The Gospel According to Matthew*. Grand Rapids, MI: Eerdmans, 1992. 745-746.

Dunn, James D.G. and J.W. Rogerson. *Eerdmans Commentary on the Bible*. Grand Rapids, MI: W.B. Eerdmans, 2003. 1062.

Robinson, Theodore H. *The Gospel of Matthew*, The Moffatt New Testament Commentary. London: Hodder and Stoughton, 1928. 237.

Jones, Alexander. *The Gospel According to St. Matthew: A Text and Commentary for Students*. London: G. Chapman, 1965. 321.

Daily Bible Readings

MONDAY
Place of Renewal
(Isaiah 2:1–4)

TUESDAY
Body Building for Baptized Believers
(1 Corinthians 12:12–13; Colossians 3:12–17)

WEDNESDAY
Lydia and Household Baptized
(Acts 16:11–15)

THURSDAY
Jailer and Household Baptized
(Acts 16:25–34)

FRIDAY
Reaching New People
(Acts 18:5–11)

SATURDAY
Matthias Chosen to Replace Judas
(Acts 1:12–17, 21–26)

SUNDAY
Disciples Called and Commissioned
(Matthew 28:16–20; Acts 1:6–8)

Teaching Tips

Words You Should Know

A. Sin *hamartia* (Gk.)—To miss the mark or target.

B. Righteousness *dikaiosune* (Gk.)—Justice, right standing, right relationship.

Teacher Preparation

Unifying Principle—Righteousness Through Christ. People sense that evil actions negatively impact their lives. Who can make amends for evil behavior? Paul told the Romans that the blood of Christ atones for all our sin.

A. Read the Bible Background and Devotional Readings.

B. Pray for your students and lesson clarity.

C. Read the lesson Scripture in multiple translations.

D. Option: Have the class work together to create a chart comparing justification by grace with justification by works of the Law. This can lead to a discussion of the great advantages we have of being under grace rather than the Law.

O—Open the Lesson

A. Begin the class with prayer.

B. Have the students read the Aim for Change.

C. Have the students read the In Focus story.

D. Ask students how events named in the story can weigh on their hearts and how they can view these events from a theological perspective.

P—Present the Scriptures

A. Read the Focal Verses and discuss the Background and The People, Places, and Times sections.

B. Have the class share what Scriptures stand out for them and why, with particular emphasis on today's context.

E—Explore the Meaning

A. Use In Depth or More Light on the Text to help provide more in-depth discussion of the lesson text.

B. Discuss the Liberating Lesson and Application for Activation sections.

N—Next Steps for Application

A. Summarize the value of recognizing we are made righteous through Christ alone.

B. End class with a commitment to pray for God to strengthen our faith in our salvation through Jesus Christ and for others to know Him.

Worship Guide

For the Superintendent or Teacher
Theme: Called to Righteousness
Song: "I Know It Was the Blood"
Devotional Reading: John 10:1–11

Called to Righteousness

Bible Background • ROMANS 3
Printed Text • ROMANS 3:21–31 | Devotional Reading • JOHN 10:1–11

Aim for Change

By the end of the lesson we will: SUMMARIZE Paul's teaching that justification is by grace and not acts of keeping the Law; REJOICE that we need not atone for our sin ourselves by works; and EXPRESS thankfulness for Jesus, our perfect Savior.

--- In Focus ---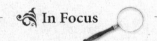

The Johnson family had been in turmoil for generations. The dynamic between family members was one wanted to be better than the other. If they didn't have the best spouse, they had to have the best children. If they were going off to college, it had to be the best, with the most amazing academic, musical, athletic, community service, or religious scholarship available. The family members had standards preset before they were born, and it sometimes was impossible to meet them. These standards did not leave room for their humanity—yet the whole Johnson family needed grace.

One particular generation had all the troubles you could imagine. Something about Thanksgiving brought their sins to the forefront. They just knew that their elders were going to condemn them, as they should have. In that moment transformation began. Each family member learned he or she was not the only one with sin and not alone in the need for grace. The family learned it was never their works that made their name great. It was the fact that they were born into this family, and loved by the family, that made their works important to the family. They did not have it all together, but they decided to work toward being better, simply because the ones who loved them believed they could.

How can we embrace and show grace toward ourselves, those closest to us, and those we do not know?

--- ## Keep in Mind ---

"Being justified freely by his grace through the redemption that is in Christ Jesus: Whom God hath set forth to be a propitiation through faith in his blood" (Romans 3:24-25a, KJV).

"Yet God, in his grace, freely makes us right in his sight. He did this through Christ Jesus when he freed us from the penalty for our sins. For God presented Jesus as the sacrifice for sin. People are made right with God when they believe that Jesus sacrificed his life, shedding his blood" (Romans 3:24-25a, NLT).

Focal Verses

KJV **Romans 3:21** But now the righteousness of God without the law is manifested, being witnessed by the law and the prophets;

22 Even the righteousness of God which is by faith of Jesus Christ unto all and upon all them that believe: for there is no difference:

23 For all have sinned, and come short of the glory of God;

24 Being justified freely by his grace through the redemption that is in Christ Jesus:

25 Whom God hath set forth to be a propitiation through faith in his blood, to declare his righteousness for the remission of sins that are past, through the forbearance of God;

26 To declare, I say, at this time his righteousness: that he might be just, and the justifier of him which believeth in Jesus.

27 Where is boasting then? It is excluded. By what law? of works? Nay: but by the law of faith.

28 Therefore we conclude that a man is justified by faith without the deeds of the law.

29 Is he the God of the Jews only? is he not also of the Gentiles? Yes, of the Gentiles also:

30 Seeing it is one God, which shall justify the circumcision by faith, and uncircumcision through faith.

31 Do we then make void the law through faith? God forbid: yea, we establish the law.

NLT **Romans 3:21** But now God has shown us a way to be made right with him without keeping the requirements of the law, as was promised in the writings of Moses and the prophets long ago.

22 We are made right with God by placing our faith in Jesus Christ. And this is true for everyone who believes, no matter who we are.

23 For everyone has sinned; we all fall short of God's glorious standard.

24 Yet God, in his grace, freely makes us right in his sight. He did this through Christ Jesus when he freed us from the penalty for our sins.

25 For God presented Jesus as the sacrifice for sin. People are made right with God when they believe that Jesus sacrificed his life, shedding his blood. This sacrifice shows that God was being fair when he held back and did not punish those who sinned in times past,

26 for he was looking ahead and including them in what he would do in this present time. God did this to demonstrate his righteousness, for he himself is fair and just, and he makes sinners right in his sight when they believe in Jesus.

27 Can we boast, then, that we have done anything to be accepted by God? No, because our acquittal is not based on obeying the law. It is based on faith.

28 So we are made right with God through faith and not by obeying the law.

29 After all, is God the God of the Jews only? Isn't he also the God of the Gentiles? Of course he is. **30** There is only one God, and he makes people right with himself only by faith, whether they are Jews or Gentiles.

31 Well then, if we emphasize faith, does this mean that we can forget about the law? Of course not! In fact, only when we have faith do we truly fulfill the law.

The People, Places, and Times

Jew. The word originally referred specifically to a member of the state of Judah (2 Kings 16:6), which was named for Jacob's fourth son. The word first occurs in 2 Kings 16:6 (KJV), when the ten northern tribes called Israel joined with the King of Aram to fight against Judah. In the New Testament, the word Jew is used to describe members of the Jewish faith and their leaders. In modern times and especially in the state of Israel, the word is used to describe ethnic birth, but not necessarily religion.

Background

The book of Romans is one of Paul's epistles, a letter he wrote to one of the earliest Jesus-following communities that formed and grew after Jesus' ascension to heaven. Paul begins the letter by describing the guiltiness of humanity, deserving God's judgment, and the power of the Gospel to save us. At the time of Paul's writing, there had been some confusion among new followers and opponents of Jesus alike, as they didn't understand the relationship between the Law that God had given to the Jews long ago and the effects of God coming to earth in Jesus, submitting to death, and then being raised again. Was it following the Law that put a person in right standing with God, or was it faith in this more recent work of God? In Romans 3, we begin to hear how God justifies us sinful human beings by the work that God has done through Jesus' death and resurrection, as opposed to the work we do in attempting to follow the Law. Here, Paul gives an explanation of the importance of each of these methods of justification (works and faith), the way that God has chosen to transition us from one method to the other, and how this is good news for each and every one of us.

Have you ever received the benefits of someone else's hard work with little to no cost to yourself? How did it feel to receive this?

At-A-Glance

1. Righteousness Through Christ
   (Romans 3:21–22)
2. Freedom From Past Sins (vv. 22–26)
3. Responding to What God Has Done
   (vv. 29-31)

In Depth

1. Righteousness Through Christ (Romans 3:21–22)

Justification was always by faith in God (Romans 4:3; Galatians 3:11; Habakkuk 2:4). In the era of the Old Testament a person expressed his faith by following God's commandments and obeying the Law that had been given to Moses. Yet the people became caught up in the ritual and the Law to maintain right relationship with God and atone for their sin. But now, God offers right relationship to all through faith in Jesus Christ who fulfilled the Law. God came to earth in Jesus Christ, died, and rose again, all for the purpose of showing God's own righteousness and faithfulness to humanity. God kept the covenant and invites us into right relationship. This flips the expected formula for right relationship with God on its head for people who had only known of the Law for all of their lives. God shows His love for humanity by coming down to earth and submitting to death on a cross as the ultimate atonement for our sin. This act of God is greater than anything we could try to do to live righteously or save ourselves from sin. Righteousness is by faith in Jesus Christ!

How does knowing that God has restored us to right relationship through Christ impact the way we reflect on the stories of the Old Testament?

2. Freedom From Past Sins (Romans 3:22–26)

Paul reminds us that though God has shaken some things up, one thing has not changed—every single person is guilty of sin. But through this new act that God has done, our sinfulness is no longer in the spotlight. Instead, it is God's own righteousness and love that are at the center of our relationship to God. Sin loses its power as a barrier between God and us.

Historically, in the event that someone disobeyed God's Law, the way to return to right standing with Him was through sacrifices and sacred offerings unto God for the atonement of sins. This is part of the reason the Roman church is confused about what religious or cultural affiliation a person needs to have to receive this gift; in the Old Testament, a person essentially needed to become a Jew and follow these practices to be in good standing with God. Paul teaches us that God no longer requires these traditional sacrifices and offerings—we are now free from this process. Instead of repeatedly needing to offer sacrifices to reconcile with God, Jesus offered Himself on our behalf, as an ultimate sacrifice to end the need for any other sacrifice. Now, we no longer lose standing with God because of our past sins, so long as we believe in the truth and power of what God has done for us through Jesus. We've received the fruit of Jesus' redemptive act simply by grace, and that fruit is made effective in our lives as we grow in faith.

How does freedom from past sins change the way you think of your future sins?

3. Responding to What God Has Done (vv. 29–31)

The Greek word for justification is the same word elsewhere translated as righteousness. Another way to understand this idea is that we learn and receive true righteousness by having faith in God's righteousness. God makes this possible through the work of Jesus Christ, freeing us from the process of needing to atone for sin through the rituals and practices that had been given to the Jews. Now, God simply asks that we have faith in God's love for us and all that He has done. But that isn't the end of it. Paul points out that this doesn't simply mean that we are free to carry on in sin or that the Law is no longer true. Instead, our love for God should drive us to holy living that aligns with the commands He communicates to us in the Law.

How do you respond to what God has done for you through Jesus Christ? What feelings do you experience? What actions do you take?

Search the Scriptures

1. Paul argues that God is righteous. What does he have to say about human righteousness (Romans 3:23)?

2. Why would God first give us the Law to follow and then send Jesus later? Do human beings gain something from this (Romans 3:21, 31)?

Discuss the Meaning

1. God's Law is not just established for the purpose of keeping order. What makes God's Law more than just a "set of rules"? How is it an experience?

2. Do you believe the rules and the law of this world are fair and just? Do you think they could contradict God's Law?

Liberating Lesson

Our world and our societies are built around the laws and systems that we create for ourselves. All communities have them, whether formal or informal; we even have them in our circles of friends and neighborhoods. Because laws are such an integral part of our daily lives, it makes sense that we would struggle to receive this gracious gift of simply being freed from past sins. We have a hard time understanding how we can be rewarded or blessed without having earned it, or how our wrongdoings could go unpunished. Our earthly communities fall into chaos when individuals choose to disobey or disregard laws—this is why we've created prisons and systems of punishment and reward. But as much as we feel comfortable with this way of maintaining community, we also see the laws and systems we've created fail repeatedly, especially when it comes to minority groups and historically oppressed peoples. But God does not have that fear. We can rejoice and find relief in knowing that God's laws are actually good for us. We don't have to be suspicious about whether something is truly for our good or if God has some sort of plan to use the Law against us. The sacrifice of Jesus is proof of God's love and goodness. All we need to do is learn to receive and believe in the gift. And as we receive this, we can begin to trust that it is God who justifies us and our neighbors, not our works, and not the laws and judgments that are passed on earth.

Application for Activation

Spend some time writing in your journal about some of the judgments that have been passed on you, particularly those that you have accepted as true. Write them down and ask God if these things align with the way that He sees you. Write out God's responses, remembering that God's voice is always loving and compassionate, not condemning or discouraging. Also consider specific people in your life upon whom you may have passed judgment. Invite God to reveal to you how He views those people. Are there individuals you feel led to reconcile with or apologize to? Are there people from whom you need to receive reconciliation or apologies? Challenge yourself—commit to beginning a conversation with one or more of the people who come to mind. Ask for God's

guidance and presence in the midst of these interactions.

Follow the Spirit

What God wants me to do:

_____

_____

Remember Your Thoughts

Special insights I have learned:

_____

_____

More Light on the Text
Romans 3:21–31

21 But now the righteousness of God without the law is manifested, being witnessed by the law and the prophets;

When Paul began his argument proving that all humanity was guilty before God, he used the phrase "for the wrath of God is revealed from heaven against all" (from 1:18). Humanity was indeed worthy of God's wrath. "But now" is a favorite expression of Paul (see Ephesians 2:11–13; 1 Corinthians 15:16–20). The apostle uses this phrase when transitioning from a gloomy, seemingly hopeless situation to something divinely wonderful: the manifestation of "the righteousness of God." As used here, God's righteousness is not a reference to His character. Paul deals with that aspect of righteousness later in verse 26. In verse 21, righteousness refers to God's gift of righteousness to all those who enter the kingdom of God (Matthew 5:19–20). By faith in Christ and His work of atonement, unrighteous sinners receive God's righteousness. This means that God forgives all their sins and provides a new "right" standing with Him. God's gift of righteousness includes victory over our sinful nature (Romans 6:12–14), separation from evil (2 Corinthians 6:14), and new eternal life under the rule of God (Romans 5:21).

God's gift of righteousness is without the Law. The word "without," from the Greek word *choris*, means absolutely apart from. God's gift of righteousness has absolutely nothing to do with the Law. Paul further states that this righteousness is witnessed to by both the Law and the prophets. The Law, in this case, refers to the Torah or first five books of the Bible, which explain the sacrificial system the Jews were to follow. When the Jews took their sin offering to the Temple, laid their hands on the bullock's head, confessed their sins, and killed the animal, they attested to their belief in a righteousness not their own (see Leviticus 4:1–4).

22 Even the righteousness of God which is by faith of Jesus Christ unto all and upon all them that believe: for there is no difference: 23 For all have sinned, and come short of the glory of God;

God freely offers righteousness to all who have "faith in Jesus Christ." One must have faith in the finished work of Jesus Christ. He is the only way (John 14:6). Paul states that God's gift of righteousness is "unto all and upon all them that believe." It appears that the apostle is repeating himself here. But in fact he is using very precise language to say that God's gift of righteousness is not universal. It does not save everyone. God's righteousness is available "unto all." His righteousness only comes to, or is "upon," "them that believe." There is a condition for receiving God's gift and that condition is faith in Christ.

The latter part of verse 22 (beginning with "for") and all of verse 23 form a parenthetical statement. Faith in Christ is the only condition for the gift and "there is no difference." The word "difference" is a translation of the Greek word *diastole* (**dee-ah-STO-lay**) and means distinction. In other words, God makes no distinction between Jews and Gentiles. He treats both exactly the same. Just as there is no difference between Jew and Gentile, there is no difference between the liar and the murderer in regard to their righteousness with God. Both are equally lost and in need of God's gift of righteousness.

To drive home his point that all the world is under sin and condemnation, Paul employs two phrases that are related to sporting events. In the phrase, "For all have sinned," the verb "sinned," from the Greek word *hamartano*, pictures a warrior's arrow or more commonly used spear falling short of its target. Sin is pictured as missing the mark of God's call for humanity. "Fall short" (Greek: *hustereo*, **hoo-STAIR-ee-o**) can point to lateness and loss. It pictures a runner losing a race. The point is that humanity fails to achieve its ultimate goal, which is the glory of God. The verb "sinned" is used in the past tense to indicate God's view of sin. The Creator looks back on all sin as an accomplished fact. He simply says, "All have sinned." The fact that all "come short" is present tense and could be read "all continuously come short." This clause refers to our practical everyday living. We all sin continuously. John, the beloved disciple, explained it this way, "If we say we have no sin [present tense], we deceive ourselves, and the truth is not in us. If we say that we have not sinned [past tense], we make him a liar, and his word is not in us" (1 John 1:8, 10).

The meaning of the phrase "glory of God," (Gk. *te doxes tou theou*) is hotly debated. The term is generally used to describe the aggregate of God's divine attributes and God's revelation of Himself (see Exodus 34:6–7). This cannot be what Paul means because humanity is not condemned because of our inferiority compared to God's attributes. Another interpretation is that in this case the glory of God means divine approval or praise, leaving us to understand that we do not receive God's approval in our sinfulness. Others believe the glory of God refers to what John mentions in his Gospel, "And the Word was made flesh, and dwelt among us, (and we beheld His glory, the glory as of the only begotten of the Father,) full of grace and truth" (John 1:14). Jesus' glory spoken of in the Gospel of John was not the out-shining of His divine attributes because He did not display that divine glory then; He had set it aside (Philippians 2:7). The glory of God referenced here is likely the operation of human beings in their God-ordained right relationship with Him and the fullness of their calling.

Paul later explains what it means to function in that fullness (Romans 8). When we are in right relationship with God, operating as children of God, our relationships flourish. Picture Adam and Eve in the Garden before sin. They were operating in their divine purpose as God's children and representatives on the earth: They had right relationship so they could stand in God's presence sinless; they were in right relationship with one another; and the Garden was flourishing. Everything in creation functions in its God-ordained purpose and is fruitful and multiplying, filling the earth. We see the revelation of this operating as children of God embodied in Christ. Jesus models perfect relationship with God as a human, without sin, and everywhere He goes He manifests the kingdom of God by destroying the works of sin in the earth that cause disease, natural and demonic oppression, wrong relationships, and ultimately death. Through the death and resurrection of Jesus Christ, by faith in His work of grace toward us, we are released from the power of sin and empowered by the Holy Spirit to live like sons and daughters of God.

24 Being justified freely by his grace through the redemption that is in Christ Jesus:

This final view would explain why humanity needs to be justified. We cannot live according to the standard set by God and modeled by Christ. Because it is impossible to live righteous lives, how can humanity ever hope to gain a right standing with God? The answer is simple: by being justified. The words "righteousness" and "justified" are spiritually linked in this epistle. Notice how the apostle clusters these words in these few verses: "Righteousness" (vv. 21, 22, 25, 26) is *dikaiosune* (**dee-KIO-soonay**) in the Greek. "Justified" (v. 24) is *dikaioomenoi* (**dee-kio-AHMEN-oy**), "just" (v. 26) is *dikaios*, "justifier" (v. 26) is *dikaiou*, and "justify" (v. 30) is *dikaiosei*. All the words share the same root *dike* (**DEE-kay**). To justify means to declare and treat as righteous. In other words, God says that we are righteous and then He treats us as if we had never sinned. Our sins are not merely forgiven or pardoned; they are wiped out! God declares us as righteous as Jesus Christ Himself. Our justification is accomplished through the redemption that is in Christ Jesus. The word "redemption" is from the Greek word *apolutrosis* (**a-paul-oo-TRO-SEES**), which means to deliver by paying a ransom. The word pictures a slave auction where people are held in bondage and are incapable of freeing themselves. Christ is portrayed as the one who sees our hopeless state and pays the ransom (Gk. *lutron,* **LOO-trahn**) for our freedom.

25 Whom God hath set forth to be a propitiation through faith in his blood, to declare his righteousness for the remission of sins that are past, through the forbearance of God; 26 To declare, I say, at this time his righteousness: that he might be just, and the justifier of him which believeth in Jesus.

The picture Paul calls to mind is that of the Exodus and being freed from the bondage of sin. It is in this context that Jesus institutes the Last Supper and becomes the ultimate Passover lamb instituting a new covenant in His blood. The thing Christ had to offer to cover this great price was His blood. When the Bible refers to blood, it means a life laid down in sacrifice (see Hebrews 9:7). In this case, "his blood" signifies the death of Christ by the shedding of His blood on the Cross. Since the life of the flesh is in the blood (Leviticus 17:11) and death is the cost of sinfulness (Romans 6:23), then only the shedding of the blood of a sinless Savior could cover the cost of our redemption.

Why was the cost of our ransom so high? Why did Christ have to die on the Cross? The most readily available answer is that God demonstrated His love for us through the death of His only begotten Son (John 3:16). However, that was not the only purpose of Christ's sacrifice on Calvary. The other reason was to declare God's righteousness in the remission of sins.

Why was it necessary for God to declare His righteousness? The phrase "for the remission of sin" is a translation of the Greek word *pareisis* (**pa-RAY-sees**), which means to overlook or suspend judgment. This explains how God dealt with sin before the sacrifice of Christ. God patiently tolerated the sins of the generations before Christ. As a result, God's holiness was called into question (Psalm 50:21). In order for God to show that He is righteous, He sent Christ to the Cross where He punished every sin—past, present, and future. This does not mean that God ignored sin in the Old Testament. It means that He did not deal with it fully and completely until Calvary. Christ's death on the Cross satisfied God's justice and frees us from the bondage of sin.

Christ thus became our propitiation. The actual Greek word for "propitiation" is *hilasterion* (**hee-las-TAIR-ee-ahn**). In secular Greek, *hilasterion* referred to sacrifices offered to pagan deities to appease their anger. However, this is not how Paul uses the word. In the Septuagint, the Greek translation of the Old Testament, *hilasterion* is translated as "mercy seat" (see Hebrews 9:5). On the Day of Atonement, the high priest appeared before the Ark of the Covenant and poured blood from a sacrifice on the golden lid of the Ark called the mercy seat (Exodus 25:17–22). This act symbolized that sin, which separated God from His people, was cleansed through the shedding of blood. So the place of judgment, the mercy seat, became the place of mercy and reconciliation. The ritual pointed to Christ's sacrificial death where God's legitimate demands for justice against sinful humanity were fully met. Therefore, He is free to show mercy to those who formally were only worthy of judgment. Christ's shed blood as our propitiation (mercy seat) allows God to righteously punish sin and at the same time show mercy and treat repentant sinners as if they had never sinned. Christ, our propitiation, allows God to be both just and the justifier.

27 Where is boasting then? It is excluded. By what law? of works? Nay: but by the law of faith. 28 Therefore we conclude that a man is justified by faith without the deeds of the law. 29 Is he the God of the Jews only? is he not also of the Gentiles? Yes, of the Gentiles also: 30 Seeing it is one God, which shall justify the circumcision by faith, and uncircumcision through faith. 31 Do we then make void the law through faith? God forbid: yea, we establish the law.

Since God provided everything necessary for our salvation, what did we do to earn our salvation that we can brag about? Paul answers the question with three short words, "it is excluded." There are two options available to anyone who wants to be reconciled to God.

445

The first is justification by works. With this option, people earn their righteousness by living according to the Law. The problem comes when one aspect of the Law is violated—then the entire Law is violated (James 2:10). So one would have to live an absolutely perfect life in order to enjoy God's fellowship. The other option is to achieve righteousness apart from the deeds of the Law. Here people are justified by faith in the life and work of Jesus Christ.

Does this void or nullify the Law? By no means; it establishes the Law by causing it to stand as a guide for human behavior. We are made righteous by faith in order that we might keep the commandments of God by His power rather than our own works.

Sources:

Bassler, Jouette M. *The HarperCollins Study Bible*: New Revised Standard Verion. Edited by Wayne A. Meeks. San Francisco, CA: HarperSanFrancisco, 1993.

Wright, N.T. *The Day the Revolution Began: Reconsidering the Meaning of Jesus's Crucifixion.* San Francisco, CA: Harper One, 2018.

Say It Correctly

Propitiation. pruh-pitch-ee-**AY**-shuhn.
Righteousness. **RIY**-chuhs-nis.

Daily Bible Readings

MONDAY
God-Given Task for Workers
(Ecclesiastes 3:9–17)

TUESDAY
The Shepherd Lays Down His Life
(John 10:11–18)

WEDNESDAY
The Value of the Law
(Romans 7:7–12)

THURSDAY
The Purpose of the Law
(Galatians 3:19–29)

FRIDAY
God Is Faithful and Fair
(Romans 3:1–8)

SATURDAY
Jesus Brings True Justice
(Romans 3:9–20)

SUNDAY
All Called to Righteousness
(Romans 3:21–31)

Notes

Teaching Tips

Words You Should Know

A. Flesh *sarkos* (Gk.)—Sinful nature.

B. Condemnation *katakrima* (Gk.)—Punishment from wrong standing, penalty.

Teacher Preparation

Unifying Principle—New Life in the Spirit. Consequences of past actions, the reality of impending death, and a sense that we cannot undo past mistakes weigh heavily on the human spirit. Where does one find relief from these pressures? Paul assures us that those who are in Christ Jesus have life in the Spirit and are free from condemnation.

A. Read the Bible Background and Devotional Readings.

B. Pray for your students and lesson clarity.

C. Read the lesson Scripture in multiple translations.

D. Option: Ask two people to prepare ahead of time to portray what it might look like to set their minds on the flesh and on the Spirit. Discuss the differences and how we can commit to the latter.

O—Open the Lesson

A. Begin the class with prayer.

B. Have the students read the Aim for Change.

C. Have the students read the In Focus story.

D. Ask students how events named in the story can weigh on their hearts and how they can view these events from a theological perspective.

P—Present the Scriptures

A. Read the Focal Verses and discuss the Background and The People, Places, and Times sections.

B. Have the class share what Scriptures stand out for them and why, with particular emphasis on today's context.

E—Explore the Meaning

A. Use In Depth or More Light on the Text to help provide more in-depth discussion of the lesson text.

B. Discuss the Liberating Lesson and Application for Activation sections.

N—Next Steps for Application

A. Summarize the value of living in the Spirit instead of our fleshly desires.

B. End class with a commitment to pray for strength to receive righteousness by grace and walk in it!

Worship Guide

For the Superintendent or Teacher
Theme: Called to Life in the Spirit
Song: "Holy Spirit Have Your Way"
Devotional Reading: Romans 6:1–14

Called to Life in the Spirit

Bible Background • ROMANS 8
Printed Text • ROMANS 8:1–14 | Devotional Reading • ROMANS 6:1–14

—————— Aim for Change ——————

By the end of the lesson we will: CONTRAST living in the flesh with living in the Spirit; DESCRIBE emptiness of trying to find life following the flesh; and SHARE what it means to have our mind set on living in the Spirit.

———— 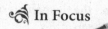 In Focus ————

Henry had run from his past for years. He couldn't tell anyone about it. The addiction was a disease. He knew that. But his actions while addicted—and the people he had hurt—were wrong. It was sinful. His 12-step program taught him to make amends with those he harmed and sinned against. That was crucial, and he did the best he could, with an awareness that he might or might not receive forgiveness from the harmed party. He worked the steps. Sober for twelve years, happily employed for eleven, saved for nine, married for seven, and three children later, he found himself here. He could not imagine why his pastor would entrust him with another young brother who was struggling with addiction. Henry had moved on and didn't want to dig up the past. But through the experience with this young man, Henry would redefine his views and be forever changed.

When he was charged with being a light, Henry found that impossible, because he had not worked his steps thoroughly the way he believed he had. When Henry went through the steps, he made amends with everybody except for one person: himself. He hadn't forgiven himself, because he hadn't acknowledged his sin against himself. Dealing with this young brother forced him to face that. He could not truly be free until he faced the reality of his sin and received God's forgiveness for himself. Henry acknowledged the sin, faced it, and was freed from the shame and power of the disease over his life.

How can being an example for others of God's grace help us receive more grace for ourselves?

—————— Keep in Mind ——————

"There is therefore now no condemnation to them which are in Christ Jesus, who walk not after the flesh, but after the Spirit" (Romans 8:1, KJV).

"So now there is no condemnation for those who belong to Christ Jesus" (Romans 8:1, NLT).

Focal Verses

KJV **Romans 8:1** There is therefore now no condemnation to them which are in Christ Jesus, who walk not after the flesh, but after the Spirit.

2 For the law of the Spirit of life in Christ Jesus hath made me free from the law of sin and death.

3 For what the law could not do, in that it was weak through the flesh, God sending his own Son in the likeness of sinful flesh, and for sin, condemned sin in the flesh:

4 That the righteousness of the law might be fulfilled in us, who walk not after the flesh, but after the Spirit.

5 For they that are after the flesh do mind the things of the flesh; but they that are after the Spirit the things of the Spirit.

6 For to be carnally minded is death; but to be spiritually minded is life and peace.

7 Because the carnal mind is enmity against God: for it is not subject to the law of God, neither indeed can be.

8 So then they that are in the flesh cannot please God.

9 But ye are not in the flesh, but in the Spirit, if so be that the Spirit of God dwell in you. Now if any man have not the Spirit of Christ, he is none of his.

10 And if Christ be in you, the body is dead because of sin; but the Spirit is life because of righteousness.

11 But if the Spirit of him that raised up Jesus from the dead dwell in you, he that raised up Christ from the dead shall also quicken your mortal bodies by his Spirit that dwelleth in you.

12 Therefore, brethren, we are debtors, not to the flesh, to live after the flesh.

13 For if ye live after the flesh, ye shall die: but if ye through the Spirit do mortify the deeds of the body, ye shall live.

NLT **Romans 8:1** So now there is no condemnation for those who belong to Christ Jesus.

2 And because you belong to him, the power of the life-giving Spirit has freed you from the power of sin that leads to death.

3 The law of Moses was unable to save us because of the weakness of our sinful nature. So God did what the law could not do. He sent his own Son in a body like the bodies we sinners have. And in that body God declared an end to sin's control over us by giving his Son as a sacrifice for our sins.

4 He did this so that the just requirement of the law would be fully satisfied for us, who no longer follow our sinful nature but instead follow the Spirit.

5 Those who are dominated by the sinful nature think about sinful things, but those who are controlled by the Holy Spirit think about things that please the Spirit.

6 So letting your sinful nature control your mind leads to death. But letting the Spirit control your mind leads to life and peace.

7 For the sinful nature is always hostile to God. It never did obey God's laws, and it never will.

8 That's why those who are still under the control of their sinful nature can never please God.

9 But you are not controlled by your sinful nature. You are controlled by the Spirit if you have the Spirit of God living in you. (And remember that those who do not have the Spirit of Christ living in them do not belong to him at all.)

10 And Christ lives within you, so even though your body will die because of sin, the Spirit gives you life because you have been made right with God.

14 For as many as are led by the Spirit of God, they are the sons of God.

11 The Spirit of God, who raised Jesus from the dead, lives in you. And just as God raised Christ Jesus from the dead, he will give life to your mortal bodies by this same Spirit living within you.

12 Therefore, dear brothers and sisters, you have no obligation to do what your sinful nature urges you to do.

13 For if you live by its dictates, you will die. But if through the power of the Spirit you put to death the deeds of your sinful nature, you will live.

14 For all who are led by the Spirit of God are children of God.

The People, Places, and Times

The Law of Sin and Death. This law represents our unsaved and condemned state before sanctification in Christ Jesus. The power and authority sin had over our flesh separate us from right relationship with God. We were unable to free ourselves from sin and death's power. It is only by the power of the Holy Spirit, called the Spirit of Life in this passage, that we are able to become free from this law. The Holy Spirit works within us to walk in new life with Jesus Christ.

What does it mean to follow the law of the Spirit?

Background

At the beginning of his letter to the Romans, Paul addresses two different methods of justification that the people have been disputing over: justification by works and justification by faith. He explains that God has transitioned us from works to faith-based justification, as Jesus' resurrection leads to justification and life for all, regardless of their nationality or background (Romans 5:18). We respond to this gracious gift by submitting to God and His commandments, out of love and faith in Jesus. Leading up to chapter 8, Paul begins speaking of the power of sin and our constant struggle to break free from this enslavement—it is easily apparent that this is something we are incapable of accomplishing as humans. We are instead set free by God for the purpose of now becoming subject to righteousness. Here in chapter 8, we hear all about the power of the Holy Spirit to free us from sin, bring life to our dead flesh, and transform us as children of God!

Have you ever been excluded from something because of your nationality, race, or past history? How did you respond to your exclusion? What might have changed if someone had stepped in on your behalf?

At-A-Glance

1. No Condemnation (Romans 8:1–8)
2. The Spirit of God Dwells in You (vv. 9–11)
3. We Are Children of God (vv. 12–14)

In Depth

1. No Condemnation (Romans 8:1–8)

Here, Paul speaks of the work that Jesus has done as a new law that frees us from the law of sin and death. At the same time, we know from the previous lesson that God's Law from the Old Testament is still important for how we respond to God's righteousness and love for us. So, what exactly does it mean that we have been set free from it? Paul breaks this down in terms of what things we set our minds on. According to the previous law, we were directed to set our minds on the things of the flesh, staying focused on all of the things that we should and shouldn't do to please God. This was important because sin had the power to keep us in our graves! But with God's new law, we are directed to set our minds on the things of the Spirit. We learn to trust the things that God has done through Jesus, rather than put our faith in what we can do as humans. The law of sin leads us to death in displeasing God, but the leadership of the Holy Spirit leads us to new life in Christ.

Sin has lost the power to keep us in our graves, but it hasn't lost all of its power. Does this change the way you think about your own sins?

2. The Spirit of God Dwells in You (vv. 9–11)

As Christians, we are no longer "in the flesh." We are now "in the Spirit" because God's Spirit lives within us. This creates an interesting dynamic for our existence here on earth. We are dead in our flesh and our humanity, yet we are very much alive because we receive the Spirit of Christ. But the two don't remain separate. Because this is the same Spirit that worked to resurrect Jesus, we, too, can believe in the resurrection of our flesh. We don't have to wait for our flesh to go away so that we can be fully alive; the Spirit is able to give life to our mortal bodies as well.

We are no longer "in the flesh," but we do still have our flesh. How does this affect the way we experience life with God?

3. We Are Children of God (vv. 12–14)

We can see that there is tension between what the previous law and the new law each means for us. Here, Paul says outright that how we live is important. We are free from the power of death, but there is an appropriate way to respond to what God has done for us. Consider the fruit of the Spirit (Galatians 5:22–23). We have received the Spirit of Christ that has the power to resurrect our dead flesh. But how do we see that this has happened or begun to happen? We see it in the way that we begin to live our lives and treat the world around us. And, of course, it doesn't happen overnight. We are like children who will always be learning, making mistakes, needing to adjust, until God makes us perfect. And we can rejoice because there is no condemnation in this. Being like children before God—teachable, playful, malleable, joyful—is an invitation and a gift from God.

What characteristics do you think of when you think of children? How might God be inviting you to be His child?

Search the Scriptures

1. Why is changing our mindset a necessity (Romans 8:6–8)?

2. What are the problems of relying on our flesh? Why is humanity flawed (vv. 3, 8)?

Discuss the Meaning

1. Do you think there are places where the things of the flesh and the things of the Spirit overlap? What tools do we have to discern between the two?

2. How do we "put to death the deeds of [our] sinful nature" (v. 13, NLT)? How are we

commanded to respond to our sins? (Think: Repentance? Reconciliation? Reparations?)

Liberating Lesson

By the power of the Spirit, we change the way we live in response to God's love. And though we repent and are free from our past sins, this does not reverse the damage that we have done to ourselves and others in our sinfulness. What responsibility do we have to make amends for the things that we've done prior to receiving the Spirit of Christ? What does a full view of repentance look like? Is it simply turning away from a particular sinful act or way of living, or are we called to rectify the damage we have done?

Consider the story of Zacchaeus the tax collector (Luke 19:1–10). After encountering Jesus, Zacchaeus says to him, "Behold, Lord, the half of my goods I give to the poor; and if I have taken any thing from any man by false accusation, I restore him fourfold" (v. 8). This is not what Jesus asks of him, rather, what he feels compelled to do as a response to his encounter with God. Might his transformation have still been complete had he not decided to repay (and in excess!) for his past sins? Can you think of situations in which you should have gone as far as repaying for past sins but were reluctant to do so? What situations can you name, personal or historical, for which reparations might be a sign of a more complete repentance of sin?

Application for Activation

Take a moment to engage in musical worship as a way of setting your mind on the Spirit. You can listen to a worship song or sing some songs together as a group (e.g., "I Surrender All" or "Be Thou My Vision"). Afterward, take a moment to silently pray to God, asking Him to speak to you about any areas in your life where you may have given power to sin. Invite God into that particular situation, repent of wrongdoing, and consider how God may be inviting you to take action as part of your repentance. If comfortable, consider sharing with the group some of the possibilities that arose.

Follow the Spirit

What God wants me to do:

_____

_____

_____

_____

Remember Your Thoughts

Special insights I have learned:

_____

_____

_____

_____

More Light on the Text
Romans 8:1–14

Prior to this passage, Paul ardently proclaims salvation and justification by faith through God's loving grace (Romans 6–7). He then addresses the constant struggle the believer has with the sinful nature ("the flesh"). Paul acknowledges that even he tries to keep the Law, but is unable to do so using his own will and efforts. Here, though, Paul preaches power! He argues that the power of the Holy Spirit changes the believer through faith in Jesus Christ. In previous chapters, Paul introduced the power of sin. Now he turns his attention to the solution: the power of the

Holy Spirit over sin. The indwelling power of the Holy Spirit offers us triumph rather than struggle. Through the "law of the Spirit of life" (Romans 8:2), the believer's faith gives the power to become the new creature God has declared him or her to be.

1 There is therefore now no condemnation to them which are in Christ Jesus, who walk not after the flesh, but after the Spirit.

Paul's theme in this chapter is centered on power in the life of the believer. The New Testament writers in general, and Paul in particular, generally write of two specific words that get translated as power in some English translations: *exousia* (Gk. **ex-oo-SEE-ah**) and *dunamis* (Gk. **DOO-naw-mees**). The first, *exousia*, means authority, and is the power equated with divine authority. Jesus refers to *exousia* when He declared to His apostles that "all power is given unto me in heaven and in earth" (from Matthew 28:18). The second power, *dunamis*, is a power that means to be able to do something. This power is the dynamic strength or wonder-working power exercised through the Holy Spirit by the believer. *Dunamis* is the power that is referred to when Jesus instructs His disciples that "ye shall receive power, after that the Holy Ghost is come upon you" (Acts 1:8). It is this latter power, this gift of the Holy Spirit, which emboldens and enables believers to live a Christian life.

Paul personalizes this very important teaching by addressing the Roman church in the first person. He has already emphasized the stronghold of sin, in general, and sinful nature, in particular: "I don't really understand myself, for I want to do what is right, but I don't do it. Instead, I do what I hate" (Romans 7:15, NLT). There is, he points out, a constant battle to subdue the sinful nature and bring it into submission. The Law, Paul explains, only seems to make him more aware of how far he is from righteousness. Paul concludes that there are two laws at work: God's law and the law of sin. In his mind, he admits, "I really want to obey God's law, but because of my sinful nature I am a slave to sin" (from v. 25, NLT).

Moving forward, Paul is adamant that there is "no condemnation to them which are in Christ Jesus." To be sure, the first-century Roman believers, to whom this letter is addressed, had an immediate understanding of the concept of "condemnation." Many of the Hebrew Christians were not citizens of Rome and enjoyed none of its privileges or protections. These Hebrew Christians were under constant and oppressive scrutiny from the Roman government. They would have been painfully aware that the tiniest infraction could result in their immediate condemnation by the Roman authorities. Found guilty of any breech of Roman laws (e.g., failing to show the proper deference to the emperor or other authority figure) could subject them to loss of property, beatings, or imprisonment.

Similarly, we should recall that even the strictest adherence to the Mosaic Law did not have the power to free man from sin. In fact, everything about the Law condemned the sinful nature. The Law could only offer a standard for righteousness. At best, it served to demonstrate how far afield humanity was from righteousness. Humanity's salvation was accomplished only through Jesus' redemptive death on the Cross. Thus, through Jesus Christ, we are free to live under grace and not the Law. To put it another way, Jesus' death and resurrection justified man, or made us guiltless before God. Through Jesus Christ, we were brought out of sin and returned to right relationship with God. Through our faith and belief that Jesus died, was buried, and rose to save us from our sins, our penalty is forever removed from our lives as believers.

2 For the law of the Spirit of life in Christ Jesus hath made me free from the law of sin and death. 3 For what the law could not do, in that it was weak through the flesh, God sending his own Son in the likeness of sinful flesh, and for sin, condemned sin in the flesh:

The spirit Paul refers to in verse 2 and the following verses must be understood to be the Holy Spirit, in Greek the *hagia pneuma* (**HA-gee-ah PNEW-mah**). Not a "thing," but rather we should understand the Holy Spirit to be a distinct person of the triune God and a significant influence in the life of believers. He is the same Spirit Jesus referred to when He told Nicodemus "except a man be born of water and of the Spirit, he cannot enter into the kingdom of God" (John 3:5).

Paul again refers to the inadequacy of the Law. The Law held only the power to condemn. It had no power to renew or change a person's desire to live a godly life. This renewal was accomplished though the resurrection of Jesus Christ. God, Paul explains, fashioned His only Son in the form of a human in order to sacrifice Him for the sins of humanity. Jesus, in flesh, died for the flesh. From that, the power of sin to condemn us to death has been nullified. God will no longer condemn us to death for our sins as the Law once did.

Here again, the reader must appreciate Paul's candor. He makes it clear that the struggle between the sinful nature, or "the flesh," and righteousness is always present in his life (indeed, in the life of every believer). It is obvious he knows that the Roman believers are struggling as he has been struggling. He wants to make it clear that God does not condemn or reject the believer for the struggle. Through Jesus Christ, we are members of God's family, and He does not kick us out because of our failures. This security was bought by Jesus' blood.

No matter what we do, as believers we have the blessed assurance that God will never reject us.

4 That the righteousness of the law might be fulfilled in us, who walk not after the flesh, but after the Spirit.

It is important to note that neither our salvation nor our justification eliminated sin itself. Sin still exists. We still wrestle against it. Paul acknowledges this constant struggle as every believer should. Some believers mistakenly believe that upon their confession of faith, God removes sin and temptation. Paul posits that the desire, or temptation, to "walk... after the flesh" will abate only after believers understand and believe that in Christ they have been made new creatures. Through the power of the Holy Spirit, believers will want to walk in righteousness rather than in the sinful nature. That which the Law was unable to legislate—the will to live righteously—the Holy Spirit empowers the believer to do.

5 For they that are after the flesh do mind the things of the flesh; but they that are after the Spirit the things of the Spirit.

The Holy Spirit does not mysteriously hover over the heads of believers, suddenly swoop down on them, bring a short period of deliverance, and then simply vanish. The Holy Spirit is not an "act." Rather, the Holy Spirit is the operative that empowers and enables the believer to live a godly life. While the Holy Spirit indwells in the life of every believer, the believer must choose to access that power. This, Paul makes clear, is an all-or-nothing proposition. The old self cannot be permitted to live because God has declared that it must die.

6 For to be carnally minded is death; but to be spiritually minded is life and peace.

Paul has already established that the worldly ("carnally minded") people cannot please God;

and that through the Holy Spirit, the believer is empowered to live righteously. The notion of "carnal" and "flesh" immediately bring to mind sins of a sexual nature. We should note, however, that as it is used here, it does not only mean the body. More specifically, Paul is addressing sins that take root in our bodies. Hence, carnally minded certainly includes obscene and lustful thoughts, but also refers to lying, jealousy, selfish ambitions, ungodly conversation, hostile and bitter feelings toward others, and perhaps the most dangerous of all, arrogance. The carnal or worldly must die so that the Spirit can reign in the life of the believer. Here, Paul makes it clear that the mind that longs for the carnal will end in death. Similarly, the spiritually minded, that is the mind of the believer empowered by the Holy Spirit, ends in life and peace.

7 Because the carnal mind is enmity against God: for it is not subject to the law of God, neither indeed can be.

Here, Paul pauses to provide the reason for the opposition he presented in verse 6. The answer lies in the Greek translation for the word enmity, *echthra* (**EKH-thrah**) meaning hatred. Paul is saying that the carnal mind hates God. Jesus Himself had taught, "No man can serve two masters: for either he will hate the one, and love the other; or else he will hold to the one, and despise the other" (Matthew 6:24). The believer, now free to choose, must decide between the old master (the sinful nature) or the new master (a spirit-filled life in Jesus Christ).

8 So then they that are in the flesh cannot please God. 9 But ye are not in the flesh, but in the Spirit, if so be that the Spirit of God dwell in you. Now if any man not have the Spirit of Christ, he is none of his.

All of the previous verses are wrapped up neatly in this one simple sentence. A sinful man cannot please God. This is at odds with the condition of the believer, who longs to please his Creator. This verse echoes a similar teaching to the Galatian church: "For the sinful nature desires what is contrary to the Spirit… They are in conflict with each other" (from Galatians 5:17). Now that Paul has drawn the line in the sand, he reminds the readers that they are not in the flesh. This happens through the grace of God, which provided the means of our salvation; through our justification in Christ Jesus our minds are renewed by the constant indwelling of the Holy Spirit.

10 And if Christ be in you, the body is dead because of sin; but the Spirit is life because of righteousness.

The conditional clause "and if Christ" at the beginning of this verse indicates that the verse is clarifying Paul's previous point. It also serves to protect the integrity of Paul's Gospel against those who would attempt to weaken it by asking, "If you're in Christ, and the penalty of sin is gone, then you can do anything you want." Here Paul argues that this is impossible since the Holy Spirit is at work in the lives of each believer. The preposition "in" carries tremendous weight in this context. The Greek word *en* (**EN**) functions to describe the Holy Spirit at rest and in a fixed position within us. The believer then is possessed by God, who resides at the center of our being. The clause that follows—"the body is dead"—is ironic. How can the believer be dead and alive at the same time? The Greek word rendered "dead" is *nekros* (**ne-KROSE**), and it describes a life that is spiritually destitute of God. Paul is using it here to support the affirmation of believers being dead to the body that would otherwise condemn us. Instead, Paul argues that our life is now a possession of the Spirit.

The Greek word for "righteousness," *dikaiosune* (**dee-kie-oh-SOO-nay**), describes a condition acceptable to God. It implies correct thinking, purity of life, virtue, and integrity from God's perspective. Paul teaches that unless the believer embraces righteousness, as given by the Spirit, then we are only left with self-righteousness. Righteousness is an important word in Scripture. It is especially significant to Paul as he uses it thirty-eight times in the book of Romans alone. It is used more in this epistle than any other time in the entire New Testament.

11 But if the Spirit of him that raised up Jesus from the dead dwell in you, he that raised up Christ from the dead shall also quicken your mortal bodies by his Spirit that dwelleth in you. 12 Therefore, brethren, we are debtors, not to the flesh, to live after the flesh. 13 For if ye live after the flesh, ye shall die: but if ye through the Spirit do mortify the deeds of the body, ye shall live.

Paul is repeating the theme of Spirit possession here. Paul stresses that the "quickening" is the power that raised Christ from the dead, and it is the same Holy Spirit power residing in each believer. This quickening revives us from the flesh to godly living.

The use of the word "therefore" indicates that Paul is now concluding the previous thought. This conclusion appears to be a call to action for the believers. Knowing that we are redeemed (a result of God's unmerited favor on our behalf), knowing the price of that redemption (the intentional sacrifice of His beloved son), and knowing the benefit of our redemption (kinship with the Father, Son, and Holy Spirit), what are we prepared to do? We are no longer enslaved to sin, Paul declares. We are free to live through the Holy Spirit for God that we might one day live and reign with Him.

14 For as many as are led by the Spirit of God, they are the sons of God.

This verse and John 1:12 share a surprising similarity and continuity of theme: "But as many as received him, to them gave he power to become the sons of God." Here and in John, the emphasis is on "the power" and the title: "sons of God." John offers that the believers are endowed with the power and the title upon their entry, or acceptance, into Christ. Here in Romans, Paul emphasizes that as the believers progress and pursue God's plan, they affirm their right to assume both the power and the adoption of God. We should note that Holy Spirit "power" characterizes our entry and our continuation in Christ.

Sources:
Bassler, Jouette M. *The HarperCollins Study Bible: New Revised Standard Version*. Edited by Wayne A. Meeks. San Francisco, CA: HarperSanFrancisco, 1993.

Daily Bible Readings

MONDAY
Believers in Jesus Have
Eternal Life
(John 5:19–24)

TUESDAY
Spirit of Christ in Our
Hearts
(Galatians 4:1–7)

WEDNESDAY
The Resurrection of the
Dead
(1 Corinthians 15:12–28)

THURSDAY
Seeing Others Through
Christ
(2 Corinthians 5:16–21)

FRIDAY
Eager Longing
(Romans 8:18–25)

SATURDAY
Sustained and Led by the
Spirit
(Romans 8:26–30)

SUNDAY
No Condemnation in Christ
Jesus
(Romans 8:1-14)

Notes

_____

_____

_____

_____

_____

_____

_____

_____

Teaching Tips

May 19
Bible Study Guide 12

Words You Should Know

A. Gentiles *ethne* (Gk.)—Word for non-Jewish people, foreign nation.

B. Reconcile *katalasso* (Gk.)—Making peace.

Teacher Preparation

Unifying Principle—Humility in Heritage. Privileged people often feel superior to others. What is the corrective to such feelings of superiority? Paul warns the Gentile believers that their acceptance into grace must not make them feel superior to their Jewish brothers and sisters.

A. Read the Bible Background and Devotional Readings.

B. Pray for your students and lesson clarity.

C. Read the lesson Scripture in multiple translations.

D. Option: Develop opportunities for the class to worship with other ethnic groups through outside services or by inviting others to class.

O—Open the Lesson

A. Begin the class with prayer.

B. Have the students read the Aim for Change.

C. Have the students read the In Focus story.

D. Ask students how events named in the story can weigh on their hearts and how they can view these events from a theological perspective.

P—Present the Scriptures

A. Read the Focal Verses and discuss the Background and The People, Places, and Times sections.

B. Have the class share what Scriptures stand out for them and why, with particular emphasis on today's context.

E—Explore the Meaning

A. Use In Depth or More Light on the Text to help provide more in-depth discussion of the lesson text.

B. Discuss the Liberating Lesson and Application for Activation sections.

N—Next Steps for Application

A. Summarize the value of humility toward the Jewish heritage of the Christian faith.

B. End class with a commitment to pray for ethnic groups other than your own, and especially people living in modern Israel and Palestine.

Worship Guide

For the Superintendent or Teacher
Theme: The Call of the Gentiles
Song: "I Need You To Survive"
Devotional Reading: Romans 10:5–13

The Call of the Gentiles

Bible Background • ROMANS 11
Printed Text • ROMANS 11:11–24 | Devotional Reading • ROMANS 10:5–13

——— Aim for Change ———

By the end of the lesson we will: ANALYZE Paul's metaphor of the olive tree with wild branches; RECOGNIZE the price Jesus paid for all to be justified; and DECIDE ways to walk in humility toward others in light of God's grace toward us.

In Focus

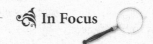

Adam knew he was the man. On paper, it was easy to see that he really was. He was Harvard-educated, hard working, and handsome. He was the youngest partner at his law firm, a generous donor to several worthy causes, and the proud owner of a black convertible Mercedes thanks to all those billable hours. However, in person, Adam's arrogance led him to share his high opinion of himself with anyone in his vicinity, including his secretary, Elaine. She was also thirty-six, but unlike Adam, she was new to the law firm. Adam would end his sentences with condescending phrases like, "But, I'm sure you don't know that, because you didn't finish college." When he told her she couldn't order lunch right because she ordered a baked potato instead of a twice baked potato, Elaine secretly started looking for other positions elsewhere.

One day, Elaine mustered the courage to ask Adam to purchase Girl Scout cookies for her daughter's troop. His response?

"Why would you think I would buy Girl Scout cookies from your daughter, Elaine?" he hissed. "I only donate to causes that benefit me. What can a bunch of girls hiking through the forest do for me?"

As he swaggered out of the room, Elaine began typing her resignation letter.

Do you know an "Adam"? How does excessive pride in worldly accomplishments contrast to God's free flowing grace to all believers?

——— Keep in Mind ———

"Boast not against the branches. But if thou boast, thou bearest not the root, but the root thee" (Romans 11:18, KJV).

"But you must not brag about being grafted in to replace the branches that were broken off. You are just a branch, not the root" (Romans 11:18, NLT).

Focal Verses

KJV **Romans 11:11** I say then, Have they stumbled that they should fall? God forbid: but rather through their fall salvation is come unto the Gentiles, for to provoke them to jealousy.

12 Now if the fall of them be the riches of the world, and the diminishing of them the riches of the Gentiles; how much more their fulness?

13 For I speak to you Gentiles, inasmuch as I am the apostle of the Gentiles, I magnify mine office:

14 If by any means I may provoke to emulation them which are my flesh, and might save some of them.

15 For if the casting away of them be the reconciling of the world, what shall the receiving of them be, but life from the dead?

16 For if the firstfruit be holy, the lump is also holy: and if the root be holy, so are the branches.

17 And if some of the branches be broken off, and thou, being a wild olive tree, wert grafted in among them, and with them partakest of the root and fatness of the olive tree;

18 Boast not against the branches. But if thou boast, thou bearest not the root, but the root thee.

19 Thou wilt say then, The branches were broken off, that I might be grafted in.

20 Well; because of unbelief they were broken off, and thou standest by faith. Be not highminded, but fear:

21 For if God spared not the natural branches, take heed lest he also spare not thee.

22 Behold therefore the goodness and severity of God: on them which fell, severity; but toward thee, goodness, if thou continue in his goodness: otherwise thou also shalt be cut off.

NLT **Romans 11:11** Did God's people stumble and fall beyond recovery? Of course not! They were disobedient, so God made salvation available to the Gentiles. But he wanted his own people to become jealous and claim it for themselves.

12 Now if the Gentiles were enriched because the people of Israel turned down God's offer of salvation, think how much greater a blessing the world will share when they finally accept it.

13 I am saying all this especially for you Gentiles. God has appointed me as the apostle to the Gentiles. I stress this,

14 for I want somehow to make the people of Israel jealous of what you Gentiles have, so I might save some of them.

15 For since their rejection meant that God offered salvation to the rest of the world, their acceptance will be even more wonderful. It will be life for those who were dead!

16 And since Abraham and the other patriarchs were holy, their descendants will also be holy—just as the entire batch of dough is holy because the portion given as an offering is holy. For if the roots of the tree are holy, the branches will be, too.

17 But some of these branches from Abraham's tree—some of the people of Israel—have been broken off. And you Gentiles, who were branches from a wild olive tree, have been grafted in. So now you also receive the blessing God has promised Abraham and his children, sharing in the rich nourishment from the root of God's special olive tree.

18 But you must not brag about being grafted in to replace the branches that were broken off. You are just a branch, not the root.

19 "Well," you may say, "those branches were broken off to make room for me."

23 And they also, if they abide not still in unbelief, shall be grafted in: for God is able to graft them in again.

24 For if thou wert cut out of the olive tree which is wild by nature, and wert grafted contrary to nature into a good olive tree: how much more shall these, which be the natural branches, be grafted into their own olive tree?

20 Yes, but remember—those branches were broken off because they didn't believe in Christ, and you are there because you do believe. So don't think highly of yourself, but fear what could happen.

21 For if God did not spare the original branches, he won't spare you either.

22 Notice how God is both kind and severe. He is severe toward those who disobeyed, but kind to you if you continue to trust in his kindness. But if you stop trusting, you also will be cut off.

23 And if the people of Israel turn from their unbelief, they will be grafted in again, for God has the power to graft them back into the tree.

24 You, by nature, were a branch cut from a wild olive tree. So if God was willing to do something contrary to nature by grafting you into his cultivated tree, he will be far more eager to graft the original branches back into the tree where they belong.

The People, Places, and Times

Gentile. This name is given to any ethnic group other than the Jewish race. The Jews looked down upon other races as barbarous and unclean. In the Old Testament, Jews referred to themselves as "God's chosen people" or "God's elect." In the New Testament, however, salvation is offered to Jews and Gentiles alike. The Law (also referred to as the Law of Moses) is the authoritative rule of conduct spelled out in the Ten Commandments and the Pentateuch (the books of Genesis, Exodus, Leviticus, Numbers, and Deuteronomy). The Lord revealed this code to Moses on Mount Sinai (Deuteronomy 5:1–2). While many of the regulations are ceremonial and procedural in nature, the moral law embodied in the Law of Moses is eternal, unchangeable (Romans 7:7–12), and fulfilled through Jesus Christ (Matthew 5:17–18).

How does remembering God's history with Israel help us be more humble?

Background

Romans 11 caps off the expositional part of Paul's magnificent summary of the Gospel. Romans 1–11 gives us the skeleton of the Gospel of grace, which then gives the Christian the foundation necessary to understand chapters 12–16, which explain the many ways to apply the knowledge that the Son of God has died to save all those who repent and rest in Him for salvation. In Romans 11, Paul, as the appointed apostle to the Gentiles, focuses specifically on how Jews and Gentiles ought to interact in the light of Christ's coming, which has reoriented, expanded, and clarified what it means to be God's chosen people.

While the rejection of Christ by many of His own people (Jews) might suggest to the outsider that God has rejected His people, Paul adamantly rejects this notion, operating from the unassailable conviction that God never retracts His Word or promises. When he writes, "God hath not cast away his people which he foreknew" (v. 2), he repeats the same language of Romans 8 in what has been referred to by theologians as the golden chain of salvation: God's foreknowledge is intimately linked to His uniting and conforming those people to Christ (Romans 8:29–20). Foreknowledge is not merely a passive recognition of a fact, but rather it is God's active work of creating a reality. To deny the centrality of the Jews in God's redemptive plan is to misunderstand that plan. In this chapter, however, Paul delves into the specifics of how that works out.

Is there a promise that God has made in Scripture that seems impossible for you to believe?

At-A-Glance

1. The Jealousy of Israel (Romans 11:11–16)
2. The Meaning of Election (vv. 17–24)

In Depth

1. The Jealousy of Israel (Romans 11:11–16)

The question looming behind this entire chapter is: Why has much of ethnic Israel rejected Christ as their Messiah? Does that mean that Israel is no longer elect? That is the import of Paul's rhetorical question: "Have they stumbled that they should fall?" (v. 11). Instead, however, the apostle tells us that his ministry to the Gentiles is for the good of the Jews as well! When they see Gentiles enjoying the benefits of union with Christ, jealousy will lead them back to Christ. Paul's continuous reasoning (from the lesser to the greater or the "how much more" argument) suggests that somehow, the Lord will work the miracle of the full inclusion of the Jews in question. Theologians have gone back and forth as to what this means, but the end of the chapter suggests that many Jewish people will come to recognize Christ before His return. None of this gives Gentiles a reason to think that they are better than the Jews or "more susceptible to the Gospel" than the Jews. Rather, Paul is unfolding God's salvific plan for both Jews and Gentiles.

In what ways might the light of your union with Christ bring others to faith? What are some of the visible aspects of a relationship with Christ?

2. The Meaning of Election (vv. 17–24)

In these eight verses, Paul revisits a favorite theme of the book of Romans and the Gospel itself: There is no reason for the Christian to boast in him/herself. Here, the method of explanation is an extended metaphor of an olive tree. Paul makes a statement quite in line with the epistle as a whole: "Do not be arrogant toward the branches. If you are, remember it is not you who support the root but the root that supports you." Paul is careful to remind those of us who are Gentiles that we are the "wild olive shoots" grafted onto the olive tree. Prophets present the image of an olive tree (Jeremiah 11:16; Hosea 14:6), but it was not a common practice to graft wild olive shoots into cultivated trees. Instead, Paul uses this image to emphasize the unnatural reality of salvation in general and salvation of the Gentiles in particular.

The Old Testament provides the image of the people of God as largely confined to the Jewish people with a few exceptions. But the work of Christ and the subsequent revelation of the Holy Spirit through the apostles reveal to us that the plan extended beyond the Jews to the Gentiles as well. For this reason, Gentiles have no reason to boast. Salvation is not anything that they, in any way, deserved. The root that nourishes and supports them is none other than Christ, the author and finisher of their salvation. To say that we are deserving of salvation is to suggest that Christ needs our support, which is wildly absurd. God is the one who grafts in and who cuts off in the case of unbelief. We remain in our salvation not because of our own merit, but because of our God's mercy. So Paul says: "Note then the kindness and the severity of God: severity toward those who have fallen, but God's kindness to you, provided you continue in his kindness. Otherwise you too will be cut off."

What events/people/gifts tempt you toward pride or its oft-misunderstood twin, self-pity?

Search the Scriptures

1. Paul encourages us in this passage to "not become proud, but fear." What does that mean?

2. Attention in this passage is drawn to both God's kindness and His severity. But Paul tells us elsewhere that both of these characteristics point humans to the same goal: repentance. What is the result of repentance in verse 15?

Discuss the Meaning

1. Think of a time when you were prideful, jealous and/or boastful. What were your thoughts and actions based on? How did others react?

2. How has God "grafted" you into His family—naturally (culturally/ethnically) or supernaturally (by faith)? What has your response been to this reality?

Liberating Lesson

Supersessionism, the idea that the new covenant has replaced the old covenant and rendered it null and void, has manifested itself in many ways, some of which have been violent and anti-Semitic. Christians must reject this way of seeing our faith and relating to Jewish neighbors; for as Paul argues it is not the will of God but the way of pride. Christians must be humble in understanding Judaism because we believe Jesus fulfills the Jewish covenants and all of the early disciples were Jews who received Jesus as the Messiah. Paul argues as a Jewish believer that Jews should not be prideful in thinking themselves more pleasing to God than non-Jews who have come to the faith. Yet as Christians, we must be driven by the fact that Christ is the identity and root from which we glean spiritual benefit. Salvation is found in Christ alone and for a human being to experience salvation it must be through Christ. The benefits of union with Christ are not confined in the life to come; rather, they permeate our earthly lives as well. The joy of that ought to bleed into our work, conversations, and every aspect of that life.

Application for Activation

All views of personal superiority, whether rooted in class, education, race, or any other factor are examples of pride. In these Scriptures, we have one of many reasons to constantly be on guard against this great enemy. Whenever you are tempted to see yourself as better than someone else, turn your eyes, prayers, and thoughts toward the Cross of Christ, where you are reminded that your gifts and opportunities are not fruits of your unending labor, but rather overflow of God's worship-worthy grace. He is worthy of all praise!

Follow the Spirit

What God wants me to do:

_____

_____

_____

_____

Remember Your Thoughts

Special insights I have learned:

_____

_____

_____

_____

More Light on the Text

Romans 11:11–24

In Romans 9:30–10:21 Paul showed that although the Israelites failed to obtain a right relationship with God because of their unbelief, God had not rejected them entirely. He used two examples to prove that God always preserves a faithful remnant, even when the situation seems hopeless (11:1–5). He then goes on to describe the way in which God does His work in the world, by choosing some and rejecting others, so that in the end all nations may receive His blessing (vv. 6–10).

11 I say then, Have they stumbled that they should fall? God forbid: but rather through their fall salvation is come unto the Gentiles, for to provoke them to jealousy. 12 Now if the fall of them be the riches of the world, and the diminishing of them the riches of the Gentiles; how much more their fullness?

In verse 11 Paul begins his explanation of how God planned to extend His salvation plan beyond Israel to include the whole world, and then, in the end, to bring Israel in as well. The meaning of the passage is elucidated by noting the contrast between stumbled (Gk. *ptaien*,

TAY-en) and fall (Gk. *pesein,* **PAY-sen**). A person who stumbles may recover himself or herself, or he or she may fall completely. Hence *pesosin* (**pay-SO-sen**) is used here of a complete and irrevocable fall (cf. Isaiah 24:20). Although the nation Israel had stumbled (9:32) through unbelief, the failure to believe had not led to their absolute ruin—Israel had not stumbled irretrievably. God had a definite purpose in allowing them to stumble. Because of their rejection of the Gospel, salvation had gone out to nations other than Israel (Gk. *ethne,* **eth-ne**, "Gentiles"). The unbelief of Israel opened the door of opportunity for the nations, and thus God's purpose in history is being accomplished. God has graciously overruled the Jewish unbelief and turned it to a means of glory for Himself and blessing to the world. Their fall was not the necessary means of the salvation of the Gentiles; certainly the Jews' unbelief could never produce faith in the Gentiles. Rather, Paul simply makes a case: The Jews, in their rebellion and obstinacy, rejected Jesus Christ and the salvation offered them in His name; the apostles then turned to the Gentiles, and they heard and believed.

The Jews themselves perceived that the Gentiles were to possess similar privileges to those that they, as the peculiar people of God, had enjoyed; they could not bear this notion and put forth all their strength in opposition and persecution. The calling of the Gentiles, which existed in the original purpose of God, became in a certain way accelerated by the unbelief of the Jews, who had forfeited all their privileges and fell from that state of glory and dignity in which they had been long placed. Through their fall (Gk. *to auton paraptomati* **ow-TAHN par-apt-toe-MA-tee**), literally, "by their false step," continuing the metaphor of *eptaisan* (**ep-TIE-sahn**) meaning to stumble, salvation comes to the Gentiles to provoke the Jews to jealousy. The phrase "to provoke them to jealousy" is Paul's interpretation of Deuteronomy 32:21, a passage that had Paul already quoted (Romans 10:19). The attitude of the Jews in rejecting the Gospel led more quickly to its spread and proclamation to the nations (Gentiles). Israel would, in turn, be stirred up to envy when they see the nations enjoying the blessings that they themselves could have had. Although Israel had stumbled, God has purposed that the result of their transgression would ultimately provide the incentive to return, that is "to provoke them to jealousy." By seeing the Gentiles turn to Christ, the Jews may be moved to jealous desire to receive the blessing of salvation. As such, the salvation of the Gentiles is divinely blessed or purposed for the salvation of the Jews.

Paul expands the thought further and argues that if Israel's misstep had brought enrichment to the world and their defeat had proved to be such a benefit for the Gentiles, it is unimaginable to think how great would be the result of their restoration. The salvation of the Jews will turn out to the fulfillment of God's redemptive purpose for all, regardless of race, ethnicity or nation.

13 For I speak to you Gentiles, inasmuch as I am the apostle of the Gentiles, I magnify mine office: 14 If by any means I may provoke to emulation them which are my flesh, and might save some of them. 15 For if the casting away of them be the reconciling of the world, what shall the receiving of them be, but life from the dead? 16 For if the firstfruit be holy, the lump is also holy: and if the root be holy, so are the branches.

Verses 13–14 constitute a parenthesis. Paul would later resume his argument in verse 15. In verse 13, Paul sought to remind his Gentile audience that his primary concern was about them by reminding them that he was their apostle and, therefore, should not assume that

what he was saying had nothing to do with them. Rather, it makes him even more zealous in his work for them. By Paul emphasizing that he was "the apostle to the Gentiles," Paul was hoping he might stir his countrymen to envy with the result that "some of them" might be saved (v. 14). He would do everything in his power for the salvation of his own people.

Paul returns to the idea of verse 12 in verse 15. If the casting away (Gk. *apobole*, **a-po-bo-le**) of Israel led to reconciliation for the world, what would "the receiving of them" their acceptance (Gk. *proslēmpsis*, **pros-lemp-sis**) mean but "life from the dead?" Paul believes firmly in the future conversion of the Jews, something he likens to a resurrection from the dead. If so great a benefit has flowed from their being cast away, a greater benefit may be expected when those who have been rejected are now accepted. Paul uses the final resurrection as an expression for all the events accompanying the end times or consummation of the age. The consummation of the age will come only when God is satisfied that His purposes for humanity have been fully achieved.

Paul then mixes metaphors to make his point. He alludes to the firstfruits offering, which required Israel to offer to God the first portion of its grain or dough (Numbers 15:17–21). The cake presented to the Lord consecrated the rest of the batch. Paul writes that if the dough offered as firstfruits was holy, then the entire batch was holy. The holiness of the firstfruits (Gk. *aparchē*, **a-par-KAY**) ensured that the entire batch would be holy. In this metaphor the "firstfruit" represents the Jewish believers who had accepted Christ (the remnant of verse 5), and the "lump" would be those who would come to believe. The metaphor then changes to a tree with its branches. If the root is holy, so are the branches. In this case the "root" represents the patriarchs (especially Abraham), and the "branches" the nation that follows. The point is that if the patriarchs were holy (and they were), so also were the Jewish people. God's rejection of the Jewish nation was neither complete (Romans 11:1–10) nor final (11:11–24). Paul seems to apply this double figure to suggest that Jewish Christian converts somehow "sanctify" the unbelieving majority of Israel.

17 And if some of the branches be broken off, and thou, being a wild olive tree, wert grafted in among them, and with them partakest of the root and fatness of the olive tree; 18 Boast not against the branches. But if thou boast, thou bearest not the root, but the root thee. 19 Thou wilt say then, The branches were broken off, that I might be grafted in. 20 Well; because of unbelief they were broken off, and thou standest by faith. Be not highminded, but fear: 21 For if God spared not the natural branches, take heed lest he also spare not thee.

Building on verse 16, Paul presumes that both Jewish and Gentile believers mutually share in (Gk. *synkoinōnos*, **sun-koi-no-nos**, "partakest") the extraordinary privilege of being nourished by the graced heritage of Israel. Both partake in the holiness of the patriarchs, the one historical root of the people of God, and in the blessings attached to it. In verses 17–24 Paul uses the figure of grafting olive trees to illustrate how the Gentiles came to share the spiritual blessings of Israel, to warn them that the arrogance of privilege would lead to their being cut off, and to remind them of God's ability to graft in the natural branches once again should they not persist in unbelief.

Paul's Gentile readers should not view themselves in any way superior to the former branches. They owed their spiritual relevance to Israel; it was not the other way around. They do not support the root; the root supports them. Believing Gentiles are correct in their understanding that unbelieving Jews were broken off so they could be grafted in. Paul said: "Well, it is true. But do not forget that they were broken off because of unbelief and your permanence depends upon your continuing faith." Therefore, Gentile believers were to be on guard and eschew any form of arrogance. After all, if God did not spare the natural branches (Israel), what possible chance was there that He would spare branches grafted in contrary to nature (the Gentiles)? Paul's point is that the church is not entirely new, nor a replacement of Israel. It is instead the continuation of God's ancient people. Thus, Paul insists that the church is no place for competition and separation but for community and continuity. Believers—both Jews and Gentiles—live by dependence on God and the ancient traditions of the people of God.

The purpose of the olive tree illustration is to prevent any false sense of security on the part of the Gentiles. While we do not lose our salvation for disobedience, we can lose our inheritance both in this life and the life to come (1 Corinthians 3:11–15). Paul's point in verse 21 is poignant and clear: If God, in His infinite justice and holiness, could not tolerate sin in the people whom He foreknew, so long loved, cherished, miraculously preserved, and blessed, believers in Christ should take heed lest He also not spare us. Rather we must know and be convinced that the same righteous principle in Him will cause Him to act toward us as He has acted toward the Jews, if we sin as they did—which is where self-sufficiency and self-confidence will soon lead us. We ought, then, to remember the branch to which we were grafted, and the hole of the pit from which He dug us out. We must incessantly and continually depend on God's free grace, that we may abide in His favor.

22 Behold therefore the goodness and severity of God: on them which fell, severity; but toward thee, goodness, if thou continue in his goodness: otherwise thou also shalt be cut off. 23 And they also, if they abide not still in unbelief, shall be grafted in: for God is able to graft them in again. 24 For if thou wert cut out of the olive tree which is wild by nature, and wert grafted contrary to nature into a good olive tree: how much more shall these, which be the natural branches, be grafted into their own olive tree?

The exclamation, "Behold therefore the goodness of God!" is frequent among the Jewish writers, when they wish to call attention to particular displays of God's mercy, especially toward those who are singularly unworthy. The Gentile believers ought to consider that God is both good and severe. "Goodness," or literally "kindness" (Gk. *chrēstotēs*, **chres-to-tes**) and "severity" (Gk. *apotomia*, **a-po-to-mia**) are aspects of the divine nature. A proper understanding of God must include both His kindness and His sternness. The two qualities must be maintained in balance. God's sternness is seen in His dealings with unbelieving Israel. He cut them off. God's kindness is seen in the inclusion into His family of those who at one time were "foreigners to the covenants of the promise, without hope and without God in the world" (Ephesians 2:12). His kindness to Gentile believers is, of course, contingent upon their continuing to respond to that kindness. A failure in this responsibility will lead to being cut off. There is no security for those who by their lives show that the grafting process of faith was apparent rather than real.

Paul said of Israel that if they did not persist in unbelief they would be grafted back into their own olive tree (v. 23). God certainly had the power to graft them in again. The only thing that stood in Israel's way was their continuance in unbelief. So, we find that their rejection took place in consequence of their willful obstinacy, but they may return into the fold, the door of which still stands open. God would never overpower their unwillingness to believe and force them back into His family.

Paul does not envision the church as a replacement for Israel, nor of separate Jewish and Gentile churches, but rather a church made up of Jews and Gentiles. The God who was able to bring Gentiles to faith is able to restore unbelieving Israel into the one people of God. If the incorporation of Gentiles into Israel is possible, how much more is the restoration of unbelieving ethnic Israel to the people of God a divine possibility? God is able (v. 23)! Although fallen and degraded, God can, in the course of His providence and mercy, restore them to all their forfeited privileges. This will take place if they do not abide in unbelief, which intimates that God has furnished them with all the power and means necessary for faith, and that they may believe on the Lord Jesus whenever they will. Paul elsewhere explains that the veil now continues on their heart; it is not a veil which God has spread there, but one caused by their own voluntary and obstinate unbelief. If or when they turn to the Lord Jesus, the veil would be taken away (2 Corinthians 3:6–18).

The logic of verse 24 is clear. The fact that God has grafted in the wild olive tree holds out good hope of success in the easier case—the grafting in of the branches that belonged "by nature" to their own olive tree. If God can take a wild olive shoot and graft it into a cultivated olive tree (as he did with the nations), how much easier it would be to graft the natural branches (Israel) back into their parent tree? The strength of Paul's argument lies in the fact that the process he describes is contrary to nature. It is a process unexpected in horticulture. Paul disarms his critics by acknowledging that he is aware of the unnaturalness of this particular kind of grafting, but this is what God has done (and will do), contrary to nature or not. Ethnic or national identity has no bearing on membership of the people of God. God has grafted wild olive branches into His cultivated tree, and He is certainly able to graft the natural branches in again.

Sources:

Achtemeier, Paul. *Romans. Interpretation: A Bible Commentary for Teaching and Preaching.* Louisville, KY.: John Knox Press, 1985.

Barnett, Paul. *Romans: The Revelation of God's Righteousness.* Fearn, Ross-shire, Scotland: Christian Focus, 2003.

Bruce, F.F. *The Epistle of Paul to the Romans.* The Tyndale Bible Commentaries. Grand Rapids, MI: Wm. B. Erdmans Publishing Company, 1963.

Greathouse, William M. and George Lyons. *Romans 9–16: A Commentary in the Wesleyan Tradition.* New Beacon Bible Commentary. Kansas City, MO: Beacon Hill Press of Kansas City, 2008.

Moo, Douglas, *The Epistle to the Romans.* New International Commentary on the New Testament. Grand Rapids, MI: Wm. B. Eerdmans, 1996.

Mounce, Robert H. *Romans,* Vol. 27, The New American Commentary. Nashville,TN: Broadman & Holman Publishers, 1995.

Say It Correctly

Consummation. kahn-suh-**MAY**-shun.
Gentile. jent-**EYEL.**
Reconciliation. re-**KUHN**-si-lee-ay-shuhn.
Severity. suh-**VER**-i-tee.

Daily Bible Readings

MONDAY
The Heritage Keepers
(Romans 9:1–5, 14–17)

TUESDAY
A Light for the Gentiles
(Acts 13:44–49)

WEDNESDAY
Life in Christ Jesus
(Colossians 2:1–10)

THURSDAY
Testimony of God's Grace
(Acts 20:17–24, 32)

FRIDAY
Israel's Rejection Not Final
(Romans 11:1–10)

SATURDAY
All Peoples Saved by Faith
(Romans 11:25–36)

SUNDAY
Salvation of the Gentiles
(Romans 11:11–24)

Notes

Teaching Tips

May 26
Bible Study Guide 13

Words You Should Know

A. Transform *metamorphoo* (Gk.)—To be continually molded, shaped, changed in a permanent way, metamorphosis.

B. Grace *charis* (Gk.)—Gift, favor, ability.

Teacher Preparation

Unifying Principle—Living Sacrifices. People often engage in a "me first" way of thinking, which results in conflict and makes cooperation difficult. How do people learn to work together? Paul compares the church to a body and encourages believers to see themselves as individual members that work in sync with other members.

A. Read the Bible Background and Devotional Readings.

B. Pray for your students and lesson clarity.

C. Read the lesson Scripture in multiple translations.

D. Option: Invite the class to analyze their gifts and abilities and to commit those to the Lord for the good of the body of Christ.

O—Open the Lesson

A. Begin the class with prayer.

B. Have the students read the Aim for Change.

C. Have the students read the In Focus story.

D. Ask students how events named in the story can weigh on their hearts and how they can view these events from a theological perspective.

P—Present the Scriptures

A. Read the Focal Verses and discuss the Background and The People, Places, and Times sections.

B. Have the class share what Scriptures stand out for them and why, with particular emphasis on today's context.

E—Explore the Meaning

A. Use In Depth or More Light on the Text to help provide more in-depth discussion of the lesson text.

B. Discuss the Liberating Lesson and Application for Activation sections.

N—Next Steps for Application

A. Summarize the value of becoming a living sacrifice to God.

B. End class with a commitment to pray for renewed minds and united love for all believers.

Worship Guide

For the Superintendent or Teacher
Theme: Called to New Life In Christ
Song: "Take My Life"
Devotional Reading: Psalm 34:1–14

Called to New Life in Christ

Bible Background • ROMANS 12
Printed Text • ROMANS 12:1–8 | Devotional Reading • PSALM 34:1–14

―――――――――― **Aim for Change** ――――――――――

By the end of this lesson we will: EVALUATE Paul's teaching about being a living sacrifice and part of the body of Christ; RECOGNIZE that being a living sacrifice is a responsibility as part of the body of Christ; and IDENTIFY our gifts that can be used as living sacrifices for God in service to the body of Christ.

――――――――― 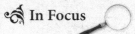 In Focus ―――――――――

The Carter family's finances were a nightmare. Randall had been laid off for six months. Still, he and his wife, Brittany, wondered how they had let it get this bad.

"We have to get our finances under control again," Randall said with a heavy sigh at the emergency family meeting. "Everyone needs to take inventory of their skills and find a job ASAP! From now on, things are going to be a lot different."

The couple's children were certainly old enough to contribute to the family budget. One by one, Brittany met with each child to determine the best plan.

The youngest, Jack, started mowing lawns on weekends and delivering papers before school. Jazmine made baked goods to sell in the neighborhood. The twins got jobs washing cars after school and on the weekends. The children reported their income to the family on a dry erase board in the living room. Each Sunday, the family paid their tithes on what was earned, saved another 10%, and managed the rest. Once everyone put their minds toward working, saving money, and managing extra income, the Carters were transformed. They became a little less trendy, more grateful, and a lot more focused on things that really mattered. After a year, two credit cards with the lowest balances were paid off, and they embraced living life on a budget.

God often reminds us that He has a unique role for each of us in His kingdom. How has God called you during different seasons of your life to work together with other believers toward a significant goal?

―――――――――― **Keep in Mind** ――――――――――

"I beseech you therefore, brethren, by the mercies of God, that ye present your bodies a living sacrifice, holy, acceptable unto God, which is your reasonable service"
(Romans 12:1, KJV).

"And so, dear brothers and sisters, I plead with you to give your bodies to God because of all he has done for you. Let them be a living and holy sacrifice—the kind he will find acceptable. This is truly the way to worship him" (Romans 12:1, NLT).

Focal Verses

KJV **Romans 12:1** I beseech you therefore, brethren, by the mercies of God, that ye present your bodies a living sacrifice, holy, acceptable unto God, which is your reasonable service.

2 And be not conformed to this world: but be ye transformed by the renewing of your mind, that ye may prove what is that good, and acceptable, and perfect, will of God.

3 For I say, through the grace given unto me, to every man that is among you, not to think of himself more highly than he ought to think; but to think soberly, according as God hath dealt to every man the measure of faith.

4 For as we have many members in one body, and all members have not the same office:

5 So we, being many, are one body in Christ, and every one members one of another.

6 Having then gifts differing according to the grace that is given to us, whether prophecy, let us prophesy according to the proportion of faith;

7 Or ministry, let us wait on our ministering: or he that teacheth, on teaching;

8 Or he that exhorteth, on exhortation: he that giveth, let him do it with simplicity; he that ruleth, with diligence; he that sheweth mercy, with cheerfulness.

NLT **Romans 12:1** And so, dear brothers and sisters, I plead with you to give your bodies to God because of all he has done for you. Let them be a living and holy sacrifice—the kind he will find acceptable. This is truly the way to worship him.

2 Don't copy the behavior and customs of this world, but let God transform you into a new person by changing the way you think. Then you will learn to know God's will for you, which is good and pleasing and perfect.

3 Because of the privilege and authority God has given me, I give each of you this warning: Don't think you are better than you really are. Be honest in your evaluation of yourselves, measuring yourselves by the faith God has given us.

4 Just as our bodies have many parts and each part has a special function,

5 so it is with Christ's body. We are many parts of one body, and we all belong to each other.

6 In his grace, God has given us different gifts for doing certain things well. So if God has given you the ability to prophesy, speak out with as much faith as God has given you.

7 If your gift is serving others, serve them well. If you are a teacher, teach well.

8 If your gift is to encourage others, be encouraging. If it is giving, give generously. If God has given you leadership ability, take the responsibility seriously. And if you have a gift for showing kindness to others, do it gladly.

The People, Places, and Times

Jews and Christians in Rome. While the Romans' power was making itself felt in the Mediterranean world at the time of the later writings of the Old Testament, it did not dominate the world then as it did during the time the New Testament was written. Because Rome was the principal city of the empire, it was inevitable that both Christians and Jews would eventually be attracted to it. By the time

Paul wrote the epistle to the Romans (around the mid-first century AD), it had already become an important church (Romans 1:8). But there are other views regarding the origin of the church in Rome. About the year AD 49, the emperor Claudius issued an edict expelling Jews from Rome. The fact that Christians were expelled as well (see Acts 18:2) indicates that at that time Roman officials did not differentiate between Christians and Jews, perhaps because the Christian community was not large enough to be significant.

Background

Romans 12 is the beginning of Paul's concentrated work of applying the Gospel of grace that he has just articulated. The first eleven chapters have given us the major themes of biblical faith: sin, judgment, faith, works, grace, justification, sanctification, and the list continues. Always in view, however, is the righteousness of God. God's righteousness reveals our sinfulness and our need of a Savior. God's righteousness in Christ is the source of our acceptance, as the Father, by His grace and mercy, unites us to the Son through faith, justifying us. But so far this understanding of salvation is largely external and entirely focused on what God has done for us. The obvious question is: "Since God has done so much for me, what does He want from me in return?" Chapter 12 is a turning point where Paul moves to discuss what the response of the Christian ought to be to such marvelous Good News. We will find that God demands no less than all of us. Each of our gifts were given to us by God not for our own benefit, but for His glory and for the edification of the body of Christ. This is not to repay Him for His grace, as such a repayment is impossible. Instead, the fullness of our joy and the shining of His glory is found in our obedience and use of our gifts.

What is the relationship between faith and practice? What are the dangers of one without the other?

At-A-Glance

1. A Living Sacrifice (Romans 12:1–2)
2. Gifts to the Body (vv. 3–8)

In Depth

1. A Living Sacrifice (Romans 12:1–2)

In chapter 12, Paul switches to a direct address as if to say, "Now that I've explained the Gospel, it's time to explain how you, as a believer, ought to feel and act as a result." Thus, Paul offers his appeal: that believers present their bodies as "living sacrifices." When Paul refers to our bodies, he does not merely refer to only our physical bodies, but rather our entire selves as embodied individuals. In other words, God does not merely want our bodies to be working for His glory, He wants our hearts and souls engaged as well. Such a demand is entirely reasonable from a God who sent His only Son to die for sinners. This was God's command in the covenant He made with Israel (Deuteronomy 6:5).

But it is not an easy one to fulfill, especially when multiple demands come from different areas of human life. So verse 2 gives us the source of motivation and strength for such an endeavor. Paul tells us not to be conformed to this world, meaning the world is not to shape us, nor is it to dictate what we do, how we feel, or what we say. Instead, we are to be transformed by the renewal of our mind, an interesting turn of phrase because it is passive. The one who does the transforming and renewing is the Holy Spirit, as He reveals God's will to us.

How does the Holy Spirit transform our minds? How do we guard against the world's constant attempt to shape us?

2. Gifts to the Body (vv. 3–8)

In the previous chapter, Paul encouraged the Gentile Christians not to boast because they were grafted in "contrary to nature" (Romans 11:24). Here, both Jewish and Gentile Christians are encouraged not to boast in any particular gifts. There are no spiritual gifts that are more inherently "useful" than others. Similar to 1 Corinthians 12, Paul uses the analogy of the body to describe the church: We are not disjointed people in a gathering, but rather we are, as Paul pointedly puts it, "members one of another" (v. 5). This means that if someone is united to Christ by faith, he or she is our brother or sister, regardless of background, education, language, or anything else. When a believer suffers, we mourn. When one succeeds, we rejoice.

This also means, however, that our greatest concern is not ourselves. Our gifts were not given to us for the sake of self-importance. Instead they are meant for the edification of the body. The gifts that Paul lists in verses 6-8 are all other-centered: Prophecy, service, teaching, giving, leading, and acts of mercy all seek to enrich the life of the hearer or recipient. Each also has practical significance. Prophecy reveals the Word of God; service, giving, and leading help people in their practical endeavors; acts of mercy help physical, emotional, and spiritual health; teaching shapes the minds of the hearers for God's glory and for the good of those involved. In each of these endeavors, the apostle encourages us to eagerly use our gifts.

What do you think your gifts are? What do you enjoy doing in the community of faith and in what have you been affirmed?

Search the Scriptures

1. Paul makes this appeal "by the mercies of God" (Romans 12:1). What mercies can you keep in your mind as you continue in the Christian life?

2. Can you think of any events in Scripture when the world had one interpretation but God, through the Scriptures, revealed what was actually going on?

Discuss the Meaning

1. Define the term "spiritual gifts" in your own words. What are yours? In which ways do these gifts equip you to serve God's kingdom?

2. Transformation is often easier said than done. In a world of ever-changing trends, how can Christians sustain their spiritual transformations over time?

Liberating Lesson

We worship God by offering ourselves as sacrifices. No act of service is too "low" or unimportant for us as Christians and no matter the act of service, we ought to engage in it joyfully. When our minds are shaped by the Holy Spirit, we are reminded of Christ, who, though He was in the form of God, did not consider His Godhood to be a reason not to take on flesh and get into the muck and mire of daily human existence (cf. Philippians 2:6–8). If our Savior undertook such radical condescension, so also we ought to be willing. We must walk with each other through the storms of life, no matter how embarrassing or messy. Is your brother or sister in Christ struggling with something considered "taboo"? The response as a fellow member of the body of Christ is not to shun, but to walk alongside him or her.

Application for Activation

When you build relationships with fellow Christians, do not be afraid to ask hard questions and to be willing to answer hard questions about your own spiritual struggles. God placed the body of Christ around you for you to serve them—and for them to support you. But that requires openness, which involves risk. While opening your lives to the people of God also risks pain, the possible reward outlined in Scripture far outstrips it. We must live as our identities in Christ mandate. We were created for such a life. Make an effort this week to spend time in prayer about how to be more open in sharing and receiving from someone you trust in Christ. The first step is usually the most difficult. Record how you feel after the exchange.

Follow the Spirit

What God wants me to do:

_____

_____

_____

_____

Remember Your Thoughts

Special insights I have learned:

_____

_____

_____

_____

More Light on the Text
Romans 12:1–8

The Christian life is not only a life of privilege and blessing but also of responsibility and service to God and others. Nothing is more important for Christians than a deepening conviction that the righteousness they have received from Christ through faith is to be demonstrated in daily living. The natural and necessary testimony to the reality of Christian experience is a Christ-like life. With the beginning of Romans 12, Paul moves to the practical implications of the Gospel for character and behavior. He will demonstrate that the proof of faith is a new kind of conduct and the purpose of God in humanity's redemption is that we might be holy and without blemish in the sight of God.

1 I beseech you therefore, brethren, by the mercies of God, that ye present your bodies a living sacrifice, holy, acceptable unto God, which is your reasonable service. 2 And be not conformed to this world: but be ye transformed by the renewing of your mind, that ye may prove what is that good, and acceptable, and perfect, will of God.

The force of Paul's ethical appeal that follows is based on Paul's earlier arguments in the letter. However, "therefore" does not only connect the reader with the preceding eleven chapters but looks forward to affirm that justification should lead to transformation. The Greek word *parakaleo* (**pa-ra-ka-LEH-oh**), translated here as beseech, means to exhort, appeal, beg, or implore as opposed to giving a legal commandment.

Paul's exhortation is in view of what Christian life is: a right standing with God effected by union with Christ through His death and resurrection. There could be no more compelling motive or incentive for giving ourselves to God other than His mercies. The appeal is made in view of God's mercy. He invites Christians to offer themselves to God as the appropriate response to God's prior demonstration of mercy. Paul's exhortation is twofold. First, although with slight modification in language, in the same manner as in Romans 6:13,

Paul commands the believers to "present their bodies a living and holy sacrifice" (12:1). Three qualities distinguish the sacrifice Paul calls for. It is to be living, holy, and pleasing to God. It is to be living in contrast to the Old Testament sacrifices, which were slain animals. We die to sin and self so that we may live wholly to Him who died for us and rose again. To live sacrificially is not heroic. In fact, we will all die sometime, whether or not we give ourselves courageously as weapons of righteousness. Our choice is not between heroism and cowardice, but for what and for whom we will live and die. Paul calls for us to offer ourselves in the service of a cause that is greater than we are. We offer ourselves as a living sacrifice so that even our dying may be living in the deep theological sense—living in the new life of the Spirit. The sacrifice is to be holy and, moreover, pleasing to God. That is, it is the kind of sacrifice God accepts as satisfying His expectations. Paul explains that such a sacrifice is not literal, but metaphorical, or better rational (Gk. *logikos*, **low-gee-KOCE**). As rational, spiritual worship, God desires to embrace the whole of our daily lives, not just the interruptions in our routine set apart for religious activities at a place of worship.

Second, Paul goes further with a prohibition for the Roman Christians "not to be conformed to this world." Instead, they should be "transformed by the renewing of their mind." Paul here calls upon the Roman Christians to make a decisive act of yielding themselves to God. The word for "be transformed" Paul uses is the source of the English word "metamorphosis." What Paul urges is not merely a change of appearance and behavior, but a change of essence. He advocates a total, radical change. This is not a matter of acting a part, but being completely different, meaning not the person we used to be. The indwelling Spirit of Christ is God's agent in effecting this inside-out transformation, reproducing Jesus in the lives of committed Christians (see Romans 8:29; 2 Corinthians 3:17–18; 2 Thessalonians 2:13).

Christians are not to be crammed or squeezed into the mold of the present world. Rather they are to seek a new model realized by the power of the transforming Spirit. The mind, freed from the power of the flesh (Romans 8:1–4), is refocused on "things which are above, where Christ sitteth on the right hand of God" (Colossians 3:1). As followers of Christ we cannot go on complacently, allowing ourselves to be stamped afresh by the whimsical fashions of the dominant culture, wherever we may be. Instead, we yield ourselves to a different pressure, the direction of the Spirit of God. We must not be conformed to the world, but transformed from it. To express this idea Paul uses two difficult-to-translate Greek words that we have taken almost sentences to express. The word he uses "to be conformed to the world" is *suschematizesthai* (**soos-khay-ma-TEED-zes-thai**); its root is *schema* (**SKHAY-mah**), which means the outward form that varies from year to year and from day to day. We are to allow ourselves to be transformed—*metamorphoo* (**meh-tah-mor-FOH-oh**)—continually remolded, remade, progressively sanctified. By this means, our present lives may more and more clearly exhibit signs and tokens of the coming age of God, the new order that has already come in Christ.

It is also significant to note that Paul's exhortation is communal in nature, not simply individual. Paul commands his Christian readers collectively to refuse the negative option and accept the positive. Apparently, communal cooperation is called for. This is not a call for rugged individualism—they all are involved. Christian living, or sanctification, for that matter is not a solo performance; it demands a choir, an orchestra, a community of saints. In urging the community to "present your bodies, (plural) as a living sacrifice (singular), holy and pleasing to God," the community, in its corporate life, is called to embody an alternative order that stands as a sign of God's redemptive purposes in the world.

3 For I say, through the grace given unto me, to every man that is among you, not to think of himself more highly than he ought to think; but to think soberly, according as God hath dealt to every man the measure of faith.

On the basis of entire dedication and consecration that Paul urged, he now makes further appeal for the translation of the ideals of righteousness to one's relational life. First, the Christian life is to be marked by humility. Humility is the immediate effect of yielding and self-surrender to God. Paul illustrates this by his own position. He speaks through the grace (Gk. *charis*, **KHAR-eece**) of God given to him as an apostle, and therefore without pride. The word for grace means gift, favor, or charism (ability), in this case God has gifted and empowered him for the apostolic work he is called to do. Each person must have proper self-evaluation. A Christian needs to have a right attitude toward himself or herself. This means without self-depreciation or mock humility. It also means that we guard against exalting ourselves and magnifying our virtues and abilities. Paul's exhortation is certainly apropos for Christendom where a penchant for titles and religious honorifics are the "in thing." A bloated ego has no room in the life of a believer. The believer is to be sober-minded, a quality that has God as its frame of reference. Our opinions of ourselves should not be based on our natural talents, capacities, or achievements but on God's gifts. If this is so we will never be boastful for we will remember that we have nothing we have not received (1 Corinthians 4:7). We do not have any reason to exalt ourselves above others, but we have every reason to appreciate what God has done for us.

4 For as we have many members in one body, and all members have not the same office: 5 So we, being many, are one body in Christ, and every one members one of another.

Christian humility has another basis. To be "in Christ" is to be incorporated into a social whole in which individualism may be overcome as we demonstrate a loving concern to serve other members of the community. As the adage goes, "no person is an island." That is especially true of the church. The church is the body of Christ, a simple analogy but with profound implications. Like the physical body, which is made up of many members with different functions, so the church is a body made up of many members, all closely related and constituting a unity in Christ, but each one having unique functions and individual responsibilities.

"In Christ" we are a corporate fellowship. Believers have varied functions, which are essential to the proper working of the body of which they are parts; there is therefore no room for anyone to think highly of themselves. The members of the body do not quarrel and compete or envy each other, nor dispute about the importance of one another. Rather, each part of the body carries out its own function as required, however prominent or humbly unseen that function may be. Whatever gift one has received marks that individual for a particular line of service, to which one must devote oneself. We must realistically assess our assets and deficits, gifts and graces, and privileges and responsibilities within the community of faith. If Jesus' disciples were repeatedly tempted to argue among themselves concerning who was the greatest, we cannot assume that this pattern of thinking has disappeared within the household of faith. But Paul gives sound advice for avoiding dissension in the ranks: First, don't waste time making comparisons. Recognize that roles, abilities and gifts come from God; leave the assessing of worth to Him. Second, focus on the abilities you have been given, and enhance each gift with the appropriate spiritual grace. Whatever gift or gifts we have received distinguishes each individual for a specific line of service, to which we must devote ourselves.

6 Having then gifts differing according to the grace that is given to us, whether prophecy, let us prophesy according to the proportion of faith; 7 Or ministry, let us wait on our ministering: or he that teacheth, on teaching; 8 Or he that exhorteth, on exhortation: he that giveth, let him do it with simplicity; he that ruleth, with diligence; he that sheweth mercy, with cheerfulness.

The apostle proceeds by highlighting the diversity of gifts in the church. Each Christian possesses gifts as dispensed by God's grace and according to His purpose, and it is the believer's obligation to use his or her gift faithfully. There is to be no competition. At times, Paul appears to state the obvious in this passage—let prophets prophesy; let teachers teach. But at the close of his list of gifts (vv. 6–8), he suggests that the quality of one's contribution is more significant that its nature or quantity. Thus, giving should be done generously, leadership performed diligently, and mercy demonstrated cheerfully (v. 8).

In several of his letters, Paul identifies various "gifts of the Spirit" (Romans 12; 1 Corinthians 12; Ephesians 4). Scholars sometimes discuss the gifts under supernatural or natural categories. To do so misses Paul's point altogether. For Paul, all the gifts reflect God's activity. Paul suggests that God is the source of all our endeavors and that even simple

tasks can be accomplished according to the grace given us (v. 6). For Paul, the distinctions between human talent and divine gifts are lost in a unified body whose members have become a living sacrifice.

As he does elsewhere, Paul provides an ad hoc list of the gifts in verses 6–8. At the head of the list is prophecy. God enables some within the community to discern and declare with clarity and conviction what God is doing among them (vv. 13–19, 29–33). As a result, others in the church are strengthened, encouraged, comforted, edified, and instructed (vv. 3–4, 31). Simultaneously, unbelievers present are convinced by such prophecy that they are sinners and that God is present in the community (vv. 24–25). Whereas Paul understands "teaching" as a gift in the same way as prophecy, prophecy probably depends directly on divine inspiration for its message. In some traditions, prophecy is treated as synonymous with teaching, thereby robbing it of its forth-telling element. This should not be the case. Although Paul would certainly desire that prophecies be weighed, he is nevertheless open to ecstatic spontaneity (1 Corinthians 14:22–25, 31, Acts 21:9-11).

Paul speaks of "ministry" (v. 7). The Greek word *diakonia* (**dee-ah-ko-NEE-ah**) is better translated as "service." It was used generally of all Christian service (11:13; Ephesians 4:12) or specifically of ministering specifically to the temporal and bodily wants (1 Corinthians 16:15). Obviously it includes ministry like Paul's (Romans 11:13; 15:25). The inclusion of service as a gift shows that every believer can do something for Christ. Perhaps a person may never have the privilege or opportunity of standing in public and proclaiming Christ, but every person can daily show the love of Christ in deeds of service.

Paul moves on to giving: "he that giveth, let him do it with simplicity." Giving is to be carried out with simple kindliness. The word that Paul uses is *haplotes* (**hap-LOW-tace**) and it connotes both simplicity and generosity. It is openhanded and openhearted generosity out of compassion and singleness of purpose. There is a giving that pries into the circumstances of another as it gives. It gives a moral lecture along with the gift, which gives not so much to relieve the need of the other as to pander to its own vanity and self-satisfaction. This gives with a grim sense of duty, which is giving always with some ulterior motive and never for the sheer joy of giving. Christian giving is with *haplotes*, the simple kindness that delights in the sheer pleasure of giving for giving's sake.

The one that ruleth (Gk. *ho proistamenos*, **hoe pro-ees-ta-MEH-noce**, "he who presides") with diligence is probably a reference to someone who leads any area of ministry rather than a distinct office. It may have referred to house church leaders. Paul's point is clear: A person who has the privilege to lead must do so with diligence or zeal. Paul says if we are so called, we must do it with zeal. We must not carry out our tasks by going through the motions. One of the daunting challenges of the church today is getting leaders in all departments of its work. There are fewer and fewer people with a sense of service and responsibility, willing to give up their comfort and leisure to undertake leadership. In many cases potential leaders plead unfitness and unworthiness when the real reason is disinclination and laziness. If a person takes on such leadership, Paul says that it is to be done with zeal. There are two ways in which a teacher may prepare a lesson—with heart and mind or in the most non-engaged way. A man may dully and drably go through some task in the church, or he may do it with the joy and thrill of zeal. The church needs leaders with zeal in their hearts. The leader not only stands in front of others to offer direction but also provides a model for followers. Paul's concern is that those who lead exercise zeal for and devotion to their managerial tasks (Romans 12:11; 2 Corinthians 7:11, 12; 8:7, 8, 16).

Lastly, showing mercy would include such helpful activities as feeding the hungry, caring for the sick, and caring for the aging. These are to be done cheerfully. Because we have received mercy, we minister with gladness—not gloom—to the needs of others. To a Christian, kindness must be a delight, not a duty. When we practice charity we must do so with a joyful heart. It has to be shown with gracious kindness, Paul says. Yet we must realize that although compassionate care should not be frivolously given, neither should it be performed with drudgery or a cavalier attitude. Showing mercy can also extend to the issue of forgiveness. It is possible to forgive in such a way that is less than gracious by demonstrating an attitude of criticism and contempt. If we have to forgive someone who sins against us, we must remember that we were once sinners. "There but for the grace of God, go I," said George Whitefield, an 18th century revivalist, as he saw the criminal walk to the gallows. Real forgiveness is always undergirded by love and never shown with an air of superiority.

Sources:

Barclay, William, ed. *The Letter to the Romans*, The Daily Study Bible Series. Philadelphia, PA: The Westminster John Knox Press, 1975.

Bence, Clarence L. *Romans: A Bible Commentary in the Wesleyan Tradition.* Indianapolis, IN: Wesleyan Publishing House, 1996.

Cornell, T. and J. Matthews, eds. *Atlas of the Roman World.* New York: Norton Publishing Co., 1982. 5-140.

Cranfield, C.E.B. *The Epistle to the Romans.* Vol. 2. The International Critical Commentary. Edinburgh: T&T Clark, 1979.

Godet, F. *St. Paul's Epistle to the Romans.* Trans. A. Cusin. New York: Funk and Wagnalls, 1883.

Grieb, A. Katherine. *The Story of Romans: A Narrative Defense of God's Righteousness.* Louisville, KY: Westminster/John Knox, 2002.

Greathouse. William M. and George Lyons, *Romans 9–16: A Commentary in the Wesleyan Tradition,* New Beacon Bible Commentary. Kansas City, MO: Beacon Hill Press of Kansas City, 2008.

Keener, Craig. *Romans.* New Covenant Commentary Series. Eugene, OR: Cascade Books, 2009.

Daily Bible Readings

MONDAY
Trust and Honor God
(Proverbs 3:1–12)

TUESDAY
The Gift of Love
(1 Corinthians 13)

WEDNESDAY
Lifestyle of Christian
Believers
(Luke 6:27–36)

THURSDAY
Seek Peace and Pursue It
(Psalm 34:1–14)

FRIDAY
Genuine Love for Each
Other
(Romans 12:9–15)

SATURDAY
Living Together in
Harmony
(Romans 12:16–21)

SUNDAY
A Living Sacrifice
(Romans 12:1–8)

Notes

_____

_____

_____

_____

_____

_____

_____

Covenant in God

This quarter will teach how Jesus fulfilled the Law in the sense that it was given full meaning. Jesus emphasized the deep, underlying messages of the Gospel and this same message is continued through the Apostle Paul and the writer of Hebrews. Relationships of faith empower us to live the covenant and spread the Gospel message.

UNIT 1 • A Fulfilled Covenant

In four sessions, this unit reveals a new sign of the covenant for Jewish and Gentile believers, as recorded in Matthew, Mark, Luke, Hebrews, and Colossians. During the celebration of the Passover, Jesus explained to the disciples that He would initiate a new covenant through His death. Paul explains that the sign of the covenant is now a relationship of the heart between God and God's people, not circumcision.

Lesson 1: June 2, 2019
Jesus Institutes the New Covenant
Mark 14:17–24; Hebrews 8:6–7, 10–12

People often make promises to one another seeking lasting, committed relationships. How can one be assured that a relationship will last? In Mark and Hebrews, Jesus is affirmed as the one through whom God's new everlasting covenant is fulfilled.

Lesson 2: June 9, 2019
Jesus Seals the New Covenant
Mark 15:6–15, 25–26, 33–39

All personal relationships encounter problems that result in division and strife. Who can heal the breaches and restore harmony? Mark describes how Jesus' crucifixion forges a new covenant and reconciles God and humankind.

Lesson 3: June 16, 2019
The New Covenant's Sacrifice
Hebrews 9:11–22

People have devised many methods to deal with the sense of moral uncleanness their misdeeds incur. How can we be definitively cleansed of guilt? Through shedding His blood and dying, Jesus once and for all fulfilled God's new covenant to forgive sins and guarantee eternal life.

Lesson 4: June 23, 2019
Hearts United in Love
Colossians 2:1–15

People bind themselves together by mutual bonds of love and commitment. How can communities avoid losing their identities while under attack? Paul urged the Colossians to be united in love in order to fully understand the rich treasures offered to them by faith so they can resist false teachings and come to appreciate their new spiritual standing in Christ.

UNIT 2 • A Heartfelt Covenant

This unit has five sessions and gives new meaning and purpose to the Law. According to Matthew, Jesus began teaching the Law in a way that gave life to the hearer and doer. Unlike other teachers of the Law, Jesus preached the transforming righteousness of the kingdom. Jesus challenged the mere external observance of God's Law without internal transformation.

Lesson 5: June 30 , 2019
Jesus Teaches About Right Attitudes
Matthew 5:1–12

Our attitudes determine how we view circumstances in our lives. How can our attitudes bring long-term benefits? Jesus' Beatitudes taught the crowd and His disciples those heartfelt values and attitudes required of anyone who seeks to be in a covenant relationship with Him.

Lesson 6: July 7, 2019
Jesus Teaches About Fulfilling the Law
Matthew 5:13–20

People express their beliefs through their actions. How do we express what we believe? Jesus teaches us that we are to do good for others and follow God's Law.

Lesson 7: July 14, 2019
Jesus Teaches Us to Love One Another
Matthew 5:21–32

Love transforms how we relate to one another. In what form does this transformation come? Jesus teaches us how to be a reflection of His light through controlling our anger, being reconciled with others, immediately dealing with sin, and being faithful.

Lesson 8: July 21, 2019
Jesus Teaches About Transforming Love
Matthew 5:38–48

Many people believe retribution is justified when they are mistreated. What is the appropriate response when people are mistreated? Jesus taught His disciples to love their enemies and pray for those who persecuted them.

Lesson 9: July 28, 2019
Jesus Teaches About Spiritual Discernment
Matthew 7:1–6, 15–23

In a complex world, many become confused in trying to cope with the diversity in beliefs and lifestyles. How can one maintain a sense of stability given such complexity? Jesus taught His disciples the spiritual disciplines of resisting the use of judgment and using discernment.

UNIT 3 • Covenant: A Personal Perspective

This unit has four sessions. It focuses on personal relationships between people in 1 Samuel, Ruth, and Ephesians. Ultimately, those relationships pave the way for the Messiah. After Christ established the New Testament church, relationships between people have been based on relationship with Christ Jesus. These relationships continue the work of Christ Jesus by spreading the Gospel message.

Lesson 10: August 4, 2019
A Covenant Between Friends
1 Samuel 18:1–5; 19:1–7

Sometimes we are challenged to compromise our loyalty to a beloved authority figure to keep a promise made to a trusted friend. Whom does one choose? Jonathan chose to keep his promise to love and protect David, his intimate friend, despite his father's insane hatred of David.

Lesson 11: August 11, 2019
A Mother-Daughter Covenant
Ruth 1:6–11, 14–18

When bonded by a strong love and commitment to one another, people who are unrelated by birth may enter into a covenant relationship. What drives and sustains this relationship? Although Naomi begged Ruth to return to her people, Ruth clung to her mother-in-law and vowed her loyalty until death.

Lesson 12: August 18, 2019
A Covenant to Marry
Ruth 3:1–6, 8–12, 16–18

Obedience and commitment to others may bring unanticipated rewards. How should loyalty be compensated? Ruth's commitment to Naomi and her efforts to obey were rewarded with favor in Boaz's eyes, marriage to a kinsman-redeemer, and the assurance of a comfortable life in the future.

Lesson 13: August 25, 2019
Marriage: A Covenant of Mutual Love
Ephesians 5:21–33

In an ever-changing and increasingly complex society, the focus on self-indulgence has endangered a healthy concept of family. How do we make commitment to God and family central to our well-being? Paul says a committed relationship must be sought in which husbands, wives, and children love, honor, and respect both God and one another.

What is Covenant?

by Bertram Melbourne, Ph.D.

Have you ever entered into a serious agreement with someone? Then you have made a covenant. Simply put, a covenant is an agreement between two individuals that forms a new relationship. In the ancient world, especially during the time of the Hittites, there were two types of covenants: *sunthēkē* (**soon-THAY-kay**), an agreement between equals as can be seen in Genesis 21:32 and 26:28; and *diathēkē* (**dia-THAY-ke**), an agreement between a superior and an inferior as between a lord and a vassal, or a sovereign king and a conquered nation. Isaiah 36:16-17 exemplifies this. The latter is the kind of agreement God entered in with His people.

Diathēkē covenants had a specific format. It began with a historical prologue that noted the past relationships between the parties. Next it named the parties to the treaty followed by the specific and the general conditions of the treaty. This was followed by the witnesses and the blessings for faithfulness and curses for disobedience. It is significant that the Decalogue or Ten Commandments is written in this format as is the entire book of Deuteronomy— chapter 27 gives the blessings for obedience, while chapters 28 and 29 denote the curses for disobedience. Yet, what necessitated a covenant relationship between God and humans?

God made humans in God's own image and gifted them with dominion over all the earth. Misled by the tempter and infatuated by desire for an existence akin to God's, humans lost their elevated status and became subject to sin and death. A holy, perfect and righteous God did not abandon them in their plight. Rather, God made a promise to them that a seed of the woman would crush the head of the serpent, though it would bruise his heel in the process. That would ultimately lead to the new covenant in Christ Jesus. A covenant was made with Noah (Genesis 6:18; 9:9, 11 and 13) before and after the Flood, and with Abraham (Genesis 15:18, 17), Isaac, Jacob and the Children of Israel (Genesis 2:24 and 6:4). Succeeding generations anticipated the seed of Eve. Indeed many women, including Eve, thought their sons were the fulfillment of this promise only to be disappointed. God's prophetic clock had not yet struck the right time.

Paul opines in Galatians 4:4 that in the fullness of time God sent forth God's Son born of a woman, born under the Law, to redeem them that were under the Law. What this tells us is that the promised Messiah came at the right time in fulfillment of God's covenant promise to Adam and Eve and as God's remedy for the sin problem. There are noteworthy elements in Paul's statement in Galatians 4:4.

First, what made the first century the fullness of time and the right time for the fulfillment of the covenant? Among many factors are the following:

1. The world was at peace. After several years of war, Augustus had ushered in the Pax Romana.

2. The world was under one government, the Roman government.

3. The world was accessible for travelers. A good road system existed along with good sea routes to all parts of the empire.

4. World travel was safe. Augustus had rid the sea of pirates.

5. There was one universal language: Greek.

6. The Bible had been made available to the world in Greek.

7. Men had become dissatisfied with their religious beliefs and were longing for something better.

8. The Jews of the diaspora had been bearing witness to the true God and knowledge of Him had been spreading as can be evidenced by the wise men who were able to recognize the star and understand its significance.

9. Messianic expectation was rife among the Jews. The situation was ripe worldwide for the Messianic figure.

Fulfilling the Covenant

At such an auspicious time, God fulfilled His covenant by sending the Son to be born under the Law to redeem those who were under the Law. Jesus was subject to human laws and regulations. His gestation was akin to that of every other human being, yet He was different from them in that He was neither born in sin nor shaped in iniquity. This does not mean He could not sin. He came as the first Adam came and was tempted in all points like we are, yet He is without sin because He overcame the tempter. Like the first Adam, He was a direct creation of God. He was the Second Adam whose mission was to redeem fallen human beings. How?

Paul informs us in the book of Romans. After identifying Jesus as the Son of God (1:1-4), Paul testifies that he is not ashamed of the Gospel (1:16-17). Why? Because the Gospel is the power of God unto salvation to all who believe—both Jews and Gentiles. He then uses the rest of chapter 1 to show the Gentiles' need for salvation. He follows up with the Jewish need in 2:1-3:9. By 3:19 he demonstrates the universal need for salvation and shows that everyone is on the brink of hell awaiting a deserved death.

At this point he introduces the notion that law-keeping or works of Law cannot make one right with God. This is Paul's critique of his Jewish past and his Pharisaic background. The function of Law is not to save but to show the need of a Savior. Yet, the Pharisees built up merits to gain standing with God. Paul says that is an impossibility. He introduces God's way of setting humans right. He shows that God, apart from works of Law yet in a manner consistent with the Old Testament Scriptures (the Torah), has provided a new means of salvation—the shedding of Jesus' blood on the Cross in contrast to the shedding of the blood of bulls and goats. Salvation can neither be earned nor merited. It is dispensed as a free gift of God through justification by faith (Romans 3:21). In keeping with God's original promise, here was now the realization of past hopes and dreams.

In this context, Paul makes a curious statement. He says the blood of Jesus is for the remission of former sins that God in God's "forbearance had passed over" (Romans 3:25, RSV). How could a just and upright God pass over sins? What does He mean? What He means is that although people received forgiveness of sins under the old sacrificial system, the blood of bulls and goats was inadequate to achieve propitiation. Such sacrifices could not effectively atone for sin. They were symbolically anticipating the blood of Jesus. Those sins were all dealt with by Jesus on the Cross to fulfill the covenant.

Jesus is God's remedy for sin, an antidote that we receive by faith. Jesus is the fulfillment

of the covenant that is effective for both Jews and Gentiles as well as all creeds, races, ethnicities and genders. The covenant was made possible through Jesus' life, but sealed in Jesus' death. As Paul points out in Romans 1:1-5, the preexistent Son of God—Jesus Christ our Lord—was made of David's seed, according to the flesh. This reference is to His earthly existence, when in fulfillment of the covenant He became one of us to save us.

Receiving New Covenant

Looking at Jesus' earthly life, what was the significance of His temptation in the wilderness if He had no sin? Was it a farce? No, that too had to do with the covenant. It is essential for us to spot the modus operandi of our foe. Fascinatingly, Malachi, the last book of the Old Testament, had predicted that God would send a messenger to prepare the way of the messenger of the covenant whom they were seeking. He would appear suddenly in the Temple (Malachi 3:1). Now we know that John the Baptist was the messenger who prepared the way of the Lord. Yet, there is more to this than the fact that the birth of Jesus took the priests by surprise and they did not even recognize Him when they blessed Him. Herein lies the significance of the second temptation. Why did the devil take Jesus to the Holy City, to the pinnacle of the Temple? He would not have done it if there was no significance. The devil tried to have Jesus throw Himself down from the Temple to prove He was the Son of God and to "suddenly appear in the Temple." Yet, that would have been failure for He would have obeyed the tempter and would thus have sinned. The devil distorts and misuses Scripture, so we have to be on the lookout if we are to be faithful to our covenant with God. But, are we modern Christians in a covenant with God?

After His ministry on earth and as He prepared for His departure, Jesus had His Last Supper with His disciples. Luke tells us that after supper, He took the cup and said, "This cup is the new testament in my blood, which is shed for you" (from Luke 22:20). This doubtlessly was a fulfillment of Jeremiah 31:31 and the promised new covenant. This is the covenant ratified not by the blood of bulls and goats but by the blood of Jesus, which would be and was indeed achieved on Calvary. This is what Paul references in 2 Corinthians 3:6 when he says we, as servants of a new covenant, are made adequate through the spirit and not by the letter—letter meaning works of the Law for salvation. There is great opposition in the writings of Paul to the Law as a means of salvation. He sees this as undermining to the sacrificial death of Jesus. Yet, how does a modern Christian become incorporated in this new covenant?

When the opponents of Paul heard his teaching that where sin abounds grace super abounds, they took it to the extreme by saying if one wanted to see God's abundant grace then one should sin since more sin means more grace. Paul countered this argument in Romans 6:1-5. He questioned how one who has died to sin could continue to live in it. He opined that baptism brings believers into a new relationship with Christ. Baptism represents a change of ownership and so demonstrates that Christians have entered a new relationship in which sin may remain but should not reign for there is one Lord—Jesus Christ. While the term covenant is not used here, it is implied in the language and change of ownership. This is a new sign of covenant rather than circumcision as the sign of the old covenant.

It is in this context and in that of salvation by faith that we should understand and exemplify Ephesians 2:11-12. Non-Jewish Christians were neither members of Israel's commonwealth nor partners in the covenant. Yet, the blood of Jesus has broken barriers and brought us near to God. The church of God is neither exclusive nor private. It is a kaleidoscopic alliance of all God's children covenanted together by love and the blood of Christ. We now have rights and privileges and are partakers of the divine nature. This was always God's plan. It is now incumbent upon us to maintain this freedom and to be inclusive. God expects each of us, as part of the new covenant, to bring others to share the joy, peace, and opportunities that are ours through the blood of Jesus.

Source:

Achtemeier, Paul J. gen. ed. *Harper's Bible Dictionary*. San Francisco: Harper, 1971.

Alexander, Desmond T. and David W. Baker, eds. *Dictionary of the Old Testament: Pentateuch*. Downers Grove, IL: InterVarsity Press, 2003.

Craigie, P.C. *The Book of Deuteronomy. The New International Commentary on the Old Testament*. Grand Rapids, MI: Wm. B. Eerdmans Publishing Co., 1976.

Freedman, David N., ed. *The Anchor Bible Dictionary*, Vol. 1. New York: Doubleday, 1992.

Heppenstall, Edward. *Salvation Unlimited: Perspectives in Righteousness by Faith*. Washington, DC: Review and Herald Publishing Association, 1974.

Bertram Melbourne, Ph.D., is Professor of New Testament Language and Literature at the Howard University School of Divinity in Washington, D.C.

Covenant In God

by Ramon Mayo, M.A.

The Bible is a collection of stories. Authors from different time periods, occupations, and social standings wrote these stories. What binds them together into one is covenant. Covenant is the agreement between two parties to follow through on their obligation. At the same time covenant is much more than a contract full of duties and consequences for violation. Covenant is about relationship.

Beyond the ceremonies and documentation that we find in the Old Testament, a covenant is a binding relationship between two parties. It's more than an agreement to do one thing in exchange for the other. Even when we dissect what most call the old covenant, it's deeper than "you scratch my back and I'll scratch yours."

The old covenant was given to Israel after the ordeal of their deliverance from Egyptian slavery. It was a sign of their relationship with Yahweh. He had fought for them with ten plagues that ravaged the Egyptian countryside. The plagues culminated in the death of the firstborn in all the Egyptian households, including Pharaoh's own.

Even after Pharaoh released the Israelites, Yahweh had to fight the Egyptian army, drowning them in the water of the Red Sea. With the Hebrews safely across and preparing to journey through the wilderness to the Promised Land, the covenant communicates one thing: These people are mine.

Now the new covenant is a sign of our relationship with God the Father through Jesus Christ. His blood shed on the Cross has sealed the covenant between the believer and God. It is this covenant that brings us forgiveness and new life in Him.

Jesus outlines the stipulations and blessings of the new covenant in the Sermon on the Mount. It is here that we see a dramatic challenge of the understanding many Jews of the time had of the old covenant. Poverty is not a result of violating the covenant but a condition for receiving the blessings of the covenant. We all are in spiritual poverty that needs God's salvation to redeem us.

This was countercultural to the first-century Jew and it is countercultural to our sensibilities, too. Under the new covenant, poverty, mourning, persecution, and suffering are not consequences of disobedience but of obedience. Not only are they consequences of righteous living, but also doorways to greater blessing.

The new covenant is not the total opposite of the old covenant; it gives us a deeper understanding of the former one. Israel was called into covenant with God because of relationship. This relationship gave them the opportunity to obey and walk out the covenant's stipulations in order to display that relationship.

In the midst of this overarching covenantal relationship we also have covenants with each other. While most of this may sound archaic to the modern mind, room does exist for covenant in the twenty-first century. There are different times when we are called into relationship and those relationships demand more from us—in fact they may demand all of us.

There are relationships of friendship, such as Ruth and Naomi. This relationship was more than just about being family. It was a covenant that Ruth pursued with Naomi. She would become a part of God's people and take Yahweh as her God. Ruth's devotion to Naomi went beyond the typical in-law relationship. Ruth renounced everything she had to be at Naomi's side.

Ruth's whole identity became attached to Naomi. Their destinies became intertwined. This covenant relationship was more than a daughter-in-law coming to live with her mother-in-law. It was a covenant relationship defined by the giving of the whole self.

David and Jonathan's relationship also highlights a covenant relationship between two people. We don't normally think of two men having this close of a friendship in the Western world. In fact, many have tried to view this as a homosexual relationship. It is nothing of the kind.

In the ancient Near East, men developed vital friendships with each other. This was necessary, as you needed to count on your neighbors and friends to help you when times were tough. There was no room for individualism. David and Jonathan's relationship is reflective of their times, not ours.

But their relationship was highly extraordinary because of Jonathan's actions. He totally gives David his whole soul and self. As the next in line to be king, Jonathan opens up and makes himself vulnerable by giving David his robe, belt, tunic, and sword. He is saying that wherever David goes he will be by his side.

The underlying message is that Jonathan knows David will be king and will not stand in his way, but instead offer him unconditional loyalty and support. The covenant that Jonathan made was a vow to love David as his own soul and self.

To have friends to call on is rare nowadays. To have friends who covenant with you on that deep of a level is almost nonexistent. But there is another area where covenants between people result in this kind of unconditional love and support: marriage.

In his letter to the Ephesian church, Paul shows us how the marriage covenant is unique among all other relationships. It is a vow to love your spouse with your entire being. This is not just a 50/50 contract. It is more like a 100/100 covenant with both partners giving 100 percent of themselves to each other.

We are to stay faithful to this marriage covenant. It is more than a contract supported by the state; it is a promise to love each other in submission to God. In fact, the covenant is more about your promise to God than to the other person.

The other person is subject to change. He or she may not always be loveable or maintain good looks or health. Your spouse may do things that will forever cause you to cringe. But your faithfulness is to the covenant you made before God and not to your spouse's fickle moods and changing behavior.

Covenant in God is about God and not us. We are humans. God is God. When He says something He will do it. When we enter into covenant with each other we are also putting our trust in God. Ultimately our covenant is not about our own trustworthiness or relationships with each other. They are a reflection of God and our relationship with Him.

Ramon Mayo, M.A., is the Digital Content Specialist at UMI and former Developmental Editor of *Precepts for Living*. He holds a masters of arts from Fuller Theological Seminary in Pasadena, California.

The Story of Shavuot

by Rabbi Jason Sobel

The Story of Shavuot

From the day after the Sabbath—the day you bring the bundle of grain to be lifted up as a special offering—count off seven full weeks. Keep counting until the day after the seventh Sabbath, fifty days later. Then present an offering of new grain to the LORD. From wherever you live, bring two loaves of bread to be lifted up before the LORD as a special offering. Make these loaves from four quarts of choice flour, and bake them with yeast. They will be an offering to the LORD from the first of your crops. … When you harvest the crops of your land, do not harvest the grain along the edges of your fields, and do not pick up what the harvesters drop. Leave it for the poor and the foreigners living among you. I am the LORD your God (Leviticus 23:15–17, 22, NLT).

The Promise of Pentecost: Revelation of Word and Spirit

As a child, do you remember the mounting excitement you felt when your birthday was approaching? I still relive it as I watch my kids with their countdown calendars. They start at about thirty days out and tick off time as each date passes. The anticipation is almost more than they can handle as the day gets closer!

You can think of this next holiday in much the same way. Shavuot, also known as Pentecost, is a celebration, and God rejoices if we brim with the anticipation of a child nearing his or her birthday. But unlike any other party, Pentecost is topped off with the greatest gift possible—God's Word and Spirit. In the Old Testament, the gift was presented on Mount Sinai in the form of the Torah. In the New Testament, the gift was presented by the infilling of the Holy Spirit (Acts 2).

The Countdown

Now, this can get a bit tricky, but buckle up and hang on.

Jesus died on Passover. On the second day of Passover, He arose on an agricultural holiday called First Fruits (Yom Habikkurim). In ancient times, an offering of the first fruits of the barley harvest was given to the Lord, which was the wave offering referred to in the Leviticus excerpt above. The first fruits of this harvest would be waved before the Lord as a sign of thanksgiving and eager expectation. Agriculturally, if you had a good early harvest, you were guaranteed to have an abundant later harvest. First Fruits was a sign of the greater harvest to come, but it also started the forty-nine-day countdown to Shavuot.

We have always acknowledged that nothing is random with God. Therefore, it is appropriate that Jesus, who died on Passover, would arise from the dead as "…the firstfruits of them that slept" (1 Corinthians 15:20, KJV). After He arose, Jesus instructed the disciples, "Do not leave Jerusalem until the Father sends you the gift he promised … John baptized with water, but in just a few days you will be baptized with the Holy Spirit" (from Acts 1:4–5, NLT). His resurrection on First Fruits started the countdown to Pentecost, which was His Father's gift—the biggest biblical God party on record, where God literally rocked the house, and there were three thousand salvations in one day!

Now, let's take a step back into the Old Testament and explore the first Pentecost on Mount Sinai.

Four Hundred Years Undone in Fifty Days

For more than four hundred years, the Jews had been the "beasts of burden" to the Egyptians. To their captors, they were objects, not people. Century upon century passed as prayers and desperate cries rose from their souls to a seemingly deaf heaven. They felt forgotten. God warned Abraham in Genesis 15 that four hundred years of affliction would befall the Jews, but who knows why four centuries had to pass before God moved. It's a question I have for Him once I'm on the other side. However, we know that God is never in a hurry, and He is also never late. Because of this protracted captivity, He needed to win back His people's trust and their love. He had to rebuild relationship. God had a big gift in store for His people, but for them to receive it in the proper way, they needed to be healed and prepared, or the gift would have no meaning.

Holy and Whole

Though the Jews' exile was primarily physical, it also had spiritual, emotional, and relational components. God took Israel out of Egypt, and now, He had to take Egypt out of Israel. They were in dire need of healing, desperate to rebuild relationship with God, but also with each other.

For the Jews to be truly free, God had to break their slave mentality. Violence,

oppression, and hatred were all the Jews knew. They had learned to deal with one another the way the Egyptians dealt with them—with verbal, mental, and physical abuse. In diametric opposition to God's way, the Egyptian method was destructive.

Because of the idolatrous environment they had lived in for so long, the Jews were also spiritually impure. Their environment eventually and sadly influenced the Jews in idolatry of their own, ultimately leading them to create the golden calf once they were out of Egypt.

Broken in body, mind, heart, and spirit, God's people needed multidimensional healing.

It's almost too hard to fathom that the undoing of four centuries of horrific abuse could happen in only fifty days! Two verses speak against this mindset, though: "For with God nothing shall be impossible" (Luke 1:37, KJV) and "Hope deferred makes the heart grow sick, but a dream fulfilled is a tree of life" (Proverbs 13:12, NLT). In His faithfulness, God overcame impossibilities and restored hope to the Jews by delivering them from Egypt, displaying His extravagant love through signs and wonders, bountifully providing for them in the barren desert, and radically healing their bodies. He wanted His people whole so He could bestow upon them the gift of His holiness and His presence.

United They Stood

And the LORD said unto Moses ... be ready against the third day: for the third day the LORD will come down in the sight of all the people upon mount Sinai ... And all the people saw the thunderings, and the lightnings, and the noise of the trumpet, and the mountain smoking: and when the people saw it, they removed, and stood afar off (Exodus 19:10–11, 20:18, KJV).

God's heart has always been for the unity of His people, and He begins a unifying process through healing the Jews after their deliverance from Egypt. When He rescued millions of people from Pharaoh, He chose to heal each and every one of them. Given the people's various ages and the inevitable number of bodies wrecked by daily toil, can you imagine the number of infirm among them? However, He brought healing to everyone so all were able to come to the mountain to hear His Word, see His natural spectacles, and encounter His presence. The word "all" from Exodus 20 signifies more than the obvious, however.

For they were departed [plural form] from Rephidim, and were come to the desert of Sinai, and had pitched in the wilderness; and there Israel camped [singular form] before the mount (Exodus 19:2, KJV).

Many symbols of unity are associated with Pentecost. Opposite to Passover during which leaven is avoided, Pentecost/Shavuot is celebrated by presenting an offering of "two loaves of bread … to the LORD" (from Leviticus 23:17, NLT). You might wonder why leaven is allowable at Pentecost but forbidden at Passover. In Jewish thought, after we have purified ourselves of the leaven and what it represents, then that which is impure is transformed and sanctified by faith, making the leaven no longer taboo.

Notice that not one but two loaves are offered! Two represents unity between Word and Spirit, heaven and earth, body and soul, Jew and Gentile. Shavuot represents not only unity but the unification of opposites, which is why the book of Ruth is read during this holiday. There was power in the unlikely marriage between Boaz, the Jew, and Ruth, the Gentile. From their union comes the lineage of Yeshua (Jesus)! The Messiah's final prayer in John 17

asks for unity among God's people just as He and the Father are one (John 17:21). The same language that Rashi, an ancient Jewish rabbi, used to describe the love and unity that existed among Israel at Sinai is the same language used in Acts to describe followers of Yeshua before, on, and after Shavuot:

They all met together and were constantly united in prayer, along with Mary the mother of Jesus, several other women, and the brothers of Jesus (Acts 1:14, NLT).
****

And when the day of Pentecost was fully come, they were all with one accord in one place (Acts 2:1, KJV).
****

The apostles worked many signs and miracles among the people. One in heart, they all used to meet in the Portico of Solomon (Acts 5:12, author's translation).

Unity is a powerful force, which is why armies march in break-step. When Roman armies marched in unison, bridges would break under them, and it has been speculated that if millions of people marched in step on the Golden Gate Bridge, the bridge would come down! God wouldn't give the gift of His Word and Spirit until all were present at Sinai, not just in headcount but in heart. Similarly, it was only when they were on one accord in Jerusalem that the promised power came!

Suddenly, there was a sound from heaven like the roaring of a mighty windstorm, and it filled the house where they were sitting. Then, what looked like flames or tongues of fire appeared and settled on each of them. And everyone present was filled with the Holy Spirit and began speaking in other languages, as the Holy Spirit gave them this ability (Acts 2:2–4, NLT).

For Messianic Jews, this Pentecost is considered a re-enactment of Mount Sinai. The booming of the wind is like the thunderings at Sinai, and the tongues of fire over the disciples' heads are akin to the cleft tongue that came out of the mouth of God when He first uttered the Commandments. According to the Targum, an ancient Aramaic paraphrase and interpretation of the Hebrew Bible, the split tongue looked like a fiery bird, which is said to have inscribed the tablets of the covenant. God again imprinted His Word on His disciples as He did on Sinai. This time, the stone of Sinai was replaced as God wrote His new covenant within them, as the prophet had foretold: "I will make a new covenant with the people of Israel and Judah … I will put my instructions deep within them, and I will write them on their hearts" (from Jeremiah 31:31, 33, NLT).

This unity of God's people, first on Sinai, then in Jerusalem, sparked the fire and wind of the Spirit, which then created a wildfire of transformation! God's presence, power, and provision are in direct proportion to the unity of His people.

Redemption and Revelation

God physically, emotionally, and spiritually redeemed Israel from Egypt to make them a whole, holy nation. We must realize that as He was preparing them for redemption, He was also readying them for revelation. Here's an important truth: Redemption without revelation can slide into reverse, regressing us to that place from which we were redeemed. In fact, the purpose of redemption IS revelation. Without a new purpose, a renewed mindset, and a fresh identity, we can easily slip into slavery to "Pharaoh" again. The Egypts in our lives can take many forms—our careers, our bank account, even our families. God freed, redeemed, absolved, and saved us so He could fully reveal to us who we are in His divine plan!

A New Creation

As God redeemed Israel, He has redeemed us through Messiah. We, too, are a new creation with a new identity and purpose. Israel was called a royal priesthood, a holy nation, on Mount Sinai. Peter declares the same for us:

Ye are a chosen generation, a royal priesthood, an holy nation, a peculiar people; that ye should shew forth the praises of him who hath called you out of darkness into his marvellous light; Which in time past were not a people, but are now the people of God (from 1 Peter 2:9–10, KJV).

Peter himself became a new creation during Pentecost. Instead of the cowering coward who denied Yeshua three times, he became Petrus (Peter), living up to the name Yeshua gave him, which in Latin means "rock." Filled with the power of *Ruach* (the Holy Spirit), he preached his first sermon and birthed the early church during this Pentecost, just as in Genesis when the Spirit hovered over the deep and God spoke the Word creating the world. As it was in the beginning, so it was on that Shavuot in Jerusalem—the union of Word and Spirit swelled the ranks of the followers of Yeshua by three thousand new creations that day. Word and Spirit always result in newness of life!

Remember, all that God has done in the past, He wants to do again in the present and the future. The past is more than events that have already happened. It reflects the heart of God and what He desires to do in and through you. Let's seek the Lord for our own personal Pentecost as individuals and as a church and watch the amazing work of transformation that comes through His Word and Spirit.

Rabbi Jason Sobel is a Messianic Jewish Rabbi and contributing writer to *Precepts for Living*® from California.

Reward The Adult Learner!

by La Verne Tolbert, Ph.D.

In the learning environment, why not reward adults? Awards and prizes are called extrinsic motivations—external rewards that encourage behavior. Of course, rewards work well with children. When they earn a gift or prize for good behavior or for completing an activity, they are encouraged to continue with that activity. Many of us memorized dozens of Scriptures and all sixty-six books of the Bible in Sunday School just to earn a sticker.

The wise adult teacher is aware that rewards also encourage adults. That's why Jesus says, "Look, I am coming soon, bringing my reward with me to repay all people according to their deeds" (Revelation 22:12, NLT). Some will even earn crowns to place at His feet!

Rewarding adults in the adult Bible class or Sunday School is not as difficult as it may seem. A $5 coffee gift card for Bible memorization, for example, will put a smile on any adult's face. Plus, it will encourage other students as well. Less expensive is a small token for arriving on time, such as a bookmark, or a thank you note, or a simple verbal acknowledgment. These examples are enough to inspire the entire class to accomplish a goal set forth by the teacher.

Extrinsic and Intrinsic Motivation

External rewards are never the end goal. The point is intrinsic motivation—being motivated internally to accomplish something. We serve the Lord, not to earn a reward, but because we love Him. This passion motivates us and it's internal, in our hearts. Receiving a reward from Jesus, now that's a bonus!

Extrinsic motivation often results in intrinsic motivation. The child who earns an A on his or her paper may learn the value of study and hard work, a lifelong value to which they may aspire. Similarly, adults, especially when learning new things, may be inspired by extrinsic rewards. Receiving a paycheck is an extrinsic reward even though some might do the same work even if they did not receive a check.

Rewards encourage learning and should not be overlooked for the adult learner. Teachers who prepare lessons in advance and who are alert to extrinsic motivation may encourage intrinsic motivation that lasts a lifetime.

Early-Riser Buttons

A teacher of an adult Bible study class wanted to encourage students to spend a few minutes every morning reading the Bible. Proverbs 8:17 provided the inspiration: "I love them that love me; and those that seek me early shall find me" (KJV). This teacher made a small investment to have buttons produced with a picture of the sun along with the Scripture's address, Proverbs 8:17.

Each week, a button was awarded to students who reported they had completed seven days of being an early riser. Imagine an entire class competing to win a simple pin-on button!

You, too, deserve a reward. I applaud you for teaching God's Word to His people and for your commitment to encourage, inspire, and educate so that the body of Christ is transformed. May God continue to bless you!

La Verne Tolbert, Ph.D., is author of *Teaching Like Jesus: A Practical Guide to Christian Education in Your Church* (Zondervan).

496

EVANGELINE CAREY

(1949-2011)

Former 'Precepts For Living' Developmental Editor

Evangeline Carey was a talented and inspiring woman of God. Her love for the Lord, excellent teaching skills, and her joy in sharing the Gospel with others were genuine gems. Her knowledge and strong prayer life will always be remembered and live in the hearts and minds of those who share in the reading of *Precepts for Living*.

She was born August 5, 1949, in Laurel, Mississippi. As a young child in Laurel, she experienced the deep and entrenched dehumanizing conditions of racial and social injustice. She knew what it was like to ride in the back of the bus, stand in lines marked by "colored only" and "white only" signs, and experience the poor educational conditions that permeated the lives of Black people. At an early age, she was determined to receive an excellent education, fight injustice, and create opportunities for others to learn. She lived this resolve through her faith and her willingness to encourage others to strive for excellence!

Her family relocated to Gary, Indiana, when she was about twelve years old. She attended Beckman Middle School and graduated with honors from Gary Roosevelt High School in 1968. When she was fifteen, she met the love of her life, Winston Carey. Their courtship continued throughout high school and they married in March 1969. They were blessed with three children and seven grandchildren during forty-two years of marriage. She truly loved her husband and family.

Evangeline Carey received her Bachelor of Science in sociology degree with a minor in psychology from Indiana University Northwest. Her pursuit for additional higher education was impacted by her failing health because she was not able to finish as quickly as she wanted. Yet, she did not give up. Even when her doctor said that she "would die from her health issues," she did not stop working toward her educational goals. Carey was a fighter who believed that her strong faith in God, much prayer, and supportive family and friends allowed her to press toward the mark of her educational prize. In May 2012, Carey received her prize, a Master of Arts degree in Biblical Studies from Moody Bible Institute.

While she worked on her Master's degree, Carey tutored her grandchildren, assisted other students with papers, researched, wrote poetry and books, and counseled those who needed her wisdom and kindness. Every time she met someone who thought that a high school level of knowledge was all they could aspire to, she

promptly let them know that "God had more for them, but they had to step out in faith, want to learn more, and do more."

Carey's deep love and appreciation for God's Word was expressed in her meticulous and diligent work as Developmental Editor for *Precepts for Living* at Urban Ministries, Inc.

It was her ultimate dream to work for a Christian publishing company. Urban Ministries gave Carey the opportunity to write and teach God's Word to thousands of people. She often stated:

"I want God's Word to reach the masses!" God allowed her to achieve her dream and to bring the Good News to so many.

She accepted Christ at a young age and believed that she should serve God's people in the church and the community. She served in the church as a Sunday School teacher, vice president of the Women of the Church of God (WCG), and a member of the Board of Christian Education. She taught various workshops, preached, and donated school supplies and gifts to children and teens who were in need. Evangeline Carey's love for Christ, people, and especially for children in need will always be remembered and cherished.

Teaching Tips

Words You Should Know

A. Mediator *mesites* (Gk.)—A go-between, or someone who tries to bring together two sets of people or individuals who are not getting along.

B. Bread *artos* (Gk.)—An unleavened flat cake eaten during the Passover.

Teacher Preparation

Unifying Principle—Covenant Fulfilled. People often make promises to one another seeking lasting, committed relationships. How can one be assured that a relationship will last? In Mark and Hebrews, Jesus is affirmed as the one through whom God's everlasting covenant is fulfilled.

A. Read the Bible Background and Devotional Readings.

B. Pray for your students and lesson clarity.

C. Read the lesson Scripture in multiple translations.

D. Option: Brainstorm ways people publicly proclaim and remember their loyalties: wearing a wedding ring, reciting the pledge of allegiance, etc. What do such acts do for those who participate in them? How do we proclaim and remember our relationship to God through Christ?

O—Open the Lesson

A. Begin the class with prayer.

B. Have the students read the Aim for Change.

C. Have the students read the In Focus story.

D. Ask students how events named in the story can weigh on their hearts and how they can view these events from a theological perspective.

P—Present the Scriptures

A. Read the Focal Verses and discuss the Background and The People, Places, and Times sections.

B. Have the class share what Scriptures stand out for them and why, with particular emphasis on today's context.

E—Explore the Meaning

A. Use In Depth or More Light on the Text to help provide more in-depth discussion of the lesson text.

B. Discuss the Liberating Lesson and Application for Activation sections.

N—Next Steps for Application

A. Summarize the value of understanding our new covenant in Christ Jesus.

B. End class with a commitment to pray for deeper reflection on the new covenant's impact on our lives.

Worship Guide

For the Superintendent or Teacher
Theme: Jesus Institutes the New Covenant
Song: "The Blood Will Never Lose Its Power"
Devotional Reading: Jeremiah 31:31–34

Jesus Institutes the New Covenant

Bible Background • MARK 14:21–31; HEBREWS 8
Printed Text • MARK 14:17–24; HEBREWS 8:6–7, 10–12 | Devotional Reading • JEREMIAH 31:31–34

Aim for Change

By the end of the lesson, we will: IDENTIFY Jesus as the initiator of the new covenant illustrated in the Lord's Supper; APPRECIATE our standing in right relationship with God because of the new covenant; and CONSIDER the Lord's Supper with reverence as the sign of new covenant in Christ.

In Focus

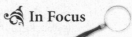

"Don't ever make a promise you can't keep," said Rita, Roxanne's mom. "In fact, you're probably too young to make promises at all. So don't."

Roxanne sobbed softly, remembering her mother's sage advice. She thought she understood what keeping her word was all about, but she was wrong. While she was at school, she made a promise to her best friend, Keisha, to help her with her math homework after school. They were preparing for a math test, and Keisha needed the extra help from Roxanne, who was an A+ math student.

But now Roxanne's mom was working late unexpectedly, and Roxanne was going to her grandmother's for the evening. She was definitely going to break her promise. The only thing she could do was call Keisha to inform her of the change of plans. To her surprise, Keisha wasn't mad all. She understood why Roxanne had to cancel and decided to study with her older brother Brandon instead.

"I guess your mom was right about making promises, huh?" Keisha said with a smile over the phone.

"I'm just not old enough to control things in my life," Roxanne replied. "But I have a feeling adults struggle with promises, too."

God's promises are unfailing compared to ours. As Christ's followers, how can we depend on Him being trustworthy? Which promise of God are you holding to dearly?

Keep in Mind

> "But now hath he obtained a more excellent ministry, by how much also he is the mediator of a better covenant, which was established upon better promises" (Hebrews 8:6, KJV).

"But now Jesus, our High Priest, has been given a ministry that is far superior to the old priesthood, for he is the one who mediates for us a far better covenant with God, based on better promises" (Hebrews 8:6, NLT).

Focal Verses

KJV **Mark 14:17** And in the evening he cometh with the twelve.

18 And as they sat and did eat, Jesus said, Verily I say unto you, One of you which eateth with me shall betray me.

19 And they began to be sorrowful, and to say unto him one by one, Is it I? and another said, Is it I?

20 And he answered and said unto them, It is one of the twelve, that dippeth with me in the dish.

21 The Son of man indeed goeth, as it is written of him: but woe to that man by whom the Son of man is betrayed! good were it for that man if he had never been born.

22 And as they did eat, Jesus took bread, and blessed, and brake it, and gave to them, and said, Take, eat: this is my body.

23 And he took the cup, and when he had given thanks, he gave it to them: and they all drank of it.

24 And he said unto them, This is my blood of the new testament, which is shed for many.

Hebrews 8:6 But now hath he obtained a more excellent ministry, by how much also he is the mediator of a better covenant, which was established upon better promises.

7 For if that first covenant had been faultless, then should no place have been sought for the second.

10 For this is the covenant that I will make with the house of Israel after those days, saith the Lord; I will put my laws into their mind, and write them in their hearts: and I will be to them a God, and they shall be to me a people:

11 And they shall not teach every man his neighbour, and every man his brother, saying, Know the Lord: for all shall know me, from the least to the greatest.

NLT **Mark 14:17** In the evening Jesus arrived with the Twelve.

18 As they were at the table eating, Jesus said, "I tell you the truth, one of you eating with me here will betray me."

19 Greatly distressed, each one asked in turn, "Am I the one?"

20 He replied, "It is one of you twelve who is eating from this bowl with me.

21 For the Son of Man must die, as the Scriptures declared long ago. But how terrible it will be for the one who betrays him. It would be far better for that man if he had never been born!"

22 As they were eating, Jesus took some bread and blessed it. Then he broke it in pieces and gave it to the disciples, saying, "Take it, for this is my body."

23 And he took a cup of wine and gave thanks to God for it. He gave it to them, and they all drank from it.

24 And he said to them, "This is my blood, which confirms the covenant between God and his people. It is poured out as a sacrifice for many.

Hebrews 8:6 But now Jesus, our High Priest, has been given a ministry that is far superior to the old priesthood, for he is the one who mediates for us a far better covenant with God, based on better promises.

7 If the first covenant had been faultless, there would have been no need for a second covenant to replace it.

10 But this is the new covenant I will make with the people of Israel on that day, says the LORD: I will put my laws in their minds, and I will write them on their hearts. I will be their God, and they will be my people.

11 And they will not need to teach their neighbors, nor will they need to teach their relatives saying, 'You should know the LORD.'

12 For I will be merciful to their unrighteousness, and their sins and their iniquities will I remember no more.

For everyone, from the least to the greatest, will know me already.

12 And I will forgive their wickedness, and I will never again remember their sins."

The People, Places, and Times

Mediator. A person who serves as an intermediary to reconcile differences between people. Under the old covenant, a priest served as the mediator between humanity and God. The ministry of Jesus, the new covenant, pronounced Him as the final and complete mediator between us and God (Hebrews 8).

Covenant. A binding agreement made between two or more people or groups; a solemn agreement or vow made between God and His people that promised His blessings in return for their devotion and obedience (Genesis 17:1–27). Some covenants were "one-sided," meaning that God declared His intent to do certain things without any obligation from the second party (Genesis 9). Jesus Christ became the mediator of a new covenant when He sacrificed His life on the Cross, reconciling people to God and bringing salvation and eternal life to all who trust in Him (Hebrews 8:1–13, 10:12–17).

Background

Our Scripture lesson causes us to review the old (Mosaic) covenant and its meaning in order to understand the new covenant in its context. The Last Supper Jesus has with His disciples before His death on the Cross occurs during the Passover celebration in Jerusalem.

The Passover was established and instituted by God through His servant Moses. God established the Hebrew calendar and delivered the Hebrews from bondage in Egypt (Exodus 12). God gave instructions on what day the sacrifice was to be set apart, the criteria for the sacrifice, and when the sacrifice was to be offered. God further gave instructions on where the blood of the sacrifice was to be placed on the households of the Israelites. The lamb that was to be sacrificed had to be roasted over fire and eaten with unleavened bread and bitter herbs.

The Lord was establishing His covenant with Israel. Moses obeyed all God commanded. On the night of Passover, the Death Angel brought death on the houses of Egypt and Pharaoh, and the Egyptians were left in unprecedented mourning and shock. God had executed judgment against the false gods of Egypt and their oppressors. Pharaoh sent for Moses and Aaron, and told them to get their people out of Egypt and go worship God as they had said.

From Exodus 12 until the time of our text, the Israelites observed the Passover as the act of God that became foundational for His covenant with Israel on Mount Sinai. God established the Passover, and Feast of Unleavened Bread, as an everlasting ordinance. In our text Jesus sent two of His disciples to go and prepare the Passover for them to celebrate together.

At-A-Glance

1. The Perpetual Promise of Passover
(Mark 14:17–24)
2. The Perpetual Purpose of the High Priest
(Hebrews 8:6–12)

In Depth

1. The Perpetual Promise of Passover (Mark 14:17–24)

Jesus, knowing that His time of sacrifice and suffering is drawing near, prepares to celebrate and reach the climax of His teaching to the Twelve with this Passover feast. Jesus has removed Himself from public view because there is a plot to kill Him and Judas Iscariot has arranged to betray Him. Jesus, knowing all this, continues in the will of the Father to reveal a new meaning to a traditional meal.

Jesus opens the table talk with a disturbing statement, "Verily I say unto you, One of you which eateth with me shall betray me" (from v. 18). All the disciples question one another and Jesus, but the only clue that Jesus gives is still veiled and vague: "It is one of the twelve, that dippeth with me in the dish" (from v. 20). All the disciples are now trying to remember who dipped their hands in the dish. Was it them?

Amid their confusion and conversation, Jesus pulls their attention back to Him and to the reason for their gathering. Jesus takes two elements from the meal and gives them new meaning. First He takes the bread, blesses it, breaks it and gives each of them some. Then he takes the cup, gives thanks and let them drink from it. Jesus tells His disciples that the bread and cup of Passover have now become His body and blood. Jesus reveals how He is related to the Passover feast for His disciples.

As we reflect on Exodus 12, when the Passover was instituted by God through Moses, God showed Moses, the Israelites, and the Egyptians that He alone was a mighty deliverer! The blood of the Passover lamb was a sign to the Israelites and the death angel that they belonged to the Lord.

By comparison, now with the new covenant, the blood of Jesus identifies those who believe in Him as Lord and Savior of their lives. Just as the blood on the doorpost spared the lives of those Israelites who were in bondage in Egypt, so likewise the blood of Jesus delivers us from the penalty and bondage of sin. We have this declaration from Jesus Christ: "This is my blood of the new covenant, which is shed for many" (from v. 24). The purpose of the great Passover Lamb Jesus was to set all who are in the bondage of sin free from the penalty of death.

What continuing experiences have you had because of the perpetual promise and purpose of salvation through Jesus?

2. The Perpetual Purpose of the High Priest (Hebrews 8:6–12)

Now on the other side of the resurrection of Jesus, we experience Him not only as the Passover Lamb, but also as our High Priest forever. Those who served as ministers of the old covenant, Aaron and his sons, also needed redeeming, for they could not redeem themselves. Jesus became the Passover Lamb that made everything new. Jesus alone is the only High Priest needed between heaven and humanity. The priests of the old covenant would offer sacrifices to God on behalf of themselves and the people. But Jesus as God in human flesh offered Himself as a sacrifice for the sins of all humanity. Now Jesus has been elevated to a more excellent ministry of High Priest, as the prophet Jeremiah foretold (31:31–34). Now we see this new covenant being established and fulfilled through Jesus. Jesus said to His disciples that He would not leave them comfortless, but He would send the Spirit of Truth. This promise extends to us today. The Holy Spirit leads us in all manner of truth (John 16:13).

Search the Scriptures

1. Who could make acceptable offerings for sin in the old covenant (Hebrews 8:6)? How is the new covenant different?

2. We see from these two passages of Scripture that God has an incomprehensible love for humanity. What does the Scripture say about God forgiving and forgetting our sins?

Discuss the Meaning

1. Typically, are you a promise keeper or a promise breaker? Under which circumstances have you been one or the other? How do you count the cost of keeping or breaking your word? How have these experiences affected your relationship with others? With God?

2. Think of a time when you needed to rebuild trust with someone or even yourself. How did you respond? Compare and contrast that with Jesus' need to make a better covenant.

Liberating Lesson

As you consider your life as a Christian, consider what this new covenant has afforded and provided you. Write down how different your life would be if you were still under the old covenant. Praise Jesus for His willingness to be our Passover Lamb and High Priest. What will you do with your liberty? Do you feel any responsibility to help others because of what Jesus has done for you? Hear and see this text in view of what Jesus says, "The Spirit of the Lord is upon me, because he hath anointed me to preach the gospel to the poor; he hath sent me to heal the brokenhearted, to preach deliverance to the captives, and recovering of sight to the blind, to set at liberty them that are bruised, To preach the acceptable year of the Lord" (Luke 4:18–19). What will you do? Whom will you help lift and liberate from sites and systems of oppression?

Application for Activation

Because of the death, burial, and resurrection of Jesus, we now have a new covenant and a High Priest who sits in the highest of heavens who is our mediator, advocating for us in the presence of God the Father. The product of sin is death, but the new covenant provides us with an opportunity to accept Jesus' sacrifice, which freed us from our sins. Today we have the opportunity not only to accept Jesus as Savior and Lord but to then share the redemptive power of Jesus with someone who needs to be saved.

This week what can you modify in your attitude, behavior, or character to express your identity in Christ?

Follow the Spirit

What God wants me to do:

_____

_____

_____

_____

Remember Your Thoughts

Special insights I have learned:

_____

_____

_____

_____

More Light on the Text

Mark 14:17–24

17 And in the evening he cometh with the twelve. 18 And as they sat and did eat, Jesus said, Verily I say unto you, One of you which eateth with me shall betray me. 19 And they began to be sorrowful, and to say unto him one by one, Is it I? And another said, Is it I? 20 And he answered and said unto them, It

is one of the twelve, that dippeth with me in the dish.

In the evening (Thursday after sunset), Jesus came to Jerusalem with His disciples fully aware that He was to accomplish the Passover in His own person.

Jesus warned the disciples of the betrayal. He announced that one of them would betray Him. Even though the betrayal described in the Scriptures was clearly foreseen by Jesus, it was a surprise to the disciples. The word "to be sorrowful" in Greek is *lupeo* (**loo-PEH-oh**), meaning to be grieved or distressed. This word points out the strong reaction of the disciples. The question they ask "one by one" shows that they did not understand that it was too late. In His answer Jesus removed all ambiguity and said that it was one of the twelve "that dippeth with me in the dish." Thus, the betrayal is revealed as all the more horrible because of the betrayer's intimate fellowship with Jesus.

21 The Son of man indeed goeth, as it is written of him: but woe to that man by whom the Son of Man is betrayed! Good were it for that man if he had never been born. 22 And as they did eat, Jesus took bread, and blessed, and brake it, and gave to them, and said, Take, eat: this is my body.

The expression of "as it is written" refers to the Scriptures in general and not a particular passage. The death of the Son of Man is in harmony with the Scriptures. Judas' betrayal is within the context of God's plan and purpose. Yet Judas was responsible for his act. Here his existence was deplored and the terrible destiny awaiting him pronounced.

The "bread" (Gk. *artos*, **ARE-toce**) usually denotes a flat cake of unleavened bread. Jesus takes the symbols of His coming death. He "blesses" the bread, in Greek *eulogeo* (**ew-low-GEH-oh**), "to bless or speak well of," and gives it to them. The bread stands for His dying. The

breaking of the bread stands for Jesus' suffering. Taking Communion—the Lord's Supper, Eucharist, or whichever name is used—is a means of participating in the covenant of Jesus. The Greek expression *soma mou* (**SO-MAH moo**), translated "my body," can mean the whole being.

23 And he took the cup, and when he had given thanks, he gave it to them: and they all drank of it. 24 And he said unto them, This is my blood of the new testament, which is shed for many.

He took the cup and after giving thanks (Gk. *eucharisteo*, **ew-kha-rees-TEH-oh**), He gave it to them. The word for giving thanks mean something closer to "giving a good gift or grace." The cup stands for blood atonement, which inaugurates a new covenant. His blood is poured out for many. "Shed for many" is probably both a reference to Exodus 24:8 and to the work of the Servant of the Lord in Isaiah. Making a new covenant is part of the mission of the Servant, whose prophecy is fulfilled by Jesus Christ (Isaiah 42:6; 49:8). "Shed" in this context is present tense but the implication in the Greek is a participle involving a near future (is being shed). "For many" probably refers to Isaiah 53 and shows the great number of the beneficiaries of the sacrifice. This phrase speaks to the reality that Jesus would shed His blood soon (within days) for His disciples, but the impact of that shed blood would reach far beyond those at the table to impact all who would respond to Jesus Christ in the future.

Hebrews 8:6–7, 10–12

A major point of the book of Hebrews is that Christians have a "high priest" in Jesus Christ (Hebrews 3:1, 4:14, 6:20, 8:1). He is the one who connects us to God and God to us (see 1 Timothy 2:5; Hebrews 8:6). Ironically, under the old covenant, Jesus would not have qualified to be a priest. Under the Law, all priests were required to be Levites, and although His mother was related to the Levites, Jesus was from the tribe of Judah (see Hebrews 7:14). However, Jesus' priestly tabernacle is heaven, and His priestly commission comes directly from God, who ordained Him for ministry.

6 But now hath he obtained a more excellent ministry, by how much also he is the mediator of a better covenant, which was established upon better promises.

A "mediator" (Gk. *mesites*, **meh-SEE-tace**) is a go-between, or someone who tries to bring together two sets of people or individuals who are not getting along. Christ is the mediator between God and humankind (1 Timothy 2:5). The Greek word *diatheke* (**dee-ah-THAY-kay**) is translated as "covenant" and is a pact, arrangement, or agreement. It can also be translated as "testament." The covenant between God and the nation of Israel is thus referred to as the Old Testament (Exodus 19:5–6). Moses was the mediator in the Old Testament. However, approximately six hundred years before Christ, God promised His people a new covenant (see Jeremiah 31:31) involving a new heart and a new spirit (Ezekiel 36:26). The word "better" (Gk. *kreitton*, **KRATE-tonn**) is found twice in this verse, and means more useful, more serviceable, or advantageous. Here, the writer implies that the new covenant—as fulfilled by the blood of Jesus—will be a far greater ministry than that of the priests under the old covenant.

7 For if that first covenant had been faultless, then should no place have been sought for the second.

If the first covenant had been faultless, then God would not have needed a second one. The phrase "have been sought" is the Greek verb *zeteo* (**dzay-TEH-oh**) and implies "seeking something out or trying to find it." Because God was dissatisfied with the Israelites for not keeping the law under the old covenant, He sought to establish a second covenant—a covenant based on grace, through Jesus Christ, who is faultless. Our human tendency to sin and the dependency on human obedience to keep the covenant made it flawed in keeping us in right relationship with God. God had to act apart from our works in order to bring right relationship. The new covenant gives us access to the benefits of righteousness through Jesus Christ who fulfilled the old covenant with perfect obedience. Hence, we now have been given a more excellent covenant by God.

10 For this is the covenant that I will make with the house of Israel after those days, saith the Lord; I will put my laws into their mind, and write them in their hearts: and I will be to them a God, and they shall be to me a people:

In the old covenant, God's agreement with the Israelites was written on stone tablets given to Moses at Mount Sinai. These stone tablets were external to the individual. In contrast, under the new covenant, God would now write His truth inside the hearts and minds of humankind. This is a fulfillment of God's Word prophesied by Jeremiah, where God's law would be in the hearts of people, coming to pass through the indwelling of the Holy Spirit in believers in Jesus Christ (Jeremiah 31:33). By the indwelling of the Holy Spirit, Christians have an internal and intimate relationship with the living God. Jesus said, "If a man love me, he will keep my words: and my Father will love him, and we will come unto him, and make our abode with him" (from John 14:23). God wants an intimate relationship with us.

11 And they shall not teach every man his neighbour, and every man his brother, saying, Know the Lord: for all shall know me, from the least to the greatest.

In the old covenant, few people could read, and instruction was primarily mediated through the priest. In other words, in order to have a relationship with God, people were dependent on another human being. However, the new covenant promises the indwelling of the Holy Spirit (v. 10), resulting in every person being able to "know" the Lord for him or herself. Here, two different Greek words are used to express the word "know." In the first instance ("know the Lord"), the word is *ginosko* (**ghee-OCE-ko**), meaning "to understand, perceive, or have knowledge." In the second instance ("all shall know me"), the Greek word is *oida* (**OY-da**), meaning "to pay attention or observe." Thus, getting to "know" God means both understanding and paying attention to what the Holy Spirit teaches from within. Everyone can "know the Lord." In fact, the very definition of having eternal life is that we might know the only true God and Jesus Christ (John 3:15–16). When we come to "know" God through His Son, Jesus Christ becomes our mediator and we receive the gift of salvation (John 1:12).

12 For I will be merciful to their unrighteousness, and their sins and their iniquities will I remember no more.

Two of the synonyms for "sin" occur in this verse: "unrighteousness" (Gk. *adikia*, **ah-dee-KEE-ah**), which means injustice, and "iniquities" (Gk. *anomia*, **ah-no-MEE-ah**), meaning contempt for and violation of the law. In the Old Testament, the people were constantly reminded of their need to atone for their sins by virtue of Levitical laws. However, here we see that God has chosen not to remember the people's sins. What great love God has for His people! Elsewhere in the Bible, we find God casting sins into the deepest sea (Micah 7:19). This is God's way of saying that our sins will never be found again. We can, therefore, take comfort in the fact that if God chooses to forget our sins, there's no point in our dredging them up again! Because of the new covenant through Jesus Christ, our sins are forgiven and forgotten by God.

Daily Bible Readings

MONDAY
The Original Passover Celebration
(Deuteronomy 16:1–8)

TUESDAY
Triumphal Entry Into Jerusalem
(Mark 11:1–10)

WEDNESDAY
Preparation for the Passover Meal
(Mark 14:12–16)

THURSDAY
The Heart-Centered New Covenant
(Jeremiah 31:31–34)

FRIDAY
The Lord's Supper Shared With Disciples
(Luke 22:14–23)

SATURDAY
Clean Feet, Clean Hearts
(John 13:2b–7)

SUNDAY
Jesus Institutes the New Covenant
(Mark 14:17–24; Hebrews 8:6–7, 10–12)

Teaching Tips

Words You Should Know

A. Prisoner *desmios* (Gk.)—A military prisoner or captive.

B. Scourge *fragellosas* (Gk.)—Beaten with a metal-tipped whip.

Teacher Preparation

Unifying Principle—Jesus is Crucified. All personal relationships encounter problems that result in division and strife. Who can heal the breaches and restore harmony? Mark describes how Jesus' crucifixion forges a new covenant and reconciles God and humankind.

A. Read the Bible Background and Devotional Readings.

B. Pray for your students and lesson clarity.

C. Read the lesson Scripture in multiple translations.

D. Option: Explore hymns that describe a believer's participation or experience of Jesus on the Cross, such as "Were You There?" or "O Sacred Head, Now Wounded." What details from Mark's Crucifixion story are reflected in these hymns? What message do these hymns communicate about the meaning of the Crucifixion for believers?

O—Open the Lesson

A. Begin the class with prayer.

B. Have the students read the Aim for Change.

C. Have the students read the In Focus story.

D. Ask students how events named in the story can weigh on their hearts and how they can view these events from a theological perspective.

P—Present the Scriptures

A. Read the Focal Verses and discuss the Background and The People, Places, and Times sections.

B. Have the class share what Scriptures stand out for them and why, with particular emphasis on a present-day context.

E—Explore the Meaning

A. Use In Depth or More Light on the Text to help provide more in-depth discussion of the lesson text.

B. Discuss the Liberating Lesson and Application for Activation sections.

N—Next Steps for Application

A. Summarize the value of knowing Jesus as the crucified Savior.

B. End class with a commitment to pray for those who feel forsaken and persecuted for their faith.

Worship Guide

For the Superintendent or Teacher
Theme: Jesus Seals the New Covenant
Song: "Were You There?"
Devotional Reading: Psalm 22:1–8, 21b–28

Jesus Seals the New Covenant

Bible Background • Mark 14:32–50; 15
Printed Text • Mark 15:6–15, 25–26, 33–39 | Devotional Reading • Psalm 22:1–8, 21b–28

—————— Aim for Change ——————

By the end of the lesson, we will: SUMMARIZE Mark's account of Jesus' crucifixion; REFLECT on the sacrifice Jesus makes; and RECOGNIZE the new covenant and reconciliation Jesus provides.

———— In Focus ————

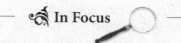

Ten years ago, Jake and Melissa were married raising two children. Now they were in the middle of a lengthy, high-conflict, my-way-or-the-highway divorce. They had both lost themselves in the prideful arguments, stonewalling, and countless disappointments.

"I just want this to be over," Melissa whispered to her attorney as they waited for the judge. "I'm so tired of fighting and getting nowhere."

Jake wasn't the perfect husband and father. He worked hard, but had lost himself in his job and the travel that it required. He came home late most nights when he was in town and had removed his financial support unexpectedly from Melissa and the kids. He wanted his family back. He just didn't know where to start.

He tapped Melissa on the shoulder in the chilly courtroom. "Can I speak to you outside for a moment?" he asked. Jake confessed to his wife that he had really put their family in a poor position but wanted to do the right thing and restore their family.

"I want to put this on hold. Would you go to counseling with me?" asked Jake.

Melissa paused for a while, thinking carefully. "You have no idea how long I've waited for you to say those words," gasped Melissa with tears in her eyes. "Of course, I will."

Some relationships are always worth saving. God's plan to restore peace with humanity reveals God's perfect holiness as a Father and Savior. How does the Cross remind us that with God nothing is impossible?

—————— Keep in Mind ——————

"And when the centurion, which stood over against him, saw that he so cried out, and gave up the ghost, he said, Truly this man was the Son of God" (Mark 15:39, KJV).

"When the Roman officer who stood facing him saw how he had died, he exclaimed, 'This man truly was the Son of God!'" (Mark 15:39, NLT).

Focal Verses

KJV **Mark 15:6** Now at that feast he released unto them one prisoner, whomsoever they desired.

7 And there was one named Barabbas, which lay bound with them that had made insurrection with him, who had committed murder in the insurrection.

8 And the multitude crying aloud began to desire him to do as he had ever done unto them.

9 But Pilate answered them, saying, Will ye that I release unto you the King of the Jews?

10 For he knew that the chief priests had delivered him for envy.

11 But the chief priests moved the people, that he should rather release Barabbas unto them.

12 And Pilate answered and said again unto them, What will ye then that I shall do unto him whom ye call the King of the Jews?

13 And they cried out again, Crucify him.

14 Then Pilate said unto them, Why, what evil hath he done? And they cried out the more exceedingly, Crucify him.

15 And so Pilate, willing to content the people, released Barabbas unto them, and delivered Jesus, when he had scourged him, to be crucified.

25 And it was the third hour, and they crucified him.

26 And the superscription of his accusation was written over, The King Of The Jews.

33 And when the sixth hour was come, there was darkness over the whole land until the ninth hour.

34 And at the ninth hour Jesus cried with a loud voice, saying, Eloi, Eloi, lama sabachthani? which is, being interpreted, My God, my God, why hast thou forsaken me?

35 And some of them that stood by, when they heard it, said, Behold, he calleth Elias.

NLT **Mark 15:6** Now it was the governor's custom each year during the Passover celebration to release one prisoner— anyone the people requested.

7 One of the prisoners at that time was Barabbas, a revolutionary who had committed murder in an uprising.

8 The crowd went to Pilate and asked him to release a prisoner as usual.

9 "Would you like me to release to you this 'King of the Jews'?" Pilate asked.

10 (For he realized by now that the leading priests had arrested Jesus out of envy.)

11 But at this point the leading priests stirred up the crowd to demand the release of Barabbas instead of Jesus.

12 Pilate asked them, "Then what should I do with this man you call the king of the Jews?"

13 They shouted back, "Crucify him!"

14 "Why?" Pilate demanded. "What crime has he committed?" But the mob roared even louder, "Crucify him!"

15 So to pacify the crowd, Pilate released Barabbas to them. He ordered Jesus flogged with a lead-tipped whip, then turned him over to the Roman soldiers to be crucified.

25 It was nine o'clock in the morning when they crucified him.

26 A sign announced the charge against him. It read, "The King of the Jews."

33 At noon, darkness fell across the whole land until three o'clock.

34 Then at three o'clock Jesus called out with a loud voice, "Eloi, Eloi, lema sabachthani?" which means "My God, my God, why have you abandoned me?"

35 Some of the bystanders misunderstood and thought he was calling for the prophet Elijah.

36 One of them ran and filled a sponge with sour wine, holding it up to him on a reed stick

36 And one ran and filled a sponge full of vinegar, and put it on a reed, and gave him to drink, saying, Let alone; let us see whether Elias will come to take him down.

37 And Jesus cried with a loud voice, and gave up the ghost.

38 And the veil of the temple was rent in twain from the top to the bottom.

39 And when the centurion, which stood over against him, saw that he so cried out, and gave up the ghost, he said, Truly this man was the Son of God.

so he could drink. "Wait!" he said. "Let's see whether Elijah comes to take him down!"

37 Then Jesus uttered another loud cry and breathed his last.

38 And the curtain in the sanctuary of the Temple was torn in two, from top to bottom.

39 When the Roman officer who stood facing him saw how he had died, he exclaimed, "This man truly was the Son of God!"

The People, Places, and Times

Golgotha. Golgotha in Aramaic, or Calvary in Latin, means "the place of a skull." It was on this hill just outside of Jerusalem that Jesus was crucified. Simon, the father of Alexander and Rufus, was from Cyrene in North Africa and he carried the cross for Jesus who was on His way to be crucified.

Crucifixion. This tortuous method of execution was commonly used by the Romans, though they did not invent it. The worst criminals, usually political dissonants, were ordered to be crucified. Crosses with the dead or dying on display would line major avenues into the city, warning passersby not to follow their ways. Crucifixion was a slow way to die, as implied in the Gospel account when Pilate is surprised that Jesus died after about eight hours (Mark 15:44). Those condemned to this death were stripped and flogged beforehand, then long nails were driven through their hands and feet (or they were tied with ropes), so they would hang exposed to the elements. When suspended from a cross, the body is unable to exhale and slowly asphyxiates.

Tradition holds that when Peter was condemned to crucifixion, he requested that his cross be hung upside-down because he felt he was unworthy of dying in the same way as his Master.

Background

Our text for this lesson focuses our attention on the scenes preceding Jesus' crucifixion. Jesus—along with his disciples Peter, James, and John—left for the Garden of Gethsemane after He instituted the new covenant at the Passover meal. Judas Iscariot had already agreed to hand Jesus over to the high priest for thirty silver coins. Judas said, "Whomsoever I shall kiss, that same is he; take him" (from Mark 14:44). Judas led a crowd carrying clubs and swords to where Jesus was and greeted Jesus with a kiss. Jesus was arrested, many of the disciples scattered, but Peter followed at a distance. Jesus was taken to the high priest where he was questioned. False witnesses testified against Him. They accused Jesus of blasphemy during the night court session. Peter, who was outside, was questioned by a servant girl as he warmed himself by the fire. He denied that he knew Jesus then remembered Jesus' words: "Before the cock crow twice, thou shalt deny me thrice" (from 14:72)

Once the high priest and the Sanhedrin council reached a decision, they arose early the next morning and delivered Jesus to the Roman governor, Pontius Pilate, to be crucified. Our text reveals the humanity of Jesus and the hatred of people without a relationship with God the Father. As we examine our text today, we will witness Jesus' commitment to fulfill God's plan to suffer and die for all humanity.

At-A-Glance

1. Dealing With Rejection of the Crowd (Mark 15:6–15, 25–26)
2. Darkness That Reveals the Commitment of Christ (vv. 33–39)

In Depth

1. Dealing With Rejection of the Crowd (Mark 15:6–15, 25–26)

All night, the high priest and the Sanhedrin council have questioned Jesus. They brought false witness after false witness, and finally charged Him with blasphemy (14:61–64). Now headed to Pilate to have Jesus die by capital punishment, the high priest and the Sanhedrin have stirred the crowd to request Barabbas' release and Jesus' crucifixion. Jesus, once a crowd favorite, now found Himself without a friend in the crowd.

Just a few days earlier, crowds had gathered to cut down palm branches and lay them in the road, saying "Hosanna; Blessed is he that cometh in the name of the Lord: Blessed be the kingdom of our father David, that cometh in the name of the Lord: Hosanna in the highest" (from 11:9–10). They called Him King of the Jews because He rode in triumph on a colt. They thought He would be the one to overthrow the oppressive Roman government. But crowds are fickle. They are with you when it seems like you are the one on top; but when trouble comes, they scatter or turn their backs on you.

Pilate recognized that Jesus was not guilty of any crime and that the high priest had brought Jesus to be crucified because of envy and jealousy. Pilate was impressed with Jesus and how He did not express any rebuttals in the face of the false charges from the high priest who was bringing Him to be crucified.

To keep peace in the land, Pilate released Barabbas, a known murderer, at the crowd's request. He had Jesus beaten and then carried off to be crucified. Jesus had endured night trials with many false witnesses and the crowd's rejection. He endured Pilate's flogging with leather straps that had sharp pieces of bone and metal that tore the flesh. He endured a crown of thorns on His head and His hands and feet being nailed to the Cross. And He endured the separation from God the Father. We must remember that sin causes a void, a deep separation from God.

Should we stand up to crowds that carry out the wishes of the corrupt, powerful, and elite in leadership? Why or why not?

2. Darkness That Reveals the Commitment of Christ (vv. 33–39)

As Jesus was hanging on the cross, darkness loomed over the land for three hours starting at noon. Jesus begins to cry out to God at about 3 p.m., saying, "My God, My God, why have you forsaken me?" In this moment, Jesus showed His humanity even while obeying the will of the Father. While Jesus was dying many gathered around to see what would happen next. Some thought He was calling for Elijah; some wanted to give Him something to drink. But Jesus took His last breath and died. Jesus' death sealed our salvation! His death destroyed the power of sin. He gave His life that we might have the opportunity by faith to have eternal life and life more abundantly. He paid the ultimate price for our sin so we may be reconciled with God. Jesus is now the mediator between heaven and humanity. The veil in the Temple where only the high priest could enter was torn from top to bottom, so Jesus is the only High Priest the believer needs.

The way Jesus died even had an impact on those who guarded the cross. One centurion confessed that Jesus truly was the Son of God. Jesus' death showed God's commitment to restoring fallen humanity to the relationship enjoyed in the beginning.

Have you been reminded of God's commitment during some of life's darkest moments?

Search the Scriptures

1. What prohibited the high priest and the Sanhedrin from crucifying Jesus without Pilate's permission (Mark 15:14–15)?

2. What is the significance of the veil in the Temple being torn from top to bottom (v. 38)?

Discuss the Meaning

1. How does the charge "King of the Jews" prove to be ironic?

2. True restoration of relationships, which are built on trust, takes an incredible amount of work and diligence. How does Jesus' ultimate sacrifice motivate you to restore relationships in your life?

3. Consider the centurion's realization that "Truly this man was the Son of God" (from v. 39). Describe how that may have impacted his life going forward.

Liberating Lesson

The example of Jesus' obedience to God— remaining faithful even though He had to die—shows us a level of commitment that is hard to match. We need to have that same level of commitment in reaching out to brothers and sisters who are on the margins of life. We must help others onto a path of productivity and progress despite current culture norms.

Can a brother or sister count on you to be present in their darkest hours of life? Will you this week stand up for someone who is being unjustly treated by the crowd, the elite, or the powerful?

Application for Activation

Jesus' death sealed the deal of our salvation! During His trial, sentencing, and execution, things seemed to be following the will of the high priest and the Sanhedrin council. They said of Jesus, "He saved others; himself he cannot save" (from Matthew 27:42). Despite their ridicule, God's plan of restoration was being completed.

This week attempt to model what Christ did for us by paying a debt that we could not pay. Buy lunch for someone you do not know. Pay for somebody's parking ticket. By performing acts of kindness while expecting nothing in return, you will show the love of Christ toward someone else.

Follow the Spirit

What God wants me to do:

_____

_____

_____

_____

Remember Your Thoughts

Special insights I have learned:

_____

_____

_____

_____

More Light on the Text

Mark 15:6–15, 25–26, 33–39

6 Now at that feast he released unto them one prisoner, whomsoever they desired. 7 And there was one named Barabbas, which lay bound with them that had made insurrection with him, who had committed murder in the insurrection. 8 And the multitude crying aloud began to desire him to do as he had ever done unto them.

The feast being described is the Passover feast, which was a reminder of God delivering the Children of Israel out of Egypt. Passover is one of the three feasts that the Israelites were instructed to keep annually in every generation. The word for prisoner is *desmios* (**DES-mee-oce**), which means someone who is a military prisoner or captive. This sort of prisoner was held because he was a political threat or had committed a crime against the state; in this case, it was someone who had been arrested in the previous rebellions.

Apparently it had become Pilate's practice to release one prisoner during the Passover as a gesture of goodwill to the occupied people of the Roman Empire. Pilate was a harsh governor, not only during Jesus' lifetime but in the years following as he tried to maintain control over Judea, a rebellious region of the empire. It is worth noting the complexity of his character: in that he was willing to allow for gestures of mercy, such as the release of a prisoner during the important Jewish feast when there would have been crowds of Jews from all around the occupied land in Jerusalem. The crowd assembled in Jerusalem was crying out for Pilate to perform his custom of releasing a prisoner.

Barabbas had committed murder during the insurrection, perhaps a Roman guard or Temple worker. The inspiration for the rebellions was likely the history and legend of Judas Maccabeus and the Maccabbean revolt. The last time Israel was an independent nation not ruled by an imperial power before Jesus' time was after the Maccabbean revolts successfully freed Judea and established an independent monarchy in Judah for the first time since the Babylonian exile. The monarchy eventually ceased to be independent and the territory was ruled by the Roman Empire during Jesus' lifetime. However, there were periodic uprisings as the Israelites fought for freedom from Roman oppression. Many Israelites believed that the Messiah would be the ultimate freedom fighter who would liberate the people.

9 But Pilate answered them, saying, Will ye that I release unto you the King of the Jews? 10 For he knew that the chief priests had delivered him for envy. 11 But the chief priests moved the people, that he should rather release Barabbas unto them.

Pilate asks the crowd if they want him to release the King of the Jews, referencing Jesus again. The title "King of the Jews" also is a reference to the role some think the Messiah is supposed to fill. The Messiah is expected by some to overthrow the empire and restore the Davidic lineage as king of Judah.

The Scripture suggests that Pilate asks this question expecting the crowd to respond that they want Jesus released. Pilate has just confronted Jesus about the accusation that He is King of the Jews, and Jesus does not deny it. Having a King of the Jews would be a direct political threat to the symbolic kingship of Herod and, if Jesus is seen as the Messiah who would lead the rebellion, a political threat to the control of the Roman Empire.

The popularity of Jesus is also a direct threat to the chief priests and elders because if Jesus holds spiritual authority apart from them, it makes them less powerful. Pilate is well aware of this dynamic (v. 10). Pilate has seen Jesus' humility, wisdom, and conviction (vv. 1–5). Jesus does not respond the way a normal rebel, criminal, or lawbreaker would because He is innocent. Pilate, who is not Jewish and does not know God, is able to tell that these accusing priests have wicked motives.

The priests continue to act out their unjust plan by persuading the crowd they should request the release of Barabbas instead of Jesus. The priests are more interested in preserving their position than doing what is just. The priests go as far as to justify the release of a violent rebel instead of the innocent Son of man. In this passage, the striking parallel is the crowd choosing the violent revolutionary instead of the true Messiah and the anointed Son of God to be their liberator.

12 And Pilate answered and said again unto them, What will ye then that I shall do unto him whom ye call the King of the Jews? 13 And they cried out again, Crucify him. 14 Then Pilate said unto them, Why, what evil hath he done? And they cried out the more exceedingly, Crucify him. 15 And so Pilate, willing to content the people, released Barabbas unto them, and delivered Jesus, when he had scourged him, to be crucified.

Pilate again places the fate of Jesus in the hands of the crowd. The madness of mob mentality has fully set in. They move from wanting the criminal released instead of Christ, to demanding that Christ be crucified.

Crucifixion was not a common death. It was a death reserved only for criminals and enemies of the state. It was intended to be not simply punishment but public humiliation, excruciating death, and a warning to all who watched. Death by crucifixion was not caused by bleeding but by a person suspended from a cross suffocating to death slowly. Its impact on the audience was much like that of a public hanging, death by firing squad or electric chair, or lynching. It was not enough that Jesus had been beaten and humiliated already.

The priests had persuaded the crowd that he needed to be killed publicly and in one of the most violent ways possible.

Pilate tries again to reason with the crowd, yet the crowd again demands that Pilate crucify Jesus. Pilate, known for violently putting down any opposition or disorder, does not want the large crowd to riot. A riot at this point could result in dozens of deaths as Roman soldiers gain control of the crowds visiting Jerusalem for the high holiday of Passover.

Instead, Pilate decides that Jesus of Nazareth must die to please the crowd and stop any unrest. This fulfills the prophesy of the chief priest that it would be better that one man die than all the nation perish (John 11:49–51). Pilate gives in to the crowd and has Jesus scourged with a whip, an intensely brutal practice, then has Him taken to be crucified.

25 And it was the third hour, and they crucified him. 26 And the superscription of his accusation was written over, THE KING OF THE JEWS.

The cycle of the Jewish day began with sunset and lasted until the following sunset, but the numbering of what hour it was began at sunrise, which was around 6 a.m. in Palestine where the crucifixion took place. Therefore the third hour would have been approximately 9 a.m. It was early in the morning when Jesus was crucified. It would have been a time when many people were around to watch and see what had happened, and yet only some in the crowd would have come out to Golgotha to watch such a spectacle, those in the city would have seen Jesus on his way to be crucified as He walked through the street struggling to carry His own cross.

The accusation written over His head was again "King of the Jews," for the audience that mocked His claim that He was the Messiah. The one who had declared He was the Messiah meant to free the people was being publicly killed and could not even free Himself. In another deeper nuance, the irony was that God Himself was the original King of the Jews and conceded to let them have a human king. Now Jesus Christ the God-Man was being openly identified for who He was, God and Messiah, yet dying on a cross in a completely unexpected death for all those who followed and believed in Him.

33 And when the sixth hour was come, there was darkness over the whole land until the ninth hour.. 34 And at the ninth hour Jesus cried with a loud voice, saying, Eloi, Eloi, lama sabachthani? which is, being interpreted, My God, my God, why hast thou forsaken me?

After three hours, the suffering was intense. Jesus cried in Hebrew, "*Eloi, Eloi, lama sabachthani,*" (**el-OY el-OY lah-MAH-ma sah-BAKH-tha-nee**) or "My God, my God, why hast thou forsaken me?" The Greek word fluidly translated "why" could more literally mean "for what thing or reason?" This is a quotation of Psalm 22:1. Jesus probably had in mind the whole psalm, a prayer of a righteous sufferer. The speaker of the psalm cries out from his pain, but also sees God's past and present faithfulness, and determines to praise and trust God still. Rather than indicating that Jesus actually thought God had abandoned Him, this cry expressed Jesus' unshaken faith in God at this horrible hour. He had faith in God's continual protection and final vindication. The scene is to be understood in the perspective of the holy judgment of God and the character of sin, which cuts the sinner off from God (see Isaiah 59:2). Jesus identified Himself completely with sinners and bore on the Cross the judgment of God upon human rebellion (see Mark 10:45; Romans 5:8; Galatians 3:13; 2 Corinthians 5:21).

35 And some of them that stood by, when they heard it, said, Behold, he calleth Elias.

Some spectators, who probably misunderstood Jesus or were mocking Him, said "Behold, he calleth Elias." They believed that he was calling Elijah to rescue him (Malachi 3:1; 4:5). There was an expectation among the Jewish people that Elijah would return before Christ came based on the prophecy of Malachi. Elijah was one of the two people in the Old Testament who ascended to heaven without dying (2 Kings 2:10–12); the other was Enoch (Genesis 5:21–24). Elijah was noted also as one of the archetypal Jewish prophets. For some then, it made sense that Jesus would be calling Elijah with expectation of Him coming off of the cross and establishing the kingdom of God on earth by overthrowing the Roman Empire.

36 And one ran and filled a sponge full of vinegar, and put it on a reed, and gave him to drink, saying, Let alone; let us see whether Elias will come to take him down.

A soldier soaked a sponge in vinegar and reached it up to Jesus' mouth on the end of a reed. It was intended to keep Him conscious for as long as possible. But some were still wondering whether there would be a last-minute miracle. They said, "Let us see whether Elias will come to take him down." According to popular Jewish beliefs, Elias (Elijah) would come to the help of the just in their time of distress.

37 And Jesus cried with a loud voice, and gave up the ghost.

Jesus died suddenly (see vv. 39, 44). He died for us (Mark 10:45, 14:24). His death was voluntary. His life was not taken, for He "gave up the ghost" (His Spirit). Jesus gave His entire life, His very last for the sake of love for humanity. Through His death and resurrection we are invited to have life more abundantly and be restored to right relationship with God.

We know as Christians that God had a plan that defied the expectations of the people through Jesus' death on the Cross. God would liberate the people not with violent revolution but humble submission and total obedience to God. The revolution freed humanity from the penalty of sin as the love of God was shown through Jesus' death on the Cross. God was restoring not just a monarchy or land, but restoring people to right relationship with Himself.

The enemy of the Jewish people (the emperor) was not defeated. Death itself—the ultimate enemy of all people—was defeated. God was empowering humanity not just to make free political decisions but empowering them, by the Holy Spirit through faith in Jesus Christ, to be agents of change in the world. The message of the Gospel of Jesus Christ did in fact change the course of history: For the first time, the followers of Jesus who were oppressed, unimportant, and unremarkable became the most influential and powerful people in history.

38 And the veil of the temple was rent in twain from the top to the bottom. 39 And when the centurion, which stood over against him, saw that he so cried out, and gave up the ghost, he said, Truly this man was the Son of God.

These final verses of the passage add a further supernatural and ultimate dimension to Jesus' death on the Cross. When Jesus gives up His Spirit, the veil in the Temple that separated the holy place from the Holy of Holies was ripped from top to bottom. The Holy of Holies was where the presence of God dwelt and the Ark of the Covenant was kept. This would have been an incredible sight and an impossible work for any human being to accomplish. The veil in the Temple was made of several layers of thick weaving, and was almost two stories high, the closest analogy would be like the curtain on the stage of a theater. A rip in this veil would take extraordinary force, and that might only cause a small rip which would happen from bottom to top. The fact that the veil was torn from top to bottom signifies that it was an act of God from heaven above.

Furthermore, this tear in the veil would have been unimaginable for the priests and Levites at the Temple. The veil not only separated the holiness of God from the interactions of humans except for one day a year (the Day of Atonement), it also protected the priests who work in the holy place from being destroyed by the awesome presence of the Almighty God. The separation—which kept God from being openly accessed by all people and kept people from being destroyed by encountering God's presence—was ripped apart.

The centurion, who was a Roman soldier designated to guard the prisoners and monitor them as they died, recognized that Jesus was divine. We can only imagine what exactly struck him about Jesus' cry and the way He took His last breath that let the centurion know that Jesus was Son of God. But when he saw the scene, the revelation of Jesus as Son of God hit him, and he confirmed the truth of Jesus' identity. The witness of the veil and the witness of the soldier simultaneously give testimony to the tremendous impact of Jesus dying on the Cross for both heaven and earth.

Say It Correctly

Barabbas. buh-**RAB**-uhs.
sabachthani. sa-bok-**THAHN**-ee.
Pilate. **PIY**-luht.

Daily Bible Readings

MONDAY
Turmoil at the Last Supper
(Mark 14:26–31)

TUESDAY
Jesus Prays While the Disciples Sleep
(Mark 14:32–42)

WEDNESDAY
Jesus Betrayed and Arrested
(Mark 14:43–50)

THURSDAY
Jesus Crucified Before Friends and Enemies
(Mark 15:16–24)

FRIDAY
Two Criminals Crucified With Jesus
(Mark 15:27–32)

SATURDAY
Faithful Women
(Mark 15:40–47)

SUNDAY
New Covenant Sealed With Jesus' Blood
(Mark 15:6–15, 25–26, 33–39)

Notes

_____

_____

_____

_____

Teaching Tips

Words You Should Know

A. Testament *diatheke* (Gk.)—Will, covenant.

B. Inheritance *kleronomia* (Gk.)—The rights, resources, and property received after the death of a person, or given to the next generation.

Teacher Preparation

Unifying Principle—The Blood Covenant. People have devised many methods to deal with the sense of moral uncleanness their misdeeds incur. How can we be definitively cleansed of guilt? By shedding His blood and dying, Jesus fulfilled God's new covenant to forgive sins and guarantee eternal life.

A. Read the Bible Background and Devotional Readings.

B. Pray for your students and lesson clarity.

C. Read the lesson Scripture in multiple translations.

D. Option: Discuss the many ways people try to assuage their feelings of guilt. Note both those that may prove helpful (at least to some) and those that are of dubious value or are harmful. Why does the writer of Hebrews claim that only the blood of Jesus can effect definitive cleansing of sin?

O—Open the Lesson

A. Begin the class with prayer.

B. Have students read the Aim for Change.

C. Have students read the In Focus story.

D. Ask students how events named in the story can weigh on their hearts and how they can view these events from a theological perspective.

P—Present the Scriptures

A. Read the Focal Verses and discuss the Background and The People, Places, and Times sections.

B. Have the class share what Scriptures stand out for them and why, with particular emphasis on today's context.

E—Explore the Meaning

A. Use In Depth or More Light on the Text to help provide more in-depth discussion of the lesson text.

B. Discuss the Liberating Lesson and Application for Activation sections.

N—Next Steps for Application

A. Summarize the value of knowing Jesus as our ultimate high priest.

B. End class with a commitment to pray for forgiveness and reconciliation.

Worship Guide

For the Superintendent or Teacher
Theme: The New Covenant's Sacrifice
Song: "The Blood Song"
Devotional Reading: Psalm 50:1–15

The New Covenant's Sacrifice

Bible Background • Hebrews 9:11–28
Printed Text • Hebrews 9:11–22 | Devotional Reading • Psalm 50:1–15

———————— Aim for Change ————————

By the end of this lesson, we will: EXPLORE the symbolism of blood in the Old Testament in relation to Jesus' work on the cross; SENSE our moral shortcomings; and REJOICE in the work that Jesus accomplished.

———————— 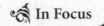 In Focus ————————

Sam's younger brother Dex was graduating from college, and Sam wanted to do something special for him. Sam suggested that they take a trip to the Bahamas and agreed to cover the cost to celebrate the momentous occasion. Dex was excited about the vacation. A month before the trip, the brothers got into a heated disagreement on the phone. Dex's temper got the best of him and, in his frustration, he said some extremely hurtful things to Sam and hung up on him. After a week, Dex calmed down and realized that he had overreacted. But by then, Sam had stopped calling Dex.

Dex wanted to call and apologize but didn't know where to start. He beat himself up for how he had talked to his brother. He thought about how he wouldn't have bought a flight for Sam if he had talked to him the way he had talked to Sam. He came to the conclusion that the trip was not going to happen, but he knew that he wanted to repair his relationship with his brother. So, he called Sam, and when Sam picked up, Dex immediately began to apologize. After hearing the apology, Sam replied, "So are you still looking forward to the Bahamas?"

Dex answered in shock, "You accept my apology? You still wanna go?"

Sam responded, "I know how you are! I forgave you a week ago. Plus, I bought the flight before we even got into it! So we better still be going!"

Have you ever been in a place like Dex, where you were forgiven but were still beating yourself up?

———————— Keep in Mind ————————

"And almost all things are by the law purged with blood; and without shedding of blood is no remission" (Hebrews 9:22, KJV).

"In fact, according to the law of Moses, nearly everything was purified with blood. For without the shedding of blood, there is no forgiveness" (Hebrews 9:22, NLT).

Focal Verses

KJV **Hebrews 9:11** But Christ being come an high priest of good things to come, by a greater and more perfect tabernacle, not made with hands, that is to say, not of this building;

12 Neither by the blood of goats and calves, but by his own blood he entered in once into the holy place, having obtained eternal redemption for us.

13 For if the blood of bulls and of goats, and the ashes of an heifer sprinkling the unclean, sanctifieth to the purifying of the flesh:

14 How much more shall the blood of Christ, who through the eternal Spirit offered himself without spot to God, purge your conscience from dead works to serve the living God?

15 And for this cause he is the mediator of the new testament, that by means of death, for the redemption of the transgressions that were under the first testament, they which are called might receive the promise of eternal inheritance.

16 For where a testament is, there must also of necessity be the death of the testator.

17 For a testament is of force after men are dead: otherwise it is of no strength at all while the testator liveth.

18 Whereupon neither the first testament was dedicated without blood.

19 For when Moses had spoken every precept to all the people according to the law, he took the blood of calves and of goats, with water, and scarlet wool, and hyssop, and sprinkled both the book, and all the people,

20 Saying, This is the blood of the testament which God hath enjoined unto you.

21 Moreover he sprinkled with blood both the tabernacle, and all the vessels of the ministry.

NLT **Hebrews 9:11** So Christ has now become the High Priest over all the good things that have come. He has entered that greater, more perfect Tabernacle in heaven, which was not made by human hands and is not part of this created world.

12 With his own blood—not the blood of goats and calves—he entered the Most Holy Place once for all time and secured our redemption forever.

13 Under the old system, the blood of goats and bulls and the ashes of a heifer could cleanse people's bodies from ceremonial impurity.

14 Just think how much more the blood of Christ will purify our consciences from sinful deeds so that we can worship the living God. For by the power of the eternal Spirit, Christ offered himself to God as a perfect sacrifice for our sins.

15 That is why he is the one who mediates a new covenant between God and people, so that all who are called can receive the eternal inheritance God has promised them. For Christ died to set them free from the penalty of the sins they had committed under that first covenant.

16 Now when someone leaves a will, it is necessary to prove that the person who made it is dead.

17 The will goes into effect only after the person's death. While the person who made it is still alive, the will cannot be put into effect.

18 That is why even the first covenant was put into effect with the blood of an animal.

19 For after Moses had read each of God's commandments to all the people, he took the blood of calves and goats, along with water, and sprinkled both the book of God's law and all the people, using hyssop branches and scarlet wool.

20 Then he said, "This blood confirms the covenant God has made with you."

22 And almost all things are by the law purged with blood; and without shedding of blood is no remission.

21 And in the same way, he sprinkled blood on the Tabernacle and on everything used for worship.

22 In fact, according to the law of Moses, nearly everything was purified with blood. For without the shedding of blood, there is no forgiveness.

The People, Places, and Times

High Priest. He was the one in charge of the Temple worship. It was a hereditary position based upon descent from Aaron. Normally, the high priest served for life. Only the high priest could enter the Holy of Holies and only on the Day of Atonement.

Book of Hebrews. Because there are references to religious sacrifices and ceremonies, the book of Hebrews may have been written after the destruction of the Temple in Jerusalem in AD 70, although others suggest it was written before the destruction. The name of the author is not given, but the person is associated with Timothy (Hebrews 13:23). The setting for the book is a period when Jewish Christians underwent severe persecution from the Romans and Jews, both socially and physically. It is clear that the author is knowledgeable about the Old Testament because there are direct quotations from it as he argues the superiority of Jesus Christ and faith.

Background

When reading the book of Hebrews, if you find yourself wanting to shout "Preach!" you are right in line with the communities that first heard these words. Although not much can be said about the author of Hebrews for certain, many scholars assert that the author is a preacher and this book is really a sermon. As you know, a good sermon weaves together ancient Scripture, sensitivity to its audience, and contemporary application. We see these marks in our focus text as the author knits the following together for his community: Hebrew Bible imagery of Tabernacle/Temple worship, the new reality of Christ's centrality for these early believers, and a solution to the community's most pressing challenge—worshiping after the destruction of the Jerusalem Temple. Many of the early Jesus followers were Jewish, and their identities were rooted simultaneously in the Temple's practices and in Jesus as the prophesied Messiah. Both seemed to be foundational for keeping their part of the covenant with God, which was most clearly established with Moses through the Torah (law). Part of the Torah included offering sacrifices of animals to God, and on the Day of Atonement (Yom Kippur) the high priest sprinkled the blood from a special offering on the people and instruments. The blood was used in the Temple to cover their sins and their commonness in order to set them apart to God.

When the Temple was destroyed in AD 70, it left this community and its members pondering who they were independently and who they were together. Who were they collectively as their way of understanding worship was obsolete? Who were they individually now that the center for atoning for their sins was wiped off of the earth? To these questions, the preacher of Hebrews suggests that the community can take their worship to another level because believers have access to the heavenly temple through Jesus. Also, the author notes that the need for a physical atonement is no longer necessary because Jesus has spiritually provided atonement through His own blood as both high priest and offering. Praise God for that!

At-A-Glance

1. High Priest: Christ Over Calves
(Hebrews 9:11-12)
2. High Production: Conscience Cleansed
(vv. 13-14)
3. High Price: Covenant Created (vv. 15-22)

In Depth

1. High Priest: Christ Over Calves (Hebrews 9:11–12)

One of the major distinctions between a high priest and the other priests is that the high priest could offer the most solemn sacrifice on the most holy day of the year—the Day of Atonement. On that day, one of the actions of the high priest was to sprinkle the blood of an innocent goat in a room that only he could enter once a year. In that room, called the Most Holy Place, he took the blood and sprinkled it on the Mercy Seat of the Ark of the Covenant, which was where God dwelt in a most special way. The high priest had to perform this ceremony every year. The preacher of Hebrews asserts that Christ came as a high priest, but He was qualitatively and quantitatively different than other high priests in terms of the caliber, place, and frequency of offering. Jesus offered His own blood in the heavenly Most Holy Place (not made with human hands) one time for all times.

2. High Production: Conscience Cleansed (vv. 13-14)

Blood may seem to be a strange cleansing agent. In the ancient world, blood was the detergent that eliminated the stains and defilement that separated people from God. The separation was strongly linked to actions that led to ritual impurity, which was significant because ritual impurity prevented people from being able to participate in Temple worship. The actions demanded physical purification by applying innocent blood. The preacher of Hebrews does not discredit that logic; instead, the preacher offers a comparison.

If physically offering the blood of innocent animals can purify flesh, one can only imagine what spiritually offering the blood of the unblemished Christ produces! It does not only remove the external wall that ritually separates people from God, but it eliminates the internal guilt that often creates a barrier for worshiping God. The blood of dead animals offered by mortal priests made temporary effects, but the blood of the living Christ offered through the eternal Spirit produces eternal redemption.

3. High Price: Covenant Created (vv. 15–22)

The preacher of Hebrews compares the covenant to a will in two significant ways. The first is that they both are inaugurated by death. This is especially true in regards to making covenants. The idiom for making covenants in Hebrew is "to cut a covenant," which refers to slaughtering animals to represent the seriousness of the commitment. The second significant comparison is that both wills and covenants link the finality of death with the opening up of new possibilities for living. Often the death of the testator or person leaving the will leads to inheritances, which potentially lead to lifestyle changes for the survivors. Similarly, Jesus' sacrifice for the covenant ushers in new relationships with the divine for believers. The blood of the covenant is powerful. It grants the believer forgiveness and release from bondage to dead works (sins) in the past. It also demands that released believers now use their new liberty to follow the path of the one who gave His life.

Search the Scriptures

1. How does the use of the word "blood" throughout this passage give us a glimpse into what the preacher of Hebrews means by "redemption" and "covenant" (Hebrews 9:12, 14, 18–22)?

2. How do you understand Jesus to be both high priest and offering (Hebrews 9:11–14)?

Discuss the Meaning

1. How does imagery from the Day of Atonement ceremony in the Hebrew Bible help you to understand how you are forgiven under the new covenant?

2. How does the new covenant demand that you follow Christ's model of self-giving? What does being forgiven demand of you?

Liberating Lesson

The past is gone. The decision was confirmed. The mistake was made. There is no need to continue to wallow in what could have been. The new covenant demands we acknowledge that outside of Christ, there is no sacrifice for our sins, errors, and failings. Allow the blood of Christ to be sprinkled on your conscience. Its eternal impact is not fazed by the problems of your yesterday but is gazing excitedly at your tomorrow. There is a release (remission) because of the blood.

This message is not only focused on individuals but also on communities. Communities may feel that they are in chaos like the first readers of Hebrews did. Church communities are dying; the political climate seems more unstable than ever before; the lives of Black and Brown boys and girls are undervalued. It may feel as though we have no way forward. But in the same way there is release for individuals, there is a way forward for our families,

communities, and nations. We must accept the atoning power of the blood, and allow it to sanctify us, making us into forward-looking agents of God's vision for the world—willing to give up our lives as Jesus gave up His.

Application for Activation

As you think about the offering of Jesus' blood as an agent that both atones for forgiveness and sanctifies for service, consider the following:

1. Where do I struggle to accept Christ's forgiveness? What is keeping me from accepting the blood applied to my guilty conscience? Try thinking of this issue while rubbing your hands under water and feel the guilt wash away.

2. Where can I follow Jesus' example of giving Himself and extend forgiveness to someone today?

Follow the Spirit

What God wants me to do:

_____

_____

_____

_____

Remember Your Thoughts

Special insights I have learned:

_____

_____

_____

_____

More Light on the Text
Hebrews 9:11–22

The ceremonial proceedings of the Levitical system were unable to clear the worshiper's conscience (Hebrews 9:1–10), the writer of Hebrews explains. He shows that Christ's sacrifice of Himself is far superior to that of animal sacrifices. The ordinances of the old covenant served a provisional purpose until the inauguration of the new covenant, but they could not facilitate intimacy with God.

Worship under the Levitical system focused on ceremonial purity and did little to reconcile people's hearts to God and enhance moral purity. Sacrifices were ultimately unacceptable to God because we are all tainted by sin. This description of worship under the old covenant of the Levitical priesthood highlights by contrast the "good things" that accompany worship under the new covenant and Christ's priesthood.

Christ's sacrifice of Himself for our sin accomplished what the sacrifices of the old covenant could not. Because of Christ's sacrifice for our sins, we can have our consciences cleansed from guilt. Indeed, Jesus is the only one who could pay the penalty for our sins. Therefore, He—and He alone—qualifies as our Redeemer!

11 But Christ being come an high priest of good things to come, by a greater and more perfect tabernacle, not made with hands, that is to say, not of this building;

Since this text was written long after the life, death, and resurrection of Jesus, the Greek phrase *genomenon agathon* (**gen-o-MEN-ohn ah-gah-THOHN**, here translated "good things to come") is the present tense and should probably be translated "the good things that are already here" as in the NLT. Although the author does not identify what these good things are, it is reasonable to conclude that this is a reference to the current and future blessings Christ affords those who by faith accept His saving grace. By referring to "a greater and more perfect tabernacle, not made with hands, that is to say, not of this building," the writer seeks to convey the heavenly and eternal nature of Christ's redeeming work and compares it to the earthly nature of ceremonial proceedings that took place in the Temple built by human hands. The Tabernacle of Moses was built with earthly and corruptible materials. The more perfect tabernacle that Christ's saving work creates within the hearts of the redeemed (Revelation 21:3) is heavenly, "incorruptible, and undefiled, and… fadeth not away" (1 Peter 1:4). This was accomplished not by the continuous flow of goats' and calves' blood, but by the once-and-for-all-time shedding of the blood of Christ, which was far superior to earthly sacrifices.

12 Neither by the blood of goats and calves, but by his own blood he entered in once into the holy place, having obtained eternal redemption for us.

Every time the high priest went into the Holy of Holies, he took the blood of goats and calves with him (Hebrews 9:7) to sprinkle on the Ark. The goats' blood symbolized the cleansing of the people and calves' blood symbolized the cleansing of the priests (Leviticus 16:15-17). In radical contrast to this annual ritual performed by the high priest, Christ "obtained eternal redemption for us" by entering "once into the holy place." When the high priest entered the Holy of Holies, it was believed that he had entered into the presence of God. The Holy of Holies, however, was built by human hands, as was the Ark upon which the blood of animals was sprinkled by imperfect priests.

In contrast to the priest, Christ did not enter the same Holy of Holies; rather, He who knew no sin entered the true sanctuary above—the heavenly sanctuary—and offered up His own blood in the very presence of God in heaven (Hebrews 8:1; see also Hebrews 9:24).

13 For if the blood of bulls and of goats, and the ashes of an heifer sprinkling the unclean, sanctifieth to the purifying of the flesh: 14 How much more shall the blood of Christ, who through the eternal Spirit offered himself without spot to God, purge your conscience from dead works to serve the living God?

Verses 13–14 form one rhetorical question. The implied answer highlights the superiority of Christ's sacrifice over the sacrifices of animals. The inadequacy of animal sacrifices under the old covenant to "purge [the] conscience from dead works to serve the living God" has been established. The blood of Christ (i.e., Christ's death) is far more efficacious than "the blood of bulls and of goats, and the ashes of an heifer."

Here the writer reaffirms the point that while animal sacrifices may have given worshipers the feeling of external cleansing, only the blood of Christ can purge our consciences and liberate us from the internal guilt of sin. God's holy character demanded a perfect sacrifice in order to achieve reconciliation for us.

The Spirit works in and with Christ, making sure our redemption is secure and we through faith in Christ are set free "to serve the living God." Christ is our Redeemer!

15 And for this cause he is the mediator of the new testament, that by means of death, for the redemption of the transgressions that were under the first testament, they which are called might receive the promise of eternal inheritance.

The writer goes on to amplify what Christ's death achieved. Central to the writer's explanation is the use of the Greek word *kleronomia*

(**klay-roh-noh-MEE-ah**), or "inheritance." Generally speaking, an inheritance is received through the will or testament of someone who died. Christ died and bequeathed redemption to us and to all those who believe in Him. Because Christ's death achieved what the old covenant could not achieve, He is the mediator of "the new testament" (i.e., the new covenant), which surpasses the old covenant.

16 For where a testament is, there must also of necessity be the death of the testator. 17 For a testament is of force after men are dead: otherwise it is of no strength at all while the testator liveth.

There is a word play in the Greek; the word *diatheke* (**dee-ah-THAY-kay**) means both covenant and will. Verse 16 affirms the fact that a testament or a will is activated only after the death of the person who made the will. Verse 17 repeats the point that without the death of the testator or person who makes the will, the will has no force. In essence, this is the writer's way of illustrating the necessity of Christ's death. The inheritance referenced in verse 15 could not have been given and received by us apart from the death of Christ. Christ had to die in order for the new covenant to be put in force. Just as a will becomes valid after the testator's death, so our eternal inheritance could only be received after the death of Christ.

18 Whereupon neither the first testament was dedicated without blood.

Having argued that death must occur in order for a will to be put in force, the writer now argues the same point from the perspective of the Law. Under the Law, blood had to be shed for sin to be forgiven. The writer reasons that just as a death was required under the old covenant, so also was a death required under the new covenant. This point will be reiterated in Hebrews 9:22: "And almost all things are by the law purged with blood; and without shedding of blood is no remission."

19 For when Moses had spoken every precept to all the people according to the law, he took the blood of calves and of goats, with water, and scarlet wool, and hyssop, and sprinkled both the book, and all the people, 20 Saying, This is the blood of the testament which God hath enjoined unto you. 21 Moreover he sprinkled with blood both the tabernacle, and all the vessels of the ministry. 22 And almost all things are by the law purged with blood; and without shedding of blood is no remission.

Verses 19–22 use an allusion to Leviticus 8-9—when Moses and Aaron begin the practice of offerings at the Tabernacle according to the Lord's command—to advance the point that it is through shedding of blood that sins are forgiven. Through the establishment of the Law of God with Israel, there was a system of sacrifices that kept people in right relationship with God's presence at the Tabernacle. However the writer of Hebrews is reminding his audience that those sacrifices and that bloodshed could only provide temporary relief to the problem of sin. The shed blood of Jesus Christ brought in a new covenant that fulfills the old covenant and also provides permanent forgiveness of sin and cleanses us.

In Leviticus 14:6 the priest is instructed to perform similar actions with the hyssop and scarlet yarn dipped in bird's blood to purify someone who suffers from leprosy. Verse 19 also holds an allusion to Jesus' death on the Cross; Jesus shed His blood and when the Roman soldier pierced His side water flowed out (John 19:34). Verse 21 is again an affirmation that everything used for serving God in the Tabernacle according to the old covenant was purified for use by sprinkling blood on it.

Leviticus 17 has an extended explanation of how blood is life, and elaborates that any bloodshed belongs to God and if blood is shed without offering to God, there is penalty. Leviticus 17:11 is really the hinge Scripture of the point that the author of Hebrews is making. It states: "For the life of the flesh is in the blood: and I have given it to you upon the altar to make an atonement for your souls: for it is the blood that maketh an atonement for the soul." Indeed Jesus Christ's blood is the ultimate blood given in exchange for our souls that purifies us and makes atonement for our sin.

Say It Correctly

Hyssop. **HIS**-uhp.

Daily Bible Readings

MONDAY
The People Promise to Obey
(Exodus 24:3–8)

TUESDAY
Aaron Performs the Atoning Sin Sacrifice
(Leviticus 16:11–19)

WEDNESDAY
Redeemed and Purified
(Titus 2:11–15)

THURSDAY
Entering the Sanctuary by Jesus' Blood
(Hebrews 10:19–25)

FRIDAY
The Time Has Come
(Hebrews 9:1–10)

SATURDAY
Christ, the Final Sacrifice for Sin
(Hebrews 9:23–28)

SUNDAY
Christ, Mediator of the New Covenant
(Hebrews 9:11–22)

Notes

_____

_____

_____

_____

Teaching Tips

June 23
Bible Study Guide 4

Words You Should Know

A. Heart *kardia* (Gk.)—In context it means either soul or mind.

B. Built Up *epoikodomeo* (Gk.)—To continue construction on an already established foundation.

Teacher Preparation

Unifying Principle—True Unity in Christ. Mutual bonds of love and commitment can bind people together. How can communities avoid losing their identities while under attack? Paul urged the Colossians to be united in love to fully understand the rich treasures offered to them by faith and so that they could resist false teachings and come to appreciate their new spiritual standing in Christ.

A. Read the Bible Background and Devotional Readings.

B. Pray for your students and lesson clarity.

C. Read the lesson Scripture in multiple translations.

D. Option: As a class, brainstorm beliefs and practices that are essential to the Christian faith. Write these on the board. Challenge the group to narrow the list to ten items. Next, narrow the list to five items. If the class could only list one item as absolutely essential to our faith, what would it be?

O—Open the Lesson

A. Begin the class with prayer.

B. Have the students read the Aim for Change.

C. Have the students read the In Focus story.

D. Ask students how events named in the story can weigh on their hearts and how they can view these events from a theological perspective.

P—Present the Scriptures

A. Read the Focal Verses and discuss the Background and The People, Places, and Times sections.

B. Have the class share what Scriptures stand out for them and why, with particular emphasis on today's context.

E—Explore the Meaning

A. Use In Depth or More Light on the Text to help provide more in-depth discussion of the lesson text.

B. Discuss the Liberating Lesson and Application for Activation sections.

N—Next Steps for Application

A. Summarize the value of uniting with other believers in Christ.

B. End class with a commitment to pray for unity in the church grounded in the truth of God.

Worship Guide

For the Superintendent or Teacher
Theme: Hearts United in Love
Song: "Make Us One"
Devotional Reading: 1 Corinthians 3:10–17

Hearts United in Love

Bible Background • COLOSSIANS 2:1–15
Printed Text • COLOSSIANS 2:1–15 | Devotional Reading • 1 CORINTHIANS 3:10–17

———— Aim for Change ————

By the end of this lesson, we will: CONTRAST the deceptive philosophies and false unity of false teachers with true faith in Colossians; EVALUATE being rooted and built up in Christ; and EMBRACE our new standing in Christ as a guard against false teaching.

———— In Focus ————

In a medium-sized city in America, there were two pastors who were passionate about God and God's people but had two very different approaches to reaching people. Pastor Jackson believed that the work of God was strongly oriented toward social justice. He was known to lead marches, challenge civic leaders, and push legislative policies that he believed would make his community better. Rev. Harris, on the other hand, had a different pastoral perspective. He believed that the church's primary job was the business of saving souls. He was confident that the most important thing that he could do was preach the Gospel from the pulpit on Sunday morning. The congregation offered a weekly dinner to homeless people in the neighborhood, and he preached during the meal.

Pastor Jackson wanted to involve Rev. Harris in his most recent campaign critiquing racial profiling by the local police department. Rev. Harris said that he was not interested, but that he was looking forward to having Pastor Jackson come over and preach at his church. Late one Saturday evening, Rev. Harris called Pastor Jackson. He told him that his son, J.T. Harris, was stopped by the police and held at gunpoint because he allegedly fit the description of a burglar. He shared with Pastor Jackson that perhaps some police officers needed their souls saved, and asked about the next meeting for Pastor Jackson's campaign.

How does a commitment to Christ demand unity that goes beyond meeting for weekly worship services?

———— Keep in Mind ————

"As ye have therefore received Christ Jesus the Lord, so walk ye in him: Rooted and built up in him, and stablished in the faith, as ye have been taught, abounding therein thanksgiving" (Colossians 2:6–7, KJV).

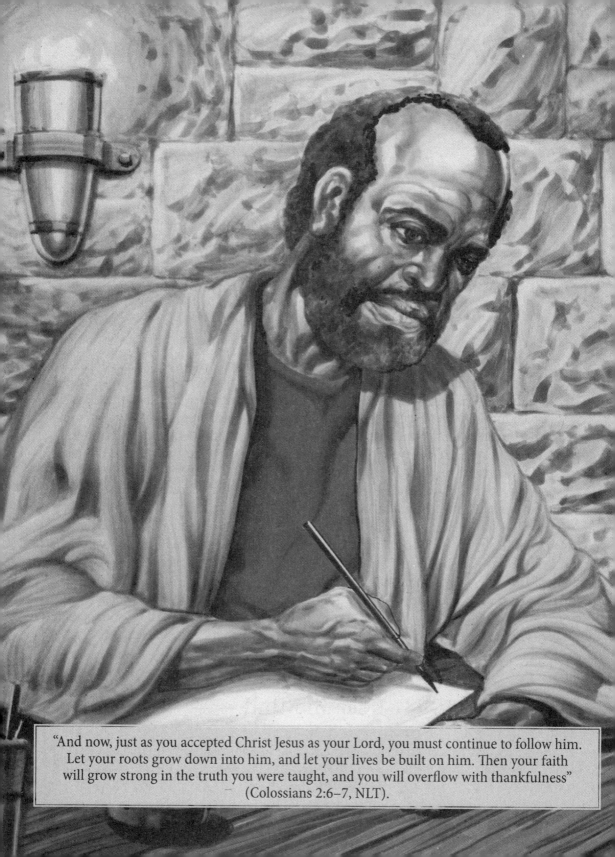

"And now, just as you accepted Christ Jesus as your Lord, you must continue to follow him. Let your roots grow down into him, and let your lives be built on him. Then your faith will grow strong in the truth you were taught, and you will overflow with thankfulness" (Colossians 2:6–7, NLT).

Focal Verses

KJV **Colossians 2:1** For I would that ye knew what great conflict I have for you, and for them at Laodicea, and for as many as have not seen my face in the flesh;

2 That their hearts might be comforted, being knit together in love, and unto all riches of the full assurance of understanding, to the acknowledgement of the mystery of God, and of the Father, and of Christ;

3 In whom are hid all the treasures of wisdom and knowledge.

4 And this I say, lest any man should beguile you with enticing words.

5 For though I be absent in the flesh, yet am I with you in the spirit, joying and beholding your order, and the stedfastness of your faith in Christ.

6 As ye have therefore received Christ Jesus the Lord, so walk ye in him:

7 Rooted and built up in him, and stablished in the faith, as ye have been taught, abounding therein with thanksgiving.

8 Beware lest any man spoil you through philosophy and vain deceit, after the tradition of men, after the rudiments of the world, and not after Christ.

9 For in him dwelleth all the fulness of the Godhead bodily.

10 And ye are complete in him, which is the head of all principality and power:

11 In whom also ye are circumcised with the circumcision made without hands, in putting off the body of the sins of the flesh by the circumcision of Christ:

12 Buried with him in baptism, wherein also ye are risen with him through the faith of the operation of God, who hath raised him from the dead.

13 And you, being dead in your sins and the uncircumcision of your flesh, hath he

NLT **Colossians 2:1** I want you to know how much I have agonized for you and for the church at Laodicea, and for many other believers who have never met me personally.

2 I want them to be encouraged and knit together by strong ties of love. I want them to have complete confidence that they understand God's mysterious plan, which is Christ himself.

3 In him lie hidden all the treasures of wisdom and knowledge.

4 I am telling you this so no one will deceive you with well-crafted arguments.

5 For though I am far away from you, my heart is with you. And I rejoice that you are living as you should and that your faith in Christ is strong.

6 And now, just as you accepted Christ Jesus as your Lord, you must continue to follow him.

7 Let your roots grow down into him, and let your lives be built on him. Then your faith will grow strong in the truth you were taught, and you will overflow with thankfulness.

8 Don't let anyone capture you with empty philosophies and high-sounding nonsense that come from human thinking and from the spiritual powers of this world, rather than from Christ.

9 For in Christ lives all the fullness of God in a human body.

10 So you also are complete through your union with Christ, who is the head over every ruler and authority.

11 When you came to Christ, you were "circumcised," but not by a physical procedure. Christ performed a spiritual circumcision— the cutting away of your sinful nature.

12 For you were buried with Christ when you were baptized. And with him you were raised to new life because you trusted the quickened together with him, having forgiven you all trespasses;

14 Blotting out the handwriting of ordinances that was against us, which was contrary to us, and took it out of the way, nailing it to his cross;

15 And having spoiled principalities and powers, he made a shew of them openly, triumphing over them in it.

mighty power of God, who raised Christ from the dead.

13 You were dead because of your sins and because your sinful nature was not yet cut away. Then God made you alive with Christ, for he forgave all our sins.

14 He canceled the record of the charges against us and took it away by nailing it to the cross.

15 In this way, he disarmed the spiritual rulers and authorities. He shamed them publicly by his victory over them on the cross.

The People, Places, and Times

Gnosticism. Gnosticism comes from the Greek word *gnosis* (**guh-NO-seese**), meaning "knowledge." The Gnostics separated physical matter from thought. They concluded that matter was evil and formulated the idea that the possession of knowledge was the only requirement for salvation. This is why they did not want to attribute humanity to Jesus Christ because to them, material things were evil. Paul stresses that in Him (Jesus Christ as He appeared on earth) "dwelleth all the fulness of the Godhead bodily"(Colossians 2:9). Jesus was truly God in the flesh (John 1:14). As a result of their philosophical concepts—that the body is evil, for example—the Gnostics ignored or diminished the significance of the historic facts of the ministry, death, and resurrection of Jesus Christ simply because they were so apparent and too easy to understand. To them, all the secrets of God were in the mind or appearing in an immaterial identity.

Circumcision. Circumcision is the cutting off of the foreskin. Jewish baby boys are circumcised at eight days old by mandate of Mosaic Law (Leviticus 12:3). Circumcision marked males as belonging to God, and it was supposed to be more than an outward

sign, signifying complete devotion to God (Deuteronomy 10:16).

When Gentiles began turning to Jesus, a big discussion arose as to whether Gentile Christian men needed to be circumcised. Paul pointed out that uncircumcised Gentiles had come to Christ simply by grace through faith. No one came to Christ through anything else. Because no one was able to keep the Law to perfection, it was obvious that the Law, including circumcision, did not save anyone.

Today, many baby boys are circumcised but not for religious reasons. Studies have shown the circumcised males are less likely to spread sexually transmitted diseases and other potential conditions, so sometimes circumcision is done for health reasons.

Background

The first readers of the letter to the Colossians fell into one of several groups of early Jesus followers attempting to determine their identity during a pretty dynamic time. The Jesus movement had provided a new lens to these believers for understanding the Torah (the Law in the Hebrew Bible), the prophets, and the traditions that had been passed down to them for generations. These traditions included rituals, such as circumcision, that went all the way back to Abraham, the first patriarch.

Also, the message of Jesus as Lord and hero/Savior challenged the boundary that separated two groups. The first group was the Judeans or Jews who understood themselves as a part of a historical lineage that included the characters in the Hebrew Bible and was linked to Torah observance, Temple worship, and the land of Israel. The second group was the Gentiles. These were families of people whose history was linked to other narratives, practices, and places. Despite their differences, the message and movement of Jesus brought together these very different tribes and made them into one community. Paul encourages this community that has chosen to eliminate the unhealthy boundary that separated them. The author also continues to urge them to adopt a radical love ethic.

Paul, however, was concerned about them developing a healthy, external boundary between the community and the forces that attempt to destroy the harmony and love that they share. Negotiating both boundaries was of primary importance, as they forged their new identity together.

At-A-Glance

1. Shared Values (Colossians 2:1–5)
2. Shared Vision (vv. 6–12)
3. Shared Victory (vv. 13–15)

In Depth

1. Shared Values (Colossians 2:1–5)

The author shares that the community has access to the true spiritual treasures of wisdom and knowledge, but those treasures are linked to the community's values. Two values resonate throughout this and other letters written by Paul: love and faith. In this passage, unity through love is the key that grants access to the best that God has to offer humanity. God's treasures are hidden in Christ and activated by individuals loving each other. The passage suggests that the treasures of true wisdom and knowledge cannot be accessed alone, but they must be sought together in community. This is directly connected to faith. The faith that the community shares is deeply rooted in Christ, but its strength is measured by how the Colossians weather challenges together.

Why is it important for us to receive God's truth in community rather than in isolation?

2. Shared Vision (vv. 6–12)

The author suggests that the Colossians should be focused on one thing: development in Christ. The passage also implies that this type of development and growth does not happen solely at an individual level. The second person plural pronouns in the Greek text, translated as "you" meaning "you all," highlight the fact that the writer is imploring the community to grow together. Two keys to growing together in Christ are the ability to ignore voices that undermine growth and to challenge traditions that prevent development. The standard for growth is Christ, which is immeasurable, because all of who God is in Christ. Therefore, that goal should prevent them from paying attention to the progress or lack thereof of others around them, because they recognize that they can only reach such a goal themselves by the power of God. Such power is available through a dedication and faith that can see the invisible and believe the impossible. That type of faith grants access to the type of power that can raise the dead. Believers know this power because it has lifted them from spiritual death into sharing Christ's life.

What does it mean to be "spiritually circumcised?"

3. Shared Victory (vv. 13–15)

The image of Christ's victory and the erasure of the record of sin against believers is particularly powerful because it takes the language of the empire and turns it on its head. Christ is portrayed as disarming the forces of oppression and triumphing over them like a Roman emperor would celebrate victory over enemies. Christ does not replace the oppression with His own but instead renders oppression itself as ineffective. Christ conquers what has attempted to conquer the community, and the community shares in that victory. This shared victory is also captured in the idea that in spite of our trespasses and sins, through faith, God has made us alive together with Christ.

The author uses the idea of "uncircumcision of flesh" to represent a very contentious issue that was used by members who had been circumcised to oppress those members of the community who had not been circumcised. The author employs this specific example to illustrate Christ's victory from cosmic forces in spiritual places to the human forces in local places. This is the victory that believers share.

How have you seen Christ's victory show up in your life?

Search the Scriptures

1. What does this passage teach us about Christ (Colossians 2:2–3)? Who He is? What He does?

2. What are some boundaries Paul encourages the community to set (Colossians 2:4, 8)?

Discuss the Meaning

1. What are some useful strategies for creating unity in Christ-centered relationships and communities?

2. How does Christ's victory relate to how believers are supposed to engage with each other and the world?

Liberating Lesson

All cries for unity are not created equal. From political discourse to church disagreements, unity is frequently evoked as the preferred position often without any justification. It is especially dangerous when unity is synonymous with uniformity. This is treacherous when calls for unity demand individuals to give up their identity, look past their injury, or to support wrong with complicity. To this end, unity should not be sought for its own sake. Unity, instead, should be a tool for promoting a cause that is working to bring about the reign of God in the world.

True unity in love looks like criminal justice reform, mentoring young people, providing healthcare for the sick, standing up for the safety of the marginalized, mobilizing disenfranchised people to wield their right to vote, etc. If a community, even a church community, cannot build unity around destroying oppression and uplifting those in need, then perhaps they are not looking for the sort of unity Jesus taught us.

Application for Activation

1. Building boundaries is important both in collective and individual life. The people with whom we choose to build community tell us about who we are. Who are the five people with whom you have the least amount of boundaries? How do you manage the boundaries? How do you keep others from infringing on those boundaries?

2. In any relationship, it is important to place boundaries to both protect and limit the relationship. Write down two relationships where you need to do a better job of managing the internal boundaries. Where do you need to improve the external boundaries that define the relationship?

Follow the Spirit

What God wants me to do:

_____

_____

_____

_____

Remember Your Thoughts

Special insights I have learned:

_____

_____

_____

_____

More Light on the Text

Colossians 2:1–15

The previous chapter ends with the purpose of Paul's labor and striving: to be able to present every man perfect in Christ with all the might given him by the power of God that works in him (1:28–29). The next seven verses express Paul's concern about the state of the church, and his wish that the members would be united in love, having a fuller understanding of the mystery of the Father and of Christ. This anxiety is based, as we shall see later in this study, on the heresy being perpetrated by false teachers. He warns the church and urges it to remain faithful in Christ (vv. 1–7).

1 For I would that ye knew what great conflict I have for you, and for them at Laodicea, and for as many as have not seen my face in the flesh;

Our passage opens with a titanic struggle. Paul speaks of a powerful inner "conflict," using the Greek word *agon* (**ah-GOAN**), from which we get our word "agony." You could say that the theme of the book of Colossians is found in 2:17: "Which are a shadow of things to come; but the body is of Christ." Paul is confronting a mixture of Jewish legalism and Gnostic teaching. Both fall short and are but "shadows," for different reasons, of obtaining the fullness of what Christ brings to His church.

We can now understand the inner struggle Paul feels for what the Colossian Christians and those at Laodicea are going through. We learn that they have not met Paul ("see one's face in the flesh" is another way of saying "see one face to face"). As a result, the apostle must rely on reports of their faith toward Christ and their love for one another. Knowing how quickly such faith can be set aside or compromised by professed believers, Paul agonizes in prayer over the Colossian believers.

We will discover in the following verses both his fondest hopes and his deepest fears concerning them.

2 That their hearts might be comforted, being knit together in love, and unto all riches of the full assurance of understanding, to the acknowledgment of the mystery of God, and of the Father, and of Christ;

The word "hearts" in the Greek is *kardia* (**kar-DEE-ah**) and refers to the soul or mind, thought by the ancient Greeks to be "the fountain and seat of thoughts, passions, desires, appetites, affections, purposes, and endeavors." The Greek translation for the phrase "might be comforted" is *parakaleo* (**pah-rah-kah-LEH-oh**), and it means "to encourage, strengthen." Paul's prayerful "agony," we see here, concerns the spiritual health of those to whom he writes.

He desires for them, first, a profound inner comfort—not a comfort founded in self-reliance or external circumstances but in hearts "knit together in love." Next, Paul prays for believers to have a solid insight into the mystery of God, describing such an understanding as "riches." We see Paul striving to articulate the spiritual wealth that comes to those who are in Christ. For after all, Christ Himself is the greatest treasure.

The point of the next phrase is that Christ is the mystery of God. God's "mystery" is not something hard to figure out; rather, it is something that had been previously unknown but now is revealed. One of the most helpful explanations of "mystery" in the New Testament comes in Ephesians 3:1–13. Christ's coming was, of course, promised time and time again in the Old Testament, but what was unknown was that Jesus would unite Jew and Gentile into one body, and that the Holy Spirit would dwell in that suffering body, the church, until Christ's delayed return. It is this mystery—and all the comfort, encouragement, power and focus it brings to those whom Christ has joined to His one body—that Paul prays for the Colossians to understand.

3 In whom are hid all the treasures of wisdom and knowledge.

This small but powerful verse taps into the longings and expectations of God's people for generations before the coming of Jesus. As pointed out by commentators focusing on Colossians 2:2–3, God's people have long considered wisdom the greatest of all treasures. In the Greek, the word "hid" is *apokruphos* (**ah-POH-kroo-foce**) and means "hidden, secret, stored up." Clearly, the Old Testament authorizes God's Law as the source of all wisdom, for it reveals God to His people, at least in a limited way. But Paul's point here is that Christ reveals God in a full, unlimited way;

Christ possesses every treasure of God, all wisdom and all knowledge that can be gained. And so Jesus Christ is "the image of the invisible God" (Colossians 1:15), the revelation of God to a people walking in darkness. It is no wonder that Paul prays for the Colossians to understand such a profound truth!

4 And this I say, lest any man should beguile you with enticing words.

In the Greek, the phrase "should beguile" is *paralogizomai* (**pah-rah-low-GEED-zoh-my**) and means "to deceive, delude, circumvent." The Greek word for the phrase "enticing words" is *pithanologia* (**pee-thah-no-low-GEE-ah**), and it refers to discussion meant to mislead others into error. It was common at the time of Paul's writing for people trained in the art of rhetoric to seek to persuade others without any regard for truth. The mere act of convincing another person of something was considered worthwhile, whether the one persuaded ended up fortified by truth or deceived by falsehood. Based on verses 4 and 8, as well as 2:20–23, we can observe that the Colossians were indeed in danger from false teachers, particularly from those who taught the dangerous mix of Jewish legalism and Gnosticism. It was these wolves in sheep's clothing about whom Paul had great concern, lest the purity of the Colossians' devotion to Christ be compromised.

5 For though I be absent in the flesh, yet am I with you in the spirit, joying and beholding your order, and the steadfastness of your faith in Christ.

"I am with you in spirit" is a phrase to be unpacked. Paul could not possibly visit all the Christian churches as the Gospel was bearing fruit and the faith was exploding throughout the Roman Empire. For him, communication through epistle was critical, to the point that he believed his carefully chosen words represented his actual presence among the hearers. So when he speaks of being "absent in the flesh" but "with you in the spirit," he is probably not focusing on the idea of being connected to them spiritually. The way he "beheld" their order and steadfastness to Christ was through the reports that disciples like Tychicus brought to him (Colossians 4:7). We should note, too, that the things which pleased Paul so deeply were not miraculous revelations or demonstrations of God's power, but the simple, ordinary work of "order" and "steadfastness."

6 As ye have therefore received Christ Jesus the Lord, so walk ye in him: 7 Rooted and built up in him, and stablished in the faith, as ye have been taught, abounding therein with thanksgiving.

We should remind ourselves that this is a letter of encouragement to the church at Colosse to remain steadfast in its belief in spite of the dangers that were threatening the church. In verse 6, Paul encourages the members of the Colossian church to continue leading a life consistent with their belief in Christ. The phrase "received" or "accepted" Christ describes the new relationship that takes place when a person comes to the knowledge of Christ. To Paul, receiving or accepting Christ is just the beginning; the follow-up is to live in Him through our lifestyle, conduct, and faithfulness.

The words "built up" translate the Greek *epoikodomeo* (**eh-poy-koh-doe-MEH-oh**), which has the idea of the continuing construction of a building of which the foundation has been laid. It is figuratively used here to describe the believer's constant increase in relationship with and knowledge of Christ. No building can stand without a firm foundation, and a foundation without a building is worthless. When both take place, then the house would be established (Gk. *bebaioo*, **beh-bye-OH-oh**) or stabilized.

To complete this four-fold cycle of victorious living (in Christ) is the exhortation to abound in thanksgiving. In several of his letters (especially in the opening sections), Paul always expresses his gratitude to God and to Christ, and urges or challenges his readers to give thanks always to God. This type of thanksgiving can be spontaneous, such as an outburst of praise, worship, and singing often found in African American or African churches, where gratitude to God is expressed based not only on what we have materially but rather on who we are in Christ and on His blessings of redemption. It comes deep from within.

This attitude of thanksgiving—resulting from the firm foundation of the increasing knowledge of Christ by faith in the Gospel—will protect the believer from all type of threats, deceptions, and falsities. This is explicitly expressed in the following verses.

8 Beware lest any man spoil you through philosophy and vain deceit, after the tradition of men, after the rudiments of the world, and not after Christ.

Paul continues with a strict warning and cautions the Colossians to be careful of the heresy that is going around. With the clause, "Beware lest any man spoil you," Paul shows his love and concern for the spiritual well-being of the Colossian brethren. "Beware" (Gk. *blepo*, **BLEH-po**) means "to take heed, or look out," as one looks out for impending danger in crossing a busy street, or looking out for dangerous snakes walking through the woods. Verse 8 employs a battle or war term: "spoil" (*sulagogeo*, **soo-lah-go-GEH-oh**), in which the defeated are carried away captives and their goods are carried away as plunder. The goods are the spiritual blessings of salvation and its benefits, which believers enjoy in Christ. Paul readily explains how one can be robbed of Christ's benefits: through philosophy and vain deceit. The word "philosophy" is a direct transliteration of the Greek word *philosophia* (**fee-low-sow-FEE-ah**), which simply means "love or pursuit of wisdom," and is used only here in the Bible. Paul uses it to describe the false theology of certain Jewish Christian ascetics. Paul insists that this philosophy is contradictory to the teachings of the Gospel based on Christ Jesus. The teachings are man-made, humanistic, and worldly rather than spiritual and Christ-centered.

Paul then adds that this type of teaching is according to the rudiments or basic principles of the world. Here Paul probably refers to the elementary rules and principles of the world system and of the Jewish religion, which tend to seek salvation through personal efforts and human wisdom rather than through faith in Christ. Although Christ's death had nullified this belief, some Jews tried to combine faith in Christ with man-made traditions and Pharisaic ordinances. The philosophy based on "the rudiments of the world" here probably also refers to the study and worship of the heavenly bodies, which would be similar to our modern astrology and new age metaphysics. These teachings contradict and fall short of what Christ offers, His works, and His teaching. They tend to take men away from Christ, weaken their trust in Him, and limit their relationship with Him.

9 For in him dwelleth all the fulness of the Godhead bodily. 10 And ye are complete in him, which is the head of all principality and power:

Paul makes a bold assertion regarding Christ, His person, and His work in relationship to humanity's redemption. Paul says in effect that in Christ alone can be found the fullness of God—the real representation of God in a bodily or physical form. The word "Godhead" (Gk. *theotes*, **theh-OH-tace**) means deity, state of being God or "God-hood." It appears only

once in Scripture and relates to the deity of God. Christ is the personal and physical manifestation of all the fullness of God's power and blessings to humanity. Therefore, God is found not in the philosophies or human traditions of the Jews and Gentiles, nor in worldly principles. In Christ, we have the entire essence of God concentrated in a human bodily form.

Since the fullness of God is resident in Christ, it makes no sense, Paul seems to argue, to look elsewhere for help or salvation. Christ is the source of all things, so we do not need any other. In Him, we have attained the full measure of all things for this life and the one to come. Since Christ is the full bodily expression of the invisible God, with all His attributes, He is therefore the head of each and every principality and power. Christ is the head in the sense of possessing supreme authority and control. All powers and principalities are subject to Him, and He controls all their activities because He is their Creator. The good angels cannot affect salvation for believers, and the bad angels are limited in what they can do to the believer. This idea is reemphasized in verse 15. It is in Christ, who is the full manifestation of the Godhead and controls all spiritual beings, that we are complete and fulfilled.

11 In whom also ye are circumcised with the circumcision made without hands, in putting off the body of the sins of the flesh by the circumcision of Christ: 12 Buried with him in baptism, wherein also ye are risen with him through the faith of the operation of God, who hath raised him from the dead.

Speaking of Christ as the head of all principality and power, Paul continues his argument, "...in whom also ye are circumcised." Paul introduces the theme of circumcision, which seems to suggest at this point that there is confusion about the subject among the Colossians. Probably, among the false teachers, were some

Jews (Jewish Christians) who were making the ritual of circumcision a condition for salvation as in the Galatian churches (Galatians 5:2–3; cf. Acts 15:1). Rather, the type of circumcision they have received is of Christ, which Paul describes as putting off (*apekdusis*, **opp-EK-doo-seese**) the sins of the flesh, i.e., laying aside the evil nature, rather than the removal of the physical foreskin.

Paul alludes to the ritual of baptism as a symbol for spiritual circumcision, which is signified by the death, burial, and resurrection of Christ. By baptism, we identify with and partake as it were, in the death, burial, and consequent resurrection of Christ. Christ's death and resurrection offers us redemption, whereby all our sins are forgiven.

13 And you, being dead in your sins and the uncircumcision of your flesh, hath he quickened together with him, having forgiven you all trespasses; 14 Blotting out the handwriting of ordinances that was against us, which was contrary to us, and took it out of the way, nailing it to his cross;

This verse describes the effect the work of God has in the life of the believer. It describes the former state of all humans, the Gentile Colossians in particular, and contrasts it with their present state after the transformation through Christ's death on the Cross. This transformation is all the work of God. They were all dead in sins but now alive in Christ. Apart from the eschatological bodily resurrection of all believers at the end time with Christ, the forgiveness of sins is a type of resurrection, symbolized by the historical, physical, and bodily resurrection of Christ, which all believers experience.

Paul employs another metaphor to describe God's work of redemption through Christ. Not only has He quickened us (i.e., brought us to life) and pardoned our sins, He has blotted out the handwriting of ordinances that was against us, which was contrary to us. Using computer language, it means to delete from existence the written document of the Law and its rigid regulations, which confront and condemn man because of man's inability to keep them. Since no one is ever able to keep the Law, both in its moral and ceremonial aspects, God in His mercy has rendered it non-binding. He annulled the Law and its demand when Christ through His death satisfied the demands of the Law and bore its curse on Calvary. It has been figuratively nailed to His Cross. Our righteousness is not dependent upon what we do, or on our efforts to keep the Law, rather it is dependent on who we are now, and on our trust (faith) in and acceptance of the finished work of Christ on the cross on which the Law has been nailed.

Christ says, "If ye love me, keep my commandments" (John 14:15). Therefore, the abolition of the Law does not imply that man's responsibility has been nullified to do right. The Law that demands that we love the Lord and our neighbor still has eternal relevance (cf. Romans 13:8–9; Galatians 5:14).

15 And having spoiled principalities and powers, he made a shew of them openly, triumphing over them in it.

Paul argues here that Satan or powerful demonic forces know humanity's inability to keep the Law, and so he uses it against them, accusing them before the Father. Therefore, the abolition of the written Law, which hitherto has been a snare to man, renders Satan's strategy against humans ineffective. Hence, Paul says: "and having spoiled principalities and powers, he made a shew of them openly, triumphing over them in it." The Greek word translated as "spoiled" is *apekduomai* (**ap-ek-DOO-oh-my**), which means "to strip off," as in pulling off clothes. It is different than the use of the word in verse 8 but similar to verse 11.

"Principalities and powers," we noted earlier, are demonic forces who war against us. Here, Paul says that by blotting out the written Law and the ordinances that entangle man, satanic forces have been stripped of their power. They have been rendered impotent and powerless. They cannot hold believers any longer to ransom and bondage because of the Law (Romans 7:5–25). They are not only disarmed, but they are also put to open spectacle and ridicule. Paul applies military language in which the defeated are disarmed and stripped of their clothes, and humiliated as prisoners of war. This is what Christ did by His death on the Cross. His death means defeat and open humiliation for the accusers of believers. The crucifixion of Christ—which enemies meant for public shame, humiliation, and ultimately death—turned out to be for their own public defeat and shame (Acts 3:15). The enemy's defeat means victory for believers, and so believers need not be afraid.

Source:

Thayer, Joseph H. *Thayer's Greek-English Lexicon of the New Testament Numerically Coded to Strong's Exhaustive Concordance*. Ada, MI: Baker Book House, 1988.

Say It Correctly

Laodicea. ley-ohd-i-**SEE**-uh.
Principality. prin-suh-**PAL**-i-tee.

Daily Bible Readings

MONDAY
Christ, the Source of Life
(1 John 5:6–12)

TUESDAY
Pursue Unity in the Church
(1 Peter 3:8–12)

WEDNESDAY
All Peoples United in Christ
(Ephesians 2:11–22)

THURSDAY
Christ, the Image of God
(Colossians 1:15–20)

FRIDAY
Paul's Ministry in the Congregation
(Colossians 1:24–29)

SATURDAY
Maintain Your Union With Christ
(Colossians 2:16–23)

SUNDAY
United With Christ and One Another
(Colossians 2:1–15)

Notes

Teaching Tips

Words You Should Know

A. Blessed *makarios* (Gk.)—In the context of the Beatitudes the word means "happy."

B. Mercy *eleos* (Gk.)—Forgiveness or compassion, kindness.

Teacher Preparation

Unifying Principle—Right Attitudes. Our attitudes determine how we view circumstances in our lives. How can our attitudes bring long-term benefits? The Beatitudes taught the crowd and the disciples the heartfelt values and attitudes required of anyone seeking to be in covenant relationship with Jesus.

A. Read the Bible Background and Devotional Readings.

B. Pray for your students and lesson clarity.

C. Read the lesson Scripture in multiple translations.

D. Option: As a class, give students time to evaluate which of the Beatitudes they struggle with and to come up with a plan for improving in that area.

O—Open the Lesson

A. Begin the class with prayer.

B. Have the students read the Aim for Change.

C. Have the students read the In Focus story.

D. Ask students how events named in the story can weigh on their hearts and how they can view these events from a theological perspective.

P—Present the Scriptures

A. Read the Focal Verses and discuss the Background and The People, Places, and Times sections.

B. Have the class share what Scriptures stand out for them and why, with particular emphasis on today's context.

E—Explore the Meaning

A. Use In Depth or More Light on the Text to help provide more in-depth discussion of the lesson text.

B. Discuss the Liberating Lesson and Application for Activation sections.

N—Next Steps for Application

A. Summarize the value of responding to the Beatitudes.

B. End class with a commitment to pray for the poor, the mourning, the frustrated, the persecuted, and those who seek righteousness.

Worship Guide

For the Superintendent or Teacher
Theme: Jesus Teaches About Right Attitudes
Song: "Blessed Are the Humble Souls
That See"
Devotional Reading: Isaiah 61:1–8

Jesus Teaches About Right Attitudes

Bible Background • Matthew 5:1–12
Printed Text • Matthew 5:1–12 | Devotional Reading • Isaiah 61:1–8

—————— Aim for Change ——————

By the end of this lesson, we will: EXAMINE the irony of the Beatitudes; DISCOVER the reversal of the world's values that Jesus teaches; and DECIDE how to live out Christ's values as we pursue God's kingdom.

————— In Focus —————

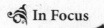

Travis was in shock. His name was called as "employee of the year," and Travis could not believe it. At his company, he simply tried to do his work and treat people well. His CEO read a statement, telling how Travis kept working hard after he returned from personal leave following the death of his son earlier that year. Travis had to attend court a few times during the criminal trial for his son's killer. He felt guilty about missing time, but tried his best to still look for the joy in each day and trust God while he mourned and worked.

Although Travis expected justice from the law, he did not have a lot of money for a powerful attorney. He wasn't sure if the things he told the state's attorney would actually help in the case. Yet he never seemed bitter when he was working or dealing with customers. He had been faithful at his company for twenty years and did so without a lot of fanfare—sometimes feeling overlooked. The CEO said Travis' commitment and spirit amid his hardship moved many in the company to reevaluate their own commitment and attitudes. The company decided to establish a scholarship in the name of Travis' son and award Travis "employee of the year" for his work in raising the company's consciousness during his darkest moments. Travis began to cry. God had seen him. God had seen how he endured. And in his lowest valley, he was blessed.

How do Jesus' words—that those most in need and persecuted are the ones who are blessed and to whom the kingdom of heaven belongs—impact how you see your life? Which of the Beatitudes rings in your spirit the loudest?

—————— Keep in Mind ——————

"Rejoice, and be exceeding glad: for great is your reward in heaven: for so persecuted they the prophets which were before you" (Matthew 5:12, KJV).

"Be happy about it! Be very glad! For a great reward awaits you in heaven. And remember, the ancient prophets were persecuted in the same way" (Matthew 5:12, NLT).

Focal Verses

KJV **Matthew 5:1** And seeing the multitudes, he went up into a mountain: and when he was set, his disciples came unto him:

2 And he opened his mouth, and taught them, saying,

3 Blessed are the poor in spirit: for theirs is the kingdom of heaven.

4 Blessed are they that mourn: for they shall be comforted.

5 Blessed are the meek: for they shall inherit the earth.

6 Blessed are they which do hunger and thirst after righteousness: for they shall be filled.

7 Blessed are the merciful: for they shall obtain mercy.

8 Blessed are the pure in heart: for they shall see God.

9 Blessed are the peacemakers: for they shall be called the children of God.

10 Blessed are they which are persecuted for righteousness' sake: for theirs is the kingdom of heaven.

11 Blessed are ye, when men shall revile you, and persecute you, and shall say all manner of evil against you falsely, for my sake.

12 Rejoice, and be exceeding glad: for great is your reward in heaven: for so persecuted they the prophets which were before you.

NLT **Matthew 5:1** One day as he saw the crowds gathering, Jesus went up on the mountainside and sat down. His disciples gathered around him,

2 and he began to teach them.

3 "God blesses those who are poor and realize their need for him, for the Kingdom of Heaven is theirs.

4 God blesses those who mourn, for they will be comforted.

5 God blesses those who are humble, for they will inherit the whole earth.

6 God blesses those who hunger and thirst for justice, for they will be satisfied.

7 God blesses those who are merciful, for they will be shown mercy.

8 God blesses those whose hearts are pure, for they will see God.

9 God blesses those who work for peace, for they will be called the children of God.

10 God blesses those who are persecuted for doing right, for the Kingdom of Heaven is theirs.

11 "God blesses you when people mock you and persecute you and lie about you and say all sorts of evil things against you because you are my followers.

12 Be happy about it! Be very glad! For a great reward awaits you in heaven. And remember, the ancient prophets were persecuted in the same way.

The People, Places, and Times

Mercy. God does not condone sin or ignore it; instead, He pours out mercy and compassion on the person who is constantly falling short. One who is merciful recognizes the state of an unbeliever and shows pity to the sinner, praying for and loving that individual, and doing what can be done to help. The merciful in the context of Jewish financial law recognized when there was lack and held off on demanding payment for a debt until the person was in a better position to repay.

What does mercy mean in our modern context?

Background

The book of Matthew is the first book we encounter when reading the New Testament. Named after its author, Matthew the tax collector, this book offers a collection of sayings Jesus uttered to small and large crowds during His ministry. We come to know Jesus as a teacher early on in this book in Matthew 5–7, best known as the Sermon on the Mount. After a crowd gathered around Jesus from neighboring cities, He climbed to a mountain top and began to speak to His disciples about societal ethics.

During this time, the Roman Empire was a hierarchal society with no middle class. A few powerful men and their families ruled. In effect, their reign influenced the values of society. As an advocate for the lower class, Jesus offered a new value system, which favored their daily experience. The word "blessed" beginning each statement spoken by Jesus in the Beatitudes signifies the ironies of life. While those in lower strata face negative circumstances daily, Jesus teaches them to not allow the negativity to affect their attitude. Instead, He instructs them on how to follow Him and grow in their relationship with Him through changing their attitudes. Jesus teaches His followers to reject the values of the world and embrace His values, thus altering their concepts of blessings and rewards. Blessings become less about material gain and social status and more about a stronger relationship in Jesus. God also promises "the kingdom of heaven" (vv. 3, 10). While our reward may be delayed, we can rejoice and be glad in the meantime knowing we are living according to the teachings of Jesus. An attitude check enables the followers of Jesus to have a new way of life.

How do you describe your attitude?

At-A-Glance

1. Reflecting on Our Attitudes
(Matthew 5:1–9)
2. Ready for Others' Actions (vv. 10–12)

In Depth

1. Reflecting on Our Attitudes (Matthew 5:1–9)

Jesus leaves the crowd, climbs the mountain, and takes a seat. The disciples follow Him, positioning themselves to hear the first of Jesus' five lessons recorded in Matthew. The first seven statements Jesus makes focus on the development of human character traits. Each statement shows the paradox between what the world believes and what Jesus is teaching. Jesus offers the disciples instruction on a different and new way of living, which is more fulfilling and rewarding than the ways of society. What society had deemed as valuable does not equate to true value in the lessons of Jesus. Jesus calls the disciples to sacrifice a value system—rooted in self-centeredness and material possessions—for one that calls individuals into closer relationships with Jesus and their neighbor. The Teacher shows us our value does not depend on our material possessions when He promises the kingdom of heaven to those who are destitute (v. 3).

In this lesson, Jesus sets the foundation for the value system that must be embraced to gain access to the kingdom of heaven. Jesus is concerned about the position of our heart, not our position in society. This is why He highlights those who mourn, the meek, those who desire righteousness, the merciful, the pure in heart and those who make peace. Jesus highlights the characteristics of a person whose attitude is not self-centered or pessimistic. Ultimately, He is describing the attitude and character of a follower.

Using these first seven statements about character traits, the disciples and readers can check their attitude. We cannot fully understand the value of the blessings associated with each character trait without checking our attitude. By taking on Jesus' new value system, our worldview shifts and our actions change.

What are some ways God reminds you to check your attitude daily?

2. Ready for Others' Actions (vv. 10–12)

The final two statements Jesus makes to the disciples address a rather weighty subject: persecution. Deciding to apply Jesus' teaching to your life does not come without a cost. Sacrificing societal values and the dominant worldview makes one stand apart from the rest. Choosing to follow Jesus means committing to living your life in a way that does not always please other people. Jesus reminds us of the cost associated with taking on this new way of life (vv. 10–12). People may revile us, make negative comments, and persecute us simply because we choose to embody righteousness. Even with the right attitude, it can be difficult to endure these types of actions. However, our focus should not be on how people negatively treat us in this world. Instead we choose to live as Jesus instructs us, because this is how we grow in relationship with Him. Changing our attitudes helps our minds remain on the rewards we will receive in heaven. Yes, this reward is delayed and can be hard to wait for. We should not allow impatience to block our blessings. Thankfully, none of the blessings Jesus talks about is temporary, unlike material things can be. These blessings strengthen our relationship with God and prepare us to receive our reward in heaven.

How do you deal with God's delay in your life?

Search the Scriptures

1. Based on the teaching of Jesus, what are some ways in which Jesus is calling His followers to move from a self-centered worldview to a communal worldview (Matthew 5:1–12)?

2. What does "blessed" mean in the context of this passage?

Discuss the Meaning

1. How do we see God's blessings in the midst of suffering and persecution?

2. Are all Christians experiencing God's blessings? Why or why not?

Liberating Lesson

During the middle of the twentieth century, racism and injustice remained deeply woven into the social fabric of American society. People of color, in particular African Americans, suffered from systemic, race-based disenfranchisement. Following in the footsteps of ancestors who blazed the trail to freedom before them, activists of different ages sought to bring about change in the face of dire circumstances. Enacting positive change required a constant attitude check. One reason the Civil Rights Movement gained success was that its initiatives were focused on community and not individuals. A communal, positive perspective fueled the desire to fight for justice and equality. Also, that value system did not reflect the prominent value system in society. As Christians, we must apply the instruction of Jesus as we follow in the footsteps of our ancestors in the fight for justice. Current circumstances cannot shape our attitudes. Following Jesus requires change.

Application for Activation

In the passage, Jesus gives His followers instruction on how to experience happiness and wholeness amid less than desirable circumstances. While our circumstances may not change, our perspectives should as God's children. We cannot live a life reflective of Christ if we allow societal values to influence how we respond to unfortunate situations. Implementing the values in Matthew 5:1–12 is not easy.

1. Identify which Beatitude you struggle with the most and why.

2. Look for biblical examples of how this value is lived out.

3. For the next week, ask God to check your attitude and change your behavior.

Remember: A reward in heaven is promised, but we must first check our attitudes. The Beatitudes are instructions on how to faithfully respond with a new attitude.

Follow the Spirit

What God wants me to do:

_____

_____

_____

_____

_____

Remember Your Thoughts

Special insights I have learned:

_____

_____

_____

_____

_____

More Light on the Text
Matthew 5:1-12

1 And seeing the multitudes, he went up into a mountain: and when he was set, his disciples came unto him: 2 And he opened his mouth, and taught them, saying,

The narrative serves as an introduction to the passage. It sets the stage for what will follow in the rest of the Sermon on the Mount. Here we learn that Jesus would be teaching from a mountain. The "and" (Gk. *de*, **DEH**, which can also be translated "now," "moreover," or "but," etc.) that begins this chapter is a conjunction and serves as a transition connecting what follows to the previous passage (4:25) and the earlier narrative. In Matthew 4 we read of Christ's ministry of teaching, miracles, and healing throughout the regions of Palestine and Galilee. These events had attracted large crowds to Him.

When He saw the multitudes, He "went up into the mountain" (v. 1). The crowd was so great that Jesus needed a higher and broader space where He could address them. Verse 1 seems to suggest that there were two different types of people in the crowd. The first represented the larger group (mentioned in 4:25), who came from different regions around Jerusalem. The people that made up the second group were Jesus' disciples, among whom were those Jesus had called earlier to follow Him (4:18-22).

The word translated "set" here is the Greek word *kathizo* (**kah-THEED-zo**) and means "to sit down, settle down, or sojourn." Jesus sat as He taught the people, which was customary for teachers in the Jewish circles (see 13:2; 23:2; Luke 4:20-21). "And he opened his mouth, and taught them" is a familiar phrase often used to introduce an important teaching, as it is here and elsewhere in Scripture (see Psalm 78:1–2; Job 33:1–2; Acts 8:35). The phrase also demonstrates a conscious and deliberate decision on the part of the Teacher to teach, seizing the opportunity afforded Him by the surging crowd to set forth the fundamental ordinances of the kingdom.

To whom is Jesus speaking? Is He teaching the disciples, the crowd, or both? To whom does the pronoun in "taught them" refer? At first glance, one might assume that the immediate antecedent is "his disciples" in verse 1. However, at the conclusion of the sermon, one observes that "the people were astonished at his doctrine" (from 7:28), implying that these teachings were addressed to the entire crowd.

3 Blessed are the poor in spirit: for theirs is the kingdom of heaven.

Verse 3 begins the second section consisting of "blessed" sayings, or more correctly, the Beatitudes (vv. 3–12). Each of the verses starts with the word "Blessed" (Gk. *makarios*, **mah-KAH-ree-oce**), which also means "happy." The word "beatitude" is derived from the Latin *beatus* (**beh-AH-toos**), the equivalent of *makarios*. Others prefer to title the passage Macarisms from the Greek. The sayings found here are reminiscent of the Old Testament form of writing found primarily in the poetical books, especially the Psalter (e.g., Psalms 1:1, 32:1–2; Proverbs 3:13; Daniel 12:12). Jesus makes references to the Psalms and other Old Testament Scriptures throughout this sermon.

Jesus begins by pronouncing blessings on or proclaiming God's favor on the "poor in spirit." As we have already noted, *makarios* may be translated as either "blessed" or "happy." If the former is the case, it means that the poor in spirit are blessed because "theirs is the kingdom of heaven." If the latter is the case, then those who are "poor in spirit" (here on earth by implication) will inherit the kingdom of heaven (God). In the parallel passage in Luke 6:20, it omits the phrase "in spirit." There, the meaning is clear: it refers to those who are

economically bankrupt on earth, deprived of earthly riches, and who will be rewarded in the kingdom of heaven. The Old Testament is full of references to the poor (Deuteronomy 15:11; Psalm 72:1–4; Amos 8:4). These passages address those who are poor in material goods and of lowly disposition, which accompanies such deprivation, rather than the poor in spirit. In these situations, God fights for the cause of the poor and delivers them (cf.1 Samuel 2:8; Psalm 34:6; 35:10; Isaiah 41:17).

Although the "poor" in the Old Testament were usually the pious (Psalm 69:29–36; Isaiah 61:1), the phrase "poor in spirit" is not found in the Old Testament. Here in Matthew, it can be interpreted in different ways: (1) The phrase refers to those who cultivate the spirit of humility and self-abasement; (2) It describes those in a need, like the poor, whose poverty is an affliction of the spirit.

The phrase does not speak of those who are faint-hearted, as some would contend, but speaks of the humble in heart. Thus, it means the humble—those who acknowledge their unworthiness before God and absolute dependence on the Lord. Both the Old Testament and New Testament speak profoundly of the rewards, benefits, and blessings of being humble (Proverbs 16:19, 29:23; Isaiah 57:15; Matthew 18:4). Here the reward is that the kingdom of heaven belongs to them, they will partake in the reign of the Messiah and enjoy the blessings He brings. Christ is the perfect example of humility and its rewards, as Paul describes (Philippians 2:6–11).

4 Blessed are they that mourn: for they shall be comforted.

While the humble or "poor in spirit" will inherit the kingdom of heaven (v. 3), those who mourn will be comforted. Who are they? What makes them mourn? Jesus is likely referring to the godly remnant who weep and lament because of the suffering and humiliation of Israel at the hands of foreign nations, which is the consequence of both personal and corporate sin against the Lord. The Beatitude here in Matthew speaks of the deplorable condition of the world, both then and now. Like Simeon, they were "waiting for the consolation of Israel," when there will be no more pain and sorrow (Luke 2:25). These first two Beatitudes are alluded to in Isaiah's messianic blessings (Isaiah 61:1–3), which are fulfilled in Christ (Luke 4:16–19). Christ says that He has come to change mourning into joy and to bestow "the oil of joy for mourning, the garment of praise for the spirit of heaviness" (Isaiah 61:3). These blessings, as yet only partially realized, will be fully consummated at the return of the Messiah (Revelation 7:17).

5 Blessed are the meek: for they shall inherit the earth.

The next group to be rewarded are the "meek." The word "meek" (Gk. *praus*, **praw-OOS**) is difficult to define. The nearest synonym is "gentleness." *Praus* refers to mildness of disposition, or gentleness of spirit. Meekness toward God is that disposition of spirit in which we accept His dealings with us as good, and therefore submit without dispute or resistance. In the Old Testament, the meek are those who wholly rely on God rather than coercion in their own strength to redress injustice. It stems from trust in God's goodness and control over the situation. A meek person is not occupied with self. As noted in 1 Peter 3:4, 14–15, meekness can signify absence of pretension but generally suggests gentleness and self-control (Matthew 11:29; James 3:13). This is a work of the Holy Spirit, not of the human will (Galatians 5:23). It is a virtue to aspire to; but to the Greeks, it was a vice because of their inability to distinguish it from servitude. Jesus is the perfect example of meekness, and Matthew throws more light

on this word when he uses the same word to describe the way Christ exercises His authority (gentle, 11:29; humble, 21:5). Meekness has to do with the way we relate to others, when we shun the arrogant and vicious ways of the strong. The meek, rather than the strong, aggressive, harsh, and tyrannical, will inherit the earth, Jesus asserts.

The verb "inherit" is often used in Scripture, especially in the Old Testament, in relation to the Promised Land (see Deuteronomy 16:20; Isaiah 57:13, 60:21). The promise here is alluded to by the psalmist in Psalm 37:11 (see also v. 9 and 29), although in the Old Testament texts, "the earth" refers to the land of Canaan to be possessed. "Earth" or "land" in this Beatitude has the broader meaning of "the realm of God's Kingdom on earth."

6 Blessed are they which do hunger and thirst after righteousness: for they shall be filled.

The next group in the Beatitudes whom Matthew congratulates are those who hunger or long for righteousness. The language is reminiscent of Old Testament themes. The verbs "hunger" and "thirst" express a strong urge or desire, a craving for something good like food and water. Here, it expresses a desire to live rightly or to have a good relationship with the Lord. Eating and drinking is used metaphorically in the Old Testament to express the desire to have a relationship with God (Isaiah 55:1–3)—a desire that only God satisfies (Psalm 107:9). Those who "hunger and thirst" for righteousness are the people who yearn for a deeper, right relationship with the Lord. Yet an alternative definition of the term "righteousness" is expressed here in the Greek word *dikaiosune* (**dee-kie-oh-SOO-nay**), which means justification or equity and is from the word *dikaios* (**dee-kie-oce**), meaning just. It carries with it the idea of justice—dealing fairly or rightly and equitably with other—with social justice as the undertone (see Acts 17:31; Revelation 19:11). Therefore, this Beatitude addresses those who hunger and thirst not only for personal righteousness (i.e., living uprightly before the Lord) but who also strongly desire that justice be done everywhere and to all mankind. They yearn for the new kingdom where there is justice, equality, and holiness (2 Peter 3:13); they are not satisfied with the status quo. They desire both personal spiritual growth and change in society.

The reward for their yearning is that they will be "filled" or "satisfied." Note that the verb "filled" (Gk. *chortazo*, **khor-TAD-zo**) is the same word used after Jesus fed the 5,000 (Matthew 14:20). They are blessed and (will be) happy because their desire and curiosity will (most likely) be fulfilled in the actualization of the kingdom.

7 Blessed are the merciful: for they shall obtain mercy.

The simplest way to talk about the Beatitude in verse 7 is in terms of reaping and sowing. The phrase "You reap what you sow" goes back at least to Paul (Galatians 6:7) and maybe earlier, and could be used here in a positive sense. The word "mercy" or its Greek equivalent (*eleos*, **EH-leh-oce**) contains the idea of both forgiveness and compassion, or showing kindness. Both understandings of mercy (forgiveness and compassion) are common themes in Matthew's Gospel (6:12–15, 12:7, 18:33–34). The reward for showing mercy is obtaining (i.e., also receiving) mercy, not necessarily from other people or from the immediate recipients, but from the Lord. The opposite is equally true: Those who do not show mercy will not be shown mercy (James 2:13). Mercy is part of God's character and is not dependent upon our merciful acts; it is in God's nature and a gift to sinful humanity.

8 Blessed are the pure in heart: for they shall see God.

"The pure in heart" seems to address genuineness of faith and those who reflect truthfulness and purity of mind without duplicity. This Beatitude is a reflection of the Psalter (Psalm 24:3–6), which poses the question of who is able to ascend to the Temple and see the Lord. In his answer, the psalmist (most likely David) replies that it is "he that hath clean hands, and a pure heart" (from v. 4). From this psalm, it is apparent that only those who relate to God and others with sincerity of mind—those who are internally clean (Deuteronomy 10:16; 30:6) as opposed to merely the externally pious—will see God (James 4:8). The Beatitude speaks of those whose thoughts are pure and free from deceit as opposed to the hypocrites (6:1–18).

To see God is to experience His presence in an intimate way, to have a close relationship with Him. Moses had this experience with the Lord when God spoke "face to face" with him in the wilderness (Exodus 33:11)—an experience the psalmist also desired and in fact had (Psalm 63:1–2). Abram (Abraham) had such an intimate relationship with the Lord that God "talked with him" (Genesis 17:3). Isaiah also had this experience, which was terrifying and yet transforming (Isaiah 6:5). These were glimpses of the revelation of God's presence, but the complete unveiling of this truth, promise, and blessing to the "pure in heart" is yet future.

9 Blessed are the peacemakers: for they shall be called the children of God.

Among those who are blessed are the peacemakers, not the peaceful. Their reward is that they will be called the children of God. The Bible speaks continually of peace in both the Old and New Testaments (e.g., Exodus 14:14; 1 Kings 5:12; Psalm 4:8; Isaiah 52:7; Luke 24:36;

Romans 12:18; 1 Corinthians 7:15; Hebrews 12:14; 1 Peter 3:11).

Isaiah prophesied that the Promised Son would be called "Prince of Peace" (9:6). Jesus is the fulfillment of Isaiah's prophecy and the supreme example of a peacemaker. He brings reconciliation between God and humanity and between people. The Greek word *eirenopoios* (**eye-ray-no-poy-OCE**), which is translated "peacemakers," occurs only here in the New Testament, but the sentiment is found in other parts of the New Testament. The people Jesus blesses here are neither the peaceful, nor lovers of peace, nor those who only speak of peace, but rather those who work actively to make or bring about peace. With God as their example, they strive to make peace at all costs (sometimes sacrificing their own peace or even their lives) and with all persons, whether friends or foes (Matthew 5:45). By imitating the Lord in peacemaking, the peacemakers demonstrate that they are the true children of God. Hence, Jesus says that God will accept them as His own at the consummation of all things.

10 Blessed are they which are persecuted for righteousness' sake: for theirs is the kingdom of heaven.

The next group to receive God's blessings are those who are persecuted for their righteousness or right deeds, probably referring to the peacemakers and those who fight for justice (v. 6). In a world that is full of hate and prejudice, the peacemakers and those who endeavor to live uprightly in the sight of God are never cherished or welcomed in society. Often, they are persecuted and receive the brunt of society's anger and hatred.

Persecution or oppression is the mark of discipleship, as Jesus reminded His disciples (John 15:18–25). Encouraging the disciples at Lystra, Iconium, and Antioch to remain true to the faith, Paul and Barnabas remind them,

"We must through much tribulation enter into the kingdom of God" (from Acts 14:22; cf. 2 Timothy 3:12; 1 Peter 4:13–14).

The promise or blessing for the poor in spirit (v. 3) is the same as here. Indeed, this Beatitude tends to tie together all the other Beatitudes, for all the virtues therein can be summed up under the theme of righteousness or right living. Some interpreters believe that the phrase "for righteousness' sake" refers to the Lord Jesus Christ, and that can be equally true (v. 11). However, it is not apparent that Jesus is referring to Himself here but to those who suffer because they choose to walk uprightly.

11 Blessed are ye, when men shall revile you, and persecute you, and shall say all manner of evil against you falsely, for my sake. 12 Rejoice, and be exceeding glad: for great is your reward in heaven: for so persecuted they the prophets which were before you.

Verses 11 and 12 are an expansion of verse 10. They deal with the attitude people or believers ought to cultivate when they face persecution and oppression because of their faith in Christ. We notice here that Jesus changes from third-person pronouns to second-person plural pronouns, which indicates that at this point He is addressing a specific group in the audience.

Jesus lists three forms of oppression that the disciples (and all those who believe in Him) would suffer because of their faith and their relationship with the Lord Jesus: revilement, persecution, and slander. "Revile" (Gk. *oneidizo*, **oh-nay-DEED-zo**), means to defame, rail at, taunt, or reproach. It also means to ridicule somebody because of what that person does, how that person acts or behaves, how that person looks physically, or what that person believes. The second opposition is "persecution," translated from the Greek *dioko* (**dee-OH-ko**). Persecution takes a variety of forms and covers a wide range of hostile actions. It would include harassment, molestation, and maltreatment in various forms. The third form of opposition the disciples will suffer is that people "shall say all manner of evil against [them] falsely" (i.e., slander or false and malicious accusation). In the parallel passage, Luke adds that they would be excluded and thought to be evil (Luke 6:22–23).

Jesus urges His disciples to rejoice with exceeding gladness even in the face of their tribulations. He gives two reasons why the disciples should have this reaction. The first is that they will be greatly rewarded for their faith, that their reward will be great in heaven. It should be noted that this reward is not a "rite of passage" into the kingdom; rather, it demonstrates that God is faithful and just to reward those who are faithful and endure to the end. The second reason the disciples can rejoice in tribulation is that they are in the same company with the Old Testament prophets before them who were likewise persecuted (cf. 2 Chronicles 24:21; Nehemiah 9:26; Acts 7:51–52; Hebrews 11:35–38). Jesus is implying that the disciples, who will share the same fate as the prophets of old are themselves prophets, persecuted in the same manner as their predecessors. Therefore, this calls for rejoicing, and the apostles understand and apply this later (Acts 5:41; cf. 2 Corinthians 4:17; 1 Peter 1:6–9).

This Beatitude does not imply that Christians or believers should seek persecution, nor does it permit them to retreat from it or exact revenge for it. Rather, it speaks of the Christian's need for steadfast faith in the Lord under any and all circumstances. Disciples must follow the Lord with humility and singleness of heart and continuing reliance on and faithfulness to God irrespective of what may come their way, whether good or bad.

Daily Bible Readings

MONDAY
Living Among Wrongdoers
(Psalm 57)

TUESDAY
Perfect God's Love Among You
(1 John 4:7–21)

WEDNESDAY
Great Rewards to Come
(Luke 6:17–23)

THURSDAY
Apostles Chosen for Ministry
(Mark 3:7–12)

FRIDAY
Do Not Judge
(Luke 6:37–45)

SATURDAY
A Life Pleasing to God
(1 Thessalonians 4:1–12)

SUNDAY
Right Attitudes for Blessed Living
(Matthew 5:1–12)

Teaching Tips

Words You Should Know

A. Jot or Tittle *iota e keraia* (Gk.)—Letter i or hook of a letter, smallest pieces of a word.

B. Fulfill *pleroo* (Gk.)—To uphold, keep, bring to conclusion.

Teacher Preparation

Unifying Principle—Fulfilling the Law. People express their beliefs through their actions. How do we express what we believe? Jesus teaches us that we are to do good for others and follow God's Law.

A. Read the Bible Background and Devotional Readings.

B. Pray for your students and lesson clarity.

C. Read the lesson Scripture in multiple translations.

D. Option: List some Old Testament passages that point to the coming of Jesus. Then explain how Jesus fulfilled these passages.

O—Open the Lesson

A. Begin the class with prayer.

B. Have the students read the Aim for Change.

C. Have the students read the In Focus story.

D. Ask students how events named in the story can weigh on their hearts and how they can view these events from a theological perspective.

P—Present the Scriptures

A. Read the Focal Verses and discuss the Background and The People, Places, and Times sections.

B. Have the class share what Scriptures stand out for them and why, with particular emphasis on today's context.

E—Explore the Meaning

A. Use In Depth or More Light on the Text to help provide more in-depth discussion of the lesson text.

B. Discuss the Liberating Lesson and Application for Activation sections.

N—Next Steps for Application

A. Summarize the value of being salt and light in our communities.

B. End class with a commitment to pray for boldness and faithfulness.

Worship Guide

For the Superintendent or Teacher
Theme: Jesus Teaches About Fulfilling the Law
Song: "This Little Light of Mine"
Devotional Reading: Psalm 119:105–112

Jesus Teaches About Fulfilling the Law

Bible Background • MATTHEW 5:13–20
Printed Text • MATTHEW 5:13–20 | Devotional Reading • PSALM 119:105–112

—— Aim for Change ——

By the end of this lesson, we will: CONTRAST the righteousness Jesus taught with that of the Pharisees; DISCUSS what it means to be salt and light in our righteousness; and IDENTIFY things that keep us from being salt and light in our communities.

—— 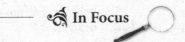 In Focus ——

Mrs. Taylor was always warm and welcoming to new families in her neighborhood. She would go out of her way to bake cookies for them and stop to talk when they would pull up to their houses while she was out in her garden. She was known for her presence at the local middle school volunteering during basketball games, and singing at the park on Sunday afternoons. When she finally reached an age where was having trouble walking and couldn't do the things she used to do, she was devastated. One day her neighbor Audrey knocked on her door, and Mrs. Taylor brought her cane to answer it.

Audrey had baked cookies for her and asked to come in and enjoy them with her. Mrs. Taylor was thrilled! Audrey asked her how she managed to always be so full of joy and to remember the little details of her neighbors' lives, such as what their kids were doing in school. Mrs. Taylor responded she made each neighbor and their family a point of prayer every night. Audrey was intrigued. She had been to church as a kid, but had stopped going some years ago and was curious to hear more about Mrs. Taylor's faith in Jesus.

How can we preach the Gospel with our actions in ways that invite people to draw nearer to hear our words about Christ?

—— Keep in Mind ——

> "Let your light so shine before men, that they may see your good works, and glorify your Father which is in heaven" (Matthew 5:16, KJV).

"In the same way, let your good deeds shine out for all to see, so that everyone will praise your heavenly Father" (Matthew 5:16, NLT).

Focal Verses

KJV Matthew 5:13 Ye are the salt of the earth: but if the salt have lost his savour, wherewith shall it be salted? it is thenceforth good for nothing, but to be cast out, and to be trodden under foot of men.

14 Ye are the light of the world. A city that is set on an hill cannot be hid.

15 Neither do men light a candle, and put it under a bushel, but on a candlestick; and it giveth light unto all that are in the house.

16 Let your light so shine before men, that they may see your good works, and glorify your Father which is in heaven.

17 Think not that I am come to destroy the law, or the prophets: I am not come to destroy, but to fulfil.

18 For verily I say unto you, Till heaven and earth pass, one jot or one tittle shall in no wise pass from the law, till all be fulfilled.

19 Whosoever therefore shall break one of these least commandments, and shall teach men so, he shall be called the least in the kingdom of heaven: but whosoever shall do and teach them, the same shall be called great in the kingdom of heaven.

20 For I say unto you, That except your righteousness shall exceed the righteousness of the scribes and Pharisees, ye shall in no case enter into the kingdom of heaven.

NLT Matthew 5:13 "You are the salt of the earth. But what good is salt if it has lost its flavor? Can you make it salty again? It will be thrown out and trampled underfoot as worthless.

14 "You are the light of the world—like a city on a hilltop that cannot be hidden.

15 No one lights a lamp and then puts it under a basket. Instead, a lamp is placed on a stand, where it gives light to everyone in the house.

16 In the same way, let your good deeds shine out for all to see, so that everyone will praise your heavenly Father.

17 "Don't misunderstand why I have come. I did not come to abolish the law of Moses or the writings of the prophets. No, I came to accomplish their purpose.

18 I tell you the truth, until heaven and earth disappear, not even the smallest detail of God's law will disappear until its purpose is achieved.

19 So if you ignore the least commandment and teach others to do the same, you will be called the least in the Kingdom of Heaven. But anyone who obeys God's laws and teaches them will be called great in the Kingdom of Heaven.

20 "But I warn you—unless your righteousness is better than the righteousness of the teachers of religious law and the Pharisees, you will never enter the Kingdom of Heaven!

The People, Places, and Times

Salt and Light. Before refrigeration, salt was used to preserve food. Meat would not keep for long unless it was salted. It meant the difference between life and death. Similarly, the followers of Christ should preserve the best traditions and morality of their societies. They are the difference between life and death in their societies. The addition of salt to food turns a bland meal into a delicious feast. Christians demonstrate to the world how a relationship with Christ adds zest to our mundane lives. It encourages unbelievers to "taste and see that the LORD is good" (from Psalm 34:8).

Christ was the original light to the world. When healing the blind man, Jesus explained to His disciples, "As long as I am in the world, I am the light of the world" (John 9:5). When He went back to heaven, He passed the obligation to illuminate to His disciples: "Ye are the light of the world." As light, we show the way. Jesus showed the way to the kingdom of heaven; we show the way to Jesus.

How should we react to the call of Jesus to be light as He was light in the world?

Background

This passage is found near the beginning of Christ's well-known Sermon on the Mount (Matthew 5-7), the first of five sermons and teachings recorded in Matthew. This beloved sermon begins with the Beatitudes, a list of statements with each beginning "Blessed are," and describing the well-being and character-istics of one who is actively following God. Christ teaches His followers that there are certain blessings—a state of supernatural bliss and happiness—that can be expected in those who choose to live with a kingdom mindset.

He then continues this sermon by quoting from certain well-known portions of the Law, further elaborating on their meanings and expressions, focusing on the kingdom of God. As Christ preaches, He often addresses the "hypocrites," emphasizing the importance of being more concerned with the attitudes of their hearts, than their actions.

These "hypocrites" would be familiar to the disciples. They were the religious experts of the day, such as the Pharisees and scribes. These men were highly respected as the protectors of the Law of Moses—the first five books of the Bible—also known as the Torah, and well-versed in the books of the prophets. As the religious and moral authorities, they were the teachers who created additional rules to follow in order to look righteous. Jesus would later

call these rules "burdens" in His seven woes to the Pharisees and scribes (Matthew 23). Throughout the Gospels, these experts would constantly challenge His authority and attempt to discourage His followers.

In what ways are some modern-day believers like the Pharisees?

At-A-Glance

1. We Are Salt and Light (Matthew 5:13–16)
2. Christ Fulfilling the Law (vv. 17–20)

In Depth

1. Christians Are Salt and Light (Matthew 5:13–16)

After addressing the personal blessings given to followers of God, Christ then tells them how they are to impact the world around them. He uses two familiar examples, salt and light. There has been some debate about Jesus' intention in using salt because of its various uses during Christ's time. It was a preservative, an agent added to fertilizer, a disinfectant, and a seasoning. At any rate, salt was accessible, valuable, and useful. Christ seems to point toward its use as seasoning. Real salt does not lose its saltiness. And if it does, it no longer serves any of its purposes, be it flavoring, disinfecting, or preserving. It is useless.

Jerusalem was considered by Jews to be the light of the world (they also called God and the Law this). Therefore, the city Jesus referenced may be Jerusalem, or simply any elevated city whose light is visible to the surrounding valley. People could know where they were by simply locating the city on the hill. Ancient Jewish homes had few windows and their oil lamps provided little light. In order to get the best coverage, lamps had to be elevated. Going through the effort of positioning the light properly, then covering it with a basket, would have been futile. Light needs to be seen in order to dispel darkness. In both illustrations, Jesus exhorts His followers to be useful, visible and impactful. They should do good works and serve the purpose for which they are on earth—to bring glory to God.

How can you be "salt and light" in your world so that people in your circle know whose you are and give God glory?

2. Christ Fulfilling the Law (vv. 17–20)

The Pharisees accused Jesus of seeking to nullify the Law. He was not opposing the Law, but rejecting their misinterpretation and expression of it, through man-made traditions. Jesus came to fulfill the Law—to complete it. His moral demands were not less than Moses'. He was the only one who could perfectly obey the Law. He fulfills the predictions. He is the Messiah that the prophets were looking for. He is perfect. As such, He is the only one who would completely satisfy the sacrificial system so that all could meet the requirements of the Law and be righteous in God's eyes (as opposed to people's eyes) by faith in Him. Jewish teachers taught that disobeying one law was equivalent to disobeying them all. The smallest infraction was problematic. Jesus reminds them this is true of the Law. The smallest letter in the Greek alphabet is the *iota*, in Hebrew it is *yod* (about the size of an apostrophe). Changing the smallest of these letters could change a meaning. God is a stickler for details, and not one thing would "pass away" until everything that He wants to accomplish is fulfilled. To further emphasize God's requirements, Jesus points to the Pharisees. Even their righteousness wasn't enough to enter the kingdom of God. This would have been unsettling to hear, because to common Jews the Pharisees were the epitome of righteousness. But Jesus wanted His followers to realize that God was far more concerned about their hearts and true righteousness than their ability to follow rules.

Is it easier to follow man-made rules rather than to submit one's heart to God? How?

Search the Scriptures

1. Jesus would continue to be a threat to the Jewish leaders. Read Matthew 7:28–29. After His Sermon on the Mount, what was said about Him? Why would this cause problems?

2. Jesus states His case against the Pharisees in Matthew 23. Read Matthew 23:1–7. What is His primary issue, as it influences all of the others?

Discuss the Meaning

1. In what ways can your presence in your family, church, and community make it better as you are salt and light there?

2. What effect does the declaration that Jesus came to fulfill the Law and not abolish it have on the way we should act as His followers?

Liberating Lesson

"This little light of mine, I'm going to let it shine..." This familiar childhood song has been hijacked in modern society, even in the church. We have forgotten the purpose of the light. Everyone wants to "shine"—to get the credit we deserve, accolades we've earned, and be acknowledged for our "righteousness," while expecting others to fall in line. Like the Pharisees, we often want our own glory. It is normal, even understandable. But wrong. We are expected to shine, and to do good things, but in doing so, we must remember that it's not about us. The purpose is "so that they (the world) may see your good works and give glory to your Father who is in heaven." A lamp shines not for the sake of itself, but the sake of the one who placed it (God) and those around it (the world). How can we be like lights that shine in our communities but point to God and not ourselves? How can we be like salt that flavors and preserves our communities for God's glory?

Application for Activation

"Therefore, since we are surrounded by such a huge crowd of witnesses to the life of faith, let us strip off every weight that slows us down, especially the sin that so easily trips us up. And let us run with endurance the race God has set before us... (Hebrews 12:1, NLT). When we think about being seen, we think about people in our circles. Not God. Not the "cloud of witnesses" who left a legacy of faith for us. Like Pharisees, we often get entangled trying to impress or please an earthly crowd. How would it look for you to "lay aside every weight" in order to run well in your relationship with God? What sin are you clinging to that needs to be released?

Follow the Spirit

What God wants me to do:

_____

_____

_____

_____

Remember Your Thoughts

Special insights I have learned:

_____

_____

_____

_____

More Light on the Text
Matthew 5:13–20

13 Ye are the salt of the earth: but if the salt have lost his savour, wherewith shall it be salted? it is thenceforth good for nothing, but to be cast out, and to be trodden under foot of men.

Verses 13–16 are still being addressed directly to Christ's followers. This is evident from the second person plural pronoun, which was first used in the previous verses (v. 11). Indeed, the subject "ye" in both verses 13 and 14 (Gk. *humeis*, **hoo-MACE**) is emphatic and can be translated "you yourselves." The emphasis demonstrates the importance of the subject and the specificity of the sayings to the disciples. Here, Jesus uses two metaphors, salt and light, to describe the disciples' calling and their responsibilities to the world. Salt and light are two common but very important and useful substances used by humankind in all generations. In what sense does Matthew use "salt" here? There are a number of ways salt was—and is—used as a preservative, as a purifying agent (2 Kings 2:20–21), and as a seasoning for food (Job 6:6). In the ancient Israelite religion, it was used especially for sacrifices (Leviticus 2:13; Ezra 6:9; Ezekiel 43:24). It is not clear in what sense "salt" is being used in this verse.

However, we know that salt plays very important roles in our daily lives, and Jesus expects His disciples to fulfill similar roles in the world. If those roles are not fulfilled, the disciples are like salt that has "lost his savour," the taste or saltiness, and is therefore worthless. The question "wherewith shall it be salted?" is rhetorical with an obvious answer: nothing! Therefore, Jesus says, it will be thrown out "to be trodden under foot of men." The phrase "to be cast out, and to be trodden under foot of men" speaks of judgment for those who do not fulfill their calling (cf. 8:12, 22:13, 25:30), whose lives fail to make a positive Christian impact in the world.

14 Ye are the light of the world. A city that is set on an hill cannot be hid. 15 Neither do men light a candle, and put it under a bushel, but on a candlestick; and it giveth light unto all that are in the house.

The second metaphor used to describe the disciples is "light." They are the "light of the world," Jesus says. He begins by emphasizing the nature and function of light, which is primarily to illumine large areas and make things visible. Lights are usually visible, and light helps people see where they are going. Jesus qualifies the analogy of light with, "A city that is set on an hill cannot be hid." The idea here is probably taken from the city of Jerusalem, which is built on a hill and can be seen from afar, especially at night when the lights from the oil lamps glow. It is also believed that many ancient cities were built with limestone, which made them gleam in the sun and therefore difficult to conceal.

Continuing with this theme, Jesus says in effect that for lamps to be useful, they must be on lampstands so that they can illumine large areas, rather than "under a bushel." A bushel refers to a basket or bowl used for measuring out a bushel of produce (e.g., wheat). People would normally light their candles and put them on lampstands so that they might give light to the whole house, not cover them with a bowl. If the flame is covered, it will die and the people will be in the dark. Therefore, the disciples have the same function as light into the world. Light is a common symbol in the Bible: The Jews saw themselves as the light of the world (Romans 2:19), and the true light is the suffering Servant (Isaiah 42:6; 49:6), who ultimately was Christ (Matthew 4:16; John 8:12; 1 John 1:7).

16 Let your light so shine before men, that they may see your good works, and glorify your Father which is in heaven.

Jesus then spells out the obvious as He drives home His point and the meaning of the metaphor. The disciples as the light of the world must show forth their "light" as it were by letting it shine. They would do this through good works, by living out their lives as set forth in verses 3–10. Although they would face all types of persecutions (vv. 10–12), that should not make them hide their light, which was for others to see so that they might give glory to their Father in heaven. This is the main objective and purpose of discipleship (1 Peter 2:12, 4:11; cf. 2 Corinthians 4:6) as exemplified by Christ Himself (John 17:4; cf. 13:31, 14:13).

17 Think not that I am come to destroy the law, or the prophets: I am not come to destroy, but to fulfil. 18 For verily I say unto you, Till heaven and earth pass, one jot or one tittle shall in no wise pass from the law, till all be fulfilled.

"The law and the prophets" is a short-hand expression for what we know as the Old Testament. Jesus prepares His listeners for what He is about to say by explaining that His teaching does not destroy, but rather fulfills the Old Testament. The Greek word translated "destroy" is *kataluo* (**kah-tah-LOO-oh**). In other contexts, it means "dissolve, disunite, subvert, demolish." Here it means "do away with, annul, make invalid." To "fulfill" (Gk. *pleroo*, **play-ROH-oh**) the law and prophets, then, would be to uphold the laws of the Old Testament, and to bring to fulfillment their Messianic and kingdom of God prophecies. The Law and the prophets are the Word of God, and God has made it clear that His Word will never fail (Isaiah 40:8; 55:10–11). Jesus is in full agreement with the Scriptures and goes to the extent of saying that not even a "jot" or "tittle" will pass away. The Greek word translated "jot" is *iota* (**ee-OH-tah**), the name of the smallest letter of the Greek alphabet. The Greek word translated "tittle" is *keraia* (**keh-RYE-ah**), and it refers to a projection or hook of a letter. Jesus was saying that not even the smallest letter— or even a small part of a letter—will ever be removed from God's Law (see also Luke 16:17; 21:33). In fact, God's Word will endure until heaven and earth pass away—an event that Jesus Himself asserts is a certainty (Matthew 24:35), but not until everything that is written comes to pass.

19 Whosoever therefore shall break one of these least commandments, and shall teach men so, he shall be called the least in the kingdom of heaven: but whosoever shall do and teach them, the same shall be called great in the kingdom of heaven.

Since Jesus' kingdom does not destroy the Old Testament Law, neither should we. The Greek word translated "break" is *luo* (**LOO-oh**) and can also mean loosen or untie. Violations of God's Law are an attack on that Law; they attempt to weaken and destroy it. Jesus uses a play on the word "least" to make a memorable point: If you break the least commandment, you will be the least. The Greek word translated "least" is *elachistos* (**eh-LA-kheese-toce**) and refers to the thing that is smallest in importance. The rabbis of Jesus' time classified the laws of the Old Testament according to their importance. Jesus uses their terminology to make a point that contradicts their practice: It is a grave error to minimize any of God's commandments. The consequence for living in deliberate violation of God's Law is being called "least" in the kingdom of heaven. What God wants is not a display of religious behavior that impresses others, but our wholehearted submission to His will. It is impossible to rise to greatness in God's eyes without a firm commitment to total obedience.

20 For I say unto you, That except your righteousness shall exceed the righteousness of the scribes and Pharisees, ye shall in no case enter into the kingdom of heaven.

The scribes and Pharisees were some of the spiritual elite in Jesus' day. The scribes were the expert teachers and interpreters of the Law. The Pharisees were a Jewish religious party whose name comes from the Aramaic word *pherisha'* (**feh-REE-shaw**), meaning "separated." Among other things, they attempted to distinguish themselves through fastidious obedience to the Law (cf. Philippians 3:4–6). However, they also added human traditions to the laws of God and modified God's laws through their interpretations and traditions. Because their lives were so dominated by conformity to their religious rules, the Jewish people highly regarded them for their outward appearance of righteousness.

Jesus' statement that our righteousness must exceed that of the Pharisees would have shocked His audience. Most of His hearers would have assumed that if anyone could make it to heaven on the basis of their good works, it would be the Pharisees. Doubtless they would have thought, "If even the Pharisees fail to be good enough, is there any hope for the rest of us?" But Jesus' point is not that we must do more than the Pharisees, but that their righteousness is not true righteousness. True righteousness would be gained only through faith in Jesus, and it is through Him that we enter and live in the kingdom of God.

Sources:

Global Study Bible, English Standard Version. Wheaton, IL: Crossway Publishers, 2012. 1326-1327.

Keener, Craig S. *The IVP Bible Background Commentary: New Testament*. Downers Grove, IL: Intervarsity Press, 1993. 53-58.

Radmacher, Earl D., ed. *Nelson Study Bible*, New King James Version. Nashville, TN: Thomas Nelson Publishers, 1997. 1582-1584.

Unger, Merrill F. *The New Unger's Bible Dictionary*. Chicago, IL: Moody Press, 1988. 997-998,1141-1143.

Walvoord, John F., and Roy B. Zuck, eds. *The Bible Knowledge Commentary: New Testament*. USA: Victor Books, SP Publications, Inc., 1983. 28-30.

Daily Bible Readings

MONDAY
Living Wisely
(Colossians 4:1–6)

TUESDAY
A Light to the Nations
(Isaiah 42:1–9)

WEDNESDAY
Christ's Sacrifice for All
(Hebrews 10:1–10)

THURSDAY
Living Humbly
(Matthew 23:1–12)

FRIDAY
Applying the Law in New
Ways
(Luke 6:1–11)

SATURDAY
Deliverance from the Law
(Romans 7:24–8:4)

SUNDAY
Interplay of Salt, Light,
and Righteousness
(Matthew 5:13–20)

Notes

_____

_____

_____

_____

_____

_____

_____

_____

_____

_____

_____

Teaching Tips

Words You Should Know

A. Adversary *antidikos* (Gk.)—Refers to an opponent in a lawsuit, enemy.

B. Fornication *porneia* (Gk.)—Refers to any type of sexual sin.

Teacher Preparation

Unifying Principle—Pure Hearts and Actions. Love transforms how we relate to one another. In what form does this transformation come? Jesus teaches us how to be a reflection of His light through controlling our anger, reconciling with others, dealing immediately with sin, and being faithful.

A. Read the Bible Background and Devotional Readings.

B. Pray for your students and lesson clarity.

C. Read the lesson Scripture in multiple translations.

D. Option: As a class discuss the difference between behavior motivated by appearing righteous and that which arises from inner convictions. What is the appeal of superficial or hypocritical religiosity? What steps can participants take to move beyond such behavior and serve God out of the inner purity that Jesus commands?

O—Open the Lesson

A. Begin the class with prayer.

B. Have the students read the Aim for Change.

C. Have the students read the In Focus story.

D. Ask students how events named in the story can weigh on their hearts and how they can view these events from a theological perspective.

P—Present the Scriptures

A. Read the Focal Verses and discuss the Background and The People, Places, and Times sections.

B. Have the class share what Scriptures stand out for them and why, with particular emphasis on today's context.

E—Explore the Meaning

A. Use In Depth or More Light on the Text to help provide more in-depth discussion of the lesson text.

B. Discuss the Liberating Lesson and Application for Activation sections.

N—Next Steps for Application

A. Summarize the impact of having pure hearts has on our actions.

B. End class with a commitment to pray for our enemies and those whom society considers enemies.

Worship Guide

For the Superintendent or Teacher
Theme: Jesus Teaches Us to Love
One Another
Song: "Blessed Are the Pure In Heart"
Devotional Reading: Genesis 2:18–24

Jesus Teaches Us to Love One Another

Bible Background • MATTHEW 5:21–32
Printed Text • MATTHEW 5:21–32 | Devotional Reading • GENESIS 2:18–24

Aim for Change

By the end of the lesson, we will: CONTRAST outward conformity of obedience to God with inner purity; REPENT of the times we have obeyed God superficially; and RESPOND to the call of Jesus to take practical steps to live righteously.

In Focus

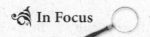

"Another African American teenager has been shot by a police officer on Chicago's South Side," the headline read on the TV screen.

"Man! When is this going to stop? Seems like every time we turn on the news, another brother is dead in the streets," said Eli. "Seriously, it's getting crazy out here." Michael looked up to see the headline and then returned to cutting Eli's hair.

"I'm telling you, I hear these news reports, and I get so angry. Then I got to go to class and sit there knowing some of those people think no more of me than that cop did of that teenager, or if I'm going to 'fit someone's description.' It's crazy!"

"So what are you doing about it?" Michael asked Eli.

"What do you mean? I'm just trying to live."

"Yeah, but do you ever go to the Black Student Union meetings or United Student Caucus? They're DOING something," Michael said. "Even better, how many police officers do you know?" Eli looked confused.

"Listen," Michael continued, "I'm not saying it's going to solve everything, but if you just get angry, it will eat you up until you do something crazy. Believe me, God is watching all of this. He knows what He's doing. We just gotta make sure we're doing what we can in the meantime."

There are situations where anger seems like the only way to react. Is there an experience where you had to take a minute to decide how you were going to respond to a situation that made you angry?

Keep in Mind

"Therefore if thou bring thy gift to the altar, and there rememberest that thy brother hath ought against thee; Leave there thy gift before the altar, and go thy way; first be reconciled to thy brother, and then come and offer thy gift" (Matthew 5:23-24, KJV).

"So if you are presenting a sacrifice at the altar in the Temple and you suddenly remember that someone has something against you, leave your sacrifice there at the altar. Go and be reconciled to that person. Then come and offer your sacrifice to God" (Matthew 5:23-24, NLT).

Focal Verses

KJV **Matthew 5:21** Ye have heard that it was said of them of old time, Thou shalt not kill; and whosoever shall kill shall be in danger of the judgment:

22 But I say unto you, That whosoever is angry with his brother without a cause shall be in danger of the judgment: and whosoever shall say to his brother, Raca, shall be in danger of the council: but whosoever shall say, Thou fool, shall be in danger of hell fire.

23 Therefore if thou bring thy gift to the altar, and there rememberest that thy brother hath ought against thee;

24 Leave there thy gift before the altar, and go thy way; first be reconciled to thy brother, and then come and offer thy gift.

25 Agree with thine adversary quickly, whiles thou art in the way with him; lest at any time the adversary deliver thee to the judge, and the judge deliver thee to the officer, and thou be cast into prison.

26 Verily I say unto thee, Thou shalt by no means come out thence, till thou hast paid the uttermost farthing.

27 Ye have heard that it was said by them of old time, Thou shalt not commit adultery:

28 But I say unto you, That whosoever looketh on a woman to lust after her hath committed adultery with her already in his heart.

29 And if thy right eye offend thee, pluck it out, and cast it from thee: for it is profitable for thee that one of thy members should perish, and not that thy whole body should be cast into hell.

30 And if thy right hand offend thee, cut it off, and cast it from thee: for it is profitable for thee that one of thy members should perish, and not that thy whole body should be cast into hell.

NLT **Matthew 5:21** "You have heard that our ancestors were told, 'You must not murder. If you commit murder, you are subject to judgment.'"

22 But I say, if you are even angry with someone, you are subject to judgment! If you call someone an idiot, you are in danger of being brought before the court. And if you curse someone, you are in danger of the fires of hell.

23 "So if you are presenting a sacrifice at the altar in the Temple and you suddenly remember that someone has something against you,

24 leave your sacrifice there at the altar. Go and be reconciled to that person. Then come and offer your sacrifice to God.

25 "When you are on the way to court with your adversary, settle your differences quickly. Otherwise, your accuser may hand you over to the judge, who will hand you over to an officer, and you will be thrown into prison.

26 And if that happens, you surely won't be free again until you have paid the last penny.

27 "You have heard the commandment that says, 'You must not commit adultery.'

28 But I say, anyone who even looks at a woman with lust has already committed adultery with her in his heart.

29 So if your eye—even your good eye causes you to lust, gouge it out and throw it away. It is better for you to lose one part of your body than for your whole body to be thrown into hell.

30 And if your hand—even your stronger hand causes you to sin, cut it off and throw it away. It is better for you to lose one part of your body than for your whole body to be thrown into hell.

31 "You have heard the law that says, 'A man can divorce his wife by merely giving her a written notice of divorce.'

31 It hath been said, Whosoever shall put away his wife, let him give her a writing of divorcement:

32 But I say unto you, That whosoever shall put away his wife, saving for the cause of fornication, causeth her to commit adultery: and whosoever shall marry her that is divorced committeth adultery.

32 But I say that a man who divorces his wife, unless she has been unfaithful, causes her to commit adultery. And anyone who marries a divorced woman also commits adultery.

The People, Places, and Times

Lust. In the midst of Jesus' Sermon on the Mount, Jesus goes through most of the Ten Commandments to clarify and intensify the interpretation in contrast to the misinterpretations of the Pharisees. The Pharisees had done the utmost to make sure people caught in adultery would be punished; Jesus asserts that to lust, passionately desire, or covet another woman was just like the sin of adultery for the married man. The Old Testament commandments naturally set up an order to not take what was not allotted to us by God, whether by stealing, adultery, or jealousy. The command to not lust is a reminder to not covet in our minds or hearts what God has not given in the covenant of marriage.

Background

The Sermon on the Mount is an extension of the preaching with which Jesus launched His ministry, "Repent: for the kingdom of heaven is at hand" (from Matthew 4:17). However, the teaching does not present the way to salvation; instead, it outlines the way of righteous living and contrasts it with the teachings of the scribes and Pharisees.

The sermon begins with an explanation of eight moral characteristics that lead to true happiness and blessings and should be true of all believers. These characteristics both demand and describe. They demand proper attitudes of believers, and they describe the blessings from the right attitudes. The demands and descriptions are given in an if/then relationship. If we are poor in spirit, then ours is the kingdom of heaven; if we mourn, then we shall be comforted; if we are meek, then we shall inherit the earth; if we hunger and thirst for righteousness, then we shall be filled; if we are merciful, then we shall obtain mercy; if we are peacemakers, then we shall be called the children of God; and if we rejoice during times of persecution, then great is our reward in heaven. After His opening, Jesus launches right into the heart of His teaching. His audience knew that righteous living was required to enter God's kingdom (Psalm 24:3–6). However, they had been taught that the religious practices of the Pharisees were sufficient. Jesus challenged that belief with the statement, "For I say unto you, That except your righteousness shall exceed the righteousness of the scribes and Pharisees, ye shall in no case enter into the kingdom of heaven" (Matthew 5:20). Those who would be followers of Christ would not just be called to a different standard of living, but a higher standard of living.

How does Jesus call for His followers to hold even higher standards than the Law of the Old Testament?

At-A-Glance

1. Abandon Unrighteous Anger
   (Matthew 5:21–22)
2. Consequence of Unrighteous Anger
   (vv. 23-26)
3. Avoid Lustful Looks (vv. 27-29)
4. Declarations on Divorce (vv. 31-32)

In Depth

1. Abandon Unrighteous Anger (Matthew 5:21–22)

Jesus calls on true believers to demonstrate a righteousness that surpasses the righteousness of the Pharisees. The phrases "you have heard" and "it has been said" do not refer to the teachings of Moses and the prophets but rather to the imbalanced interpretations of the scribes and Pharisees. The phrase "But I say" reveals Jesus' superiority to all past interpreters. The Old Testament prophets spoke for the Lord and began their pronouncements with the phrase "Thus saith the LORD" (e.g., 2 Samuel 7:5; Isaiah 56:1). Jesus, on the other hand, did not simply quote God as instructed, He spoke with the authority of God. In His discussion of the futile religious system of the Pharisees, Jesus gives six examples of how the Pharisees failed to fulfill the Law and how believers are to succeed in fulfilling it. In the first example, Jesus quotes the sixth commandment: "Thou shalt not kill" (Mathew 5:21; Deuteronomy 5:17). The Law said that any person who took the life of another would forfeit their life in return (Leviticus 24:17) and then be subject to judgment (Matthew 5:21). To the scribes and Pharisees, the act of killing meant the actual taking of a life. But Jesus says that anything leading to murder is wrong. Not only must the act of murder be avoided but the attitudes and emotions that lead to it are condemned. The physical act of murder is simply the last step in the process that began with envy, greed, anger, hatred, or fear in our hearts and minds.

How do you respond when someone makes you angry or offends you?

2. Consequence of Unrighteous Anger (vv. 23–26)

Verses 23–25 give an illustration to amplify Jesus' message on letting go of anger and not letting it turn into sin that leads to death. He instructs that before anyone gives an offering to God to take care of any ongoing conflict with their neighbor. Jesus is making radical statements with a practical point via a common teaching method used by rabbis to make points and draw attention to the force of God's commands. God desires that we be in right relationship with our neighbor before we even enter into His Temple to worship. God would rather we forgive offenses and release anger or seek forgiveness for wrongdoing before we end up in court, jail, hurt, or dead because of a conflict (Leviticus 19:17–18). We would be wise to apply this to ourselves today in understanding that we cannot worship and serve God with a pure heart at church gatherings while we hold grudges, offense, anger, and bitterness outside church meetings. Our worship is tainted by our festering conflict with our neighbor. Jesus argues that if we let it continue until we are in a court battle, we deserve to pay every penalty if we lose the case.

Do you have an experience of going through the religious motions when you knew you needed a change in your heart toward God or another person? Why did you go through the motions?

3. Avoid Lustful Looks (vv. 27-29)

The second issue Jesus confronts is again taken from the Ten Commandments: "Thou shalt not commit adultery" (Matthew 5:27; cf.

572

Deuteronomy 5:18). He clarifies the meaning by saying, "But I say unto you, that whosoever looketh on a woman to lust after her hath committed adultery with her already in his heart" (Matthew 5:28). The word adultery refers to a marriage breaking, the breaking of one's covenant vows. Before Jesus explained the true meaning of the law, people believed they could remain true to their spouses by refraining from the physical act while entertaining tantalizing fantasies of illicit relationships. The "look" that Christ condemns here is not the notice of a person's attractiveness or the sudden thought that the enemy might bring to a person's mind. This lustful look is the approval of an immoral thought or desire. It is the contemplated desire for sexual pleasure that leads to the physical act of adultery. Therefore, the sin actually begins with the thought and ends with the act.

Why is entertaining lustful thoughts a problem for followers of Jesus Christ?

4. Declarations on Divorce (vv. 31–32)

After explaining how a person breaks the marriage vow through adultery, Jesus turns His attention to the subject of divorce. All any husband (not wife) had to do was write a bill of divorcement charging the wife with uncleanness (see Deuteronomy 24:1). Jesus argues that any man who divorces his wife for any cause except immorality "causeth her to commit adultery: and whosoever shall marry her that is divorced committeth adultery" (Matthew 5:32). Jesus squarely places the onus for the adultery on the divorcing husband. He "causes" her to commit adultery. By divorcing her, the husband is forcing her to break the marriage vow. The point Jesus makes gets to the hearts of the hearers: Marriage is a life and death covenant that God takes seriously, and divorce is just as serious a teaching that Jesus expands on later in the Gospel (Matthew 19:1–12). If the people were getting divorced to be with

someone else, it was just as bad as committing adultery in the first place; our hearts cannot lust for someone else and then use a technicality in the Law to justify our sin. Fortunately God gives grace and can heal those who have experienced the cutting pain of adultery and divorce. Yet Scripture presents the institution of marriage as the spiritual fusion of two people (male and female) into one. Jesus teaches that fusion should be permanent (Matthew 19:6).

How can we respond to Jesus' teachings about divorce with such high divorce rates in our society?

Search the Scriptures

1. What emotion did Jesus compare to murder (Matthew 5:22)?

2. How is it possible to commit adultery without actually engaging in illicit sex (v. 28)?

Discuss the Meaning

1. In moments of frustration, have you learned to channel your energy into something that is more positive? What are some ways?

2. What is a time when you have had to "lay down" an issue?

Liberating Lesson

Jesus challenges us to look at the motives behind our actions and thoughts. Having the wrong heart toward God and others gives birth to sin. We often are hurt and surprised when it gets to the point of obvious individual and collective sin such as murder or systemic racism. But what Jesus challenges us to do is deal with our sinful thoughts and feelings toward our neighbors before we see the sinful action. Much of the murder, adultery, lying, stealing, cheating and so on we see around us can be traced back to lack of love and respect for God's ways, and lack of love and value for ourselves and for other people. What are some motives behind sins you see in your community? How are they not Christ-like? How can we work to serve as examples of living according to Jesus' teachings?

Application for Activation

Take time this week to evaluate where you may struggle with sin. Ask yourself, "Am I spending too much energy trying to do just enough to get by in my relationship with God, or am I really letting God deal with my heart in the matter?" Is there someone you are holding a grudge against? Is there someone you need to ask forgiveness? Are you acting in hurtful ways toward other people and still acting as though you can worship God guilt-free? Pray about how to approach those ongoing conflicts and listen to God. Let God show you where you are cultivating sin in your heart so it can be dealt with before it becomes actions that hurt you and other people. Pray for God to help you have a clean heart so you can worship in spirit and in truth with clean hands.

Follow the Spirit

What God wants me to do:

_____

_____

_____

_____

Remember Your Thoughts

Special insights I have learned:

_____

_____

_____

More Light on the Text

Matthew 5:21–32

21 Ye have heard that it was said by them of old time, Thou shalt not kill; and whosoever shall kill shall be in danger of the judgment: 22 But I say unto you, That whosoever is angry with his brother without a cause shall be in danger of the judgment: and whosoever shall say to his brother, Raca, shall be in danger of the council: but whosoever shall say, Thou fool, shall be in danger of hell fire.

Although the Law was to remain in force, Jesus called His disciples to move from external obedience to internal submission to the Law written in their hearts. He begins by explaining some of the basic tenets of the Law. The first principle He explains is the law against murder (Exodus 20:13; Deuteronomy 5:17). The Lord uses the phrase "Ye have heard" because most of the common people of His time knew the Law only by its public reading and the exposition of the scribes that accompanied the readings. To them the scribes' interpretation carried the same authority as Scripture itself. The phrase "but I say" speaks with greater authority than other Jewish teachers and scribes claimed because they would generally cite another authority.

Jesus teaches that the external act of murder results from an inner emotional state and describes three degrees of offense and respectively three different degrees of punishment. Silent rage, described as unjustified anger, was punishable by judgment. The Law of Moses provided for the appointment of judges (Deuteronomy 16:18). This tribunal was known as the judgment, and they were elders who determined the case of the manslayer (see Joshua 20:2–5). In determining the manslayer's case the elders might confine the man in one of the cities of refuge, or order him stoned to death. The second degree was contemptuous speech, such as calling someone *Raca* (Gk.

rah-KAH). This word is an expression of contempt of uncertain derivation thought to mean "empty-headed" or heretic. This internal act of murder was punishable by a trial before the Sanhedrin, or council. The Sanhedrin was the chief court of the Jews, and common people held it in great awe. The third degree was bitter reproach as evidenced by calling someone a "fool." To the Jews a fool is not a person who is mentally deficient but one who is morally perverse. David described the fool as a corrupt person who does abominable deeds and no good works. Worst of all, He denies God in his heart (Psalm 14:1).

The third punishment goes beyond human jurisdiction. It is the final punishment—being cast into hell. *Gehenna* (*geʼenna*, **GEH-en-nah**), the Greek word translated "hell," is derived from the name Hinnom—a deep, narrow valley, lying southeast of Jerusalem. The Greek word *Gehenna*, which we translate as hell, is first mentioned in Joshua 15:18 (in the Septuagint). It is the place where idolatrous people worshiped the god Molech by offering human sacrifices in the fires of Molech. Two Jewish kings burned their children in the valley as sacrifices (Ahaz, 2 Chronicles 28:3; and Manassah, 33:6). This horrible practice of human sacrifice caused the valley to be associated in the mind of the Jews with sin and suffering and led to the application of its name which, in the Greek form, is the place of final and eternal punishment. Human sacrifice to Molech was entirely destroyed by King Josiah, who polluted the entire valley making it unfit for even heathen worship (2 Kings 23:12–14).

The key to this passage is that while sin has stages, God takes note of it from the time it first begins to evolve in the heart, and a person's soul is put in danger long before his feelings bear their fruit of violence and murder.

23 Therefore if thou bring thy gift to the altar, and there rememberest that thy brother hath ought against thee; 24 Leave there thy gift before the altar, and go thy way; first be reconciled to thy brother, and then come and offer thy gift.

The altar in question here is the Temple altar, and the gift is the offering being brought for sacrifice. This teaching underscores the priority of forgiveness in two ways. First, it warns us against the hypocrisy of pretending to be at peace with God when we are at odds with others. If our faith is genuine, God's forgiveness of us in Christ transforms us and makes us willing to pursue reconciliation with others. Secondly, Jesus is saying forgiveness is so important that we need to pursue reconciliation, even in situations when others—not ourselves—are the angry ones. Note that it is not the worshiper who is harboring unforgiveness; it is a brother. And Jesus doesn't even discuss whether or not the brother's anger is justified. Unforgiveness is so dangerous that we are responsible to make sure we don't tempt our brother to sin by leaving conflicts unresolved. This is not to condone abuse or suggest a relationship with those who pose danger to us. But we must do everything in our power to eradicate the poison of resentment from our lives as well as the lives of others God has called us to be in relationship. Our faithfulness to do so is far more important than even the most solemn act of worship.

25 Agree with thine adversary quickly, whiles thou art in the way with him; lest at any time the adversary deliver thee to the judge, and the judge deliver thee to the officer, and thou be cast into prison. 26 Verily I say unto thee, Thou shalt by no means come out thence, till thou hast paid the uttermost farthing.

Jesus ends His interpretation of the sixth commandment by discussing the urgency and wisdom of forgiveness. The Greek phrase translated "agree with" (*isthi eunoon*, **EES-the ew-no-OHN**) is a two-part verb. One part communicates an imperative command; the other part means "to be peaceable or amenable to." The Greek word translated "adversary" is *antidikos* (**an-TEE-dee-koce**) and refers to an opponent in a lawsuit. Because of the preceding verses, we know that Jesus is not speaking only of legal affairs, but is using a legal situation as an example to make His point. He is talking about our need to reconcile as quickly as possible in a conflict. Just as in the preceding situation with the brother, who is right and who is wrong is irrelevant. The word translated "farthing" is *kodrantes* (Gk. **koh-DRAN-tace**), and it referred to the smallest Roman coin. Unresolved conflict creates situations in which others may seek to get every last penny from us. Failure to reconcile quickly can have dramatic, painful, and even permanent consequences. It is a foolish and unnecessary risk to let a matter wait. The best time to attempt reconciliation will always be right now!

27 Ye have heard that it was said by them of old time, Thou shalt not commit adultery: 28 But I say unto you, That whosoever looketh on a woman to lust after her hath committed adultery with her already in his heart.

Jesus returns to the Ten Commandments for His next teaching. As in the case with murder, Jesus again teaches against the thought that motivates the act. Lust here, in the Greek *epithumesai* (**eh-pee-THOO-meh-sie**), means to desire or long after. Therefore, the look of lust is a leering stare with immoral intent. The seedbed of sin is the heart and the seed bag of the heart is the eye. Those who allow lustful leers to lead them to immoral imaginings and lustful desires are just as guilty before God as if they had committed the act. The teaching

method Jesus is using is called "building a fence" around the Torah or Law, in other words putting rules in place that keep one from even getting close to disobeying God. The declaration is intentionally intense to force the listener to take it seriously and obey the teachings of God. The natural result of disobeying God or committing sin is death, the same way that the natural result of walking off a cliff is to fall. According to the Old Testament, sin ultimately negatively affects everyone in the community, not just the individual (Leviticus 16:15–17; Ezekiel 11:2–12).

31 It hath been said, Whosoever shall put away his wife, let him give her a writing of divorcement: 32 But I say unto you, That whosoever shall put away his wife, saving for the cause of fornication, causeth her to commit adultery: and whosoever shall marry her that is divorced committeth adultery.

In His next teaching Jesus refers to Deuteronomy 24:1. Under Jewish law in the time of the Pharisees adultery only referred to the woman's illicit behavior, not the man's. Jesus' teaching on adultery, where He specifically refers to the man's adultery, proves that He did not share or endorse their view. Because the specific law He is dealing with here refers to the woman, Jesus deals only with the issue of the wife. The law of divorce permitted the husband to put away the wife when he found "some unseemly thing" in her (Deuteronomy 24:1). Jesus explained that the divorced woman is forced into a state of adultery. The mere fact of divorce did not make her an adulteress, but it brought her into a state of disgrace from which she invariably sought to free herself by contracting another marriage. This other marriage, which was due to her humiliating situation, drove her into a state of adultery.

"Fornication"—from the Greek *porneia* (**por-NAY-ah**), from which we derive our

English word pornography—refers to any type of sexual sin. In a marriage, this fornication (extramarital sex) would be considered adultery. Jesus' words here are as strict as in verses 27–28, and continue those verses' focus on adultery. Jesus' exception here for the case of fornication could be interpreted as not to give a justified cause for divorce, but to give the reason for the wife becoming an adulteress. She could have become an adulteress by her own action, or by her husband divorcing her.

Jesus would later explain that this law was given by Moses on account of the hardness of the people's heart; that is, to prevent greater evils (Matthew 19:3–12). In that discussion, Jesus more clearly limits the right of divorce to cases of fornication. It is implied that divorce for marital infidelity breaks the marriage bond, and it is therefore held almost universally that the innocent party to such a divorce can marry again. Of course, the guilty partner could not. No one is allowed by law to reap the benefits of his or her own wrong.

Sources:

Baltes, A.J., ed. Biblespeech.com. http://biblespeech.com (accessed May 29, 2010).

Beers, V. Gilbert. *The Victor Handbook of Bible Knowledge*. Wheaton, IL: Victor Books, 1981. 374–76, 389, 390–91.

Brand, Chad, Charles Draper and Archie England, gen. eds. *Holman Illustrated Bible Dictionary*. Nashville, TN: Holman Bible Publishers, 1998. 596.

Doriani, Daniel M. *Matthew*. Reformed Expository Commentary, Vol. 1. Phillipsburg, NJ: P&R Publishing, 2008. 138–49.

The ESV Study Bible. Wheaton, IL: Crossway Bibles, 2008. 1828–29.

Henry, Matthew. *Concise Commentary on the Whole Bible*. Nashville, TN: Thomas Nelson, n.d. 864–66.

Merriam-Webster Online Dictionary. Merriam-Webster, Inc. http://www.merriam-webster.com (accessed May 8, 2010).

Morris, Leon. *The Gospel According to Matthew*. Grand Rapids, MI: William B. Eerdmans, 1992. 106–17.

Daily Bible Readings

MONDAY
Obey Judicial Rulings at Once
(Deuteronomy 17:8–11)

TUESDAY
Handling Temptations
(Mark 9:42–48)

WEDNESDAY
Living With Neighbors
(Leviticus 19:11–18)

THURSDAY
Living With Believers
(1 Thessalonians 5:12–18)

FRIDAY
The Unbreakable Marital Bond
(Mark 10:2–9)

SATURDAY
Let Yes Be Yes; No, No
(Matthew 5:33–37)

SUNDAY
Commit to Love Each Other
(Matthew 5:21–32)

Notes

Teaching Tips

Words You Should Know

A. Evil *poneros* (Gk.)—In the context of this lesson means mischief, harm, or misdeeds.

B. Perfect *teleios* (Gk.)—Complete, full, or mature.

Teacher Preparation

Unifying Principle—Love Our Enemies. Many people believe retribution is justified when they are mistreated. What is the appropriate response when people are mistreated? Jesus taught His disciples to love their enemies and pray for those who persecuted them.

A. Read the Bible Background and Devotional Readings.

B. Pray for your students and lesson clarity.

C. Read the lesson Scripture in multiple translations.

D. Option: Have groups of students create and present skits that demonstrate loving your enemy.

O—Open the Lesson

A. Begin the class with prayer.

B. Have the students read the Aim for Change.

C. Have the students read the In Focus story.

D. Ask students how events named in the story can weigh on their hearts and how they can view these events from a theological perspective.

P—Present the Scriptures

A. Read the Focal Verses and discuss the Background and The People, Places, and Times sections.

B. Have the class share what Scriptures stand out for them and why, with particular emphasis on today's context.

E—Explore the Meaning

A. Use In Depth or More Light on the Text to help provide more in-depth discussion of the lesson text.

B. Discuss the Liberating Lesson and Application for Activation sections.

N—Next Steps for Application

A. Summarize the value of loving our enemies and seeing them as human.

B. End class with a commitment to pray for those who society deems as "enemies."

Worship Guide

For the Superintendent or Teacher
Theme: Jesus Teaches About Transforming Love
Song: "A Heart That Forgives"
Devotional Reading: Romans 12:9–21

Jesus Teaches About Transforming Love

Bible Background • MATTHEW 5:38–48
Printed Text • MATTHEW 5:38–48 | Devotional Reading • ROMANS 12:9–21

——— Aim for Change ———

By the end of the lesson, we will: IDENTIFY what it means to love one's enemies; CONSIDER how loving our enemies can be a witness of Christ's love to them; and PRAY that God would work through us to show His love to our enemies.

——— 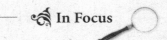 In Focus ———

John did not like his new project manager, Ida. He never agreed with her decisions, wouldn't answer her emails, and often used harsh and belittling language during meetings.

Ida noticed John's behavior, but she was determined to make her project a success. When John did achieve a task, she would write him a personal email expressing her gratitude for his efforts, and tried her best to affirm John. One day, right before a strategy meeting, Ida noticed John on the phone. He was pacing back and forth and looking really worried. When he got off the phone, he angrily walked toward the office.

"Are you OK?" Ida asked.

"Yeah," he replied and sat at the table. All of a sudden he blurted out...

"It's just, my kid keeps messing up in school. They keep telling us if he doesn't get it together, they're going to have to suspend him or even worse expel him!" Ida could see how torn John was feeling. "My wife and I, we just can't afford one of those fancy prep schools, ya know. We're at our wit's end!" For the first time, she understood why John had been so disconnected all the weeks prior. She now felt a sense of empathy toward him.

"Hey John, let's reschedule our prep meeting for tomorrow. Maybe today we'll just go for coffee instead..."

How can seeing our "enemies" as humans help us to demonstrate the love of Jesus Christ to them?

——— Keep in Mind ———

> "Ye have heard that it hath been said, Thou shalt love thy neighbour, and hate thine enemy. But I say unto you, Love your enemies, bless them that curse you, do good to them that hate you, and pray for them which despitefully use you, and persecute you (Matthew 5:43–44, KJV).

"You have heard the law that says, 'Love your neighbor' and hate your enemy. But I say, love your enemies! Pray for those who persecute you!" (Matthew 5:43-44, NLT).

Focal Verses

KJV **Matthew 5:38** Ye have heard that it hath been said, An eye for an eye, and a tooth for a tooth:

39 But I say unto you, That ye resist not evil: but whosoever shall smite thee on thy right cheek, turn to him the other also.

40 And if any man will sue thee at the law, and take away thy coat, let him have thy cloak also.

41 And whosoever shall compel thee to go a mile, go with him twain.

42 Give to him that asketh thee, and from him that would borrow of thee turn not thou away.

43 Ye have heard that it hath been said, Thou shalt love thy neighbour, and hate thine enemy.

44 But I say unto you, Love your enemies, bless them that curse you, do good to them that hate you, and pray for them which despitefully use you, and persecute you;

45 That ye may be the children of your Father which is in heaven: for he maketh his sun to rise on the evil and on the good, and sendeth rain on the just and on the unjust.

46 For if ye love them which love you, what reward have ye? do not even the publicans the same?

47 And if ye salute your brethren only, what do ye more than others? do not even the publicans so?

48 Be ye therefore perfect, even as your Father which is in heaven is perfect.

NLT **Matthew 5:38** "You have heard the law that says the punishment must match the injury: 'An eye for an eye, and a tooth for a tooth.'

39 But I say, do not resist an evil person! If someone slaps you on the right cheek, offer the other cheek also.

40 If you are sued in court and your shirt is taken from you, give your coat, too.

41 If a soldier demands that you carry his gear for a mile, carry it two miles.

42 Give to those who ask, and don't turn away from those who want to borrow.

43 "You have heard the law that says, 'Love your neighbor' and hate your enemy.

44 But I say, love your enemies! Pray for those who persecute you!

45 In that way, you will be acting as true children of your Father in heaven. For he gives his sunlight to both the evil and the good, and he sends rain on the just and the unjust alike.

46 If you love only those who love you, what reward is there for that? Even corrupt tax collectors do that much.

47 If you are kind only to your friends, how are you different from anyone else? Even pagans do that.

48 But you are to be perfect, even as your Father in heaven is perfect.

The People, Places, and Times

Enemy. An enemy in the context of Jesus' Sermon on the Mount was a person with whom strife existed for the hearer. This could include a member of the oppressive class such as a Roman soldier, a direct enemy or rival who lived in the community with the hearer, or someone with whom a person had a dispute or lawsuit. The enemy in this context would not be a spiritual enemy such as a demon, but a person living in the same vicinity who could have adversarial interactions with a person.

Background

The book of Matthew is based on the recording of Matthew the tax collector. His account of the Gospel characterizes Jesus as a teacher to the disciples and many crowds that gathered around to listen. In Matthew 5, Jesus climbs to the top of a mountain and begins to teach the disciples lessons about present and future ethics of society. Ultimately, Jesus' teaching offered a different perspective on how one can live in the Roman Empire's society. Opposed to following the customary value system and way of living, Jesus instructs His listeners to live a different life by following Him. In Matthew 5:38–43, Jesus teaches on two major subjects: retaliation and love for enemies. Jesus takes the time to clarify a law that was misinterpreted by the Pharisees. He uses relatable examples to teach the disciples the difference between the meaning behind God's law on retaliation and the Pharisees misinterpretation of revenge. This lesson on retaliation feeds into a lesson on loving our enemies. Jesus instructs the disciples to love and pray for their enemies. He draws comparisons to show that He knows this is not easy, yet He still instructs them to love their enemies. Each lesson calls us to a higher standard.

Given this Scripture, how do we define love?

ethical codes. Jesus teaches on this important subject because He is aware of the Pharisees' false teachings and misinterpretations. The laws in the Old Testament about retaliation did not permit people to retaliate and seek vengeance against anyone unless a relative was murdered (Leviticus 24:18–21). The purpose of the retaliation laws in the Old Testament were to privilege civil justice, not individual revenge. Jesus teaches the disciples a method of de-escalating conflict through several examples (vv. 39–42). Turning our cheek and giving more than asked, whether materially or through our efforts, are ways by which we can mitigate the desire to retaliate. "Resisting evil" is a key phrase to focus on, because one can easily misinterpret what Jesus is requiring of us. In this context, resist does not mean meet violence with violence. Instead, it means to stand against any wicked deeds that are intended to cause harm or mischief. We stand against evil through love. Jesus aims to alleviate any confusion on the idea of retaliation to prepare His disciples and followers for a higher calling. He calls the disciples and us to a higher standard of love.

Why do you think Christians struggle with retaliation when the Lord promises us "vengeance is mine" (Romans 12:19)?

At-A-Glance

1. A Lesson on Retaliation
(Matthew 5:38–42)
2. A Lesson on Loving Your Enemies
(vv. 43–48)

In Depth

1. A Lesson on Retaliation (Matthew 5:38–42)

Jesus begins this lesson on retaliation by recalling what the disciples may have been taught based on society's official or unofficial

2. A Lesson on Loving Your Enemies (vv. 43–48)

Verse 43 also begins with Jesus recalling another lesson known throughout society regarding hating our enemies. While the first clause ("love thy neighbour") aligns with biblical teachings, the second clause ("hate thine enemy") is not how God intends for us to treat our enemies. The Scripture does not instruct us to hate our enemies anywhere in the biblical text. Beyond simply not hating them, Jesus now instructs His audience not only are they to love their enemies, but also pray for them.

Performing these two actions is one way to show the world we are children of God. Loving an enemy appears hard or impossible to most people, because we compare "loving our enemy" to loving a loved one or friend. When we view love as solely an emotion, we miss its meaning as an action verb. Love is filled with a deep generosity we often overlook. Even God generously treats believers who seek righteousness as kindly as people who do evil by allowing the sun to shine on all of us equally (v. 45). If God can be generous with something as magnificent as sunshine and rainfall, then the least we can do as God's children is treat our enemies with generosity as well. Love in action, especially toward our enemies, demonstrates our choice to rise above society's norms. Jesus points out by asking numerous rhetorical questions that it is easy to love and treat well people who love us back. Again, Jesus calls us to a higher standard of "perfection" or mature and complete relationship with Him. In sum, we love because Jesus loves!

What does God's equal generosity toward the righteous and evildoers make you think about loving your enemies?

Search the Scriptures

1. Why do you think Jesus teaches about retaliation before calling His followers to love their enemies?

2. Considering the rhetorical questions Jesus poses (vv. 46–47), how should His followers' understanding of love differ from tax collectors' and Gentiles' understanding?

Discuss the Meaning

1. How does grace operate when it comes to dealing with those who have used or wronged us?

2. How can we apply this difficult teaching of Jesus to love our enemies and pray for those who persecute us?

Liberating Lesson

On June 17, 2015, one of the most heartbreaking events in our most recent history took place. Dylann Roof walked into a Bible study at Emanuel AME Church in Charleston, South Carolina, and opened fire on innocent parishioners, sadly killing nine victims. Globally, many people mourned and perceived Roof as an enemy. We found it hard to love this man because of his violent action. Many believers showed Roof conditional love due to his disregard for Black life and disrespect for sacred ground. However, family members of the victims chose to accept Jesus' call to live and love at a higher standard. They embodied and exemplified what Jesus meant when stating, "Love your enemies and pray for those who persecute you" (Matthew 5:44). In the courtroom, they showed Roof love by asking God to have mercy on his soul and expressing forgiveness.

While still holding Roof accountable for his deplorable actions, the family members chose to love their enemy. By choosing love and forgiveness, they freed their hearts to experience liberty from hurt and pain. Realistically, liberation and healing is a process, but it starts with loving our enemies.

Application for Activation

Honestly, loving your enemies is not easy. Accepting Jesus' call requires practical steps. Listed below are a few steps toward loving your enemies:

- Identify the people who fit into the category of "enemies."
- Determine and write down how each person has offended you.
- Pray to God to clear any rooted bitterness, hurt, or pain from your heart.
- Forgive them for their wrongdoing. Ask God to open your heart to loving the other person.

- Pray for and love your "enemies" each day.

Jesus' call to act toward our wrongdoers differently is doable! All we need is love.

Follow the Spirit

What God wants me to do:

_____

_____

_____

_____

Remember Your Thoughts

Special insights I have learned:

_____

_____

_____

More Light on the Text

Matthew 5:38–48

38 Ye have heard that it hath been said, An eye for an eye, and a tooth for a tooth: 39 But I say unto you, That ye resist not evil: but whosoever shall smite thee on thy right cheek, turn to him the other also.

Jesus continues the antitheses He has been teaching throughout the latter part of Matthew 5. He deals with the problem of retaliation, restitution, and forgiveness. Although the old principle, "an eye for an eye" and "a tooth for a tooth" (Exodus 21:24; Leviticus 24:19–20) seemed to advocate vengeance and retaliation, it was given not for that purpose. Indeed, it was given explicitly to limit or eliminate excessive retaliation and vengeance. It was given, as is

revealed in the Old Testament, as a judicial guideline for fair punishment for committed offenses—the punishment should be commensurate to the offense committed—neither too heavy nor too light. Rather than retaliation, Jesus says to His disciples to "resist not evil." The word translated "resist" is the Greek verb *anthistemi* (**an-THEESE-tay-me**), which means to withstand, to stand against, or oppose. It has the idea of violence. Contrary to society's norm or standard of meeting violence with violence, Jesus opposes such a norm. "Evil" (Gk. *poneros*, **poe-nay-ROCE**) here does not mean evil as related to the devil, which the Bible says that we must also resist (James 4:7), but instead the idea of harm, malice, mischief, or wicked deeds. Rather than meeting such wicked deeds with other wicked deeds (i.e., meeting violence with violence) or retaliation, we are to meet the evil with generosity and love.

40 And if any man will sue thee at the law, and take away thy coat, let him have thy cloak also. 41 And whosoever shall compel thee to go a mile, go with him twain. 42 Give to him that asketh thee, and from him that would borrow of thee turn not thou away.

Jesus now gives examples of the evils and how we ought to react to them. "Whosoever shall smite thee on thy right cheek," He says, "turn to him the other also. And if any man will sue thee at the law [in court], and take away thy coat, let him have thy cloak [shirt] also. And whosoever shall compel thee to go a mile, go with him twain [two]." The idea here refers to the Roman soldiers who would intimidate the Jews or other subjects by forcing them to give up their garments, administering to them undue punishment, or forcing them to carry their belongings far distances. Earlier in this chapter (vv. 10–16), Jesus called those who suffered persecution without retaliating blessed. Continuing His teaching on generosity, Jesus advocates giving to the person who asks us and not refusing or turning away anyone who would borrow from us. This ideal community was what the Lord wants for His people.

43 Ye have heard that it hath been said, Thou shalt love thy neighbour, and hate thine enemy.

The last set of antitheses deals with love and hatred. The theme of generosity, which is the practical dimension of love, is continued in this segment. The command "Thou shalt love thy neighbour" summarizes the Old Testament law (from Leviticus 19:18), but the antitheses, "and hate thine enemy," is found nowhere in the Scriptures. Rather the Law says that we should love even strangers (Leviticus 19:34). Indeed, the Old Testament commands that we be generous to our enemies (Proverbs 25:21; cf. Romans 12:20). Where then did Jesus get this quote? It must have been a common practice, and as natural during Jesus' time as it is now for people to love their neighbors but hate their enemies. Other reasoning is that since God advocates love for the "neighbor," then hatred for the "enemy" is implicit and perhaps sanctioned in the Leviticus passage, which is of course a misinterpretation and found nowhere in Jewish rabbinical literature. The story of the Good Samaritan in the Gospel of Luke (10:25–37) defines the extent of the category of "neighbor."

44 But I say unto you, Love your enemies, bless them that curse you, do good to them that hate you, and pray for them which despitefully use you, and persecute you; 45 That ye may be the children of your Father which is in heaven: for he maketh his sun to rise on the evil and on the good, and sendeth rain on the just and on the unjust.

Rather than hating your enemies, Jesus advocates that you "love your enemies, bless them that curse you, do good to them that hate you, and pray for those who despitefully use you" (e.g., v. 41), and for those who "persecute you." Again, instead of hating or planning evil against your enemy, which would seem to be a justified thing to do, Jesus gives a new but radical dimension of the law about loving others. Jesus says that we should "do good to them," which means do something that will benefit them. Although they may curse us, we should bless them instead. Not only should we love, bless, and do good to those who hate us, but also to those who "despitefully" use us (i.e., accuse us falsely or treat us abusively) or persecute us; we are also commanded to pray for them.

All of this is related to God's own activity in the world. God's generosity is demonstrated by His making the sun rise on both the evil and the good, and the rain fall on the just as well as the unjust. Thus, we ought to follow our heavenly Father's example. By dealing generously with those who hate us, we demonstrate that we are the children of God. Children will often resemble their father or mother. The resemblance is not always usually in the physical appearance, but rather in character and behavior. In most cases, a person's character can be traced back to their family background. The idea here is not only that the child resembled the parent in appearance, but also that he or she behaves like the parent in character. Thus, Jesus calls on us to resemble our heavenly Father in being loving and generous toward others, even our enemies. Doing this would not only demonstrate our filial relationship with the Father, but also would bring glory to Him (Matthew 5:16).

46 For if ye love them which love you, what reward have ye? do not even the publicans the same? 47 And if ye salute your brethren only, what do ye more than others? do not even the publicans so?

Jesus reemphasizes this teaching with a number of rhetorical questions. These rhetorical questions point to the fact that Christ's disciples, both then and now, should live their lives and love in a way that is superior to the normal way of the world around them. They are to go beyond the usual or normal patterns of doing things. For example, it is normal to love people who love you (v. 46) or to "salute" only those who are related or friendly to you. If we only do the same, Jesus asks, "what reward have ye?" or "what reward do you get?" and "what do ye more than others?" since even the tax collectors do the same. The word "reward" here is the Greek word *misthos* (**meese-THOCE**), which means pay or wages for service done. It can be used in the sense of both bad or good rewards, but is especially used of the rewards that God bestows, or will bestow, upon individuals for good deeds and endeavors. Although the Greek verb *echete* (**eh-KEH-tay**), meaning "you have" or "you get," is present tense, it is no doubt futuristic also (e.g., Matthew 6:19-21; we will see this again in our next lesson). It is also worthy to note the KJV translation for verse 47 uses the word "publicans" or tax collectors for the Greek noun *telones* (**teh-LOW-nace**) while the NLT uses "pagans" for the noun *ethnikos* (**eth-nee-KOCE**). On the one hand, *telones* is usually translated "publican" (i.e., a tax collector).

Tax collectors were usually Jews appointed by their Roman lords to collect taxes. They were therefore despised by other Jews, perceived as traitors, unclean because of their association with Gentiles, and corrupt because of the dubious ways they collected the taxes (cf. Luke 19:1-9). They were generally regarded as sinful and associated with harlots and other public sinners. Yet, they loved those who loved them—their friends, family members, or fellow tax collectors. They would be similar to a corrupt government official today. On the other hand, *ethnikos (***eth-ni-KAHS***)*, from which we get the word "ethnic," refers strictly to non-Jews, hence, Gentiles. In the eyes of Jews, Gentiles were pagans, and were regarded as sinners and despised. Therefore, translations of "pagans" or "Gentiles" are preferred translations of the Greek *ethnikoi* (**eth-ni-KOY**) . If Christ's audience "salutes" (a mark for courtesy and respect) only their own brethren—those who are close to them or, indeed only other fellow disciples—they do not go beyond the status of the pagans, whom they despise. So they need to rise above the status quo if they want to show that they are different and "the children of their Father which is in heaven" (v. 45).

48 Be ye therefore perfect, even as your Father which is in heaven is perfect.

This call for distinction, and indeed the thought of the whole passage, is summarized and capped in this last verse—"be... perfect... as your Father which is in heaven is perfect." It concludes the antitheses (vv. 21–47). The word "perfect" is derived from the Greek *teleios* (**TEH-lay-oce**), which means complete or full grown and mature, with the idea of completeness (cf. Ephesians 4:13; Hebrews 6:1). The idea is borrowed from the Hebrew *tamim* (**taw-MEEM**), meaning without blemish or spot, complete, full, or undefiled, as in the sacrificial animal (Exodus 12:5). It speaks of being upright and committed to the Lord (Genesis 6:9; Deuteronomy 18:13; 2 Samuel 22:26). No place in the Old Testament is God referred to as being "perfect," though we read that He is perfect in knowledge (Job 37:16) and perfect in His ways (Psalm 18:30). Instead, He is called "holy" in many passages of the Scripture. Probably, the thought of this last verse is derived from Leviticus 19:2, where "holy" is used rather than "perfect." Hence, the verse can equally be understood as "Be ye therefore holy, even as your Father which is in heaven is holy."

We recognize as finite humans we could never be perfect, but are always being perfected. We can walk in sanctification being made more perfect by the power of the Holy Spirit. We can be holy by reflecting the character of God in love, in the way we deal with other people, and the way we lead our lives. Our righteousness must surpass that of the scribes and Pharisees (v. 20). We are to show favor and not retaliate against those who mistreat us maliciously (vv. 38–42). We are to love our enemies and pray for our persecutors (vv. 43–45); such love should surpass that of the tax collectors and Gentiles (vv. 46–47). When we do these things, we do not only demonstrate that we are the children of our heavenly Father (v. 45) and inherit "the kingdom of heaven" (v. 20), but we will be regarded as perfect (holy)— just as our heavenly Father is holy—and as imitators of God (v. 48). This ultimate goal is what a true child of God should pursue.

Say It Correctly

Persecute. **PUR**-si-kyoot.

Daily Bible Readings

MONDAY
Restrain Your Anger
(Leviticus 24:16–22)

TUESDAY
Filled With Grace
(Acts 6:8–15)

WEDNESDAY
Transformed Giving and Praying
(Matthew 6:1–6)

THURSDAY
The Lord Honors Patience
(Lamentations 3:25–33)

FRIDAY
Love Your Neighbors
(Romans 13:1–10)

SATURDAY
The Greatest Commandments
(Matthew 22:34–40)

SUNDAY
Practice Love Toward All
(Matthew 5:38–48)

Notes

_____

_____

_____

_____

Teaching Tips

Words You Should Know

A. Judge *krino* (Gk.)—To pronounce an opinion or verdict often with the intent to criticize or condemn.

B. Discernment *diakrisis* (Gk.)—To distinguish, decide, pass sentence on.

Teacher Preparation

Unifying Principle—Discern Instead of Judge. In a complex world, many become confused in trying to cope with the diversity in beliefs and lifestyles. How can one maintain a sense of stability given such complexity? Jesus taught His disciples the spiritual disciplines of resisting the use of judgment and using discernment.

A. Read the Bible Background and Devotional Readings.

B. Pray for your students and lesson clarity.

C. Read the lesson Scripture in multiple translations.

D. Option: Have students compare and contrast discernment and judgment. Discuss why Jesus endorses one and condemns the other. You can use a board, computer, or other visual aid to chart the comparison.

O—Open the Lesson

A. Begin the class with prayer.

B. Have the students read the Aim for Change.

C. Have the students read the In Focus story.

D. Ask students how events named in the story can weigh on their hearts and how they can view these events from a theological perspective.

P—Present the Scriptures

A. Read the Focal Verses and discuss the Background and The People, Places, and Times sections.

B. Have the class share what Scriptures stand out for them and why, with particular emphasis on today's context.

E—Explore the Meaning

A. Use In Depth or More Light on the Text to help provide more in-depth discussion of the lesson text.

B. Discuss the Liberating Lesson and Application for Activation sections.

N—Next Steps for Application

A. Summarize the value of knowing the difference between judgment and discernment.

B. End class with a commitment to pray for good discernment and the humility to not judge others.

Worship Guide

For the Superintendent or Teacher
Theme: Jesus Teaches About Spiritual Discernment
Song: "Perfect People"
Devotional Reading: Galatians 5:16–26

Jesus Teaches About Spiritual Discernment

Bible Background • MATTHEW 7:1–6, 15–23
Printed Text • MATTHEW 7:1–6, 15–23 | Devotional Reading • GALATIANS 5:16–26

Aim for Change

By the end of this lesson, we will: CONTRAST judgment with discernment and distinguish between them; REFLECT on the consequences of practicing discernment rather than judgment; and MODEL discernment instead of judgment.

In Focus

"Did you hear about that guy coming to speak at the community college next week?" Travis asked Regina.

"No, what is he coming to speak about?" Regina responded.

"He is teaching people how to use the power of their minds to unlock their potential and get rich in less than a year!"

"That sounds a bit unrealistic, Travis." Regina remarked.

"But I saw a video online with all of this research he did. It seems to work for some people!"

"Do you know anyone it has worked for? Or who those people are and how they are doing after a year?"

"No."

"Well, how about instead you come to this career fair where Jackie Malone is speaking."

"Didn't she go through a divorce a few years back? I heard she had an affair…"

"She did get a divorce, but that has nothing to do with her helping people prepare for work and to find jobs. She's been a very successful business woman."

"I don't know…" Travis responded uncertainly.

It can be difficult to decide who to listen to and associate with when there are so many ideas, ways of living, and problems in our lives. How do you determine the difference between being judgmental and being discerning?

Keep in Mind

"Beware of false prophets, which come to you in sheep's clothing, but inwardly they are ravening wolves. Ye shall know them by their fruits. Do men gather grapes of thorns, or figs of thistles?" (Matthew 7:15-16, KJV)

"Beware of false prophets who come disguised as harmless sheep but are really vicious wolves. You can identify them by their fruit, that is, by the way they act. Can you pick grapes from thornbushes, or figs from thistles?" (Matthew 7:15-16, NLT)

Focal Verses

KJV **Matthew 7:1** Judge not, that ye be not judged.

2 For with what judgment ye judge, ye shall be judged: and with what measure ye mete, it shall be measured to you again.

3 And why beholdest thou the mote that is in thy brother's eye, but considerest not the beam that is in thine own eye?

4 Or how wilt thou say to thy brother, Let me pull out the mote out of thine eye; and, behold, a beam is in thine own eye?

5 Thou hypocrite, first cast out the beam out of thine own eye; and then shalt thou see clearly to cast out the mote out of thy brother's eye.

6 Give not that which is holy unto the dogs, neither cast ye your pearls before swine, lest they trample them under their feet, and turn again and rend you.

15 Beware of false prophets, which come to you in sheep's clothing, but inwardly they are ravening wolves.

16 Ye shall know them by their fruits. Do men gather grapes of thorns, or figs of thistles?

17 Even so every good tree bringeth forth good fruit; but a corrupt tree bringeth forth evil fruit.

18 A good tree cannot bring forth evil fruit, neither can a corrupt tree bring forth good fruit.

19 Every tree that bringeth not forth good fruit is hewn down, and cast into the fire.

20 Wherefore by their fruits ye shall know them.

21 Not every one that saith unto me, Lord, Lord, shall enter into the kingdom of heaven; but he that doeth the will of my Father which is in heaven.

22 Many will say to me in that day, Lord, Lord, have we not prophesied in thy name?

NLT **Matthew 7:1** "Do not judge others, and you will not be judged.

2 For you will be treated as you treat others. The standard you use in judging is the standard by which you will be judged.

3 And why worry about a speck in your friend's eye when you have a log in your own?

4 How can you think of saying to your friend, 'Let me help you get rid of that speck in your eye,' when you can't see past the log in your own eye?

5 Hypocrite! First get rid of the log in your own eye; then you will see well enough to deal with the speck in your friend's eye.

6 Don't waste what is holy on people who are unholy. Don't throw your pearls to pigs! They will trample the pearls, then turn and attack you."

15 "Beware of false prophets who come disguised as harmless sheep but are really vicious wolves.

16 You can identify them by their fruit, that is, by the way they act. Can you pick grapes from thornbushes, or figs from thistles?

17 A good tree produces good fruit, and a bad tree produces bad fruit.

18 A good tree can't produce bad fruit, and a bad tree can't produce good fruit.

19 So every tree that does not produce good fruit is chopped down and thrown into the fire.

20 Yes, just as you can identify a tree by its fruit, so you can identify people by their actions.

21 Not everyone who calls out to me, 'Lord! Lord!' will enter the Kingdom of Heaven. Only those who actually do the will of my Father in heaven will enter.

22 On judgment day many will say to me, 'Lord! Lord! We prophesied in your name and cast out demons in your name and performed many miracles in your name.'

and in thy name have cast out devils? and in thy name done many wonderful works?

23 And then will I profess unto them, I never knew you: depart from me, ye that work iniquity.

23 But I will reply, 'I never knew you. Get away from me, you who break God's laws.'

The People, Places, and Times

False Prophets. The time in which Jesus lived could be viewed as a marketplace of religion. There had been a number of (mostly political) Jewish and Gentile "messiahs" who promised their followers freedom from Roman rule. There were also a large number of sects and wandering prophets, including mystery cults, idol worshipers, philosophical schools, and state-sanctioned temples around the empire. Every group fought for followers, and all promised that their own form of belief was superior. The groups that professed to follow the Law of God and yet led people astray were identified as false prophets in this context.

Background

Matthew 7 is the last chapter in what is traditionally known as the Sermon on the Mount (Matthew 5–7). The Sermon on the Mount contains several prominent Scriptures including the Beatitudes (Matthew 5:3–12) and the Lord's Prayer (6:9–13). The sermon is a collection of sayings where Jesus teaches His disciples about discipleship. However, due to His miracles and teachings throughout the land, crowds from all over have gathered to follow Jesus. Early on in Matthew 5, Jesus explains that He has come to fulfill the Law and that they are to go beyond exercising the letter of the Law to practicing the heart of it. The heart is love for everyone, including your enemies. In Matthew 6, Jesus focuses on spiritual disciplines such as fasting and praying, and taking care of the needy. He emphasizes that their personal piety is for growing closer to God, not for public admiration like the scribes and Pharisees. Finally Jesus lets them know that they can trust God to take care of them.

Why are all of these topics so crucial to discipleship and how do they set a foundation for discernment? How are these topics still crucial for discipleship today?

At-A-Glance

1. Examine Yourself (Matthew 7:1–6)
2. Examine the Fruit (vv. 15–20)
3. Be Obedient to God's Will (vv. 21–23)

In Depth

1. Examine Yourself (Matthew 7:1–6)

Through Jesus' teachings we learn that judgment is a slippery road with more than one bad end. The first bad end is when we make ourselves judge, we will be judged not with grace and mercy but by how we judge others. While we are digging a grave of judgment for others, we are actually digging one for ourselves. Another end of the road of judgment is hypocrisy. Hypocrisy makes us blind to ourselves, our sins, and our need for transformation. We miss the new life that is available through Christ because we are too busy straining and focusing on what someone else has done. Yet Christ commands us to resist such hypocrisy. He instructs us to work to remove the sin out of our lives. That opens the door for us to rightly help our brother or sister remove the sin out of theirs. Also, Jesus lets the listeners know that what they have been given is sacred and valuable, and instructs them to be wise with whom they share their gift or grace. It is not about them keeping this to themselves, but not giving it over to those who reject the kingdom.

How does judgment and hypocrisy hurt the church?

2. Examine the Fruit (vv. 15–20)

In every movement for good there will always be people who join in and try to lead others away. The same was true for Jesus' movement. Jesus instructs His disciples to watch out for false prophets. He warned them that they will look and sound like real prophets but their fruit will be different. It is of the utmost importance to pay attention to the fact that both trees produce fruit. It is not the quantity of the fruit that makes a tree good or bad but the quality. The same is true for real and false prophets. The size of one's following does not dictate if one is a true or false prophet. False prophets will lead people down the road of destruction (v. 13). True prophets will lead people down the road to life that goes beyond abundant life on earth—the road to everlasting life with Christ.

What false teachings are people settling for instead of receiving everlasting life with Christ?

3. Be Obedient to God's Will (vv. 21–23)

Just like false prophets, there are false disciples. These are people who appear to do the Lord's work on the outside but actually are disobedient to God. There are those who will prophesy in Jesus' name, cast out demons in His name, and perform miracles in His name. These are all good works, but they are not the only works that Jesus has for His disciples. Jesus is telling them not to just do the public works, but do the private works and apply all the teachings that He has shared. Signs, wonders,

and miracles do not necessarily mean a relationship with God or integrity in obedience to God's commandments.

What activities have some church groups focused on that keep them from following all of Christ's teachings?

Search the Scriptures

1. Why does Jesus caution against judging others (Matthew 7:2)?

2. What offense are those who are told they won't enter the kingdom of heaven guilty of committing (vv. 21, 23)?

Discuss the Meaning

1. It can be a lot easier to point out other people's sins and shortcomings than to identify our own. How can we keep each other accountable as followers of Jesus without judging one another?

2. There are many people who proclaim to have found the truth and higher understanding in our modern time, are quick to discredit Christian tradition, but fully believe philosophies and religions they have just discovered through friends or on the Internet. Some of these individuals or groups use parts of the Bible to justify themselves. How can we tell false teachers in our digital society from those who are really speaking truth?

Liberating Lesson

Unrighteous judgment has a negative effect on individuals, the church and society. Too often groups of people are judged to be inferior because of social difference. Or more correctly, that social difference is exploited to justify war, oppression, and evil. All of this has economic, social, educational, physical, mental, emotional, and spiritual consequences. It comes as no surprise then that a basic request of historic and current freedom movements is for all people's humanity to be recognized and respected.

Freedom fighters demand treatment free of unrighteous judgment.

What response does this require of us? The church is the body of the forgiven. God has decided to judge us based on the redemptive work of Christ rather than our works alone. As a result of this grace, the church should be a voice for freedom for all who are oppressed under unrighteous judgment. How should we extend the grace that we've received from God to others?

Application for Activation

• Write down ways that you have been hurt in church due to judgment and hypocrisy. Collect those cards and pray over them as a class that the Lord would heal the group from these hurts.

• Pray for God to provide your church with an opportunity to minister to people who have been hurt by hypocrisy in the church.

• Identify an area where God has delivered you and pray for an opportunity to share that with someone who is struggling this week.

• Join with a coalition of individuals that is fighting for justice in your community.

• Pray that people are delivered from false prophesy and that false prophets would repent and turn to God's truth.

Follow the Spirit

What God wants me to do:

_____

_____

_____

_____

Remember Your Thoughts

Special insights I have learned:

_____

_____

_____

_____

More Light on the Text
Matthew 7:1–6, 15–23

Matthew 7 concludes the Sermon on the Mount that began in chapter 5. Jesus starts a new section of the sermon with the subjects that deal with interrelationship. He speaks about and warns against the danger of being judgmental (vv. 1–5), or finding fault in others and leaving our own fault unattended. He talks about how to deal fairly with one another (v. 12), and concludes with a call for eternal decision and commitment to enter the kingdom of heaven. He then warns us about false teachers, describes how we can recognize them, and warns about the consequence of their falsity.

7:1 Judge not, that ye be not judged. 2 For with what judgment ye judge, ye shall be judged: and with what measure ye mete, it shall be measured to you again.

The chapter begins with a negative command as in the preceding chapter (6:19, 25, 31, 34). While the preceding imperatives deal with an individual's attitude toward oneself (for their good and benefit) and how to deal with stress, the instructions that follow deal with one's relationship to others—how to deal with others' problems and faults. The verb "judge," (Gk. *krino*, **KREE-no**) has a wide range of meaning and usage. For example, "judge" can be judicially used as in the court of law (i.e., summoned to trial so that one's case can be examined and verdict passed upon it). It can also mean to pronounce an opinion either right or wrong, or to pass judgment on the deeds and words of others with the purpose of condemning—criticizing wrongly.

What does Jesus mean here? He does not have in mind the judicial judgment; neither does He forbid judging or discernment of any kind, nor correcting people when they are wrong. The Scriptures demand in several passages that we make right judgments and corrections (John 7:24; cf. 1 Corinthians 5:5; Galatians 1:8–9). Indeed, Jesus refers to some people as dogs (v. 6) and cautions His disciples against false prophets (vv. 15–20), as we will see later. The command "judge not" used here, therefore, forbids being judgmental or critical against others. We recall from the beginning of the sermon that Jesus was addressing a mixed crowd of people (4:25–5:2). The crowd probably included some scribes and Pharisees who were noted for their self-righteousness (cf. 5:20; 12:22–30) and condemnation of others. He therefore addresses them here and warns His disciples not to follow their example if they have the kingdom of heaven in view. This verb *krino*, used here is the same and has the same force as Paul and James use it in Romans 14:10–13 and James 4:11–12, respectively.

Why should we desist from judging others? Jesus gives the answer: so that "you will not be judged." In other words, those who judge will likewise be judged; not necessarily by men, but by God, the great judge of all. Jesus explains this further in verse 2. Using a number of metaphors in the following verses, He warns them of the absurdity of criticizing or judging people's small failings and cautions about the danger of doing so. First, he uses the metaphor of measurement with the idea of measuring or portioning food or grain to people. The metaphor is already explained in the first part of verse 2: "with what judgment ye judge,

ye shall be judged." It refers to trying to claim God's judgmental authority (Romans 14:10) and consequently falling under God's ultimate divine judgment.

3 And why beholdest thou the mote that is in thy brother's eye, but considerest not the beam that is in thine own eye? 4 Or how wilt thou say to thy brother, Let me pull out the mote out of thine eye; and, behold, a beam is in thine own eye? 5 Thou hypocrite, first cast out the beam out of thine own eye; and then shalt thou see clearly to cast out the mote out of thy brother's eye. 6 Give not that which is holy unto the dogs, neither cast ye your pearls before swine, lest they trample them under their feet, and turn again and rend you.

Jesus states the second metaphor rhetorically, which puts everyone on the same level of unworthiness, and therefore incapable of judging or condemning other people. The word "mote" is a translation of the Greek noun *karphos* (**KAR-foce**), which can be any tiny foreign matter like sawdust or a small grain of sand. The "beam" (log or plank) translates the Greek word *dokos* (**doe-KOCE**), with the picture of a two-by-four or big log, highly exaggerated here. Jesus is not saying that it is wrong to help people, or to tell or correct people (in a friendly way) when they are wrong or at fault. Indeed, the Bible says that if a brother (or sister) is "overtaken in a fault," those who are spiritual should restore the other "in the spirit of meekness" (from Galatians 6:1). Rather, it is wrong to point out people's faults when in fact we have similar or even worse faults. How would one with a hyperbolically big log in one's eyes be able to see the speck or sawdust in another person's eyes without first removing the plank in his own eyes? The answer here is clear—it is not possible. It is hypocrisy of the highest order. It makes sense, therefore, that we judge or examine ourselves first, then we are able to correct our brother's or neighbor's fault in a spirit of meekness. We will then see clearly enough to help the other person with his or her own problem.

The next wisdom given through example in this section is to understand and be careful about whom you entertain and share important things. When something is supposed to be used for God, that which is holy, it should not be given to those who do not know how to handle holy things. When something valuable like a pearl is possessed, it should not be given to those who do not recognize its value. They will waste it and then hurt the one who shares it. In addition to being good general wisdom about recognizing the value of what we possess and with whom we share it (not talking about giving of resources, which Jesus instructs we should do boldly in the same sermon), Jesus lets His hearers know the value of what is being offered to them: the kingdom of God. This passage speaks about the kingdom of God and the people of God over the false authority of the Pharisees and scribes. The kingdom of God is the most valuable thing Jesus could offer, and He reminds the crowd that as it is shared with them, those who can not handle it because of their unrighteous agenda (the dogs) will not receive it. Likewise those who do not know God (the pigs) will not receive the kingdom either. The ones who receive the kingdom in this life and the life to come are those who know God and recognize the value of the gift of God.

are ravening wolves." The caution is that the audience should be watchful for false prophets or teachers who go about falsifying the truth. They do not come in their true colors; rather they disguise themselves and pretend they are genuine in order to deceive people. At first glimpse they look authentic, sound orthodox, show spiritual piety, and are usually difficult to distinguish from the true prophets. The issue of false prophets was not a new occurrence in the New Testament, but also an Old Testament problem (cf. Deuteronomy 13:1–5; Jeremiah 6:13–15; Ezekiel 13). Certainly Jesus must have faced this problem, and He knew that it would continue in the future of the church (Acts 20:29; 2 Corinthians 11:11–15; 2 Peter 2:1–3).

Just as Deuteronomy suggests ways to identify false prophets, Jesus uses a different metaphor, a tree, to indicate how to recognize the false prophets: by the fruits they bear (v. 16). John the Baptist used the fruit imagery when he called on the people to repent of their sins (Matthew 3:8, 10). The rhetorical question here allows the readers or listeners to supply the answer, which of course is obvious: Men cannot gather grapes from thorns, neither can they gather figs from thistles. Thorns and thistles are used synonymously here. "Thistles" (Gk. *tribolos*, **TREE-bow-loce**) are prickly wild plants that hurt other plants. They can produce beautiful flowers, but never good fruits. The beauty of their flowers can easily deceive, but their fruit can be poisonous and deadly. So is the case with false prophets.

15 Beware of false prophets, which come to you in sheep's clothing, but inwardly they are ravening wolves. 16 Ye shall know them by their fruits. Do men gather grapes of thorns, or figs of thistles?

Jesus warns the audience to "beware of false prophets" who disguise themselves, figuratively speaking, in sheep's clothes, "but inwardly they

17 Even so every good tree bringeth forth good fruit; but a corrupt tree bringeth forth evil fruit. 18 A good tree cannot bring forth evil fruit, neither can a corrupt tree bring forth good fruit. 19 Every tree that bringeth not forth good fruit is hewn down, and cast into the fire. 20 Wherefore by their fruits ye shall know them.

The inference is made clear in verse 17. The subject seems to be so important to Jesus that He repeats it negatively (v. 18). The tree and fruit imagery is mentioned again later in Jesus' ministry (Matthew 12:33–37; cf. James 3:12; Galatians 5:22–23) and they reveal the type of character one possesses. Evidently, what we do or say will eventually disclose who we are. It may take some time, but surely our true nature will always come to light through our actions (12:33–37; Luke 6:45).

The outcome of such false prophets or the consequence of their action is again described using the tree metaphor. This is akin to John's teaching (3:10). Just as the tree with bad fruit will be cut down and thrown into the fire, so will every false prophet whose aim is to deceive people be judged; they will be cast into the everlasting fire. Although Jesus does not explain what type of falsehood these prophets would teach, the evidence of their falsity is widespread, in the Old Testament, to the time of Jesus and the apostles, and very much in our own time. From the context, we know that their main purpose is to lure people away from the strait gate and narrow way that leads to life, into the wide gate and broad road that leads to destruction (vv. 13–14). The evidence of false prophets/teachers and preachers is everywhere. Just as Jesus says, they come in different forms, as true and quinine preachers and teachers who draw large crowds, but never show their true colors as deceivers. Just like their master the devil, they come as angels of light and suffer the same fate (2 Corinthians 11:13–15). They speak eloquently, articulately, convincingly, and with great conviction, but inwardly they are deceitful.

It is important to note that trees take time to grow and mature, then they bear their fruits. The point is that it takes time. In the same way, it may take (and oftentimes takes) a long time to discern false prophets and their teaching.

However, as time goes on, their actions and words will betray them. Examples of such people in the last two or three decades are not difficult to cite. The call here is that children of God should be alert and watchful, for false prophets are always around.

21 Not every one that saith unto me, Lord, Lord, shall enter into the kingdom of heaven; but he that doeth the will of my Father which is in heaven. 22 Many will say to me in that day, Lord, Lord, have we not prophesied in thy name? and in thy name have cast out devils? and in thy name done many wonderful works? 23 And then will I profess unto them, I never knew you: depart from me, ye that work iniquity.

Jesus is making a point that it is not simply calling Jesus Lord that gets someone into the kingdom of God. It is not even performing miracles, prophesying, and doing works that makes someone fit for God's kingdom. It is by faith in Jesus Christ evidenced in doing the will of God that we enter into the kingdom of God. Jesus was speaking another word of conviction to the listening crowd.

It is remarkable to note here again that Jesus refers to God as "my Father" as opposed to simply God declaring that Jesus has authority and intimacy as God's Son, which the scribes and teachers that the crowd was used to hearing did not. Jesus also reaffirms His identity as Lord, stating that people will refer to Him as Lord and yet still not enter the kingdom of heaven. This indictment strikes at the heart of the hearer as Jesus ends this portion of His Sermon on the Mount. It is not simply knowing that Jesus is Lord that makes a person fit for the kingdom of God, or being able to be used by God. God uses whoever He chooses to do His will. It is in hearing the Word of God and obeying Him that we are made fit for the kingdom. The importance is the relationship and the obedience.

For Christians today this is an important reminder that our actions must line up with God's will, and that we are called to be in obedient covenant relationship with God, not simply to do "spiritual works" seen by others. Indeed, Jesus will say to those who try to read their spiritual resumes to Him that He never knew them—they did what was sinful and thought their "spiritual works" would cover them. Jesus tells His hearers that God is interested in obedient relationship more than empty words and flashy works.

Say It Correctly

Thistle. **THIS**-uhl.

Daily Bible Readings

MONDAY
Walk by the Word and Prosper
(Psalm 1)

TUESDAY
Godly Trust Leads to Fruitful Life
(Jeremiah 17:5–8)

WEDNESDAY
Settle Differences Face to Face
(Matthew 18:15–20)

THURSDAY
How Believers Judge Grievances
(1 Corinthians 6:1–6)

FRIDAY
Asking and Receiving Fairly
(Matthew 7:7–14)

SATURDAY
Hearing and Doing
(Matthew 7:24–29)

SUNDAY
Discerning Faith and Action Together
(Matthew 7:1–6, 15–23)

Notes

_____

_____

_____

_____

Teaching Tips

Words You Should Know

A. Soul *nephesh* (Heb.)—Refers to mind, spirit, and total person.

B. Knit *qashar* (Heb.)—To join or bind together, to league together in this context.

Teacher Preparation

Unifying Principle—Godly Friendship. Sometimes we are challenged to compromise our loyalty to a beloved authority figure to keep a promise made to a trusted friend. Whom does one choose? Jonathan chose to keep his promise to love and protect David, his intimate friend, despite his father's insane hatred of David.

A. Read the Bible Background and Devotional Readings.

B. Pray for your students and lesson clarity.

C. Read the lesson Scripture in multiple translations.

D. Option: As a class or individually compose a poem, song, or story praising loyalty and friendship.

O—Open the Lesson

A. Begin the class with prayer.

B. Have the students read the Aim for Change.

C. Have the students read the In Focus story.

D. Ask students how events named in the story can weigh on their hearts and how they can view these events from a theological perspective.

P—Present the Scriptures

A. Read the Focal Verses and discuss the Background and The People, Places, and Times sections.

B. Have the class share what Scriptures stand out for them and why, with particular emphasis on today's context.

E—Explore the Meaning

A. Use In Depth or More Light on the Text to help provide more in-depth discussion of the lesson text.

B. Discuss the Liberating Lesson and Application for Activation sections.

N—Next Steps for Application

A. Summarize the value of having strong friendships.

B. End class with a commitment to pray for our friends and those who need stronger godly friendships.

Worship Guide

For the Superintendent or Teacher
Theme: A Covenant Between Friends
Song: "Blessed Be the Tie That Binds"
Devotional Reading: John 15:12–17

A Covenant Between Friends

Bible Background • 1 SAMUEL 18–20
Printed Text • 1 SAMUEL 18:1–5, 19:1–7 | Devotional Reading • JOHN 15:12–17

——————— Aim for Change ———————

By the end of the lesson, we will: SUMMARIZE Jonathan's plan to protect David; APPRECIATE how the bonds of covenant friendship can surpass the demands of outside forces; and EXAMINE our own relationships to commit to honesty and loyalty in the sight of God.

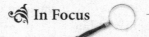 In Focus

Natalie and Iesha became friends during their first years as undergraduates studying journalism. Natalie wanted to be a news anchor and Iesha was a promising producer. They always had each other's back personally and professionally. From the beginning Natalie's star was on the rise and many other students felt threatened by her popularity and skill. During senior year, Natalie was offered the chance to cover a big story about the new ultra-conservative candidate for governor. The head producer knew politics wasn't Natalie's strongest area, and he was not a fan of Natalie. It almost seemed like he purposefully picked her to cover the topic.

Iesha saw what was going on and decided she would do everything she could to help Natalie prepare for the interview. It was a difficult situation for Iesha—in order to help her friend she would have to take on extra time, energy, and test her loyalty to the head producer who was very influential at the station. Iehsa knew that the head producer could make the rest of her days at the station difficult if he found out, but she thought her loyalty to Natalie was more important. Much to the head producer's dismay, Natalie did a great job with the story, and it became one of her main portfolio pieces when she applied to networks after graduation.

How do you determine whether to risk your own comfort for the sake of a friend or loved one?

——————— Keep in Mind ———————

"And it came to pass, when he had made an end of speaking unto Saul, that the soul of Jonathan was knit with the soul of David, and Jonathan loved him as his own soul" (1 Samuel 18:1, KJV).

"After David had finished talking with Saul, he met Jonathan, the king's son. There was an immediate bond between them, for Jonathan loved David" (1 Samuel 18:1, NLT).

Focal Verses

KJV **1 Samuel 18:1** And it came to pass, when he had made an end of speaking unto Saul, that the soul of Jonathan was knit with the soul of David, and Jonathan loved him as his own soul.

2 And Saul took him that day, and would let him go no more home to his father's house.

3 Then Jonathan and David made a covenant, because he loved him as his own soul.

4 And Jonathan stripped himself of the robe that was upon him, and gave it to David, and his garments, even to his sword, and to his bow, and to his girdle.

5 And David went out whithersoever Saul sent him, and behaved himself wisely: and Saul set him over the men of war, and he was accepted in the sight of all the people, and also in the sight of Saul's servants.

19:1 And Saul spake to Jonathan his son, and to all his servants, that they should kill David.

2 But Jonathan Saul's son delighted much in David: and Jonathan told David, saying, Saul my father seeketh to kill thee: now therefore, I pray thee, take heed to thyself until the morning, and abide in a secret place, and hide thyself:

3 And I will go out and stand beside my father in the field where thou art, and I will commune with my father of thee; and what I see, that I will tell thee.

4 And Jonathan spake good of David unto Saul his father, and said unto him, Let not the king sin against his servant, against David; because he hath not sinned against thee, and because his works have been to thee-ward very good:

5 For he did put his life in his hand, and slew the Philistine, and the Lord wrought a great salvation for all Israel: thou sawest it, and didst

NLT **1 Samuel 18:1** After David had finished talking with Saul, he met Jonathan, the king's son. There was an immediate bond between them, for Jonathan loved David.

2 From that day on Saul kept David with him and wouldn't let him return home.

3 And Jonathan made a solemn pact with David, because he loved him as he loved himself.

4 Jonathan sealed the pact by taking off his robe and giving it to David, together with his tunic, sword, bow, and belt.

5 Whatever Saul asked David to do, David did it successfully. So Saul made him a commander over the men of war, an appointment that was welcomed by the people and Saul's officers alike.

19:1 Saul now urged his servants and his son Jonathan to assassinate David. But Jonathan, because of his strong affection for David,

2 told him what his father was planning. "Tomorrow morning," he warned him, "you must find a hiding place out in the fields.

3 I'll ask my father to go out there with me, and I'll talk to him about you. Then I'll tell you everything I can find out."

4 The next morning Jonathan spoke with his father about David, saying many good things about him. "The king must not sin against his servant David," Jonathan said. "He's never done anything to harm you. He has always helped you in any way he could.

5 Have you forgotten about the time he risked his life to kill the Philistine giant and how the Lord brought a great victory to all Israel as a result? You were certainly happy about it then. Why should you murder an innocent man like David? There is no reason for it at all!"

rejoice: wherefore then wilt thou sin against innocent blood, to slay David without a cause?

6 And Saul hearkened unto the voice of Jonathan: and Saul sware, As the Lord liveth, he shall not be slain.

7 And Jonathan called David, and Jonathan shewed him all those things. And Jonathan brought David to Saul, and he was in his presence, as in times past.

6 So Saul listened to Jonathan and vowed, "As surely as the Lord lives, David will not be killed."

7 Afterward Jonathan called David and told him what had happened. Then he brought David to Saul, and David served in the court as before.

The People, Places, and Times

Jonathan. Jonathan was the oldest son of King Saul and rightful heir to the throne of Israel after Saul's death. He was a courageous warrior who by God's intervention defeated a Philistine army camp with only the help of his servant who went with him to the battle. Jonathan became David's closest friend, and after dying in battle in the same war his father Saul was killed in, David cared for Jonathan's descendants in the palace.

Background

In the previous chapter (1 Samuel 17), David had accomplished a feat that no one in Israel, not even the strongest and most experienced soldiers, could do. He had just killed Goliath of Gath, the strong man of the Philistines. The Philistines had mustered their armies to battle against the armies of Israel. Goliath, a skilled nine-foot soldier, fully armed with every kind of military weapon and regalia, had come out and challenged all of Israel. He dared them to choose one person among their forces to a one-on-one combat against him. Whoever won, the other person and his nation would serve him and his people. For forty days, Goliath defied the whole of Israel, their army, and their God. No one in Israel had the guts to face this man. But David, a young and inexperienced youth, volunteered despite being dismissed by

Goliath, King Saul, and even his older brothers. Armed only with a shepherd staff, five smooth stones and a sling (a common distance weapon at the time) in his hand, David stepped forward to face Goliath. Armed foremost with "the name of the LORD of hosts, the God of the armies of Israel" (v. 45), David defeated and killed Goliath and he gave victory to Israel. The Philistines fled and Israel pursued and slaughtered them.

After the victory, David returned. Abner, King Saul's commander, brought David with Goliath's head to King Saul. Amazed, the king asked David about his family background. David answered, "I am the son of thy servant Jesse the Bethlehemite" (17:58).

At-A-Glance

1. Friends' Covenant is Crafted (1 Samuel 18:1–5)
2. Friends' Covenant is Challenged (1 Samuel 19:1-3)
3. Friends' Covenant is Confirmed (vv. 4-7)

In Depth

1. Friends' Covenant is Crafted (1 Samuel 18:1–5)

David has just given a speech to explain to Saul who he is, where he comes from, what he has been through, and most importantly how he has had faith in God. It would be much like David sharing a testimony of his triumph over Goliath, acknowledging that only God could have caused a young shepherd boy from an unimportant family to have victory over the giant champion who had threatened the armies of Israel. Jonathan is so moved by David's testimony of courage and faith that he felt like he was meeting his long lost twin. Jonathan had also single-handedly gone to battle against the Philistines and seen God give him triumph over them (1 Samuel 14). King Saul is so impressed with David that he makes him a prince in his house; David moves from the sheep's pasture to the palace in an instant.

Jonathan is so moved that he feels like David is his kindred spirit, and wants to make their bond of friendship and brotherhood official by cutting a covenant to always protect and show love for one another. Jonathan then gives David the royal clothes off his own back, prophetically acknowledging that God has called David to be royalty alongside him. Jonathan himself was next in line for Saul's throne. David and Jonathan are young men who make a covenant of friendship and kinship with one another; although they were not born blood relatives, they would live and protect each other as though they were one blood and spiritual brothers from that day forward. Jonathan's love for David foreshadows the words and actions of Christ: "Greater love hath no man than this, that a man lay down his life for his friends" (John 15:13).

2. Friends' Covenant is Challenged (1 Samuel 19:1–3)

Some time later, Saul calls together his servants and Jonathan his son because he has become jealous of David's popularity with the people. David has at this point led many successful battles against Israel's enemies and has become the talk of the town. Although Saul receives the glory for the victories as king of Israel, David's growing popularity has begun to make Saul so insecure that he tried to put David in higher ranks, which meant riding out in front of troops and more likely to be killed. Saul is upset that despite his attempts to place David in harm's way, God keeps delivering and protecting His anointed. Saul plots with his servants and Jonathan, who all love David, to kill David. Jonathan, however, has made the covenant with David to protect him as though he was protecting himself, a relationship Saul no doubt knew about. Jonathan informs David of the plot and tells him to hide while Jonathan tries to talk Saul out of his murderous thoughts. The tension is real for Jonathan between siding with his father, his own blood, or siding with his covenant brother and the will of God. Jonathan chooses what is right before God and protects his best friend David.

3. Friends' Covenant is Confirmed (1 Samuel 19:4–7)

Jonathan takes the opportunity to spend time with his father near the field where David is hiding in order to talk him out of trying to kill David. Jonathan makes two important arguments about why killing David is against God's will. First, David is an innocent man; he has done nothing to threaten Saul and killing him would be spilling innocent blood, which is against the will of God. Second, David has been a faithful servant who has brought glory to God and Saul by leading Israel into battle. To kill him would be standing against someone whom God has clearly anointed to bring glory to Himself. Saul listens to Jonathan and decides not to have David murdered. He then swears a very serious oath in God's name that he will not kill David, and David is restored to serving in Saul's house. Sadly, Saul quickly breaks his oath before God and tries to have David killed later. But as the oath proclaimed, David is not killed as long as God lives, which is of course eternally. David dies of natural causes later in life rather than being killed in battle despite his many wars. God protects him even more than his friend Jonathan had protected him.

Search the Scriptures

1. What inner difficulty did Jonathan face as his father Saul plotted to kill David?

2. In what ways does God show that David is His anointed servant?

Discuss the Meaning

1. Have you ever been in a position where you were willing to make a sacrifice for someone whose relationship you really valued? How did you make the decision?

2. What are the qualities of a true friendship? What are situations where your friendships have been tested?

Liberating Lesson

In our society today it is increasingly common for people to lack healthy friendships or for adults to state they have very few close friends. With the rise of social media and globalization, the average American working multiple jobs for longer hours, and time spent tending to family and home, it is even more likely that people lack supportive friends with whom they can spend time. The U.S. Surgeon General has stated many times that one of the biggest health threats of our current era is isolation. This reality calls us as Christians to reexamine the lesson from David and Jonathan and take seriously the need for positive friendships. Jesus taught His disciples that friendship was one of the deepest relationships they could have with Him (cf. John 15:15). How can we as Christians seek to be friendly, build friendships, and maintain them? How can we follow Jesus in love, care for ourselves and one

another, and model to the world how to build healthy relationships? With many people in our communities seeing relationships built only on necessity, power, pleasure, or convenience, it is important that we as believers build friendships that protect one another, consider others before ourselves, and demonstrate God's love.

Application for Activation

This week consider the friendships in your life and the friends who have healthy relationships with God and positive relationships with you. Think of ways to invest in those friendships. Spend time with a friend, whether in person or with a simple phone call. If you do not recognize any friendships like that, ask God to send you supportive friends who have healthy boundaries and can help you grow in Christ. Remember to cultivate your friendships and be a friend—the responsibility is on you to do so and show the love of Christ.

Follow the Spirit

What God wants me to do:

_____

_____

_____

_____

Remember Your Thoughts

Special insights I have learned:

_____

_____

_____

_____

More Light on the Text

1 Samuel 18:1–5, 19:1–7

18:1 And it came to pass, when he had made an end of speaking unto Saul, that the soul of Jonathan was knit with the soul of David, and Jonathan loved him as his own soul.

Chapters 18 and 19 continue the narrative of 1 Samuel 17. The phrase, "And it came to pass," the Hebrew *hayah* (**HAW-yaw**), which means "it happened" or "it follows" used here as emphasis, begins chapter 18. The conjunction "And" connects the last verse of the preceding chapter as a continuation of the story. It appears that this conversation is not just a short question-and-answer discussion as the preceding verse (17:58) tends to indicate. It is rather a protracted conversation between the two, King Saul and David, with a number of people present. What David had done is no secret (the news has spread everywhere); Captain Abner, who led the troops and witnessed the battle, had come to report back to Saul with his bodyguards. The king's advisers and members of his advisory board must have come together to celebrate and congratulate Saul for the victory. Any victory won in a battle was always attributed to the sitting king. This one was no different. David had won the battle, but King Saul took the glory (18:6). What David had done so thrilled and amazed the king that he wanted to know more about him, his family background, and whose son he was. Saul and David had previously met before David went to fight Goliath (17:31–39). David had probably given the history of his family and further explained in detail what happened and how his faith in the Lord helped accomplish what he did (see 17:37, 45–17) to the audience present.

Among those present at this briefing is King Saul's first son, Jonathan, who logically was to be the heir to his father's throne. We first met Jonathan in 1 Samuel 14; he is an amazingly courageous young man of faith "who initiated a one-man war against the Philistines" (14:6). It is thought that David and Jonathan were similar in many ways. They were about the same age. They were both very courageous young men with great faith in the living God; both had genuine relationships with the Lord God of Israel. Jonathan is so fascinated by David's story and his recent accomplishment that his soul was attracted to David. The word "knit" is the Hebrew *qashar* (**KAW-shar**), which means to "join or bind together" or to "league together." Soul is the translation of the Hebrew *nephesh* (**NEH-fesh**), which refers to the mind, spirit, or the total person. The soul is the seat of emotion. That means both Jonathan and David were spiritually and emotionally attracted to each other. There was an immediate, strong bond of love between the two, and Jonathan's love is so strong that the narrator adds the clause, "and Jonathan loved him as his own soul." We will discover later that Jonathan and David's love for each other was as strong as two brothers' love. Lamenting later over Jonathan's death, David calls him "my brother" (2 Samuel 1:26). This is not a sexual love, but the love for a kindred spirit. That's how strong and genuine was their love and friendship.

2 And Saul took him that day, and would let him go no more home to his father's house. 3 Then Jonathan and David made a covenant, because he loved him as his own soul. 4 And Jonathan stripped himself of the robe that was upon him, and gave it to David, and his garments, even to his sword, and to his bow, and to his girdle.

After learning all about David and his family, King Saul decided to keep David, and would not let him return to his father's house. The Lord instantly changed David's status from a poor shepherd boy to a prince at the king's palace to serve in the king's household.

Throughout his reign as king, Saul and Israel engaged in bitter wars with the Philistines, so Saul had the habit of drafting strong and brave men whenever he saw one (14:52). Jonathan and David made a covenant to seal their trust and friendship with each other.

The word "covenant" is a translation of the Hebrew *berit* (**beh-REET**), which means treaty, alliance, or league. Used together, the phrase "made a covenant" more literally means to "cut a covenant" because it is made by passing through pieces of flesh. God cut a covenant with Abram (Abraham) by instructing him to offer several three-year-old animals in a sacrifice and cut them in half (Genesis 15:9–10). God required Abraham and his descendants to circumcise by cutting the foreskin of every male child on the eighth day after birth as a covenant with Him (Genesis 17). This is still practiced in the Jewish and many other cultures today. Jonathan's rationale for making the covenant with David was "because he loved him as his own soul," reemphasizing what was said earlier (vv. 1, 3).

To show the authenticity of his commitment of friendship to David, Jonathan stripped himself of all his princely regalia and armor and gave them to David. These included his robe and garment, his sword, bow and girdle. He put them on David. Beyond demonstrating his genuine friendship, Jonathan seems to recognize that David is the one the Lord has chosen as Israel's next king (20:16–17, 42; 23:16–18). He happily relinquishes his hopes for the throne in respect to God's choice—David. The robe is usually a symbol of authority. Jonathan's action here symbolizes passing or bestowing of the royal authority, which rightly belonged to him, on David. This symbol was common among the Old Testament Jews. We know that Joseph's coat was a symbol of his authority (Genesis 37:3, 23). Before his death, Aaron removed his priestly garment and put it on his son, Eleazar

(Numbers 20:22–28). Elijah placed his mantle on his successor, Elisha, as a symbol of transfer of authority (1 Kings 19:19–21).

Jonathan and David demonstrate genuine love and friendship. It has been observed that their friendship is one of the deepest and closest recorded in the Bible. Above all, their friendship is based on their commitment to the Lord, not just to each other, and it lasted to the end. This type of love foreshadows Christ's love for us: He gave up His own life so that we might live, became poor so that we might be rich, and set aside His position so that we might be in right position with the Father.

5 And David went out whithersoever Saul sent him, and behaved himself wisely: and Saul set him over the men of war, and he was accepted in the sight of all the people, and also in the sight of Saul's servants.

David now lives in the royal palace; he is fully submitted to Saul and obediently serves him. He acts with wisdom in whatever work assigned to him. He is successful in everything he does, and Saul promotes him and "set him over the men of war." It appears this means he was put in charge over a section of the army, because Abner was still the commander of the army. David, though still very young, grew quickly in ranks. "All the people," from the troops to Saul's servants, accepted him as their commander. David became very popular among the people, and they praised him.

The women went out to welcome Saul; they sang and danced with joy in his honor. But their song: "Saul hath slain his thousands, and David his ten thousands" (18:7) infuriated Saul. Envy and jealousy set in; David was becoming more popular than Saul. One would think that Saul's motive for promoting David (v. 5) was good, and that he was happy for David's victory over Goliath. But Saul's actions seem to indicate the opposite. Saul's promotion of David was diabolical. Army commanders in those days didn't command from behind, rather they led in front of the troops. That was why all the people accepted him (v. 5). It therefore can be reasoned that Saul's motive was to put David at harm's way so that he would be eliminated (see 2 Samuel 11:14–17). But David "behaved himself wisely" (Heb. *sakal*, **saw-KAL**), which means circumspectly, insightfully, prudently, or cautiously. He went wherever Saul sent him with wisdom and caution (v. 5). Because David was becoming more popular than he, Saul became envious and angry. Saul also knew and was nervously afraid that David would one day replace him as king instead of his own son. Consequently, he tried several times and many ways to kill him (18:11, 17, 27). Saul's attempts to kill David (more than fourteen times) occupy a great part of the rest of the book.

19:1 And Saul spake to Jonathan his son, and to all his servants, that they should kill David. 2 But Jonathan Saul's son delighted much in David: and Jonathan told David, saying, Saul my father seeketh to kill thee: now therefore, I pray thee, take heed to thyself until the morning, and abide in a secret place, and hide thyself: 3 And I will go out and stand beside my father in the field where thou art, and I will commune with my father of thee; and what I see, that I will tell thee.

Although David is obedient and serves him sincerely, Saul is unhappy with him—David is becoming more popular. Saul's mind was so filled with hatred for David that he wanted to eliminate him. But all his attempts to do so himself failed; he tried to solicit help from his son, Jonathan, and the servants. Saul probably called together his aides, his court attendants and Jonathan to a special secret meeting. The only agenda was the assassination of David. Fortunately he called the wrong group of people—his servants who liked and accepted

David's leadership, and Jonathan, David's best friend who loved David as himself and made a covenant with him for protection (18:1–4).

Saul was backing the wrong horse, because his son Jonathan delighted much in David and his servants loved David (18:22). Why would Saul ask Jonathan to kill his best friend? It sounds strange that he would ask Jonathan to do such a criminal act, knowing full well the relationship between the two. Probably he thought that Jonathan would be as envious as he and kill David so that Jonathan would be heir to the throne. Or probably he was asserting his parental privilege and authority or God's commandment (Exodus 20:12). When hatred, envy, and jealousy take control of a man's mind, he loses all his senses. That is unfortunately what happened with Saul. Filled with envy and hatred, he lost common sense. He had forgotten how irrevocable and binding covenants are; Jonathan had made one with David. Rather than tow the same road as his father, Jonathan devised ways to save David's life. He informed David of Saul's diabolical plot to kill him and warned him to be careful.

It was already evening, and Jonathan asked David to be cautious and hide until the next morning (v. 2). Jonathan probably was not sure who among the king's servants would comply with the king's orders, though they accepted David (18:5). He therefore asked David to go into a secret place and hide himself till the next morning. In addition to instructing David to hide, Jonathan devised another plan to save David's life. He planned to go the next morning and chat with his father concerning David. He tells David, "I will go and meet my father in the field near where you are hiding; and I will speak with my father concerning you; after I will let you know the outcome of our conversation." That's what friends are for—loyal to and protective of each other. A friend is one who has the interest of another at heart even when it is against parental interest—and especially when a man's will conflicts with God's will and purpose. Jonathan knew that David was God's chosen heir to the throne; eliminating David would mean putting Jonathan on the throne, which plausibly belonged to him. But such thought was far from Jonathan; he wouldn't be a party to challenging God's plan. For Jonathan, family pressure could not come between him and David or God's will. Additionally, Jonathan greatly "delighted" (Heb. *chaphets*, **KHAW-fates'**) in David. That means he was "pleased with" and "took pleasure" in having him as his friend, and therefore he would never do anything to tarnish that relationship. Moreover, such a wicked act would mar his relationship with God.

4 And Jonathan spake good of David unto Saul his father, and said unto him, Let not the king sin against his servant, against David; because he hath not sinned against thee, and because his works have been to thee-ward very good: 5 For he did put his life in his hand, and slew the Philistine, and the Lord wrought a great salvation for all Israel: thou sawest it, and didst rejoice: wherefore then wilt thou sin against innocent blood, to slay David without a cause?

As he promised, the next morning, Jonathan approached his father to intercede on behalf of David. He spoke well about David to him and pleaded with him not to harm David. Jonathan presented two arguments why it was wrong to harm David. The first was that David was innocent and didn't deserve to die. The second was that David had been good to Saul and served him faithfully. Indeed David helped make Saul who he was—he won many battles against Saul's enemies.

Jonathan reminded his father the many victories the Lord wrought through David. He reminded Saul how David risked his life and faced the Philistine and "the Lord wrought a great salvation for all Israel." The Philistine referred here was Goliath of Gath, whom all of Israel dreaded, but was defeated by David. The expression "he did put his life in his hand" means that David took a great risk when he faced Goliath, but God granted Israel victory. Saul witnessed it and invited David to serve in his house and even promoted him (18:5). Then Jonathan went further and asked another question that was difficult for Saul to answer given his present state of mind. Jonathan said something to the effect, "Why then should you murder an innocent man like David, without a cause? There is no reason for it at all!"

6 And Saul hearkened unto the voice of Jonathan: and Saul sware, As the Lord liveth, he shall not be slain. 7 And Jonathan called David, and Jonathan shewed him all those things. And Jonathan brought David to Saul, and he was in his presence, as in times past.

After reasoning with his son Jonathan, Saul seemed to listen and he concurred with him. He swore an oath not to harm David. Using a common formula of making a serious pledge, Saul promised Jonathan using the name of the Lord, "As the Lord liveth, he shall not be slain." Using this formula, "as the Lord lives" makes such an oath binding. The Israelites believe that Yahweh is eternal—He lives forever and is unchallengeable, therefore any promise made in His name was taken seriously and was binding. It is comparable with cutting a covenant. Therefore Saul made a solemn and solid promise to Jonathan that nothing would harm his friend David. He was right because God protected David throughout his life—he was never slain, but died peacefully of a natural cause (1 Kings 2:1–10). But as the rest of the book will reveal, Saul's oath was an empty promise; he would make several attempts to slay David, but failed. Saul was never a trustworthy person.

He was well known for breaking promises and he did the same in this case (1 Samuel 14:24, 44).

Meanwhile, Jonathan trusted his father and called David to tell him how everything went with his father. Believing that all had been settled and David would be safe in the house, Jonathan invited David back home and he served Saul as he did before. Jonathan and David's love and friendship epitomize the type of friendship that ought to exist between friends and members of Christ's church. It is a type of Christ's supreme example of love, which He demonstrated by coming down, humbling Himself, and relinquishing His position as God to take the form of man and servant, and die on the cross to save us from sin and death (Philippians 2:6–8).

Sources:
Biblesoft's New Exhaustive Strong's Numbers and Concordance with Expanded Greek-Hebrew Dictionary. Copyright © 1994, 2003, 2006 Biblesoft, Inc. and International Bible Translators, Inc.
Blue Letter Bible, OT, Online.
Interlinear Transliterated Bible. Copyright © 1994, 2003, 2006 by Biblesoft, Inc. All rights reserved.
Life Application Study Bible NIV. Carol Stream, IL: Tyndale House Publishers, Inc.; and Grand Rapids, MI: Zondervan.
Zondervan NIV Study Bible, Copyright © 1973, 1995, 2002, 2008. Grand Rapids, MI: Zondervan.
"The Biggest Threat Facing Middle-Age Men Isn't Smoking or Obesity. It's Loneliness." *The Boston Globe.* BostonGlobe.com, March 9, 2017. www.bostonglobe.com/magazine/2017/03/09/the-biggest-threat-facing-middle-age-men-isn-smoking-obesity-loneliness/k6saC9FnnHQCUbf5mJ8okL/story.html.

Daily Bible Readings

MONDAY
Saul Fears David
(1 Samuel 18:10–16)

TUESDAY
David Marries Saul's Daughter
(1 Samuel 18:20–24, 28–30)

WEDNESDAY
Michal Helps David Escape
(1 Samuel 19:8–12)

THURSDAY
David and Jonathan Enter Covenant
(1 Samuel 20:12–17)

FRIDAY
Jonathan and David Plan Rendezvous
(1 Samuel 20:18–23)

SATURDAY
David and Jonathan Separate in Peace
(1 Samuel 20:35–42)

SUNDAY
Covenant Between Two Friends
(1 Samuel 18:1–5, 19:1–7)

Say It Correctly

Goliath. guh-**LAHY**-uhth
Jonathan. **JON**-uh-thuhn.
Philistine. fi-**LIH**-steen.

Teaching Tips

August 11
Bible Study Guide 11

Words You Should Know

A. House *bayit* (Heb.)—In this lesson means household or family.

B. Deal *'asah* (Heb.)—To put in order, to attend to.

Teacher Preparation

Unifying Principle—Loyalty and Commitment. When bonded by a strong love and commitment to one another, people who are unrelated by birth may enter into a covenant relationship. What drives and sustains this relationship? Although Naomi begged Ruth to return to her people, Ruth clung to her mother-in-law and vowed her loyalty until death.

A. Read the Bible Background and Devotional Readings.

B. Pray for your students and lesson clarity.

C. Read the lesson Scripture in multiple translations.

D. Option: Have the class write notes of affirmation for people in vulnerable situations who they may know.

O—Open the Lesson

A. Begin the class with prayer.

B. Have the students read the Aim for Change.

C. Have the students read the In Focus story.

D. Ask students how events named in the story can weigh on their hearts and how they can view these events from a theological perspective.

P—Present the Scriptures

A. Read the Focal Verses and discuss the Background and The People, Places, and Times sections.

B. Have the class share what Scriptures stand out for them and why, with particular emphasis on today's context.

E—Explore the Meaning

A. Use In Depth or More Light on the Text to help provide more in-depth discussion of the lesson text.

B. Discuss the Liberating Lesson and Application for Activation sections.

N—Next Steps for Application

A. Summarize the value of strong relationships between women, and between generations.

B. End class with a commitment to pray for natural and spiritual mothers and daughters.

Worship Guide

For the Superintendent or Teacher
Theme: A Mother-Daughter Covenant
Song: "Loyalty"
Devotional Reading: Ruth 4:13–17

611

A Mother-Daughter Covenant

Bible Background • Ruth 1:1–18
Printed Text • Ruth 1:6–11, 14–18 | Devotional Reading • Ruth 4:13–17

Aim for Change

By the end of the lesson, we will: IDENTIFY the relationship between Ruth and Naomi; EMPATHIZE with those in vulnerable situations; and COMMIT to demonstrating godly loyalty to our family members.

In Focus

Shortly after graduating from Hampton University, Jessica got a job in Indianapolis. She was really excited but adjusting was challenging, and the office culture was not inclusive. She felt isolated and alone, like she was living in a foreign world.

Jessica was in the cafeteria when she noticed an older woman sitting in the corner, reading a newspaper.

She approached the table. "Hi ... do you mind if I sit here?" The woman barely looked up from the newspaper, but Jessica sat anyway. "Hello, my name is Eileen Moxie," the woman said. "I've seen you around. How have the first few weeks been?" Over the next few months the two became friends. Jessica valued Eileen as a friend and maternal figure.

One day, Jessica sat down to talk to Eileen, who looked distant. "They've let me go," Eileen said. "One more year to retire with benefits, and they've let me go. I'm widowed and never had kids. This job was everything I had," Eileen said softly. Jessica felt so heavy. The first few months had been so difficult for Jessica, but Eileen had been there to guide her through the process.

Jessica stared at Eileen a long time, not knowing exactly what to say. After a few moments, she reached out and grabbed Eileen's hand. She knew that it was her time to listen.

How can we show care to those who have shown care for us?

Keep in Mind

"And Ruth said, Intreat me not to leave thee, or to return from following after thee: for whither thou goest, I will go; and where thou lodgest, I will lodge: thy people shall be my people, and thy God my God" (Ruth 1:16, KJV).

"But Ruth replied, "Don't ask me to leave you and turn back. Wherever you go, I will go; wherever you live, I will live. Your people will be my people, and your God will be my God" (Ruth 1:16, NLT).

Focal Verses

KJV **Ruth 1:6** Then she arose with her daughters in law, that she might return from the country of Moab: for she had heard in the country of Moab how that the Lord had visited his people in giving them bread.

7 Wherefore she went forth out of the place where she was, and her two daughters in law with her; and they went on the way to return unto the land of Judah.

8 And Naomi said unto her two daughters in law, Go, return each to her mother's house: the Lord deal kindly with you, as ye have dealt with the dead, and with me.

9 The Lord grant you that ye may find rest, each of you in the house of her husband. Then she kissed them; and they lifted up their voice, and wept.

10 And they said unto her, Surely we will return with thee unto thy people.

11 And Naomi said, Turn again, my daughters: why will ye go with me? are there yet any more sons in my womb, that they may be your husbands?

14 And they lifted up their voice, and wept again: and Orpah kissed her mother in law; but Ruth clave unto her.

15 And she said, Behold, thy sister in law is gone back unto her people, and unto her gods: return thou after thy sister in law.

16 And Ruth said, Intreat me not to leave thee, or to return from following after thee: for whither thou goest, I will go; and where thou lodgest, I will lodge: thy people shall be my people, and thy God my God:

17 Where thou diest, will I die, and there will I be buried: the Lord do so to me, and more also, if ought but death part thee and me.

18 When she saw that she was stedfastly minded to go with her, then she left speaking unto her.

NLT **Ruth 1:6** Then Naomi heard in Moab that the Lord had blessed his people in Judah by giving them good crops again. So Naomi and her daughters-in-law got ready to leave Moab to return to her homeland.

7 With her two daughters-in-law she set out from the place where she had been living, and they took the road that would lead them back to Judah.

8 But on the way, Naomi said to her two daughters-in-law, "Go back to your mothers' homes. And may the Lord reward you for your kindness to your husbands and to me.

9 May the Lord bless you with the security of another marriage." Then she kissed them good-bye, and they all broke down and wept.

10 "No," they said. "We want to go with you to your people."

11 But Naomi replied, "Why should you go on with me? Can I still give birth to other sons who could grow up to be your husbands?

14 And again they wept together, and Orpah kissed her mother-in-law good-bye. But Ruth clung tightly to Naomi.

15 "Look," Naomi said to her, "your sister-in-law has gone back to her people and to her gods. You should do the same."

16 But Ruth replied, "Don't ask me to leave you and turn back. Wherever you go, I will go; wherever you live, I will live. Your people will be my people, and your God will be my God.

17 Wherever you die, I will die, and there I will be buried. May the Lord punish me severely if I allow anything but death to separate us!"

18 When Naomi saw that Ruth was determined to go with her, she said nothing more.

The People, Places, and Times

Bethlehem-Judah. This city is five miles south of Jerusalem. Its hyphenated name is to distinguish it from the town of the same first name in the area of Zebulun. Bethlehem translates to "house of bread." It was previously known as Bethlehem-Ephrathah. Therefore the people were called Ephrathites. This is the city Ruth and Naomi traveled toward when they left Moab. Ruth would eventually become the great-grandmother of King David. David and his ancestors lived in Bethlehem (1 Samuel 16:1–5), so it is also known as the city of David. This is the lineage into which Jesus was born.

How have you seen God provide in the midst of loss or hardship?

Background

We are introduced to a family set in the time when judges presided and governed over the children of Israel in the early days of the nation. Elimelech, the patriarch, was from Bethlehem, a province of Judah. Elimelech left his homeland with his wife Naomi and two sons, Mahlon and Chilion, to escape famine in the land. The family settled in the country of Moab. The people of Moab were descendants from the incestuous relationship between Abraham's nephew Lot and his oldest daughter (Genesis 19:37); therefore, Moabites were distant relatives of the Jewish people. As the Children of Israel made their journey to the Promised Land, the Moabites sent Baalam to curse the Israelites (Numbers 22). From this and other contentious interactions, the Law of Moses prohibited Moabites from the Lord's assembly, the worshiping community made up of men, for ten generations if not forever (Deuteronomy 23:3–6). Moab was an also an idolatrous nation; one of their gods, Chemosh, was worshiped with child sacrifices.

In Ruth 1:3–5, Elimelch dies while living in Moab and his sons Mahlon and Chilion marry Moabite women, Orpah and Ruth. Ten years after their unions to these women both sons died childless. We are not told the circumstances surrounding the death of these men, but the three women are now widows. Naomi suffers the greatest having lost her husband and two sons. In this culture women without men were at the mercy of extended family and community to care for them.

How could Naomi and her daughters-in-law go on after enduring such losses?

At-A-Glance

1. A Mother's Farewell (Ruth 1:6–11)
2. A Daughter's Response (vv. 14–18)

In Depth

1. A Mother's Farewell (Ruth 1:6–11)

After the death of her sons, Naomi, an older woman, was left with no one to care for her. The text does not give the span of time between the passing of her sons and the decision to move forward. Traditionally, a Jewish burial takes place within twenty-four hours of death because the Torah says, "His body shall not remain all night … but thou shalt in any wise bury him that day" (Deuteronomy 21:23). Further, ancient Jewish culture dictates that after the death of a husband the sons were to care for their mother. A widow was considered blessed to have sons because they inherited the father's possessions and his tie to land. To have lost her husband and ten years later to have no sons was a mark of shame, and it weighed heavily on Naomi. She had no choice but to go back to Judah to reconnect with extended family members and her community. The people would know her story upon return. As the three women made their way toward Judah broken and in mourning, Naomi stopped during their trek and implored her daughters-in-law Orpah and Ruth to return to their own mothers to start over. Her daughters-in-law would also need to be cared for in this culture. Naomi encouraged them to go back to the security of their own people. However, she also spoke the blessing of the Lord over her daughters-in-law. She prayed that the Lord would deal kindly with them as a reward for their love for her sons as well as the kindness extended to her. After the death of their husbands, Orpah and Ruth could have immediately returned to their families and left Naomi to grieve alone. However, they showed great honor for their husbands' memory and their mother-in-law by caring for her and refusing to leave her side.

Naomi made the case to the two women that no hope existed for them if they remained with her (vv. 12–13). Naomi would be unable to have more sons for them to marry but if they returned home, they could possibly find husbands and marry again because they were young. Naomi was reeling in the bitterness of her losses and felt forsaken by God, but tried to offer hope for a future for her daughters-in-law.

Have you tried to offer hope to others while in a dark place?

2. A Daughter's Response (vv. 14–18)

Orpah reluctantly listened to her mother-in-law's logic and with a gut-wrenching cry said goodbye, but tearful Ruth decided to stay with or "cling to" her mother-in-law. Naomi again pleaded with Ruth to return to her family and her gods like Orpah, but Ruth refused. In this moment Ruth became more than a daughter by marriage but a daughter birthed in the spirit as she literally comes into a covenant relationship. Ruth responded emphatically that she did not want to leave Naomi's side and that she wanted to continue the journey. Ruth honors her husband's memory in declaring to remain with her mother-in-law, not wanting to dishonor her by leaving her to travel alone. Ruth becomes one with Naomi by proclaiming

that where she lives, she will live. She would become one with her people and worship her God. Where Naomi is buried, she would also be buried; she accepts that if she does not keep her word and stay by her side, she would leave it to God to judge her. To seal the deal Ruth vows that nothing but death will separate her from her mother-in-law. When Naomi saw how resolute Ruth was about moving forward with her, she said nothing more. When love in action is that strong and committed, it requires no further argument and nothing more is to be done but to receive it. Ruth, a Moabite woman, displays such great love and honor for a woman she highly esteems, leaving all that is familiar to start a new life.

Can you see the picture of God's love for His people and His church to not allow anything or anyone to separate them from His love? How do we respond to such a love?

Search the Scriptures

1. Why was it important for Naomi to leave Moab, a place of such pain, and return to Judah to be among her people?

2. Compare and contrast Orpah's and Ruth's responses to Naomi's plea for them to return home. Why was Ruth so determined to stay with Naomi?

Discuss the Meaning

1. Have you ever been in an unfamiliar situation? Who did you turn to for guidance?

2. What are times when you feel God has tested your strength? How did you react?

Liberating Lesson

We are called to show one another deep love and commitment to God and His people. When one of us hurts, we all hurt. Nothing hurts more than the death of a loved one. Many churches make a resolution to care for members when they suffer such loss. With churches all around, communities across the country have been touched by gun violence that has ripped the hearts of mothers, fathers, grandparents, siblings, extended family, and friends. How can our churches be first responders to provide hope and healing? How can we stay in touch in the days and weeks to come?

Application for Activation

As you receive news through your medium of choice, pray for families who are experiencing the pain of loss. Pray for peace in our communities. And if your community or a surrounding community hosts a prayer vigil, join in or convene one. Volunteer your time and seek to partner with other institutions to end violence in our communities. Be a beacon of hope and a reflection of God's love by asking the Holy Spirit to present you (or your small group/congregation) with opportunities to provide comfort to those who grieve.

Follow the Spirit

What God wants me to do:

_____

_____

_____

_____

Remember Your Thoughts

Special insights I have learned:

_____

_____

_____

_____

More Light on the Text
Ruth 1:6–11, 14–18

Various writers and scholars have described the story contained in the book of Ruth in many different ways. Some writers describe its theme as "from emptiness to fullness," "from poverty to riches," or "from tragedy to triumph." All these describe the plight of the chief characters of the story, especially Naomi and Ruth. It is a story that begins with having nothing and ends with abundance; it goes from poverty to prosperity, and from tragedy of death to triumph of life. Indeed, the best way to view the story of Ruth is to see it through the lens of God's providential intervention in the affairs of His people, those who would choose Him as their God. The story illustrates the act of God in rewarding the faithfulness of those who put their trust in Him. No matter how one looks at this story, one thing is certain: God has made His plan of salvation available to all of His creation from the beginning of time, whether Jews or Gentiles.

Due to famine and the death of their husbands, the world of Naomi, Orpah, and Ruth collapsed around them. Still, they displayed strength of character that is worth emulating. They showed love, faithfulness, selflessness, and concern for each other that should be named among all believers. Instead of a negative mother-in-law report about Naomi, the text portrays her as a godly woman, who in spite of her own suffering and loss is concerned about the well-being of her daughters-in-law, Orpah and Ruth. Life had dealt Naomi a devastating hand: Not only had her husband Elimelech died, but ten years later, her two sons—Mahlon and Chilion—passed away as well (Ruth 1:1–5). Yet, Naomi was not so caught up in her own grief that she could not see the needs of her two daughters-in-law.

617

6 Then she arose with her daughters in law, that she might return from the country of Moab: for she had heard in the country of Moab how that the Lord had visited his people in giving them bread. 7 Wherefore she went forth out of the place where she was, and her two daughters in law with her; and they went on the way to return unto the land of Judah.

Verse 6 serves as a transition; it concludes the introductory part and sets the stage for what follows. The author seems to give a glimmer of hope amidst the rather grim and tragic circumstances that have so far dominated the first part of the story. He does this by relating the news that "the Lord had visited his people in giving them bread," which prompted Naomi to decide to return to Bethlehem, her homeland. However, as we shall see, Naomi does not see any bright future beyond her present bitter situation (vv. 19–22). In any case, she decides to return home.

"Then she arose" (Heb. *kum*, **KOOM**) means "to stand up" or "to arise." It carries the idea that Naomi had made up her mind to venture home. This construction is similar to the construction found in Christ's New Testament parable of the prodigal son arising and returning home. The purpose of Naomi rising is that she might return from Moab. Note the use of the preposition "for" (Heb. *kiy*, **KEE**). The reason for Naomi's decision to return to Bethlehem is that she had heard the Lord had given them bread. How did she hear this news? The narrator does not tell us, although the most likely theory is that she heard the news through rumor. Jacob heard there was food in Egypt and sent his sons to buy some, without saying how he heard (Genesis 42:1). The writers in both instances do not deem it necessary to reveal how Jacob or Naomi got the news. Yet with her situation in a foreign land, Naomi was all ears to hear news about her home country. The

news is "that the Lord had visited his people" by giving them bread. The verb "visited" (Heb. *paqad*, **paw-KOD**) is used in a number of ways in the Old Testament and can mean to attend to, muster, reckon, punish, care for, or commit for care. Here, as in many other instances the visitation produces a beneficial result: the return of "bread" (Heb. *lechem*, **LE-khem**), which also refers to food in general.

So Naomi, along with her two daughters-in-law, set out from Moab where she had been living. The second clause, "they went on the way to return unto the land of Judah," implies that they went toward Judah. Her daughters-in-law, ignorant of where she is going, accompany her. As they turn onto the road that leads to Judah, Naomi turns to them and asks them to go back to Moab, their country of origin.

8 And Naomi said unto her two daughters in law, Go, return each to her mother's house: the LORD deal kindly with you, as ye have dealt with the dead, and with me. 9 The LORD grant you that ye may find rest, each of you in the house of her husband. Then she kissed them; and they lifted up their voice, and wept.

It is interesting that Naomi tells them to go back to their "mother's house," rather than the expected advice to return to their father's house. This could be because of a family system where their mothers were one of many wives, or their mothers were single, divorced, or widowed as well. We can definitely see this through a womanist perspective recognizing the importance of relationships between women as the focus of the book of Ruth. Naomi, however, might also have used "mother's house" in a generic or general sense to mean their homeland of Moab, especially considering her later statement to Ruth: "Behold, thy sister in law is gone back unto her people…" (v. 15).

In verses 8–9, the word "house" in Hebrew (*bayit*, **BAH-yeet**) means "household" or "family." In the ancient world, there was almost nothing worse than being a widow, living without blood-related family to provide or take care of you. This was the lot of Naomi, Orpah, and Ruth. Their husbands were all dead. Who would care for these women in their dire situation? They could be taken advantage of, ignored altogether, or swallowed up in poverty. Therefore, Naomi tells them to return to their birth families so they would have someone to look after them.

Because Orpah and Ruth had dealt kindly with her, Naomi also blessed them. She said, "The LORD deal kindly with you" (v. 8). The word "deal" in Hebrew is *'asah* (**aw-SAW**) and means to attend to, or to put in order, and "kindly" is *checed* (Heb. **KHEH-sed**), meaning loving-kindness, goodness, favor, and mercy. In other words, because Orpah and Ruth had shown goodness, favor, and mercy toward Naomi and her dead sons, she asked that God show them the same as they returned to their people. In addition, she wanted the Lord to bless them with "rest" (Heb. *manokhah*, **maw-NOisakh**), meaning quietness, a resting place, or comfort. The phrase "may find" in Hebrew is *matsa'* (**maw-TSAW**), meaning attain, or encounter. Naomi knew that with the loss both she and her daughters-in-law had experienced, all three of them needed a place where they could rest, regroup from their sorrows, and receive nurturing and care. She was confident that the three of them could find this when they returned home to their own people.

After blessing them, the three women "wept" (Heb. *bakah*, **baw-KAW**), which means they cried loudly and shed tears. Since they had already experienced great loss and now they could be separated from each other for the rest of their lives, they had much to cry about. The sadness of their predicament overwhelmed them.

10 And they said unto her, Surely we will return with thee unto thy people. 11 And Naomi said, Turn again, my daughters: why will ye go with me? are there yet any more sons in my womb, that they may be your husbands?

Naomi had the mindset for them to return to their own people; however, Orpah and Ruth had the mindset to go with Naomi to Judah—to return with Naomi to Naomi's people. They were at an impasse. Since Naomi had acted so selflessly toward them, Ruth and Orpah returned the kindness by acting selflessly toward her—they followed Naomi's example. Naomi sowed the seeds of love and kindness and reaped love and kindness in return. Since her daughters-in-law would not relinquish their desire to go with her, Naomi reminded them of her own sad situation. She feared that she would not be able to provide or find provision for them. She was past the normal age to bear children they could marry as husbands, and if she was able to find refuge among her own people there was no certainty that her foreign daughters-in-law would be welcomed or able to remarry.

14 And they lifted up their voice, and wept again: and Orpah kissed her mother in law; but Ruth clave unto her. 15 And she said, Behold, thy sister in law is gone back unto her people, and unto her gods: return thou after thy sister in law. 16 And Ruth said, Intreat me not to leave thee, or to return from following after thee: for whither thou goest, I will go; and where thou lodgest, I will lodge: thy people shall be my people, and thy God my God: 17 Where thou diest, will I die, and there will I be buried: the LORD do so to me, and more also, if ought but death part

thee and me. 18 When she saw that she was stedfastly minded to go with her, then she left speaking unto her.

After listening to a long, persuasive plea and a convincing argument by Naomi for her daughters-in-law to return to their people, Orpah goes back, "but Ruth clave unto her." Then Naomi goes through another passionate plea for Ruth to return with her sister-in-law (v. 15), but Ruth determinedly commits herself to go with Naomi back to Judah. She does this through one of the most beautiful and poignant statements of human loyalty and commitment in all of Scripture.

The English translation of the phrase "and Ruth said" does not seem to bring out the force and emotion of the statement that follows. "Said" (Heb. *'amar,* **A-mar**) is used more than 5,000 times in the Old Testament with a variety of meanings, including "promise, command, pledge, or vow" as well as simply "stated." In light of the mundane nature of the dialogue it makes Ruth's insistence more unexpected and that much more powerful.

In her reply, Ruth asks Naomi: "Intreat me not to leave thee, or to return from following after thee," which in simple English means, "do not ask me or urge me to leave you." The word translated as "intreat" is the Hebrew word *paga'* (**paw-GAH**), often meaning "to meet, encounter, or strike." In this case, it means "to encounter with a request." It seems to be a gentle but determined objection to Naomi's effort to dissuade Ruth from following her to Judah. This objection translates into an absolute

committed loyalty, which Ruth expresses in a beautiful poetic form. Ruth's commitment and allegiance to Naomi extends beyond a commitment to one individual; it transcends the boundaries of nationality and ethnic religion. Her resolve to follow Naomi to the end is expressed as a matter of both life and death.

In many cultures, especially in Africa and the Jewish culture, people may decide to live among another tribe or people, but at death they always want to be buried in their homeland, among their people. But Ruth implicitly declares her allegiance to the Jewish community, culture, and religion. She invokes God's covenant name and seals this declaration with an oath. In it, she pronounces a curse on herself if she fails to keep this promise or fails to do what she has pledged. In its Hebrew context it means something like, "May the Lord deal with me ever so severely." Ruth says that not even death would be able to separate her from Naomi. She says that the only thing that could keep her from fulfilling her vow to Naomi was if she died first. A covenant oath of this nature in Hebrew is taken very seriously and is binding, especially when the name Yahweh is invoked.

Naomi understands the degree of Ruth's commitment and determination to go with her, and she entreats her no longer (v. 18). When she saw that she was determined to go with her, she stopped urging her to return to Moab. The rest of the chapter summarizes their return to Bethlehem and the reception Naomi received from the women there (vv. 19–22).

Say It Correctly

Orpah. **OR**-pah.
Moab. **MOE**-ab.

Daily Bible Readings

MONDAY
Protecting Widows
(Deuteronomy 24:17–22)

TUESDAY
Continuing the Family Line
(Deuteronomy 25:5–10)

WEDNESDAY
Ruth, Mother of David and Jesus
(Matthew 1:2–6, 16)

THURSDAY
Naomi Loses Her Husband and Sons
(Ruth 1:1–5)

FRIDAY
Ruth and Naomi Return to Bethlehem
(Ruth 1:19–22)

SATURDAY
Boaz Welcomes Ruth to His Fields
(Ruth 2:5–13)

SUNDAY
Intimate Family Ties
(Ruth 1:6–11, 14–18)

Notes

_____

_____

_____

_____

Teaching Tips

August 18
Bible Study Guide 12

Words You Should Know

A. Kindness *chesed* (Heb.)—Compassion, loyalty, mercy.

B. Winnow *zarah* (Heb.)—To fan, scatter, a part of the harvest process separating wheat.

Teacher Preparation

Unifying Principle—Commitment. Obedience and commitment to others may bring unanticipated rewards. How should loyalty be compensated? Ruth's commitment to Naomi and her efforts to obey were rewarded with favor in Boaz's eyes, marriage to a kinsman-redeemer, and the assurance of a comfortable life in the future.

A. Read the Bible Background and Devotional Readings.

B. Pray for your students and lesson clarity.

C. Read the lesson Scripture in multiple translations.

D. Option: Have students brainstorm ways they could show kindness to people whether they deserve it or not, as Boaz did for Ruth and Naomi. Plan a "random acts of kindness" day to carry out the ideas.

O—Open the Lesson

A. Begin the class with prayer.

B. Have the students read the Aim for Change.

C. Have the students read the In Focus story.

D. Ask students how events named in the story can weigh on their hearts and how they can view these events from a theological perspective.

P—Present the Scriptures

A. Read the Focal Verses and discuss the Background and The People, Places, and Times sections.

B. Have the class share what Scriptures stand out for them and why, with particular emphasis on today's context.

E—Explore the Meaning

A. Use In Depth or More Light on the Text to help provide more in-depth discussion of the lesson text.

B. Discuss the Liberating Lesson and Application for Activation sections.

N—Next Steps for Application

A. Summarize the value of seeking godly counsel in Christian marriages.

B. End class with a commitment to pray for married couples and those who want to pursue marriage.

Worship Guide

For the Superintendent or Teacher
Theme: A Covenant to Marry
Song: "Love"
Devotional Reading: Hebrews 13:1–8

622

A Covenant to Marry

Bible Background • RUTH 1:6–18; 3–4; MATTHEW 19:1–12
Printed Text • RUTH 3:1–6, 8–12, 16–18 | Devotional Reading • HEBREWS 13:1–8

—— Aim for Change ——

By the end of the lesson, we will: SUMMARIZE the actions that led to the marriage of Boaz and Ruth; IDENTIFY the strong trust between Ruth and Naomi; and CONSIDER ways to honor marriage and courtship whether we are married or not.

In Focus

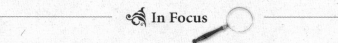

Last year, Kerry ended a sour relationship and moved to a new city. She had many of the things she'd always desired, but she still felt incomplete. Her mom suggested she start dating again.

"Dating? Why would I do that? That's the thing that got me off track in the first place!"

Her mother also suggested that Kerry stop partying so much. "Think about it, Kerry. When you're not at work, you're partying. You aren't doing the things you really like doing. Be open, that's when you'll find a partner." Kerry was silent. "Just pray on it."

"Pray? For what?"

"That God will guide you to the right man. You're working on yourself, so God will find someone who wants to work with you."

"I never really thought of it that way."

"All relationships are work, especially your relationships with men. Just like He presented you with this job opportunity, He'll present the right partner."

That night, Kerry thought about what her mother had said. She closed her eyes and said a quick prayer, "Lord, thank you for letting me have a fresh start. Thank you for my family and friends. I am ready for what is next. I want to walk toward the one you have for me. Amen."

What relationships are you currently working on building or re-creating?

—— Keep in Mind ——

"And he said, Blessed be thou of the Lord, my daughter: for thou hast shewed more kindness in the latter end than at the beginning, inasmuch as thou followedst not young men, whether poor or rich" (Ruth 3:10, KJV).

"The Lord bless you, my daughter!" Boaz exclaimed. "You are showing even more family loyalty now than you did before, for you have not gone after a younger man, whether rich or poor" (Ruth 3:10, NLT).

Focal Verses

KJV **Ruth 3:1** Then Naomi her mother in law said unto her, My daughter, shall I not seek rest for thee, that it may be well with thee?

2 And now is not Boaz of our kindred, with whose maidens thou wast? Behold, he winnoweth barley to night in the threshingfloor.

3 Wash thyself therefore, and anoint thee, and put thy raiment upon thee, and get thee down to the floor: but make not thyself known unto the man, until he shall have done eating and drinking.

4 And it shall be, when he lieth down, that thou shalt mark the place where he shall lie, and thou shalt go in, and uncover his feet, and lay thee down; and he will tell thee what thou shalt do.

5 And she said unto her, All that thou sayest unto me I will do.

6 And she went down unto the floor, and did according to all that her mother in law bade her.

8 And it came to pass at midnight, that the man was afraid, and turned himself: and, behold, a woman lay at his feet.

9 And he said, Who art thou? And she answered, I am Ruth thine handmaid: spread therefore thy skirt over thine handmaid; for thou art a near kinsman.

10 And he said, Blessed be thou of the Lord, my daughter: for thou hast shewed more kindness in the latter end than at the beginning, inasmuch as thou followedst not young men, whether poor or rich.

11 And now, my daughter, fear not; I will do to thee all that thou requirest: for all the city of my people doth know that thou art a virtuous woman.

12 And now it is true that I am thy near kinsman: howbeit there is a kinsman nearer than I.

NLT **Ruth 3:1** One day Naomi said to Ruth, "My daughter, it's time that I found a permanent home for you, so that you will be provided for.

2 Boaz is a close relative of ours, and he's been very kind by letting you gather grain with his young women. Tonight he will be winnowing barley at the threshing floor.

3 Now do as I tell you—take a bath and put on perfume and dress in your nicest clothes. Then go to the threshing floor, but don't let Boaz see you until he has finished eating and drinking.

4 Be sure to notice where he lies down; then go and uncover his feet and lie down there. He will tell you what to do."

5 "I will do everything you say," Ruth replied.

6 So she went down to the threshing floor that night and followed the instructions of her mother-in-law.

8 Around midnight Boaz suddenly woke up and turned over. He was surprised to find a woman lying at his feet!

9 "Who are you?" he asked. "I am your servant Ruth," she replied. "Spread the corner of your covering over me, for you are my family redeemer."

10 "The Lord bless you, my daughter!" Boaz exclaimed. "You are showing even more family loyalty now than you did before, for you have not gone after a younger man, whether rich or poor.

11 Now don't worry about a thing, my daughter. I will do what is necessary, for everyone in town knows you are a virtuous woman.

12 But while it's true that I am one of your family redeemers, there is another man who is more closely related to you than I am.

16 When Ruth went back to her mother-in-law, Naomi asked, "What happened, my

16 And when she came to her mother in law, she said, Who art thou, my daughter? And she told her all that the man had done to her.

17 And she said, These six measures of barley gave he me; for he said to me, Go not empty unto thy mother in law.

18 Then said she, Sit still, my daughter, until thou know how the matter will fall: for the man will not be in rest, until he have finished the thing this day.

daughter?" Ruth told Naomi everything Boaz had done for her,

17 and she added, "He gave me these six scoops of barley and said, 'Don't go back to your mother-in-law empty-handed.'"

18 Then Naomi said to her, "Just be patient, my daughter, until we hear what happens. The man won't rest until he has settled things today."

The People, Places, and Times

Kinsman. During Bible times, "kinsman" described a person's nearest male relative. He had certain responsibilities according to the law. For example, the kinsman acted as an avenger. A wrong done to one member of a family was considered an offense against the entire group. Kinsmen were obligated to punish the wrongdoer. Also, the kinsman was obliged to act as redeemer and handle financial matters on family members' behalf. These responsibilities could include redeeming property a relative might have sold due to poverty (Leviticus 25:25), ransoming (buying back) his kinsman who may have been sold into slavery (25:47–49), or acting as a go-between in case a person wanted to make restitution to a relative. The role of the kinsman-redeemer also included taking responsibility for the extended family. When a woman's husband died, the law provided she could marry a brother of her dead husband (Deuteronomy 25:5–10). If there were no brothers, the nearest relative to the deceased husband could become the kinsman-redeemer and marry the widow. If he chose not to, the next nearest relative could marry the widow. In order to provide for those widows who did not remarry, the "gleaning laws" were established (Leviticus 19:9–10).

What situations cause people to take on responsibility for others' well being in our society today?

Background

At the end of Ruth 1 and into chapter 2, Naomi and Ruth arrived in Bethlehem in time for the harvest of the barley fields. The whole town was abuzz at Naomi's return with her Moabite daughter-in-law. Naomi shared her losses with the women of the community and the story of Ruth's care for her mother-in-law spread throughout the town. Ruth took the initiative to provide for the two of them by setting out to glean behind the reapers. It was custom as a form of charity to allow the poor, widows, orphans, and foreigners to follow behind the harvesters to gather the leftover grain (Leviticus 19:9-10; Deuteronomy 24:19). Through God's providence, Ruth happened to glean the fields owned by Boaz, a relative of Naomi's late husband. Boaz was a noble man of means and he took notice of this unfamiliar young woman. He inquired of her background and learned that she was the Moabite woman who returned with Naomi. After making the familial connection, learning further details of Ruth's story and hearing of her hard work, he approached Ruth. Boaz implored her to stay close to his young women and to not move to another field. He also spoke a blessing of reward for Ruth because of how she honored her mother-in-law, and left her own people to live with Naomi. Boaz further blessed Ruth by making sure she was protected as she worked, she was nourished, and that she could earn a good living to take care of her household. At the end of her workday, Ruth was excited to tell Naomi of her success and learned that the man who blessed her was a relative of Naomi's. Ruth and Naomi settled in, and Ruth continued to work in Boaz's field with the rest of the young women through the barley and wheat harvest season.

How can reputation and location be key to new opportunities in life?

At-A-Glance

1. Partners in Covenant (Ruth 3:1–6)
2. An Interest in Covenant (vv. 8–12)
3. Waiting on Covenant (vv. 16–18)

In Depth

1. Partners in Covenant (Ruth 3:1–6)

In ancient Middle Eastern culture a woman without a husband had little to no public standing, was not secure, and thus needed protection. Out of concern for Ruth's future, Naomi advises Ruth on how to secure a husband by expressing interest in Boaz, who was by marriage her next of kin (Ruth 2:20). Naomi returns Ruth's love and protection, because as an older woman she was secure and would be taken care of (Deuteronomy 14:29, 24:19), but she wanted to ensure Ruth's standing, protection, and provision in the community. There are different schools of thought on Naomi's suggested approach to Ruth. But the planned end result of her advice was in line with the Hebrew levirate marriage custom: In order to keep the deceased man and his inheritance in the family line, the next of kin or kinsman-redeemer would marry his widow (Leviticus 25:25, 48–49). Naomi advises Ruth to get cleaned up, put on her best scented oil, a nice outfit, and to stealthily go to Boaz in the night. She further counsels Ruth to wait until he has retired from his work. She knew that after eating and drinking, he would be good and relaxed, so it would be a good time to make her move. Ruth followed Naomi's counsel as the older woman is teaching the younger one how to ensure their survival by connecting with this man. To some, Naomi and Ruth's plan may appear forward, but in the story of Tamar (Genesis 3) we have another example in Scripture of a woman who also enacted a plan using the same custom to secure her future. Both Tamar and Ruth end up in Jesus' family lineage.

Why is learning from someone who has experience in our pursuit important?

2. An Interest in Covenant (vv. 8–12)

Boaz awakened to find a woman lying at his feet and discovered that it was Ruth. This suggestive move, to appear in a man's presence at the threshing floor, was a bold one because she was not sure how he would receive her. Ruth asked for Boaz to spread his cloak over her for he was the nearest kinsman or next of kin. The spreading of the cloak signified the desire for acquisition through marriage. His relation to Ruth was not direct but due to her connection to Naomi's family. The love and loyalty shown to Naomi placed Ruth in a position to make such a plea. Boaz was overcome with her gesture and stated how this act of loyalty was better than the first: Ruth could have pursued the application of levirate law with someone younger, rich or poor, or with someone out of her husband's bloodline, but she chose him. Boaz acknowledges her virtue and tells her that the community viewed her not as a foreigner but a worthy woman. He seeks to further protect her purity by committing to do what she has asked, but there was another male relative who would be the actual next of kin. Upon their first meeting, Boaz spoke a blessing over Ruth because of her love and devotion to Naomi (v. 12). God's masterful orchestration fulfilled this word; Boaz had no idea that he would be that blessing in the beginning.

What role does acting at the right time have in us receiving what God wants for us?

3. Waiting on Covenant (vv. 16–18)

After spending the night at the threshing floor with Boaz, Ruth leaves before anyone can recognize her. Boaz goes through great lengths to protect her reputation in the community because it was against custom for a woman to appear at the threshing floor. He commits to meeting with the men of the community, which includes the actual next of kin to see if he will make the claim or serve as the next of kin (v. 13). Ruth returns to her mother-in-law with her cloak filled with grain because Boaz does not want her to return to Naomi empty-handed. Naomi asks Ruth for a report of what happened just as a trusted friend and confidant would. As Ruth shares the exchange between her and Boaz, Naomi offers her next pearl of wisdom on how to manage the situation. She instructs Ruth to sit tight and wait until she receives word of the outcome. Naomi knew that Boaz had already made the commitment to be the next of kin because of how he already sacrificed and extended himself to protect and provide, as a good man would. She was confident that Boaz would keep his word and that the matter would be settled by the end of the day.

The book of Ruth can be seen as a picture of God's love for us expressed through His Son Jesus Christ as our next-of-kin redeemer. We have to take the step of receiving God's salvation by trusting in the finished work of Calvary, accepting Jesus into our heart, and living for Him.

How do you manage waiting on God when in a time of transition or seeking a new opportunity?

Search the Scriptures

1. Why was it important for Naomi to secure Ruth's future (Ruth 3:1)?

2. What was the significance of Ruth's approach to Boaz and his response to her plea (vv. 9–12)?

Discuss the Meaning

1. Think of times in your life when you've noticed God guiding you through a transition. What were some of the things that you noticed?

2. What are times when you've felt you had to work on yourself and make a dramatic change to your routine?

Liberating Lesson

The Ruth/Boaz story is often romanticized as a picture of how a woman should wait for a man to notice her to be chosen to marry. However, what is often not highlighted in this story is Naomi's advice on how to capture his attention and express interest. This often overlooked part of the story is a direct challenge to many societal norms that force women to wait idly for men to pursue romantic relationships. The book of Ruth itself highlights the importance of women building relationships with one another and honoring each other as important and worthy. Although in the end Ruth waited for Boaz's decision to marry her, she expressed interest when she encountered him. The older woman provided instruction, and the younger woman followed the advice to make herself known. Once she did it was up to the man to take action. When God illuminates a person for pursuit of a marriage relationship, it is best to do so with wise counsel to discern and accountability to make good choices. Ruth decided to serve the God of Israel, positioning herself to work to survive and take care of herself, identify a potential mate, and then act on Naomi's advice to courageously present herself to Boaz. These decisions were so impactful that it allows this once marginalized woman to become an important part of the lineage of Jesus Christ.

Application for Activation

Having the reputation as a noble man or a worthy woman opens the door for God to bless and reward beyond what one can ask or imagine. The church community can be the conduit to cultivate organic covenant relationships worthy of God's stamp of approval by providing safe and accountable spaces to make kingdom-minded connections. This week consider how you make your church community a space where healthy relationships can form and marriages can be encouraged and cultivated. If you have been married for a long time, how can you encourage younger couples? If you are unmarried and desire marriage, how can you seek wise counsel before pursuing marriage? If you are single and part of the community, how can you affirm and support healthy romantic relationships around you?

Follow the Spirit

What God wants me to do:

_____

_____

_____

_____

Remember Your Thoughts

Special insights I have learned:

_____

_____

_____

_____

More Light on the Text

Ruth 3:1–6, 8–12, 16–18

1 Then Naomi her mother in law said unto her, My daughter, shall I not seek rest for thee, that it may be well with thee?

Naomi's desire for each of her daughters-in-law, Ruth and Orpah, had long been that they have husbands and a place to rest (1:9). Their kindness was a blessing that Naomi wanted the Lord to repay to them by giving each a husband and a home. Ruth and Naomi traveled to Bethlehem. While in Bethlehem, Ruth gleaned from the crops to feed herself and her mother-in-law. Gleaning is picking up the leftover crops after they have been harvested. Leaving crops for foreigners and the poor is what God declared that the Israelite landowners must do. Gleaning was not a new concept. It is not an act of charity for the Israelite landowners as others practiced. Gleaning is based on God's holiness. The landowners, who are Israelites, are required by God to leave crops for the poor, foreigners, and those living on the margins of life (Leviticus 19:10; Deuteronomy 24:19–22). God's love is not rooted in the desires of others to be kind or not; it is rooted in God's nature and is unconditional. Naomi was determined to find a home for Ruth. While waiting for their new home, Ruth chose to work. She did not sit idly by and wait for someone to feed and care for them. She had asked Naomi if she could glean. Her work meant they would have food to cook and eat.

2 And now is not Boaz of our kindred, with whose maidens thou wast? Behold, he winnoweth barley to night in the threshing floor.

Ruth had asked in chapter 2 if she could glean wheat after the reapers and had been granted permission (2:2). Boaz was a relative of Elimelech, Naomi's husband, and the owner of the land where Ruth and the other handmaidens picked the grain after it was cut by the reapers. Boaz, whose name means "swiftness," was a man of status and wealth. He was a man of integrity that others listened to and respected. The reapers knew that Ruth was a Moabite. Boaz learned this and more when he spoke directly with Ruth (vv. 8–13). Her kind responses and demeanor caught Boaz's attention. Boaz would remember her kindness.

Ruth shares with Naomi her encounter with Boaz. Naomi believed that the meeting and conversation between Ruth and Boaz was an opportunity to secure a future for Ruth. Naomi's question to Ruth, about Boaz's relation to the family, points to him as the kinsman-redeemer (3:2). The kinsman-redeemer or guardian redeemer (Heb. *ga'al*, **gaw-ALL**) is based on laws in the Torah and had the responsibility or honor of intervening on behalf of the family member (i.e., Leviticus 25:25–55; Ruth 3:12–13).

The Scriptures describe Naomi and Ruth as widows. Neither had children who could take care of them. Therefore, Naomi needed redemption of her husband's land because they did not have children or any living male relative. Consequently, Boaz could buy the property as the relative, the kinsman-redeemer, and Naomi and Ruth would not become slaves because of debt owed on the property. Naomi

realized here was an opportunity for Ruth to have a home and a husband. Naomi devised a plan for Ruth to establish a covenantal relationship with Boaz that could lead to marriage.

Naomi knew that Ruth would need to speak with Boaz when others were not around. The harvesting process of the barley would allow this. After the barley was harvested, various steps were involved to prepare it to sell. Nighttime was a good cover for Naomi's plan to begin. Her plan was an undercover move to help secure Ruth's future. Would the plan work? Naomi's plan for Boaz and Ruth to marry could happen, if careful planning, explicit details, following directions, and Boaz's unknowing cooperation occurred. Ruth was willing to participate in Naomi's plan. Naomi could not control Boaz's actions, but she could guide Ruth in securing a future for both women. If Ruth and Boaz were married, Ruth would have a home and a husband and become a surrogate mother for Naomi. A child born from the marriage of Ruth and Boaz would be the heir for Naomi to keep her family alive and growing. Also, Boaz, who would purchase the land, would retain the land in trust for the family's probable future heir.

3 Wash thyself therefore, and anoint thee, and put thy raiment upon thee, and get thee down to the floor: but make not thyself known unto the man, until he shall have done eating and drinking. 4 And it shall be, when he lieth down, that thou shalt mark the place where he shall lie, and thou shalt go in, and uncover his feet, and lay thee down; and he will tell thee what thou shalt do. 5 And she said unto her, All that thou sayest unto me I will do. 6 And she went down unto the floor, and did according to all that her mother in law bade her.

Naomi instructed Ruth how to prepare for her upcoming encounter with Boaz (vv. 3–5).

Boaz would be sleeping on the threshing floor to protect the crop from robbers. The threshing floors were away from the village where the men lived. Naomi told Ruth to bathe and anoint herself with fragrances that would appeal to Boaz. Ruth's fresh bath, clean dress, and sweet smelling perfume would attract him.

Verse 4 is a very controversial topic. There are two points of debate. Some scholars believe that Naomi's instructions to "uncover" Boaz implied a sexual interpretation in Hebrew because the words uncover (Heb. *galah*, **gaw-LAW**), feet (Heb. *margelot*, **mar-guh-LOTE**), and lay down (Heb. *shakab*, **shaw-KOV**) all have sexual meanings. Other scholars state that the uncovering referred to his limbs, which include legs, thighs, and feet (Daniel 10:6). Ruth waited until Boaz laid down and then went onto the threshing floor and laid near him. This allowed Ruth access to him during the cover of night. Naomi cautioned her to wait until he was finished eating and drinking. Boaz would relax and fall asleep. This would provide Ruth a chance to see where he was sleeping and position herself near Boaz without his knowing that she was present.

Naomi assured Ruth that Boaz would tell her what to do. Ruth would need to follow his instructions. Ruth agreed that she would obey all that Naomi had told her to do, then went to the threshing floor and did it (v. 6).

8 And it came to pass at midnight, that the man was afraid, and turned himself: and, behold, a woman lay at his feet. 9 And he said, Who art thou? And she answered, I am Ruth thine handmaid: spread therefore thy skirt over thine handmaid; for thou art a near kinsman. 10 And he said, Blessed be thou of the LORD, my daughter: for thou hast shewed more kindness in the latter end than at the beginning, inasmuch as thou followedst not young men, whether poor or rich. 11 And now, my daughter, fear not; I will do to thee all that thou requirest: for all the city of my people doth know that thou art a virtuous woman. 12 And now it is true that I am thy near kinsman: howbeit there is a kinsman nearer than I.

The darkness was a shield for both of them. Ruth's presence could become a problem if anyone knew they were together. Boaz's reputation would be tainted and Ruth an outcast or looked down upon (v. 14). The other men who had been sleeping on the various threshing floors were either already asleep or chose to ignore any sounds or movements that were non-threatening. The threshing floor was also known as a place for men to frequent with prostitutes and drink wine (Hosea 9:1–2).

As Naomi had instructed, Ruth uncovered Boaz by folding back his long tunic. The night air or the feeling of someone's presence may have awakened him. Once he was awake, Ruth would have the opportunity to have a private talk with him. When he awoke, Boaz was startled to see someone was lying near him. The text does not say where she was lying, but it was close enough for him to see someone was near, but too far to fully recognize who. The darkness of the night shielded her. Boaz asked who was there and Ruth answered by stating her name, her status, and asked if he would spread his garment over her because he was their family's closest kinsman-redeemer (vv. 8–9).

Ruth deviated from the plan that Naomi had given her. Ruth decided for whatever reason to state why she was there. In essence, Ruth had requested for Boaz to marry her and take care of any debt that she and Naomi had. This was not a part of Naomi's initial plan. Boaz had not forgotten their earlier conversation. He had inquired who she was before the two ever spoke, and then had the opportunity to expand and deepen the relationship. Ruth's integrity and faithfulness were highly respected by Boaz. She was considered a virtuous woman. Ruth was free to marry the family's kinsman-redeemer. The beginning stages of this relationship could lead to a covenant of marriage.

Marriage is a special and honorable event. Boaz knew marriage was created and ordained by God (Genesis 2:24). The sacredness of marriage is addressed in the New Testament by Jesus after the Pharisees tried to trap him with a question about divorce (Matthew 19:4–9). Jesus emphasized that God created marriage and that unless the wife commits sexual immorality, a man should not divorce his wife. If Boaz agreed to cover Ruth with his garment, he was agreeing to marry her (Ezekiel 16:8). He was willing to accept the responsibility, financial needs, and the sacredness of marriage.

Before Boaz agreed to marry Ruth by spreading the garment over her, he spoke about her character and how well he and others thought of her. Boaz praised Ruth's kindness (Heb. *khesed*, **KHEH-sed**), referring to the kindness, compassion, faithfulness, loyalty, mercy, and love she had shown (1:8; 2:11, 20). Additionally, Boaz stated that she did not choose the younger men, whether they were rich or the poor, stronger or energetic. This obviously pleased Boaz. Ruth was a woman of integrity. Her character and her discipline demonstrated this.

Ruth must have shown or indicated that she was afraid because Boaz told her not be afraid (v. 11) in her request for him to become the provider, protector, and to marry her. If the kinsman-redeemer who is the closest relative to the family does not marry Ruth, Boaz agreed to honor her request and marry her. The name of this close kinsman-redeemer is not given in the text. Yet, Boaz is aware of whom he is and must speak with him before moving forward with any plans of buying the property or marrying Ruth. Boaz demonstrated his integrity

and respect of Ruth because he did not want her reputation ruined, and he respected the family and tradition processes of kinsman-redeemer (vv. 11–14). Although he agreed to marry Ruth, he was willing to abide by the established tradition.

Naomi's return to Bethlehem, and Ruth traveling with her and gleaning in Boaz's field are examples of the Lord's interaction before the relationship began. Their covenantal relationship would unfold as the story continues. The future marriage between Ruth and Boaz is part of the divine and historical lineage that Jesus, the Messiah, would be born into. Ruth and Boaz would have a son named Obed, who was the father of Jesse, and Jesse would become the father of David. David would become one of the greatest kings of Israel. Each of these ancestors are named in the lineage of Jesus (Matthew 1:5–6; Luke 3:31–32).

16 And when she came to her mother in law, she said, Who art thou, my daughter? And she told her all that the man had done to her. 17 And she said, These six measures of barley gave he me; for he said to me, Go not empty unto thy mother in law. 18 Then said she, Sit still, my daughter, until thou know how the matter will fall: for the man will not be in rest, until he have finished the thing this day.

It is interesting to note Naomi's initial question, "Who art thou, my daughter?" which in this context would be akin to asking "Are you Mrs. Boaz?" Ruth laid at the feet of Boaz until the early morning as he had asked (v. 14). Before the sun rose, Ruth left and returned home to her mother-in-law. No one else would know that she was in the threshing floor area with Boaz except for her mother-in-law, Naomi. Ruth did not leave empty-handed. Boaz asked her to give him the veil or shawl that covered her head. As she held this piece of fabric, Boaz put a large amount of barley, "six measures," into it (vv. 15, 17). He wanted to make sure that she returned home with a gift for Naomi. The barley was a gift of substance and one both women would use and remember Boaz for his generosity. The amount and the weight of the barley were so great that Boaz had to place it on Ruth's shoulder (v. 15).

First, Ruth showed Naomi the large amount of barley that Boaz gave her as a gift for Naomi. He did want her to return home empty-handed. Secondly, after hearing Boaz's response, Naomi tells Ruth to wait until Boaz completes what he needs to do. Naomi is confident that Boaz will take the necessary actions to solidify the relationship. Naomi believed that he would not stop until he had done so.

The initial meeting of Ruth and Boaz was the beginning steps of a covenantal relationship that would develop into a marriage. Ruth, Boaz, and Naomi were integral parts of God's plan. Although God does not speak in the book of Ruth, His handiwork is evidenced throughout the book of Ruth.

Sources:

Attridge, Harold, W. *The Harper Collins Study Bible, New Revised Standard Version*. New York, NY: Harper One, 2006. 382-383, 386-387.

Cabal, Ted et. al., *The Apologetics Study Bible*, Holman Christian Standard. Nashville, TN: Holman Bible Publishers, 2007. 401-402.

Block, Daniel I. *The New American Commentary: Judges and Ruth*. Nashville, TN: B&H Books, 1999. 686.

Carson, D.A, gen. ed. *NIV Zondervan Study Bible*. Grand Rapids, MI: Zondervan, 2015.

Van der Mass, Ed M. *Halley's Bible Handbook: Deluxe Edition* (25th Edition). Grand Rapids, MI: Zondervan, 2007. 195.

Blank, Wayne. "Winnowing." Bible Study - Winnowing. http://www.keyway.ca/htm2001/20010626.htm.

"BibleGateway." Ruth 3 KJV - Bible Gateway. https://www.biblegateway.com/passage/?search=Ruth 3&version= KJV.

"Agriculture - International Standard Bible Encyclopedia." Bible Study Tools. http://www.biblestudytools.com/encyclopedias/isbe/agriculture.html.

"Ga'al - Old Testament Hebrew Lexicon - New American Standard." Bible Study Tools. http://www.biblestudytools.com/lexicons/hebrew/nas/gaal.html.

Strong's Hebrew: 5115. (navah) - Home. http://biblehub.com/hebrew/5115.htm.

The Kinsman-Redeemer. BibleHub.com. http://biblehub.com/library/maclaren/expositions_of_holy_scripture_h/the_kinsman-redeemer.htm.

Charles Halton. "Seduction on the Threshing Floor." BibleOdyssey.org. http://www.bibleodyssey.org/people/related-articles/seduction-on-the-threshing-floor.aspx.

"Gleaning (Leviticus 19:9-10)." TheologyOfWork.org. https://www.theologyofwork.org/old-testament/leviticus-and-work/holiness-leviticus-1727/gleaning-leviticus-19910.

"Boaz." Boaz Dictionary Definition | Boaz Defined. http://www.yourdictionary.com/boaz.

Daily Bible Readings

MONDAY
God's Chosen Bride
(Ezekiel 16:8–14)

TUESDAY
Status of Divorced Women in Israel
(Deuteronomy 24:1–4)

WEDNESDAY
Sustain Marital Love and Fidelity
(1 Corinthians 7:1–11)

THURSDAY
Husbands and Wives, Joint Heirs
(1 Peter 3:1–9)

FRIDAY
Boaz Buys Naomi's Property
(Ruth 4:9–12)

SATURDAY
Ruth and Boaz Marry; Obed Born
(Ruth 4:13–17)

SUNDAY
Support and Protect Marriage
(Ruth 3:1–6, 8–12, 16–18)

Teaching Tips

Words You Should Know

A. Love *agapao* (Gk.)—Unconditional love, usually comes from God; in today's lesson the love husbands and wives should aspire to.

B. Nourish *ektrepho* (Gk.)—To provide sustenance; to provide for the necessities of life.

Teacher Preparation

Unifying Priniciple—Godly Marriage. In an ever-changing and increasingly complex society, the focus on self-indulgence has endangered a healthy concept of family. How do we make commitment to God and family central to our well-being? Paul says a committed relationship must be sought in which husbands, wives, and children love, honor, and respect both God and one another.

A. Read the Bible Background and Devotional Readings.

B. Pray for your students and lesson clarity.

C. Read the lesson Scripture in multiple translations.

D. Option: Invite volunteers to read Mark 10:42-45; John 13:3-5, 12-17; and 1 Corinthians 7:3-4. How do these passages apply to relationships in marriage? Based on these passages, how should we read the commandment for wives to "be subject" to their husbands? What should husbands do with respect to this verse?

O—Open the Lesson

A. Begin the class with prayer.

B. Have the students read the Aim for Change.

C. Have the students read the In Focus story.

D. Ask students how events named in the story can weigh on their hearts and how they can view these events from a theological perspective.

P—Present the Scriptures

A. Read the Focal Verses and discuss the Background and The People, Places, and Times sections.

B. Have the class share what Scriptures stand out for them and why, with particular emphasis on today's context.

E—Explore the Meaning

A. Use In Depth or More Light on the Text to help provide more in-depth discussion of the lesson text.

B. Discuss the Liberating Lesson and Application for Activation sections.

N—Next Steps for Application

A. Summarize the importance of mutual love and respect in marriage.

B. End class with a commitment to pray for married couples and families.

Worship Guide

For the Superintendent or Teacher
Theme: Marriage: A Covenant of Mutual Love
Song: "All I Need Is You"
Devotional Reading: Hebrews 12:7–13

Marriage: A Covenant of Mutual Love

Bible Background • EPHESIANS 5:21–6:4
Printed Text • EPHESIANS 5:21–33 | Devotional Reading • HEBREWS 12:7–13

—— Aim for Change ——

By the end of the lesson, we will: SUMMARIZE the relationship Paul describes as proper between a husband and wife; APPRECIATE the holy relationship between husband and wife that is natural and spiritual; and COMMIT to creating a culture where holy marriages can flourish in our church communities.

—— In Focus ——

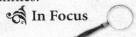

"You still think that we should wait on this?" Emily sat looking very perplexed. "What do you mean? We've been waiting … we've been waiting for like a year."

Langston and Emily had been dating for some time, and when Langston saw things getting serious, he wanted to be thoughtful about the relationship, including abstaining from sex. Emily equally cared for Langston, but felt they were more than ready to have a sexual relationship, especially because neither of them were virgins. This debate had been coming up in their relationship for a few months. Langston didn't want Emily to feel as if he didn't want her; he wanted to be clear about his intentions.

"Emily, I desire you so much that I want to build my entire life with you, as husband and wife. Believe me, waiting is extremely difficult for me. But I trust that God is leading us to exactly where we need to be."

Emily was really taken aback. She had never heard a man speak to her so clearly about his intentions. She had felt that Langston could be her husband, but she never allowed herself to believe that he felt so strongly about her. She decided at that moment that she would be more patient with Langston and their relationship. She wanted him to know that they were in this together, as partners.

How can Christian couples focus on submitting to God first in order to effectively submit to one another?

—— Keep in Mind ——

"Submitting yourselves one to another in the fear of God" (Ephesians 5:21, KJV).

"And further, submit to one another out of reverence for Christ" (Ephesians 5:21, NLT).

Focal Verses

KJV **Ephesians 5:21** Submitting yourselves one to another in the fear of God.

22 Wives, submit yourselves unto your own husbands, as unto the Lord.

23 For the husband is the head of the wife, even as Christ is the head of the church: and he is the saviour of the body.

24 Therefore as the church is subject unto Christ, so let the wives be to their own husbands in every thing.

25 Husbands, love your wives, even as Christ also loved the church, and gave himself for it;

26 That he might sanctify and cleanse it with the washing of water by the word,

27 That he might present it to himself a glorious church, not having spot, or wrinkle, or any such thing; but that it should be holy and without blemish.

28 So ought men to love their wives as their own bodies. He that loveth his wife loveth himself.

29 For no man ever yet hated his own flesh; but nourisheth and cherisheth it, even as the Lord the church:

30 For we are members of his body, of his flesh, and of his bones.

31 For this cause shall a man leave his father and mother, and shall be joined unto his wife, and they two shall be one flesh.

32 This is a great mystery: but I speak concerning Christ and the church.

33 Nevertheless let every one of you in particular so love his wife even as himself; and the wife see that she reverence her husband.

NLT **Ephesians 5:21** And further, submit to one another out of reverence for Christ.

22 For wives, this means submit to your husbands as to the Lord.

23 For a husband is the head of his wife as Christ is the head of the church. He is the Savior of his body, the church.

24 As the church submits to Christ, so you wives should submit to your husbands in everything.

25 For husbands, this means love your wives, just as Christ loved the church. He gave up his life for her

26 to make her holy and clean, washed by the cleansing of God's word.

27 He did this to present her to himself as a glorious church without a spot or wrinkle or any other blemish. Instead, she will be holy and without fault.

28 In the same way, husbands ought to love their wives as they love their own bodies. For a man who loves his wife actually shows love for himself.

29 No one hates his own body but feeds and cares for it, just as Christ cares for the church.

30 And we are members of his body.

31 As the Scriptures say, "A man leaves his father and mother and is joined to his wife, and the two are united into one."

32 This is a great mystery, but it is an illustration of the way Christ and the church are one.

33 So again I say, each man must love his wife as he loves himself, and the wife must respect her husband.

The People, Places, and Times

Saul. Saul (later known as Paul) was a Jew—and not just an ordinary Jew. A single man, Saul was educated under Gamaliel, one of the foremost rabbis of the first century. Saul was a "Jew of Jews," meaning that he was highly educated in Jewish law and very devout. He followed Jewish law zealously and vigorously persecuted the followers of Christ (Acts 22:1–4). After Saul's dramatic conversion, God called him to minister specifically to the Gentiles (vv. 14, 21). In that day, it was against Jewish law for a Jew to associate with a Gentile in any way (Acts 10:28). The Jews of that day were highly offended by Paul's association with Gentiles, especially since Paul taught that circumcision and other Jewish laws were not binding on the Gentiles. Paul's experience with a crowd of hostile Jews in Jerusalem nearly cost him his life and resulted in a four-year imprisonment at Caesarea and Rome. This imprisonment was a direct result of his ministry to the Gentiles. It is for this reason that Paul reminds the Gentiles, with no rancor, that he is a prisoner for their sake (Ephesians 3:1).

Why is it important to receive wise counsel as we navigate marriages?

Background

The book of Ephesians has one prevailing theme: union with Christ. This is, in fact, the central fact of Christian identity. We are justified, sanctified, and ultimately saved because we have been united to Christ by faith through the Holy Spirit. Union with Christ is the reality by which we are considered righteous and that ought to color each of our personal relationships. As Paul explains, it is "in Christ" that God has blessed us with every spiritual blessing; it is "in Christ" that we were chosen to be holy and blameless; and it is "in Christ" that we have been adopted as sons and daughters (Ephesians 1:3; Colossians 1:22; Galatians 3:26).

In the end of Ephesians 5 and the beginning of chapter 6, we gain a glimpse into the closest human relationship possible, which offers a special glimpse into the reality of union with Christ: marriage. In fact, Christ's relationship with the church is the archetype for the relationship between a husband and wife, as Paul will explain in these verses. One also finds in these verses distinct commands to husbands and wives, adding more credence to the biblical understanding of marriage as a relationship between a man and a woman and as the righteous context for sexual expression.

How does unity between Christ and the church relate to unity in marriage?

At-A-Glance

1. Wives and Mutual Submission (Ephesians 5:21–24)
2. Husbands, Love Your Wives (vv. 25–30)
3. Christ and the Church: The Model for Marriage (vv. 31–33)

In Depth

1. Wives and Mutual Submission (Ephesians 5:21–24)

Paul begins this explanation of household codes with the matrix in which everything that follows takes place: mutual submission. Each of the family and work environments outlined in the coming verses takes place under the umbrella of reverence for Christ. All members of the family submit to Christ and mutually to one another in covenant. But Paul still has particular commands to particular family members, often personalized to keep in mind specific temptations that husbands and wives need to guard against.

Beginning with wives, Paul encourages them to submit to their own husbands. It must be noted that this is not a command rooted fundamentally in gender, but rather in the relationship. He does not say, "Women, submit to men" but rather "wives, submit to your own husbands." The reason for this is that the husband is the head of the household and the one whom God holds responsible. This does not mean that wives are to be doormats for their husbands, but it does mean that wives are to gratefully accept the love, care, and leadership of their husbands.

2. Husbands, Love Your Wives (vv. 25–30)

It is often suggested that the paradigm of wifely submission and the headship of the husband lends itself to abusive relationships. Such a connection cannot be made if the husband is obedient to the apostle's command that he love his wife as Christ loved the church. The command to the man is total and uncompromising: The Son of God gave up His life for His church. Husbands ought to do the same for the sake of the growth of their wives. Husbands must remember and constantly affirm the great worth of their wives in any and all situations. Paul extends the analogy of the body, saying a husband should be willing to sacrifice himself for his wife and then nourish, provide for, and wash his wife with the Word in the same way Christ cares for the church. A reasonable person would not harm or deprive his or her own body; how much more would a righteous man intentionally and lavishly care for his wife?

What cultural trends and narratives from the world make these commands difficult? What life situations make this difficult?

3. Christ and the Church: The Model for Marriage (vv. 31–33)

Paul's commands to husbands and wives are intense, all-encompassing, and intended toward a permanent, lifelong relationship. Wives are to submit in all things and husbands are to give up their lives for their wives "till death do us part." How is this possible? Even Paul refers to it as a profound mystery. It is possible because a heavenly model exists for the relationship that husbands and wives can look to, and the Creator of the universe has a vested interest in the health of Christ-centered

marriages. The husband looks to Christ's work of nourishing and cherishing the church as he considers how to nourish and cherish his wife, and the wife looks to the church's work and history of submitting to the loving rule of Christ to determine the ways in which she can wisely submit to her husband's leadership. These commands are separated by gender not because of any underlying ideas of inferiority and superiority, but because our human relationships beg for structure and order. For this need, God has provided this solution in creating boundaries to guide Christian marriage.

If you are married, what is the hardest part of being married? If you look to be married, what do you think will be hardest for you in marriage? If you are single, what do you think Paul would have you glean from the relationship between Christ and His church?

Search the Scriptures

1. When you read Paul's commands to husbands and wives, what Scriptural echoes do you hear? What does this have to do with Genesis 3 (v. 31)?

2. Why should husbands and wives submit to one another (v. 21)?

Discuss the Meaning

1. How can we demonstrate submission to the Lord in covenant marriages?

2. It appears that single people are left out of these verses, but they make up a significant portion of the population of the church. Do Paul's commands to married couples have any bearing on single people?

Liberating Lesson

Marriage is a hotly debated issue in our world today. But as Christians, we must seek not to conform to the world around us; instead we are to have our minds renewed and our spirits transformed. As such, we must be willing to operate within the boundaries that God has set for us in our marriages. The Scripture speaks of covenant marriage between a man and woman as mutual submission with ultimate submission to Christ. As with the Gospel more broadly, it is a call to a better, more fulfilling life in submission to Christ and covenant with one another. Whatever a couple's status, the apostle's message is the same: Marriage should have boundaries, respect, and love that glorifies God. Such expression is even more fulfilling within a marriage with the elements that Paul has just described: The husband loves his wife like Christ loves the church and the wife submits to her husband as the church submits to Christ; and both submit to one another in sacrifice for each other as one united body representing the body of Christ in unity and love.

Application for Activation

Talk about the realities and temptations within marriage with your brothers and sisters in Christ. As much as discussions of sex may make you squeamish, the body of Christ ought to be the safest place to talk about such things. It is one of the reasons that intergenerational relationships are so important to build: Younger married couples have much to learn from older married couples. Young singles have much to learn from older singles. There is wisdom to be gleaned from experiences of others in the body of Christ on how to walk in love and submission God's way. Make the bold step of asking for wisdom where you need it, sharing wisdom with those who ask, and most importantly being vulnerable enough to communicate with those you are in relationship with about God's call for the relationship.

Follow the Spirit

What God wants me to do:

_____

Remember Your Thoughts

Special insights I have learned:

_____

_____

_____

_____

More Light on the Text
Ephesians 5:21–6:4

These verses espouse and present a unifying principle of building strong family ties. These strong family ties are built in order to help families live together in the home as believers serving one another in the name and spirit of Jesus Christ. Family life was originated and ordained by God in the Garden of Eden. He set the first man, Adam, in a family with his prototypical marriage to Eve and bearing of children (Genesis 1:26–28; 4:1–25). God encouraged and tutored His people, in both the Old and New Testaments, to value strong family networks and live in harmony and peace with all loved ones. However, as believers, this idea of a healthy family life cannot be achieved without submission to one another and reverence to Christ.

21 Submitting yourselves one to another in the fear of God. 22 Wives, submit yourselves unto your own husbands, as unto the Lord. 23 For the husband is the head of the wife, even as Christ is the head of the church: and he is the saviour of the body.

24 Therefore as the church is subject unto Christ, so let the wives be to their own husbands in every thing.

Some scholars have argued that the phrase "submitting yourselves one to another in the fear of God" seems to be unexpected. They comment on how it probably does not fit into this context, since it grammatically belongs to a discourse on worship.

It is, however, not illogical. The key word in the text is "submission" (Gk. *hupotasso*, **hoo-poe-TOSS-so**), and it lays a framework for a discussion on how to discharge Christian duties in dynamic relationships of mutuality, in an act of true Christian spirituality. This idea, put forth in the text, suggests the potential danger that individualism poses against a true community life or fellowship. It becomes very serious when individualism is expressed without an intentional desire to willingly bear one another's burdens for the sake of Christ. Whenever there is a true submission for the sake of the Lord, it leads to a frame of heart and an attitude that is penetrated with a deep sense of obligation. True submission seeks not to repudiate or dominate others in a relationship. It is within this context of understanding that the word "submission" sets an agenda for reverence to God and His divine principles. This is done as a means to cultivate a submissive spirit, which values and seeks to unselfishly support, love, and respect others for the sake of Christ. Thus, Paul laid this framework for his teaching regarding the marriage relationship and true harmony in the home.

Paul underscored how a husband and a wife, through devotion for the sake of Christ, must dutifully exercise love and respect for each other in a marriage. The quality of the nature of relationship that should exist between husbands and wives was primarily illustrated by Paul, when he drew on the analogy of Jesus Christ and the church. The key verb "submit," from the Greek, connotes an understanding of voluntarily placing under, or ordering oneself under, a leader or an authority. The church, out of love, gratitude, and reverence, subjects itself to the Lord Jesus Christ as its head. It does this to comply with God's authority. In the same vein, wives are instructed to submit, in the marriage relationship, to the husband.

It is important to note the agency of both parties in this relationship. Wives should submit to acknowledge that God ordained the husband as the leader of the household. This divine arrangement is for the sake of producing ordered household conditions, which are necessary to bring glory to God's name as well as peace and productivity in family life. This is God's pattern of true governance or leadership.

The contextual meaning of the word "head" (Gk. *kephale*, **keh-fah-LAY**) in this passage, in reference to a husband's relationship with his wife, has generated different interpretations among scholars. While some claim that the word "head" denotes an idea of a source, others choose to explain it as portraying leadership. Another interpretation is to see head as the topmost part, the point, as in an arrow or in a Roman military formation. The Roman military would attack in a *cuneus* (**KYOO-nee-us**), which was a triangular formation. The soldier at the point would be first to encounter the enemy, but be held up by the supporting soldiers to his right and left. This soldier was often the leader of that unit. Thus, the husband faces any danger or new territory first in the household. A wife, out of love and humility, submits to the husband. In conjunction, the husband must seek the holistic welfare of his wife and the entire household. He does this out of reverence for God and the position God has given him.

The interpretation as "source" carries an understanding of delegated authority from a higher being or power, which must be exercised with great responsibility and knowledge. In other words, it does not imply that the wife should act like a slave and be a mindless person in the relationship.

The third interpretation of *kephale* as leader in this context has its foundation on ability to provide good leadership. This is accomplished by loving others, who are followers. We love them by listening and respecting them. We also love them by carrying out given responsibilities in a manner that considers the feelings of others.

The fourth interpretation is to view head as literal top of the body. This would be an honored part of the body, containing the face, with the wife completing the rest of the body in that analogy. It is important to note that during the time of Paul's writing, people did not know what the brain did within the head. Aristotle had the popular interpretation and believed the brain was a cooling organ for the head. It was not hypothesized that nerves (and still not the brain) controlled the body until the physician Galen about 100 years later, so to place husband (head) in control over the wife (body) would be out of context.

25 Husbands, love your wives, even as Christ also loved the church, and gave himself for it; 26 That he might sanctify and cleanse it with the washing of water by the word, 27 That he might present it to himself a glorious church, not having spot, or wrinkle, or any such thing; but that it should be holy and without blemish. 28 So ought men to love their wives as their own bodies. He that loveth his wife loveth himself.

The Greek word *agapao* (**ah-gah-PAH-oh**), used in verse 25 for "love," is rooted in an understanding of a person who has unconditionally subordinated his or her own desires, inclinations, and personality for the benefit of others in a relationship. It expresses an idea of an intention and activities that are based on virtues that encourage people to act by saving, building, and restoring others in love. This word for love is frequently used in the New Testament to describe God's love toward humanity (John 3:16). Jesus Christ expressed this kind of love to the church when He vicariously laid down His life so that the church could be born, developed, and expanded. Paul states that Christ restrained Himself unselfishly from engaging in a lifestyle that would put personal glory above God's purpose: Christ, out of love and devotion, had to make "himself of no reputation" (Philippians 2:7) so that He could fully serve God's purpose for the church. The key motivation for His life was to fulfill God's purpose, by serving the ultimate needs of God's people, through a shameful death on the Cross.

In the same way, husbands are admonished to follow the example of Christ to unconditionally and sacrificially serve the holistic—spiritual, physical, psychological, emotional, economic, and material—needs of their wives. This analogy or concept of how to sacrificially express love for the sake of others should not be misunderstood in the marriage relationship as a requirement for wives to over-depend on their husbands for everything. This is because although Christ loves the church, gave Himself for it, and still serves consistently its needs, God has also given the church spiritual and moral responsibilities with agency.

These must be carried out with great maturity and decorum. After all, the Scriptures teach that as a result of the grace of Christ's redemptive work of love believers must act as "workers together with Him" (2 Corinthians 6:1). In principle, the church must see itself as forming and building a team with Christ, aiming to fulfill God's purpose on earth. In the same vein, wives must not overrely on their husbands for everything in life, since both the former and latter must work as a team to fulfill the needs of a healthy home. This means that wives must learn to complement responsibly their husbands' efforts. This is done through their God-given gifts and graces to mutually establish a home or household that is full of peace, progress, and order.

The love that Christ expressed to fulfill God's divine purpose on earth is presented as being motivated by the "sanctifying and cleansing" of the church (vv. 26–27). The sanctification and cleansing of the church of Christ will lead to its glorification and splendor in the midst of a world system that is characterized by sin and darkness. This implies that in a marriage, it is important to work toward values of purity and true spirituality of thoughts and actions, just as Christ purposed for the church. In verse 28, the Apostle Paul reemphasizes the basic foundations that God put in place for Adam and Eve (Genesis 2:23–25). This imagery of the marriage relationship, in which Adam declared Eve as the "bone of my bones, and flesh of my flesh," proclaims forcefully a unique kind of spiritual and bodily union. It also declares an identification in which Adam's heart was prepared to love his wife despite her weaknesses and failures.

29 For no man ever yet hated his own flesh; but nourisheth and cherisheth it, even as the Lord the church: 30 For we are members of his body, of his flesh, and of his bones.

The two key words in these verses are "nourisheth" (Gk. *ektrepho*, **ek-TREH-fo**) and "cherisheth" (Gk. *thalpo*, **THAL-po**). The word "nourisheth" can be defined, in a generic sense, as providing sustenance and attending carefully to others' necessities of life so that they might mature. It means that the husband has been endowed with the godly responsibility of participating in the personal life of his wife. He is to meet her holistic needs in a manner

that progresses the marriage relationship, as ordained by God. Indeed, we are called to act in a way to specially feed and care for our lives. This idea does not mean that the wife is socially, psychologically, or economically inferior to the husband. The author is simply emphasizing the husband's responsibility to play his role as a God-ordained head of the family or household. Second, by using the word "cherisheth" the writer is referring to a husband's promise to his wife to nurture, protect, and shelter her emotionally, physically, psychologically, and spiritually in all situations.

31 For this cause shall a man leave his father and mother, and shall be joined unto his wife, and they two shall be one flesh. 32 This is a great mystery: but I speak concerning Christ and the church.

Verse 31 seems to be the central and organizing phrase in the text of verses 22–33. These verses focus on marriage life and building authentic relationship in a family context based on true love. The key phrases "shall a man leave," "joined unto his wife" and "shall be one flesh" are grounded on Genesis 2:24. It requires characteristics of devotion that inspires transactions of self-sacrifice, deep affection, and total commitment. The new bond and obligation that marriage involves transcend any attachment or commitment to other forms of relationships that are outside the marriage. There must be a "leaving" of anything (except God) that stands between the love relationship between husbands and wives. The "joining," in this context, is a work of God's grace.

Finally, Paul connects the marriage relationship with the "great mystery" of God's plan of salvation. This plan was concealed, but was later unfolded through the redemptive work of Christ and the ministry of His apostles. The Greek word used for "mystery" is *musterion* (**moos-TAY-ree-on**). Its use in this context denotes some particular deep truth about Christ's great love and concern for the church that cannot be fully grasped by the power of the mind, without the help of the Holy Spirit.

33 Nevertheless let every one of you in particular so love his wife even as himself; and the wife see that she reverence her husband.

Paul summarizes the quality of marriage relationship necessary for building a healthy Christian home by, once again, admonishing the husband to "love his wife" and the wife to "see that she reverence her husband." Some commentators have wondered why the teachings in this passage did not specifically mention that wives should "love their husbands" and that husbands should "reverence their wives." Perspectives on this issue sometimes present different views. However, it is important to state that this line of reasoning is sensible and a need exists for a human response to another's love. But since biblical presentation made a connection between Christ's mysterious love for the church and a husband's love for his wife, the emphasis was put on the husband to love his wife. This is the model that Christ laid down in the Scriptures. In any case, the Scripture is clear; husbands and wives are to live in love and unity under the authority of Jesus Christ, modeling the love of Christ to one another and the world around them.

Daily Bible Readings

MONDAY
Partners From the Beginning
(Genesis 2:18–24)

TUESDAY
We Will Serve the Lord
(Joshua 24:14–18)

WEDNESDAY
Capable Wife and Supportive Husband
(Proverbs 31:16–31)

THURSDAY
Live as Children of Light
(Ephesians 5:6–20)

FRIDAY
Parents and Children Together
(Ephesians 6:1–4)

SATURDAY
Masters and Slaves Together
(Ephesians 6:5–9)

SUNDAY
Marriage: A Covenant of Mutual Love
(Ephesians 5:21–33)

Notes

_____

_____

_____

_____

A

Abomination: A foul and detestable thing

Affliction: Anguish, burden, persecution, tribulation, or trouble

Angel: A messenger of God, not eternal or all-knowing; specific types include cherubim and seraphim

Ascension: Raising up in authority or physical place. Can especially refer to the event forty days after Jesus' death, burial, and Resurrection, when He went returned to heaven to sit at the right hand of the Father (Acts 1:9–11)

Atone: To propitiate, satisfy the demands of an offended holy God; or reconcile to a holy God after sin

B

Baptize: To dip, immerse, or submerge

Blameless: Irreproachable, faultless, flawless

Blessedness: Happiness, joy, or prosperity, to be well spoken of by God or others

Bless the Lord: To bend the knee in praise to God

Blood of the Lamb: The blood that Jesus shed on the Cross that redeems humanity

Bowels: To ancient Middle Easterners, the place of emotion, distress, or love

C

Called by God: Appointed or commissioned to fulfill a task

Charge: Admonish, order, command

Chosen: To be approved and selected by God

Christ: The Anointed One, the expected Messiah the Jews hoped for and whom Christians believe came as Jesus of Nazareth

Commandments: God's mandates; the entire body of Laws issued by God through Moses for Israel

Conduct: Manner of living

Confess: To acknowledge or fully agree

Consider: To determine or make out

Covenant: An agreement or promise between God and humanity based on God's character, strength, and grace

Crucifixion: A method of Roman execution in which a criminal was hung on a cross

D

Decalogue: From "ten words" in Greek; the Ten Commandments

Desolation: The state of being deserted or uninhabited

Disciples: Learners, students, followers

Dominion: Rule or reign

Dwelling place: A person's refuge or home

E

El: The Hebrew word for "god" or "mighty one"

Evil: Bad, unpleasant, or displeasing things

Evil doer: A malefactor, wrongdoer, criminal, troublemaker

Evil spirits: Messengers and ministers of the devil

Exalt: To raise up to the highest degree possible

Exhortation: Giving someone motivation to change his or her behavior either by rebuke or encouragement

F

Faithfulness: Steadfastness, steadiness

Fear of the Lord: Reverence or awe of who God is, resulting in obedience to Him and abstaining from evil

G

Glory: Splendor, unparalleled honor, dignity, or distinction; praise and worship

God's bride: The church

God's own hand: God's strength, power

Gospel: The Good News of Jesus the Messiah's arrival and presence of His kingdom

Graven image: An idol cut (often from stone, wood, or metal) and worshiped as a god

Great Tribulation: A time of great suffering that has not been experienced since the world began (Matthew 24:21, Revelation 7:14)

H

Hallowed: Consecrated, dedicated, or set apart

Hear: Listen to, yield to, or obey

Hearken: Pay attention to, give attention to

Heart: The figurative place of emotion and passion

Heathens: The Gentiles, all those who are not a part of the people of God

Holy: Anything consecrated and set aside for sacred use; set apart from sin

Honor: To revere or value

Host: An army or vast number

I

Idolatry: The worship of anything other than God

Infidel: One who is unfaithful, unbelieving, and not to be trusted

Iniquity: Perversity, depravity, guilt, sin

J

Just: Righteous, that which is right and fair

Justice: Righteousness in government

K

Kingdom of Christ: The rule and reign of Christ as King both now and in the age to come

L

Law: Either the Mosiac Law or any human law; synonyms include commandments, ordinances, statutes, legal regulations, authoritative instructions, and teachings

Logos (LOG-os): (Gk.) Word; the Word of God, either the Bible or Jesus

M

Manna: Food from heaven baked into a kind of bread, which God miraculously gave to the Israelites in the wilderness

Messiah: The Anointed One

Minister: A servant, an attendant, one who executes the commands of another

Mosiac Law: The law passed down by Moses from God to the Hebrew people at Mt. Sinai

O

Omnipotent: All powerful

Omnipresent: All present, being everywhere

Omniscient: All knowing

Ordained: Established and founded by God; founded, fixed, or appointed

P

Parousia (par-oo-SEE-ah): (Gk.) presence, appearing; Christ's Second Coming

Peace: Wholeness, quietness, contentment, health, prosperity; more than an absence of conflict or problems, but every part of life being blessed

Pentateuch: The first five books of the Old Testament

Power: Boldness, might, or strength, especially God's

Prophets: People filled with the Spirit of God and under the authority and command of God, who pleaded His cause and urged humanity to be saved

Profit: To gain or benefit

Prosper: To succeed, especially in spiritual things; to move forward or succeed in one's efforts

Proved: Examined, tested, tried

Psalm: A piece of music or a melody, especially one dedicated to God or a god

Purity: Sinlessness, without blemish spiritually

R

Ransom: To buy back or pay a price for a person, buying their freedom

Redeem: To ransom or purchase

Refuge: A shelter from rain, storm, or danger; stronghold or fortress; a place to run to and be secure when the enemy threatens

Repent: To turn back from sin and turn to God in faith

Righteous: To be declared not guilty

Righteousness: Justness, rightness, especially God's, which He works as a gift in His people; the right way to live as opposed to a lifestyle that treats others unfairly or unjustly

S

Sabbath: From "ceasing (from work)" in Hebrew; the day set aside to worship God

Sanctuary: The holy place, either in the Tabernacle or the Temple

Salvation: Rescue, safety, or deliverance, especially from eternal punishment

Satan: A fallen angel who is opposed to God and His people

Savior: Defender, rescuer, or deliverer; a term applied to Christ as the rescuer of those who are in bondage to sin and death

Scribes: Secretaries, recorders, men skilled in the Law during Jesus' day

Selah (SEE-lah): (Heb.) A pause in singing to allow for an instrumental musical interlude or silent meditation

Septuagint: "Seventy" in Latin; the Greek translation of the Hebrew Old Testament made by 70 Jewish scholars beginning in the third century BC

Servant: A slave, subject, or worshiper

Shalom (sha-LOME): (Heb.) Peace, prosperity, blessing

Shekinah Glory: The awesome presence of the Lord; His honor, fame, and reputation

Shofar (sho-FAR): (Heb.) A ram's horn; commonly used in celebration, as well as in signaling armies or large groups of people in civil assembly

Soul: The immaterial part of a person (what leaves the body after death), or the whole being, the self, one's life

Stiffnecked: Obstinate and difficult

Strengthen: To secure, make firm

Strive: To struggle, to exert oneself

Supplication: Seeking, asking, entreating, pleading, imploring, or petitioning

T

Tabernacle: A tent; the name of the portable temple constructed by Moses and the people of Israel

Tetragrammaton: YHWH; the four consonants of God's name, as the Jews would often write it

Torah: (Heb.) Law, instrument, or direction; the first five books of the Old Testament

Transfiguration: A change or transformation. Often refers to Jesus' transformation while on the Mount of Olives with His disciples Peter, James, and John, when His face shone like the sun and His clothing was white as snow (Matthew 17:2; Mark 9:2; Luke 9:29)

Transgression: Sin, rebellion, breaking God's Law

Try: In the sense of a test: refined or purified

Trumpet: A ram's horn or simple metal tube used in celebration as well as in signaling armies or large groups of people in civil assembly

V

Vanity (vain): A waste, a worthless thing, or simply emptiness

W

Wisdom: Prudence, an understanding of ethics

Woe: Grief or sorrow

Worship: Bow down deeply, show obedience and reverence

Wrath: Burning anger, rage

Y

Yahweh: God's name, often spelled with consonants only (see Tetragrammaton)

Notes